State of Doom

STATE OF DOOM

Bernard Brodie, the Bomb, and the Birth of the Bipolar World

Barry Scott Zellen

continuum

2012

Continuum International Publishing Group
80 Maiden Lane, The Tower Building,
New York, 11 York Road, NY 10038 London, SE1 7NX

www.continuumbooks.com

Library of Congress Cataloging-in-Publication Data
A catalog record for this book is available from the Library of Congress.

ISBN: 978-1-4411-2462-3 (paperback)
         978-1-4411-5984-7 (hardcover)

Typeset by Newgen Imaging Systems Pvt Ltd, Chennai, India
Printed and bound in the United States of America

Contents

FOREWORD

Rethinking the Unthinkable: Bernard Brodie's Continuing Relevance

Peter R. Lavoy

As the Cold War retreats ever further into the past, its bipolar order is increasingly looked back upon with some nostalgia, mainly for its seeming simplicity—a world divided by two super-powers whose vast nuclear arsenals induced an unprecedented mutuality of caution in their behavior. So dangerous was this world, so high the cost of strategic miscalculation, that a stable nuclear peace emerged—one that many believe was the inevitable outcome of the balance of terror.

With the last decade, defined largely by the global war on terror, globalization, the growth of new military powers, and daunting riddles of asymmetry arising in every region of the world, the clarity and symmetry of the earlier bipolar era can seem preferable to the complexity we now face. But this is a terribly deceptive notion. While it is true that the international system of the Cold War was largely bipolar, at least in terms of military capability and influence, we should not forget how dangerous this era really was, as the two great nuclear-armed rivals stood at the very precipice of an apocalyptic showdown that never came, and all of us living in the shadow of a mushroom cloud.

When the World War II drew to a close, U.S. defense planners were compelled to grapple with a pair of emergent problems, each of which suggested its own solution, but taken together they posed an unprecedented security challenge. First, the enormous destructive power of the newly invented atomic weapon, and the lack of any foreseeable defense against its use, made future wars unthinkable, and thus prompted calls for world government and full military dis-armament. The second challenge, the emergence of the Soviet Union as an implacable global adversary, made these schemes unacceptable to U.S. policymakers, and instead stimulated pro-posals to prolong and exploit America's nuclear monopoly, and possibly even to launch a preven-tive war against the Soviet Union before it could acquire its own nuclear arsenal. But these ideas risked turning the budding Cold War into yet another world war.

Recognizing the inevitability of superpower competition, and the likelihood that any con-flict between the United States and the Soviet Union would quickly escalate into an unimagina-bly horrible war fought with the *absolute* weapon, a group of realist thinkers proposed a novel strategy of nuclear deterrence to bring order to this dangerous predicament. One of the era's greatest thinkers was Bernard Brodie, an innovative theorist of war whose early work was on naval strategy and the effects of technological change on sea power, completed on the eve of World War II just as America took to the high seas to roll back the forces of tyranny from its shores.

As Brodie came to understand, deterrence can be hard to maintain, but it is necessary. It was a constant challenge to implement a strategy that could sustain such a balance between two ideologically opposed, and mutually distrustful, superpowers. Some, like Albert Wohlstetter, came to believe it was at heart a "delicate balance." But Brodie disagreed; he saw much reason for hope, especially as the years went by and general war was avoided. For the duration of the Cold War, the United States and the Soviet Union jointly pursued their deterrence policies, and succeeded in avoiding general war, and with it the specter of a true apocalypse.

But there was a great deal of learning that went on, and a lot of close calls along the way, including the Cuban missile crisis, the Berlin crises, as well as two very unpopular limited wars—Korea and Vietnam—that were fought for limited objectives and with limited means. The superpowers, aided by a new breed of civilian strategists, like Brodie, gradually improved their deterrence policies as a result of lessons learned from the many crises and conflicts that punctuated the Cold War. Each time they stepped closer to the abyss, they managed again to step back, with the strategists gaining new insights at each critical juncture on how to survive in a nuclear world.

The global system that came to define the Cold War was largely bipolar in structure, especially in terms of strategic military power, but it was not a static system. Instead it was a system that dynamically changed, and over time became increasingly dangerous as weapons technology continued its inexorable advance. As a consequence, the bipolar world was not a simple world by any definition, but was instead a world that was every bit as complex as our world today.

Driving these changes, and increasing the dangers, was an unprecedented surge in scientific knowledge—one that would give birth to not just the atomic age, but also the space age and the digital age. From the first atomic test at Trinity in July 1945, to the first thermonuclear explosion at Bikini Atoll in November 1952, to the emergence of the international continental ballistic missile (ICBM) in 1957, and later the multiple independently targetable re-entry vehicle (MIRV) in 1970, technology continued to accelerate and with it the destructiveness, speed and accuracy of these new, unimaginably lethal weapons. Because of this increasing lethality, Brodie would remain firm in his belief that general war between the nuclear powers must never be fought. He recognized this as early as 1946, when he wrote in *The Absolute Weapon* what became one of his best known precepts for the nuclear age: "Thus far the chief purpose of our military establishment has been to win wars. From now on its chief purpose must be to avert them. It can have almost no other useful purpose."

In Brodie's time, the vertical proliferation of nuclear weapons by the superpowers posed the greatest danger—and it was this challenge he focused on. Although this threat diminished substantially with the demise of the Soviet Union and end of the Cold War, Brodie's contributions on deterrence, escalation, nuclear targeting, limited war, and related strategic concepts are worth reacquainting ourselves with, because Russia and China are now modernizing their nuclear arsenals and associated delivery systems, and thus we are entering a new phase in strategic nuclear competition.

Deterrence theory also has relevance to the new set of states that have joined or are trying to break into the nuclear club. In 1969, when the Nuclear Non-Proliferation Treaty was signed, only five countries possessed nuclear weapons: the United States, the Soviet Union, China, France, and Great Britain. Later, Israel, South Africa, India, Pakistan, and North Korea developed their own nuclear weapons capabilities. Driving this continued horizontal proliferation—at the pace of one or two new nuclear nations each decade—has been a mutuality of insecurity by states that face dangerous external threats. Some countries pursue nuclear weapons not to offset a nuclear threat, but rather to offset a conventional military threat. For example, India started its nuclear bomb program in the aftermath of war with China, and then accelerated this effort when China conducted its first nuclear explosive test in 1964. Pakistan launched its nuclear weapons program after losing to India in the 1971 war over East Pakistan (now Bangladesh) and stepped it up after India tested its first nuclear explosive device in 1974. And now Iran points to an alleged Israeli nuclear threat to justify its own attempt to develop the technology and materials needed to produce nuclear weapons. So, as a result of the persistence of insecurity to so many states, nuclear weapons continue to have appeal.

Some argue that having first developed nuclear weapons, and then integrating them into a global military strategy, with deployments in multiple continents and on a variety of sea- and air-based platforms, the United States is responsible for their further proliferation to other countries. Brodie himself realized, reluctantly, at the dawn of the nuclear age that the United States could not afford to give up its nuclear arsenal. But the United States never fired a nuclear weapon in anger since 1945, nor has it even been quick to issue explicit nuclear threats. Ample evidence shows that it is not the U.S. possession of nuclear weapons, or even the existence of a U.S. military force as awesome as it is today, that drives most countries to pursue nuclear weapons or other weapons of mass destruction. It is their own regional adversaries, their neighbors in many cases, which cause them to seek nuclear weapons. More often, in fact, it is U.S. force that helps persuade other countries not to pursue weapons of mass destruction. U.S. security commitments, backed up by a credible U.S. nuclear deterrent, ultimately persuaded Taiwan and South Korea, for example, to abandon their nuclear weapons development programs in the 1970s. Washington was able to provide security commitments to them, so they concluded they did not need nuclear weapons, and instead chose to rely upon the U.S. deterrent much the way Western Europe did throughout the Cold War. This served as the bedrock of European security, and a policy, as Zellen reminds us in the pages that follow, that Brodie strongly advocated throughout the Cold War period.

Just as Brodie realized over a half-century ago, even if the United States did get rid of its nuclear weapons, it would be idealistic—and unrealistic—to believe that other countries would not pursue them anyways, knowing their destructive potential, and thus their potential to offset conventionally superior opponents and to deter larger nuclear powers. And if the United States is going to maintain its own nuclear capacity, its nuclear arsenal might as well be useable as well as safe and secure. It would be too simplistic to believe that if the United States had nuclear weapons, it should not continue to do things to improve their capability and maintain them over time. Our world is much too complex, its dangers much to real, to do so. We must, quite simply, continue to think about the unthinkable—and plan for the unthinkable as well. Bernard Brodie was one of the first to do so. While his colleague, Herman Kahn, is perhaps more famously remembered for authoring a book entitled *Thinking About the Unthinkable* in 1962, it was Brodie who was the first to do so some seventeen years earlier, writing in November 1945, "war is unthinkable but not impossible, and therefore we must think about it."

Nuclear weapons cannot be dis-invented. The most reasonable approaches to the nuclear problem today are the ones Brodie identified at the dawn of the nuclear era: efforts to reduce the insecurity that drives states to pursue their own nuclear deterrent, and failing that, efforts to stabilize deterrence relationships among nuclear-armed states. The renewed international interest in the elimination of nuclear weapons is largely based on the success of measures to achieve these two conditions.

In the case of India and Pakistan, the pursuit of a stable nuclear peace has been particularly vexing. When each country openly tested nuclear weapons in May 1998, there was a widespread hope—articulated most explicitly by India's prime minister Atal Behari Vajpayee—that the prospect of mutual annihilation would induce each side to adopt stabilizing deterrence strategies and treat each other with unprecedented caution. However, less than a year later, India and Pakistan were again at war, this time for control of mountainous terrain near the town of Kargil on the Indian side of the Kashmir Line of Control. After two months of intense fighting at altitudes ranging between 12,000 and 17,000 feet, during which both sides lost several hundred soldiers, Pakistan ordered its forces home, and the crisis ended. Although the Kargil conflict did not come close to causing a nuclear war—each side observed strict limits on the geographic scope of the conflict as well as on the troop levels and military equipment used—it defied the accepted wisdom that nuclear-armed states cannot fight one another. And in the aftermath, rather than moving toward an explicit acceptance of the status quo secured through arms control and implicitly or explicitly restrained deterrence strategies, as the United States and the Soviet Union eventually did after the Cuban missile crisis, India and Pakistan suspended all bilateral dialogue, ramped up their production of nuclear weapons and missile delivery systems, and accelerated preparations for conventional war, which nearly occurred in early 2002.[1] At the same time, they gave new attention to developing robust, survivable nuclear strike capabilities that could be used to deter the outbreak of major war. (Their strategic relationship, like the dynamic between the superpowers, does not lend itself to simple generalizations.)

The military rivalry between India and Pakistan, much like the ongoing strategic rivalries among other new or aspiring nuclear-weapons states, shows that deterrence is not easy or automatically stabilizing. Just as the U.S. armed forces preferred war-fighting and damage-limiting strategies over more restrained policies based principally on deterrence for much of the Cold War (for some, these measures were intended to make deterrence more credible), new nuclear nations are themselves learning how to think about their own strategic competition and survival in the nuclear world. The strategic debates taking place in these countries probably resemble the volatile discussions that Brodie and other Western strategists engaged in throughout the Cold War.

Back to the American experience, as others sought more bellicose responses to the dangers of the nuclear world, advocating wars of prevention, or highly destructive nuclear conflicts, Brodie stayed the course—working hard to ensure that peace—the goal of deterrence—was never forgotten. He also insisted that the price of maintaining deterrence never exceeded the bounds of rationality or proportionality, which meant during peacetime investing in weapons systems designed never to be used but never at so high a cost as to imperil the national economy, and during times of conflict waging limited wars well below our own military capabilities, restraining our instinct to let war escalate to its limit where we traditionally enjoyed many advantages over our opponents.

Brodie and his colleagues—all in the first generation of nuclear strategic thinkers—are seldom read any more by Western students of international relations and strategic studies, much less by analysts in the new or aspiring nuclear nations. Indeed, when the author of this book, Barry Zellen, was conducting his research and visiting the Bernard Brodie Papers in the UCLA Special Collections in 2008, he was the first to do since the collection's last researcher signed in—in 1991. But this decline in interest in these foundational thinkers of the nuclear era does not mean their ideas are obsolete, culturally irrelevant, or even that the world had changed too fundamentally since their time. It is more a reflection of a shift in American strategic priorities, away from the absolute weapon to more precise tools now in use, such as special forces, drones, and other tools of counterterrorism, more fine-tuned and better suited to the current threats than nuclear weapons. In the absence of a military peer comparably armed, our current strategic focus is sensible, but not necessarily forward thinking. As Russia reemerges, China rises, and with other presently unseen dangers lurking over the horizon, we would be well advised to continue to study the works of these original "wizards of Armageddon," as Fred Kaplan called them a generation ago.

And as more states contemplate joining the nuclear club, and develop nuclear forces of increasing variety and destructive power, their strategic thinkers also would be well advised to study the first generation of nuclear theorists, such as Brodie. For the challenges they faced, and the solutions they imagined, were borne of necessity and designed to help ensure survival in a dangerous world—conditions that remain with all countries existing under a nuclear shadow, even if in a markedly different form.

Of course, there are those that maintain the only sure path to survival is through the total elimination of nuclear weapons. As appealing as this option might be, it is no more feasible now than it was in Brodie's day. In fact, perhaps the best chance the world had for nuclear disarmament was right after the introduction of nuclear weapons. It was then that the United States came up with a plan, the Acheson-Lilienthal Plan, which later was presented by Ambassador Bernard Baruch as the Baruch plan to eliminate nuclear weapons. But the sheer difficulty of doing that was and remains the way the world is configured—and so it probably will always be. This confounded that first effort to denuclearize the world at the very beginning of the atomic era, and we are still confronted with those same challenges. Brodie recognized right at the outset that the world was not united enough for such a solution to be practical, and that for better or worse, we had to find another path toward peace and security in a nuclear world. Brodie's solution was deterrence, a strategy that could survive not only the vertical proliferation of nuclear capabilities, which he correctly predicted would continue to accelerate, but one that continues to offer us hope, even in our current, asymmetrical world with new and aspiring nuclear weapons states.

And so it is with great pleasure that I introduce this fascinating portrait of one of America's greatest strategic thinkers, *State of Doom: Bernard Brodie, the Bomb, and the Birth of the Bipolar World*. Beyond his pioneering work on deterrence, many of Brodie's contributions are quite relevant to today's strategic problems and puzzles. His characterization of the broad sweep of military history and the constant influence that technological change has had—and continues to have—upon its flow is worth recalling in our age that is even more rapidly being transformed by technological innovation. His focus on strategic planning, not simply in the context of current threats, but more in terms of likely developments one or two decades hence also is worth understanding and emulating. And his warning during the Vietnam War that there are many political and military contexts in which American technological superiority can turn out to be less valuable than expected, and sometimes even dysfunctional, is worth reacquainting ourselves with in this era of unconventional warfare and asymmetric threats.

Bernard Brodie stands in rare and distinguished company, on par with such great strategic minds as Carl von Clausewitz of the Napoleonic era, and even the ancient philosopher of war, Sun Zi, from China's warring states era. Like both of these great strategic thinkers, Brodie has abundant wisdom to share with future generations, especially, as Zellen chronicles, about the supreme importance of never losing sight of one's ultimate objectives in war—nor letting the means that are employed become disproportionate to those ends, which ultimately define war's very purpose and thus gives it meaning.

Note

[1] See Peter R. Lavoy, ed., *Asymmetric Warfare in South Asia: The Causes and Consequences of the Kargil Conflict* (Cambridge: Cambridge University Press, 2009).

CHAPTER ONE

Before the Bomb: Brodie's Early Thoughts on War and History

This book presents an in-depth exploration of the theoretical evolution of Bernard Brodie, his strategic and philosophical response to the nuclear age, and his lifelong effort to reconcile the classical strategic theories of Carl von Clausewitz to the newfound challenges of the nuclear era.

A foundational architect of American nuclear strategy and one of the twentieth century's greatest strategic minds, Bernard Brodie helped not only to reintroduce a new generation of American sailors to the fundamentals of naval strategy on the eve of World War II, but to later guide the evolution of U.S. military doctrine through the nuclear age while also helping to bridge the gap between civilian theorists and military strategists. His life spanned a period of unprecedented global disorder, upheaval, and war—from the collapse of Europe's balance of power system in the killing fields of World War I, through the even more convulsive and first truly global total war of World War II, to the calmer but more dangerous peace of the Cold War period. During Brodie's lifetime, the technology of war advanced dramatically, with a cresting wave of innovation and wizardry as creative as that century's almost endless warfare was destructive. Brodie was something of a renaissance man when it came to the many disciplines required to truly comprehend the complexity of modern war, with expertise in technology and innovation, history and philosophy, as well as the more traditional military arts of strategy and tactics. He was, through his unique combination of expertise, one of America's most important philosophers of war and a principal architect of America's Cold War strategy of deterrence. And yet, while his theoretical contributions were on a scale shared by very few across history—brilliant minds like that of Clausewitz and Jomini in an earlier age whose formative experiences were forged in war—Brodie came to the art of war from the academic realm, making him one of the first defense intellectuals to cross over from academia to the military world.

In addition to his pioneering work on nuclear strategy—and intimately interconnected to both his theoretical work on the strategic implications of the splitting of the atom and his historical work on the strategic implications of technological change—Brodie was a pioneer in the field of Clausewitz studies, and an important contributor to America's rediscovery of Clausewitz in the post-World War II era. Brodie could fairly be described as "America's Clausewitz"—a title claimed by others of his generation, including, by some accounts, his long-time colleague and later rival, Herman Kahn. Whereas Kahn became known for his bold theories of nuclear warfighting and his unsentimental imagination of the "day after" deterrence failed, Brodie was a true believer in the strategic and moral imperative of deterrence as a strategy, and as the optimal underlying architecture of the Cold War's international order. Brodie's first influential strategic efforts were in the field of naval strategy, with his first book, *Sea Power in the*

Machine Age (Princeton University Press, 1941 and 1943), and his second, *A Layman's Guide to Naval Strategy* (Princeton University Press, 1942, later renamed *A Guide to Naval Strategy* at the Navy's request, which went on to enjoy multiple printings), positioning him for immediate recognition in the aftermath of Japan's dawn raid of the U.S. Pacific Fleet at Pearl Harbor. But Brodie's most lasting strategic impact would come after the end of World War II, in the emergent field of nuclear strategic thinking, as he took an early lead in conceptualizing and articulating precepts that would guide the emergence and evolution of U.S. strategic doctrine for the post-Hiroshima world—refining his thoughts as technology continued to evolve, and as the military balance consequently shifted throughout the Cold War era.

The aim of this book is to introduce a new generation of students and scholars to one of the most important strategic theorists of the twentieth century whose work transcends the Cold War era. It presents an in-depth examination of his bountiful written works, including his published books, reports, chapters, and articles, as well as his many memoranda, letters, and speeches. It also provides a theoretical framework for understanding Brodie's contribution to American strategic thought, embedding his work within the Clausewitzian tradition and showing how Brodie's fascination with Clausewitz contributed to the emergence his own theoretical style—one that made his work both more sophisticated and enduring in its relevance. And, it sheds light on Brodie's efforts to bridge the civil–military divide and to educate American students and scholars on the importance of Clausewitz.

This book explores Brodie's evolution as a theorist, and his response to the technological innovations that transformed warfare from the period just before World War II through to the Cold War's nuclear arms race, up to his death just after the Vietnam War. It places Brodie's theoretical development within a Clausewitzian context, noting that Brodie came to be an apt student of the famed Prussian strategist and a key player in the movement to bring Clausewitz studies to America—partnering with leading Clausewitz scholars including Peter Paret, Michael Howard, and Raymond Aron in their ambitious but only partly successful Clausewitz Project, which famously yielded the widely read Princeton translation of Clausewitz's *On War*. Brodie took Clausewitz's approach to the study of war, his embrace of complexity, and his important interconnection of war to politics, to heart, and embedded his own pioneering work in nuclear strategy in a framework that was in form and substance inherently Clausewitzian. This conscious effort at emulation, combined with his distinct theoretical elegance and analytical rigor, made Brodie more deserving of the mantle "America's Clausewitz" than any other strategic thinker of his generation.

*   *   *

Despite Brodie enormous theoretical contribution to American nuclear strategy and his prolific and multifaceted contribution to the strategic studies literature from the years immediately preceding the nuclear age right up to the end of his life in 1978, there have been just a few scholarly works fully dedicated to Bernard Brodie and his legacy. Most comprehensive is Barry Steiner's exhaustively researched *Bernard Brodie and the Foundations of American Nuclear Strategy* (University Press of Kansas, 1991), which chronicles with the greatest of historical detail Brodie's contribution to the evolution of military doctrine and his military influence during his lifetime. Included in his 1991 book on Brodie was Steiner's earlier article and working paper, "Using the Absolute Weapon: Early Ideas of Bernard Brodie on Atomic Strategy"—enhanced by what he described in his introduction to the 1991 book as "minor changes"—which was published in the December 1984 *Journal of Strategic Studies*, and earlier that year as ACIS Working Paper, No. 44, by UCLA's Center for International and Strategic Affairs. The timing of Steiner's book, which came to press just at the close of the Cold War when interest in the architects of the Cold War would fade from the public mind with the winding down of that generational conflict, and marked the endpoint, to a significant degree, of Brodie's profound theoretical and doctrinal influence in America and his contribution to the very creation of the bipolar world order that defined the half-century of the Cold War period. But now that we're two decades into the post-Cold War era, with several new and emergent nuclear states enlarging their arsenals and contemplating their own strategic nuclear doctrines and even stateless terror groups aspiring their own nuclear capability, the timing is ideal to reintroduce to a new generation of students and scholars the work of this great and pioneering theorist of war.

Indeed, it's Brodie's contribution to the evolution of strategic *theory* (and not just nuclear doctrine) that provides relevance to our own era, which continues to struggle with new conflicts, new opponents, and new technologies of war. As Steiner has observed, "One of Brodie's major postwar accomplishments was to legitimate the study of military strategy for civilians lacking a military background," bringing to the study of war and strategy what Brodie described as a necessary *"genuine analytical method,"* in part because "the magnitude of disaster which might result from military error today bears no relation to situations of the past."[1] Echoing Steiner, Marc Trachtenberg—another member of the dedicated community of Brodie scholars whose work has helped to chronicle Brodie's influence and to analyze his voluminous if at times seemingly contradictory body of strategic analysis to ensure future generations grasped his subtleties and the full complexity of his thinking—described: "In the 1950s, strategy emerged in the United States as a new field with a distinct intellectual personality. A small group of men— Bernard Brodie, Thomas Schelling, Albert Wohlstetter, and a handful of others—working mainly at the RAND Corporation, had moved into an intellectually barren 'no-man's land' traditionally neglected by both military officers and students of international politics. The body of thought they created was very different from anything that had come before. Their ideas would prove enormously influential, and their style of analysis in large measure became the sophisticated way of approaching nuclear issues in the United States."[2]

While the number of books, monographs, articles, and chapters focusing exclusively on Brodie is limited, there are numerous works that have taken various levels of inspiration from Brodie— including at least one that was explicitly dedicated to him, an anthology of conference papers from the Bellagio Conference on deterrence held in December 1985 at Villa Serbelloni, Bellagio, Italy that first appeared as a special edition of *The Journal of Strategic Studies* in December 1986 and was later published in book form by Frank Cass & Company in 1987: *Dilemmas of Nuclear Strategy*, edited by Roman Kolkowicz. As Kolkowicz , who like Trachtenberg and Steiner have helped bring attention to Brodie's important theoretical and doctrinal contributions, wrote in his introductory essay, "It is fair to say that the guiding intellectual spirit of the Bellagio conference and its proceedings was that of Bernard Brodie, to whom this volume is dedicated. Brodie was a pioneer of modern strategic studies in the nuclear era whose work has powerfully influenced generations of strategists and decision-makers. He was the first to perceive and publicly articulate the revolutionary implications of nuclear weapons for war and peace and for the management of international politics in a dangerous world. At the very dawn of the nuclear era, in 1946, he defined the essential paradox and inescapable truth of the nuclear condition: 'Thus far, the chief purpose of our military establishment has been to win wars. From now on, its chief purpose must to be avert them. It can have no other useful purpose.'"[3] Kolkowicz observed that with "his lifelong concern for the intellectual integrity and policy relevance of strategic studies in the nuclear era, Brodie insisted that 'we need people who will challenge and dissect the prevailing dogmas' of strategic fashions and fads. Above all, reflecting the teachings of Clausewitz whom he greatly admired, Brodie urged the 'need to stress the superior importance of the political side of strategy to the simply technical and technological'. He considered 'the most important single idea in [Clausewitz's] *On War . . .* the one that makes it great, is the idea that war must never be an act of blind violence, but must be dedicated to achieving the supreme goal of statecraft.' "[4]

Kolkowicz noted that the discussion that unfolded at the Bellagio conference "pointed out the resistance after the Second World War to Brodie's revolutionary formulation of the nuclear condition and his advocacy of deterrence-only, non-military use of nuclear weapons" by those who "advocated an American strategy that was similar to that of the pre-nuclear era" and who thus "considered victory rational and obtainable," in marked contrast to Brodie, who believed "the idea of actually using these weapons was not thinkable," and that "military victory in nuclear war was not possible," views that became "accepted in the 1960s by the official defense community and decision-makers and became the foundation for American strategic policies."[5] This was illustrated by former Defense Secretary McNamara in his 1983 *Foreign Affairs* article, "The Military Role of Nuclear Weapons: Perceptions and Misperceptions," but as recounted therein, he came to finally believe America couldn't "avoid serious and unacceptable risk of nuclear war until we recognized . . . that nuclear weapons serve no military purpose whatsoever. They are totally useless—except only to deter one's opponent from using them," capturing a sentiment that is at heart Brodien, and which soundly refuted his earlier notions of flexible response that captivated the best and the brightest throughout the Kennedy–Johnson years.[6]

In 1991, the same year Steiner's book on Brodie's legacy came to press, Marc Trachtenberg brought to press his own book-length manuscript that focused largely, but not entirely, on the Cold War period (with an additional chapter revisiting the causes of World War I, whose tragic runaway escalation from isolated act of terror to general war was a sobering reminder to the nuclear theorists what was at stake when reflecting on escalation): *History and Strategy*, as part of the Princeton Studies in International History and Politics series published by Princeton University Press. Its first chapter was a modified version of his 1989 *Political Science Quarterly* article, with the self-same title and which also appeared in the final volume in his multivolume anthology, *Development of American Strategic Thought: Writings on Strategy*: "Strategic Thought in America 1952–1966," which focuses heavily upon Brodie's contribution to American strategic thought in this period that immediately followed the arrival of thermonuclear weapons, based on a special public release by RAND of fourteen hitherto unpublished papers by Brodie written in nearly the identical period (1952–1965).

Trachtenberg's discussion sheds much light upon the ambiguity of Brodie's written work, which evolved over time—and in response to a rapid series of dizzying technological innovations from the splitting of the atom to the perfection of fusion bombs and their successful coupling to intercontinental missiles—and contains, as a result, some unavoidable contradictions, particularly on the topic of limited war and the battlefield use of tactical nuclear weapons. These seeming contradictions reflected the natural tension between two paradoxical responses to the new nuclear reality of the post-Hiroshima world: as Trachtenberg explained, this "basic tension" that permeated the evolution of nuclear strategic thought "was as though the coming of the hydrogen bomb in 1952 had released two great shock waves in the world of strategic thought," the first being once both superpowers "had obtained survivable and deliverable strategic forces, all-out war . . . would become an absurdity," while the second was the "equally basic notion that the threat of nuclear war could be used for political purposes that went well beyond deterring the use of nuclear weapons by an adversary."[7] The resulting doctrinal clash between these two schools, sometimes referred to as the "assured destruction" and "warfighting" (or "war-winning") schools, would define much of the literature and suggest a theoretical polarity that clashed with the more ambiguous reality, where strategies were pulled like a pendulum between the two, sometimes showing much overlap in pursuit of the same end goal: peace and survival in the nuclear world. As Trachtenberg noted, "It was not that separate factions rallied around each of these two poles: the history of American strategic thought during this period cannot be summed up as a dispute between those who believed in 'simple deterrence' and those who wanted nuclear forces to play a more far-reaching political role. Strategic discourse was during this period was not sectarian or doctrinaire: the striking thing was that the same people were attracted to both approaches, often at the same time."[8] Adds Trachtenberg, "these two basic ways of approaching strategy were in obvious conflict with one another. The fundamental question was whether there was any way this conflict could be resolved."[9]

Such would be the challenge that Bernard Brodie would face in his four-decade-long journey that started on the eve of World War II, as America rose to the heights of superpower status, and carried him past the humbling setback in Vietnam where American power—and its theories of limited warfare, escalation, and bargaining—were put to the test. In addition to the many works of Cold War intellectual history where Brodie played a prominent role, there are even more works where he was but one member of a larger cast of characters contributing to a conversation that stretched from 1945 until the Cold War's sudden end. In 1981, Lawrence Freedman authored one of the most comprehensive intellectual histories of the nuclear age, *The Evolution of Nuclear Strategy*, published by St. Martin's Press, followed the next year by Colin Gray's *Strategic Studies and Public Policy: The American Experience*, published by the University Press of Kentucky. Then in 1983 came Fred Kaplan's widely read intellectual biography of the nuclear era's greatest thinkers, the *Wizards of Armageddon*, based on his doctoral thesis for the Massachusetts Institute of Technology (MIT) Department of Political Science, was published by Simon & Schuster (to be reissued in 1991 by Stanford University Press as part of its Nuclear Age Series)—with colorful (and apocryphal) recollections of Brodie and his contributions to the emerging field of nuclear strategic thought, along with the other principal contributors like Herman Kahn among others. Soon after Kaplan's widely read 1983 work, Gregg Herken authored *Counsels of War* (Alfred A. Knopf, 1985, republished by Oxford University Press in 1987) covering ground quite similar to that covered by Kaplan but with greater attention to Brodie's theoretical development as one of many characters in the atomic drama, following up his earlier *The Winning Weapon* (also published by Knopf) in 1980, which had barely mentioned Brodie (and when doing so misspelled his first name as Bertrand in the index!) and instead focused more on the policymakers of the era. Also in 1985, Princeton University Press published *Makers of Modern Strategy from Machiavelli to the Nuclear Age*, edited by Peter Paret, a sequel to Earle's famed 1943 anthology with nearly identical title and much shared content; the new edition included a chapter by Lawrence Freedman, "Nuclear Strategists," that included Brodie among the key players, a topic he covered in great depth in his widely read 1981 work, *The Evolution of Nuclear Strategy* (St. Martin's Press), now in its third edition (now under the imprint of Palgrave, 2003). Brodie had played just as central a role in Trachtenberg's 1991 *History and Strategy*, especially his first chapter, "Strategic Thought in America."[10] While the literature focusing exclusively on Brodie is limited, he has nonetheless been an enduring, and indeed often central, character in numerous journal articles and book chapters while also being included among the cast of leading characters in many of the intellectual histories of the Cold War, most famously perhaps in the aforementioned *Wizards of Armageddon* authored by Kaplan and similar works by Gregg Herken, Lawrence Freedman and Colin Gray, among others.[11]

Steiner, along with Trachtenberg and Kolkowicz, demonstrates a rare depth and breadth of knowledge of Brodie's writings and their impact on both the theoretical and doctrinal development of nuclear strategy, and when the study of Brodie enjoys its much-deserved renaissance, these scholars and their pioneering contributions will be recognized as the foundation. Just as Steiner provides us with a unique and probing depth of insight into Brodie's thought, Trachtenberg provides us with a unique and searching breadth with his very unique anthology of preserved facsimiles of original Cold War documents in his multivolume reference set, *The

Development of American Strategic Thought: Writings on Strategy, with a total of 73 papers, articles, and reports presented in chronological sequence, including several of Brodie's lesser known articles and hitherto classified RAND papers. The first part, *Writings on Strategy 1945–1951*, includes seven Brodie chapters among its ten in total; the three-volume second part of the series, *Writings on Strategy 1952–1960*, includes eight Brodie chapters out of nine in total in volume one; six Brodie chapters out of 15 total in volume two; and two Brodie chapters out of 14 total in volume three; and in the third part of the series, *Writings on Strategy 1960–1969 and Retrospectives*, Brodie's chapters comprise 12 out of a total 25 chapters, which includes the four "Retrospectives" (two of which were authored by Brodie). While this anthology is not widely held by academic libraries, and as a complete set is now found in just a handful, it affords a rare glimpse into the lesser known Brodie, not just the Brodie of *The Absolute Weapon* or *Strategy in the Missile Age* or even his later *Escalation and the Nuclear Option* and *War and Politics*, or even his early works on naval strategy, *Sea Power in the Machine Age* and *A Guide to Naval Strategy*, the writer of heavy and enduring tomes that present as a collective a body of work on a scale that has been inhabited by an august few, theorists of war like Mahan and Clausewitz—but instead the prolific essayist and public speaker who wrote for and spoke to the lay public, and at the same time an equally prolific writer of classified reports and memoranda read primarily by America's top political and military leaders as they grappled with the new challenges of the nuclear age. Brodie's output was bountiful, even if many of his works were read by only a small audience and in the end, popular celebrity escaped him. And more importantly, as Steiner, Trachtenberg, Kolkowicz, and others have noted, Brodie's influence was felt far and wide, from the epic naval clashes of World War II through to the new challenges of the post-Hiroshima world, including the challenges of sustaining the Western alliance, up to and beyond the humbling strategic set-backs of the Vietnam War era.

Given Brodie's pioneering, indeed pivotal, role among the leading intellectuals of the bomb from the very inception of the nuclear age, a role faithfully chronicled by Kaplan in his widely read *Wizards of Armageddon*, it seems odd that when Kaplan revisited this era in his more recent *1959: The Year Everything Changed* published in 2009, he paid tribute to Herman Kahn's influence with his very own chapter, but largely neglected Brodie, who appears only tangentially in the chapter on his colleague (and rival) Kahn—even though it was Brodie's magnum opus, *Strategy in the Missile Age*, that came to press in that transformative year of 1959, and which was described without any exaggeration by Colonels William P. Snyder and John A. MacIntyre, Jr. in their 1981 article in *Parameters*, detailing Brodie's unique contribution to strategy as "the most important book on American national strategy to appear in the decade of the 1950s"— though Kahn was at that point traveling the country presenting his infamous slide show that would become, in narrative form, his best-selling 1960 *On Thermonuclear War*. While Kahn has received much recent attention by publishers, including Harvard University Press and Lexington Books, which have contributed to the recent revival of Kahn in the literature, Brodie by com-parison has remained overlooked thus far. One reason could be that Brodie's influence was more *theoretical* than *doctrinal*; another that he was something of a strategic maverick, going against the grain and thus rubbing those in power the wrong way. As Booth has commented, "At several important points in his career Brodie was a dissident" and "did not avoid professional discom-fort," nor "think it threatening to change his mind;" as well, he "did not defer to the authority of air force commanders when he believed them wrong," nor did he "believe that his colleagues at RAND had discovered timeless truths about strategy," and he thus "challenged the conventional wisdom," and "most unusual of all for an American strategist of his day, he did not believe that his own country was always right."[12] And so, Booth observes, "it is not surprising that Brodie's direct influence on the making of American strategy . . . was limited," but as he further reflects, "does influence matter? Who now worries whether Clausewitz had any influence? What counts is the enduring worth of what he wrote."[13] Booth describes Brodie's influence "as indirect rather than direct, and philosophical rather than technical," less "a 'maker' of modern strategy in a direct sense, like von Schlieffen"—and more like Clausewitz.[14]

But Brodie's own bountiful contribution to the literature more than makes up for the lack of literature about him. His works span all manner of formats, from scholarly books bearing Princeton University Press' august imprint to popular trade books published by Dell and Macmillan, and from newspaper op-eds and magazine articles to academic scholarly and military journal articles, and from public lectures and speeches to his many classified reports, working papers, and research memoranda for the military while at RAND and lectures to the service academies.[15]

Brodie's approach to nuclear strategy was distinct in its sophistication, his willingness to embrace the inherent uncertainties of war unique among his peers, placing his approach to theorizing firmly in the Clausewitzian tradition, a tradition that was beyond the reach of most strategic studies scholars whose approach to war was much more *linear*, less nuanced, and less willing to embrace war's ambiguity or honestly confront its dangers while recognizing its uncertainties. But we must go beyond merely matching up Brodie and Clausewitz as likeminded philosophers of war, unparalleled in their intellect and insight, for the connection that binds Brodie to Clausewitz across a more than a century of profound historical change is truly multilayered. As such, Brodie is best understood through a Clausewitzian lens on many levels, not just for his theoretical imitation of Clausewitz but also for his role fostering the revival of Clausewitz studies in the Anglo-American strategic studies community, helping to catalyze interest in the Prussian among a new generation of scholars, exposing students and scholars to the full richness and complexity of Clausewitz's thought, thereby fostering a more nuanced understanding of war in the modern world, particularly in the nuclear era when Clausewitz's theoretical construct of absolute war first became a reality. Unmatched among his peers for his rich and diverse range of expertise—from military history to classical philosophy to the technology of war—Brodie stepped up and filled a giant's shoes left empty ever since Clausewitz's untimely death, for a new generation that was confronted by the gravest military challenge of all time: the splitting of the atom by fallible man and his creation in the laboratory of a technology capable of realizing Clausewitz's hitherto theoretical construct of *absolute war*. Brodie's distinct style, his recurring references to Milton, his early ruminations on Socrates, his successful effort to reintroduce America to its very own "Clausewitz of the sea," Admiral Mahan, his subsequent rediscovery of and inspiration from Clausewitz himself, led to a richness in theorizing that would set him apart. But along the way, this very sophistication would alienate him from the very community he hoped to influence—as less complex thinkers better-suited for the formulation of doctrine than the more complex challenges of theory promised simplicity to an era engulfed by a cloud of fear and worry and which did not want to wade deeply into a shadow world of complexity and ambiguity, and who would, for their promise of simplicity, come to dominate the field of American nuclear strategy.

Looking back to the Napoleonic era and the duel that followed between the *Jominian* and *Clausewitzian* theoretical responses, the former which dominated military academies for a century, stretching from the American civil war when Jomini was widely read on both sides, to World War I and its tragic stalemate, through to the German and Japanese success with land- and sea-based blitzkrieg, quickly overrunning much of the world with bold, aggressive lightning strikes. But once the nuclear stalemate set in, and later the failed application of the Jominian linearity of escalation theory to Vietnam, Clausewitz was rediscovered—and Brodie was one of the theorists dedicated to that rediscovery. Brodie's interest in Clausewitz was not strictly academic; Clausewitz became in part a metaphor for the very complexity of war in a dangerous time, and the frustration felt by the philosopher of war who recognized this complexity, its danger, and its many ambiguities, and who did not reduce it to simpler catchphrases. The Jomini–Clausewitz rivalry—a battle of ideas that would take place long after Clausewitz's own death—presents us with a lens to understand Brodie, who was similarly confronted by more popular rivals who would achieve greater influence in his time, such as the best-selling pop-sensation Herman Kahn—and also the Nobel Prize-winning presidential adviser Henry Kissinger.

Brodie brought to the study of war an understanding of philosophy, history, psychology, and technology—dynamic and fluid forces where change was the only constant. And this provided him with the ammunition to articulate a complex, nuanced theory of war and the place of nuclear weapons in the modern world, one that demanded restraint and understanding, and sometimes inaction instead of action. All unpopular precepts for a more muscular world that favored bold and confident action. In a world predisposed to tough talk and bold action, Brodie's ideas ruffled feathers and left him on the sidelines of a field where his ideas, ironically, were superior to those offered up by most of his peers, and which evolved in lockstep with the times from the early era of American atomic monopoly to the world of overkill that would define the latter years of the Cold War. Brodie first thought about naval strategy in the prenuclear world, the impact of technology change on the conduct of war across the ages, and the fundamental ambiguities inherent in digesting the past and interpreting it and applying it to the emergent future. Brodie looked first at Socrates, and saw in the great philosopher the riddle of his uncertain legacy. When he later looked to Mahan, he helped resurrect interest in the central but neglected importance of sea power to history, just in time for America to take to the high seas, and rollback the wave of Imperial Japanese expansion in the Pacific and to establish the foundation for an American century.

In Clausewitz, Brodie found riddles similar to those he found in Socrates—and in his own remarkable if not always fully appreciated contribution to strategic theory in the nuclear era, he would leave his own legacy of riddles, rising to a rare and distinguished level as one of the truly great strategic minds of all time, joining a Pantheon of great thinkers, even if that meant becoming isolated from the world of mortal man. With Brodie's death now more than three decades in the past, and the Cold War itself part of history for over two decades, we find our world is again at war, and as we navigate this current world of conflict, we witness a new clash between the apostles of simplicity, and the more nuanced interpreters of complexity; as these two tidal forces array against each other, a re-examination of the last generation's greatest theorist of complex war, and his clash with simpler minds, can offer us important lessons for our own time—and for all time. We will in the pages that follow turn to the writings of Bernard Brodie that span a tumultuous half century, from the years just before World War II to those just after America's humbling Vietnam experience; in so doing, we will come to understand Brodie's pivotal place in the evolution of strategic theory and the philosophy of war, as strategic thinkers grappled not only with the cataclysmic destruction brought by total war, but the potential extinction of humanity courted by the architects of the new, nuclear order as they wrestled with how to harness the bomb without being destroyed by it.

Early on, Brodie enjoyed what Ken Booth has described as "the knack of being in the right place at the right time," and after being "drawn into the young subject of international relations" during the 1930s after studying philosophy at the University of Chicago, he stayed on for his doctorate and "studied under Quincy Wright, whose own work was making him one of the unquestioned masters of his subject" and who was "approaching the end of his mammoth project, *The Study of War*," for which Brodie's component served as his doctoral project examining "the impact of naval technology on diplomacy in the nineteenth century," which he completed, with perfect timing, in 1940.[16] In addition to Wright's influence, Booth notes Brodie "also greatly benefited from Jacob Viner, a member of the economics department" who was also "an impressive thinker about international relations and in time became an early and original contributor to thinking about the atomic bomb."[17] Brodie next went to Princeton, "where he took up a research fellowship, helped by Wright's contact with Edward Meade Earle," who like Brodie's mentor "was at the forefront of his field and was overseeing a book, *The Makers of Modern Strategy*, which would become a milestone."[18] At Princeton, Brodie "adapted his dissertation into his own first book,"[19] *Sea Power in the Machine Age*, whose success led Princeton University Press to commission Brodie to write another book on sea power, which he quickly finished, *A Layman's Guide to Naval Strategy*, which was published in 1942. Brodie's early success and positive publishing experience suggested "the strategic theorist might be valued by the practitioner," and that "civilian theorists could be appreciated by military professionals," helping precipitate the birth a new field; but Booth notes that these early successes would face later setbacks and disappointments that would suggest such acceptance "was the exception rather than the rule," at least for Brodie whose theoretical and intellectual rigor, and its embrace of complexity and contradiction, could rub some the wrong way.[20]

Early Reflections on an Uncertain World

It's illustrative to look back to the very earliest work of Bernard Brodie, when still a student, over a decade before he rose to prominence first as an expert first of naval strategy and later as one of the first and certainly one of the most insightful of the nuclear wizards. The young Brodie, while still an undergraduate student at the University of Chicago in December 1932, penned his own thoughtful reflections on Socrates and the riddle of his legacy for Course 101 of the Department of Philosophy, titled "In Quest of Socrates—Man and Philosopher." Today, we remain confronted by the lingering a riddle of Socrates' legacy, still unsure about who the real Socrates was, or how to assess the dueling interpretations of this founding father of philosophy. Brodie's early effort to reconcile these contending interpretations, and to synthesize from their ambiguous parts a coherent whole, is an early indicator of his abilities to grapple with complexity, and to find order where others might only see chaos.

Brodie's paper on Socrates earned him the following comments from his professor, Thomas Vernor (T. V.) Smith, who served as dean of the University Chicago from 1922 to 1948: "Excellent Work. This is delightfully written and shows an admirable knowledge of the sources." In the paper, one can almost sense anticipation in the heart of the young and ambitious Brodie for achieving a comparable level of philosophical greatness to that Socrates had achieved. Consider how Brodie introduced his essay on Socrates: "A happy thought to fill an idle hour is the reflection on the diversity of traits on which men are borne to greatness. Unhappily for us duller ones, genius seems an indispensable ingredient, but the consideration of the qualities that may adorn genius—or encumber it—is an intriguing one."[21] Brodie further reflects on the nature of genius: "We love the purity and earnestness of a Milton, but that his youthful wife found his table dull and wearisome is hard to forgive. We admire the salubrious abstemiousness of a Thoreau, but we hate the man whose arm to take one would easier say 'no' than 'yes'. Of a Stevenson, let us say, we delight in a soldierly heart and a cheery soul, but—tho we will subtract nothing from the loveable R. L. S.—we may reluctantly admit that there have been his betters in depth of thought. Now suppose that from those I have mentioned we abstract the admirable and good—the Miltonic earnestness and purity, the Thoreauian asceticism, the Stevensonian indomitableness and happy spirit—suppose we compound them in our retort, add a liberal dose of Voltairian wit, and stand off to catch the distillate. We infuse it into a human form, and we have one with "The elements; So mixed in him that Nature might stand up; And say to all the world 'This was a man.'" Such a man, I think, was Socrates. What a happy task to go in quest of him."[22]

This quest necessitates a "long journey" back over two millennia to Athens at its peak, "a city of a beauty-mad people, a city throbbing with activity and political turmoil, yet singularly free of the din and clatter and confusion of our own day," one that is "laid round a hill, atop which are set the noblest structures that have ever been struck against a blue sky," marred by but "one atrocity—slavery," that "gives a life of tranquility and leisure for reflection to those who are not slaves." Noting Athens "is a city with a noble convention of deliberative discourse," Brodie writes that "[o]nly such a city could have harbored and nurtured Socrates, for the Attic genius was not a genius but a climate." Brodie confronts one of the riddles of Socrates, noting "we must search for the imprint of his person in the documents of the time," where "[w]e discover at once that their (sic.) is nothing from his own hand," and speculating in his footnotes, "I wonder if Plato is hinting at why Socrates didn't write in *Phaedrus 257*."[23] Brodie reflects, "We think for a moment on the deluge of printed pulp that pours down upon us today and reflect almost sardonically that a Socrates did not write. Nor are we disappointed; somehow, it seems in keeping with the man, even as he first takes form in our imagery. We feel at once a disdain of fame, we feel a spirit of one who lived only for the living round him."[24] But "[s]ince he did not write, we look to those of his day who wrote of him," finding "him drawn by the pens of three men, a strangely contrasting three—a comic poet, a gentleman of letters, and one whose thought has been the dazzling glory of the ages. Each draws him or paints rather—and it is a vastly different picture that comes from each."[25] Brodie considers Aristophanes' "grotesque, horribly caricatured sketch," which he concludes "we dismiss at once," though he adds Aristophanes seems to be "lampooning Socrates undoubtedly not as a person but as representative of an institution he hated"—though this lampooning had hurtful consequences, evident in "Socrates' reference to the damage of this play on his reputation in *Apology*."[26]

Brodie turns next to the portrait of Socrates penned by "the gentleman of letters,"[27] Xenophon, who was much, much more than a man of letters, becoming one of the classical world's greatest military historians who sought to complete the history Thucydides began but never finished, and whose adventure in Persian regime change nearly changed history, and even in failure contributed to one of the most dramatic and heroic strategic withdrawals known to military history when he led the 10,000 free men of Greece out of Persia. Noting, "If we have by chance already stolen a glimpse at the third one," the image of Socrates presented by his student Plato, "we will perhaps purse our lips at this one,"[28] and "will likely turn the pages of Xenophon's *Memorabilia of Socrates* somewhat impatiently, for here will be portrayed a man who, [though] rather shrewd to be sure, is constantly engaged in prosaically exhorting others to virtue."[29] Brodie adds in a footnote that he believes "Professor T. V. Smith's oral characterization of Xenophon's portrait as that of a 'stupid good man' ("stupidly good is the Miltonic phrase) represents a sacrifice of some degree of veracity for the admirable succinctness of epigrammatism. Of course the Xenophonic Socrates is a far duller man than the Platonic one; but 'stupid' is a very strong word, and I am afraid I cannot agree with its application in this case. For, after all, I feel even Xenophon's Socrates to be a brighter man than I."[30] Brodie writes, "Whether Xenophon was himself dull, or whether he was fitting his eulogy to dull readers, we are not quite sure—we suspect the former. Only here and there do we sense shining thru the mocking, subtlety and wit of what we feel, from our stolen glance, to be the true Socrates—the man, for instance, who would teach the courtesan the art of loving 'if (when she called at his house) another more acceptable than you be not within.'"[31] Brodie believes "the value of Xenophon's description is not to be ignored," particularly when "in trying to delineate the philosophy of Socrates, we must sift Socrates from Plato," when Xenophon's contrary assessment "will be of inestimable usefulness. If his picture is lacking in color, it has at lest (sic) the sharpness of an etching. We can cut from it an outline of the man to superimpose upon the less sharply outline, more 'impressionistic' form of our third picture" drawn by Plato, who "will provide us color aplenty."[32]

Brodie next considers his third and final image of Socrates, commencing with a reference to Emerson who wrote, "Of Plato, I hesitate to speak, lest there should be no end."[33] First Brodie considers the friendship of teacher and student, of which the "mere thought entrances us, what a drama."[34] Brodie imagines the beginning of this powerful friendship: "We muse for a moment on how they must have first met. We have a vision of the youthful Plato, stirred and prodded by the ebullition of his expression-seeking genius, yet perplexed for choice of a channel into which to pour it. He notices one day in the Lyceum a small group gathered round a single elderly man who is discoursing with them. The youth saunters over; unobtrusively he finds a place in the outer circle. At once he is enthralled."[35] As Brodie further describes this historic encounter: "Here at last is play for his restless brain; here is sagacity to match his brilliance, and character to fit his youthful ideals. In his eagerness he lets slip into the discussion a word or two; Socrates takes notice of the newcomer, his eyes shining with delight. Perhaps (if our musing holds) we see the two alone at a later time. They are walking in the street together, the quick, graceful, finely-clad, aristocratic youth measuring his pace to the deliberate walk of the poor, ill-clothed, homely man beside him. The elder man's face is perhaps earnest, that of the younger man's is glowing; they are talking together. For ordinary men to meet on their lower common level is a simple matter, but when since, in the knowledge of the world, have two other such peerless geniuses been in like communion?"[36]

Brodie further reflects on this "peerless communion" of two of history's greatest minds: "In the youth of almost any man's life there comes a meeting with another, an older man, in whom he sees embodied the consummation of his highest ideals," writes Brodie, who then cites C. H. Cooley's *Human Nature and the Social Order,* "'Every outreaching person has matters in whose . . . presence he drops resistance and becomes like clay in the hands of the potter, that they may make something better of him. He does this from a feeling that the master is more himself than he is; there is a receptive enthusiasm, a sense of new life that swallows up the old self.'"[37] Adds Brodie: "That Plato, with his unsurpassed discernment of human character, should have so taken the man for his pattern in life, and, after the man was dead, cherish all his own long and eventful life the living image of him in his memory, round which he was to carve his great work into a monument to him, is itself a mighty tribute to Socrates. It is such a thundering salute that the peals of it will never cease to be heard so long as books are read."[38] Brodie adds that this "is a monument unique in all literature and art," and in a footnote adds, "With the possible exception of Jesus, i.e., of the gospels built around him."[39] Brodie finds that "[i]n Plato Philosophy reaches her loftiest sweep, never again to attain those heights; in him Philosophy and Art walk, not arm in arm, but interfused—one. It is a philosophy of speculative brilliance, and an art of poetic loveliness. Cast in the mold of drama, speculation becomes a setting for character, and character for speculation. In all the dialogues"—with the exception, Brodie notes, of *Laws,* and perhaps the "minor role" in *Statesmen* of the "'young' Socrates"— Socrates is "a central figure, painted as he was in life."[40] And yet, asks Brodie, "how can we trust in the realism of the portrait?"

Brodie suggests we can trust in the accuracy of Plato's portrait "[m]ostly because of the singularity of the figure, and of the consistency of the singularity," and in addition, "there is an honesty in the pens of great writers; we feel that a Plato would shy from an untrue stroke as a musician from a false note. That the artistic nature of Plato should have refrained entirely from embellishments we need not maintain; but of marked idealism or caricature there seems to be none. His painting has rotundity, depth, and trueness."[41] And while Plato's Socratic dialogues are "preeminently philosophy of course," Brodie notes they "are also human dramas," since "[l]ike the classic landscapers, Plato felt even the grandest vista to be incomplete without a touch of the human," like "the deft touch of the master artist."[42] Brodie further elaborates his theme of Plato as the master portrait artist: "And all this genius of artistry, all this vitality of expression, finds outlet in his portraits; for Plato is the portrait painter supreme. Now with the pulsating exuberance of a Rubens, here with the bold, broad strokes of a Hals, there with the restrained elegance of a Van Dyke, mostly with the Rembrandtian softness of shading in lights and shadows, he plays on a mood now in this character, expressing himself thus on another; on his central figure he plays them all by turn and then together. In one place we see the tacit admiration in the murmurs of the youthful Lysis, or the gentle praise by Laches; then, with characteristic Platonic jest, the most sustained and extravagant praise of Socrates in the dialogues is placed in the mouth of a drunken reveler."[43] Mixing both Xenophon's and Plato's portrait, Brodie crafts his own distinct synthesis: "What is this composite figure that emerges? A catching figure indeed! He is a short and thick man, one who with mock lament bemoans his pot-belly. A face of almost startling ugliness, like the mask of Silenius (sic.), yet in a sense attractive. Large protruding eyes, broad features, a stubbed nose 'with nostrils looking toward heaven,' thick lips, a white beard—a face attuned to the changing mood of the discourse, the cheeks twitching in sallies of repartee, the countenance downcast in mimicked disconsolation at an argument gone askew, always a sober earnestness staring out of the buldging (sic.) eyes—it is a face that in the supreme moment can glow in transcendent nobleness. . . . He would have beauty in all things, but most of all in the soul."[44]

Brodie notes Socrates "was the constant mocker, the comic sometimes the buffoon," and "[y] et there will slip into this clownishness a moment of seriousness, and we have a confession of faith, citing *Meno*: 'Some things I have said of which I am not altogether confident. But that we shall be better and braver and less helpless if we think that we ought to inquire, than we should have been if we indulged in the idle fancy that there was no knowing and no use in searching after what we know not; that is a theme upon which I am ready to fight, in word and deed, to the utmost of my power."[45] And, Brodie concludes, "Where this creed carried him the world well knows. He might have preferred to forego the glory of martyrdom, but when offered alternatives he can see no choice. In perhaps the most serious hour of his life, *still* not without his jest, he explains to the judges of Athens that for Socrates there can only be one way of life. He is the 'gadfly' of the Athenians—his 'inner voice' wills it. Must he live without examining life? Then let him examine lifelessness."[46]

In a two-part appendix to his paper, Brodie presented his own "APOLOGIA" to Professor Smith, "The foregoing paper represents the product of a mature 'incubation'. I enjoyed writing it immensely. However, the unexpected shortening of the available time prevented the like development of a more technical approach to the Socratic and Platonic philosophies. In the next several pages I am presenting some fragmentary ideas I played with. They represent mental abortions, and are to be taken indulgently." The first, "Appendix A," is "The Daemon of Socrates," in which he recalls a friend riding a swiftly galloping horse, and "with my apprehension over her safety quite overshadowed by admiration of her boldness, she turned to me, and with a lovely and complete ingenuousness remarked, 'this damned horse won't stop!' It was such a horse that Socrates rode—his Daemon. Not a perverse animal to be sure, but a spirited and noble steed it was, headstrong, and unwaveringly carrying his rider down the course, though it led into certain mishap."[47] Brodie further probes his analogy: "But perhaps my analogy is an unhappy one. Perhaps of the two the daemon was the rider. No, we must forego the horse altogether; it was an automobile, with Socrates at the wheel, and the daemon was the back-seat driver. Whether this was his playful appellation for an imperious voice of conscience, or whether Socrates actually was a potential psychiatric patient, may remain an eternal bait for scholarly squabbles. It is perhaps more curious than significant. In the gravity of the *Apology* it seems to be something real enough. But in the *Phaedrus* it is invoked to guide an action of trifling pleasantry; that is, to guide it straightway into farce—yet he explicitly calls it a 'voice in my ear.' Somehow, an orthodox and self-respecting voice would never take part in banter. There are the two extremes. One may take one's choice."[48]

Beyond Appeasement: "Peaceful Change" and the Prevention of War

The ambiguous riddle explored by Brodie as an undergraduate at Chicago in 1932 of finding Socrates from the few portraits left to us by his students and contemporaries was for Brodie a "happy hazard." But by 1938, now a doctoral student there, he began to grapple with far more potentially harmful sorts of hazards, those associated with war and its prevention—the fundamental challenge that would define his work for another forty years. In the spring of 1938, Brodie wrote a term paper titled "Can Peaceful Change Prevent War?" for submission to his Political Science 363 course, taught by the famed scholar of war Quincy Wright, Brodie's mentor and perhaps Brodie's most important advocate as he would soon embark upon his first job quest as a young scholar. In this paper, which examined the argument, gaining strength in some quarters before World War II erupted in full fury—but an argument that Quincy Wright would passionately oppose, as a thinker and as an activist—that peaceful territorial concessions and boundary revisions could prevent war, a view later pilloried (and harshly judged by history) as appeasement to aggression but which many theorists, largely within the idealist tradition (who would soon be displaced by the harder-nosed realists) before the war hoped would prevent the escalation of violence and thus forestall the descent of Europe into another fratricidal, continental-wide contagion. In Brodie's analysis, both in its breadth and subtlety as well as its thoughtful discussion of the peaceful change advocates' effort to prevent war, one can gain a foretaste of his future theoretical development of deterrence theory, which bore many parallels with his earlier analysis of peaceful change, and can be viewed in many ways as Brodie's response to it, modifying it to reflect the darker world view of the realists, and to achieve war avoidance not by naïve hope alone, but by a more realistic mutuality of fear of the risks and dangers of nuclear destruction.

Fred Kaplan, one of just a few scholars who discuss Brodie's early, unpublished work dating back to his student years, recalls in *Wizards of Armageddon* that Brodie was "Quincy Wright's star student in his graduate student days" and when he started work on his dissertation in 1939, he "won the department's only fellowship, an award of $350, and was assigned to assist Professor Wright, then in the final phase of his leviathan," and Wright was so well taken with Brodie that he would send out "well over a dozen letters to acquaintances in top-notch colleges across the country advertising 'an A-number-one man, Bernard Brodie'" the next year.[49] In addition to learning much from Brodie, Kaplan notes Brodie "also greatly admired Jacob Viner of the economics department," and who brought to Chicago "a course new to the field of economics—the politics of international economic relations."[50] Like Wright, Viner embraced interdisciplinarity, and in contrast to so many of his generation who embraced econometrics, he came to "see the true nature of economics as an interdisciplinary subject—and one dominated by considerations of political power."[51] And so, as Kaplan observes, from Quincy Wright and Jacob Viner "Brodie learned some valuable lessons that Brodie's contemporaries in other universities were, in the main, not getting even by the end of the 1930s. From Wright, Brodie learned about the multiple causes and complexities of war" and "picked up a well-blended mix of realism and idealism," and a "view that peace relies on more than provisions of international law," counterbalanced by an understanding instilled by Wright, who had said "opinions and ideas are an element in political power no less, and perhaps more, important than armies, economic resources and geographic position."[52] Kaplan notes that Wright had "founded the Study of War project on the belief that by better understanding war one could better ensure the keeping of peace" while "[a]t the same time, he had a *Realpolitik* view of national security and was no pacifist when it came time to defending what he saw as national interests" and was a "major figure in the Hyde Park branch of the Committee to Defend America by Aiding the Allies, an anti-appeasement organization of some influence in 1939 and 1940 that favored repealing the Neutrality Act"[53]—a view that Brodie's early writings would reflect, and which would influence the younger Brodie to embrace not only realism, but to reject the moral underpinnings of appeasement, then known as *peaceful change*.

Brodie's 1938 wrote a paper for Quincy Wright's class "Can Peaceful Change Prevent War?" was on a topic, then "a popular thesis of the day," that postulated, in the face of "the decay of the postwar settlements of 1919 and a resurgence of international violence, a method must be devised of establishing procedures for allowing changes in the international system, of avoiding war by accomplishing peacefully the ends for which nations might otherwise despairingly resort to war," and thereby "serve the cause not only of peace but also of justice."[54] The peaceful change advocates would, however, become stigmatized by another word that would long haunt their effort to engineer preventive re-adjustments to international boundaries to prevent war: appeasement. As Brodie wrote in this paper, as cited by Kaplan, in a "particularly Viner-esque passage, Brodie responded: 'If change is to be effected to correct an injustice, or to rectify disequilibrium, it necessarily follows that states will find themselves called upon to make material concessions without receiving any material compensation, which they cannot be expected to do willingly.'"[55] And, importantly, using the often unspoken word *appeasement*, Brodie added, "Are we to expect the state yielding its territories to be entirely appeased by the proud contemplation of the generosity of its contribution to world order? These are questions which cannot be glossed over. If the problems they entail cannot be satisfactorily solved, we need concern ourselves no further with the idea of peaceful change."[56] Strong words, from a young man influenced by realists who approached appeasement with a healthy, and soon to be historically verified, skepticism. But after the atomic bombings in the final hours of World War II upped the ante considerably, raising the price of violent changes to the international system, Brodie would in many ways reprise his original views rejecting peaceful change so decisively, and in time would incorporate into his views on nuclear deterrence elements that would embody the arguments put forth by the advocates of peaceful change who like Brodie sought to prevent the all but certain calamity of total war as experienced, seeming without purpose, after World War I, embracing not the metaphor of Munich but that earlier haunting vision of cascading systemic collapse whose spark took place at Sarajevo.

As for the lessons Brodie learned from Viner, Kaplan writes that these "reinforced those of Wright's and added a new dimension. Power, thought Viner, could be surrendered only to something more powerful still. Governments will not lay down their swords before a world government simply out of good will or in the name of international cooperation."[57] Viner would also play an influential role later, one when Brodie was trying to make his mind up about an essential dilemma of the nuclear age: would atomic weapons stabilize or destabilize the international order? As Kaplan recounts, "On the question of whether the A-bomb would deter or foster war between the great powers, Brodie had still not made up his mind" by September 1945, a month after the historic atomic bombings of Hiroshima and Nagasaki and Tokyo's subsequent surrender, when he attended a conference at the University of Chicago and presented his thoughts, based on a "three page outline summarizing" his thoughts that would be elaborated later that fall and published as his first monograph on the implications of the atomic bomb, his 28-page November 1945, paper "The Atomic Bomb and American Security". But his old mentor Viner "had made up his mind" and during his conference talk in Chicago, he argued that the A-bomb "makes surprise an unimportant element of warfare" since now, "Retaliation in equal terms is unavoidable and in this sense the atomic bomb is a war deterrent, a peace-making force."[58] Viner, like Brodie, understood that cities "were the only efficient target of an atom-bomb attack," to which Viner added the logical argument that any atomic-armed nation would "certainly retaliate with an atomic attack of its own" if so attacked, neutralizing any advantage of striking first.[59] Kaplan cites Viner's remarks before the

American Philosophical Society in Philadelphia on November 16, 1945: "What difference will it then make whether it was Country A which had its cities destroyed at 9 a.m. and Country B which had its cities destroyed at 12 a.m., or the other way around?" This "logic was indeed unassailable, and Brodie was finally convinced."[60]

Brodie's views would soon take on their own uniqueness, distinct from those of his inter-war mentors, and after the nuclear era began his strong advocacy of deterrence and consistent rejection of more bellicose viewpoints that he believed brought greater risk by undermining the all-important goal of deterring the outbreak of nuclear war would come to reflect some similarities with the *peaceful change* school that he had initially approached, in his student years, with the same skepticism expressed by his mentors Wright and Viner. Brodie's approach to deterrence, nuanced as it was, would be perceived by some of his critics as sounding weak, in marked contrast to the more bellicose rhetoric of the warfighting school, as discussed by Fred Charles Iklé below, and epitomized Herman Kahn's hyperrealism (bordering on surrealism), as noted by Raymond Aron, the philosopher of war and student of Clausewitz whose approach to the study of war had more in common with Brodie, and who in 1970 wrote of Kahn, "He imagines, invents, and describes with minuteness bordering on unreality, dozens of situations of conflict reduced to simplified schemes, and the decisions that suit these situations. Failing science fiction, what other name but strategic fiction could one give to this form of literature?"[61] In contrast to this surrealism seen in Kahn's hyperbolic approach to nuclear war, Brodie's approach to deterrence was marked from the get go by the very same realism that had led his mentors to become skeptics of peaceful change, and all too aware of its descent from noble intention to the all too tragic consequences of appeasement.

In the pages below we will consider Brodie's early views on peaceful change in greater detail. But first, let us consider briefly the genesis of the term, its original aspirations during the interwar years, and its ultimate conflation in the popular mind with policies of appeasement, which after Munich would be largely repudiated. In his article on peaceful change in the *Max Planck Encyclopedia of Public International Law*, Hisashi Owada explains that "the term peaceful change came to acquire its specific sense in the context of the Covenant of the League of Nations, referring to the process contained in Art. 19 [of the] League Covenant," and citing I. L. Claude Jr.'s *Swords into Plowshares: The Problems and Progress of International Organization*, he notes a "conceptual line of distinction came to separate the general problem of pacific settlement from the specific problem of peaceful change," with peaceful change coming "to be regarded as denoting 'a somewhat specialized concept' that referred to 'the problem of substituting amicable for forcible methods of resolving disputes' that arose 'out of demands for alteration of the legally established status quo'. Thus peaceful change as the specific term became popular in the political and legal milieu of the interwar period."[62] Owada recalls that "during the interwar period a few incidences of peaceful change to the status quo were moderately successful, albeit not by virtue of the invocation of Art. 19," such as "during the Washington Conference of 1924" when "a diplomatic compromise was reached regarding the restoration to China of former German holdings of the Shantung Peninsula which had been given to Japan by the Versailles Peace Treaty. Similarly, the United States of America and Great Britain were able to reach agreement regarding the control of the Canton–Enderbury Islands."[63] However, Owada notes that in "these cases, however, it was not the procedures of peaceful change that accounted for these results, but the political will of the parties involved," and citing Frederick S. Dunn—whom Brodie discussed in detail in his paper on peaceful change, and who would author the introduction to *The Absolute Weapon*, "The Common Problem," the pioneering book edited by Brodie in 1946 on the challenge of nuclear weapons—"It was said on these instances that, '[i]f the will to find a settlement is present, almost any kind of procedure will do. If the will is not there, no procedure will work, no matter how elaborate.' "[64]

However, Owada notes "the resort to institutional mechanisms of peaceful change can backfire if the political will for peaceful change is not there," citing as an example, "the Agreement concluded at Munich on 29 September 1938 between Germany, Great Britain, France and Italy," known to posterity as the Munich Agreement or by just the haunting metaphor, *Munich*, which "could apparently be said to be an attempt to resort to the procedure of negotiated settlement for change, but it could not be regarded as a genuine case of peaceful change and brought about an opposite result."[65] Again citing Dunn, Owada writes that "World War II was blamed on a 'resort to procedures of peaceful change, especially the procedures which led up to the settlement at Munich.' While 'the statesmen who engineered that particular alteration of the status quo confidently believed that they were avoiding a war', it turned out to be a disastrous move because 'it disturbed the existing security system, such as it was, and turned the balance in favour of the aggressor State without gaining any comparable advantage for the Allied nations.' "[66] As Owada explains, "The Munich Agreement epitomized the danger of indiscriminately regarding any attempt for peaceful change as panacea for preventing conflict and ensuring international peace and security. It would be fair to say that the unsuccessful efforts at moderating Axis policies through diplomatic appeasement were wrongly characterized as peaceful change, since they were, in fact, based on illegitimate arbitrary decisions emanating from the desire for 'peace at any cost,' resulting in territorial amputations. Whatever the characterization of this unhappy event, it is clear that resort to procedures of peaceful change cannot effect a change that ensures sustainable peace, unless the situation emerging from such procedures is one that is endowed with legitimacy endorsed as such by the international community."[67]

Brodie starts his analysis off by noting, "In recent years, with the progressive decay of the settlements of 1919 and the alarming resurgence of violence or the threat of it to hasten this decay, or to effect other changes deemed by some states to be desirable, we have been hearing a great deal about the inevitable necessity of instituting procedures for effecting peacefully changes in the status quo."[68] He added, in what one might call Clausewitzian fashion, that "[i]n so far as they have attempted to distinguish the causes of war from the conditions in which it occurs, students of international affairs, and protagonists of world order generally, have argued the simple logic that to avoid war one must first of all seek to accomplish by other than warlike measures the ends for which states despairingly resort to it," and while this may seem "simple and reasonable enough," Brodie notes that the "only anomaly is that these thinkers apparently withhold their approval when a statesman devotes himself to the principle with such forthright ardor as does Mr. Neville Chamberlain."[69]

Brodie explains the "reasoning typical of the advocates of 'peaceful change' is, superficially at least, somewhat in this wise: territorial revision historically has with relatively few exceptions come as the eventuation of a war," and that it thus logically "follows that if needful revision could be accomplished by processes essentially peaceful, war would be unnecessary, and its suppression would cease to be so overwhelming a problem," adding that "propounders of this doctrine are finally confirmed in their views by the observation that the states today most threatening to the peace are those dissatisfied with the status quo and which feel themselves to have suffered the most damaging and humiliating wrongs in the last great territorial reallocations, that is, in the peace treaties following the World War."[70] Further supporting this view was the "negative attitude towards international cooperation to maintain the peace demonstrated by certain states which profited most extravagantly in those settlements, such as Poland, and even Italy."[71]

While Brodie finds much to criticize in the logic of the argument put forth by the peaceful change advocates, it is interesting to note their effort to prevent war by addressing its root cause (and thereby prevent the calamitous losses brought on by war) is reminiscent, to a certain degree, of the motivation, post-Hiroshima, that deterrence theorists would bring to their efforts to prevent war through the underlying threat of nuclear retaliation, and to thereby prevent an even greater calamity. The peaceful change theorists sought to avoid war by pre-emptively modifying territorial boundaries, nipping the causes of war in the bud and thereby preserving order, whereas the deterrence theorists would later seek to avoid war by mutually affirming the permanence of the post-war division of Europe (and much of the rest of the world, albeit in a less orderly fashion), and thereby pledge not to violate the new, post-armistice territorial boundaries that defined the post-war division of Europe. It may thus seem ironic that the younger Brodie, many years before digesting the full strategic implications of the splitting of the atom and the weaponization of the unlocked forces of creation, takes the peaceful change advocates to task for their logical inconsistencies, and asserts that "we can criticize this proposition on purely logical grounds,"[72] As he explains, their error "compromises, it would seem, two false assumptions: first, that war follows from the need of revision rather than merely the desire for it; second, that the revision which might be effected by a consultation of disinterested Powers based on considerations of justice would be so like the revision sought by war as to obviate recourse to it. But we know that in fact a state will go to war to effect a change not especially enjoined by considerations of justice, and that it will, if victorious, dictate a revision quite at variance with that which the above described conference would be likely to propose. War usually results from, among other things, a desire on at least one side for territorial or other aggrandizement, whether justified or not. The territorial revision follows because its provisions are considered advantageous by the victor and because the objections of the vanquished are for the time being of no consequence."[73]

Thus, Brodie observes, war "serves the eminently useful end, for purposes of conference, of nullifying the claims of one of the parties," and this explains "why the settlements following major wars are always so far reaching."[74] Brodie believes the "fallacy" of their position "to suppose that by 'peaceful change' we avoid change by violence, because the kind of change produced in the latter case is reasonably sure to be different from that of the other, unless, indeed, the 'peaceful' change is nothing other than an obeisance to the threat of force."[75] Brodie extends his criticism to "even so considered a thinker as Mr. F. S. Dunn, whose work *Peaceful Change* is so excellent an appraisal of some of the pertinent problems" and yet who "will inadvertently betray himself into referring to such *faits accomplis* as the Japanese conquest of Manchuria, the Italian conquest of Ethiopia, and the German re-militarization of the Rhineland as bearing evidence that 'no peace system can be expected to work for any length of time unless it contains adequate provisions for bringing about changes in the status quo as required by changing conditions.'"[76] Brodie further notes "[t]he Japanese rejection of the Lytton report, and Japan's retirement from the League because of the Assembly's acceptance of that report, are on the other hand incontestable proof that disinterested proposals for revision, even when striving for the utmost in conciliatoriness, will not stay the hand of the conqueror."[77]

As for "Italy's claims to revision," Brodie believes these "would certainly never be seriously entertained by a tribunal basing its decisions on principles of justice."[78] Brodie cites Gilbert Murray, who in his chapter "Revision of the Peace Treaties," in the 1933 volume edited by L. Woolf, *The Intelligent Man's Way to Prevent War* suggested that "[i]f revision on grounds of justice and self-determination were ever to be realized, the first change would be some large surrenders by Italy; a great part of the South Tyrol should go back to Austria; some Slovene districts at the head of the Adriatic to Yugoslavia; and the Dodecanese, where Italian rules has been particularly oppressive, to Greece." Brodie adds: "This was of course written before the Ethiopian venture."[79] As for the case of Germany, Brodie concedes that "[t]he principle of the demilitarized zone in the Rhineland was, to be sure, vitiated by its one-sidedness, which, with its implied perpetuation of the humiliating 'war guilt' charge, could not but chafe the pride of the German people," but he suggests that "an international committee seeking an equitable adjustment of the problem would advocate any such solution as that reached by Herr Hitler is more than questionable."[80] Brodie adds, citing Quincy Wright, that: "In justice, it is necessary to point out that the idea of 'peaceful change' as it is ordinarily conceived by writers comprises two distinct elements, of which territorial revision is often the subsidiary one. Frequently the concept foremost in their minds is of the peaceful revision of existing international law. Thus, Professor Quincy Write explicitly states that: 'Two types of political change have been and will be from time to time necessary, change in the general principles of international law and change in territorial boundaries and status.' (Wright, Q. *The Causes of War and the Conditions of Peace*, 1935, 103.) None, certainly, would quarrel with the first of these attitudes of approach, and, for that matter, scarcely with the latter either, provided there is a sufficiency of clear thinking on what is involved in the proposal to institute procedures, other than those that already exist, for the peaceful alteration of territorial status, and provided also that not too much is claimed for it as a final preventative of war."[81]

Brodie suggests that, "Most thinkers would agree, for example, with Professor Rappard's appraisal of the international anarchy that prevails as deriving in large part from the absence of any pacific means of modifying international law without the consent of all states concerned," as a result of which "[i]nternational law ... crystallizes and perpetuates many injustices, or tends to do so."[82] Thus, as Brodie explains, "Rappard conceives the international community as being 'in the position of a State whose constitution would refuse to allow for legislation by majority and which contained no provisions permitting its own amendment.' "[83] Brodie adds that "[a]ll would concur also in his affirmation that many phenomena of international importance are at present still beyond the orbit of international law. Nor would anyone dispute that it would serve the cause of peace to amend such glaringly unjust territorial distributions as have resulted from the prostration in a recent war of one of the claimants."[84]

"That," Brodie contends, "surely, is problem enough, and proposals beyond that must be regarded very critically," something Wright "undoubtedly [had] in mind in the above quoted passage, as it is implied in the statement immediately following, which reads: 'as yet states which are dissatisfied with treaties and boundaries, such as Germany, Italy, and Hungary, are not convinced that these (existing) procedures are adequate to effect even such changes as commend themselves to the general public opinion of the world.' "[85] Brodie cautions that "[o]ne can speak altogether too glibly of the necessity of formulating some peaceful procedures for accomplishing whatever changes may from time to time in the future be required, or of the potency of such a system in the expunging of war."[86] Brodie contends, as he would later in life when assessing the impact of atomic weapons on international security, that "any consistently negative approach to the problem of peaceful change must necessarily be inadequate," as "[i]n the history of human institutions and relationships, of whatever nature, from the political to the aesthetic, the reality of change has been the most persistent characteristic." He thus cites Henry B. Brewster, who was cited by Steed, H. W. in *Vital Peace* (p. 318): "The subtitle of man's history might be: Annals in the Discomfiture of the Orthodox," with Brodie suggesting "The 'Orthodox' we may interpret as meaning those who have too pervasively adjusted themselves to the status quo."[87] Brodie asserts that "Change in territorial political status we will have, since, as a glance at any historical atlas will indicate, change we most certainly have had," and consequently, "[t]he changes to be expected in the future need be neither so rapid nor so violent as those that have characterized the past. It is indeed the purpose of this paper to argue that stability in the international order must depend on reducing such change in degree and frequency, and especially on deflating its importance."[88] On the cusp of World War II, Brodie articulates a theory on the dangers of rapid change and the necessity to reduce both its degree and frequency. Only a few years later, amidst the smoldering ruins of Hiroshima and the start of what would soon evolve into the bipolar, post-war, nuclear order, Brodie would extend his thoughts on rapid and uncontrolled change and its inherent dangers to the fragility of the nuclear peace.

As he noted in 1938, "there is little reason to suspect that boundaries will ever become wholly static. And since change purchased at the price of major wars of gigantic devastation and ruin is far more dearly priced than any civilization can afford to pay, the problem of devising procedures for the peaceful establishment of territorial equilibrium, where that equilibrium is indisputably lacking, is one that must resolutely be faced."[89] Much of his post-Hiroshima theoretical work would be devoted to this very challenge.[90] Brodie worked his way through the concept on the eve of World War II, when the imagination of destruction was shaped by the devastation of World War I. The specter of nuclear destruction would greatly exceed this, creating the very mechanism that did not exist in 1938, one of absolute, unanimous, and ubiquitous fear that the price of war was one too high to pay. Brodie argues that: "we must first understand that since the peaceful change of territorial status by voluntary cession or incorporation already exists and has long existed, any discussion of new procedures of peaceful change necessarily implies constraint by the community of nations of the state that must make the requisite sacrifice. Most criticism of Article 19 of the Covenant, we ought notice, is not that it amplifies unduly the claims marked by a threat to the peace of the world, but that the decision of the Assembly must have an unanimity embarrassingly difficult to attain, and that it is only advisory and not coercive. If change is to be effected to correct an injustice, or to rectify disequilibrium, it necessarily follows that states will find themselves called upon to make material concessions without receiving any material compensation, which they cannot be expected to do willingly."[91]

If not, then we find ourselves "at once face to face with a number of questions of primary importance," such as, "What means of persuasion are intended to be employed? What is to guarantee that the changes proposed and enforced are not at the disproportionate expense of the weak states?"[92] Brodie notes that "[h]istory, even the most recent, is markedly barren of instances that would support such expectations," so "[w]hat is to prevent the disaffection of the state making the sacrifice from being quite as great an element of disruption in our international order as that of the state whose grievance is thereby to be remedied? Are we to expect the state yielding its territories to be entirely appeased by the proud contemplation of the generosity of its contribution to world order?"[93] Brodie suggests that "[t]hese are questions which cannot be glossed over," and that "[i]f the problems they entail cannot be satisfactorily solved, we need concern ourselves no further with the idea of peaceful change. It is clearly enough to give one pause, whether of faint-heartedness or mere caution."[94] A very similar set of questions would pertain to the post-Hiroshima world, though instead of world order being sustained through selfless generosity, it would instead rely upon a more prudential self-preservation.

Brodie adds that "[a]ssuming these obstacles may be overcome, it is necessary to establish our objectives in instituting our procedures of peaceful change," which he notes is intuitively obvious, as the very "term 'peaceful change' itself indicates that our primary motive in the establishment of such procedures is the prevention of war."[95] Brodie considers the prevention of war from both the long- and the short-term perspective, noting that the issue of justice is tantamount to the former but not necessarily essential to the latter: "Our presumption has been that in the long term point of view this can be secured only when the initial emphasis is on the principle of justice. But from the short term point of view the avoidance of war and the dispensing of justice may easily be antithetical."[96] Brodie proposes that by "d[i]viding the principle of the pursuit of justice into differing categories according to whether our ends are bold or modest, our objectives may be posited as being three in number."[97] These are: "first, the rectification of conspicuous injustices in the existing situation, particularly those brought about as the result of recent wars; second, the pursuit of an ideal equilibrium founded on previously deduced and generally recognized principles of justice and responsive to the recurrent need of new adjustment; third, the immediate avoidance of threatened war."[98] These three objectives would, with some modification, bear an intriguing similarity to those of nuclear deterrence, with the third perhaps being most salient in the short term, the second being longer term in nature and essential to the endurance of deterrence as a system of war-avoidance, and the third emerging only later, at the end of the Cold War, when the inherently conspicuous injustices of Soviet rule were very rapidly, and to most analysts unexpectedly, rectified, though the many proxy wars in peripheral theaters of the Cold War suggest lower-risk efforts to rectify injustice could regularly be made far from the central front, as Soviet- and Chinese-sponsored revolutionary movements sought to redress colonial grievances within a global system that could tolerate such efforts at rectification along the periphery so long as equilibrium was maintained at the center.

On his first objective, "the correction of glaring injustices," Brodie explains that "that emphasis" thus far in his analysis "was directed to those of recent origin," and that claims rooted in more distant historical wrongs lose saliency in part for reasons of "common sense," noting that "[n]o one can question that the seizure by the United States of Mexican territory in the war of 1847 was clearly a wrong as many decried on the continent of Europe in the same century. Yet who in his senses would advocate the restoration of that territory today?"[99] And further, "Such a problem as the restoration of Poland was unquestionably compromised by the century and a quarter of the non-existence or subjection of that state," just as "'righting the wrong of 1871' in respect to Alsace-Lorraine after almost fifty years was very far from being clearly unwrong in itself,' One must remember that the French refused, on rather casuistic grounds, the plebescite (sic) besought by the Germans."[100]

Brodie also suggests that "[t]he re-annexation by Denmark of the northern zone of Schleswig was similarly embarrassed by the long interim that had elapsed since 1864," and "[o]nly the unusual and far-sighted restraint of the Danish Government of 1919 prevented undue aggravation of the issue."[101] Brodie argues that "[n]ew political dominion over a territory creates a situation to which institutions tend in the long run to adjust, and often after a lapse of time 'natural' circumstances plead as much against a change as did those prevailing at the time the current regime was established."[102] Brodie further explains that "[t]his tendency varies considerably with the territory and the character of the political control, but it always exists, and itself argues powerfully against over-readiness to disturb the status quo. It is fatuous to reopen the case of a humiliation that has long since ceased to smart."[103] Brodie believes "'Historic' claims generally have been given altogether too much consideration," and that "[t]hey merit consideration only so far as an existing maladjustment can be explained by them."[104] He recalls a "recent Czechoslovakian visitor to this country commented ruefully on the European habit of beginning all disputes with references to the Year 800!"[105]

In our own time, efforts to frame contemporary conflict through a lens of historic grievances, such as we've seen in the Balkans, as well as throughout the Middle East, including the incessant conflict between Israeli and Palestine, and even American claims against Saddam Hussein (Iraqi president) from decades earlier, illustrate Brodie's point nicely. But Brodie does conceded that "we must recognize that boundary settlements of some antiquity may have caused disturbances of a serious economic character surviving undiminished into the present day" and these "surely deserve attention even, or rather particularly, when not challenged by threats of resort to violence to secure revision."[106] Brodie suggests that when "approaching the problem of the correction of obvious injustices, we must observe that they show themselves surprisingly elusive," and he considers several historical cases that illustrate some problems associated with the rectification process, and points out that "[w]e must remember that in these instances, and in many others, the same powerful considerations would have to be taken into account in any attempt at revision and would clearly militate against it. Any change, moreover, might very well cause as much discontent as it healed."[107] Brodie has found that where such "dispositions have proved ill, the remedy indicated is more frequently the revision of principles of law, both of the international and the municipal categories, than of territories," as "[t]he problems are such as would remain, in one form or another, regardless of how the territories were reallocated."[108] "Furthermore," notes Brodie, "when one in investigation uncovers a case of flagrant injustice in the post-war territorial settlements, it is as likely as not to be one about which the world as a whole hears little," and "[s]uch is not ordinarily considered as threatening to world peace, except possibly indirectly."[109] Brodie also suggests that "it is well to remember that righting ancient wrongs sometimes has embarrassing results," citing the case of Poland to illustrate his point.[110]

Brodie concludes that "[s]entimentalism may prove a good deal more disastrous in international matters than it usually does even in private affairs, and to say that there is considerable room for the development of ethical practices in the relations between nations is not to argue that every act of international brigandage committed in the last three centuries needs to be dug up and undone."[111] Further, he adds that "it may happen that what was obviously a wrong when brought about would even if of recent perpetration, be equally a wrong to adjust."[112] Brodie closes his discussion of the first objective of peaceful change by noting, "These are but a few of the difficulties bound to be met in the attempt to adjust what appear at first hand as obvious injustices," and his "close study of the various proposed changes reveals only a few of them, of relatively minor importance, to be indisputably deserving of consummation."[113] And, he adds, "This omits entirely consideration of the practical difficulties of carrying out such a procedure, which are stupendous."[114]

With regard to the second objective, "that of pursuing a maximum equilibrium responsive to changing conditions," Brodie cautions that "we must be prepared to encounter even more appalling obstacles."[115] First among these, he explains, is that "we must realize the arbitrary and changing nature of our criteria of boundary delimitation. Considered together they are inevitably found to be conflicting, yet none may be disregarded."[116] Brodie adds that "until we are certain we have eliminated war from the pattern of international relations we cannot ignore the imperative demands of strategic considerations in drawing our frontiers," and he recalls that "[i]t was not possible to disregard them in 1919."[117] As Brodie observes, "Yet strategic, or 'natural', frontiers rarely coincide with nationality or linguistic ones," and notes that the "outline of the Bohemian and Moravian provinces of Czechoslovakia was influenced considerably more by strategic than by historic or even economic claims, and it created the misfortune of the inclusion in that state of Sudeten Germans. Italy's insistence on the strongest possible military frontier resulted in the inclusion within her territories of the quarter million Tyrolese Germans, whose lot has been particularly difficult under the rigorous Fascist endeavors to 'Italianize' them. . . . Fear of future military attack and demands for precautionary frontier delimitations have created irridentas over all Europe."[118]

Brodie also considers "the question of creating economic unities," noting such frictions between states as those caused by "[n]ationalistic impediments to international trade," which "have become a most omnipresent and disjoining reality, and the total expunging of them appears quite beyond the horizon of expectable events."[119] As well, Brodie considers "the bitter striving for political domination of areas of rich natural resources," noting "[t]hat an area not so great as Connecticut and Rhode Island with a population but little larger could cause as much trouble in Europe as did Alsace-Lorraine is explained in good part by reference to the coal and the enormously rich Minette iron region in Lorraine as well as the great potash deposit in Alsace," and that "[t]he bitter dispute over Upper Silesia is a similar case, and the partition of it on the basis of an over-meticulous regard for nationality frontiers was one of the conspicuous scandals of the Peace."[120] As well, "Poland's acquisition of the eastern part is more easily explained from the circumstances below the surface of the soil than above it."[121]

As for issues of language and ethnicity, Brodie writes that "[w]hen we approach such questions as that of language, and particularly those of nationality and 'race,' we begin to have such stuff as dreams are made on. Yet these phantasmagorical elements have caused scarcely less bloodshed in Europe than the acquisitive ambitions of dynasties, and are likely in the future to completely transcend all other causes."[122] He adds that "[e]ven scholars who decry the irrationality of it in their philosophic moments are prone to accept completely the ascendancy of linguistic and nationality considerations in the less analytical portions of their discourse. And, to be sure, as the basic elements upon which peoples insist on differentiating themselves from others, they are not to be lightly dismissed."[123] But as Brodie describes, "Race, in Europe at least, is a myth, and 'nationality' a very ethereal something, yet there are a few things people are supposed to be more loath to discard or adulterate. As one journalist recently put it, every miserable back yard in Europe insists on maintaining its own 'historic' culture. So far as conserving a distinctive culture is concerned, the fact is that people do not really want to conserve it half as much as they think they do."[124] Indeed, Brodie observes that: "Culture is a kaleidoscopic thing, its trains are undergoing constant diffusion and development. Peoples are continually accepting from their neighbors, more or less eagerly, the ideas of new modes of life. The process is a direct function of the stage of communication reached by the civilization. If things are inherently good because they are 'natural,' then surely change towards the confluence of cultures is good, because it is natural. It is the attempt to hinder this process, to augment isolation rather than to break it down, that is inherently evil. The effort to make political frontiers coincide as much as possible with 'ethnic' ones is the attempt to add political factors of isolation to the existing geographic and linguistic ones. 'In applying the principle of nationality at the Peace Conference, the statesmen were using a principle already outmoded, unless combined with something else.' "[125] Adds Brodie, "Geography, the imperfections and inadequacies of communication, ancestral inheritance, will always preserve enough of regional variation of culture for those who think it necessary. It is certainly not worth any wholesale blood spilling."[126] But as Brodie points out, "Thus we see that in the matter of territorial status, the attempt to institute procedures of adjustment to the requirements of changing conditions brings us at once face to face with the fundamental problem of altogether unresolved criteria of boundary delimitation. Those we have been accustomed to consulting are mutually conflicting. When we have decided upon our principles we are likely to lack our facts."[127] And yet, when "we come to the consideration of change to prevent immediately threatened war—the type of change Mr. Chamberlain has been so assiduously cultivating at the expense of weaker states—we are not troubled by the difficulties of indeterminate criteria of revision. The recalcitrant and threatening state has ordinarily made its wants fairly plain, and it is simply the satisfaction of these wants that bring the desired end. The question is, is this *peaceful* change?"[128]

This question, more a riddle, and one that would in many ways mock Brodie well into the nuclear age, when doctrinal battles—between advocates of deterrence and those who would be described as "warfighters" for their imagination of, and preparation for, a time when deterrence failed—raged, and what Brodie called the "cogency of steel" loomed uneasily in the imaginations of both, forever unresolved: "If peaceful change is to mean anything in the implementing of a system of collective security and order, it must rigorously exclude any kind of settlement that while perchance disposing of the immediate problem only invites the final day of reckoning through placing a premium on the cogency of steel. This may, of course, leave us with the basic dilemma of peaceful change: if the use of arms is excluded, how may change be effected at all? But there is no gain in toying with an idea or a phrase if we are to employ it merely as a euphemism to characterize a procedure with which we are already too familiar. Any established procedure of change intended to promote an enduring order of peace must avoid the possibility of rewarding those governments which have threatened to upset it."[129]

Brodie suggests that the "idea of stabilizing the status quo territorially has perhaps not been given a fair hearing," and he believes the League of Nations "been criticized unjustly and excessively as a device of maintaining the status quo."[130] He adds, "Doubtlessly, the present arrangement is not an ideal one, and some few changes are in order. The few flagrant injustices ought to be rectified, and unquestionably the way must be kept open for the graduation into independent status of entities now administered as mandates or colonies. But the question remains: can the present League, or any league of nations, exist at all except on the basis of stabilizing some sort of territorial status quo?"[131] Brodie expects that "so long as there are such vast differences in kinds of government frontiers will never become unimportant," and continues: "At present, the side of a boundary an individual lives within may make an enormous difference in his possession of liberties and in his mode of life. But where is the objective norm to determine when a form of government is good or evil, when the state is well or ill governed; and who is to decide thereupon? We can no more take frontier regions from a state because we dislike the Communism, or the Fascism, of its municipal code than we can from another because we do not agree with the monarchic principle. Whether one is born to live under the relative freedom of a democracy or the regimentation of a totalitarian state depends on providence, and perhaps on the political wisdom of his forbears. Besides, what is today the most reactionary form of government and the most despotic may tomorrow make room for the most enlightened."[132]

Brodie cites the work of Professor Frederick S. Dunn, author of the 1937 work *Peaceful Change*, and as noted above, author of the introduction to *The Absolute Weapon*, "The Common Problem," who "has pointed out the ubiquitousness of the considerations of power, prestige, honor, and self-sufficiency in any suggestion or revision,"[133] to which Brodie adds: "We have already discussed the matter of strategic frontiers. These indicate very clearly the absolute and necessary *priority* of establishing a *state of peace* before we can even begin to discuss peaceful change. The maintenance of a state of peace is not concomitant with peaceful change, and most certainly does not result from it, but must precede. Else we cannot dispose of these anomalous and troublesome considerations of power . . . Certainly paradoxical would be endeavors to promote peace by proposing changes in which the likelihood of war demands first consideration."[134] Brodie next turns to classical philosophy, and the ideas of Plato, whose well-crafted image of Socrates was discussed in his earlier paper, noting that: "Plato's conception of reality residing in ideas essentially unchanging and everlasting was motivated, we must remember, in good part by his profound abhorrence of the political instability of his day. To approach the divine patterns of unchangeable perfection, in which wars were embodied the good, the true, and the beautiful, required of the philosopher unceasing effort in the contemplation and the practice of the good. We need not accept Plato's metaphysics, as few of us do, but his observation of human nature was as good as any man's and he was a far way from thinking that a 'static' political order would be likely to result in the stagnation of culture. Moreover, if we could conceive of a France, or an England, or any other state, whose outline as a state and whose pattern as one ideally governed were permanently laid up in heaven, it would give politicians on earth determined to approach that reality no time for stagnation."[135]

Brodie closes his discussion by reasserting that "we must stress again that the doubts expressed in the foregoing relative to the feasibility or the desirability of instituting new procedures of peaceful territorial change are not to be construed as ignoring those instances of injustice which do survive objective analysis as noxious to world order and offensive to our sense of decency,"[136] and that "[e]fforts surely ought to be expended on their melioration with the hope and expectation of strengthening thereby our proposed structure of world order."[137]

"But," concludes Brodie, "we cannot expect these changes to be important either in scope or in results," and that's because "[t]he accidents of history, and by that we mean mostly of war, have given us our heritage, and if we were to attempt to change its aspect we should scarcely know where to begin. History, as a great anthropologist has reminded us,[138] is a ghost with but a single story. We cannot imagine what that story would be like, were it different from what it is. Historical accident, we may be certain, will continue to resolve our changes for the future, and at best we can only hope and strive with all our beings to assure that henceforth historical accident will be less synonymous with war."[139]

The Age of Global Sea Power

Coping with the complexities of new weapons technology—even as transformational as the atomic bomb—came naturally to Brodie, whose earlier work on sea power forced him to confront the continuous evolution of doctrine, strategy, and policy, and the dynamic impact of technology change on world politics. He was fully aware of how, on the eve of World War II, there was a vocal debate over the relative supremacy (or looming obsolescence) of sea power vis-à-vis air power. On the eve of Pearl Harbor, Brodie recalls, "curiously, at that particular moment it became most fashionable to decry that apostle of modern sea power, Admiral Mahan, as a false prophet," as the "general conviction was that while sea power in the past had been invariably decisive in war and had determined the course of history, . . . it was now a clearly obsolescent factor," having been displaced by air power.[140] But as Brodie notes, "Unfortunately for Mahan's memory, he is much more often criticized than read," a fate that resembles that other great theorist of war, Clausewitz—as noted by the well-known Clausewitz scholar, Christopher Bassford, who observed that *On War* is "much more often quoted than read or understood."[141]

With regard to Mahan, the first great theorist of war whose writings Brodie came to master, Brodie points out that "in his first chapter of his most famous work he pointed out that 'the unresting progress of mankind causes continual change in the manner of fighting,'" and thus "would have been the first to welcome the modern airplane to the arsenal of naval weapons; and he would have been the first to reject doctrines which confuse the aims of military power with the tools for carrying them out."[142] Indeed, Brodie notes that the "air forces which so vitally aided the Japanese armies in their quick conquests of Malaya, the East Indies, and Burma operated from airdromes which in almost every instance had been seized by Japanese armies landed from ships," as "[t]heir local air superiorities, in other words, were derived from sea power."[143] Brodie further noted, "Many of the aircraft involved, especially the fighter planes, and all their fuel, cargoes, and maintenance crews and supplies were brought to the scene of operations in ships," as were "[m]ost of the materials that went into the construction of the British aircraft which hurled back the Luftwaffe in the Battle of Britain."[144] Thus, concluded Brodie: "It does not therefore detract in the least from the marvelous power of air forces to say that command of the sea is still as likely as formerly to be decisive in great wars, and that in fact the greatly increased quantity and complexity of equipment used in modern war has made control of the sea lanes more important than ever before."[145]

At least, Brodie later reasoned, with the equalizing effect of atomic weaponry, which would enable even a landlocked power to deliver the same retaliatory strike as the mightiest of sea powers; but even then, his initial thoughts on the sudden obsolescence of sea power would be amended, and in later editions of *A Guide to Naval Strategy*, he would acknowledge the reinvigorated role of naval power in the nuclear era. For instance, he noted that the Polaris subprogram, which as of his fifth printing in 1965, was "well on its way to completion" and which now constituted "a large and important portion of the United States strategic bombing capabilities," and which in conjunction with the hardening of land-based silos ensured that U.S. strategic missiles were now "enjoying a high degree of safety from surprise enemy attack"—thus alleviating any "pressure for 'going first' in the event of serious troubles."[146] And as the Soviet Union continued a "further retreat from a surface fleet . . . and a greater than ever concentration on submarines," Brodie postulated that the U.S. Navy "could thus anticipate the disappearance of rival surface navies," with U.S. surface forces required for both "possible limited wars" and for "showing the flag."[147] In all, Brodie concluded, "[t]he situation for American seapower at the end of the first score years of the atomic age has thus been greatly clarified," as a "totally new role has been combined with the traditional ones," and a "deep involvement in strategic retaliatory capabilities . . . combined with the traditional role of manifesting the American presence in far-off and deeply troubled regions. The fact that enemy surface navies have largely disappeared has altered the character of, but not greatly reduced the burdens on, American seapower."[148] Recalling his thesis from his first work, *Sea Power in the Machine Age*, Brodie noted the Napoleonic maxim that "the moral is to the material as three is to one," and while not always the case, evidence from history showed on many occasions that "weak ships and strong men have triumphed over strong ships and weak men," suggesting that even as "the tools of war become ever more complex and more deadly, . . . the net result of those changes on the personnel factor is to place even greater demands on the spirit and intelligence of the men who plan to wage battles."[149] So even though Americans "take such pride in (their) technological skill and . . . tremendous productive capacity," Brodie counseled that we "must beware of relying too much on the material alone."[150]

Brodie, in his final chapter of *A Guide to Naval Strategy*, examined boldness in a manner reminiscent of Napoleon and his interpreters, who like Frederick the Great concerned themselves with genius and the coup d'oeil, and like Machiavelli considered the collision of *virtu* and *fortuna* on the outcome of war. Brodie likewise embraces boldness in command, but cautions again recklessness. Again citing Napoleon, Brodie writes: "Napoleon was a firm believer in boldness."[151] Noting the tendency for commanders to be acutely aware of the danger faced by their troops while discounting or remaining unaware of the fear felt by their enemy, Brodie observes that "Napoleon recognized the universality of this feeling among leaders, and in one of his many maxims on the subject urges the general caught by surprise in a bad position not immediately attempt a retirement but adopt a menacing attitude toward the enemy in order to disconcert him and make him wonder whether he was right in assuming he had an advantage."[152] Such a bold response in the face of danger has been practiced by great generals across history, including the famed U.S. Civil War general, Grant, and the infamous Japanese World War II admiral, Togo. But Brodie acknowledges that "[o]n the other hand, a too doctrinaire belief in the merits of boldness may be exceedingly dangerous,"[153] and reconciles these views by concluding, in a manner that Machiavelli might have once uttered, and perhaps Clausewitz as well, "It is true that the gods favor the bold, usually, but they are notoriously harsh with the reckless."[154] One might, when considering the doctrinal debates that would emerge during the nuclear era, recognize this discussion on boldness, which traces its way all the way back to the classical philosophers and which was taken up in turn by all the great modern theorists of war, as especially pertinent, and one that helps to frame the otherwise ambiguous debate between the advocates of deterrence and the warfighters, who agreed on so many things, but who fundamentally disagreed on the issue of boldness, and the danger excess in this area can bring when fortune turns away.

Rather than unmitigated boldness, Brodie calls for thoughtful reflection and analysis, noting with some disappointment that "[t]he history of most of our wars has been marked by the gradual evolution of fine leadership, but only at the cost of a long, costly period of the elimination of incompetents."[155] Indeed, he notes that "Mahan's career, it might be observed, was hindered rather than promoted by his penetrating and scholarly studies,"[156] and much the same can be said of Clausewitz, who went to great effort to hide his scholarly work from his peers, writing anonymously and insisting his classic tome, *On War*, was not viewed by the public until after his death. Machiavelli had showed himself incompetent in command and spent much of his diplomatic career in lonely exile, and Jomini was wildly successful but also largely shielded from the responsibilities of command; Clausewitz, knowing that learned men earned little respect from officers, thus sought to keep his scholarly work under wraps. The path of the strategic theorist can be a lonely one, though in recent years this has begun to seem less so, a trend noted by Brodie early in the Cold War. As he wrote in *A Guide to Naval Strategy*, "Things have changed since Mahan's time, but that does not mean we can rest in our efforts at improvement," and while a "capacity for original thinking is indeed valued" this is true "only if it is combined with a fine sense of tact," a combination that then, and now, and perhaps always did "not always run together," hence the court martial of Billy Mitchell, the prophet of air power who predicted an armed clash between Japan and the United States many years before hostilities erupted. With regard to the Navy, the focus of this particular work by Brodie, but a point that could be applied across the services, he wrote "[i]ndependent and incisive thinking therefore rarely receives the preferment it deserves."[157] Hence Brodie calls for "[o]penmindedness and insistence upon vigorous thinking ought to reach down to the very beginning of the officer's career."[158] Noting how "[b]ecause of defective eyesight, the great German strategist General von Schlieffen would never have gained admission to the peacetime officer corps of any of the American armed forces," nor would "[p]oor Nelson, with a patch over one eye and with but one arm," Brodie argues that "[a]n uncommonly good brain should be ample compensation for slight physical defects," and counsels that "[w]e must remember always that the basic element of strength in any nation is not its machines but in its manhood."[159]

Such a view of manhood as a stately virtue may seem obsolete in our gender-neutral age, but at the time of Brodie's writing was hardly controversial, and much more refined than much of the neo-Darwinian thinking from the generation prior. Indeed, an equally independent-minded theorist of naval strategy from the very dawn of the twentieth century, Frederick T. Jane, authored a controversial and colorful treatise on sea power titled *Heresies of Sea Power* in which he argued that an inherent "fitness to win" overshadowed strategy itself. Jane devotes his concluding chapter to a discussion of "fitness to win," in which he elaborates upon his thesis that a natural predisposition to victory appears to trump strategical superiority, as witnessed by both Rome's defeat of Carthage and by Sparta's defeat of Athens. Jane admits that "some definition of 'Fitness to Win' should perhaps be attempted, though it must be confessed that it is a singularly elusive thing to define. So elusive indeed, that it was originally intended not to make the attempt, but to leave it at that vague conception which most of us hold of the qualities entailed. This, however, is hardly satisfactory, consequently an attempt is here made, if not to define very exactly what it is, at least to indicate to some extent what it is not."[160] Jane adds: "It has been shown throughout this work that in every war almost the only solid fact common to all is that 'the fittest to win' were the eventual victors. It has been shown that these victors often lacked technical skill equal to that of their opponents, or were tactically inferior, strategically inferior, or had not such good ships or weapons. But they always had the 'fitness to win' quality which made up for every other deficiency and brought certain victory at the last. The 'fittest to win' have never gone under before superior materiel or before superior weapons."[161]

Jane notes that, "Sometimes, as in the case of the Romans against the Carthaginians, their original deficiencies in materiel have been enormous; sometimes, as in the case of the Japanese against the Russians, they have started with a superiority (more or less) in materiel, but the eternal verity of 'fitness to win' is at once obvious if we imagine sides to have been changed."[162] And yet, "if we ask ourselves 'Why?' we certainly cannot give a clear and direct answer, we can do little if anything more than answer 'Because the Japanese were Japanese—because the Russians were Russians.' Allowing that; can we draw any real lessons of value from what the Japanese did with Japanese ships? As suggested in an earlier chapter, if Togo and his men had changed fleets and positions with Rogestvensky and his men the lessons of Tsushima would be the exact opposite of what they now are; and in similar case the lessons of Trafalgar. No one can prove this logically, but no one is likely to try to prove it otherwise."[163] Jane considers what these qualities are that ensure victory in war and observes that a "crude desire to 'kill the enemy' seems ever to have been a most valuable asset. Nelson, when he said that a good English officer should 'hate a Frenchman like the devil' was very crude, but very far-seeing. However shocking ethically, to hate the enemy with a living personal hatred is undoubtedly a most valuable practical asset."[164]

Indeed "To go further back-back to perhaps the very greatest man who ever lived—Hannibal. Hannibal was reared from early childhood to hate the Roman with all his strength. In the power of that hate, over obstacles and difficulties of the most tremendous nature, Hannibal marched to the ruin of Rome and never met with failure till the attractions of a petticoat swamped the single-mindedness of his hate, and he was no longer able to infuse into his legions the desire to kill the enemy as the mainspring of their action."[165] Thus Jane speculates, "It is probable that Fitness to Win embodies little else besides the fixed desire to kill the enemy. Good seamanship, good gunnery, good torpedo, good engineering—all these things may aid it, but apparently all are not absolutely essential. If essential, or in so far as they are essential, the desire to kill the enemy will produce them."[166] Jane's thesis is controversial in its suggestion that strategy and tactics are of far less consequence in the outcome of war than most believe and that the inherent fitness to win of the victor is the key to victory, so much so that a switch of positions, from one fleet to the other as in the case of the Japanese defeat of the Russians in 1905, would not affect the outcome, even if such a switch led to a material disadvantage of the original victor. But there is nonetheless something compelling about his thesis, and his admission by way of the title of his work, that such a view is heretical.

A less heretical perspective on naval strategy is presented by Bernard Brodie, who was known, during World War II, as a neo-Mahanian and whose works helped to educate American seamen on the broad sweep of naval history, and the fundamental principles of naval strategy. His doctoral thesis, which examined the impact of technology on naval history and was part of Quincy Wright's massive Study of War project at the University of Chicago, was published by Princeton University Press, updated by substantively unchanged, as *Sea Power in the Machine Age*, and was just one of his two book-length works on naval strategy. The other, humbly titled *A Layman's Guide to Naval Strategy*, would later be retitled at the U.S. Naval War College's request ever since it had become a handbook for America's war-time seamen, and was thus renamed *A Guide to Naval Strategy* so as to not embarrass the fighting men who depended upon this work for an introduction to naval theory, as noted by Kaplan among others.[167] In *Sea Power in the Machine Age*, Brodie starts out with a brief excerpt from Milton's *Paradise Lost*, as he did in his 1947 article "The Atomic Dilemma"—a fuller version which would later adorn the frontispiece of his 1959 *Strategy in the Missile Age*. Though many have perceived a distinctly separate pre-Hiroshima and a post-Hiroshima strategic persona in Brodie—with Kaplan famously quoting him as saying to his wife Fawn on August 7, 1945 upon reading of the incineration of Hiroshima the day before, "Everything that I have written is now obsolete"[168]—one can see a more continuous thread connecting his early work on naval strategy up to the World War II period with his post-Hiroshima strategic thinking, with his embrace of *deterrence*, the primary objective of both Mahanian-influenced American naval strategy as well as the slightly more nuanced Corbettian naval strategy as practiced by the British in the era of their long decline, planting the conceptual seed that would undergird Brodie's nuclear theories and which would drive a wedge between his own approach to the bomb and that of the military services tasked with planning for nuclear war (which would embrace a warfighting strategy that had operational plans for a failure of deterrence).

While controversial naval theorist Fred T. Jane, author of the aforementioned turn-of-the-century *Heresies of Sea Power*, had controversially swept aside most law of war, focusing on a neo-Darwinian conception of "fitness to win" as a military extension of the evolutionary battle in the "survival of the fittest," he did embrace the importance of applying our current knowledge and views of the past to the future, without which our tactics and strategies would surely become obsolete (as happened to the Carthaginians in their defeat by the lesser-skilled Romans). And it was Brodie who followed in this path, applying his pre-Hiroshima conceptions of world order, which was sustained through sea power, to his post-Hiroshima conceptions of the nuclear order, which was sustained through the mutuality of deterrence (not naval, but nuclear). It turns out that the thermonuclear-tipped intercontinental ballistic missiles (ICBMs) that were central to Brodie's *Strategy in the Missile Age* were in fact that fanciful naval innovation that Jane pondered of a sort which was beyond his generation's ability to comprehend, that wedded an expansion of radius with a global extension of the reach of artillery, making the finite naval operational radius obsolete in the face of the global strike provided by ICBMs.

W hether based on submarines or in silos on dry-ground mattered naught; a fleet of nuclear missiles would in essence turn the interior heartland of a nation into a massive, immobile air-craft carrier that did not need to move anywhere to reach its targets, fusing the essence of land war and naval strategy. Continents, islands, naval platforms, all merged, becoming launching pads for nuclear payloads capable of pinpoint accuracy anywhere on earth. It was thus naval thinking that paved the way for nuclear strategic thought, providing a framework and a legacy of global stability to pacify the horror of the bomb and render it into a tool for order, peace, and stability. Thus Brodie's inclusion (and expansion) of Milton's *Paradise Lost* illustrates the conti-nuity that he saw between the age of sea power and the nuclear age. In *Sea Power in the Machine Age*, Brodie would also cite a segment from Book Six of *Paradise Lost,* with the full support of his editor—a work he would look to for metaphorical guidance throughout his career: "Perhaps more valid Armes, Weapons more violent, when next we meet, May serve to better us, and worse our foes, Or equal what between us made the odds, In Nature none: . . . He who therefore can invent With what more forcible we may offend Our yet unwounded Enemies, or arme Our selves with like defence, to mee deserves No less than for deliverance what we owe."[169]

Brodie's first chapter of this seminal work, "Sea Power and the New Technology," notes how the "machine age came late to the navies of the world." Indeed, Brodie observes: "When the nineteenth century was approaching its halfway mark, the capital ship that ruled the seas still differed very little from its predecessor of Cromwell's time. . . . Not all the implements of sea power were unaffected by the new technology, for perhaps a fourth of all vessels of war could propel themselves by steam. But these were only the whelps of the battle fleet. The ship of the line with its towering masts was still uncorrupted by funnel or fire box. Yet before the century drew to a close, the sail of the line dissolved into history and legend. Its place was taken by a monster of steel carrying huge ordnance, propelling itself by steam, and capable of hurling destruction upon antagonists miles away. What is more, sea warfare had entered a third dimen-sion measured in depth below the surface. Each of these changes in the character of the warship and in the means of naval attack had its effect on tactics and strategy, and each influenced the relative capacities of nations to wage maritime war."[170]

Brodie, who would later in his career emerge as a modern day Clausewitzian, took his Napoleonic-era rival Jomini to task for failing to anticipate the dynamic nature of strategic change, noting that "Jomini's dictum that changes in weapons affect the practice but not the principles of war is perhaps the most reiterated pronouncement in the whole field of military lit-erature. 'Methods change, but principles are unchanging.'" And while he find this is "a doctrine reminiscent of the 'ideas' of Plato," he notes that it's "also an unassailable statement of truth, but constant repetition, as with most truths, makes it border dangerously on cant. As a dogma it has often impeded full recognition of the changes wrought by the changing implements of war."[171] Brodie suggests that it's in fact "specious to separate too sharply the principles from the methods of war. The conduct of war is not an exercise in metaphysics—it is a practice. As a practice it involves the use of certain machines, and the pursuit of military ends has always been deter-mined by the inherent potentialities or limitations of the machines with which war is waged."[172]

Thus, Brodie writes: "To speak of a naval invention as having revolutionized maritime war is not to imply that it has affected the purposes of naval warfare or even that it has altered the basic process by which those purposes are achieved. One may mean only that it has drastically changed the means of execution. These do not, however, undergo radical change without introducing wholly new circumstances and new problems in the pursuit of hostilities at sea and in preparation for them, new circumstances which affect different states very differently. However little the advance of technology has affected man's elemental human nature or the basic mores of his culture, it has transformed his mode of life, and it has similarly transformed the conduct of his quarrels."[173] Brodie adds that it's "frequently enough asserted in a general way that warfare has been revolutionized by changes in the weapons with which it is waged, but little effort has been made to determine the effect of specific inventions and to clarify their impact on world politics, past or present. It is, of course, dearly impossible to isolate the effects of a single invention from the whole current of change. It seems a little absurd to consider how naval war would be carried on today if, for example, other things remained as they are but machine propulsion were absent. Yet the endeavor to do just that may not be without value. It brings sense, integration, and perception into one's confused awareness of constant change."[174]

These words, *brings sense, integration, and perception into one's confused awareness of constant change*, captures in a nutshell what it was that Brodie, as a theorist grappling with not only technological change but the very evolution of strategic thought in response to that change, sought to achieve throughout his career, overcoming the inherent uncertainties that shroud this always-changing world—piercing the cloud of ambiguity that he first recognized many years before as student grappling with the ambiguous legacy of Socrates, applying his own instincts to a riddle forever shrouded by the mists of history. From the mists of history to the fog of war, Brodie followed a linear path, one that swapped the inconsequential study of history with the greatly consequential process of securing the future. By way of illustration, Brodie examines the early years of the steamship, when Britain feared it might place the island-state in jeopardy: "The steam warship during the early years of its existence gave rise to apprehension among the British that it had 'created a bridge across the Channel' for hostile forces. But it had, on the contrary, removed the possibility that a chance shift of wind would favor an effort at invasion. As Winston Churchill told the House of Commons on June 4, 1940, 'In the days of Napoleon . . . the same wind which would have carried his transports across the Channel might have driven away the [English] blockading fleet. There was always the chance, and it is that chance which has excited and befooled the imaginations of many Continental tyrants.' The new Continental tyrant who was stimulating Mr. Churchill's eloquence on that day also had in his mind's eye a bridge across the Channel, one made by machines which Napoleon could only have dreamed of and which were quite unaffected by mere shifts of wind. Whether these machines, roving some above the surface of the sea and others below it, could indeed create the bridge which the steam warship had failed to make was not then clear. But neither was it clear that such a bridge was still necessary to bring proud England to submission. The strangle hold of blockade would do just as well."[175] Brodie separates in his mind the short-term tactical advantages gained by the first adopter of a new technology in war-time with the longer-term strategic advantages that are associated with broader sweeps of technological change, often helping the inventor (who aspired for an immediate tactical boost) less than his opponent. As Brodie observes: "The history of warfare from antiquity to the present records innumerable attempts to secure by some new contrivance an immediate tactical advantage, perhaps a decisive one. In such inventions the essential purpose is to obtain one's end before the adversary can bring counter-measures to bear. It is the time interval that counts. The small boats introduced by the Syracusans in the Peloponnesian Wars to get under the oars of the Athenians and shoot arrows at the rowers, the bridge-like *corvus* introduced by the Romans in the Punic Wars to . . . overcome Carthaginian superiority in seamanship, the harpago used by Agrippa in the Sicilian War against Pompey for much the same purpose, and, in modern times, the Q-boat and the submarine—trawler devices used in the anti-U-boat campaign [of] the World War—these were inventions of surprise. They were also the offspring of Necessity.[1] Such examples are the romances of history—instances of cunning being joined with brawn to overcome a strong enemy."[176]

Brodie sets out for himself an ambitious goal, one he believes few are equipped intellectually to pursue, elevating himself, in his mind, to the level of Mahan, the famed Clausewitz of the sea, his first step along the road of becoming America's Clausewitz of the nuclear age. In so doing, Brodie recognizes a unique role for the theorist as distinct from the practitioner, one that is not without its own shortcomings. As Brodie describes: "One cannot begin to tell the story of the technological revolution in naval materiel without some attempt to evaluate a whole host of inventions according to relative importance. There are many traditional appraisals at hand, but one must be cautious of accepting them. Errors in these matters tend to be self-perpetuating. Historians rarely possess the knowledge of technology and of military science necessary to make such judgments for themselves, and are hence prone to accept without criticism the dicta of their predecessors. Even military experts are likely to be of little aid. Those concerned primarily with materiel are not often equipped with the scholarship and the historical insight of a Mahan. Excursions into history by writers on strategy, particularly naval strategy, have usually shown remarkable indifference to the implements with which the campaigns they analyze were carried on—the result, perhaps, of undue subservience to the doctrine of unchanging principles.[2]"[177]

Brodie explains that in order to "determine which inventions were 'most important' it is necessary to scrutinize the whole development of naval technology during the period under review and to analyze the strategic and political consequences that flowed from each major innovation."[178] He adds that the "word 'invention' should suggest a process of change, yet oddly enough it usually implies the opposite. It carries the inference that one state of equilibrium is displaced by a new equilibrium. The continuing change which any invention introduces *is* overlooked. It is impossible, as a rule, to declare that an innovation appeared at a certain time and was followed by certain specific results, since a new device no sooner appears than it proceeds to change its character."[179] This was the case in the introduction of iron armor to warships, which led to more powerful guns capable of breaching, ultimately limiting the objective of the armor itself to the ship's core systems but not the personnel, who were no longer protected by the armor from incoming fire. Thus, Brodie argue, "A military invention cannot therefore be isolated either in time or in relation to other military instruments. Moreover, the improvement of an accepted weapon may result in the appearance of a wholly new one, terrible in its potentialities. When first introduced as a military arm, the airplane served only as a valuable instrument of reconnaissance. Subsequent development of weight-carrying capacity brought forth the bomber, which serves a quite different purpose."[180] Because any effort to "describe at all completely the technological advances in the world's navies since the beginning of the industrial revolution would require an encyclopaedia of several volumes," Brodie is forced to be selective, and considers only advances that illustrate an "exclusively naval character of an invention," and which also illustrate "the relative importance of a technical development." Hence his book "considers only the 'revolutionary' inventions of the period covered" and thus omits a "host of subsidiary naval innovations which in the aggregate mount up to considerable importance."[181] In just a few short years, Brodie would devote his full attention to one, new revolutionary technology of war: the bomb.

In Chapter 21 of Brodie's *Sea Power in the Machine Age*, he discusses "Naval Invention and National Policy," in which he starts out his discussion by noting the importance of prestige, and of what Jane had called the "fitness to win," but which Brodie attributes not to nationalistic or racial characteristics but to culture and tradition: "In the politics of power, military prestige is the medium of account, and nothing gives a nation greater prestige than past military victories. The political, economic, and most of all technological conditions under which those victories were won may have changed, but this counts for little except among the most discerning few. Foreign policy tends to run along channels determined by tradition, and Powers which have been great are considered great until they are proved otherwise."[182] Adds Brodie: "To some extent this may be fortunate. For one thing, the strategic consequences of military and naval inventions—and undoubtedly other changes as well—have often been miscalculated by those living in the period in which they occur. This was true of the steam warship and to a lesser degree of the submarine; it may yet prove true of the airplane. But even more important is the fact that such a handling of national policy implies the recognition of certain non-material factors which should be considered."[183]

While his research looked back on the century of invention that preceded the world wars, he deduced a recurring theme of deterrence, as well as its underlying principles, which in a few short years he would nimbly apply to the nuclear age. While he is said to have greeted with bombing of Hiroshima with the resignation that his past work was suddenly obsolete, the parallel between his pre-nuclear naval thinking and his post-Hiroshima strategic thought is striking, with more than *Paradise Lost* connecting his 1941 *Sea Power in the Machine Age* to his 1947 article "The Atomic Dilemma" through to his 1959 *Strategy in the Missile Age*. Most students of Brodie see something of a firebreak between his early naval work and his later nuclear work, but in fact, the two works that epitomized each era were very closely connected.

Foreshadowing his own later neo-Clausewitzian conversion, Brodie addresses the fog of naval invention: "The unpredictability of the consequences of new developments in military technology must also be considered. One of the most ironic features in the history of naval inventions is the frequency with which new devices proved disadvantageous to those very countries which had most energetically furthered their progress. This may be due to one or more of three reasons: first, a mistaken interpretation of the tactical or strategic consequences bound to eventuate from a specific invention; second, failure to predict correctly the technical progress of the invention; and third, erroneous conclusions respecting the identity of the enemy country in the next war."[184] All of these reasons would rear their heads during the Cold War era and present challenges to Brodie's thinking about the bomb. Brodie notes how a new naval "development is often said to have rendered existing materiel 'obsolete,' when it merely presents a certain degree of superiority in performance or entails a new departure in design," and points out that it "is exceedingly rare that the advent of a military invention at once renders existing equipment obsolete in the sense that it is no longer worth considering in the summation of relative power among nations."[185] Hence, a "new type of warship, however radical its improvements, does not make existing ships entirely useless until it exists in such numbers that older types have no military functions left to perform. . . . Regardless of how necessary the rebuilding of the fleet may become as a consequence of a revolutionary invention, until it is rebuilt the existing fleet remains the repository of maritime power. This truism is frequently ignored in references to military inventions."[186] Brodie recalls how, "In all the ensuing competition, through the rest of the century, whenever there sailed abroad a single warship that apparently outclassed any single vessel in their own navy, Englishmen lamented the impotence of their fleet."[187] Adds Brodie: "Historians, far from exposing the absurdities in this kind of thinking, have generally tended to perpetuate them. The *Merrimac* is usually regarded as having threatened to lift the blockade of the South before being checkmated by the *Monitor*—as though it possessed a pair of seven-league-boots or a magic carpet enabling it to be everywhere at once. Much of the course of diplomacy in the immediate pre-World War period is written in terms of the *Dreadnought,* which is supposed to have rendered pre-dreadnought types of little or no use—as though those types suffered a sudden extinction of firing power and mobility."[188] Brodie further observed, "The

lexicographer's distinction between the words 'obsolete' and 'obsolescent' is useful in this connection. In the modern world, machines, whether of war or of peace, are in a state of developing
obsolescence from the moment they are completed. Old arms may still be 'valid arms,' even
though 'weapons more violent' are constantly being evolved to change the character of war."[189]

Brodie briefly considers the confidence fostered by the emergence of a secret weapon, and
the belief it may be a game-changer in the event of war, thereby inducing recklessness on the
path to war. It is interesting that upon the advent of nuclear weapons, Brodie becomes a principal theorist of nuclear caution, erecting a theoretical and doctrinal framework of restraint,
embedding the *absolute weapon* into a framework of mutual deterrence, and countering the less
cautious ideas of his colleagues, including Herman Kahn who approached the waging of nuclear
war with much less caution and restraint. "It is clear, however, that the possession of a secret
weapon, or of a new weapon against which the potential adversary is felt to be without countering agents, may be very influential in reducing the caution with which a Power would otherwise
pursue its aims. . . . Yet it makes a very great difference to the world what tools have been placed
in the hands of the potential aggressor. If the instruments at his command have given him the
means of pushing to a quick decision in war, it is obvious that all concepts of national security
must be revised. 'Defense' must then take on a more active and a more anticipatory attitude.
It was Machiavelli, too often 'taxed for his impieties,' who pointed out that to delay a war may
not always redound to the advantage of the state which wishes to avoid its greatest evils. The
tragedies of 1939 and the years following were the tragedies of a world which stood hypnotized
by the eyes of the serpent, not knowing with what terrible swiftness it could strike or how inevitably it would do so."[190]

And yet while the world "stood hypnotized by the eyes of the serpent" as much of Europe
was conquered, Brodie notes that on the sea, the situation remained less volatile: "War at sea is
ancillary to war on land, and changes in naval materiel have not been such as to affect fundamentally the relationship of sea power to land power. Even on the sea itself, much is unaltered.
The indomitable spirit at the helm and off, and the effectiveness of the combination is vastly
greater than either one would be by itself. On the other hand, it is true that the danger of aerial
invasion or at least raiding of an island like Great Britain does mean that the British Fleet can no
longer guarantee almost by itself the security of the British Isles, though the continuing importance of its protection is generally underrated."[191]

Brodie articulated a similar sentiment in his 1946 *Foreign Affairs* article, "New Tactics in
Naval Warfare," in which he observed that in World War II "sea power reached the culmination
of its influence on history" and that the "greatest of air wars and the one which saw the most
titanic battles on land was also the greatest of naval wars—not alone in the magnitude of naval
operations but also in the degree to which those operations contributed to final victory."[192] This,
Brodie explains, "could hardly have been otherwise in a war which was truly global, in which
the pooling of resources of the great Allies depended upon their ability to traverse the sea"
and to project power to "remote theaters which could be adequately serviced only by sea."[193]
So while "the land-based airplane was the original cause of the threat, the nature of the crisis
which Allied sea power met and overcame cannot be adequately described merely in terms of
ship versus aircraft," which understates the underlying and reciprocal naval dimensions of the
conflict.[194]

Even with air forces taking flight as independent military services, the interconnection of
air power to sea power endured. A full half century after Brodie wrote, air power still remains
(albeit not without some vociferous debate from air power theorists) to a substantial degree an
adjunct to sea power broadly defined, with aviation still responsible for only a small fraction
of world commerce, of which the lion's share still travels by the merchant fleet. Missile power,
however, came to offset sea power as the primary means by which the superpowers asserted

their strategic might—though ultimately the last, best guarantor of a retaliatory capability would become the stealthful ballistic nuclear submarine, and America's continued economic primacy would continue to be sustained by its unrivaled naval power on the world ocean, a naval supremacy that has endured through our time even as a new peer rises in the Far East.

In a review in the December 1944 edition of the *Pacific Historical Review*, it was noted that Brodie's *Guide to Naval Strategy*—which had first appeared in September 1942 "under the title *A Layman's Guide to Naval Strategy*," and that the "cordiality with which it was received necessitated several reprintings and the rapid unfolding of naval actions invited revisions"—that the "present edition, though following the general lines of the author's original interpretations, represents a complete rewriting, with the classic lessons of Trafalgar, Tsushima, and Jutland supplemented by illustrations drawn from battle actions as recent as the invasions of Saipan and Normandy."[195] It further noted: "Air power, Mr. Brodie freely admits, has revolutionized naval warfare," but Brodie "insists, however, that the surface ship and particularly the battleship still has the fundamental role, and certain pronounced advantages, and that the basic principles of naval strategy have not been invalidated by the addition of carriers and planes."[196]

As Brodie reflected in the pages of *Foreign Affairs* in 1946, the U.S. Navy "proved during World War II that it had the resiliency to overcome a menace of scarcely imagined magnitude," even if this "achievement lay mostly in redeeming past errors of omissions" that led to the preventable tragedy at Pearl Harbor; but the "[s]trategic and tactical doctrines which have been conclusively validated in the war just ended must nevertheless be reviewed constantly to see if they remain valid.... In that respect the atomic bomb merely accentuates the necessity for flexibility in tactical conceptions" and also "introduces the possibility that in another general war the utility of navies will be decided ashore rather than at sea," since a "nation which has had its entire economy destroyed may be able to put a fleet to scant use," and this means "traditional concepts of military security which this country has developed over the past fifty years—in which the Navy was correctly avowed to be our 'first line of defense'—must be reconsidered," as unpopular as that may have sounded to fleet commanders still rightfully proud of their "indubitably superb accomplishment in the greatest of all naval wars."[197]

Ironically, Brodie's thinking on sea power would very soon be overlooked by many scholars, who in their zeal to reconsider those traditional concepts of military security, would look to Brodie as one of the founding architects of the new nuclear order; but the clarity of his naval thought, and its endurance after half a century and more, continues to provide us with compelling reason to revisit his pre-nuclear thinking. In the end, as we will see in the pages below, Brodie's most enduring contribution to strategic studies is not that made by his study of sea power, nor to his pioneering contribution to the study of strategic nuclear power and sophisticated development of deterrence as a theory and a strategy, but to his contribution to understanding the broader sweep of military history and the constant influence that technological change has had—and continues to have—upon its flow. Brodie's expertise in sea power would provide him with insights from the naval services that would serve him especially well as he grappled with the implications of the atomic bomb after August 6, 1945, and a few years after that with the even more daunting thermonuclear superbomb. Sea power, in contrast to land power and even air power, was an especially subtle realm of military power, one that more intuitively comprehended the complex workings of deterrence, which was rooted in both material and nonmaterial forces. As Brodie would observe in his 1959 *Strategy in the Missile Age*, in his concluding discussion of "The Problem of Stability," that deterrence "after all depends on a subjective feeling which we are trying to create in the opponent's mind, a feeling compounded of respect and fear," and he cautions that it may be "possible to overshoot the mark," and to make the opponent "fear us too much, especially if what we make him fear is our over-readiness to react."[198] Brodie counsels that the "effective operation of deterrence over the long-term requires that the other party be willing to live with our possession of the capability upon which it rests," noting that this "issue is an old one" and was "implicit in the phrase 'sabre rattling,'" or "[a]s Admiral A. T. Mahan observed: 'Force is never more operative than when it is known to exist but is not brandished.'"[199] Or as Brodie extracts from Mahan's naval insight, "Conspicuous aggressiveness in the handling of armaments does not always pacify the opponent."[200]

Brodie's thinking about the enduring relevance of sea power in a world that, at the time, seemed more enthralled by the rise of air power and its promise transform modern war, took place in those ominous years as Hitler's power and ambitions grew, and after Japan's surprise attack on Pearl Harbor would help catapult him to an impressive level of military influence during World War II, particularly for a civilian strategist—one of the first civilian defense intellectuals of the World War II era who would define a new pillar of strategic influence for the nascent world power that would come to be known under various monikers including the "best and the brightest," the "civilian–scientific strategists," and later on as the "wizards of Armageddon." Brodie's book would become ubiquitous on America's ships of war and in the Navy's ROTC classrooms as his once-titled *A Layman's Guide to Naval Strategy* was rechristened *A Guide to Naval Strategy* and provided to thousands of America's wartime seamen, providing an early renown that would carry him across the atomic threshold into the new nuclear world, one of the first strategic thinkers to comprehend the revolutionary implications of the shocking incineration of Hiroshima, and who would presciently respond to the new challenges that were to follow, from the inevitable end to America's brief atomic monopoly to the dangerous thermonuclear stalemate of his latter years. Brodie's willingness to transcend the specificity of the now and to instead probe for deeper, more enduring truths about so fundamental an issue of world order ensured that his work would remain relevant not only to his time, but to our time as well—and beyond.

Technologies evolve, world orders rise and fall, but the fundamental relationships of technology to war, and of war to policy, remain constants in a world of dynamic change. And central to Brodie's body of work was the enigmatic but all-important relationship of war to politics, and it was the determination and sophistication of his lifelong effort to illuminate this complex interrelationship that would set him apart from his peers, and elevate him to a distinguished status shared by only a small handful of strategic thinkers across the ages—and which would justify his being remembered as America's very own Clausewitz of the nuclear age.

After Hiroshima: "Everything that I Have Written is Obsolete"

Fred Kaplan, in his *Wizards of Armageddon*, recalls an incident on August 7, 1945, the morning after Hiroshima was destroyed by a single atomic bomb. Half a world away, newly appointed Yale political scientist Bernard Brodie was out driving with his wife Fawn to purchase that morning's *New York Times*, and when he saw its banner headline, it "riveted his attention: 'First Atomic Bomb Dropped on Japan; Missile is Equal to 20,000 Tons of TNT,'" with smaller headlines proclaiming: "New Age Ushered," "Day of Atomic Energy Hailed by President, Revealing Weapon," "Hiroshima is Target," "'Impenetrable' Cloud of Dust Hides City After Single Bomb Strike." As Kaplan recounted, "Brodie read just two paragraphs of the story that followed, looked up for a few seconds, turned to his wife and said, 'Everything that I have written is obsolete.'"[201] Brodie had started at Yale just a week before, on August 1, Kaplan added that "Brodie was not the only one for whom everything turned obsolete that morning. The whole conception of modern warfare, the nature of international relations, the question of world order, the function of weaponry, had to be thought through again. Nobody knew the answers; initially, not many had even the right questions. From these ashes an entire intellectual community would create itself, a new elite that would eventually emerge as a power elite, and whose power would come not from wealth or family or brass stripes, but from their having conceived and elaborated a set of ideas."[202] And "[i]n those first months following Hiroshima and Nagasaki, Yale University would become a prime mover on the thinking about how to live with the bomb, and Bernard Brodie was at the center of that movement."[203] On the threshold of the nuclear age, Brodie was best known for his popular books on naval strategy and as Kaplan recounts, the title to his 1942 *A Layman's Guide to Naval Strategy* (which in later printings, at the request of the Navy which assigned it to its ROTC courses, was shortened to *A Guide to Naval Strategy*). Then, with the dropping of those two atomic bombs, the world had suddenly changed. As Kaplan recounted, "When Brodie came to his office . . . the next day, Bill Fox greeted him with the same question Brodie had essentially posed to himself only a few seconds after glancing at the front page of the newspaper earlier that morning. 'Where does this leave you with your battleships?' Fox asked. Brodie, still somewhat baffled, just shrugged."[204]

Notes

[1] Barry Steiner, *Bernard Brodie and the Foundations of American Nuclear Strategy* (Lawrence, Kansas: University Press of Kansas, 1991), 7 citing Brodie, "Strategy as a Science," *World Politics* 1 (July 1949).

[2] Marc Trachtenberg, "Strategic Thought in America, 1952–1966," *Political Science Quarterly* 104, No. 2 (1989), 301.

[3] Roman Kolkowicz, ed., *Dilemmas of Nuclear Strategy* (London: Frank Cass, 1987), 5.

[4] Kolkowicz, ed., *Dilemmas of Nuclear Strategy*, 5. As Kolkowicz further described: "He found Clausewitz's metaphor 'War has its own language, but not its own logic' to be the 'single most important idea in all strategy' because the use of military force must at all times be determined by political decision and rational purpose. He asserted therefore the need to be aware of the 'inevitable limitations and imperfections of scientific method in strategic analysis and decision-making' and to understand that 'the most basic issues of strategy often do not lend themselves to scientific analysis . . . because they are laden with value judgments and therefore tend to escape any kind of disciplined thought'. In other words, 'war would only be senseless destruction if it were not in pursuit of some valid political objective'. Brodie, like Clausewitz before him, was concerned lest strategy became an abstract, excessively theoretical science of war and thus became detached from its guiding and constraining political context. Above all, Brodie asserted, before leaders consider the use of military force, they must ask 'De quoi s'agit-il?' Can nuclear weapons still be considered military usable and politically rational? He asked, 'Should we abandon deterrence strategies in favor of war-winning strategies? But what does this mean?'"

[5] Kolkowicz, *Dilemmas of Nuclear Strategy*, 6.

[6] Robert McNamara, "The Military Role of Nuclear Weapons: Perceptions and Misperceptions," *Foreign Affairs* 62 (1983): 59–81; 79.

[7-9] Marc Trachtenberg, *History and Strategy* (Princeton: Princeton University Press, 1991), 4.

[10] In 1992, Herken authored *Cardinal Choices: Presidential Science Advising from the Atomic Bomb to SDI* (Oxford University Press, 1992), which extended his examination of the Cold War's greatest minds to the efforts by scientists to influence presidential policy starting with the atomic scientists who lobbied successfully for the Manhattan Project during World War II, and which breathed institutional momentum into the new partnership between civilian advisors and the makers of American defense and security policy, a partnership that Brodie was both part of, and which Brodie wrote about, throughout his career. A decade later, Herken authored *Brotherhood of the Bomb: The Tangled Lives and Loyalties of Robert Oppenheimer, Ernest Lawrence, and Edward Teller*, published by Henry Holt in 2002, which covered ground similar to that covered by Herb York in his 1976 *The Advisors: Oppenheimer, Teller, and the Superbomb* (W. H. Freeman & Co., reissued by Stanford University Press in 2009) among other works covering the H-bomb's creation and the epic political battles and debates that led to the superbomb or 'Super.' In 2007, Peter D. Smith authored *Doomsday Men*, published by St. Martin's (paperback in 2008 from Penguin) examining the scientists of the Manhattan Project more broadly; and in 2008, Alex Abella's *Soldiers of Reason* that recounted the history of the RAND Corporation was published by Houghton

Mifflin (paperback in 2009); David Hoffman's Pulitzer Prize winning *The Dead Hand* examining the Russian side of the strategic nuclear community was also published in 2009, by Anchor Books. Interest in the nuclear era appeared to be on the rise once more. In 2005, Harvard University Press published Sharon Ghamari-Tabrizi's *The Worlds of Herman Kahn: The Intuitive Science of Thermonuclear War* and Herman Kahn's best-selling 1960 tome, *On Thermonuclear War*, was brought back into print by Transaction in 2007, with *On Escalation: Metaphors and Scenarios* following in 2009, with a new foreword by Thomas Schelling. And a new anthology of Herman Kahn's 'classic' writings was published in 2009: Paul Dragos Aligica and Kenneth R. Weinstein, eds. *The Essential Herman Kahn* (Lexington Books, 2009). These works have contributed to a revival in interest in Herman Kahn's work, and this suggests there is much potential for a similar renaissance of interest in Brodie's theoretically more elegant and rigorous work. More recently, in 2009, Fred Kaplan's *1959* was published by Wiley—focusing on this often overlooked year that immediately preceded the tumultuous decade of the 1960s but which played a pivotal historical role that Kaplan believes proved transformative, and thereby enabled the phenomenon of the sixties to transpire—with a chapter on Herman Kahn that drew heavily from Ghamari-Tabrizi's work as well as his earlier *Wizards of Armageddon*, but which offered no such chapter on Brodie's work, even though it was in 1959 that Brodie's seminal *Strategy in the Missile Age* was published.

[11] Articles and chapters that focus on or at least prominently feature Brodie include: Bevan M. French, "Brodie Discusses 'Limited' Conflicts, Says All-Out War is 'Meaningless'," *The Dartmouth* CXV, No. 126 (March 20, 1956), 1; John W. Chapman, "American Strategic Thinking," *Air University Review* (January–February 1967); Fred Charles Iklé, "When the Fighting Has to Stop: The Arguments about Escalation," *World Politics* 19, No. 4 (July 1967), 692–707; Richard L. Curl, "Strategic Doctrine in the Nuclear Age," *Strategic Review* 3 (Winter 1975), 46–56; Reginald C. Stuart, "Clausewitz and the Americans: Bernard Brodie and Others on War and Policy," in Brian Bond and Ian Roy, eds, *War and Society: A Yearbook in Military History* (New York: Holmes & Meier Publishers, 1977), 166–72; Thomas Schelling's obituary of Brodie upon his death in 1978, "Brodie (1910–1978)," *International Security* (Winter 1978), 23; a similarly laudatory tribute on Brodie's passing in *Arms Control Today*, "Bernard Brodie 1910–1978," *Arms Control Today* (February 1979), 10; William P. Snyder and John A. MacIntyre, Jr., "Bernard Brodie: America's Prophetic Strategic Thinker," *Parameters* XI, No. 4 (1981); Jeffrey D. Porro, "The Policy War: Brodie vs. Kahn," *The Bulletin of the Atomic Scientists* 38, No. 6 (June/July 1982), 16–19; Craig D. Wildrick, "Bernard Brodie: Pioneer of the Strategy of Deterrence," *Military Review*, October 1983, 39–45; Barry Steiner, "Using the Absolute Weapon: Early Ideas of Bernard Brodie on Atomic Strategy," ACIS Working Paper No. 44 (January 1984), Center for International and Strategic Affairs, UCLA (which also appeared in the *Journal of Strategic Studies* 7, No. 4 (December 1984), 365–93) and which, as noted above, became Chapter 2 in Steiner's 1991 book-length monograph, *Bernard Brodie and the American Study of Nuclear Strategy*; Gregg Herken, "The Not-Quite-Absolute Weapon: Deterrence and the Legacy of Bernard Brodie," in Roman Kolkowicz, ed., *Dilemmas of Nuclear Strategy* (London: Frank Cass & Co., 1987), 15–24; Marc Trachtenberg, "Strategic Thought in America: 1952–1966," *Political Science Quarterly* (Summer 1989), 301–34, which first appeared as his concluding retrospective at the end of his multi-volume anthology, *The Development of American Strategic Thought* (New York and London: Garland Publishing, 1987–1988) and which became, in extended form, his first chapter in *History and Strategy* (Princeton: Princeton University Press, 1991) and whose knowledge of Brodie's writings, published and unpublished, is extensive; William Huntington, "Clausewitz and Strategy in the Missile Age: A Critique of Bernard Brodie's Strategic Thought," a paper submitted to Foundations of National Security Strategy, National War College, October 9, 1990; Ken Booth, "Bernard Brodie" in John Baylis and John Garnett, eds., *Makers of Nuclear Strategy* (London: Pinters Press, 1991), for which Kaplan's *Wizards of Armageddon* served as a major historical source, and whose position as the first chapter of this anthology signifies Brodie's foundational role at the forefront of nuclear strategy (this chapter is also referenced in the literature occasionally as "Bernard Brodie: The Absolute Strategist," a fitting title); Michael Howard, "Brodie, Wohlstetter and American Nuclear Strategy," *Survival* 34, No. 2 (Summer 1992), 107–16; and of course, Barry Steiner's 1991 book, *Bernard Brodie and the Foundations of American Nuclear Strategy*, focused in its entirety on Brodie's evolving and enduring strategic influence.

[12-14] Ken Booth, "Bernard Brodie," in John Baylis and John Garnett, eds, *Makers of Nuclear Strategy* (London: Pinters Press, 1991), 51.

[15] See the chronological listing of Brodie's works, including his books; papers, reports, lectures, and chapters; and articles, located just after the Bibliography.

[16-18] Booth, "Bernard Brodie," 19.

[19-20] Booth, "Bernard Brodie," 20.

[21-43] Bernard Brodie, "In Quest of Socrates: Man and Philosopher," Paper Submitted to Course 101, Department of Philosophy, University of Chicago, December 1932, 1, Bernard Brodie Papers (Collection 1223), Department of Special Collections, Charles E. Young. Research Library, UCLA, pages 1–2; 2; 2; 3; 3; 3; 4; 4; 4; 4; 5; 5; 5; 5–6; 6; 6; 7 ,7 8; 10–11, respectively.

[44] Brodie, "In Quest of Socrates: Man and Philosopher," 11–12. Socrates is further synthesized by Brodie: "There is in him a total, almost disconcerting freedom from vanity; he remains unabashed by the most brilliant display of splendor. Abstemiousness is not only convenient for a poor man, he says, but good in itself. To be inurred (sic) to hardships is not to suffer from them. We have Xenophon's charming remark that 'he took only so much food as he could eat with a keen relish; and, to this end, he came to his meals so disposed that his appetite for his meat was the sauce to it.' Nevertheless, on occasion, for conviviality's sake— discussion being the only luxury he cannot dispense with—he can be the gourmand; he can be the one who, having drunk more than anyone in the company, will cast his glance about at the recumbent figures on the floor, and, going out to meet the rising sun, will pass the day as usual. The son of a midwife, he is himself a 'midwife of other men's ideas'. The same lips that discourse on poetry will continually call to witness the cobblers, the horse-trainers, and the pack-asses. He is an argument-mad man. He can be led about by the bait of proffered argument like 'a cow after a bucket of grain.' He is a stranger to the refreshing countryside, for his love of learning will not suffer him to leave the city's gates. If Phaedrus will threaten to withold (sic) all discussion in the future unless Socrates compiles with his wishes, the capitulation of 'this poor lover of discourse' is immediate. Like argument, so beauty. His love for music will bring him to learn the harp in his old age, tho the other pupils will laugh at him and call their teacher 'grand-papa's master'."

[45-6] Brodie, "In Quest of Socrates: Man and Philosopher," 16–17, 17, respectively.

[47-8] Brodie, "In Quest of Socrates: Man and Philosopher," Appendix A, i, i–ii, respectively. In his "Appendix B, The Ethics of Socrates," Brodie revisits the thorny challenging of separating Plato from his Socrates: "On the question, in the Platonic dialogues, of precisely where Socrates' philosophy ends and Plato's begins, there has been a general, and I think healthy, unanimity of disagreement," and Brodie concludes that it's "only from an extended and close reading of the dialogues that one can begin to *intuit* the distinction. One can begin to sense where Plato speaks [through] Socrates, or where the words of Socrates seem to ring joyously true. That the words of other scholars whom one has read may lie in the back of one's mind to warm one's own conclusions is unquestionably true. That one's demarcation may be wholly erroneous is also more than possible. Let the student recognize the difficulty and take his chances; it is at worst a happy hazard." Brodie, "In Quest of Socrates: Man and Philosopher," Appendix B, iv–v.

[49-60] Fred Kaplan, *The Wizards of Armageddon* (Stanford: Stanford University Press, 1991), p. 14; 14; 14; 15; 15; 15; 15; 16; 15; 27; 27; 27 respectively.

[61] Raymond Aron, "Modern Strategic Thought," tr. J. E. Gabriel, *Problems of Modern Strategy* (New York: Praeger, 1970), 31. As cited by Barry D. Watts, *The Foundations of U.S. Air Doctrine: The Problem of Friction in War* (Maxwell AFB, Alabama: Air University Press, December 1984), 103, n. 91.

[62-7] Hisashi Owada, "Peaceful Change," *Max Planck Encyclopedia of Public International Law*, Section 3, www.mpepil.com/sample_article?id=/epil/entries/law-9780199231690-e1452&recno=19&, citing I.L. Claude Jr., *Swords into Plowshares: The Problems and Progress of International Organization* 4th edition (New York: Random House, 1971), 222; Section 17; Section 17, citing F. S. Dunn, "Law and Peaceful Change," *American Society of International Law Proceedings* 38 (1944), 65; Section 18, citing F.S. Dunn, "Law and Peaceful Change," *American Society of International Law Proceedings* 38 (1944), 63; Section 18 citing F. S. Dunn, "Law and Peaceful Change," *American Society of International Law Proceedings* 38 (1944), 63; Section 19, respectively.

[68-105] Bernard Brodie, "Can Peaceful Change Prevent War?" Term Paper Submitted to Political Science 363, Spring 1938, University of Chicago, 1; 1; 1–2; 2; 2; 2; 3; 3; 3 (citing Dunn, F. S., *Peaceful Change*, 1937, 2); 3; 3–4; 4; 4; 4–5; 5; 5 (citing Rappard, W. E., "The Beginnings of World Government," in *Problems of Peace, Fifth Series*, 16); 5; 6; 6; 6; 6–7; 6–7; 7; 7; 7–8; 8; 8; 8; 8; 8; 8–9; 9; 9; 9; 9–10; 10; 10; 10, respectively.

[106] Brodie, "Can Peaceful Change Prevent War?" 10. Brodie writes one "telling example is the boundary between Belgium and Holland which gives the latter control and jurisdiction of the lower Scheldt, Belgium's great highway and only real outlet to the sea. Yet this line was fixed in the sixteenth century, when the strong Dutch were able to advantage themselves at the expense of a weak Spain in delimiting the northern

boundary of the Spanish Netherlands. It was confirmed in the Treaty of Westphalia (1648) and, for 'historic' reasons, was chosen as the logical boundary between the two countries in the Treaty of 1839. This has always caused the Belgians much dissatisfaction, on cogent economic grounds, but it was impossible to satisfy Belgium on this matter in 1919 because obviously Holland was not one of the defeated Powers." From Brodie, "Can Peaceful Change Prevent War?" 10–11, citing Haskins, C. H., and Lord, R. H., *Some Problems of the Peace Conference*, 1920, 62 ff.

[107-9] Brodie, "Can Peaceful Change Prevent War?" 12; 12; 12–13, respectively.

[110] Brodie, "Can Peaceful Change Prevent War?" 13. Brodie further noted, "During the Nineteenth Century, expressions of sentimental commiseration for the poor oppressed Poles never ceased to trickle from the pens of high-minded and moral authors, and, considering the quality of the Czarist government at least, there was good reason for it. In the war years, the trickle became a deluge. President Wilson himself was particularly soft on this very issue, giving it a hallowed prominence among his Fourteen Points. But the paeans of rejoicing that resounded through the press and the drawing rooms of the world at the renascence of that state whose people were universally adjudged as so preeminently gifted must at recollection bring blushes to the cheeks of their authors. No one now would wish that the restitution of Poland had never been accomplished—she remains, for the time being, an invaluable buffer state between the gloweringly hostile states of the Soviets and the Nazis—but neither would anyone deny that she early proved herself the *infant terrible* of the Peace Conference. Even at present her cooperation in the collective effort to maintain the peace is far from gratifying." Brodie, "Can Peaceful Change Prevent War?" 13–14.

[111-25] Brodie, "Can Peaceful Change Prevent War?" 14; 15; 15; 15; 15–16; 16; 16; 16 (citing Lore, L., "Tyrol Germans Don't Count," *The Nation*, May 21, 1938); 17; 17–18; 18–19; 19; 20; 20 (citing Webster, *loc. cit.*, pp. 18 f.), respectively.

[126] Brodie, "Can Peaceful Change Prevent War?" 21. Indeed, as Brodie observes on page 22: "Complete national unity is impossible to attain and dangerous to strive for, and we ought to remember that it might not be intrinsically desirable if it were attainable. The need is of such limitations and controls upon national sovereignty that a minority may be permitted to conserve its language, if it thinks that overwhelmingly essential, without necessarily altering the political dominion. Linguistic boundaries, especially in the open country, change remarkably little, even through several centuries." Brodie adds, "if our proposed future adjustments are nevertheless going to be concerned with realignment according to possible changing linguistic or ethnic conditions, we shall be encouraging ruthless assimilation of minorities as well as iron bars on immigration, the very phenomena we wish to avoid. Complete assurance of maintaining the territorial status quo would be certain at least to result in the more liberal treatment of minorities."

[127-8] Brodie, "Can Peaceful Change Prevent War?" 25; 25, respectively.

[129] Brodie, "Can Peaceful Change Prevent War?" 27. Brodie elaborates: "Limiting ourselves to a consideration of efforts towards change otherwise motivated than by threats of violence, we find ourselves wondering if we are not pursuing a fanciful vision. We have not even attempted to analyze the practical difficulties of providing means of effecting territorial revisions in peacetime. We have found ourselves sufficiently impeded by an attempt to resolve our principles. We find that even the modestly ambitious project of ameliorating conspicuous injustices presents ideological difficulties. When we set our goal somewhat higher we are beset by a confusion of mutually contradictory principles of determination and a poverty of pertinent, impartial information."Peaceful change on the basis of justice, moreover, even if we could accomplish it, would not obviate resort to force on the part of governments to whom justice is a principle of no great compulsion in their conduct of foreign policy. Besides, the situation in Europe being what it is, no maximum objective justice could be attained without certain states nevertheless feeling themselves to have been unjustly treated. When we consider in addition to this the periodic excrescence of such doctrines as that now promulgated by the Nazi Government that all peoples of "German nationality" must be included in the German Reich, regardless of whatever other minorities are thereby included, it is difficult to see how the propounders of the idea of peaceful change can expect so much of it." Brodie, "Can Peaceful Change Prevent War?" 27–8.

[130-3] Brodie, "Can Peaceful Change Prevent War?" 28; 28; 29–30; 30, respectively.

[134] Brodie, "Can Peaceful Change Prevent War, 30. Brodie cites Dunn, *Peaceful Change*, 1937, 11 ff: "The things which nations value most highly and for which they are prepared to go to war are the things which bear upon their power to make war . . . Any proposed change which would noticeably alter the existing

power ratio to the disadvantage of any state is fairly certain to be resisted tenaciously, regardless of the justice of the claim or of its bearing upon the general welfare of the community." He then comments: "Certainly paradoxical would be endeavors to promote peace by proposing changes in which the likelihood of war demands first consideration."

[135-9] Brodie, "Can Peaceful Change Prevent War?" 33; 33; 34; 34 (citing Dr. Alexander Goldenweiser, "in a popular lecture at the University of Chicago"); 34, respectively.

[140] Bernard Brodie, *A Guide to Naval Strategy* (New York: Praeger, 1965), Fifth Edition, 2. Originally published as *A Layman's Guide to Naval Strategy*. Princeton: Princeton University Press, 1942.

[141] Brodie's comment from Brodie, *A Guide to Naval Strategy* (New York: Praeger, 1965), Fifth Edition, 2. Originally published as *A Layman's Guide to Naval Strategy*. Princeton: Princeton University Press, 1942; Bassford's comment is from Christopher Bassford, "Review Essay: Carl von Clausewitz, *On War* (Berlin, 1832)," posted online at: www.clausewitz.com/readings/Bassford/DefAnReview.htm, originally published in *Defense Analysis*, June 1996.

[142-59] Brodie, *A Guide to Naval Strategy*, 2; 3; 3; 3; 245; 246–7; 248; 248; 254; 253; 255; 257; 263; 263; 263; 263; 264, respectively.

[160-6] Frederick T. Jane, *Heresies of Sea Power* (London: Longmans, Green, 1906), 321; 321; 322; 322–3; 324; 325; 326, respectively.

[167-8] Fred Kaplan, *Wizards of Armageddon*, 9, 10 respectively.

[169-91] Brodie, *Sea Power in the Machine Age* (Princeton: Princeton University Press, 1941), 2; 3; 3–4; 4; 4; 4; 5; 7 (Brodie notes in this paragraph, note number one, that: "In that portion of his poem from which the frontispiece of this book is taken, Milton depicts an incident in the war in Heaven which perfectly illustrates this type of invention. To overcome the advantage of the loyal angels, Satan invents the field gun, and he proceeds to employ it in a manner calculated to reap the maximum benefit of surprise. Bk. VI, lines 438–669"); 8 (in note 2, Brodie adds: "Note 2: A notable exception is Admiral William L. Rodgers. See his *Greek and Roman Naval Warfare* (Annapolis, 1937) and his *Naval Warfare Under Oars, Fourth to Sixteenth Centuries* (Annapolis, 1939)"); 8; 8; 9; 9; 431–2 (In the language of the day, Brodie's discussion of the non-material factors of war echoes Jane's conception of the fitness to win at the dawn of the century: "For, despite what sociologists tell us about the ambiguous and loose thinking by which 'racial' traits are usually discovered in nations—and they are no doubt right—the events of 1939 to 1941 have proved that there are some nationalities which can persistently win battles against odds and others which as consistently lose even when the odds are on their side. True, it is culture and tradition rather than race which accounts for it, but it is nevertheless a factor, and one which may upset estimates based on appraisals of material strength alone. It was easy to say in the summer of 1940 that Great Britain could not possibly win against the odds that faced her, and that her decisive defeat before the end of the year was to be expected. Yet somewhere deep down in the national heritage was a trait which refused to admit defeat—a trait which had somehow survived more than a century of industrial revolution and a generation of political disillusionment." Brodie would later become familiar with the language of Clausewitzian theory, and its own vocabulary to describe the non-material factors, known as the *frictional* dimensions of war); 431–2; 441; 441–2; 442; 443; 443; 445; 446–7; 447–8 (indeed, Brodie adds "The fact that the British Isles were not invaded in 1940 could hardly be due exclusively to a British air force, which was far inferior in power to the German Luftwaffe, nor could it be due to a British army which was disorganized and virtually disarmed. The question of whether the airplane will eventually replace the surface merchant vessel as the carrier of the bulk of ocean commerce needs also to be answered, though there has been a good deal of rank nonsense written on the subject. If such a change should occur, sea power as we have known it in the past will no longer have any reason for being. The most that can be said today, however, is that such a change, if it is at all possible, is still far in the future"), respectively.

[192-4] Bernard Brodie, "New Tactics in Naval Warfare," *Foreign Affairs* 24, no. 2 (January 1946), 210; 210; 210, respectively (in the Winter 1943 edition of *Isis*, Whittier College's Alfred Romer observed that in *Sea Power in the Machine Age*, "Brodie has traced the detailed history of the five great, essentially naval, inventions which produced it: the steam warship, armor and great ordnance, submarine modes of warfare, and naval aircraft," and that it was, overall, a "thorough study well-documented and indexed, and written with professional detachment." He noted Brodie's sweeping effort illustrates that, "Politics and technology were curiously mixed in the introduction of the new devices"—perhaps the seed from which Brodie would, by 1945 (at least tentatively) and by the early 1950s both more forcefully and frequently, link to the famous

Clausewitzian dictum that war is a continuation of politics by other means. Alfred Romer, "Review: Sea Power in the Machine Age," *Isis* 34, No. 3 (Winter 1943), 230–1.

[195-6] Pacific Historical Review, "Review: A Guide to Naval Strategy," *Pacific Historical Review* 13, No. 4 (December 1944), 484; 484, respectively.

[197] Brodie, "New Tactics in Naval Warfare," 223.

[198-200] Brodie, *Strategy in the Missile Age* (Princeton: Princeton University Press, 1959), 397; 397–8; 398, respectively.

[201-4] Kaplan, *Wizards of Armageddon*, 9–10; 10; 10; 22–3, respectively.

CHAPTER TWO

After the A-Bomb: Restoring Order in the Age of Absolute War

While still in his early thirties, Brodie would briefly join the faculty of Dartmouth from 1941 to 1943, where, as Ken Booth recounts, "he organized a course called 'Modern War, Strategy and National Policies'"—which included one notably Clausewitzian lecture titled "War as a Continuation of Politics"—and whose course syllabus has been described by Booth as having "a remarkably contemporary ring" and could "claim to be the first modern syllabus course in what later became strategic studies,"[1] one of many efforts by Brodie to help nurture the emergence of a new science of modern strategy. But Brodie "discovered at Dartmouth that energy and ability do not always lead to success in academic life," and despite his early renown, and his laudable publishing accomplishments, Brodie's "achievements failed to earn him the support of some of his immediate colleagues, and his contract was not renewed."[2] So he left the academy, working for the U.S. Navy through to the end of World War II, and thereby gaining "first-hand experience of government in Washington and contact with the military establishment at a high level. He soon began to learn that the relationship between civilian experts and the military could be unsatisfactory, as well as important."[3]

Brodie's work soon came to the attention of Yale's Institute of International Studies, among whom could be found "some of the key figures . . . in the development of 'realist' thinking about international relations"—including the institute's Frederick S. Dunn, William T. R. Fox, and Arnold Wolfers, who would later collaborate with Brodie on the widely celebrated 1946 treatise, *The Absolute Weapon*, along with their colleague, Percy E. Corbett, a work that Booth describes as "remarkable" and "of exceptional quality" and a "book of considerable analytical clarity and technical expertise," exhibiting both a "sophisticated application of the ideas of political realism" as well as "extraordinary prescience"—so much that there would be "no comparable works for over ten years."[4] They invited Brodie to join the institute, where he had planned to continue his work on sea power, only to soon learn of the dramatic events unfolding in the skies of Japan, which "quickly changed the direction of his study."[5] While "greatly impressed by the revolutionary character of the new weapon," Booth recalls that Brodie was at first "'tentative' on the question of whether the atomic bomb would deter or provoke tension,"[6] as evident in his November 1945 essay, "The Atomic Bomb and American Security" that preceded his chapters in *The Absolute Weapon* the next year. But Booth notes in the "intervening months Jacob Viner had helped him to make up his mind," and Brodie "came to accept Viner's argument that the bomb would be stabilizing since no promise of victory would be worth the price if devastating retaliation was certain."[7] This would become the foundation not only of American nuclear strategy, but the theoretical framework of structural realism during the Cold War period, also known as neorealism. Brodie would encapsulate in just a few enduring words what would become the foundation of both neorealism and the strategic nuclear order, first presented in his 1945 paper and which worked their way into *The Absolute Weapon*, "tucked away on page seventy-six," soon becoming "a compulsory quotation for the age of nuclear deterrence (as did Clausewitz's famous aphorism about war as a continuation of politics for the age of the classical European states' system)," that: "Thus far the chief purpose of our military establishment has been to win wars. From now on its chief purpose must be to avert them. It can have almost no other useful purpose."[8]

Together, the group of theorists who contributed to *The Absolute Weapon*, known as the "Yale group," articulated a distinct nuclear realism that rejected both the "warfighting" or "war-winning" school of thought that was articulated forcefully in 1946 by William Borden, author of *There Will Be No Time* and later by the prolific Herman Kahn, as well as the nuclear idealism of those who advocated world government as the solution to the new nuclear danger. The Yale group believed "the bomb was revolutionary but that states would not put their security in the hands of an international organization. As a result, the great powers could not return to old-style wars, but neither could they move forward to world government. They therefore had to live with the bomb but without war; this meant living in a world of competitive arms building and deterrence. So it was that the 'reality' of the postwar strategic confrontation was in part created out of the realist images of the Yale group and other early contributors to the atomic debate."[9]

Brodie's early consideration of the accidents of history that so profoundly shaped man's odyssey, and the value in the effort to ameliorate conditions of injustice which, if left festering, could result in war, *with the hope and expectation of strengthening thereby our proposed structure of world order*, as he described in 1938 in his writings on the prevention of war through peaceful change, resonate even more strongly in the immediate post-Hiroshima era, when the high price of accident and the unique fragility of the emergent world order, allow for a logical and natural progression, from considering the merits of "peaceful change" to articulating a philosophy and a strategy of deterrence, which one can think of as an update to the peaceful change argument for the new, exceedingly dangerous, nuclear era. It is thus no small coincidence that Brodie was among the first to turn his full attention to the unique challenges of the post-Hiroshima world, taking the lead in conceptualizing deterrence, embracing it, and taking the first steps toward operationalizing it.

Indeed, Brodie's contributions to the foundational 1946 book on nuclear strategy, *The Absolute Weapon: Atomic Power and World Order*, helped to establish the theoretical principles that underlay America's emergent strategy of deterrence, and his later work, *Strategy in the Missile Age*, updated his thinking to take into consideration the loss of America's atomic monopoly, the increase in destructive yield as thermonuclear weapons entered the arsenals of the superpowers, and the enhancement of the reach and accuracy of delivery vehicles, most notably the intercontinental missile. Brodie is perhaps best known for his conclusion, articulated most famously in his 1946 contribution to *The Absolute Weapon*—but first presented in his 1945 article that preceded it, "The Atomic Bomb and American Security," published by the Yale Institute of International Studies as Memorandum 18 in November 1945—that: "Thus far the chief purpose of our military establishment has been to win wars. From now on its chief purpose must be to avert them. It can have almost no other useful purpose."

Strategic Ambiguity Redux: Lessons for the Atomic Age

Brodie had long recognized an essential ambiguity inherent in naval power: "A navy thus has defensive and offensive uses, which are sometimes indistinguishable and always mutually reinforcing."[10] This would also be true of nuclear weapons, resulting in what would remain a complex and never truly resolved ambiguity with regard to defensive and offensive weapons systems, or in the parlance of the nuclear strategists, with regard to the credibility of deterrence versus warfighting—and whether warfighting capabilities, doctrines, training, civil defense measures, and declaratory statements would augment or undermine deterrence; and if the tools required to win major wars in the nuclear age would likely precipitate such wars, or in fact (and contrary to intuition) decrease their likelihood. Over and again, from the simplicity and glaring inadequacy of massive retaliation strategies, *Sunday Punch* strikes and other plans designed to deliver a *knockout blow* that later came to be known as *massive retaliation*, to the more refined but equally ambiguous strategies of *flexible response* for an era of *brushfire wars* fought to let off steam and reinvigorate deterrence while avoiding *general war*, this most elemental strategic ambiguity would never go away, or be fully resolved with clarity.

And so the nuclear doctrinal and theoretical debates would continue for nearly half a century, with Bernard Brodie leading the charge by articulating so clearly the fundamentals of nuclear deterrence and elucidating the requirements for strategic stability in the nuclear age. Brodie was driven by the singular goal of ensuring that nuclear war never be fought, as the price paid in death and destruction would dramatically overshadow any potential political, economic, or strategic benefits of war. However, as it would turn out, his view was not the only one, and a competing doctrine would emerge that postulated that nuclear wars could not only be fought, but they could be won, and preparing for nuclear victory was thus a necessity. One of the most well known and outspoken advocates of this competing school of nuclear warfighting was Herman Kahn, an equally prolific former RANDite just like Brodie, but Kahn came to the opposite conclusion on the wisdom of fighting nuclear wars, rejecting the Brodien presumption that fighting a nuclear war was tantamount to national suicide. Kahn and his fellow warfighters came to believe atomic weapons, and later thermonuclear bombs as well, were primarily an incremental advancement in military power, an efficient means of delivering explosive power but not necessarily a transformative one and most likely not Apocalyptic in their consequences. But to Brodie, atomic weapons, even in their earliest, low-yielding form, were truly transformative and inherently revolutionary, so much so that he would initially accept the term *absolute* to describe them.

According to Frederick S. Dunn, director of the Yale Institute of International Studies and prominent theorist of peaceful change cited by Brodie in his graduate work, in the foreword to Brodie's November 1, 1945 Memorandum No. 18 published by the institute, "The Atomic Bomb and American Security," it was now "obviously necessary to know as much as possible about the nature of this new weapon and its strategic and political implications. For these are so revolutionary that it would be very easy, by looking just at some aspects and ignoring others, to be led unwittingly into errors of catastrophic proportions."[11] Dunn offers that Brodie's analysis "should be helpful alike to policy-makers and laymen, whatever program for domestic or international action they may favor as the best means of harnessing this most startling threat to future peace and stability."[12]

It was within just 75 days of the unprecedented destruction of Hiroshima and Nagasaki, each by a single bomb dropped by a single aircraft, that Brodie published "The Atomic Bomb and American Security," a remarkably prescient analysis that foresaw not only the unique attributes of the new weapon as a deterrent, and the spread of nuclear weapons to other powers, but also the operational challenges confronting the traditional armed services in the face of such a destructive new military technology and the risk of nuclear sabotage and terrorism—over a half century before the War on Terror made fears of nuclear terrorism widespread. Brodie was struck, like many, by the awesome destructiveness of the weapon: "The introduction . . . of an explosive agent which is several million times more potent, on a pound per pound basis, than the most powerful explosives previously known heralds a change not merely in the degree of destructiveness of modern war but in its basic character."[13] As Brodie observed, "From the viewpoint of human welfare, the fearful accomplishment of the bomb itself makes the promise of possible eventual benefits resulting from the peacetime use of nuclear energy seem irrelevant and unimportant," as "the rewards of the end result inevitably appear meager against the bare fact that a few pounds of substance can blast whole cities into oblivion."[14] From the extraordinary destructive magnitude of the bomb emerged two distinct propositions: "The first proposition which must be brought home, no less to the statesmen of the world than to its soldiers, is that the atomic bomb, which in the scope of its effects defies comparison with any military innovation of the past, is not just another and more destructive weapon to be added to an already long list" and "is something which threatens to make the rest of the list relatively unimportant."[15] And the "second proposition of comparable importance is that it is wholly vain to expect scientists or engineers to fashion any counter or 'answer' to the atomic bomb which will redress the present disequilibrium of offense *versus* defense to any degree worth mentioning."[16]

Before the bomb would so drastically and permanently "alter the basic character of war"[17] Brodie had imagined "a future war between great powers could be visualized as one in which the decisive effects of strategic bombing would be contingent upon the cumulative effect of prolonged bombardment efforts which would in turn be governed by aerial battles and even whole campaigns for mastery of the air," and "older forms of warfare on land and sea would exercise a telling effect not only on the ultimate decision but on the effectiveness of the strategic bombing itself" and the "strategic bombing would (as in the war against Germany just ended) influence or determine the decision mainly through its effects on the ground campaigns."[18] But no longer; "The atomic bomb seems, however, to erase the pattern described above."[19] As Brodie observed, "A world accustomed to thinking it horrible that wars should last four or five years is now appalled at the prospect that future wars may last only a few days."[20] And—foreshadowing the missile age that would not come for more than another decade—Brodie predicted "the power of the new missile completely alters the considerations which previously governed the choice of vehicles and the manner of using them," as a "rocket far more elaborate and expensive than the V-2 used by the Germans is still an exceptionally cheap means of bombarding a country if it can carry in its nose an atomic bomb."[21]

And—foreshadowing the post-9/11 concerns about the specter of nuclear terrorism—Brodie anticipated that "[a]nother and possibly even more revolutionary change in the character of war produced in the atomic bomb lies in the unprecedented potentialities which it gives to sabotage."[22] Before the bomb "it was hitherto physically impossible for agents to smuggle into another country, either prior to or during hostilities, a sufficient quantity of materials to blow up more than a very few specially chosen objectives" and as a consequence, "[t]he possibility of really serious damage to a great power resulting from such enterprises was practically nil. Far different is the situation where such materials as U-235 or plutonium-239 are employed, for only a few pounds of either substance is sufficient to blow up the major part of a great city."[23] And while "the engine necessary for utilizing the explosive, that is, the bomb itself, seems from various hints contained in the *Smyth Report* to be a highly intricate and fairly massive mechanism," Brodie also suspects it to be "also probable that a nation intent upon perfecting the atomic bomb as a sabotage instrument could work out a much simpler device, something which permitted the major part of the materials used to be gathered and prepared locally in the target area."[24] Brodie speculated that "the war of the future might very well take the form of a revelation by one nation to another that the latter's major cities had atomic bombs planted in them and that only immediate and absolute submission to dictate would prevent them from going off,"[25] a scenario that senior Al Qaeda operative, Khalid Sheikh Mohammed—the mastermind of the 9/11 attacks on the United States—says had been implemented when he claimed under interrogation in Guantanamo Bay that Al Qaeda had hidden a nuclear bomb in Europe to be detonated if Osama bin Laden was ever killed or captured, thereby unleashing what he described as a "nuclear hellstorm"—perhaps the first effort by a nonstate terror group to deter the world's great powers from launching an attack upon their leader. Also anticipating some of the civil liberty issues that would arise during the War on Terror, Brodie wrote that for "a community alerted to national danger the F.B.I. or its counterpart becomes the first line of defense, and the encroachment on civil liberties which would necessarily follow would far exceed in magnitude and pervasiveness anything which democracies have thus far tolerated in peacetime."[26]

Brodie considered possible methods of defense against nuclear attack, writing that a "nation which has developed strong defenses against invading aircraft, which developed reliable means of interfering with radio-controlled rockets, which has developed highly efficient counter-smuggling and counter-sabotage agencies, and which has dispersed through the surrounding countryside substantial proportions of the industries and populations normally gathered in urban communities is obviously better prepared to resist atomic bomb attack than a nation which has neglected to do these things," but also points "out that progress is not likely to be confined to measures of defense. The use of more perfect vehicles and of more destructive bombs in greater quantity might very well offset any gains in defense. And the bomb already has a fearful lead in the race."[27] Indeed, "Scientific knowledge today embraces no hint of a possibility of neutralizing the atomic bomb; it *does* contain signposts pointing to the possible exploitation of other and equally horrendous means of destroying human life, such as radio-active 'gases.' "[28]

Brodie next considered the "Military Role of the Traditional Armed Forces," observing that: "Obviously, the relative importance of the army and navy in wartime would be considerably diminished if not eliminated by a device which could be operated more or less independently of them and which was capable of producing havoc great enough to effect a decision by itself. And in so far as the atomic bomb is delivered to the target by means of rockets rather than aircraft, the same would be true of the air forces as we now know them. But it is likely that decisions will be won without the traditional forces being taken into account? If there is reason to doubt it, those forces clearly remain important. The problem then becomes more pragmatic—that of discovering the degree and direction of the changes necessary to adapt them to the atomic age."[29] While tests were forthcoming on the effects of atomic bombing on naval warships using the Japanese battleship *Nagato* "and possibly other warships of various types" but despite the "certain usefulness" of tests like this, Brodie pointed out that "they can provide no answer to the basic question of the utility of sea power in the future."[30] During an anticipated though finite period of atomic bomb scarcity, Brodie expected that "ships at sea are among the least attractive of military objects as targets for atomic bomb attack," as "[t]heir ability to disperse makes them wasteful targets for bombs of such concentrated power; their mobility makes them practically impossible targets for super-rockets of great range; and those of the United States Navy at least have shown themselves able (with the assistance of their own aircraft) to impose an impressively high ratio of casualties upon hostile planes endeavoring to approach them. But it is still possible for navies to lose all reason for being even if they themselves prove completely immune."[31]

Brodie recalls how "in the main sea power has throughout history proved decisive only when it was applied and exploited over a period of considerable time, and in atomic bomb warfare the time may well be lacking. Where wars are destined to be short, superior sea power may prove wholly useless."[32] Brodie noted the irony that America emerged as a world power, and as "the unrivalled first sea power of the world" just as "all this mighty power seems to have become redundant . . . at least in the opinion of some commentators."[33] Brodie could, however, envision one "possibility, admittedly slight, that a system of international machinery for the suppression of the atomic bomb can be set up and endowed with such vigor as to enable it to function even through another major war," or more likely that "neither side will dare to use the bomb even though both possess it," and in this circumstance, "navies might have an important role to play," and "what is true of navies is even more true of armies and air forces."[34] Brodie would elaborate the possible future role for a navy in the nuclear world in the months and years ahead as he struggled to determine if all his prior work on naval strategy was now obsolete—but already he sensed that if atomic weapons could in fact be neutralized by the mutual fear of their use, there would indeed be a continuing military role for the traditional armed forces in the nuclear era.

In a footnote, Brodie invokes Clausewitz—one of his earliest discussions of the Prussian strategist—writing: "Regardless of technological changes, war remains, as Clausewitz put it, an 'instrument of policy,' a means of realizing a political end"[35]—a view Brodie would soon come to question before again circling back to his first instinct that war *was*, and *would continue to be*, a continuation of policy by other means—and as the atomic era would, a few short years later, yield to the thermonuclear era, Brodie would strenuously add the word *must* to Clausewitz's old dictum, making it much more than an observation, and even more than a prescription; to Brodie, it became a *commandment*. His earlier point, expressed in late 1945, on the enduring interconnection of war to policy no matter what the technology was, was Brodie's first articulation of what would become a sacred point to him, that was in the nuclear era would continue to obey the logic—and what would soon amount to the moral imperative—of Clausewitz. Brodie would extend the Prussian's logic to suggest that if, as in the case of nuclear war, there could be no rational end to war, then such a war could not, and must not, be fought.

One could argue that Brodie was in the process of elevating an *observation* of the Prussian beyond a *prescription*, in some ways *ideologizing* what for Clausewitz was mere theorizing (with a healthy dose of prescription woven into his Hegelian structure, with synthesis the ultimate objective), harnessing it into a normative prescription on the permissibility, or in this case the impermissibility of nuclear war. Or if Brodie senses in Clausewitz a shared horror of war in its absolute form, and a shared normative commitment to preventing absolute from erupting beyond the ideal form of its theoretical description into an orgy of real, physical, and human destruction. While Brodie's first, tentative comment is buried in a footnote, it shows that Brodie as early as 1945 was thinking about Clausewitz, and while of the belief that Clausewitz's teachings still applied even after the nuclear age had begun, he had not yet realized how central they would become—and endeavored in the years ahead to introduce Americans to the long-ignored theorist, and to share his wisdom and insight in the hope that his precepts would be embraced by others just as Brodie was beginning to. So what started as a footnote penned at the dawn of the nuclear age would blossom into a lifelong inquiry into the enduring wisdom of Clausewitz and how best to apply his lessons to the new age.

It appears prescient that the context in which Brodie addresses Clausewitz and his enduring relevance is not to address the question of whether or not war in the nuclear age can be waged in a manner that honors the Clausewitzian dictum that war is a continuation of politics by other means, but the narrower question of war termination after atomic bombs are used and the role of traditional armed services in postattack military operations, a topic that would enjoy much attention by a later generation of escalation theorists who would debate the escalatory (and potential de-escalatory) nature of the bomb: "It as already been suggested," he writes, "that a nation which suddenly attacked another with atomic bombs would find it imperative to follow up its initial blow with rapid invasion and occupation, at the very least for the purpose of minimizing retaliation in kind."[36] He adds that to "obviate retaliation with atomic bombs to any considerable degree, the invasion would have to be incredibly swift and sufficiently powerful to overwhelm instantly any opposition."[37] But in the same footnote where Brodie reflected on Clausewitz's relevance, he observes that "[c]ertain scientists familiar with the atomic bomb have argued privately that in any future war invasion and occupation would probably not be necessary at all," but with the World War II experience still fresh and with it that war's necessity for a surrender every bit as total as the war itself, Brodie argued otherwise: "Quite apart from the likelihood of direct retaliation with atomic bombs, this view is wholly untenable. A nation which had inflicted enormous human and material damage upon another would find it intolerable to stop short of eliciting from the latter an acknowledgement of defeat implemented by a readiness to accept control. Wars, in other words, are fought to be terminated, and to be terminated decisively."[38]

Brodie's earliest published thoughts on nuclear deterrence appeared in this very 1945 essay, in a section titled "Is the Atomic Bomb a Deterrent from War?" Brodie considers the value of the atomic bomb as a deterrent, a preliminary analysis that explores both sides of an issue and in which he does not yet take sides: "Hope mixed with horror has provoked the exclamation on some hands that the atomic bomb 'makes war impossible!' In the sense that war is something not to be endured if any reasonable alternative remains, it has long been 'impossible.' But for that very reason we should suspect that the atomic bomb does not make war impossible in the narrower sense of the word. Even without it the conditions of modern war should have been a sufficient deterrent to aggression but proved not to be such. Realism therefore dictates the assumption that war remains possible, however more horrible the consequences."[39] Adds Brodie: "However, a change so fundamental in the character of war cannot but change drastically the degree of probability of the recurrence of large-scale war within any given period," though Brodie remembers all too vividly how during the 1930s "a deeper and probably more generalized revulsion against war than in any other era of history," and "[u]nder those circumstances the breeding of a new war required a situation combining dictators of singular irresponsibility with a notion among them and their general staffs that aggression would be both successful and cheap. The possibility of madmen again becoming rulers of powerful states is by no means ruled out for the future. But can there exist again the notion that aggression will be cheap?"[40] It is this latter point that will propel Brodie to embrace deterrence as the only logical response to the unprecedented dangers of the bomb: "If the atomic bomb can be used without fear of substantial retaliation in kind, it will clearly encourage aggression," but this strikes Brodie as quite unlikely, and "[f]or this reason, the atomic bomb may prove in the net a powerful inhibition of aggression. It would make little difference is one power had more bombs and were better prepared to resist them than the opponent. It would in any case undergo tremendous destruction of life and property."[41] One situation "where fear of retaliation is at a minimum" is "where one side has the bombs and the other lacks them entirely," but Brodie even as far back as 1945 was confident this "special situation is bound to be short-lived."[42]

Brodie speculates that the fear of atomic destruction will be uniformly great even if it varies by culture or nation in relative intensity; as he observes, "It goes without saying that the governments and populations of different countries will show very different levels of apprehension concerning the effects of the bomb," and while "[i]t may be argued that a totalitarian state would be less unready than would a democracy to see the destruction of its cities rather than yield on a crucial political question," Brodie surmises that the "real political effect of such a disparity, however—if it actually exists, which is doubtful—can easily be exaggerated. For in no case is the fear of the consequences of atomic bomb attack likely to be low. More important is the likelihood that totalitarian countries can impose more easily on their populations than can democracies those mass movements of peoples and industries necessary to disperse urban concentrations."[43]

Brodie remains unsure at the time of this writing, in the fall of 1945 just a few short months after the leveling of Hiroshima and Nagasaki, whether the bomb will restrain or unleash the more aggressive instincts of states—and he even considers how it may not stop crises from erupting with the potential to escalate. As he writes: "But even if one is to assume that in the net—that is, barring the special situations outlined above—the atomic bomb will act as a powerful deterrent to aggression against great powers, that fact may not be overwhelmingly important with respect to the political crises out of which wars generally develop. In a world in which great wars become 'inevitable' as a result of aggression by great powers upon weak neighbors, the important question is whether the existence of the atomic bomb will cause a greater restraint on the part of great powers in all their dealings with other nations, whether the latter be great or small. It may easily have the contrary effect. Hitler made a good many bloodless gains by mere blackmail, in which he relied heavily on the too obvious horror of modern war among the great nations which might have opposed him earlier. A comparable kind of blackmail in the future may actually find its encouragement in the existence of the atomic bomb. Horror of its implications is not likely to be spread evenly, at least not the form of over expression. The response may be a series of *faits accomplis* eventuating in that final deterioration of international affairs in which war, however terrible, can no longer be avoided."[44] This image of faits accomplis is reminiscent of the years before World War II erupted, when a preference for *peaceful change* placed the diplomatic and strategic premium on avoiding war at all costs, even if that meant allowing for the sacrifice of the sovereign independence of smaller states; indeed, the bifurcation of the international system, along an "Iron Curtain," revealed the existence of a recognized limit of Western diplomatic and military influence, essentially enabling such a blackmail situation to transpire across Eastern Europe as Soviet power oppressed numerous formerly independent nations without a hint of opposition from the West; but within the free world, a countereffect ensured that Soviet power could not be so applied on the Western side of this new frontier. It was thus a precarious balance, predicated upon a mutuality of blackmail that would be enforced by the decreasingly delicate nuclear balance.

In this first effort to flesh out the many consequences of the bomb, Brodie is not yet ready to place his bet on deterrence or on the stability it might provide, and even suggests that he holds a contrary view which he would, within the year, substantially modify: "Finally, and perhaps most important, the anxiety which the atomic bomb itself induces, and which is likely to become more intense as the number of bombs and of the states producing them increases, will remain a powerful but wholly unpredictable factor in world affairs. It may stimulate a sense of urgency which will make feasible correctives far more drastic than any that are possible today. It may, on the other hand, breed national neuroses manifested in the urge for a 'preventive' war,"[45] which would in fact prove to be a prescient forecast in the years to come when calls for *timely action* were raised by some who feared the loss of opportunity enjoyed first during the four-year atomic monopoly and later during the very brief ten-month thermonuclear monopoly—calls that were fortunately not heeded. Adds Brodie: "The doctrine that the only possible defense is a vigorous anticipatory offense may even acquire some military plausibility if the number of bombs in existence greatly increases, but it will be the 'solution' of total despair."[46]

An Absolute Weapon?

When first grappling with the riddles of the new nuclear era, Brodie was especially sensitive to the unprecedented totality of warfare, and the prospects of atomic obliteration. As he wrote in the opening words of his chapter, "War in the Atomic Age," in his widely acclaimed 1946 edited volume, *The Absolute Weapon*, "Most of those who have held the public ear on the subject of the atomic bomb have been content to assume that war and obliteration are now completely synonymous," and that the "state of obliteration" might be the "future fate of nations which cannot resolve their disputes," as a "few degrees difference in nearness to totality is of relatively small account."[47] Brodie speculates that a "war with atomic bombs would be immeasurably more destructive and horrible than any the world has yet known," a fact that is "indeed portentous, and to many . . . overwhelming."[48]

In his second chapter in *The Absolute Weapon*, Brodie discusses the military implications of the bomb and argues that now an "aggressor state must fear retaliation," as "it will know that even if it is the victor it will suffer a degree of physical destruction incomparably greater than that suffered by any defeated nation of history," more so than that faced by defeated Nazi Germany, and by Brodie's calculation, "no victory . . . would be worth the price."[49] From the horrific destruction promised by atomic weapons, and the assured retaliation that would have to be absorbed by an aggressor in the atomic age, Brodie anticipates not chaos but order, not war but a sustained stability—as if having magically created gold from nonprecious metals through some sort of nuclear alchemy.

Only if the bomb could "be used without fear of substantial retaliation in kind" would it "clearly encourage aggression," so Brodie argues that we should endeavor to "make as nearly certain as possible that the aggressor who uses the bomb will have it used against him," even if this means an inevitability of the "multilateral possession of the bomb."[50] So long as "such arrangements are made," and any atomic aggressor will inevitably face an atomic retaliatory strike, "the bomb cannot but prove in the net a powerful inhibition of aggression," even "if one power had more bombs" or was "better prepared to resist them."[51] Brodie suggests that the "first and most vital step in any American security program for the age of atomic bombs is to take measures to guarantee to ourselves in case of attack the possibility of retaliation in kind."[52] Here, Brodie famously reiterated: "Thus far the chief purpose of our military establishment has been to win wars. From now on its chief purpose must be to avert them. It can have almost no other useful purpose."[53] This becomes the heart of Brodie's strategic philosophy for the nuclear age, with its central dependence upon deterrence as its pillar. In later years, many would disagree, resulting in the bifurcation of the emerging field of nuclear strategy into two broad categories: the deterrers and the warfighters, and their fundamental disagreement over this singular issue, whether averting war rather than winning wars should be the "chief purpose" of American military power; and even if so, whether it was possible to avert war without being prepared to win them. In the end, successful deterrence might depend on an opponent's belief that its enemy was preparing not only to fight a nuclear war, but to win one, forever obscuring the clarity evident in Brodie's original analysis in a subsequent cloud of irresolvable strategic ambiguity and doctrinal debate.

On June 10, 1946, *Time* magazine published a favorable review of *The Absolute Weapon*, an indicator of how important this early effort to grapple with the implications of the atomic era was considered beyond the hallowed halls of academia. As *Time* wrote, "Since Hiroshima, thinkers have started one chain reaction after another about The Bomb," and " 'To clear away the hysteria,' five of them published *The Absolute Weapon* . . . all members of the Yale Institute of International Studies," and they "have produced the best overall job yet on the atom's actual political implications. They make it more real by frankly presupposing that the only two powers likely to engage in an atomic-armament race are the U.S. and Russia."[54] The review considers the "Threat of Retaliation," noting: "Whether or not a world atomic agreement is reached, the authors round the globe. While some scientists think that an atomic-arms race is the most dreadful thing that could happen, *The Absolute Weapon*'s text argues that it would be still more dreadful for only one nation to have bombs—for only then could they be used with impunity. 'In the atomic age the threat of retaliation is probably the strongest single means of determent.' "[55] The review next considers the "Threat of Stalemate," noting: "In developing this theme *The Absolute Weapon*'s text refutes the rather silly title. The atom can and will be fitted into military and political strategy, like all other weapons. A surprise atom-bomb attack could make Pearl Harbor look like a mere raid, but continental areas such as the U.S. and Russia are too great for immediate knock-out blows. A surprised but still surviving nation with atomic stockpiles could in its turn destroy the aggressor's cities and industries. After the first heavy devastation, both sides would have to fight minus most of their production; the war might well degenerate into a long stalemate with neither side able to launch a successful long-distance invasion."[56] *Time* further notes, "More dangerous than the atom itself is the idea that a quick atomic blitz would defeat any great nation. No possible atomic aggressor would be able to think that if other great nations are automatically prepared. In mutual atomic war, even the 'victor' will suffer 'destruction incomparably greater than that suffered by any defeated nation in history. . . . Under those circumstances no victory, even if guaranteed in advance—which it never is—would be worth the price.'"[57]

Only one day earlier, in the pages of the New York Times, this pioneering work enjoyed similarly broad exposure to the lay public—further testimony to both the importance of the subject matter in the public mind as to the esteem merited upon the authors. But in great contrast to the Time review, the article in the New York Times was absolutely scathing. Authored by none other than the Chancellor of the University of Chicago, Robert M. Hutchins, the review starts out with all guns blazing directly at the otherwise distinguished authors of this work: "This book, in which five distinguished scholars take part, is confused and contradictory in its thinking, and unimaginative and defeatist in its conclusions."[58] As Hutchins critically observes, "After showing that neither international agreements, inspection, nor the fear of retaliation can prevent atomic war, it recommends that we rely on a combination of all three to save civilization. Of the three measures, the authors look with the most favor upon the fear of retaliation. Freedom from fear is no longer an aim toward which America should strive, they seem to suggest; only a world living in fear can be safe."[59] Rejecting the authors' consensus on the logic of deterrence, and citing Frederick Dunn's introductory comment that the "atomic bomb is one of the most persuasive deterrents to adventures in atomic warfare that could be devised," Hutchins suggests—as many critics of neorealism would similarly do during its theoretical reign at the end of the Cold War—that "[a]t this point it would seem that we could adjourn and go home, because if the atomic bomb itself is going to prevent war none of us needs to do anything about it, except that we should urge our Government to distribute its supply of bombs all over the world. Then every nation would enjoy the pacifying influence of the fear of retaliation"[60]—a controversial premise that the father of neorealism, Kenneth Waltz, himself would later suggest. "But this the authors of this book do not propose. They do not even advocate making our knowledge of the technique of bomb manufacture available to other nations now."[61] Hutchins holds back some fire on Brodie, saluting his "useful list of the military qualities and consequences of the atomic bomb," finding only two faults with it, the first being Hutchins' belief that Brodie's five-to ten-year estimate for the end of the American atomic monopoly might be excessive, citing a competing viewpoint that Russia would be capable of manufacturing atomic bombs "in about three years," a time frame that proved more accurate than Brodie's; but Hutchins also suggests that Moscow will then also become capable of producing atomic bombs "at a far higher rate than we can," which turned out not to be the case.[62]

Hutchins also disputes Brodie's contention that "the possibilities of sabotage by atomic bombs are greatly exaggerated," finding a more persuasive case made for the dangers of nuclear terrorism by National Bureau of Standards director and atomic bomb expert E. U. Condon.[63] However, with the passage now of over half a century since publication of The Absolute Weapon, no case of atomic sabotage has yet to take place—not even in the chaotic post-9/11 world nor during the even more chaotic collapse of the Soviet Union. But apart from limited praise for Brodie's analysis, Hutchins takes aim once more at Brodie's embrace of deterrence, writing: "After making his military diagnosis, Mr. Brodie goes on to discuss its implications for military policy," and it is here that "we meet again with the fear of retaliation. Mr. Brodie says that if the aggressor state must fear retaliation, no victory . . . would be worth the price."[64] Hutchins finds that Brodie is "highly unconvincing when he sets out to show how we may counter-attack and fight on after an atomic assault upon us," and finds that Brodie "overlooks the great fact about the atomic bomb, even though it appeared on his list of its qualities and consequences; and that is the fact that there is literally no defense against it."[65] And so, if "as we are told on high authority, 40,000,000 Americans could be killed in a single night of atomic explosions; if in the same period all our cities could be destroyed and all our transportation and communications disrupted, how could we carry on anything that would look like organized warfare?"[66] With "no faith in a purely military solution," Brodie "merely wants to have us get ready to fight so that we shall not be a tempting target," and if we comply, Brodie suggests that as a nation we'll be able to "pursue actively that progressive improvement in world affairs by which alone it finds true security," a contention that Hutchins rejects as nonsensical: "The elaborate measures urged by Mr. Brodie are more likely to divert us from the task of improving world affairs than they are to encourage us to tackle it," and may very induce an opposite reactions, resulting instead in the "progressive deterioration in world affairs."[67]

Hutchins directs even more hostile fire at Brodie's co-authors, describing Arnold Wolfers as "unintelligible"; taking Percy E. Corbett to task for joining his colleagues "in saying that the fear he wishes to overcome offers the greatest hope for peace"; and finding fault with all five authors for being "scornful of world government," and repeatedly challenging their embrace of perpetual fear of retaliation as a foundation for peace.[68] He sees a glimmer of reasonableness in William T. R. Fox's observation that a "world in which two or more states were sitting on powder kegs powerful enough to destroy every major city on earth would be a world of half-peace at best"—a conclusion Hutchins finds to be "so obvious that one wonders why Mr. Fox is the only one of the five authors who ever shows signs of seeing it," and wondering "why he did not confide in his colleagues and why the reader is not told until the third page from the end."[69]

In a more formal—and favorable—academic review in the January 1947 edition of the *Annals of the American Academy of Political and Social Science*, University of Pennsylvania's Robert Strausz-Hupé writes that in "this book five members of the Yale Institute of International Studies investigate the problems of atomic war, its conduct and prevention," and "[a]lthough the authors eschew the doomsday rhetoric which the general public has learned to expect from experts on atom politics, they succeed in presenting the most impressive analysis of the terrible dilemma which thus far has appeared in print," and "are agreed that the political problem of the atom bomb, superimposed on the staggering problems of pre-atomic world politics, cannot be isolated from the syndrome of international crisis; that control of atomic energy as a weapon is tantamount to the imposition of political, not merely technical, controls; that the United Nations offers the most practical alternatives now available for averting 'a clear-cut polarization of power around . . . the Soviet Union and the United States,' the tendency toward which is fraught with the most immediate threat of war, atomic or old-fashioned; and that the best defense of the United States against the threat of atomic attack, although not against terrible destruction once that attack has been launched, is determent-power, i.e., capacity for instant retaliation."[70] And he also observed how, "Paradoxically, *The Absolute Weapon* is a valuable contribution to the controversy on Man and the Atom just because it rejects absoluteness as a basis of discussion," and "[s]ince the authors are apparently agreed that capacity for retaliation is the factor most likely to deter a would-be aggressor, they contend implicitly, it seems, that the effectiveness of atomic weapons is relative, i.e., relative to other atomic weapons"—an impression that is "strengthened by Dr. Brodie's two chapters on the strictly military implications of atomic energy."[71]

Summarizing Brodie's contribution, Strausz-Hupé notes Brodie's first chapter presents a "synopsis of the views expressed by various physicists," in which Brodie, "leaning heavily on the Smyth report, argues that military and naval supremacy in the traditionally accepted sense no longer furnishes protection against attack by atomic missiles," and "agrees with those scientists who assert that there is no 'secret' and that other nations will be able, in a few years, to break our monopoly of atomic weapons," after which he "proceeds to speculate brilliantly on the technical aspects of large-scale atomic warfare" and "proposes for the United States a military establishment which will be independent of urban centers of supply" and whose mission is "that of averting, rather than winning, wars."[72] And in contrast to "the proponents of international control as the one and only alternative to inevitable destruction," Strausz-Hupé observes that Brodie "has the intellectual courage to investigate the case that failure of international control schemes compels us to devise a unilateral policy of national security."[73] Strausz-Hupé concludes that *The Absolute Weapon* is "an important book because the authors combine thorough under-standing of technical problems with a strong sense of what is and is not feasible politically," and "[w]hile principally concerned with the latest threat to our battered civilization, Dr. Brodie and his scholarly companions have contrived to expand a book on an atrocious gadget into an extremely interesting introduction to world politics."[74]

In the December 1946 edition of *Pacific Affairs*, R. G. Cavell, chairman of the National Executive Committee of the Canadian Institute of International Affairs, observed that he "should like to feel certain that this small volume, which deals so ably with the subject 'Atomic Power and World Order', will be read by all statesmen and others upon whose work and deci-sions, over the next few years, will depend the peace of the world."[75] Cavell concludes that *The Absolute Weapon* is a "constructive book which should be widely read; its reading by the right people might help to clarify their minds and thus avoid further misery to those millions, par-ticularly in the Far East, who suffer so terribly now, largely because the Great Powers fear and distrust one another."[76]

Ken Booth, in his biographical chapter on Brodie in *Makers of Nuclear Strategy*, described *The Absolute Weapon* as "a landmark in the story of thinking about nuclear weapons" but none-theless clarifies that this "is not to say that it was an influential or widely read book," and much like Brodie would himself describe Clausewitz, Booth observes: "Like several of the key works in strategic theory, it has been referred to more frequently than actually read, and in hindsight its reputation has become more significant than in the late 1940s. Even today it is unlikely that most members of the strategic profession know more about it than a couple of much-repeated quotations."[77] In a footnote, Booth elaborates on the book's overstated influence, arguing the "book's landmark status when it was first published is exaggerated by Herken and Kaplan," and that "Freedman's verdict is correct," that "the book stands out only in retrospect" but was "'peripheral' to the main professional concerns of the late 1940s, the implications of atomic bombs for strategic bombardment."[78] Nonetheless, Booth does recognize that *The Absolute Weapon* "was the first comprehensive exposition of American strategy for the age of nuclear deterrence," and that it was "a remarkable book," notable for being both "[q]uickly produced" and "of exceptional quality" even if its influence is somewhat more ambiguous, and certainly less immediate than history now commonly suggests.[79]

The Security Problem in Light of Atomic Energy: Some Basic Propositions for the Atomic Age

While Brodie's contribution to *The Absolute Weapon* is often presented as the starting point of his nuclear strategic thinking, with his earlier Yale memorandum less well known, he was actually quite prolific in the first years of the atomic era with many conference presentations, book chapters, and articles to his credit. Indeed, just a month after the favorable review in *Time*, he participated in the 22nd Norman Wait Harris Memorial Foundation lectures held at the University of Chicago in July 1946, presenting a paper titled "The Security Problem in the Light of Atomic Energy" that starts out by noting—as he would again more famously in his "Strategy Hits a Dead End" article in *Harper's* a decade later—that "strategy seems to have lost its entire reason for being. Certainly, the famous remark of Clausewitz, that 'war is a continuation of policy,' has now become a complete absurdity."[80] Brodie would a few years later reprise his early thoughts on Clausewitz's obsolescence, finding new relevance as the atomic era gave way to the more dangerous thermonuclear era—and given Brodie's long interest in Clausewitz it is fascinating to observe him invoke the Prussian so early on and in a manner so contrary to both his later efforts to integrate Clausewitzian theory with nuclear strategy and to his first instinct captured in his aforementioned footnote less than a year earlier.

As Brodie explained: "In a war in which both sides use the atomic bomb it is hardly conceivable that the victor, if there is one, can derive any benefits, even negative ones, at all commensurate with the costs. Whether that was true or not before is arguable; it is now inescapable."[81] America's strategy through to its victory in World War II was "the age-old policy, which has always been basic to strategy, of destroying the enemy's armed forces—and there again we see one of the basic tenets of strategy collapsing."[82] As the nuclear era began, Brodie suggested that there are three things that we will want to know: "whether the atomic bomb does nor does not facilitate aggression"; what are the "minimum requirements of any international system for the control of atomic energy"; and "whether there is any useful course of defense policy left to us in the event of a failure to attain a system possessing those minimum requirements."[83]

Brodie proceeds to list a "few basic propositions" he had hitherto discussed elsewhere, including his first, that "in the atomic bomb we have a weapon of which one to ten units is sufficient to destroy any city in the world."[84] He noted one colleague's objection "to our use of the term the 'absolute weapon' in speaking of the atomic bomb,"[85] which Brodie explained by saying: "When you have a weapon as effective as this one is, it does not make much difference whether you succeed in devising one which is more effective," a point he would later revisit when the thermonuclear leap in destructiveness became apparent; but at this early juncture, he still remains "completely unimpressed by the discussion that this bomb is only a beginning and that ten or twenty years from now we shall have one a hundred times more powerful," not because this was unlikely—indeed, the H-bomb would yield a punch a thousand times greater than the A-bomb; but because he does not believe "the order of difference between that situation and the present one is at all comparable to the difference between the atomic bomb and the preatomic-bomb era."[86] Indeed, "with air forces no greater than those which existed in the recent war, it is at least physically possible for any power to destroy all, or at least most, of the cities of any other great power," and "industry as now organized would be the first casualty of such an attack."[87]

Brodie's second proposition is "that no defense against the atomic bomb is known, and the possibilities of its existence in the future are exceedingly remote"; and while Brodie acknowledges that we "certainly cannot be dogmatic about the future," he adds that "what we can say very definitely is that the experience of the past, which superficially leads one to believe that aggressive weapons have always been successfully countered, breaks down under analysis as misleading or irrelevant. . . . What we have always had in the past is an adjustment to new weapons which tended to qualify those weapons, and such adjustments will not be sufficient in terms of the atomic bomb."[88] Indeed, London's successful response to the German V-1, which on their "banner day" succeeded in downing 97 of 101 missiles launched, would have seemed less a victory had they been tipped with atomic warheads: "then the survivors in London would have had little cause to congratulate themselves."[89] This leads to Brodie's third proposition, "that superiority neither in numbers of bombs nor in numbers of air forces, let alone armies and navies, is sufficient to guarantee security," and even an inferior air force stands a reasonable probability that it "can succeed in penetrating"[90] its opponent's air space, and the consequence is that the "concept of command of the air . . . breaks down."[91]

Brodie reflected on Britain's long experience in maintaining a naval balance of power and participating in foreign wars, some imperial while "others were designed to *maintain on an economical level* those defenses which Britain found sufficient to her security," which Brodie conceived as the very "purpose of the balance-of-power principle."[92] Until the atomic era, Brodie argues, the "British experience is certainly relevant to the American case," and the United States "prior to the atomic bomb could have felt some assurance that . . . had a fairly effective guaranty against devastation, or invasion of its homeland."[93] But with the atomic bomb, everything had now changed.

Brodie next discussed the "effect of the atomic bomb on the ranges even of existing aircraft, not to mention long range rockets, which are certain to be developed within the next several decades."[94] He noted, as he had elsewhere, that the bomb enabled aircraft to extend their range "to practically its entire straight-line cruising radius without payload," albeit at the "sacrifice of the plane and crew"—far greater than the current conventional bombing range for an aircraft of on average "one-quarter or less of its straight-line cruising radius."[95] In effect, an atomic bomb-equipped aircraft would become a manned cruise missile whose mission was in effect a one-war suicide mission, since it was "not likely that belligerents using the atomic bomb and delivering it by aircraft would be particularly interested in getting back after each mission the particular plane or crew which delivered it."[96]

Brodie turns to his fifth and last proposition, that it was "pretty clear by now that there is no question at all of world-wide scarcity of the materials for producing the bomb," and that "[r]elative to the tremendous destructive powers of the bomb, such materials are not scarce" even if "their distribution is still incompletely known."[97] Hence, "we all know that it is only a matter of time before there is multiple possession of the bomb among the great powers," and while how much time remained a matter of conjecture, Brodie noted that "estimates range from three to about twenty years."[98]

Brodie puts all these propositions together, coming to "the conclusion that military forces can no longer defend a territory in the sense of offering protection; the only defense possible is of the deterrent type. In other words, defense becomes synonymous with measures to guarantee the ability to retaliate if attacked and also of measures to diminish the ease with which the enemy can overwhelm the country by his attack."[99] Brodie recalled the controversy this view had precipitated, including the "violence against this suggestion, not least [by] the chancellor of the University of Chicago," and concedes that "a defense based on deterrence is of less than no value if it fails to deter," and that a "reign of mutual fear which such a system implies would unquestionably would produce psychoses, which, in turn, would have effects, the direction and magnitude of which are unpredictable, almost unimaginable."[100] But he points out that on "the other hand, I think we should not for those reasons too readily write off the real deterrent value of the ability to retaliate against an aggressor, provided that that ability is somehow maintained."[101] And so Brodie pragmatically, and realistically, embraces deterrence as our last, best hope for peace.

Sea Power in the Atomic Age?

Brodie considers some other consequences of the nuclear era, including his realization that "in an atomic-bomb war there would be almost no scope whatever for sea power,"[102] extending a bridge to his earlier work on sea power while at the same time emphasizing the break with history precipitated by the advent of the bomb, adding that it was "a matter of no consequence at all that a navy is completely immune to the atomic bomb if the whole reason for its existence collapses,"[103] which would be the consequence of nuclear war, since the navy would thenceforth be "operating from a country which has lost its entire industry," and would consequently "lose both its ability to operate and its reason for operating."[104] With subsequent advances in missile technology and the deployment of ship- and submarine-launched missiles, Brodie would later come to recognize that sea power would become an essential component of an assured retaliatory capability—restoring sea power from this predicted obsolescence. But at this early stage of the atomic era, Brodie believes sea power to be past its historic peak. As he explains, this "is an issue of tremendous significance for the United States," which "has just inherited from Great Britain the mantle of leading sea power of the world. I think also, contrary to the opinions of a great many observers, that sea power reached its apogee in the war just ended. It was often spoken of as an obsolescent force, of less importance than other forces, especially air power. I can think of no war in history in which sea power played a greater role."[105] Indeed, Brodie suggests that "the Allied air attack on Germany . . . and Japan would both have been impossible without British–American command of the seas."[106] Added Brodie: "The ability of the three major powers to marshal and combine their forces and choose first one enemy to concentrate against and then the other was also a function of their command of the seas; and, of course, a large amount of the relatively high degree of security which the United States enjoyed was the result of its great sea power."[107] But now, in the atomic age, "geographical distance loses much of its importance as a barrier against attack," so much so that the long geographical isolation between the United States and the Soviet Union that provided an "impedance or obstacle to any outbreak of conflict" was, if not "entirely obliterated by the appearance of the atomic bomb" was at least "vitally affected."[108]

New Dangers of Appeasement

With the emergence of the atomic bomb, Brodie observes, comes "the collapse of the threat of war as an instrument of policy on the part of responsible governments"—but at the same time comes its "much greater instrument in the hands of irresponsible governments."[109] This concerns Brodie, as the "threat of war . . . on the part of responsible governments has had a tremendous utility in the past," and while its threat "obviously has not prevented war," Brodie suspects that "it probably did reduce the frequency of wars."[110] While Brodie does not allude to his early reflections on the dangers of appeasement, he does confront the specter of a new nuclear appeasement arising should an aggressor become a nuclear power, lacking the same sense of responsibility to its own people as a more responsible state: "Now we have the situation in which a government comparable to the Hitler government could pursue a line of policy comparable to that pursued by the Hitler government in 1938, and the cards would be stacked even more in its favor than was true in the past. In other words, the war with atomic bombs becomes so unthinkable that a government possessed of its senses and possessed also of some feeling of responsibility both to its own people and to the world could be nothing but appalled at even the thought of using a threat of force, in the knowledge that such a threat, if realized, might provoke an atomic war."[111] And so we find a bridge, directly interconnecting Brodie's thoughts on, and concerns about, peaceful change advocates and the corrosive dangers of appeasing a hostile power, as articulated during the interwar years that preceded World War II, and the more dangerous era of nuclear arms, when the threat of war made by a similarly aggressive state would certainly cause a more responsible government to pause, and perhaps once again accept the moral compromise that led down a very slippery slope toward continental conquest by a very dark regime. Brodie confronted such riddles, as he did before the advent of atomic weapons, and dared to think about what he himself described as 'unthinkable" many years before others would make "thinking about the unthinkable" a household phrase.

The End of Absolute Security

In the discussion that followed Brodie's presentation, his colleague Leo Pasvolsky suggested that there was "no such thing as security in an absolute sense," and as a result "[t]here is always an element of insecurity" and that it was a "question of degree," a view Brodie echoed: "I agree entirely with Mr. Pasvolsky's remark that there is no such condition as absolute security today," adding he "would go further and say that relative security as we have known it in the past no longer exists."[112] And echoing a comment from Cornelis W. DeKiewiet, Brodie said that he agreed "there is no longer any such thing as strategy"—a view he would reiterate a full decade later in his article "Strategy Hits a Dead End"—and consequently, "nations are bound, in so far as it does not look too ridiculous to them, to pursue their security in somewhat accustomed paths."[113] Brodie adds this does not mean his "approval or disapproval," but instead was meant "merely as a statement of fact," noting that Britain was thereby "justified in feeling that a domination of the entire European Continent by Russia means less security than she has today, even if what she has today is very little indeed."[114] Brodie added that the "very expansionist character" of the Soviet Union "prevents the working of the United Nations."[115]

Quincy Wright noted the hitherto unprecedented 8,000-mile range of airplanes delivering atomic weapons put "practically every large city in the world" within "that radius" from "the mainland of the United States" and that "reciprocally, practically every large city would be included from the Soviet territory," a point with which Brodie concurred—and to which Brodie added: "Practically all the great cities of the world are in the Northern Hemisphere, and especially when you consider that, in a Soviet–American conflict, the United States would probably have bases in northern Canada and the Soviet Union in northern Russia and Siberia, there is no question there."[116]

A Realist Critique of International Atomic Energy Control

In his Norman Wait Harris Memorial Foundation paper, Brodie lauded the innovation and ambition of the Lilienthal plan, which proposed internationalizing the control of atomic energy, as "a sample of human ingenuity applied to a great social and political problem" that was "not only an admirable achievement but a magnificent one," but he added a dose of realism by cautioning that "before we lose ourselves in rejoicing, we should consider that many aspects of that plan are of such nature that one can hardly be optimistic concerning acceptance of the plan on the part of certain powers whose co-operation is indispensable."[117] Brodie adds that he "can think of no issue more likely to provoke suspicion than our proposal that we and a number of other countries send representatives into the Soviet Union to conduct large-scale industrial, exploratory, and even policing operations."[118] Nor, adds Brodie, does it "help one bit that while we make that proposal we have in our left hand a sizable quantity of atomic bombs and are also continuing to produce them."[119] Brodie also expressed concerned with the "possible collapse of a system which is put into operation."[120] While challenging, such problems had to be confronted, boldly wading forth into the *unthinkable*, years before Herman Kahn, who rose to celebrity status in part for his willingness to think out loud about the *unthinkable*, made doing so famous. "To put the issue epigrammatically, war is unthinkable but not impossible, and therefore we must think about it."[121]

One conference attendee, Mr. Price, commented critically on what he described as Brodie's casual rejection of an international atomic control agency: "I thought Mr. Brodie dismissed the possibility of a real international agency to control the bomb a little bit too casually."[122] Brodie defended his view, praising the ambition if not the viability or practicality of the Lilienthal plan: "The mere fact that we have evolved this plan does not in itself give us cause for great rejoicing. I think it was a great accomplishment of ingenuity. I think it looks like the kind of plan which would be workable, if accepted. I was simply giving reasons for restraint of optimism for its acceptance."[123] Brodie added the plan, which was "in substance . . . the official American proposal, is only the bare outline of a plan; and in filling in that outline numerous great problems arise which, so far as I can see, we have not even explored in our own minds. . . . But the basic point is that the plan involves large-scale activities within Russia on the part of an international authority, of a nature which our experience this far in comparable issues does not lead us to have extravagant hope will be acceptable to them."[124]

Quincy Wright asked if the UN or the "atomic development authority" might be viewed by its members as " 'us' rather than as a foreigner," not unlike how Illinois may "not regard it as invasion if the federal government establishes a post office or even maintains federal troops here," though he cautions that it may be more like "the reaction that some of the inhabitants of western Connecticut had to the invasion of the United Nations" which "is not entirely hopeful on this."[125] Brodie added to this, noting of the Connecticut citizens who opposed the UN's arrival in New York, "And they are all mild men, too."[126] The Soviets, one could venture, would be much less mild and their opposition to invasive inspections that much more vehement. Indeed, in an earlier discussion on great power relationships, Brodie commented on Soviet Russia: "Whether or not the Russian government has abandoned the idea of world revolution as an abstract ideal, it seems not to have abandoned at any time the hypothesis that the Soviet Union is not secure in a capitalist world, which means that her recent experience would only augment, rather than diminish, the urge to capitalize on present instability."[127] Indeed, Brodie later predicted that in the event of an end to America's atomic monopoly and successful pursuit of the bomb by Stalin, "a radical change in thinking would take place in this country. I think there would be an even greater feeling of urgency and even of desperation."[128]

During the discussion of general security that followed Brodie's presentation, William T. R. Fox returned to the Lilienthal plan, noting: "It seems to me an admirable feature of the Lilienthal-Baruch proposals that it gives to the atomic development authority a monopoly of all kinds of atomic energy activities," and hence the "[m]ere performance of uranium extraction and any of these other things convicts the power."[129] Brodie responded: "I think you can put that another way and say that the great merit of the plan is that it minimizes the inspection problem, which otherwise appeared to a great many persons, especially some of the physical scientists, as an insuperable one. However, it does not by any means obliterate the inspection problem. A very sizeable inspection function remains."[130] While minimized, nations must "permit foreign agencies . . . to carry on large exploratory, industrial, and even policing activities within its country, which is an enormous abatement of sovereignty. However desirable such abatement may appear in the abstract, the question is: Is a nation like Russia prepared to relinquish that much of its authority?"[131] Brodie lauds the plan for its reliance on an international authority to conduct inspections, stating "that is why the plan has such merit. . . . I say, the great merit of the plan is that it minimizes those sources of friction."[132]

In a later part of the discussion, Brodie observed, "I don't think anyone would suppose for a moment that we should not try earnestly and patiently to secure its adoption" but that we must nonetheless "analyze the minimum requirements inherent in that plan and decide what we can afford to yield without yielding the essence of the plan," adding that he believed it was "heartening . . . that the reception in this country, including . . . Congress, has been, on the whole, distinctly favorable," and likewise "that thus far we have no categorical rejection on the part of the Russians."[133] But Brodie remains most comfortable with deterrence and its reliance on logic, and the mutuality of fear and of the desire to survive—and not any one state's good will: "under the atomic bomb, assuming reciprocal use on the part of at least two belligerents, you have a condition which you have never had before, namely, that even the victor would suffer far greater destruction and devastation than any defeated country has ever suffered in recorded history."[134] He added: "With the atomic bomb you have a condition under which war becomes universally destructive. You might say that that margin of difference is not enough to give you great anxiety concerning the elimination of the bomb, but I think it is an important margin of difference."[135]

Brodie addressed the challenges of disarmament, noting "you have a greater promise of success if you press for limited objectives. Our history of the pursuit of disarmament in general has not been an especially fortunate one."[136] Adds Brodie: "In the case of the atomic bomb we have not only a limited objective but a new and cosmic force which we have reason to suppose will cause nations to feel differently concerning its limitation from the way they have felt concerning the limitation of more orthodox arms, and I think the reception, at least in this country, is indicative of that fact. In other words, our problem is 'merely' that of making the Russians see it as we do."[137]

Quincy Wright suggested that rather than eliminate the atomic bomb, perhaps mankind would instead eliminate war since with "the knowledge of atomic weapons general, any country that starts a war by traditional methods will know that the way will probably develop into an atomic war," so if "the anxiety to avoid atomic war has been sufficient to achieve effective measures to prevent a sudden use of atomic weapons, it might be sufficient to induce measures adequate to prevent war altogether."[138] Brodie agreed, since this is the operating mechanism of deterrence; "if we succeeded in eliminating the production of the atomic bomb universally, we would have that benefit, namely, the removal of immediate fear plus the benefit that the deterrent value of the bomb is still there."[139]

Brodie again revisited the Lilienthal plan at the end of the discussion of general security, again lauding its merits but cautioning that we must not overstate its likelihood of success. It proponents "have argued that the great merit of the plan is that it also combines with the inspection function the positive function of research and distribution of the benefits of peacetime use."[140] He continued: "It seems to me that we are justified in solacing ourselves with the fact that atomic energy does furnish promise of peacetime uses, but I think we should not deceive ourselves by it. It seems to me, if we accept the most optimistic predictions on what it will mean in welfare, in terms of combating disease as well as in producing energy, power, and heat, that the whole sum total of it is unimportant compared to the fact that we have the material of which a few pounds can blow up a whole city. . . . we've got to consider the security angle first and the welfare angle only as it fits into it."[141]

Limits of International Laws and Treaties

Brodie was asked about the ability of international law to pacify nuclear-armed mankind through treaties limiting arms or committing nations to their non-use. In the atomic era the dangers are so great that: "Each nation has to be sure, or as sure as human ingenuity permits it to be, that there is no violation or evasion. In other words, the evasion or violation has to be practically *impossible*, not merely *improbable*, and that is a very different situation from what we have had before."[142] He added that "the only really effective disarmament programs of the past have pertained to naval disarmaments, and those, of course, are units which are extremely difficult to hide, battleships especially."[143] Brodie also notes the successful use of treaties to ban the use of gas in World War II, adding that "there is another issue there, especially in relation to gas. You have a very different order of military utility between gas and atomic bombs."[144] And in the case of gas, there were "other instruments which were not barred by law, such as tanks of gelatinous gasoline" which proved as effective and were as easily transported by air.[145] Also differentiating poison gas from atomic weapons, Brodie noted "in the case of gas you have such things as gas masks and decontamination units," providing not only "the ability to retaliate but also actual protection," the latter which atomic weapons lacked.[146]

Rethinking World Government

During the discussion of general security, William T. R. Fox challenged Brodie's faith in deterrence: "Mr. Brodie suggested that defense can be thought of only in terms of deterrents," noting that "[t]here has been considerable objection in certain quarters to erecting a system of atomic energy control on the substratum of retaliation."[147] Fox also reiterated the venomous reaction to Brodie's proposal by the chancellor of the University of Chicago: "Mr. Brodie mentioned in his remarks the book review which Chancellor Hutchins published in the *New York Times* and which is written from the point of view of world government. The Chancellor championed the argument that only world government can help. I cannot see how that would help very much, because, in order to establish world government, one has to compel the powers which are not willing to accept the authority of world government to accept this authority; therefore world government would be nothing else than, to use a historical term, *Pax Romana*. World government would be possible only if the power which has the monopoly of the atomic bomb would really use this monopoly, or would threaten to use this monopoly, against governments which would not accept world government."[148]

Brodie responded to criticisms leveled at him by proponents of world government, noting: "I think a great deal can be said against the idea. I will confine myself to only one remark. I think that the preaching of world government as a solution to the problem is really a rejection of the problem, because even the proponents concede, as Mr. Hutchins did in that article . . . that this is, after all, a long-term proposal, not a short-term one. I am not interested in whether or not it is a valid even for the long term. I am thinking only of the proposition which I think the late Lord Keynes originated, that in the long term we are all dead. I would also now add to that: In the short term we may all be killed. So it seems to me much more profitable to consider solutions which, if possible at all, can be attained within the next two decades, let us say."[149] On the proposition that world government could only be achieved by conquest, Brodie noted "at present only two powers appear to have anything like the strength necessary to effect such a conquest, and of those two only one appears prepared to carry through with the administration and policing of conquered territories, especially if those territories are world-wide. It is prepared and to some degree equipped to do so. I obviously do not have in mind the United States, which is having trouble enough staffing its occupation armies in Germany and Japan."[150]

From Balance of Power to Balance of Terror

Mr. White turned back to the topic of the balance of power, suggesting the concept's obsolescence only occurs if there's "a monopoly of the bombs" held by one power; but if "the bombs are fairly equally distributed among the great powers," he suspects they will "tend to offset each other in terms of destruction of each other's cities, populations, and so on, much as high-powered air power has done."[151] Brodie disagrees, pointing out that: "Except that under the old system you could always depend on a certain duration of time, a rather long time, before your instruments could take decisive effect," and "[e]ven if you had a monopoly of air power, you could not depend on bringing a great power to its knees within a term of weeks; you would need a lot more time, during which all sorts of other things could happen."[152] The experience of World War II showed that it took several years to achieve command of the air over Germany: "You could never expect a war to begin with a greater monopoly," as "it took a pretty long time to destroy her industry, even if we consider only the period during which the most effective bombing was carried on—which was the last year. During that year a nation might conceivably, if it had the resources, be able to marshal those resources and resist the attack."[153] All that changed after the emergence of atomic weapons: "Where you have a situation in which the decisive phases of the war may take only days or hours, you have something new and almost completely unknown. I don't think I would approach a solution of what would happen under such circumstances by a study of past situations. One would have to start anew to think it through."[154] Brodie speculates on the dynamics of a post-attack conflict, suggesting that "even if you imagine a situation in which both sides have, let us say, their cities wiped out, you certainly don't have equality. You have all kinds of factors entering into the situation, such as relative degrees of panic and disintegration. In one case, you might have a readiness to capitulate on the part of those who remain who have the authority to do so; on the other side, you may have a readiness to conduct guerrilla warfare, which would require an invasion."[155] Quincy Wright commented that he "was very much interested in Mr. Brodie's introduction of the time element, which seems to me the crucial thing."[156]

In the discussion session, Brodie examined the question, posed by Quincy Wright, if "the invention of the atomic bomb has rendered the balance of power more stable or less stable than it was before."[157] Brodie observed that it was "not only likely to be less stable but that it has become a much more ambiguous concept; that is, the old calculus of what constitutes power largely falls to the ground. Certainly, industrial strength does not mean a great deal if you assume that the industry of a nation will be the first thing to go, that is, if that assumption is valid. Size of population ceases to have the importance it had before. Various other factors which it has lately become fashionable to add up in a calculus of power have to be considered completely anew."[158]

Changing Course: Rethinking 'Traditional Paths'

Brodie noted there remains a certain momentum in foreign policy that propelled states to seek security along "traditional paths," just as Britain did with regard to its preoccupation with who possessed the Low Countries, even this became less critical to British security after the arrival of steam power; he thus concluded as the atomic era began: "This suggests that we might take stock of our foreign policy in respect to distant bases and see what it is that we are striving for which means a lot of friction with others countries but which may have no intrinsic benefit in terms of strategic use for the future."[159] Considering various configurations of the international system in the atomic age, Brodie notes "with the distinction between monopoly as against multilateral possession, it seems to me that in one case you have a clear instance not only of lack of deterrent value but also of a positive incentive to aggression; and that is something we always have to bear in mind in relation to any minimum requirements for an international system. The worst kind of system—one which would be worse than no system—would be one in which an aggressive state could by evasion gain a monopoly; and in such a case aggression would be far cheaper than it has ever been in the past, and the kind of calculation . . . on the part of the Japanese war lords would be not only much more likely to be made but also would be accurate."[160]

And though it was only 1946 when Brodie participated in the 22nd Norman Wait Harris Memorial Foundation lectures, he already imagined the forthcoming "missile age" that he would christen about a decade later: "The Bureau of Ordnance of the Navy has developed some so-called guided missiles, some of which depend on infra-red rays and some on radar, which are used for short-range bombing. It is no secret now. . . . Possibly that kind of technique might be devoted to very long-range rockets. And also we have to consider the fact . . . that, with the atomic bomb, you have a premium on the development of long-range rockets such as you have never had before—and from the point of view of physics it is theoretically possible to build, even with existing fuel, a rocket capable of a few thousand miles' range. . . . I should imagine a nation which had, let's say, four thousand-mile rockets which had the capacity of being guided accurately would be in a somewhat better position than a nation which depended on aircraft. How much better depends on what kinds of variables."[161]

The War in Heaven

Five years before the arrival of the H-bomb, Brodie would turn again for metaphorical, and one might add doctrinal, inspiration—just as he did in his 1941 *Sea Power in the Machine Age*—to the epic story of the war in Heaven as described in Book VI of *Paradise Lost* in his January 1947 article "The Atomic Dilemma" in the *Annals of the American Academy of Political and Social Science*.[162] Here he further elaborated on Milton's haunting but prophetic allegory, from which Brodie coined the term "super-absolute weapon," suggesting something more fearsome than the "absolute" weapon of the immediate post-Hiroshima period.

It is intriguing that five years later, such "super-absolute" weaponry would indeed emerge in the arsenals of man, and that it would be initially called the "superbomb" or "super" by most before the more sanitary term H-bomb came into vogue. Then, the atomic era, with its menacing increase in the totality of war toward what looked to be the equivalent of Clausewitz's theoretical abstraction of "absolute war," would experience another jarring leap in destructiveness only a five years after *The Absolute Weapon* came to press, as fusion weapons, long known to be theoretically possible, quickly became practically possible as well—with expectations gaining currency throughout 1952 that forthcoming tests of the new thermonuclear "superbomb" were expected to be successful, which proved to be the case when on November 1, 1952, America detonated the very first hydrogen bomb—more like a small factory than a working bomb since it weighed over 62 tons and stood nearly 20 feet tall—code-named "Ivy Mike," yielding between 10 and 12 megatons of explosive blast, and generating a fireball over three miles in width.

Revisiting the epic war for Heaven, Brodie recounts: "After a day of fighting, Raphael relates, the issue is still in doubt, although the rebellious angels have received the more horrid injury. . . . Satan is persuaded that their inferiority is one of weapons alone, and he announces that he has already invented the instrument which will shift the balance. . . . The following day the rebel seraphs, exploiting to the utmost the benefits of tactical surprise, secretly bring up their field pieces and commit them at a critical moment to action. At first the infernal engines wreak dreadful execution. But the loyal angels, not to be surpassed in the application of science to war, seize in the fury of the moment upon the 'absolute' weapon. Tearing the seated hills of Heaven from their roots, they lift them by their shaggy tops and hurl them upon the rebel hosts. Those among the latter who are not immediately overwhelmed do likewise. In a moment the battle has become an exchange of hurtling hills, creating in their flight a dismal shade and infernal noise. 'War,' observes Raphael, 'seemed a civil game to this uproar.' Heaven is threatened with imminent ruin, and the situation is resolved in the only way left open-the intervention of God himself, who introduces what the modern radio announcer would unquestionably call the 'super-absolute weapon.' "[163]

Brodie explains that this epic war for Heaven "casts into its ultimate dramatization the chief dilemma which confronts modern man and which, while commonplace, has with the coming of the atomic bomb reached truly tragic if not catastrophic proportions—the dilemma of ever widening disparity in terms of accomplishment and of magnitude of consequences between man's physical inventions and his social adaptation to them."[164] Brodie is troubled that "even in the most favorable of contexts and with an omniscient and all-powerful God as a directly interested party, these nearly perfect celestial beings were unable to prevent the outbreak among themselves of a civil war which was saved from being suicidal only by the ulterior circumstance that angels cannot die,"[165] in contrast to mortal man. With man as fallible as he is mortal, the particular destructiveness of the atomic bomb deeply worries Brodie, who discounts the virtues of peacetime atomic energy and medical uses of radiation for treating cancers when confronted by the sheer dangers presented by the bomb: "We may be solaced by the promise, but we should not be deceived by it. Cancer is a horrible disease, and the radioactive materials generated in uranium piles may carry us far towards alleviating or even eradicating it. But under modern conditions of sanitation, neither cancer nor the whole complex of known diseases even remotely threatens the basic fabric of our civilization, as the atomic bomb clearly does."[166] Adds Brodie: "In terms of power, nature has already bountifully endowed man with fuels to turn his machines and propel his vehicles. The increasing efficiency of those machines and vehicles has been generally assumed to be a good thing, and the use in them of atomic fuels—to the degree that such fuels prove adaptable will no doubt greatly accelerate the trend towards higher mechanical efficiency in the tools of peacetime pursuits. But the rewards of the end result inevitably appear meager against the bare fact that a few pounds of substance can blast whole cities into oblivion. The scientists who worked on the bomb must have felt that intuitively, for Professor Smyth tells us that many of them wished during 1943 and 1944 that the experiments upon which they were engaged would fail."[167]

In addition to the medical and energy promises of atomic energy, Brodie considers the hopes among many that the advent of the bomb would motivate mankind to embrace world government, dismissing such a outcome as highly improbable: "Another miracle, the expectation of which has now become widespread among an extraordinary number of otherwise sophisticated people, is represented by the symbol 'world government.' I use the word 'symbol' advisedly, because my own limited experience with proponents of the principle is that few of them have in mind a blueprint for a system which would make sense to themselves, let alone others. Their entire intellectual capital in this respect is an insistence that mankind will now be united by an intensification of the kind of fear—the fear of one another—which has always thus far had the opposite result."[168] Brodie notes that "[p]rominent among those who are determined to bring our politics abreast of our physics, in other words to institute 'world government,' are many of the leading scientists who assisted in the production of the atomic bomb" who were "understandably enough, gravely shaken by the appalling miracle they have wrought. They are also aware of their limitations as producers of further miracles in their own field. None of them, so far as I am aware, has any confidence in the ability of science to devise some agent which will counter the bomb and rob it of its terrors. They find it more profitable, therefore, to enter a field in which they have no specialized knowledge to encumber them in their designs, to mitigate the effect of their earlier work."[169] Brodie takes these scientists to task for presuming they could tame the chaos of world politics when they proved impotent to tame the inherent lethality of their atomic creation, plutonium: "It is really unfortunate that these scientists have not been consistent in their methodology. If they had used in the laboratory the same kind of reasoning they have demonstrated in the political forum, we should not now have the atomic bomb to worry about. The physical scientist learns at the very outset of his career to analyze the properties of his materials and to adjust his techniques completely to those properties. He has, to be sure, created elements not previously found in nature; but even plutonium, once created, showed itself to be a true child of nature in having a will of its own concerning its proper behavior as Element No. 94. It has specific characteristics which determine its utility, and in order to exploit that utility the physicist had to adjust to all the peculiar manifestations of its coy and spritely individuality. The physicist would never dream of exhorting an element to behave like something which it was not, and it is only because he wastes no time doing so that he is able to accomplish such marvels. The physicist might therefore be expected to appreciate the fact that the cure for the world's ills does not lie in exhorting men, or the states into which they have become organized, to behave in a way which the facts of day-to-day events indicate to be utterly foreign to their natures."[170]

In a world of "two giants," the United States and the Soviet Union, "an agency with superior power not only does not exist but cannot be manufactured out of existing ingredients, even if the genuine will to do so existed, unless that will goes to the extent of preparedness on the part of the United States and of Soviet Russia to dismember themselves. Splitting the United States and splitting Soviet Russia seem to present a more difficult problem than splitting the atom proved to be."[171] Brodie rebukes University of Chicago Chancellor Hutchins, who "asserts that world government is 'necessary, therefore possible,'" noting that "one might overlook the non sequitur and reply that what is manifestly impossible it is a waste of time to regard as necessary. What is necessary is in any case not world government but control of the atom bomb, by whatever means are possible."[172] (Brodie further notes, in a subtle and indirect reference to Hutchins' rebuke of Brodie in an earlier review of *The Absolute Weapon* published by the *New York Times* in which Hutchins—as described by Brodie's mentor Quincy Wright, "championed the argument that only world government can help," a view that Wright, like Brodie, rejected—how, "in the same article Chancellor Hutchins admonishes certain persons, whose negative views on world union he regards as reprehensible, to 'read *The Federalist*'—thus bringing in the inevitable example of the American Union—one might refer him especially to the second of the papers known by that name."[173]) Brodie instead "urges realism," adding that it "behooves the political scientist to set about analyzing the problem of atomic-age security in a two-power world. It is a world in which the polarity of power is matched by a polarity of ideologies, and in which the ordinary barriers to human communication and sympathy, difficult enough to scale at best, are many times augmented by deliberate state policy on the part of one of the two primary powers. If the scholar insists on speaking in terms of an ideal world wholly different from that which confronts him, he is merely rejecting his problem."[174] Thus, Brodie concludes, "The business of devising and pursuing a sound national policy in a desperately dangerous world is something which demands all our intelligence as well as our moral strength. If the words 'national policy' sound too narrow, I submit that national policy is the only policy upon which we can hope to exercise any influence, and is our only channel for affecting international policy."[175]

Early Thoughts on Limited War in the Atomic Age

Brodie next presents a discussion of various proposals with regard to "limited warfare" rooted in a realist approach to the new nuclear world that "are at least based on the determination to work with the materials available rather than those we would like to have," rejecting the notion proposed by famed British strategic theory, Liddell Hart, "who takes the position that since it seems impossible to eliminate war, we should at least attempt to restore to war the limited character it possessed in the eighteenth century," which Brodie finds "[a]t first blush" to seem "fanciful" but which "has at least the virtue of representing a situation which did actually obtain historically" and which was furthermore "in part reflected in the proposed draft convention presented by Mr. Gromyko before the Atomic Energy Commission, which on the surface is primarily a convention for the outlawry of the atomic bomb," which like Liddell Hart's proposal was "essentially a plan to limit the nature of wars, differing essentially, however, from previous proposals along such lines in the tight system of guarantees incorporated in it."[176]

Brodie points out, however, that the "limited-warfare characteristic of the period between Grotius and Napoleon was never a matter of deliberate restraint of power in the sense that a renunciation of total warfare would be today, for the concept of total war did not exist, and under the circumstances prevailing could not exist. The limitations obtaining were imposed in part by material considerations," including the fact that "campaigns were fought by mercenaries, who would desert if pressed too hard," and that it was also "necessary to restrain their avidity for plunder partly as a matter of discipline, partly out of fear of retaliation in an era when all territories were at one time or another subject to the passage of enemy armies, and partly out of desire to refrain from offending a population which was not necessarily predisposed to hostility."[177] Additionally, warfare was "the calling of the aristocracy, whose lopsided code of morals, however deficient in other respects, permitted no compromise with the code of the duel," and as consequence was "an art governed by tradition and managed by conservatives."[178] It took "the plebeian Napoleon, exploiting the nationalistic fervor of the French Revolution, who involved the populations in war and who, especially in Iberia, plunged hostilities back into the bestial character of the Thirty Years' War"[179]—and whose contribution to the history war marked the arrival of total war, or war without limits. Ever since, Brodie observes, "all the sanctions making for limited war have collapsed—moral, social, and economic. Whether or not the two great wars of this century were in fact 'total wars' (and there were in fact important qualifications to 'totality' in each belligerent country even during the recent war), the fact is that the basis for total warfare may now be considered firmly established."[180] That's because total warfare "stems from total mobilization, and total mobilization could have no meaning prior to the industrial revolution when there existed no great margin of resources to be converted to war" and which as a technique "had to be discovered, evolved, and perfected," and Brodie suggests that it "would be much easier to expunge from the human race the knowledge of how to produce the atomic bomb than the knowledge of how to produce total mobilization."[181]

Brodie refutes the logic of the argument put forth by some advocates of "outlawing the atomic bomb" that we should take solace in knowing that "poison gases were not used during the recent war" as "poison gas and atomic bombs represent two wholly different orders of magnitude in military utility," and "unlike gas, the atomic bomb can scarcely fail to have fundamental or decisive effects if used at all."[182] And while this would reduce both the logic and likely effectiveness of efforts to similarly outlaw the bomb, Brodie concedes such efforts are not without value (much as future, protracted arms control talks) since the very effort "might prove the indispensable crystallizer of a state of balance which operates against use of the bomb. But without the existence of a state of balance—in terms of reciprocal guarantees against manufacture of the bomb or reciprocal ability to retaliate in kind if the bomb is used—any treaty purposing to outlaw the bomb in war would have thrust upon it a burden far heavier than such a treaty can normally bear."[183]

Thus any effort—whether the Lilienthal plan then under negotiation, or a subsequent endeavor—by the U.S. government to control these new weapons of mass destruction must be pursued within a realistic framework, and "will need at every turn the criticism and support of a sober and informed public opinion; and one may earnestly hope that specialists in the field of political science will assume their proper function of leadership in the instruction of that public opinion," demonstrating "tough minds as well as soft hearts" and a willingness to "to reject as incompatible with science the standards of Hollywood, where all stories must have a happy ending."[184] Adds Brodie, "For the scientist it is better to arrive at truth than at an optimistic conclusion which is false—though, incidentally, I should regard as the most pessimistic of all possible conclusions the notion that our safety depends on a complete revolution in the hearts and minds of men."[185] In this vein, Brodie advises that "the political scientist must reject as meaningless and useless the frequently expressed appeal in support of a given plan—repeated even in the Lilienthal report—that 'the alternative is catastrophe.' Since that appeal has already been made in support of several different plans, it cannot be wholly true of any of them," and the "alternative to any magnificent plan which fails to work or win acceptance is always another plan, which may be less magnificent and less generous in its promises of security but which may have a better chance of working—so long as we do not deceive ourselves as to its actual content of security. The pursuit of security has always been an unending one, in which, like Keats's lover on the Grecian Urn, we are never more than 'winning near the goal.' Absolute security against the atomic bomb lies irretrievably in the past, and neither panic nor incantations will help us to reinvoke it."[186]

War Department Thinking on the Atomic Bomb

During the summer of 1947, Brodie published back-to-back articles in *The Bulletin of the Atomic Scientists* that examined and critiqued the response by the U.S. Army and Navy to the bomb— addressing an official policy statement, "The Effects of the Atomic Bomb on National Security (An Expression of War Department Thinking)" that had been submitted to Congress and later published in the April 12, 1947 *Army Navy Journal*, and then reprinted by *The Bulletin of the Atomic Scientists* in June 1947. Fred Kaplan, in *Wizards of Armageddon*, suggests that Brodie was the primary influence on the development of the *official* thinking of the U.S. War Department, citing a survey of military thinking about the new weapon conducted by Brodie preserved in the Bernard Brodie Papers, whose lessons were synthesized and presented in *The Bulletin of the Atomic Scientists*, first in June 1947 ("War Department Thinking on the Atomic Bomb") and then in July 1947 ("Navy Department Thinking on the Atomic Bomb").[187] In the introduction to the first of the series in the June 1947 edition of *The Bulletin*, its editors write that the second article to come, "Navy Department Thinking on the Atomic Bomb," was authored by Brodie "while in the part-time employ of the Legislative Reference Service" of the Library of Congress and that the War Department report was "prepared by the Army" but had been "patterned upon" Brodie's report on Navy thinking. So Brodie's ideas worked their way into both documents, directly or indirectly, and reflect many of the same arguments he had made in his 1945 article and further developed in his 1946 contributions to *The Absolute Weapon*.

As in Brodie's 1945 article, "The Atomic Bomb and American Security," the 1947 War Department report began with a discussion of the new weapon's capabilities as well as limitations imposed in part by its enormous destructive power: "The atomic bomb is not an all purpose weapon; in fact, it is rather narrowly limited in its employment due to its great destructive power (which is not significant reducible at present), and its relative high cost as a single weapon. In a restricted sense, it is just another bomb, particularly suited for purposes of destruction of major targets, such as cities, industrial concentrations and major military targets. In a broader and more accurate sense, it is a 'decision in a package,' providing a means of wiping out large segments of civilization."[188] While at the time, the bomb was deliverable only by means of "long-range heavy bomber type aircraft, or to surreptitious transportation to, placement on, and detonation at a target,"[189] looking ahead, it was expected that "[f]uture deployments will likely make possible the employment of atomic explosives by such other means as pilotless aircraft, and as war-heads in guided missiles and torpedoes."[190] Even dirty bombs were foreseen: "Such weapons might make use of radioactive effects of particles dispersed by means other than explosion, thus providing the radiation effects without the accompanying blast and heat effects."[191] It was also foreseen that "satisfactory international control of atomic energy provides the only alternative to a future atomic armament race with attendant world-wide day-to-day fear of atomic attack," the latter which would come to define the early Cold War era with concerted efforts at arms control to only gain momentum once the nuclear balance had stabilized, along with a global nonproliferation effort to limit the spread of nuclear weapons to other states, and while the War Department pledged full support of "present efforts to establish such international control," it also recognized that at best these would deliver "a period of approximately one year in which to prepare for a full-scale atomic attack" and because of this, "we must retain indefinitely . . . our knowledge and industrial capacity to produce atomic weapons."[192]

The War Department report considers "The Importance of Time," noting that it was expected to take "several years" before "any other nation" would develop an atomic bomb and "an additional period of several years" before they would have "a significant number of bombs," with "perhaps as many as eight to fifteen" years during which "only the U.S. will possess atomic bombs in significant quantities," after which "other nations will possess atomic bombs in significant quantities."[193] Before such a time, "our strategy, tactics, weapons, and political and military requirements, must undergo gradual evolution, in such a manner that we will attain the advantages of accelerated development and acceptance of the new, while simultaneously retaining the full security afforded by the old. Time is an all-important factor in our military posture."[194] Echoing Brodie's first strategic assessment of the new weapon, the War Department report suggests that the "end of an atomic war may find both victor and vanquished in a state of almost complete ruin," and it thus "follows that winning the war may well not be preserving national security."[195] Indeed, America would now confront a new vulnerability: "The development of long-rage aircraft and guided missiles, however, coupled with the introduction of atomic explosives now makes the U.S. vulnerable to the destructive effects of total war and leaves us in the position of no longer being able to count so heavily on our geographical location for the protection of our homeland."[196] Additionally, the "'cushion of time,' which we have historically enjoyed for the mobilization of our resources, both manpower and industry, is lost";[197] and the loss of this cushion increases the value of allies as well as "far-flung bases" since the "shock of a powerful aggressor, with modern weapons, including the atomic bomb, can be better absorbed by a number of nations than by a single nation."[198] Also required is an "effective intelligence services," as well as measures for civil defense: "War today is total war. Since a future attack on the U.S. will be an attack of our industry and the communities serving our industry, we must be prepared to reduce to a minimum the damage, casualties, and dislocation resulting from such an attack."[199]

The War Department report also echoes a theme that would remain one of Brodie's most cherished: that of the important partnership between the military and the new generation of civilian scientists who contributed so much to the war effort: "The atomic bomb is the successful result of history's greatest example of the cooperative effort of science, industry, and government to produce a weapon of war" and the "lesson it teaches is the extreme importance of continuing research and development efforts in the interest of National Security," as "[o]ur own research and development leading to the production of the bomb has taught us that it is possible for a nation to adapt scientific and industrial progress to warfare in such a manner as to affect decisively the outcome."[200] Going forward, it will now be "necessary to have forces in being capable of providing instantaneous defense against air attacks or surface forays against us, of minimizing the effects of such attacks, and of concurrently launching counterattacks against vital enemy targets, including the bases, launching sites, and industrial facilities which support an enemy atomic attack and are invulnerable to our aerial counterattack."[201] In addition to "defensive forces capable of intercepting and destroying aircraft and/or guided missiles," the War Department report identified that the "most important aspect of the absence of a preparatory period is that our counter-attacking forces must be ready for instant retaliation," including "strategic bombers, and . . . long-range guided missiles when they are developed, to carry atomic explosives to those installations, probably deep in enemy territory, which are vital to the continuation of his early attacks on us or which are necessary to his general war effort."[202] Central to strategy in the new era will be strategic bombing, and the War Department report asserts the "belief now that strategic bombardment either by piloted aircraft or by guided missiles of one form or another provides the single most important element of our military capabilities."[203] As the atomic bomb favors the offensive, balanced forces in being are required; "[u]nless we provide adequate means to reduce our vulnerability we may find in the moment of emergency that we are unable to launch our own atomic offensive," including a "minimum degree of such protection essential to the preservation of our retaliatory counter-offensive power."[204] And while dispersion of industrial assets would enhance America's military security, the report notes—as Brodie's earlier article had—that the "pattern of U.S. life, social and industrial, will never permit the degree of dispersion which military strategy makes desirable," though it is possible to "disperse the bulk of our critical military stockpiles" and "some of our vital industry, particularly new plants."[205] But the dispersion of our cities "appears beyond our capabilities" not because of financial considerations "but because of the political resistance of our people against being regimented, uprooted, and forcibly moved," adding, in language that echoes Brodie's: "Our strategy must be based on realism, and the all-out dispersion of industry can only be classed as a militarily desirable but unattainable measure."[206]

The War Department report concludes that the "Atomic Bomb is Not Enough," and "[w]hile the inherent offensive value" of the new weapon was "unquestioned, it would be shortsighted to believe that even during the interim period it was sufficient in itself. A large measure of security comes to the U.S. from the very existence of its military strength which is evidenced in its conventional force in being, as well as such unorthodox weapons as the atomic bomb," and "[t]o retain our strength in terms understandable to all nations, we must continue in existence certain of the forces which clearly spell power to the potential aggressors. These forces include Fighter and Bomber units, Infantry Divisions and Aircraft Carriers; in short, the conventional forces that the man on the street can recognize anywhere in the world."[207] Additionally, the War Department report argues that "tactics are relatively unaffected by the advent of the atomic bomb," and until the bomb could "achieve a decision by itself (and the certainty that it can has yet to be demonstrated), conventional military operations will continue to be employed, using, for some time to come, substantially the tactics of the end of World War II, characterized by constantly increasing speed of movement and more concentrated power," and the "principle of dispersion to limit the effects of Air action will be of greater consequence."[208] The bomb would present a new challenge to the principle of concentration, as "[m]assing of forces can be effected only with the full realization of the risks involved in offering a profitable target for the employment of the atomic bomb," which necessitates the formation of new tactics "to evolve methods of quickly massing for offensive action."[209] The advent of the new weapon will "only add to the burden borne by all peoples and all nations in the interest of National Security," and has thus "not given the U.S. an inexpensive substitute for a balanced Military establishment"—and in fact "has made the defense of the nation more difficult, more expensive, and less certain of attainment."[210]

In the following month's issue of *The Bulletin of the Atomic Scientists*, Brodie presents a summary of Navy thinking titled "Navy Department Thinking on the Atomic Bomb" based upon interviews he conducted "with Admiral Nimitz and senior naval officers."[211] Navy planning considered "three wholly different situations," including "1. Peacetime, when the Navy's functions, apart from augmenting preparedness for war and thereby guarding the peace, are taken up with policing obligations"; "2. A war in which the atomic bomb is either not used at all or introduced only substantially after the onset of hostilities, or perhaps used only by us and not by our enemies"; and "3. A war in which atomic bombs are available in substantial numbers to both sides and in which reciprocal resort to their use may occur at any time."[212] Conceding that "the forces required to fight a war say fifteen years from now may be very different from those existing today," the Navy Department also noted that "the forces which would be needed to fight a war today or in the near future are those which on the naval side represent pretty much the kind of fleet which we have and are trying to keep," and which "operate as a deterrent to aggression anywhere in the world."[213] And, "Thus, for the 'intermediate' era of the relatively near future as well as for the present," four "general types of naval forces will be required," including "1. Mobile tactical air forces, embodied in aircraft carrier groups"; "2. Amphibious forces" including "specialized transports, escort craft, supporting ships . . . and tactical air forces"; "3. General escort forces, including anti-aircraft and anti-submarine craft"; and "4. Submarine forces, including submarines for coordinated attack, for bombardment, for reconnaissance, for sea air rescue, and for special purposes, including the launching of new weapons."[214] The report affirms that the "present United States active and reserve fleets, which already comprise the types of forces described above, appear suitable for the kind of hostilities likely to prevail over at least the next ten years."[215] As the War Department report had noted, "under the conditions of war in which atomic bombs are available to a possible enemy, the importance of depriving the enemy of bases near one's own shored and preferably of acquiring and maintaining bases close to his territory remains at least as great as before."[216]

One area where the Navy Department erred was in its belief that it was "a wholly reasonable and safe assumption that rockets with atomic warheads capable of thousands of miles of range are not to be expected for at least another twenty-five years," and that "[d]espite the prevalence of romantic predictions concerning 'push-button' warfare, presumably carried on with rockets capable both of great accuracy and of some four or five thousand miles range, experts in the field of supersonic guided missiles—including civilian scientists so engaged—are practically at one in their conviction that such missiles cannot be considered to be in the offing."[217] In fact, the missile age would come much sooner than expected, by the better part of a decade. Another predictive misfire was in the area of defensive measures, which at that time looked promising, just as was experienced during World War II—in part because of the earlier error with regard to the missile threat, when slower-moving and more easily interdicted aircraft were the primary offensive threat: "The large subsonic bobig aircraft . . . operating at extreme range, cannot be considered a sufficiently reliable means of delivering scarce and expensive atomic bombs against a strong and well-alerted enemy," the Navy Department believed, and the "present technological trend is decidedly in favor of the defense as against the offense in ordinary strategic bombing," with jet aircraft then believed to be "much more suited to short-range fighter planes than to large, long-range bombers."[218] However, the Navy Report did acknowledge that "such trends may reverse themselves in the future as they have in the past," but noted that "the present trend is the only one we can see in operation," a trend that "decidedly favors—as against the recent past—the defense of large centers of population and industry."[219]

But on the other hand, the Navy Department recognized that the "solution from the offensive side is the resort to short-range but very high speed jet-propelled bombers or preferably to supersonic missiles representing an evolutionary development of V-2," and even if intercontinental-range missiles were still in the realm of science fiction, it was conceivable to envision "increasing the range of the V-2 by a factor of perhaps two and arming it with an atomic warhead," but this would require basing close to enemy territory, whether an advanced base on a "distant territory" or potentially in "the form of a ship, including submersible types."[220] As for fleet protection, the Navy Department believed that in "most respects defense of naval craft against atomic bomb attack involves simply a further development of the types of defenses already erected against ordinary aerial attack," though "[t]here will of course be an even greater premium than in the past upon downing enemy aircraft at a distance from one's ships rather than close in," and "[s]o long as the enemy is obliged to sacrifice a large proportion of his planes in order to reach the inner defenses, he must regard his aircraft as an unreliable and wasteful means of delivering atomic bombs, especially against targets which by their ability to disperse can greatly limit the amount of damage suffered by any one bomb."[221] It is in recognition of this capacity of naval forces, to employ tactical dispersion to increase fleet security from atomic attack, the Navy Department observes that the "problem of dispersion, especially, involves strategic as well as tactical considerations which, while by no means wholly new, pose a different order of urgency from that experienced in the past," a problem reinforced by the experience at Pearl Harbor where even before the nuclear era the dangers of fleet concentration were tragically revealed.[222] While "with non-atomic weapons it was exceedingly rare that a single missile—whether bomb, shell, or torpedo—should hurt more than one ship, and to inflict damage at all it had to achieve either a direct hit or a very close miss. And only a very modest amount of dispersion in space was sufficient," atomic weapons posed new challenges that would require further study of both tactical and strategic dispersion in order to assess the new problems of fleet protection, personnel protection, as well as the dispersion of naval industries.[223] On the matter of fleet protection, the Navy Department recalls how, "Except for fleeting moments in the history of naval development, no warship has ever been wholly invulnerable to the weapons of its time," and that naval architecture had evolved to become "a study in compromises, based mainly on the most thoroughgoing scrutiny of the experience of battle."[224] And recent data from the Operation Crossroads tests of the effects of atomic explosions on naval ships at the Bikini Atoll in the summer of 1946 "indicate that the amount of protection already built into modern first-class naval vessels as a counter to bombs, shells, and torpedoes provides a very high degree of immunity to atomic blasts as well," especially with regard to "underwater protection."[225] It was found that "in each test the radius from the center of blast within which important ships suffered mortal or crippling structural damage was much less than was generally expected" and "a good deal less than the radius of 'total destruction' of building structures at either Hiroshima or Nagasaki," though "certain changes are definitely indicated" including strengthening "essential light structures above decks, especially those supporting gun directors and radar antennas," while "[b]elow decks everything must be rendered as shock-proof as possible" and a need for "sufficient barriers in the flues to prevent atom bomb blasts from wrecking boilers."[226] It was noted that "the blast effect of the atomic bomb, while tremendous in magnitude, is by no means as sharp as a close-in blast from ordinary explosives" and that it's "been estimated that a superstructure designed to withstand a typhoon with a 50-percent margin of safety would be sufficient for all practical purposes against atomic bomb blasts."[227] With regard to personnel protection, the Navy Department acknowledges that the "great problem is the protection of exposed personnel above decks, especially those manning anti-aircraft guns," and while the guns can be protected from blast and heat, "shielding of above-decks personnel against destructive radioactive rays is a much more difficult matter," though the report notes with some relief that, "[f]ortunately, the effects upon personnel of excessive radioactivity are generally delayed and by no means always mortal," with one solution being "having complete spare crews to relieve those exposed."[228] And as there's "no thought of protecting ships or their personnel from the effects of very close blasts from atomic bombs," then the "only feasible and legitimate aim is to reduce the radius of destruction of any one bomb, and to depend upon one's active defenses as well as upon maneuverability and tactical dispersion of the individual units to increase the unattractiveness of our naval craft as targets for the enemy's atomic bombs."[229]

As with the War Department report, which noted the loss of the "cushion of time" introduced by atomic weapons, the Navy Department observed that "the greatest impact of the atomic bomb on the Navy pertains to the time scale of preparations," and that it was "now far more necessary than ever before that we maximize the force available at the outset of hostilities"; consequently, "[f]or the longer-term point of view, the Navy is not in favor of perpetuating anything that has actually become obsolete," nor to "hang onto something after its usefulness is gone."[230] But that notwithstanding, it reaffirmed its belief that "the Navy is life insurance now and will remain such until conditions are radically changed from those prevailing today," something not immediately anticipated: "For the next ten years, and possibly much longer, we will need naval forces comparable to those which the Navy is trying to keep now."[231] As always, "We must keep our philosophies flexible," and remain committed to its "main task for the future" which is "to resurvey the world situation, to decide who our most probably enemy will be, and to make and revise our plans accordingly," and if those "plans call for the abandonment of any type of ship, or any other implement of war, or the development of new weapons, then the Navy must lead the way in making the necessary changes." By the same logic, if "our most up-to-date plans require a large fleet, we must get one—if we can."[232]

A Critique of Official Thinking: A "Flexible Philosophy is Necessary"

Though Brodie's survey lays the foundation for the Navy Department report on its thinking about the atomic bomb, which in turn influenced the War Department's report on the same topic (which showed a greater parallel with Brodie's own thoughts and expectations on the strategic consequences of the new weapon), Brodie differentiates his own views from the official views of both the Navy and War departments, and thus presents in the subsequent issue (August 1947) of *The Bulletin* a critique of both departments and their thinking on the bomb, in an article titled, appropriately enough, "A Critique of Army and Navy Thinking on the Atomic Bomb." As the editors of *The Bulletin* noted in their introduction to Brodie's August 1947 critiques, Brodie "prepared a critical analysis" of the official views that he had prepared of the "summaries of Army and Navy Thinking on the problems posed by the advent of atomic weapons," which was being reprinted "for the first time" with the permission of the Legislative Reference Service of the Library of Congress for whom it was originally prepared.

First up is Brodie's critique of Navy thinking. Brodie found "[e]specially cogent and significant" the Navy's view that its "plan for the future must cover at least two radically different but equally conceivable situations—i.e., a war in which atomic bombs are used reciprocally on a substantial scale and one in which they are not so used"; that "the kind of force necessary to fight a war fifteen or more years hence would not necessarily be suitable for one which might occur a good deal sooner"; that "guided rockets of ranges measured in thousands of miles can by no means be considered to be 'around the corner'"; and that "for shorter-range rockets like the V-2 or for bombing aircraft the fleet itself might provide ideal launching platforms."[233] He also found "persuasive" the Navy's "argument that a fleet, especially when under way, is already a highly unattractive target for atomic bombs" as compared to onshore targets and that "measures are feasible which will increase that relative immunity."[234] But Brodie does challenge some of the other thinking of the Navy and the "validity of some of the other arguments" which he finds depend upon "certain unexpressed assumptions, which deserve at least to be pointed out."[235] Among these questionable views include the fact that "a major part of the Navy's presentation seems to rest on the assumption that atomic bombs will remain for a rather long time to come a very scarce and expensive commodity of war," as "reflected most clearly in the idea that unescorted long-rang bombing planes" traveling at subsonic speeds "will not be a sufficiently 'reliable' means of delivering atomic bombs," which Brodie explains is "an idea which implies that atomic bombs will remain too scarce to permit any appreciable wastage."[236] As Brodie had explained in detail in his contribution to *The Absolute Weapon*, and reiterated here in briefer form, it is in fact "easy to demonstrate that if available in sufficient numbers, *atomic bombs need not require nearly as 'reliable' a means of delivery as ordinary bombs.*"[237] So while conventional strategic bombing attacks could sustain losses of around ten percent and still retain their necessary punch, Brodie estimates that it was "conceivable that a 90 per cent rate of loss of carriers might not be at all excessive," so long as "atomic bombs were plentiful enough."[238] Once a sufficient stockpile of atomic bombs had accumulated, "the degree of reliability demanded for any carrier of atomic bombs is an extremely variable figure" and which falls within a range "far greater than is true for manned aircraft carrying ordinary bombs"—and Brodie is convinced that the period during which the current scarcity of the bomb will continue has been overstated, when in his view, exactly "[h]ow long it is destined to remain so is a crucial but unsettled question," and that the "[v]arious predictions pertaining to this question have been gratuitously offered to the public."[239] While detailed information on the availability of the necessary components such as "purified fissionable materials necessary for a bomb" remain "highly secret," making it impossible to disprove the Navy's assumption, Brodie adds that "we are entitled to the opinion that the Navy's atomic bomb philosophy . . . may evaporate a good deal faster than the Navy expects."[240]

Brodie also questions the Navy's assumption on the need for fixed bases, noting that bombers such as the B-36 already existed with a one-way range of 7,500 miles that suggests the Navy "greatly exaggerates the utility of fixed bases for the detection and interception of long-range bombers or even for ships bent on attack," since the fixed bases may well simply be by-passed, and "[s]o far as long-range bombers based on Europe or Siberia are concerned, bases for their interception would have to extend over a very wide arc indeed, and would have to be especially prominent in the Arctic. The Marianas bases and other bases in the Pacific and the Atlantic would simply not be in the picture."[241] However, Brodie agreed with the Navy's assessment of the "indispensability of advanced bases as staging areas for *invasion*" and noted in the cases were invasions were launched from far afield during the last war it was "against relatively weakly held enemy outposts, where enemy strength was either small in quantity or necessarily dispersed," whereas a major invasion such as Normandy "could simply not have been launched from a base two thousand miles away."[242] But Brodie cautions the Navy must nonetheless begin thinking now about its needs even as far ahead as fifteen years, and even though its focus on the current needs over future ones is "valid," Brodie notes the "needs of fifteen years hence must surely require some measure of planning *now*."[243] And that the Navy must address current areas of known vulnerability, such as its "concentration of facilities within" its larger bases that it acknowledged to be "points of known vulnerability," as well as issues of "docking and port facilities" necessary for the projection of military power across the seas for "military operations on foreign soils."[244]

Brodie closes his critique by noting that a "Flexible Philosophy is Necessary" for both the Army and the Navy going forward, and challenging their "argument for continued preparation along traditional lines largely if not predominantly on the thesis that destruction from the air, however devastating, is in itself not enough" and that—much like Brodie argued in November 1945 before later changing his view—that "invasion and occupation are also necessary to consummate victory, or at least to wring from the enemy the acknowledgement of defeat."[245] Brodie asks some hard questions that he had himself only recently begun to fully grapple with, such as "how are mass armies and their even more massive equipment to be shipped from ports in which docks and railroad terminal facilities have been largely destroyed?" While the Navy "recognizes that amphibious operations must be modified to permit a more thinly spread approach," Brodie believes the issue and others are nonetheless "deserving study, and the present can hardly be too soon to begin."[246] Brodie believes that the "most fundamental question of all is of course the degree to which the Navy can be depended upon to guarantee for itself that flexibility of philosophies which it now recognizes as of paramount importance for the future," and that its "assertion 'we must keep our philosophies flexible,' however sincerely intended, must be accepted as an expression of hope rather than a promise," and that it may prove to be a struggle to overcome its own natural institutional inertia—"especially after a great war which it has fought with brilliant success" and which would logically foster "an enormous vested interest in the experience which it has acquired with so much pain and labor," making all the harder to "feel spontaneous sympathy with the suggestion that that experience may be of very diminished applicability for the future."[247]

"Revolutionary in the Extreme"

Brodie next turns his attention to the War Department's thinking as expressed in the report he helped to compile and which was published in the June 1947 issue of *The Bulletin of the Atomic Scientists*, finding at a general level that "one cannot logically take exception to any of these points" but that there nonetheless "many questions may be appropriately asked because of the vague manner in which these principles are presented and the absence of any indication of how the Army proposes to implement them."[248] But despite the absence of clarity on how the Army "proposes to proceed toward their implementation," Brodie acknowledges the principles are nonetheless "revolutionary in the extreme and imply gigantic problems of reorganization."[249] Interestingly, Brodie challenges the Army on its "continuing devotion to the 'principle of the offensive'" even though he would in time come to recognize a futility to the defense in the face of the new weapon's offensive advantages—distancing himself from his early view expressed in November 1945 favoring the defensive; at this point in time, Brodie is still inclined to argue for the defensive, writing "it is now clear that we must devote a higher percentage of our national resources than ever before to defensive measures—if only to guarantee our ultimate ability to take the offensive,"[250] a view he would later modify, shifting from defensive measures to protective measures to ensure offensive forces can survive a surprise attack and maintain their retaliatory capacity—thereby ensuring the stability of deterrence, but nonetheless recognizing that the principle of the offensive had regained its stride. Brodie also argues at this point in time that "since it is politically and economically unfeasible to retain in being forces sufficient to discharge all requirements of an atomic war, 'there remains a vital need for rapid mobilization of manpower as well as industry,'" even if not to the full extent or with the full cushion of time witnessed in World War II.[251] He would later rethink this issue as well, and come to agree that in being forces must be developed that are sufficient to meet the requirements of deterrence since the cushion of time hitherto available, owing in large part to America's geographical isolation, would be neutralized by the unprecedented speed, global reach, and destructiveness of atomic war. Brodie does largely agree with the realistic assessment by the Army on the unfeasibility of dispersing the American populace and its industrial base, but challenges the Army's suggestion to disperse military-critical industries, noting this too is "a problem of Gargantuan proportions" and one requiring closer study.[252] He also agrees with the Army's assessment that the "very existence of her military strength as evidenced by conventional forces in being considerably contributes to the security of the United States" and that "if we want to be sure to impress all interested observers with our strength we must be strong in all departments, including the old as well as the new."[253] But as for the Army's contention that the ability of the bomb to "achieve a decision by itself . . . 'has yet to be demonstrated,'" Brodie points out that the opposite is just as true, that "'the certainty that it *cannot* has yet to be demonstrated'"—and this means "there is no need to favor either slant" since "how decisive the atomic bomb will be in a future war is not definitely known at present."[254] But Brodie goes on to argue that "the numbers of bombs used and the tactical circumstances governing their delivery will be the chief determinants of the character and outcome of any war in the future," and—here is where he errs in his prediction—the "number of bombs used is a far more important consideration than the possible increase in power of the individual bomb."[255] Brodie's error is that he does not anticipate an increase in a single bomb's destructive power by an entire order of magnitude as would soon be experienced with the advent of the thermonuclear *superbomb* in just four years' time; so he still views the atomic bomb as the absolute weapon, and can't conceive it will soon be eclipsed by a weapon of vastly greater destructive power. The increase in yield from the conventional to the atomic would be of a comparable leap in magnitude as the increase in yield from the atomic to the hydrogen bomb—and as Brodie realized early on, the "increase in power of the individual bomb" mattered quite a lot when that first leap was made, just as it would at the start of the next decade. But Brodie's main argument was that it was quite impossible to know how decisive the bomb would be in the wars of tomorrow—an argument that would remain true at least until the truly absolute weapon would emerge a few years hence with arrival of the thermonuclear weapon—at which point he would agree that the new superbomb was intuitively capable of achieving a decisive decision with finality on its own.

Brodie closes by noting the War Department's paper presents a disappointing lack of originality—even though in large measure the ideas reflected in its thinking echoed many of Brodie's own early ideas. But Brodie wants to see more originality of thought from the department, writing that its "paper does not materially assist in the advancement of thinking on the military impact of the atomic bomb" and that "[m]ost of the conclusions and deductions contained in it are to be found in earlier writings available to the public"[256]—such as Brodie's 1945 article, "The Atomic Bomb and American Security," and his 1946 chapters in *The Absolute Weapon*. But this may be "of no moment if the Army has earnestly engaged itself with the task of refining the conclusions which it has accepted and of laying plans for the implementation of the policies indicated by those conclusions."[257] Nor does it overshadow the importance of the fact that the "implications of the arguments advanced in the War Department paper are revolutionary in the extreme"—illustrating "an elasticity of thought and a readiness to consider new ideas" and a "commendable minimum of visible attachment to the *status quo ante Hiroshima*" for which it "clearly deserves some credit."[258]

Unity of War and Politics in the Atomic Era: "The Atom Bomb as Policy Maker"

In his October 1948 *Foreign Affairs* article, "The Atom Bomb as Policy Maker," Brodie continues his examination of the unfolding strategic transformation in world politics, and the central place of nuclear weapons in the emergent bipolar order.[259] He noted that it was "now three years since an explosion over Hiroshima revealed to the world that man had been given the means of destroying himself," and that each of the eight atomic detonations achieved thus far "was in itself a sufficient warning that the promise of eventual benefits resulting from the peacetime use of atomic energy must count as nothing compared to the awful menace of the bomb itself. The good things of earth cannot be enjoyed by dead men, nor can societies which have lost the entire material fabric of their civilization survive as integrated organisms."[260] But despite this unprecedented danger to humanity, Brodie notes the continuing relevance of realism, as the "dilemma nevertheless faces us that the enforcement of tolerable behavior among nations will continue for an indefinite time in the future to depend at least occasionally upon coercion or the threat of it, that the instruments of coercion against Great Powers will most likely be found only in the hands of other Great Powers (who can dispense with them only by acknowledging their readiness to forfeit whatever liberties they may happen blessedly to possess), and that those instruments appear fated, largely because of those same imperfections of our society that make power necessary, to include the atomic bomb and perhaps other comparable instruments of mass destruction."[261] Taking a swing at idealists who deny this unsavory reality, Brodie writes: "Individuals may retreat from this dilemma behind a barrage of high moral protestation, usually combined with glowing predictions of a better world to be. Such retreat is rendered doubly sweet because it is more often than not accompanied by applause, especially from the intellectual wing of our society. But the nation as a whole cannot retreat from the problem, and those who desert simply leave the others to think it through as best they can."[262]

Brodie observes that American policy during the first three years of the atomic era "has thus far been evidenced most clearly in the almost frantic effort to secure the adoption of a system of international control of atomic energy," noting critically that it's "difficult if not impossible to find an historical precedent for the eagerness with which this nation has pursued an endeavor which, if successful, would deprive it of the advantages of monopoly possession of a decisive military Weapon,"[263] and while he admits this "monopoly is bound to be temporary" such a fate "has always been true of new weapons, the monopoly possession of which has usually been jealously guarded for as long as possible,"[264] as evident in the historical lessons of naval history that he explored in *Sea Power in the Machine Age* a decade earlier. Brodie contends that America's effort to internationalize the control of atomic energy was not driven by a "national generosity" but instead a "well-warranted fear of living in a world which morally and politically is little different from the one we have known but which in addition is characterized by multilateral possession of atomic weapons," a fearsome prospect even to those nuclear realists unwilling to, in Brodie's words, either *retreat* or *desert* from the new nuclear challenges.[265] Brodie notes that "the fear which engendered the pursuit of international control also provoked the resolve that any control scheme must contain within itself practically watertight guarantees against evasion or violation," which "greatly reduces the chance of securing the requisite agreement," and which after two years of unsuccessful diplomatic effort "leaves us . . . with the unwanted bomb still in our hands, and, so far as we know, still exclusively in our hands," while "also under the compulsion to go on building more bombs, and better ones if possible."[266] This sober nuclear realism leads Brodie to suggest that "we must also begin to consider somewhat more earnestly and responsibly than we have thus far what it will mean for the nation to adjust to an atomic age devoid of international controls"—adding that that the "ramifications of that adjustment process are legion, but certainly they involve above all a continuing reconsideration of the effects of the bomb upon our plans for the national security."[267]

Brodie challenges the internationalists who believe that nuclear weapons renders the concept of *national* security obsolete in the face of the bomb's *global* consequences, adding that America's security was now, "for all practical purposes synonymous with world security" and that "large-scale war without American participation borders on the inconceivable."[268] Moreover, Brodie adds, national security remains "the only policy upon which we as citizens can hope to exercise any direct influence, and it is our only channel for affecting international policy" while "world security, on the other hand, is an abstraction which gains meaning—at least meaning sufficient to induce him to pay a price for it—only to the extent that he is persuaded that American security is enhanced thereby."[269] Brodie considers four propositions that "are basically unaffected by the existence of the atomic bomb" and which argue against internationalizing control over atomic weapons: "International organization at its existing level of development is obviously inadequate to guarantee either world or American security"; "a highly reliable and effective mechanism for the collective guarantee of security can hardly be deemed to lie within the range of conditions reasonably to be expected within our time"; the "pursuit of security against war—the objective which takes precedence above all others in the modern world—is not inevitably identical with the pursuit of smoother and more intimate international cooperation, the two being especially divergent where the latter holds out little promise of significant success"; and for the "the purpose of threat or warning, adequate national strength is indispensable. The statesman who possesses it can choose whether to appease or warn; the one who lacks it can only appease."[270]

Brodie turns his attention the emergent bipolar structure of world politics, noting that the Soviet Union remained the "only foreign Power whose defeat would require great exertions on our part," and this uniqueness—the Soviet Union's substantial military might—that accounts for the new post-war bipolarity; as one unnamed admiral cited put it, "there would still be a problem to concern us even if the Soviet Union were something other than what it is; and that the fact that the power system of today is a bipolar one has dominant implications of its own. The main trouble with a bipolar system, as a colleague has so tersely put it, is that the target is all too unambiguous."[271] Brodie explains that the "admiral's statement reminds us also that concern with security is a concern with possibilities, and not necessarily with high probabilities or certainties. Nevertheless, if the reason which the admiral gave were the only one which counted, there is no doubt that our attitudes and our efforts concerning security would be profoundly more relaxed than they are" and that "special reasons residing in the character of the Soviet state (or, if one insists, in the difference between our two systems) and in the events resulting from that character (or difference in characters) which account for the special dangers and the present acute degree of tension."[272]

But for all Moscow's military might, and its willingness to use force in pursuit of its objectives, Brodie finds that a "saving grace of the Soviet philosophy so far as international relations are concerned is that, unlike the Nazi ideology, it incorporates within itself no time schedule"—and even if Moscow was "convinced that ultimately there must be war between the Communist world and they call the 'capitalist' one," a such a war was not necessarily imminent, and America could thus endeavor "to persuade them each time the question arises that 'The time is not yet!' "[273] Brodie thus turned his attention to the "problem of how to accomplish this act of persuasion in an atomic age, when the already precious objective of peace is made immeasurably more precious by the immeasurably enhanced horror of the alternative," a problem that Brodie would continue to wrestle with for the next thirty years.[274] Ever the realist, Brodie adds that "since preoccupation with the horror has brought us nothing positive thus far, and offers exceedingly little promise of doing so in the future, it is time for a shift to a more sober position. There are a large number of questions pressing for an answer, and consideration of many of them requires appraisal of the atomic bomb as an instrument of war—and hence of international politics—rather than as a visitation of a wrathful deity."[275]

Revisiting his thesis presented in 1946's *The Absolute Weapon*, Brodie recalls how before the atomic era, "it was as nearly certain as any military prediction can be that a conflict between the two major centers of power would be a prolonged one—comparable in duration to the two world wars—and not promising the same finality of decision achieved in each of those instances"; but the "atomic bomb has changed all that."[276] It was now "difficult to see how the decisive phases of a war fought with substantial numbers of atomic bombs could be anything but short."[277] With the inevitable loss of America's atomic monopoly—which would take place just a year after this article's publication—"the atomic bomb has deprived the United States of what amounted almost to absolute security against attack upon its continental territories," and "has in military effect translated the United States into a European Power."[278] Alluding—as he did in *The Absolute Weapon* and would again in *Strategy in the Missile Age*—to Milton's *Paradise Lost*, Brodie adds: "However, though Heaven is lost, not all is lost."[279]

The Coming Age of Atomic Vulnerability: Learning to Live with the Bomb

To confront the dangers of America's emergent atomic vulnerability, Brodie challenged the "frenetic pursuit of international control of atomic energy at almost any cost, including the cost of neglecting to consider any possible alternatives," noting how it was an earlier generation's effort at arms control, in the form of the Washington Naval Treaty of 1922, that "made the Pacific phase of World War II possible, for it assured to Japan something much closer to naval parity with the United States than would have been anywhere near her reach in any real building competition ensuing from the absence of such a treaty"; and even if the treaty did succeed in postponing a " 'costly' naval building competition," he suggests that war with Japan was "immeasurably more costly," asking rhetorically: "would Japan have dared embark upon a war against an America boasting a naval power which was—as it easily could have been, without any untoward strain upon the American economy—two or three times her own?"[280] Brodie thinks not, suggesting that at least the Pacific War could have been avoided had America sought to *deter* Japanese aggression by maintaining a decisive military advantage, and not surrendering to the false temptation of parity through arms control. It would thus be the deterrence of future major wars between great powers that would come to define Brodie's contribution to the stra-tegic riddles of the nuclear age, reuniting strategy with policy in the tradition known to many as *Clausewitzian*.

The underlying mechanism of deterrence, Brodie writes, undergirded the long Pax Brittanica, which ultimately depended upon the maintenance of British naval supremacy; thus, Brodie writes: "Those to whom armaments competition appears disastrous as well as wicked are somewhat inconsistent when they look back nostalgically on the relatively peaceful nine-teenth century and on the marvelous role played by Great Britain in helping to preserve that peace," especially when they "speak vaguely of Britain's invulnerability as a contributing fac-tor, as though that invulnerability were something handed down from on high. It was indeed Britain's invulnerability at home which enabled British statesmen to play such an active and on the whole beneficent part in helping preserve the peace of Europe, but it was not simply the accident of the Channel which made Britain invulnerable. It was her clear-cut naval superiority over the Channel and adjacent seas, *the impairment of which Britain would not brook,* which gave her that enviable position."[281]

The coming Pax Americana would thus depend as much upon deterring war as Pax Brittanica did, and while not often noted, Brodie firmly connected the lessons learned from age of sea power to the emerging challenges of the atomic era. And so, "Returning again to the atomic bomb, the issue is not whether our country ought to seek to maintain its present superi-ority in atomic armaments but whether it has any chance at all of succeeding in such an effort. It has been argued by some (including at one time the present writer) that it was in the very nature of atomic armaments that the kind of clear and decisive military superiority that was feasible in the past—conspicuously in the case of naval armaments—could no longer be realized."[282] Brodie notes this argument, as he advocated in *The Absolute Weapon*, was "based fundamentally on two considerations: first, that there was 'no defense against the atomic bomb,' and second, that when a nation had enough bombs to overwhelm its opponent in one surprise attack and was willing to make such attack, it would make little difference whether its opponent had two or three times the number."[283] But in the two years since he first put pen to paper and grappled with the nuclear riddle, his thinking had evolved in lock step with both the horizontal and the vertical proliferation of atomic weapons—and would continue to evolve with each new phase of the nuclear age. As of 1948, Brodie found that there was "now reason to believe that the situation is not so simple as all that. A great deal depends on the total number of bombs which it will be possible for the various Great Powers to make in any given period of time. Clearly, a three to one superiority in numbers of bombs would mean one thing if the numbers of bombs on each side were numbered at most in the scores or hundreds, and something quite different (and much less significant) if they were numbered in the thousands. Information which would enable private citizens to make intelligent estimates concerning rate of bomb production has not been made public, but there appear to be hints in various quarters that the maximum feasible rate of bomb production is substantially less than was being generally assumed two years ago. It is also clear that the richer of the known deposits of uranium and thorium are much more accessible to the United States than to the Soviet Union."[284]

Imagining the world to come in just a few short years, Brodie considers the technological dimensions of the atomic era, starting with the "enormous technological lead which the United States has over the Soviet Union—and which shows no conclusive signs of diminishing," which Brodie expects "is bound to mean a great potential advantage for the United States in the design of the instruments for using the atomic bomb. The bomb by itself has no military utility. It must be delivered to the target in some kind of vehicle which, unless it is a free-flying rocket, is subject to various kinds of attack. Marked superiority in the vehicle or in the means of shoot-ing down the enemy's vehicles may be no less important than superiority in numbers of bombs, especially if those numbers are something less than gigantic. If those several types of superiority are concentrated on the same side, the disparity in atomic fighting power may be sufficient to warrant comparison with outright monopoly."[285]

Even with the Soviet Union's efforts to advance its military technology, Brodie remained confident that America's "lead in types of aircraft, in the ordnance of combat aviation, and in anti-aircraft materiel should, or rather could, be as great during the next 20 years as it was in the recent war"—adding that the "only question is whether we will make the necessary effort to keep in the lead in our military technology. That the Soviet Union will spare no effort within her capabilities to over take us goes without saying."[286] Brodie recalled that "We are often told that our monopoly of the atomic bomb is a wasting asset," and observed: "It is, to be sure, in the sense that some day it is bound to end and we are constantly getting closer to that day. But is our superiority similarly a wasting asset? In one respect, at least, we know that it is not, for our fund of bombs is increasing steadily during the period in which the Soviet Union remains without any. On the day that the Soviet Union produces its first bomb, we will have many more than we do at present. What happens thereafter depends on a large number of variables. But looking forward from the present, we may say with a good deal of assurance that our present superiority in atomic armaments will increase considerably before it begins to wane, that it may continue to increase even after the Soviet Union is producing bombs, and that it may be a long time in waning thereafter. At any rate, we know that merely to distinguish—as is usually done—between the monopoly period (in which we are safe) and the post-monopoly period (in which we are lost) is not enough."[287]

But even if the end of America's atomic monopoly need jeopardize America's military superiority over the Soviet Union, Brodie is nonetheless concerned with the American political and military leadership's capability to effectively wield American power in the atomic era. As he puts it, "Concerning the effects of the atomic bomb upon our military organization and strategic plans, we must recognize first of all that, to paraphrase Clemenceau, the matter is much too important to be left to the generals—or to the politicians either for that matter."[288] Not only do political leaders tend to gravitate toward what is "politically safe," but Brodie finds that they have "neither the time nor the inclination to preoccupy themselves with the long-term significance of changes in military technology, and rarely the competence to make anything of it if they do," and must therefore "rely upon the advice of their military aides, who belong to a profession long recognized as markedly conservative" with "vested service and personal interests which influence them consciously or unconsciously, whose talents are not primarily dialectic, and who are saddled with tremendous responsibility."[289] As a consequence, Brodie thought it unlikely "to find military leaders, or the civilian officials whom they advise, accepting readily upon the advent of some revolutionary military device that drastic adjustment which free and objective inquiry may indicate as necessary or at least desirable."[290]

Brodie suggests that, "If we consider national defense policy in its broader aspects, and look beyond the period of American monopoly of atomic weapons, we see that recognition of the loss of American invulnerability to overseas attack and expectation of quick decisions in the event of war will no doubt entail a violent wrench to our defense traditions."[291] But traditions can be hard to change, particularly military traditions, and as of Brodie's writing in 1948, he concluded that "our military planners are thinking of an atomic bomb which is an 'important military capability' but nevertheless only an ancillary rather than a decisive weapon. The chief danger is that the inevitably transitory nature of the conditions presumed will not be recognized sufficiently or in time."[292] Added Brodie, "Regardless of what the Soviet Union may accomplish in the field, our own production of atomic bombs is proceeding apace, and the justification for regarding the weapon as an ancillary one is bound to evaporate as our stockpile accumulates."[293] Once the revolutionary nature of the new weapons becomes evident to war planners, Brodie expects that "[p]reparedness in the old sense of the term, which meant mainly provision for great expansion of the military services and of military production after the outbreak of hostilities, will appear even less adequate than it has been charged with being in the past. What will that mean for the costs of military preparedness? Unquestionably the costs will increase, as they have already begun to."[294] Brodie notes there is the "problem of avoiding military expenditure which is improvident not only because it is too large but also because it is misdirected,"[295] such as the proposal to disperse American cities to reduce their vulnerability—an issue that he first examined in *The Absolute Weapon*: "We have heard much, for example, of the business of dispersing our cities as a defense against atomic attack. It is clear that such dispersion would result in a tremendous loss of fixed and sunk capital and, in all probability, in a less efficient spatial arrangement of industries than previously existed. Thus, even if one should make the wholly untenable assumption that wholesale dispersion of our cities and the losses resulting would be tolerated by the public, the project might still appear to be militarily wasteful. A great many combat airplanes could be provided with what it would cost to disperse even a relatively small city." [296] Brodie concedes that "[t]hese observations are of course not very reassuring to those who, like the present writer, deplore the necessity of spending on military protection even so substantial a portion of our national income as we are spending today," and the "limits referred to are fairly flexible and we are still far from having reached them. And what will occur in this country when the conviction settles upon it that the Soviet Union is producing atomic bombs is the big question of the future."[297]

Brodie concludes with a note of guarded optimism on our prospects for living in a nuclear world, and preventing the unthinkable from transpiring: "Our problem now is to develop the habit of living with the atomic bomb;" and he finds some comfort knowing that "the very incomprehensibility of the potential catastrophe inherent in it may well make that task easier."[298]

Notes

[1-9] Ken Booth, "Bernard Brodie" in John Baylis and John Garnett, eds., *Makers of Nuclear Strategy* (London: Pinters Press, 1991), 20; 20; 20; 21; 20; 23; 23; 23–4; 25, respectively.

[10] Brodie, *A Guide to Naval Strategy*, 5.

[11-12] Brodie, "The Atomic Bomb and American Security," Memorandum No. 18, Yale Institute of International Studies, November 1, 1945, i, i, respectively.

[13-46] Bernard Brodie, "The Atomic Bomb and American Security," in Philip Bobbitt, Lawrence Freedman, and Gregory F. Treverton, eds., *U.S. Nuclear Strategy: A Reader* (London: Macmillan, 1989), 65; 64–5; 65; 65; 66; 67; 67; 67; 67; 68; 68–9; 69; 69; 69; 70–1; 71; 71–2; 72; 72; 72; 73; 73; 93 (n.3); 73; 73; 93 (n.3); 77; 77; 77; 77; 79; 79–80; 80; 80 (Brodie footnotes this sentence, suggesting—as he would later more assertively argue—that "[i]f the number of bombs in both of two rival camps should become very large, it might not only raise doubt of the possibility of fending off attack but also stimulate hope on the part of either party that a sudden attack upon the other would be so overwhelming as almost to eliminate the latter's chances for effective retaliation," 93, n.6.)

[47-48] Bernard Brodie, ed., *The Absolute Weapon*. New York. Harcourt, Brace and Company. 1946. Part I: The Weapon. Chapter One. "War in the Atomic Age," 21; 21, respectively.

[49-53] Brodie, "Implications for Military Policy," *The Absolute Weapon*, 74; 75; 75; 76; 76, respectively.

[54-7] *Time* Magazine, "ATOMIC AGE: Absolute Weapon?" *Time*, June 10, 1946, www.time.com/time/magazine/article/0,9171,793035,00.html.

[58-69] Robert M. Hutchins, "Scholarly Opinions on Atomic Energy—and its Control," *New York Times*, June 9, 1946, 6; 6; 6; 6; 6; 6; 6; 6; 6; 6; 27, respectively.

[70-4] Robert Strausz-Hupé, "Review: The Absolute Weapon by Bernard Brodie," *Annals of the American Academy of Political and Social Science* 249, Social Implications of Modern Science (January 1947), 177; 177–8; 177; 177; 178, respectively.

[75-6] R. G. Cavell, "Review: The Absolute Weapons, edited by Bernard Brodie," *Pacific Affairs* 19, No. 4 (December 1946), 450 (also on page 450). Cavell notes the book "is written by five members of the Yale Institute of International Studies under the editorship of one of them, Bernard Brodie, an authority on modern armaments," and that "Brodie divides into two sections a comprehensive chapter entitled 'The Weapon,'" and in his first, "'War in the Atomic Age', he discusses very realistically, the effect of the bomb on the character of war" while in the second, "'Implications for Military Policy', he goes into problems of attack and defence and stresses the fact that 'military authorities will have to bestir themselves to a wholly unprecedented degree in revising military concepts inherited from the past'." Cavell also notes Brodie "outlines the possibilities of defence against this new weapon," and points out that, "So far he sees no evidence that American military authorities have begun really to think in terms of atomic warfare."); 451, respectively.

[77-9] Booth, "Bernard Brodie," 21; 52 (n.17); 21, respectively.

[80-111] Bernard Brodie, "The Security Problem in the Light of Atomic Energy," in Quincy Wright, ed. *A Foreign Policy for the United States* (Chicago: University of Chicago Press, 1947), 89; 89; 89; 90; 91; 91; 91; 92; 92; 92; 92; 93; 93; 93; 93; 93; 93–4; 94; 94; 94; 94; 94; 94; 94–5; 95; 95; 95; 95; 95; 95; 96, respectively.

[112-16] "Discussion of General Security," in Quincy Wright, ed. *A Foreign Policy for the United States* (Chicago: University of Chicago Press, 1947), 101; 101; 101; 102; 103, respectively.

[117-21] Brodie, "The Security Problem in the Light of Atomic Energy," 90; 90; 90; 90; 91, respectively.

[122-6] "Discussion of General Security," in Quincy Wright, ed. *A Foreign Policy for the United States* (Chicago: University of Chicago Press, 1947), 103; 104; 104; 104; 104, respectively.

[127] "Discussion of Great-Power Relationships," in Quincy Wright, ed. *A Foreign Policy for the United States* (Chicago: University of Chicago Press, 1947), 37

[128-61] "Discussion of General Security," in Quincy Wright, ed. *A Foreign Policy for the United States* (Chicago: University of Chicago Press, 1947), 114; 111; 111; 112; 112; 118; 120; 121; 121; 121; 121; 124; 125; 112; 112; 113; 113; 113; 104; 107; 108; 108; 108; 108–9; 109; 109; 109; 110; 111; 107; 107–8; 115; 124; 124, respectively.

[162-86] Bernard Brodie, "The Atomic Dilemma," *Annals of the American Academy of Political and Social Science* 249, Social Implications of Modern Science (January 1947), 32–41; 32; 32; 32; 33; 33 (citing Henry D. Smyth, *Atomic Energy for Military Purposes* (Princeton: Princeton University Press, 1945), 224.); 33; 34; 34; 35; 35 (Quincy Wright, *A Foreign Policy for the United States* (Chicago: University of Chicago Press, 1947), 107.); 36; 36; 36; 36–37; 37; 37; 37; 37; 37–8; 38; 41; 41; 41, respectively.

[187] See: Fred Kaplan, *Wizards of Armageddon* (Stanford: Stanford University Press, 1991), 395, the sixth note listed from page 34 on the topic of "survey of military thinking." Brodie's survey of military thinking available in Box 3, Bernard Brodie Papers, Special Collections, UCLA Library.

[188-210] "War Department Thinking on the Atomic Bomb," *The Bulletin of the Atomic Scientists*, June 1947, 150; 150; 150; 150; 151; 151; 151; 151; 151; 151; 152–154; 152; 153; 153; 153; 154; 154; 155; 155; 155; 168; 168; 168, respectively.

[211-32] Bernard Brodie, "Navy Department Thinking on the Atomic Bomb," *The Bulletin of the Atomic Scientists*, July 1947, 177; 177; 177–8; 178; 178; 178; 179; 179; 179; 179; 180; 180; 198; 198; 198; 198; 198; 198; 198; 199; 199; 199, respectively.

[233-58] Bernard Brodie, "A Critique of Army and Navy Thinking on the Atomic Bomb," *The Bulletin of the Atomic Scientists*, August 1947, 207; 207; 207; 207; 207; 207–8; 208; 208; 208; 208; 209; 209; 209; 209; 209; 210; 210; 210; 210; 210; 210; 210; 210; 210; 210; 210 (indeed in a February 1956 presentation to the Naval War College nearly a full decade later on the topic of the "Influence of Mass Destruction Weapons on Strategy," Brodie was still pondering the revolutionary implications of nuclear weapons (as he would continue to do for another 22 years thereafter), presenting several propositions on their impact: The first is that the changes to be expected are profound rather than marginal, and profound to a completely unprecedented degree. Words like "revolutionary," which have been debased by too-common and too-loose usage, inevitably understate the case. In our efforts at intellectual adaptation to the needs of the future, we must literally be prepared for anything. My second proposition is that the influence we're talking about is, on the whole, not subtle or abstruse but simple and, with reflection, inescapable, of the "two plus two equals four" variety. I am tempted to use the word "obvious," but that cannot be obvious which is disputed by obviously intelligent men. When I say that the changes to be expected from the new weapons are simple and inescapable, I mean among other things that they do not hinge on special items of secret information, or on day-to-day

technical developments. For that reason among others I have made this lecture unclassified. I think it worth stressing that the most important issues confronting us both as citizens and as professional students of war can be debated to the fullest limits of our wisdom without benefit of classified information. Unfortunately, only we who have access to classified information can be quite sure that it is so. My third proposition, is not quite so elementary as the other two. It is that the influence on strategy of mass destruction weapons—by which I take it we mean nuclear weapons—is that they must force a shift in our area of discourse from a strictly military context—which was always too narrow, but for certain purposes acceptable in the past—to a wider one which is predominantly political and social. You remember the famous remark of Clemenceau that "war is too important to be left to the generals." Let us not worry about whether or not he meant it disparagingly. Disparaging overtones, if any, are immaterial to the profound truth of the statement. War has long been something that involved the whole nation deeply and often desperately, and its proper governance with respect to fundamentals has always been the responsibility of the political leaders of the state—as Clausewitz, himself a general, so earnestly stressed. But the political and social context is now of much more immediate and direct influence upon military affairs. This change greatly accentuates the twin problems of (a) developing the appropriate skills and insights among the military, and (b) developing the means by which the political leaders of the state may furnish sound and relevant political guidance to the military planners and commanders. The latter is in my opinion much the more difficult problem to solve, that is, the problem of getting correct guidance. Bernard Brodie, "Influence of Mass Destruction Weapons on Strategy," Naval War College, February 6, 1956. This lecture was slightly updated and presented under a different title, "Nuclear Weapons and Changing Strategic Outlooks," to the U.S. Army War College on February 20, 1956 at Carlisle Barracks, Pennsylvania. The latter title was used for a composite of the two lectures published as RAND Paper P-811 on February 27, 1956 and also published in the February 1957 edition of *The Bulletin of the Atomic Scientists*, 56–61. A lecture on the same topic and with the latter title, "Nuclear Weapons and Changing Strategic Outlooks," was presented to Dartmouth College's "Great Issues" course in March 1956.)

[259-98] Bernard Brodie, "The Atom Bomb as Policy Maker," *Foreign Affairs* 27, No. 1 (October 1948), 17–33; 17; 17; 17; 17; 18; 18; 18; 18; 18–19; 19; 19–20; 21; 21; 23 (Brodie describes Moscow's ideological enmity to the West as "a cardinal doctrine of their faith" and suggests "we can probably do nothing within the present generation to alter it"—implicitly suggesting such an alteration of their core ideological tenets might be possible over a longer period. Just such a transformation would take place four decades later, as a new generation rose up, challenging Moscow's "cardinal doctrine" with one that was at heart *Western*); 23–4; 24; 25; 26; 26; 26; 27; 27; 27–8; 28; 28; 28–9; 29; 30; 30; 30; 30; 32; 32; 32; 32; 33; 33; 33; 33, respectively.

CHAPTER THREE

After the H-Bomb: Preserving Order in the Age of Apocalyptic War

America would lose its atomic monopoly on August 29, 1949, and little more than three years later, on November 1, 1952, it would lead the way forward into the thermonuclear era with its first successful H-bomb test. As the complexity and potential destructiveness of the nuclear era increased, Brodie would revisit his assumptions as first expressed in "The Atomic Bomb and American Security" and in his subsequent chapters in *The Absolute Weapon* and test his faith in deterrence, and in the process would become something of an advocate of limited war. As the number of nuclear states increased—as he had long predicted would happen, and as the yields of nuclear weapons increased by an order of magnitude, Brodie's thinking reflected a recontextualization of the totality of atomic warfare, allowing for relative and not absolute considerations to come into play. Thermonuclear weapons, which peaked with the Soviet testing of Tsar Bomba in 1961 with a theoretical yield of 100 megatons and a dialed-down yield of only 50 megatons to reduce fallout (twice the yield of the United States' maximally destructive device), which resulted in one of the cleanest nuclear detonations of the nuclear age, altered the strategic (and indeed existential) landscape, making the range of atomic obliteration in actual fact a relative thing, and carving out in Brodie's mind not only the possibility of waging limited nuclear wars, but establishing something of a moral and strategic imperative to explore such doctrinal and strategic possibilities. Thus while his colleague Herman Kahn would later become renowned for *thinking about the unthinkable*, Brodie was doing precisely this from the very dawn of the atomic age. But while Kahn would, like a showman, radiate a persona that knew no fear, Brodie would embrace fear, and confront the inherent horror of nuclear warfare. So while he thought no less about the unthinkable, he never once trivialized the dangers faced.

As recounted by Fred Kaplan in *Wizards of Armageddon*: "Living with the bomb suddenly became more awkward, difficult and perturbing than ever," and even prior to the Soviet acquisition of a nuclear capability, Brodie had written in 1948 that, with the rapid demobilization of American forces after World War II, "the fact remains that the atomic bomb is today our only means for throwing substantial power immediately against the Soviet Union in the event of flagrant Soviet aggression," and the precarious international situation "requires appraisal of the atomic bomb as an instrument of war—and hence international politics—rather than as a visitation of a wrathful deity."[1] Kaplan cited "[a]n epigram Brodie had composed two years earlier" that now seemed "immediately relevant: 'War is unthinkable but not impossible, and therefore we must think about it.' "[2] Again it is Brodie at the forefront of "thinking about the unthinkable," even though later generations would often attribute that epigram to the controversial Herman Kahn. Kaplan commented that "it seemed that one of Brodie's main assumptions in *The Absolute Weapon* was now unraveling—the notion that superiority in atomic weapons offered no strategic advantage."[3]

Lessons of Strategic Bombing: A Scientific Assessment

With atomic weapons assuming "enlarged importance in American policy," and with the "supposed condition of even greater atomic scarcity than previously imagined," Kaplan writes: "the question of how to use the bomb" and "which targets to strike, in what order, for precisely what desired effects" had "suddenly emerged, at least in Bernard Brodie's mind, as a vexingly pertinent problem." This became all the more important once the Soviet Union joined the nuclear club in 1949.[4] Finding a "shockingly shallow" level of strategic thought in military circles with regard to the bomb, Brodie considered the effects of strategic bombing in World War II, looking to history for guidance, something he had been doing since his very first work of scholarship, *Seapower in the Machine Age*. He found from his study of the United States Strategic Bombing Survey and from interviews with participants that American forces "had given very little systematic thought to the problem of target selection" until late in the war; that area bombing of cities proved wasteful in terms of both bombs and lives; and that precision bombing was often undermined by the selection of "illogical points at which to aim."[5] With the scarcity of atomic bombs and the questionable results of World War II's strategic bombing, Brodie concluded that "the bombing of cities for its own sake . . . should not dominate the strategic bombing of World War III."[6] Brodie presented his "preliminary thoughts in the August 15, 1950 issue of *The Reporter*"—the new journal of liberal opinion published by Max Ascoli since 1949, and which would continue publishing for the next twenty years—"under the title 'Strategic Bombing: What It Can Do.'"[7]

Five years to the day after World War II came to its formal conclusion, less than one year after the Soviet Union joined the nuclear club, and just under two months after frustrating the Korean War got under way, marking the start of the limited war era, Brodie published his article on strategic bombing in *The Reporter*, revisiting the lessons of the Allied strategic bombing effort during World War II, and the implications for the future of war—not just limited wars of the sort unfolding on the Korean peninsula, but total wars as well. Brodie noted that "what is most distinctive about Korea is that there are practically no targets outside the transportation system for strategic bombing forces," and while "B-29's are not useless in Korea" that "they would seem to be among the weapons we need least."[8] Brodie added that that "detractors of strategic bombing are certainly going to have a field day—but even so our nation as a whole is not likely to fall into the delusion that perimeter war is the only kind we ought to be worrying about. It is worth repeating that in a war directly with the Soviet Union, strategic bombing would be our chief offensive weapon" since the Soviet Union was "as immune as we are to naval blockade, and has on two historic occasions shown that it can absorb great enemy armies and destroy them."[9] And while a "strong, well-equipped army supported by a powerful tactical air force is obviously indispensable for the containment of the Soviet armies," and "western Europe and other key areas can be defended," Brodie writes that "defense alone will not win the war. Soviet power must be shattered by an offensive" and in the years before the advent of intercontinental ballistic missiles (ICBMs), "strategic bombing offensive present[ed] fewer technological and logistic difficulties than any other kind."[10] And although the "strategic bombing lessons of the last war would not automatically apply to another one" as "the technological circumstances and the character of the target would be very different," Brodie argued it as " nonetheless important to know whether our bombing of Germany was a success or, as the dissenters cry, a failure."[11] Brodie believed without hesitation that it was a success, and that "our strategic bombing knocked the German war economy flat on its back," though he notes "this great result came too late to have anything like its full effect on the battlefields" and that "the decisive results achieved by bombing could have come much sooner."[12] He observes that "the biggest single factor in delaying usual results was the effort devoted to 'area' or urban bombing—which simply did not payoff militarily,"[13] and though he challenges those who argue that area bombing actually boosted German morale, he finds the impact was more subtle: morale was undermined but the effect was diluted across the whole of society, including many nonessential industries, where the decrease in morale did not thereby undermine Germany's war effort, thereby diminishing the strategic effects of urban bombing and suggesting to Brodie that a more targeted approach would be more effective, one he would continue to strongly argue during the nuclear era.

Critics point to findings in the U.S. Strategic Bombing Survey that Germany's "war production in almost all categories increased drastically between the middle of 1942 and the middle of 1944," but Brodie points out that this "is quite beside the point, because the decisive bombing results we are talking about had barely begun by mid-1944."[14] Brodie further points out "it wouldn't matter whether or not production as a whole diminished at all if the Germans were denied one indispensable war commodity—such as oil or liquid fuel," and that "in the final stages of the war, is just what happened" when "Allied bombers knocked out two essential German industries—liquid fueled and chemicals."[15] In May 1944, Brodie recounts: "German oil-production facilities were chosen as a top priority target," and "[i]mmediately German oil production dropped precipitously," from 662,000 tons per month on average to 80,000 in less than a year, and Brodie adds: "As for aviation and motor gasoline, our results were even better," with a "tremendous" effect on the Luftwaffe, though a "somewhat slower" effect on ground operations.[16] And while Germany's chemical industry was "never singled out as a target," because "most of the chemical industry was closely integrated with synthetic-oil production, attacks on the latter served to dispatch the former as well" and so by August 1944, these indirect "attacks on chemicals were threatening Germany's ability to carry on the war."[17] Brodie notes that the German transportation sector "became a strategic target system in March, 1944," and that "heavy attacks did not start until September, 1944," yet by the end of the next month, "carloadings were declining rapidly and showing immediately effects in overall production.[18] By late November and early December all munitions production had been severely affected by the failure to move critical materials" and as "the Strategic Bombing Survey put it: 'Even if the final military victories that carried the Allied armies across the Rhine and the Oder had not taken place, armaments production would have come to a virtual standstill by May; the German armies, completely bereft of ammunition and of motive power, would almost certainly have had to cease fighting by June or July.'"[19]

Even though the results came late in the war, Brodie believes "a strong case that our strategic bombing was decisive anyway," with "the fact that from the time of our Normandy landing onward our ground forces did not have to contend with any significant enemy air opposition, while our own planes were making things very rough" for the German armies, owes a great deal to our strategic bombing.[20] And undeniably the shortage of materials, especially oil, which our bombing was imposing on the Germans did in fact hasten the final collapse of their armies."[21] But "the fact remains" that "[b]y the time those results were making themselves felt in a really big way, the Battle of the Bulge was a thing of the past and the Allied armies were well into Germany;" but had those results "come six months or so earlier, no one could say that our strategic bombing of Germany had no significant effect upon the outcome of the war."[22] Of course, had the Allies made an earlier commitment to strategic bombing, Brodie points that that they "might have suffered fewer casualties," but at the same time, "the Russians might have made a separate peace" or "[i]f they had gone on fighting, it would have been their armies and not ours which would have liberated western Europe."[23]

While Brodie at this stage in his writing does not often refer to Clausewitz, he does talk about the necessity of balancing military means with the political and diplomatic ends of war, and notes that while a "directive of June 10, 1943, gave both Allied air forces the primary objective or preparing the way for the invasion of France," which he describes as an "entirely proper objective," as "was the derivative conclusion that the first priority was the elimination of the Luftwaff as an effective force."[24] But he explains that "the selection of the proper objective does not guarantee the choice of the proper target system," and it was the process of determining through trial and error amidst the fortunes of war that ultimately hampered the effectiveness of the strategy: "We now know that the attack upon the German aircraft industry was a failure," forcing Germany to "disperse their facilities, which proved relatively easy to do," in contrast to the oil industry.[25] Brodie also finds the failure to select the chemical industry, which ultimately collapsed under the collateral pressure of Allied bombardment of the oil industry, to be "[a] nother great failure," as was, Brodie believes, the deliberate bombing of German cities, which "turns out to have been an inordinate waste of bombs and of bombing effort," even though cities were both "easier to find and hit," particularly in unfavorable weather conditions, and were also home not only to civilian populations but also much industry.[26] But because the "chief objective of the deliberate attacks on urban areas was enemy civilian morale," which "of course suffered— the arguments that bombing heightened the enemy's will to resist are simply not supported by the evidence—but the effect of that diminished morale on production was spread out over all industrial enterprises, including nonessential ones, and in the end was trivial compared to the results of knocking out vital industrial complexes."[27] Brodie concedes that "[t]hese conclusions about city bombing and the morale factor may have no relevance for the future" as the "atomic (or hydrogen) bomb may give a wholly new and horrible meaning to city bombing,"[28] and in his later work, particularly on the strategic and tactical consequences of the H-bomb, would endeavor to apply the lessons from World War II's strategic bombing experience to the new nuclear realities.

Brodie concludes by reiterating, "But let no one say that strategic bombing was a failure against Germany. The facts disprove it."[29] Indeed, Brodie adds, "We know for a fact that the destruction of the German economy was achieved with a minute percentage of the bombs actually dropped on Germany," and as a consequence, "[w]e may therefore conclude that given only a moderate improvement in our use of the means at our disposal, the decisive effects of strategic bombing could have come soon enough to make a great, rather than only a marginal, difference in the outcome."[30] The challenge, of course, is how best to apply this lesson to the next conflict. Brodie points out some major differences between Nazi Germany and the Soviet Union, noting the latter has a "far less resilient and more thinly stretched" economy, "especially in terms of transportation," and that "it is also much farther away, and much greater penetration would be necessary to hit at vital targets;" but this more challenging geography would be partly offset by the increased destructiveness of nuclear weapons, enhanced by the "promise of a fairly long-range jet bomber, of perfected instrument bombing, and of guided bombs."[31] Brodie's concern, felt since he first turned his thoughts to this new, seemingly absolute, weapon, was that there was "no guarantee that a strategic bombing campaign would not quickly degenerate into pure terroristic destruction," and that the "atomic bomb in its various forms may well weaken our incentive to choose targets shrewdly and carefully, at least so far as use of those bombs is concerned. But such an event would argue a military failure as well as a moral one, and it is against the possibility of such failure on the part of our military that public attention should be directed."[32] But despite these new dangers, Brodie reaffirmed that with the lessons "we have learned from the German experience," if we "had to do the business all over again with the same weapons, we could do in a few months what in fact took us two years," and "with far less destruction of urban areas and of civilian lives than occurred in Germany," and losing "far fewer lives among our own combat men, both in the air and on the ground." In short, "Strategic bombing can be a way of saving life in war as well as of destroying it."[33]

Anticipating the H-Bomb: Must We Shoot from the Hip?

Brodie authored an internal RAND working paper, "Must We Shoot from the Hip?" on September 4, 1951, a year before America's first thermonuclear test but well after its forthcoming arrival had been anticipated by many within the strategic community. The title may seem somewhat casual, but the content was deadly serious—fully rebuking the then-current Air Force strategy known in some circles as "Sunday Punch," a full and total strategic nuclear assault of the enemy in the event of war. With the H-bomb on the horizon, such a massive assault would soon be excessively disproportionate, and shooting from the hip would be inherently un-Clausewitzian, even if not yet so described. While applying lessons learned from World War II's strategic bombing efforts, the lessons applied by the Air Force were contrary to those Brodie had himself derived from his analysis of the experience. While the Air Force looked to the aerial assault on Japan as the salient experience, which defanged a potentially vicious opponent without the need for a land invasion (and thus giving credence to Brodie's later argument in his 1950 article in *The Reporter*, "Strategic Bombing: What It Can Do?"), it did not, according to Brodie, properly integrate the lessons of the European air war, which demonstrated the decisive strategic benefits of precision targeting of military-industrial targets but questioned the value of urban bombing—in contrast to the Pacific air war, in which urban bombing was primarily practiced, including the two atomic bombings. The Air Force embraced the metaphor of Tokyo's surrender, while Brodie found greater value in Berlin's.

Anticipating the greater risks that would accompany the crossing of the thermonuclear threshold, Brodie addressed the emergent strategic transformation that would be realized a year later. In subsequent years, Brodie would revisit and largely reiterate his argument as presented in late 1951. In Brodie's "Statement of the Problem" at the top of his report, he writes that the "spacing or scheduling or atomic air strikes in the event or war has thus far been considered by the Air Force as strictly an operational problem to be left to Strategic Air Command for resolution according to its maximum delivery capabilities," and whose "prevailing attitude is that the more rapid the delivery or our atomic stockpile (or at least that major portion or it allocated to Phase I operations), the better," as "compressing and pushing forward in time a campaign disposing of a given number of bombs will mean, according to this conception, more bombs on target *and also* more effectiveness per bomb," adding, "that unlike most other biases with which RAND has had to contend, this one is practically universal within the Air Force and for that matter within the Military Establishment," and while "there are differences in fervor" there nonetheless "appears to be no important officer or party within the Military Establishment who seriously questions that principle" resulting in its "universality" within the service.[34] Illustrating this, Brodie cites a classified staff memo "prepared by Col. H. R. Maddux for Lt. Gen. Edwards" that states "Explicit in Air Staff thinking has long been a philosophy of strategic bombing which firmly believes the effectiveness of the strategic bombing offensive will be greatly increased, provided a saturating number of atomic bombs are released simultaneously over all important targets. This destruction time over target should be as early in the conflict as is practicable with achieving maximum effects" with a specific "goal of dropping 1,000 atomic bombs simultaneously over the Soviet Union if possible on the day—or the day after—the Soviet Union launches World War III."[35]

But Brodie strongly disagrees with the proponents of the *Sunday Punch*. Brodie notes that the "methods of use which have brought the atomic weapon its greatest triumphs to date are the methods which, under existing biases, we would abandon in the event of war. Insofar as the explosions at Hiroshima and Nagasaki hastened the end of World War II, as they undoubtedly did by some unknown margin, it was not the two expended but the threat of more to come which tipped the balance."[36] And so it would always be; expending the full or even a substantial part of the arsenal in a single concentrated attack would severely undermine the deterrent power that remained: "The damage done by those two explosions was, in terms of remaining overall enemy capabilities, literally nothing; the demonstration value was everything. Similarly, in the post war period we have kept the Soviet Union in check almost exclusively through the threat of our growing and much publicized atomic stockpile—at least through nothing else that is visible to us."[37]

So "to seek to expend almost all we have as quickly as we can" as the Air Force then planned, required "that the results will be absolutely decisive" when it remained unclear "[w]hat grounds we have for expecting such decisive results."[38] Adds Brodie, "One hears in the Pentagon assertions that so powerful and early an attack as that now planned by SAC [Strategic Air Command] would 'break the back' of the Russian economy, which, whether true or not (and I think not), still leaves open the question whether such physical and economic results will cause political changes within the Soviet Union which will induce their leadership to surrender or seek a negotiated peace on terms favorable to us, or whether they will not be offset and possibly even nullified by the Soviet conquest of the economy of Western Europe."[39] Brodie notes that "[o]ne encounters references to the psychological and political results which will follow from the crushing impact of the initial blow, but these references are always extremely vague and often naive in terms both of realities of the Soviet governmental structure and of existing knowledge, however meager, about human psychological and political behavior in disaster situations," and he believes instead that "we have no right to expect" that "political and psychological conditions highly favorable to us" will necessarily "follow," and that furthermore, "our techniques of bombing have scarcely been chosen to exploit such effects, let alone maximize them."[40]

Brodie logically suggests that "[o]ne would think that the aim of producing important psychological and political results would demand above all the capacity to continue exerting pressure in some way comparable to that exploited in an initial blow," but by concentrating the attack on the initial blow, it will lose its primary source of pressure.[41] Moreover, the "kind of mass attack envisioned for the opening period of the war will leave an urban population completely unnerved, distraught, and for the most part benumbed," and "will be preoccupied with personal loss and with bare problems of existence," a situation not unlike that experienced by the bombed-out cities of Germany and Japan, and if the "World War II experience is any guide, such a population is politically apathetic," so much so that we can "have no valid grounds for supposing that the governmental structure, with all its coercive apparatus, will be critically impaired."[42] Or as Brodie puts it: "it is not too much to say that we shoot our bolt and then wait for something to happen, being then quite unable to affect what will happen," and in a fashion that suggests the logic of Clausewitz while not directly attributing the famed Prussian theorist, Brodie explains that "[w]e permit ourselves little or no opportunity for coordinating bombing attacks with political warfare. We permit ourselves no means of tying our attacks, especially on cities, to specific war acts of the Russian government and armed forces in a manner calculated to impress the Russians, first, that the sole responsibility lies with their government and; secondly, *that they have an alternative to being destroyed*."[43] Moreover, "the compressing of the campaign in time leaves no opportunity for gauging the strategic as opposed to the physical effects of our earlier strikes," and thus "leaves untouched the question of what effect the actual destruction is having upon the enemy's economy and political structure, and upon his capacity to survive and to wage war."[44] Adds Brodie, "These considerations suggest that one cannot wisely select targets or target systems on a comprehensive basis without some knowledge (or control) of the sequence in which will hit and of the collateral pressures to be exerted."[45] A full decade ahead of many of his peers, Brodie recognizes the need for developing what would later be called a *flexible response*, and which Brodie described as follows: "In other words, the relationship between the target on the one side and a time and method of attack on the other is properly a reciprocal and not a one-sided one. One must leave some room for playing by ear according to previously-prepared but flexibly-held concepts. That is the way we would fight a war if we did not previously bind ourselves to another way, which is what we are in danger of doing."[46]

Brodie concedes that on "the operational side, there is no doubt much to be said for the importance of hitting while the hitting is good," but questions "the assumption that that pertains only to the opening stages of the war,"[47] and suggests there may be "questions concerning this proposition which seem not to have been considered" but which, given the nature of war, its inherent uncertainties, and its interactive nature, merit a close look.[48] One could view Brodie's questions as inherently Clausewitzian, an effort to firmly anchor strategy in the unfolding realities of war in the atomic age, and to learn from the strategic interactions that do take place how both sides in the conflict adapt to the frictional dimensions that so clearly separate war on paper from war in reality. With an eye on the lessons learned from World War II, where strategic bombing was practiced in earnest for the very first time, Brodie further suggests that: "We need to know, among other things, the minimum size cell for any attacking force if disproportionate losses are to be avoided, the utility of isolating geographical areas within the target region and taking them one at a time, and the ways in which techniques of approach can be varied through a campaign to give the defender a maximum of confusion."[49] Further, Brodie reminds us that "the operational factor is after all not the only one that matters," and while "[i]t gives us the limits of the possible," Brodie explains that"[w]ithin those limits, the operational factor becomes one input among several—a vitally important one to be sure, but nevertheless subject to other considerations;" and, in a Clausewitzian fashion, he adds that the "ultimate payoff is the only thing that counts, the forces involved being a means to that end (and an expendable one at that)."[50]

Brodie—as he tended to do during those first years after graduate school after penning his lengthy doctoral thesis and subsequent books on sea power, looked to the naval realm for insight; in the beginning, he found a long history of deterrence as strategy that would shape his thinking about the new *absolute* weapon, and later he would mine from his vast knowledge of naval matters' metaphorical insight that remained relevant well into the atomic era—observed that the this new Air Force "doctrine of 'Don't divide the attack' is reminiscent of the similar doctrine of 'Don't divide the fleet' which betrayed Admiral Halsey at Leyte Gulf and committed him to the absurdity of hurling ninety ships at sixteen inferior ones while leaving the essential area unguarded," an incident that Brodie would frequently cite in his effort to persuade Air Force officials of the folly of their concentrated Sunday Punch strategy, but which may have provoked greater resistance to his ideas due to the interservice biases that were the quite strong. Brodie notes that "Halsey lost only a gambit and not a war; in one sense he did not even lose the battle, and he was able at the end of his service to retire with honors," adding that in marked contrast, "We are dealing here with far greater risks, and also with a situation in which the strategic bombing campaign must perforce play a far greater role in our overall strategy than Halsey's isolated action could possibly have done."[51] More generally, Brodie derives from the experience of both world wars an importance insight: "One might also point out that the predictions concerning the two World Wars which proved almost universally wrong were the predictions concerning their duration," and that "in each or those wars, the side which made the most telling early blows and the farthest advances was the side which ultimately lost."[52] While Brodie concedes that there is "certainly no necessary connection in those events" he believes they do "suggest some qualification to the doctrine of always 'getting thar fustest with the mostest,'" to which he adds, "Incidentally, it was a Confederate general (Forrest) who originally made that crack, and the Confederates also lost."[53]

Brodie next discusses the material and non-material results of nuclear warfare, noting that the psychological dimension is a necessary element in assessing whether or not victory was possible through strategic bombardment alone, and suggesting it "may be that we cannot achieve our objectives unless we rise above the purely hardware conception of strategic bombing. The question of whether steel or electric power is the better system to attack becomes relevant only after a number or other questions have been answered."[54] He looks at the heavy Soviet losses sustained during Germany's invasion, and suggests that the "achievement of such results by strategic bombing would no doubt be considered very good. . . . Yet despite these great losses, and despite the fact that great attritional land battles were going on concurrently . . . the Russians managed to stop the huge German armies and subsequently to launch an offensive which contributed enormously to the common victory."[55] And while the war was fought with conventional arms, Brodie notes that "if horror be a necessary ingredient, the German provided that in plenty."[56] When also considering the great suffering experienced by Russia in the decades prior to World War II, from its violent civil war through its economic collapse and famine that preceded that Nazi attack, Brodie suggests that "[o]ne might well wonder whether the A-bomb destruction we are presently capable of inflicting in the Soviet Union would actually overshadow the horrors which that country has already experienced under its present regime and which that regime easily survived."[57]

Brodie has found implicit in Air Force target selection an implicit interest in the psychological and political effects of bombardment, an interest that is "much more often implied than mentioned."[58] As Brodie explains, "Capacity to fight effects willingness to fight and visa [sic] versa, and faith or lack of faith in ultimate victory certainly affects the efforts which will be directed towards restoration of damaged industries; but that is by no means the whole story."[59] But Brodie adds that even "[m]ore important is the fact that psycho-political results cannot be divorced from economic ones, so that it is impossible to rule them out in effect even when we are indifferent to them in theory."[60] The trick is that "the results we achieve on the political front may be the opposite to those we desire and may tend to offset to some extent the favorable economic results. Both categories are after all only means to an end, that end being the early and favorable conclusion of the war, and on a basis that will make the peace at least livable."[61] And this ultimate objective, the "goal of securing a final and favorable conclusion to a war usually argues a basic change in the psycho-political climate in the enemy country," which Brodie believes should remain at the forefront of our targeting strategy in the nuclear era: "Psychological objectives can no doubt be to some degree independently targeted from economic ones;" with psychological objectives in mind, we "might concentrate on cities," while the pursuit of economic objectives "would concern itself with vertical systems with small regard to the urban or non-urban location at individual targets."[62] Brodie suggests our "choice at targets may be much less important than methods at attack," and that the oft-debated "question of whether or not we go after cities would be quite secondary to the question at whether or not we introduce some system at warning . . . the resident population," and further that "the spacing of attacks, and the propaganda exploitation to those already made and those to come, will make more difference in psychological impact" than the particularities of the target itself.[63] Ultimately, Brodie argues that it *"cannot be too much stressed that there is no essential conflict between economic objectives and psychological ones."*[64]

Brodie has often been portrayed as especially sensitive, attuned to the underlying psychological issues but perhaps a tad squeamish when it came to the hard, military realities of warfare in the nuclear age, less muscular in his approach, and in his rhetoric, when compared to his colleague Herman Kahn who shot to fame for *thinking about the unthinkable* without blinking. But a close look at Brodie's discussion of human casualties, in a section titled "Are Human Casualties a Bonus?", seems particularly Kahnian, or perhaps one might say, Strangelovian and reveals Brodie was no less willing to think about the unthinkable than Kahn, and no less willing to embrace the notion that the collateral slaughter of millions of people could in fact be construed to be a strategic advantage to the attacker, a bonus of sorts in addition to the strictly material effects of strategic bombardment. While not using the term, he certainly embraces the concept, of *megadeath*. And while in a RAND report and not in his publicly published books and articles that sought to cultivate a more benign impression, it is nonetheless telling to see Brodie wading into the raw, unpolished world of nuclear warfare and not shrinking from the task, and shows that Brodie was not so different from, say, Machiavelli in the Renaissance who whispered in the ear of his would-be Prince forgiveness for the necessary brutality, counseling the strategic supremacy of fear over love: to court the powerful, in this case the nuclear-armed military services, he talked tougher than he tended to talk to the lay public. This is a very different Brodie from the general impression imprinted in the minds of most scholars, such as Ken Booth, Fred Kaplan or Gregg Herken who emphasize Brodie's torment. Brodie, at least at the dawn of the thermonuclear era, did not seem at all tormented by the gravity of the decisions that must be made.

As he writes, "Among the basic questions which appear not to have been clearly resolved either in Air Force doctrine or in RAND studies concerning strategic bombing" is this question: "is it desirable to maximize human casualties or to minimize them, or is it a matter of relative indifference how many casualties result from the destruction of targets selected on other grounds? The answer adopted by the Air Staff, and I believe by most of RAND for that matter, is the one which embraces indifference but which regards slaughter of people attending destruction of an economic target as a 'bonus'."[65] In an especially Kahnian passage (one might venture to say Machiavellist), Brodie adds: "Let us be clear that for the purpose of the present discussion we are not concerned with moral considerations *per se*. Agreed that no one wants to kill people uselessly, and that the war we are talking about would be one in which the stake is nothing less than sheer survival, the question whether we should maximize, minimize, or disregard human casualties in our strategic bombing campaign can be put on a plane where the sole criterion is whether we thereby help or hinder our program towards victory and the achievement of our national objectives. Certainly it is intrinsically an important enough question to be considered in itself."[66]

RAND's prior studies of this seemingly unthinkable question were "usually from the point of view of economic consequences alone" premised on the idea that "people, especially in cities, represent certain skills, and that to deprive the enemy of those skills may be a very good supplement to or even substitute for depriving him of his industry."[67] Brodie adds there was "no unanimous agreement on the matter among RAND staff members in both the Social Science and Economics Divisions" but that "there does seem to be some consensus on the view that highly developed war essential skills are rather thinly distributed in a population even within a city; that people, unlike buildings, can hide or flee; and that some measure of warning is likely even if the attacker does not offer it,"[68] all presenting tactic obstacles to achieving any meaningful success from purposeful human targeting. Brodie observes that "these questions are considered almost exclusively in terms of economic results is only another example of the heavy economics bias which has prevailed in this area of thought since World War II," which emerged from the realization that the devastatingly destructive "morale attacks on cities were or appeared to be a complete bust."[69] That notwithstanding, Brodie, in a bold Kahnian departure from the conventional wisdom, writes: "The question now is whether we should not be ready to revisit our thinking in view of the radically new conditions created by atomic and other weapons, of the availability of new methods of attack, and of the great difference in political climate between Nazi Germany and the Soviet Union."[70] Without saying it, Brodie suggests it was now time to think about the unthinkable, and to do so with a hitherto unprecedented boldness—and a balanced Clausewitzianism that never lost sight of the fundamental link binding war to politics (and thus political objectives). Brodie notes the Soviet system was entirely different from that of Nazi Germany, marked by a notable lack of public support; as he recalls, "There was very little basis for distinguishing between the people and government in Nazi Germany because of our knowledge that Hitler had the fervent support of the overwhelming mass of the German people," in contrast to the Soviet Union where intelligence "indicates a very different state of affairs" that suggests the merits of considering "whether and how we could exploit that situation in our strategic bombing"[71]—a question that Brodie commences exploring, and which he will continue to explore in the coming years.

Brodie observes that "[a]lmost all references to psychological results of a bombing campaign reflect the quite unexamined assumption that such results are increased only through killing more people," but a closer look presents several "considerations which would seem to suggest the opposite, that is, the desirability of minimizing casualties—or at least of appearing to wish to do so."[72] In a description that echoes the Kahnian (or Strangelovian) style Brodie has rarely been associated with, he notes "a corpse presents no problems other than disposal. All his anxieties are liquidated as are those of his family concerning him. Liquidated too are all his potential hostilities to the regime which governs him. A corpse makes no demand for food or shelter."[73] Further, he notes, "Fear and flight of survivors are the maximum dissolving agent, especially if the regime proves powerless to provide for fugitives and if we provide incentives to the population to bring pressure to bear upon the regime. To do so requires some connection between our bombing and our stated war aims, and presentation of that connection in a form which can be translated into operational demands."[74] Brodie also notes "it would probably require far fewer bombs per thousand head to create fugitives than to create an equal number of corpses."[75] Brodie also suggests that "indiscriminate bombing of populations will very likely have a disproportionate affect upon the ruled as against the rulers, since the latter will enjoy the prompted internal warnings and the deepest air raid shelters" whereas the ruled will suffer disproportionately—when perhaps a reversal of this would better serve American interests, particularly since "intelligence indicates overwhelmingly that the Russian people do not love their regime," and if Russian populace "become convinced that we want to kill Russians rather than destroy Communism, all the value of that potential disaffection is destroyed,"[76] much like what happened to the Nazis, who were initially greeted as liberators when they invaded the Ukraine but who squandered this opportunity by their poor treatment of the populace. Lastly, in perhaps the most Kahnian point raised by Brodie, he writes: "There are in any case far too many Russians for us to kill. It is not too much to say that we need Russians in order to defeat Russians."[77] All these points raised by Brodie, he writes, are "intended only to be suggestive of points which deserve further study" but which "suggest things we could do (or avoid doing) without serious cost and with the possibility of great profit," but which, even if still speculative, suggests that "we have no justification for regarding whatever large scale slaughter results from our bombings as a 'bonus'" as it may well prove "harmful to our strategic and political goals."[78]

Brodie concludes that much potential benefit will come from making an effort to spare civilian populaces from nuclear annihilation: "If we do not know that it is a bad thing to kill Russians indiscriminately, that is not the same as saying that we know it to be a good thing."[79] And so Brodie counsels that if "we find ourselves obliged for a variety of reasons to bomb targets situated within cities—as seems almost inevitable—it may becomes [sic] a matter of great urgency so to space our attacks and to attend them with such warning that the Russian population will not inexorably conclude that we are solely bent upon their destruction, denying them all opportunity of reprieve or escape."[80] And "it might be a very important factor in helping us to decide such problems as whether the centers of cities or industrial concentrations within cities" should be targeted for attack.[81] While the long, hard fight to "the very end of her capacity" by Nazi Germany may have been on the minds of many war planners in the ascendant United States armed forces at the dawn of the Cold War, Brodie suggests this may have been "an exception," and points to the "surrender to Italy and Japan in the same war, and to Germany and especially of Russia in the previous war," which "show that the will to resist may collapse long before the physical capacity to do so—provided that that will is properly conditioned by the conqueror and that the seeds of disaffection already exist in the target population. The Soviet Union looks like a perfect setup for the attack which exploits psychological weapons, and the atomic bomb looks like the perfect weapon for psychological exploitation. Why not bring these two things together?"[82]

In Quest of Sound Strategy

In a lecture delivered to the Naval War College on March 17, 1952, Brodie returned to a more traditional Clausewitzian discussion of strategy, picking up on some of the themes he developed in his 1949 *World Politics* article, "Strategy as a Science." His lecture, titled "Characteristics of a Sound Strategy," started off with an apology of sorts, as Brodie confessed that the "lecture title assigned [to] me is at once convenient and embarrassing—convenient, because it gives me a very wide latitude indeed; and embarrassing, because it implies on my part pretensions to oracular wisdom," to which he added, "I don't think I can describe the characteristics of a sound strategy except, perhaps, in the most general and abstract terms. I think I can, however, occasionally recognize an unsound strategy when I see one, as I believe I sometimes do. I shall, therefore, for the legitimate purpose of being specific rather than abstract, talk more about unsound strategies than about sound ones. In other words, I shall take a leaf from the revivalist preacher and point the way to the good life by preaching against sin."[83] Brodie had begun to preach against sin a year earlier, challenging the dogma that underlay the Air Force's concentrated *Sunday Punch* strategy. In this lecture, he would more directly address the problem of dogma, weaving together the specific criticisms that he had about current strategy with his deeper misgivings on the dangers of an unreflective approach to strategic thinking. As Brodie explains, "my views here, too, tend to be somewhat negative" and "may perhaps conflict with those current here, but that is all to the good in an academic institution, for argument is after all the stuff of learning. If we all thought alike we should all be infinitely wise or, more likely, very stupid."[84]

Brodie dives straight into a critique of the so-called principles of war, making an argument that he would restate but never truly deviate from across the spanse of his career. He tells his audience, "Now, if by Principles of War we mean that group of maxims or axioms which are usually presented in a list of 7 to 10 or more numbered items and which are supposed to be unchanging despite the most fantastic changes in everything else, then my feeling about them is not that they are wrong or useless but that we tend to be altogether too respectful of them. And if our respect becomes so extreme that we enshrine them as dogmas, as sometimes happens, then I think they become positively dangerous."[85] He adds, "You have, no doubt, heard or will hear references to bad strategies of the past where the badness is summed up in terms of its being a violation of this or that Principle of War," and suggests "it is equally true that one could point to the most egregious blunders of past actions (and I fear also of present planning) which have been committed in the name of this or that Principle of War."[86] He notes that the "so-called principles of war . . . were first formulated systematically by Jomini and developed later by subsequent writers," and that "they are essentially common sense propositions," with "all the virtues of common sense propositions," as well as "the limitations of common sense propositions, including the limitation that occasionally a strict adherence to them will be extremely offensive to common sense."[87]

Sounding much like the Roman poet Ovid, who was for the art of love what Machiavelli was for the art of politics and war, Brodie compares the art of strategy with that of courtship: "Now, because the principles of war are really common sense propositions, most of them apply equally to other pursuits in life—including some which at first glance seem to be pretty far removed from war. For instance, if a man wishes to win a fair and virtuous maiden and if he is not too well endowed with looks or money, it is necessary for him to clarify in his mind exactly what he wants of this girl—that is, the principle of the objective; and then to practice rigorously the principles of concentration of force, of the offensive, of economy of forces, and certainly of deception."[88] Referring to his "analogy of the way of a man with a maid," Brodie notes that the man "may know that he has to concentrate all his available resources on achieving his objective. In fact he is automatically driven to do so by a deep impulse of nature, but he needs deeper intuitions to tell him just how to apply those resources. He may take her to symphony concerts—when she is not that kind of a girl at all."[89] And so it is with the art of war. To illustrate this view, he discusses the concept of "economy of effort," as defined by the Canadian Armed Forces, which is "a balanced employment of forces and a judicious expenditure of all resources with the object of achieving an effective concentration at the decisive time and place."[90] The challenge is in understanding how this proper balancing is achieved: "if we had the wisdom to know what a balanced force should properly be in the present day with all the new weapons and techniques that are crowding upon us; if we really knew what was meant by judicious expenditure of resources for the sake of achieving an effective concentration; and, if we knew what a decisive time and place was—how to recognize one and choose one—then, I should say people endowed with that wisdom would more or less intuitively know how to put those factors together in the way suggested here. Mind you, I'm not saying this particular idea is unimportant—one can point to instances in the past where it has been overlooked, to the sorrow of those who did so."[91] But the trick is in the doing; such was the realization of German grand admiral Karl Doenitz, who after "becoming a captive of the Allies," had "written an essay on 'The War at Sea' from the German point of view of World War II" in which he "points out that the German submarines in the first year of the war were ten times as effective per day at sea as they were in the second year of the war. One therefore gathers (though he doesn't make this point) that if Germany had started the war with some 300 submarines instead of 60, they would have stood a very good chance of winning the war at sea, and therefore the whole war—and relatively early."[92] Asks Brodie pointedly, "why didn't they have those 300 submarines? Well, one reason is that they were enamored of the idea of a balanced force and devoted a good deal of their naval resources (which had to be limited in view of their ground and air force needs) to surface vessels, including battleships. That gave them what according to a static conception was a balanced force. The trouble was that it was highly unbalanced for a war with Great Britain. This is only one example of where the word 'balance' denotes no ready answer. The balance must always be thought of in terms of strategic needs against the particular prospective enemy."[93] The salient question now was, "What is balanced force in an atomic age? . . . It is certainly the great problem of our time."[94]

As he did in his 1951 RAND working paper, "Must We Shoot from the Hip?", Brodie again turns to the Battle of Leyte Gulf to illustrate the dangers of following the so-called principles of world unthinkingly, as dogma—with the principle in the case being the admonition never to divide the fleet, which would violate the principle of concentration. Fortunately, Admiral William Frederick Halsey, Jr., commander of the Third Fleet, recognized in the middle of the battle the danger of following this dictum to the letter, narrowly avoiding disaster. As Brodie explains, "The purpose of the principle of concentration of force is to suggest that one should so allocate one's forces that one can hope to be superior to the enemy somewhere, preferably in the most important place, or at least minimize one inferiority in the decisive place. I submit that the Commander of the Third Fleet had forces so overwhelmingly superior to those of the enemy that he could have divided his forces between San Bernardino Strait and the north and have remained overwhelmingly superior locally to each enemy force. And when you are overwhelmingly superior—how much more superior do you want to get?"[95] This would be a salient question throughout the nuclear era, as a stable structure for ensuring mutual deterrence was sought—and in its pursuit, the notion of overkill emerged. As Brodie concludes, "So much for the principles of war which, to repeat, are useful as far as they go—but which simply don't go very far at all. The real military problems facing us today are problems for which the principles of war not only offer little or no guidance but in some instances are positively misleading."[96] While Brodie firmly rejects an approach to strategy that he defines as Jominian, he does not yet affirm in response a Clausewitzian approach; the elements are there, but not yet the attribution. By the end of the decade, he would embrace Clausewitz not only in principle but in name, and dedicate his scholarship to the revival of the great Prussian theorist's influence. But at this moment, he is still battling the ghost of Jomini.

Brodie, in addition to rebuking Admiral Halsey, challenges other principles of war that became elevated to dogma, including the previous century's tactical axiom, "The ram is the most formidable of all the weapons of the ship," which became "a dogma which prevailed for half a century and which never had any real substance in fact."[97] He similarly dethrones a principle attributed to the French theorist of the nineteenth century, Charles Jean Jacques Joseph Ardant du Picq, whose famous slogan postulated that "He will win who has the resolution to advance," which "which encouraged the school of the offensive a outrance in France, which cost the French so very dearly in the first weeks of World War I."[98] Returning to the lessons of Leyte Gulf, Brodie suggests Admiral Halsey nearly fell victim to a "slogan which was relatively new, but which had certainly become firmly fixed—'The enemy's main force is where his carriers are.'"[99] As Brodie observes, "In that battle the enemy's main force comprised in fact his battleships. That would have been clear except for the existence of the slogan. The slogan is objectionable for the same reason that an undue deference to the principles of war is objectionable—it acts as a substitute for thinking, and any substitute for thinking is usually a bad substitute. Worse still, it introduces a rigidity of thought which is, after all, its purpose. This may prevent the realization of the absurdly obvious."[100] Such a "slogan may represent a brilliant insight of the past, but as a rule only at its first utterance. When it becomes common currency, it is likely already to be counterfeit. I submit, therefore, that one of the first tests for a sound strategy is freedom from the dominance of slogans."[101]

Instead, Brodie offers that "an intelligent strategy" should be based on "the sound appreciation of existing realities, which will then enable us to make predictions which have real planning values—and that is easier said than done. It is a very big order."[102] Strategic matters, Brodie notes, concern "a major portion of the entire field of human knowledge," and thus "to be covered by those responsible for strategic decisions, the military profession would have to be far and away the most learned of all professions."[103] But "other characteristics are desired in the commander—ability to lead, forthrightness, and ability to make decisions," and these may be "incompatible with the contemplative way of life"—creating a challenging dilemma for professional military education that "is only partially and very unsatisfactorily served by specialization."[104] Brodie considers the role that social science can play, noting from his time at the National War College in 1946 that he "had some misgivings at the very great amount of time, relatively, which was being spent on what one might call the social sciences," but wondered, "who is going to do the intensive study which the situation requires in matters concerning the proper utilization of new weapons, the changes in techniques indicated by those new weapons, the problem of proper targetting for strategic bombing, and the like?"[105] Brodie found that the "problem is that more and more fields of knowledge are becoming more and more intimately related to strategic decisions," such as the place of psychology in military operations: "For example, we are becoming aware of the tact that the use of weapons in war can be manipulated to have greater or less psychological effect," particularly in the "use of fire power to maximize the psychological effects of that firepower on the enemy. This is obviously a requirement for military intelligence, for military analysis."[106] But psychology remains a "field of knowledge" that "happens to be quite poorly developed" and as a consequence, there remained "a vast universe of things we don't know about the psychological effects of weapons. Nevertheless, our first priority problem is not our deficiencies in knowledge (which we can leave to the researchers), but rather the intelligent, imaginative and comprehensive application of the knowledge we do have. What we need is a steady awareness of what we know and, more important perhaps, a steady awareness of what we do not know. Above all, we need that simple but rare and indispensable thing called 'logical reasoning.'"[107]

He illustrates this need for—and challenge of—logical reasoning with a topic that has been on his mind at least since the end of World War II, namely, "if we must say that we do not know whether a certain proposition is true—that does not mean that we know the opposite to be true. I refer here to some different schools of thought on strategic bombing. One of the things that we don't know about strategic bombing is whether it is politically and militarily desirable to maximize human casualties, to minimize them, or to choose targets which show indifference to casualties. We don't know that it is a bad thing to maximize casualties, but that is not the same as saying we know it to be a good thing to maximize casualties."[108] Thus it remains essential to challenge dogma with logic: "The winning of a war (and I would add of the subsequent peace) is more important than that some doctrine should be realized in practice, such as the doctrine of balanced force or the doctrine of strategic bombing, or whatever doctrine you like—good, bad, or indifferent."[109] And so "if all one's assets are to be committed to a particular plan, I should expect that one would have a reasonable prognosis of the military and political consequences of executing that plan. That, I have found, is a most unreasonable expectation. I have seen studies which thought they were attempts at war plans, but which ended simply with putting bombs on targets."[110]

Sounding very much the disciple of Clausewitz, Brodie observes that "war is a very complex thing indeed and interpretations of past wars, upon which our planning for future wars have to be in some part based, is not easy," and "any monistic interpretation, any interpretation which finds the answer in one particular thing, is likely to be wrong simply because it is monistic."[111] He suggests "humbly" that all "easily available knowledge which is relevant should be absorbed," and that we resist dogma wherever it arises: "Now, if our staff planners diligently follow the few precepts I have mentioned, we would have fewer of those studies which so beautifully bear out the words of our great and good friend, Uncle Joe Stalin, and I quote: 'Paper will put up with anything that is written on it.'"[112] Brodie identifies "some of the touchstones for finding a plan wrong," noting "if the assumptions are clearly unrealistic, or at least unstudied, we can suspect a poor foundation for the study."[113] He also cautions that "there may be many important assumptions which are implicit in the plan but which are not recognized as such by the authors," as well as "internal contradictions of a significant character" and "factual data presented" that "may be susceptible of being proven incorrect."[114] To avoid these touchstones, Brodie encourages a wide exposure to critical minds and opposing views—he notes that "war planning is the only important function of government—perhaps the most important function of government—which is carried on entirely without benefit of criticism from the outside, of criticism from the public"[115]—and thus to "so far as possible avail themselves of the insights and novel points of view of persons who would not ordinarily be drawn into the planning process."[116]

Brodie closes his seemingly Clausewitzian rebuke of the Jominian mindset permeating war planning by at last invoking the famed Prussian strategist: "I want, finally at the end, to say a few words about national objectives—particularly in view of the age in which we live. We are living in an age in which atomic weapons already exist in substantial numbers, in which the numbers are steadily and rapidly growing, and which may at some future time include new and even more deadly weapons. If we look ahead only five years from now, we see a world in which war—if it comes—must mean a devastation (assuming that present principles are carried into practice) such as the world has never seen to any degree of approximation."[117] Brodie turns to Clausewitz for guidance in these dangerous times: "As you all know, Clausewitz somewhat over a hundred years ago made a statement in his famous book which has since been very often quoted, namely: 'war is a continuation of policy by other means.' I confess that for a very long time I was convinced that that statement had no meaning. To me, modern war was so different, so much more violent than diplomacy, that I could not conceive of it in terms of its being a continuation of diplomacy. To a degree that is true, but I have now become convinced that what Clausewitz said has profound meaning. What he was saying by implication was that war should follow a planned procedure for the sake of securing certain political and social objectives. By implication, too, the procedures and the objectives should be rational and to some degree at least appropriate to each other."[118] Once a skeptic who thought Clausewitz had become obsolete, Brodie now found relevance—and he would increasingly turn to Clausewitz for answers and guidance in the years to come. And so Brodie concludes:

> Now, the political objectives of war can not be consonant with national suicide and there is no use talking about large-scale reciprocal use of atomic weapons (including those of the future) as being anything other than national suicide for both sides. I would ask, then, is it enough to say that our armed forces exist to prevent war if possible. and to win the war if it comes? In the future it will be difficult indeed to define what you mean by winning a war and in any case the winning of a war is not an end in itself, but a necessary means to an end. We also have to ask ourselves, 'To win for what purpose?' And that will oblige us to ask, 'To win how?'

> Our national aims are a defense of the free world in order to enable it to remain free. Those objectives can be defended only by methods which include a readiness to wage war when the aggressor presents a military challenge. That proposition is well known and really provides the present basis for American foreign policy. But deterrents do not always deter. What, then? Are we obliged to commit ourselves to techniques of waging war which, if they provoke in the enemy (as they must) an equal and opposite reaction, will effectively destroy what they are designed to protect? Perhaps the chief problem of the future is to find some means of controlling events even after hostilities begin—not to let them get out of hand. The price of control, if it is possible to achieve it at all, must clearly include not only limitations in the means of waging war—but also limitations upon war objectives. Total victory, like total war, may well become an obsolete concept.

> It seems to me that with these new mass destruction weapons, the science of war ceases to be such. Destruction becomes all too efficient, all too easy. But there is an enormous area for wisdom and science in determining what to hit as well as what *not* to hit: in determining what can be achieved by war, and in what way, other than by unloosing destruction on an unlimited basis.[119]

In the coming months, the atomic age would give way to the even more dangerous thermonuclear era, Brodie continued to grapple with the consequences of the increasing destructiveness of the new weapons in a frantic effort to help American strategic thinking catch up to the new strategic realities. He had already launched a steady assault on the dangers of dogma, the reliance on outmoded and inflexible slogans, and the need to look beyond simple principles of war to fully grasp its underlying complexity.

In his lecture, "Changing Capabilities and War Objectives," presented to the Air War College on April 17, 1952, Brodie extended his discussion of realism as the theoretical foundation for modern military strategy, discussing Clausewitz as well as the classical Greek strategist and historian Xenophon. In his discussion of Xenophon, Brodie recounts how, "[i]n the beginning of the 4th century B.C., an army of some 13,000 Greek mercenaries under a committee of generals of whom one was Xenophon—who has handed the story down to us—was hired by Cyrus, a prince of Persia, who intended to use these troops along with some of his native contingents for the purpose of unseating his elder brother, Artaxerxes, from the throne of Persia."[120] After marching "some 1,100 miles across Mesopotamia into the heart of the Persian Empire, fighting some battles on the way," this mercenary army, "at a place called Cunaxa, near Babylon, met the vastly superior armies of the great king and administered to those armies a decisive defeat,"[121] but "during the battle, in a moment of vainglory, Cyrus quite unnecessarily got himself killed, thereby depriving the Greeks not only of a leader but of an objective. Without Cyrus there was no longer any point in trying to unseat the King. So on the very next day this victorious army began o negotiate with the enemy for the purpose of getting the opponent to permit it to depart in peace. It was not going to lay down its arms, mind you, but it wanted to leave; and the bulk of Xenophon's story is the saga of the passage of this army through the deserts and the mountains, through many hostile lands in which they had to fight many battles, back to the shores of Greece."[122] Brodie explains that "[o]ne of the things that impressed me about the story was that in every battle the Greeks fought, in every maneuver they performed, many of them aggressive, they had only one objective; and their strategy and tactics adhered to that one objective, and that was to bring their army intact back to the shores of the Black Sea," adding that "[s]ix months ago I should not have appreciated that particular lesson in Xenophon. There are many other things in it that would have been interesting, a cognizance for example of what we call the principles of war long, long before these principles were codified. But the principle of tailoring the operation to match the objective is something I'm afraid I should not have appreciated."[123] Brodie admits that he had "read this book only on the trip here this time without any idea of using it for this particular talk," but made the important connection linking Xenophon's laser-like focus on the strategic objective during his historic—and in the end successful—retreat from Persia over two millennia ago to the current strategic nuclear challenges, and the often overlooked necessity, in Brodie's mind, of balancing the means of war with the ends reflected in the national political objective.[124]

Brodie reflects on how "six months ago I could and in fact did deny in print that famous, often-quoted statement of Clausewitz's, 'War is a continuation of policy by other means,' could have any meaning for modern times," and "felt that modern war, modern total war, is much too big, much to [sic] violent to fit into any concept of a continuation of diplomacy," and "that war by its very outbreak must create its own objective—in modern times, survival—in comparison with which all other objectives must hide their diminished heads."[125] Brodie adds that he has "since come to believe that Clausewitz was in fact saying something very profound," and in so doing was very much still relevant: "What he was saying, it now seems to me, is that war is violence—to be sure, gigantic violence—but it is planned violence and therefore controlled. And since the objective should be rational, the procedure for accomplishing that objective should also be rational, which is to say that the procedure and the objective must be in some measure, appropriate to each other."[126] Brodie notes that "Clausewitz was himself a general, and it is interesting to notice that he insisted that the policy maker, by which he meant essentially the civilian policy-maker, must be supreme even in war," and "argued that where the general resents the intervention of the politician, it is not the intention which he should resent but the policy itself if it is in fact bad policy—that is, it is the policy and not the intervention which should be the subject of criticism."[127] Brodie observes how, "after developing these thoughts I went back to Clausewitz, and I'm now doubly satisfied that that is in fact what he really was saying."[128] He adds that Bismarck, the great Prussian unifier, "must have taken his leaf from Clausewitz when he remarked in a letter of advice to the King of Prussia that 'Wars must be fought in such a way as to make a good peace possible.'"[129] Adds Brodie: "Notice, it is not merely that the objective is good peace, but that the war should be fought in such a way as to make a good peace possible. Bismarck's own wars, even though aggressive, provide on the whole an excellent example of procedures being tailored to meet the objective," as the "century between Waterloo and 1914, as you all know, has often been called a peaceful century"—and was certainly one where war remained limited, linked in a balanced manner with the political objectives being sought, after the balance of power had been restored at the Congress of Vienna and the specter of total war that Napoleon had unleashed returned to the bottle from which it came, at least until the orgy of bloodshed unleashed by the total wars in the twentieth century.[130] In the era of limited wars between Napoleon's defeat and the outbreak of World War I, Brodie points out that "with one exception all these wars were fought for limited objectives," with the "one exception" being "the American Civil War"—"and civil wars are by definition wars in which one side seeks the political extinction of the other. Therefore, they cannot be limited in terms of objective."[131] Brodie finds, however, that "even the American Civil War was limited in terms of military procedures" and that the U.S. Army's "Manual of 1861 happened to present the first codification of the laws of war, that is, restrictions upon the use of force" a "tradition" that "continued at least through the Spanish-American War" when it was "the American Admiral Sampson who, when he fished Admiral Cervera out of the waters off Santiago Bay after destroying his fleet, remarked to him, 'My dear Admiral, you understand there is nothing personal in this.'"[132] Though Brodie does seem to gloss over General William Tecumseh Sherman's methods on his infamous March to the Sea—which included the burning of crops and cities in an effort to bring the war to the enemy's heartland and population centers, a precursor not only to total war but the very sort of counterpopulation warfare that Brodie would decry in the nuclear period.

After discussing the horrific outbreak of total war in World War I, he turns his attention to the even greater horror of total war in the atomic age, writing that the "A-bomb struck us as a horribly destructive weapon when it was first used in 1945," and explaining that "[n]othing has happened since to make it less so. Quite the contrary. We've merely gotten used to it—too much so in many respects," as the "A-bomb produced a real strategic change in the conditions of war."[133] But with the H-bomb on the horizon—Operation Ivy Mike would take place later that year, on November 1, and while not weaponized, it demonstrated the viability of a fusion weapon—Brodie recognized that the A-bomb, the once seemingly *absolute* weapon, but now "conventional nuclear fission weapon—is not so absolute a weapon that we can disregard the limits of its destructive power."[134] Indeed, Brodie explains that the "problem of target selection, for example, is still important. It is important because the numbers of weapons are still too limited to warrant our throwing them around. It is important also because attrition rates to the bombing forces, operational losses, navigational and gross aiming errors, may mean that well under 50% of the bomb sorties reach the so-called proper bomb release point."[135] And while "[t]here has been some unhappiness in certain sections of the Air Staff about the targets we have been selecting," Brodie believes that "[w]e have yet to develop a target philosophy suited to the Atomic Age. The concepts most often applied are those developed under World War II conditions with HE," or high explosive.[136] With A-bombs, Brodie writes, we still "have to be concerned about bombing-accuracy"[137] and "with the physical vulnerabilities of the target selected," and Brodie adds that "[o]ne detects also certain unsophisticated attitudes towards the psychological and political results to be derived from any bombing plan."[138]

And while Brodie expected the number of atomic weapons being produced was going to be shortly ramped up significantly, noting "our atomic weapons are increasing in numbers, and from all the build-up of the facilities we've been hearing about, they are either already or shortly will be increasing at an accelerating rate," and as their numbers rise, Brodie suggests that "military planning can anticipate these changes in at least two ways. We can find more and more targets in the strategic bombing category on which to expend our greater numbers of bombs, or we can allocate an increasing proportion of them to tactical usage."[139] But an even greater increase was expected—not in number of devices, but in their yields: "As you know, the President made an announcement that we were going to go ahead with the H-bomb, and that announcement was made about two years ago. Only last week or maybe the week before, Senator McMann stated publicly . . . that we were continuing to work on the H-bomb."[140] Brodie noted that the "newspapers have also used that magic factor of 1000 by which the 'H' is supposed to be superior to the Nagasaki bomb," and "Since the Nagasaki was a 20 KT bomb," he proposed that we "consider what might happen with a 20 megaton weapon, if and when it is delivered."[141] Brodie and his colleagues had "done some quite rough-and-ready computations" and "came out with some rather interesting conclusions. First of all, CEP no longer matters— that is, up to two miles it no longer matters. If your CEP is two or three times what the present official estimation of it is, we still get the targets. Physical vulnerability of the target selected no longer matters—at least not as much."[142] Indeed, "Even the combination of these, physical vulnerabilities and CEP, matter astonishingly little. One might even be tempted to say that attrition rates no longer matter."[143]

And, in an analysis that showed a certain antiseptic or callous nature, one might intuitively expect more from Brodie's colleague Herman Kahn who leapt to fame on his willingness to *think about the unthinkable*, Brodie writes: "Our computations indicated to us that some 55 bombs of the kind I have indicated could eliminate the 50 largest Russian cities, including the practically complete destruction of most of the industry gathered in those 50 largest cities. And after you had done that much destruction, everything else would be quite marginal, in fact useless. Eliminating the 50 largest Russian cities would mean destroying upwards of 35 million people (dead, rather than casualties), assuming that they were in the World War II type of shelters. Notice that this business could literally be done overnight, so that if you didn't want them to escape they probably could not escape."[144] Added Brodie, "We found that picking targets with the idea of minimizing casualties, that is, picking industrial complexes which were important but which would minimize casualties, would bring the enemy dead down to something like 10 or 11 million. Of course, this assumes that the enemy will not have a chance to warn his people and that we ourselves will not seek to warn these target populations."[145]

Brodie finds that "All this makes strategic bombing very efficient—perhaps all too efficient. We no longer need to argue whether the conduct of war is an art or a science—it is neither. The art or science is only in finding out, if you're interested, what not to hit."[146] Indeed, Brodie adds that the "least this H-bomb would do, if and when it comes, is greatly reduce the force requirements for strategic bombing," and "[t]he reduction of your requirements for strategic bombing coupled with the build-up of our stockpile inevitably makes large nuclear resources and the delivery capabilities available for tactical use. Notice that if we're going to have the H-bomb, we will also at that time have a much large number of the conventional A-bombs than we have today."[147] He continued: "We seem to be destined or doomed, whichever word you prefer, to a permanent inferiority in numbers of men on the ground in Western Europe. Inferiority of numbers has always traditionally been compensated for by superior mobility, if available; superior cleverness, if you have it; and superior firepower, if available. It's quite clear that weapons of this sort plus the conventional nuclear weapon introduce a fantastic augmentation of firepower. This would be an area weapon, large area, and with such a weapon the traditional arguments against the use of nuclear weapons against troops in the field fall to the ground."[148] Indeed, Brodie reflects, in what we may describe as a seemingly Kahnian fashion, "Strategic bombing has been defined as that action which destroys the war-making capacity of the enemy, but I have the feeling that burning up his armies, if you accomplish it, does the same thing. One may be as easy as the other, and certainly we shouldn't have to do both."[149] He adds that "this bombing business, strategic bombing and no doubt tactical as well, is not going to be a one-way affair. The chances of its being so are over for good."[150] And as a consequence, "The dilemma of our age is that in order to preserve the things we wish to preserve we must stand ready to meet a military challenge, and unless the ensuing business is handled most skillfully, the things we have moved to defend will surely perish."[151]

And it is from this that Brodie derives his first articulation of his "*No Cities*" strategy, so described in his own handwriting on a declassified copy of his lecture notes as marked up for delivery, presented in Marc Trachtenberg's edited anthology of original Cold War documents in his multi-volume *Writings on Strategy: The Development of American Strategic Thought* published in 1987 and 1988. Brodie contemplates the failure of deterrence, and asks what might happen "if through some misjudgment, some misconception, we get involved in what might be called a full dress war?"[152] He observes that he's "been toying with an idea about that," adding: "If I had heard it from anyone else I'd have called it a crackpot idea, but I offer it to you for what it may be worth. The atomic bomb thus far has achieved really great successes," adding, "it helped end the Pacific War, and it has so far deterred the Soviet Union from aggression."[153] As he points out, "Notice that the deterrent value has resulted from the threat value. I submit that even the ending of the Pacific War resulted not from the two cities we destroyed, but rather from the threat value of the nonexistent additional bombs which the Japanese didn't know we didn't have—from the threat of more to come."[154] But, "According to our present concepts, this threat value of the atomic bomb is the thing we plan to throw away the moment that hostilities open."[155] Brodie cautions that "[a] bomb which has been used no longer has threat value. A city which has been destroyed is no longer worth entering into negotiations with. I submit that if we decide through intensive study of the situation that our nuclear weapons would actually enable us to break and burn the Soviet armies on the ground wherever they might commit aggression, we might decide that it was possible to secure our objectives without bombing enemy cities. And provided we communicated that idea in advance and provided we retained a powerful and invulnerable SAC to lay down the ground rules and make sure that they were observed, we could say, 'We will not bomb your cities except in retaliation.' This, of course, would be sacrificing the prospect of total victory, but for the future that might be a small price to pay for the sake of avoiding total war."[156] In his 23 January 1953 RAND working paper, "A Slightly Revised Proposal for the Underemployment of SAC in an H-Bomb Era," Brodie reiterates his No Cities proposal, and strongly argues, "If it is possible to control the course of events in a possible future war by some sort of self-denying ordnance as that described above, that possibility must be pursued to the uttermost."[157]

Unlimited Weapons and Limited War

One of Brodie's first published analyses available to the public after America crossed the thermonuclear threshold came in his January 1954 *Foreign Affairs* article, "Nuclear Weapons: Strategic or Tactical," which presented to the public many of his ideas as presented in recent RAND working papers and lectures to the service academies. He recalled Truman's 1953 State of the Union address, which "dwelt on the thermonuclear tests at Eniwetok in the preceding November," in which he had explained that mankind had moved "into a new era of destructive power, capable of creating explosions of a new order of magnitude, dwarfing the mushroom clouds of Hiroshima and Nagasaki," and in which a future war "would be one in which man could extinguish millions of lives at one blow, demolish the great cities of the world, wipe out the cultural achievements of the past—and destroy the very structure of a civilization that has been slowly and painfully built up through hundreds of generations."[158] So destructive were these new weapons that what was deemed only a few years earlier to be the *absolute* weapon was now already relative, and this, Brodie notes, led President Eisenhower, later that year to differentiate "between 'conventional' types of atomic weapons and more advanced types," that latter which could potentially induce "the possible doom of every nation and society."[159] Because of the veil of secrecy on nuclear matters, Brodie had little more in the way of detail other than that "we have been told quite explicitly that a new phase of nuclear weapons development has now opened, and that it points potentially to weapons of a power 'far in excess' of the type which even in its most primitive form was enough to cause the horror of Hiroshima. We are thus faced with the necessity of exploring the implications of the new type when we have not yet succeeded in comprehending the implications of the old."[160]

Brodie concedes that there are "extremely grave and far-reaching limitations" inherent in nuclear weapons, but these "lie not in the costliness of the weapons, in the difficulty of delivering them or in the finite boundaries of their destructive power," but rather in their "excessive destructive power."[161] And as "stocks of thermo nuclear weapons increase, civil air defense as we now think about it will be almost meaningless, as will any active air defense which fails to achieve the very highest levels of enemy attrition. This may be the kind of war we have to fight if and when we have a major war, but it ought not be the kind which we make inevitable through our own military acts and policies."[162] This creates for Brodie a "dilemma of our age," which is "in order to preserve those things which we hold inviolable we must stand ready to meet a military challenge, and unless the ensuing business is handled most skillfully the things we have moved to defend will surely perish. It is self-evident that national objectives in war cannot be consonant with national suicide. But for the future there is no use talking about an unrestricted mutual exchange of nuclear weapons as involving anything other than national suicide for both sides."[163]

And, ironically, strategic bombing, only recently "deprecated on grounds of its presumed ineffectiveness, may in the future have to be restrained because it has become all too efficient. The ability to destroy the enemy's economy and some 30,000,000 or 40,000,000 of his people overnight might be inharmonious with our political objectives in war even if it could be done with impunity; but if we have to suffer such a blow the fact that we can also deliver one may be of small advantage and smaller solace."[164] That's why Brodie concurs with Truman's assessment that "[s]uch a war is not a possible policy for rational men."[165] Or as Brodie described it elsewhere the next year: strategy hits a dead end. Brodie is concerned that the very irrationality of nuclear war might induce a reaction reminiscent of the peaceful change advocates, who unwittingly fueled Hitler's rise and thus the inevitability of general war in Europe, despite their best intentions: "The standard political answer to such a horrible issue is that war must at all costs be avoided. But this is not a sufficient answer. War may in the net be less likely as a result of the new atomic developments, but there is not a sufficient guarantee against its occurrence. We have not yet discovered any substitute for force as a means of controlling blatant aggressions by powerful states, whose rulers may conceivably find in the universal fear of atomic war a stimulus to evil acts rather than a restraint upon them. There must also be a military answer, a second line of insurance, one which maximizes the chances that even a resort to arms will not mean an immediate pulling of all the stops."[166] Because "[u]niversal atomic disarmament . . . is clearly not possible," Brodie argues that we "need to maintain and develop further our strategic striking power, even if our only use of it in a war of the future is to command observance of the ground rules we lay down. And we should probably need to use nuclear weapons tactically in order to redress what is otherwise a hopelessly inferior position for the defense of Western Europe."[167]

Brodie suggests that if his "conception of unlimited atomic potential coupled with limited wartime use thereof appears fanciful, let us look again at what happened in Korea," which despite the imposition by the UN of "greater restrictions upon both its use of means and its strategic and political objectives than the circumstances demanded" resulting in what Brodie felt was a "deplorable stalemate," he nonetheless found it "noteworthy that narrow limits were imposed, and that it was the obviously stronger Power which imposed them and made them stick," evidence that war could remain limited in an era of unlimited weapons.[168] "These facts alone render dubious some of the easy generalizations of our time concerning the inevitable totality of modern war, or for that matter of the inexorable necessity to achieve total victory rather than more limited and modest goals."[169] This leads Brodie to urge that we "proceed to rethink some of the basic principles (which have become hazy since Clausewitz) connecting the waging of war with the political ends thereof, and to reconsider some of the prevalent axioms governing the conduct of military operations," so that "suitable political objectives" as well as "suitable military measures for bringing them about" are developed, in addition to "available instrumentalities for assuring that military action does not proceed beyond the suitable."[170] As Brodie explains: "The time to begin such rethinking is right now, under urgency."[171] That's because, even if we remain "far away from push-button war, as we are so often reminded," Brodie found that we were nonetheless "living right now in a situation in which the flashing of certain signals, possibly ambiguous signals, would in effect push buttons starting the quick unwinding of a military force which has been tensed and coiled for total nuclear war."[172]

Brodie synthesizes his thinking about the arrival of the H-bomb and its impact on war and strategy in a prescient article in the November 18, 1954 edition of *The Reporter* called "Unlimited Weapons and Limited War," where he not only anticipated the forthcoming "era of plenty" for both H-bombs as well as A-bombs, but also the coming of the ICBM. At the start of "Unlimited Weapons and Limited War," Brodie writes, quite engagingly, "Only day before yesterday the atomic bomb came along, and until yesterday we had a monopoly on it. Today we have lost the monopoly and we have in addition the inconceivably powerful H-bomb to reckon with. Tomorrow, we are told, the era of plenty will begin for hydrogen as well as atomic weapons. Perhaps day after tomorrow guided missiles with ·atomic warheads will be hurled from one continent to another. What changes in our strategy do these present facts and future probabilities entail?"[173] Citing the recent observations of the U.S. president, Brodie believes that "War would present to us only the alternative in degrees of destruction. There could be no truly successful outcome."[174] Brodie adds that the "conclusion seems inescapable that our government can use the threat of unlimited war to deter only the most outrageous kind of aggression," and that "[m]oreover, the more appalling the power of the new weapons, the more extreme must the aggression be. If the deterrent fails to deter, one can foresee only mutual devastation, leaving each side far too weak to 'impose its will' upon the other."[175]

Brodie revisits an earlier discussion of preventive war addressed in confidential RAND working papers in 1952 and 1953, but with less sympathy than he showed in his earlier writings where he at least appreciated the effort to inject a bona fide, if not necessarily logical or wise, national objective to nuclear strategy, noting that "[o]ne possible strategy has been urged *sotto voce* since the coming of the A-bomb: preventive war," and notes that "apart from the question of whether it would accomplish its designed objective, one simply cannot see our President adopting it," adding that it was "fantastic to assume, as advocates of this 'solution' usually do that a program of 'educating the public' could ever generate enough popular pressure to have it adopted."[176] Even "its advocates insist" that preventive war "has a time limit" and that it can be waged "only as long as the Soviets do not have a powerful strategic air arm," which "will shortly be passed, it is said," though Brodie suspects that "there probably never was a time when preventive war would have been technically—not to say politically—feasible. When we had the atomic monopoly, we did not have enough power; and when we developed the necessary power, we no longer had the monopoly."[177]

And so he turns to a more viable strategy, that of the "blunting mission" as it is known, or "a blow aimed at the enemy's strategic air force to prevent his striking at us," on the premise that even if it was "unthinkable that we start an unrestricted nuclear war, it is conceivable that an enemy provocation might make us trigger-happy," adding that "[t]here are conditions when it would make good sense to be trigger-happy, as well as conditions when it would be insane."[178] Brodie notes that a blunting mission is "sometimes spoken of as the primary mission of our own Strategic Air Command," which he concedes "makes sense if we are to do strategic bombing, but let us beware of assuming that what rates top priority in planning will necessarily be easy or even feasible to carry out."[179] Brodie describes blunting as "air defense attained by taking the offensive" and explains that "[p]recisely because it stresses offensive action it is more congenial to a profession whose education always stresses the merits of the 'offensive spirit.'"[180] But the appeal is not limited to the American side. Brodie expects that, "[a]s the Soviet capability to deliver nuclear weapons increases, we may be quite certain that a blunting mission must enjoy at least the same degree of priority among Soviet strategic planners that it does among ours. No conception could be more spontaneously congenial to the military in any country; and besides, knowing where our major and almost exclusive offensive strength lies, and knowing also how heavily we rely on it, the Soviets have every possible incentive to adopt the blunting attack idea. Thus, we undoubtedly have a situation where the strategic bombing forces of each side (which, incidentally, will not necessarily be confined to long-range bombers but may include also submarine-launched missiles) plan to eliminate each other at the first sign of war."[181]

Even though "[t]his symmetry in aspiration will not necessarily accompany a symmetry in actual power or in the success derived from it,"[182] Brodie thinks that what's "most likely" is that "neither side may be able to achieve a successful blunting mission even if it has all the initiative and surprise that it could reasonably hope for" and that "[c]ertainly thermonuclear weapons make it possible for whatever portion of a bombing force survives a surprise attack to wreak tremendous retaliation upon the aggressor."[183] Brodie likens the situation of the "blunting-mission game" to "a gunfighter duel, Western frontier style," where the "one who leads on the draw and aims accurately achieves a good clean win. The other is dead," but points out that in the "thermonuclear age," it's "going to require unheard-of recklessness on the part of a government to launch an attack in the expectation that the success thereby achieved will enable it to escape 'massive retaliation' or counter-retaliation."[184] He adds that in a "situation . . . that neither side can hope to eliminate the retaliatory power of the other, the restraint that was suicidal in one situation becomes prudence, and it is trigger-happiness that is suicidal."[185]

Brodie looks with some sympathy to the British, who "stand ready to use atomic weapons with full force and without restraint from the first moment of hostilities," knowing that "an atomic attack upon the United Kingdom would be utterly disastrous to the British," because this remains the only way they can "avert war," and thus their "position rests everything on deterrence."[186] Brodie notes this "at least has the merit of acknowledging the disastrous consequences of nuclear attack," even if it seems "a little bizarre, as well as novel, to see military leaders advocate a strategy which they agree will be suicidal if executed."[187] In contrast, Brodie writes that the Americans appear to be "ignoring Soviet nuclear capabilities as a reality to be contended with in planning," with the presumption being that "it is we, not they, who will do the striking, and they, not we, who will do the suffering."[188] Brodie is troubled by the assumption that "a disaster of overwhelming proportions is something that simply 'can't happen here',", and despite the existence of "loud whispered asides of alarm," he notes that "unlike the stage whispers of Shakespeare, there do not seem to enter into the plot."[189] Brodie reflects on how the "ultimate argument in diplomacy has usually been the threat of force," noting that "now the penalties for the use of total force have become too horrible. This means that our present-day diplomacy based on the deterrent value of our great atomic power is in danger of being strait-jacketed by fear of the very power we hold."[190] And while there is "[n]o doubt the enemy himself is in a comparable strait jacket," Brodie observes that "all in all the situation is one that puts a premium on nerves. Perhaps the Russians. as they conduct their tests, will become more frightened at their own bombs than they have thus far appeared to be at ours. But this is a rather insecure basis for what Churchill called 'the balance of terror.' "[191]

So while a "provision must still be made for that 'massive retaliation' which indisputably remains the only answer to direct massive assault," Brodie observes that "it seems unarguable that a diplomacy that concerns itself with aggressions of considerably less directness and magnitude will have to be backed by a more 'conventional' and diversified kind of force—a kind that the diplomat can invoke without bringing the world tumbling about his ears."[192] Rather than just a mutuality of fear, Brodie suggests that a "reciprocity of restraint, whether openly or tacitly recognized, will have to be on the basis of mutual self interest," noting as "fanciful" as this may sound, that the "Korean War was fought that way, and inadvertently too,"[193] illuminating a path toward stability that emphasizes not massive retaliations but more limited responses—much like he had earlier intimated in his nostalgia for limited war and his hope that the thermonuclear era would witness a recommitment to a similar mutuality of restraint. As Brodie puts it, "Rather than asking what, if anything, needs to be added to strategic air attack, we must consider what we can substitute for it."[194] Now, he adds, "We must therefore explore ways of limiting those conflicts we may be unable entirely to avoid" even if the "difficulties in the way of limitation—on both sides—are immense."[195] Brodie invokes the Prussian strategist Clausewitz and ponders that "these difficulties" of restoring limits "may be more in the minds of men than in the nature of things" and notes that "[w]e live in a generation that has identified itself with slogans Clausewitz would have regarded as preposterous—that every modern war must be a total war; that wars must be fought for total victory, 'unconditional surrender,' and the like—slogans that utterly negate the older conceptions of war as a "continuation of [presumably rational] policy.' "[196] Thus Brodie concludes that "[e]xisting national security policies cannot be justified on the grounds that the A-bomb and H-bomb may turn out to be less fearsome than is predicted by those who know these weapons best," but instead "can be justified only on the grounds that there are important alternatives to unrestricted nuclear war," and adds that if "total war is to be averted, we must be ready to fight limited wars with limited objectives—if for no other reason than that limited objectives are always better than unlimited disaster. A limited war does not necessarily mean war without victory: but the terms must be short of unconditional surrender and give the vanquished a chance to negotiate on a reasonable basis."[197] Brodie notes it was "amazing how we spontaneously acted on these propositions in Korea, and how our errors of comprehension because of the novelty of the problem caused us to show too much rather than too little restraint."[198]

Brodie explores in more detail, in a sidebar to his article. "What Clausewitz Meant," noting that the famed Prussia strategist is "to military strategy what Adam Smith is to economics or Isaac Newton to physics," but despite his importance "has been rarely read, more rarely understood, but abundantly quoted," a theme Brodie would echo for the next three decades even as he worked to introduce America to Clausewitz, and to bring an end to his being "rarely read."[199] Making Clausewitz less accessible even to those who endeavor to read him is that, "[u]nfortunately he was a follower of Hegel's method of presenting thesis, then antithesis, followed by synthesis, where the balanced conclusions are put forward," resulting in some confusion, especially if read in parts and not the whole.[200] "In his monumental work *On War*," Brodie notes, "he first describes war in theory as subject to no limitations of violence, only to develop immediately thereafter the opposite point that qualifications in practice must check the theoretical absolute."[201] And so Clausewitz writes such seeming justifications of total war as: "War is an act of force, and to the application of that force there is no limit," and "In affairs so dangerous as war, false ideas proceeding from kindness of heart are precisely the worst. . . . He who uses force ruthlessly, shrinking from no amount of bloodshed, must gain an advantage if his adversary does not do the same."[202] As Brodie comments, "These and like remarks have been seized upon and quoted (and not by the Germans alone) as a justification for absolute violence in war."[203] But if you read further, you will find that "Clausewitz takes pains to show that the above remarks apply only in a kind of theory which has no place in the real world. 'War is never an isolated act' is one of his subheadings. If war were followed to its logical but absurd extreme of absolute violence, 'the result would be a futile expenditure of strength which would be bound to find a restriction in other principles of statesmanship.' This leads him directly to his most famous and most misunderstood remark of all: "War is a mere continuation of policy by other means.'"[204]

Brodie explains Clausewitz's "meaning of this famous statement becomes clear if we read the seldom-quoted sentences that precede it: 'Now if we reflect that war has its origin in a political object, we see that this first motive, .which called it into existence, naturally remains the first and highest consideration to be regarded in its conduct. . . . Policy, therefore, will permeate the whole action of war and exercise a continual influence upon it, so far as the nature of the explosive forces in it allow.' This is in fact the leading idea of the whole work, and to it Clausewitz returns again and again. It is also the theme that governs the meaning of his famous definition of the object of war as being 'to impose our will on the enemy.' He indicated that the 'will' must have reasonable limits: 'If our opponent is to do our will, we must put him in a position more disadvantageous to him than the sacrifice would be that we demand.' In other words, according to Clausewitz, a defeated enemy, far from having unconditionally surrendered his will, must have a will of his own."[205] And it is recognition of this fact, a mutuality of will, that provides Brodie with a glimmer of hope, that should deterrence fail, that a mutuality of restraint will set in—one rooted not only in fear, but also in hope that in the age of thermonuclear weapons, war can remain limited, as efforts are made on both sides to balance the means of war with its ultimate ends—the political objective.

Brodie recalled that the "history and rationale of attempts to limit wars suggest that limitations on the character and use of weapons, wherever they have been attempted, always stand up best in wars that are also limited regionally," and that of the wars "limited regionally by deliberate intent of both parties there is a long catalogue in history."[206] Added Brodie, "Even wars within Europe have been geographically circumscribed by great-power participants, as for example the Spanish Civil War that preceded the Second World War, and the Greek Civil War that followed it. However, history suggests that Europe is a good place not to have a war if one wants to keep it reasonably manageable. We ought therefore to begin reconsidering some of the ideas we have thrown about lately concerning what we would do in the event of another peripheral challenge like that in Korea."[207]

Brodie recalls how on January 12, 1954, U.S. Secretary of State Dulles "presented before the Council of Foreign Relations in New York what was to be a famous pronouncement on this subject," with his famous massive retaliation speech: "We have since had a really fabulous spate of corrections, clarifications, counterassertions, and restatements, with the result that confusion has become worse confounded and the original declaration almost nullified."[208] Brodie explained that the "basic idea of the January 12 pronouncement was not new," noting that "[o]n several occasions during the previous Administration, one of them a public one before the Committee for Economic Development in New York, Thomas K. Finletter, then Secretary of the Air Force, asserted that the next time we were presented with a Korean-type challenge we should meet it not by local military response but by what he called 'diplomatic action.' If he meant anything effective by that phrase, he could only have meant an ultimatum to the Soviet Union, or possibly to Communist China, or both. That, of course, must also have been the essence of Mr. Dulles's reference to picking 'places and means of our own choosing.' Neither Finletter nor Dulles actually used the word 'ultimatum,' though we cannot doubt such a conception was present in their thoughts."[209] Brodie argued that "[w]hat made the Finletter-Dulles proposal weak was that it was based primarily on military rather than on political considerations—and on pseudo-military ones at that," as "Finletter argued explicitly, as Mr. Dulles did by implication, that we simply could not afford to disperse our strength in meeting Koreas, but must keep it concentrated for the main event. Here we have another case of excessive deference to a classic strategic principle, in this instance the principle of concentration."[210]

As Brodie explains, "Certainly one should not give up peripheral areas in order to keep concentrated for a central challenge that may not come for ten or twenty more years," and even if one was tempted to keep one's military capabilities concentrated, Brodie suggested that "one may doubt whether the forces we committed to Korea would have amounted to very much in a European war; and SAC, the chief deterrent to Soviet aggression in Europe, was not even committed,"[211] staying out of that fight in anticipation of a Soviet move on the central front that never materialized. Brodie concedes that "Korea-type wars are individually disagreeable, inconvenient, and in comparison with tranquil peace," much as America would again experience a decade later in Vietnam; as Brodie points out, "Americans are temperamentally and culturally indisposed to messing around" and it may thus appear to be "certainly tempting to short-circuit little wars by threatening big ones, especially if one does not expect to have to follow through."[212] Brodie suggests there are "at least two essential questions to ask about the Finletter-Dulles idea," the first being, "Will our government have the courage to make the necessary ultimatum at the critical time, and will it have the necessary support at home and abroad?"[213] Brodie suggests that "the history of the Korean War itself and of our more recent handling of the Indo-China affair, one feels disposed to doubt it," and "[i]f our leaders and our Allies have not yet mustered the courage to be bold, then let us not ask them to have the stomach to be rash."[214] Brodie's second question for them is, "If we do manage to screw our courage to the sticking place, are we quite sure the Russians or the Chinese will yield before our ultimatum and halt their local aggressions?"[215] Brodie suggests that if this is the case, "then we are basing the argument not on the military needs of concentration and on the evils of dispersion, but on a forecast of Russian or Chinese behavior before our threats."[216] He posits that while "we may theoretically prefer having one big war to fighting a series of little ones" in fact "the chances are overwhelming that we will not be the ones who will choose to fight the one big war. If we were clear on that point, we should be better prepared to handle the peripheral challenges with adequate diplomacy and adequate strategy to avoid war if possible and to fight it if necessary," much as America did, even without great enthusiasm, in Korea; indeed, Brodie notes that America's "handling of the Korean War was vastly affected by the conviction of both the Truman and Eisenhower Administrations that it was 'the wrong war at the wrong time in the wrong place,'" and Brodie adds that "General Omar N. Bradley used those words concerning the possible extension of the war against China, but by implication they applied to the whole affair. It was General James Van Fleet who insisted, on the contrary, that if there had to be a showdown with Communist China and Russia, Korea was for us the right war at the right place at the right time. If he was correct, we settled for far too little, thereby incidentally leaving in our own mouths a taste of futility and frustration that helped stop us altogether from seriously considering intervention in Indo-China."[217] It is ironic that America's initially bitter foretaste of Indochina's "futility and frustration" would erode, and that America would be drawn into another peripheral war that was limited both geographically and militarily, and like Korea would maintain these limits—but unlike Korea, would result in a humbling defeat for the reluctant superpower caught in a trap of its own creation, fighting a limited war with limited means only to experience a decline in commitment to that war, an echo of Korea but with a more tragic outcome. At least in Korea, the republic in the south was saved and became for coming generations a powerful beachhead for American economic, diplomatic and military influence in Asia.

Brodie suggests that "perhaps we should be grateful to Mr. Dulles for his pronouncement of January 12" since in making his bold speech, "[a]n idea that had been tossing around inside closed organizations for two or three years was suddenly exposed to public scrutiny and debate," and "subsequent Administration statements that purported to clarify the originally proposed policy actually resulted in changing it," since once "the wraps were finally taken off, and utter deflation followed," the country was "treated to . . . a rare demonstration of the democratic process, in the best sense of the term, at work on essentially strategic ideas."[218] Brodie believes that "[i]f such a thing could happen" more often, "some remarkable results might follow," as "[i]deas representing doctrines and orthodoxies of various kinds would be scrutinized by persons who were uncommitted to those orthodoxies" and even if we "could not expect really novel strategic ideas from such a process," Brodie holds out hope that "perhaps we could get reasonable departures from doctrines that had outlived the circumstances to which they were adapted."[219] Importantly, Brodie speculates that we may even "get a new emphasis on having our strategy serve our diplomacy, and seeking to widen rather than restrict the area of choice of that diplomacy," helping to reunite war and politics in the normative Clausewitzian fashion: "Too often history has seen the opposite happen."[220] Brodie concedes that it is possible "the diplomatist may completely mess up the broad choice that a wise strategy makes available to him," and as such he admits "[i]t is impossible to guarantee wisdom in high places at the critical time. But it is the business of the soldier to be sure he is wise in his own sphere, which is today a sufficiently difficult task to spare him the temptation of prescribing wise policies for other spheres."[221] Brodie thus invokes the esteemed Prussia strategist in his final paragraph, noting: "Of course strategy and diplomacy cannot be separated; the union between them should in fact be much closer than it is today. But if the old Clausewitzian idea of strategy being the handmaiden of diplomacy—that is, the subservient partner—can no longer be entertained in a world of such frightening military risks as we face today and shall face increasingly in the future, let us at least not rush to invert the old relationship."[222] As Brodie concludes, "It will perhaps be of some help to remember that the answers to our dilemmas, if there are any answers, cannot-be found in the area of military strategy alone. Strategy cannot determine the ultimate end that war is to pursue—particularly when strategy has at its disposal the ultimate weapon."

Strategy Hits a Dead End: All Out War Now 'Meaningless'

One of Brodie's most widely read articles during the period that followed the successful tests of the H-bomb, in a special section on "How War Became Absurd" published by *Harper's Magazine* in October 1955, was "Strategy Hits a Dead End." *Harper's* editors introduced Brodie's article by noting, "Behind President Eisenhower's remark that 'there is no alternative to peace' lies the sober, cold-blooded estimate of professional strategists that warfare, as they have known it, is no longer practical."[223] They presented "three articles" that "suggest the reasons why. Written independently, each of them explores a different aspect of our military future."[224] Marc Trachtenberg starts off his seventh and final chapter of *History and Strategy*, "Making Sense of the Nuclear Age," with a discussion of this seminal Brodie article, noting: "With the coming of the hydrogen bomb, he argued, the strategy of unrestricted warfare had become obsolete; indeed, 'most of the military ideas and axioms of the past' no longer made sense in a world of thermonuclear weapons. But it was not enough to allow these 'old concepts of strategy' to 'die a lingering death from occasional verbal rebukes.' What was needed, he said, was a whole new set of ideas, a comprehensive and radically different framework for thinking about strategic issues. And over the next decade that was exactly what took shape. Strategy as an intellectual discipline came alive in America in the 1950s. A very distinctive, influential and conceptually powerful body of thought emerged."[225]

As if dutifully handed the baton from Clausewitz in a relay against his long-time opponent, Brodie commences his *Harper's* article with a quotation from Jomini that had enjoyed great endurance, but which had—as Brodie had pointed out on several occasions—at long last become, in the face of nuclear weapons, obsolete: "One of the commonest slogans in strategic literature is the one inherited from Jomini, that 'methods change but principles are unchanging'."[226] As Brodie explained, "Until yesterday that thesis had much to justify it, since methods changed on the whole not too abruptly and always within definite limits. Among the most important limits was the fact that the costs of a war, even a lost one, were somehow supportable. At worst only a minor portion, literally speaking, of a nation's population and wealth would be destroyed. Even the two world wars did not go beyond this limit, despite their horrendous magnitude."[227] Prior to nuclear weapons, Brodie continued, "There could therefore be a reasonable choice between war and peace. There could also be a reasonable choice among methods of fighting a war, or 'strategies'. However unrestricted they were intended to be, wars were inevitably limited by the limited capabilities (as we now see it) of each belligerent for heaping destruction on the other. Indeed, there were even slogans insisting that the application of force in war *must* be unrestricted."[228]

But all that began to change a decade earlier with the atomic devastation that befell both Hiroshima and Nagasaki by a single bomb. As Brodie put it, "If the time has not already arrived for saying good-by to all that, it will inevitably come soon—depending only on when the Soviets achieve and air-atomic capability comparable to the one we already have. For unless we can really count on using ours first and, what is more, count on our prior use eliminating the enemy's ability to retaliate in kind—and surely the combination would deserve long betting odds—we can be quite certain that a major unrestricted war would begin with a disaster for us, as well as for them, of absolutely unprecedented and therefore unimaginable proportions."[229] For salvation, Brodie ultimately turns to the wisdom of Clausewitz, which should come as no surprise to those familiar with Brodie's lifelong interest in, and inspiration from, the famed Prussian strategic philosopher: "The key to the dilemma, if there is one, must be found in discovering the true sense for modern times of the old axiom of Clausewitz that 'war is a continuation of policy'. War is rational, he argued, only insofar as it safeguards or carries forward the political interests of the state. Certainly no one can dispute that, but it also seems at times that no idea could be further from the minds of people who presume to discuss national policy and strategy. One trouble is that even ordinary politicians and journalists feel impelled to utter resounding through meaningless platitudes when the phrase 'national objectives' is mentioned, so that almost everything said on the subject is likely to be unrepresentative of what really lies in the minds and hearts of people at large."[230] But as Brodie observes,

An unrestricted thermonuclear war is to the national interest of no nation. In view of the direction in which we are moving and the speed at which we are going, it seems absolutely beyond dispute that we and our opponents will have to adapt ourselves mutually to ways of using military power which are not orgiastic. The Great Deterrent will have to remain as the Constant Monitor, and its efficiency in that role should never be subject to doubt. But to argue that its efficiency requires it always to be straining at the leash is to uphold an argument today which—if we are actually intent on preserving the peace—we are bound to abandon tomorrow.

At a time when the opponent will be able to do to our cities and countryside whatever we might threaten to do to his, the whole concept of "massive retaliation"—and all that it stands for in both military and political behavior—will have to be openly recognized as obsolete. It is not enough to let a strategic idea die a lingering death from occasional verbal rebukes, leaving behind only confusion in public and professional opinion—including confusion about whether or not it is really dead. It is not enough to say that an unrestricted thermonuclear war cannot happen anyway because both sides will recognize its folly. There are various positive steps we must take to prevent its occurring even when military force is resorted to in disputes between nations.

In a world still unprepared to relinquish the use of military power, we must learn to effect that use through methods that are something other than self-destroying. The task will be bafflingly difficult at best, but it can only begin with the clear recognition that most of the military ideas and axioms of the past are now or soon will be inapplicable. The old concepts of strategy, including those of a Douhet and of World War II, have come to a dead end. What we now must initiate is the comprehensive pursuit of the new ideas and procedures necessary to carry us through the next two or three dangerous decades.[231]

Brodie would continue to focus on the imperative of limiting warfare during the coming years and preventing what he would describe as the "meaningless" folly of total war in the thermonuclear era, with the now absolute destructive potential of the superbomb weighing heavily on his mind. Rather than dig in to defend his earlier views on the impossibility of war in the atomic age to retain its Clausewitzian balance, Brodie's views would continue to evolve and adapt to the emergent thermonuclear realities, and Clausewitz would continue to guide him. Consider an article in *The Dartmouth* published on March 20, 1956 with the telling title, "Brodie Discusses 'Limited' Conflicts, Says All-Out War is 'Meaningless'" written by Bevan M. French, who later worked for many years at NASA and is currently with the National Museum of Natural History at the Smithsonian Institution.[232] The article discussed Brodie's visit to Dartmouth, where he had earlier taught, to present a lecture to the Great Issues course there; before the lecture, he was interviewed by French, and in the interview he discussed Clausewitz and his importance for helping us frame our strategic choices, and to balance the objectives of war with the new, and most menacing, means of waging war. As French cited Brodie, "With the development of thermonuclear weapons for use in warfare, a limited war without their use is both possible and necessary."[233] French wrote that Brodie "spoke to a Great Issues course last night on 'Nuclear Weapons and Changing Strategic Outlooks,'" the title of a speech he would deliver to several campuses that year including the Naval War College and the Army War College. As French recounts, "In an interview before his speech, Brodie cited the theories of Karl von Clausewitz, a Prussian general who wrote that war should be a continuation of diplomatic policy, and that the objectives of war should be political. 'Some use of force seems to be necessary in modern diplomacy,' Brodie continued, 'but the presence of mass-destruction weapons makes it important that its use should not get out of hand.'" French adds that "[t]he 46-year-old University of Chicago graduate emphasized, however, than an all-out war is 'meaningless'" as "[t]here would be no objectives in an all-out war,' he continued slowly, 'that would make it worth fighting.'"[234] French noted that "Brodie went on to cite the Korean conflict as an example of a 'limited' war," and that he commented, "We had objectives in the conflict and from that point of view, it made sense to do what we did in Korea."[235] Brodie would further develop his thoughts on the strategic implications of the new thermonuclear weapons on total war, and to reinforce his strengthening belief that total war was indeed now "meaningless" in any Clausewitzian sense, as evident in his discussion in his July 7, 1957 RAND paper, "Implications of Nuclear Weapons in Total War," as prepared for publication in the Fall 1957 issue of the *Royal Canadian Air Force Staff College Journal*.[236] Once the destructive power of the H-bomb was demonstrated, Brodie recalls that "AEC Chairman, Rear Admiral Lewis L. Strauss, stated on that occasion that the H-bombs that the United States could build and deliver would be individually capable of wiping out any city in the world!"[237] In addition to the unprecedented explosive power of the new weapon, it also produced an "unexpectedly large amount of radioactive debris, which was deposited as 'fallout' of dangerous and even lethal intensity over thousands of square miles," adding to the weapon's Apocalyptic capabilities.[238]

With such a deadly weapon in the arsenal of modern states, Brodie writes that it now "became apparent that certain controversial military questions that had remained pertinent in the fission-bomb era were no longer worth tarrying over. Chief among these were the questions inherited from World War II concerning the appropriate selection of industrial target-systems. Industrial concentrations are usually associated with cities and vice versa, and since a thermonuclear bomb exploded near the center of a city would as a rule effectively eliminate the industrial activities associated with that city, there is hardly much point in asking which industries should be hit and in what order, or which particular facilities within any industry."[239] The targeter's dilemma, for the moment, was now resolved: "once we are embarked upon an unrestricted nuclear war, the question of what to hit is all too simple to answer. We simply select the enemy's cities, which constitute the easiest targets to find anyway."[240] Moreover, Brodie suggests that "since many major enemy airfields are bound to be near cities, the distinction in priority" between *counterforce* and *countervalue* targets "is in such instances likely to be an academic one. It is idle to talk about strategies being counter-force strategies, as distinct from counter-economy or counter-population strategies, unless we actually find ourselves taking deliberate measures to refrain from injuring cities," which Brodie would in fact come to counsel as the one viable path to limiting warfare in this new, deadly thermonuclear age.[241] As Brodie notes, "It can hardly matter much to the populations involved whether the destruction of cities is a by-product of the destruction of air fields or vice versa."[242]

Brodie discussed the introduction, in the British *Defence White Paper* of 1954, of a new concept and "expressive phrase 'broken-backed war' to describe what presumably would happen after the first huge exchange of thermonuclear weapons, assuming the exchange itself failed to be decisive,"[243] and in a footnote cites the document's description of this scenario and how it would unfold: "In this event [global war], it seems likely that such a war would begin with a period of intense atomic attacks lasting a relatively short time but inflicting great destruction and damage. If no decisive result were reached in this opening phase, hostilities would decline in intensity, though perhaps less so at sea than elsewhere, and a period of broken-backed warfare would follow, during which the opposing sides would seek to recover their strength, carrying on the struggle in the meantime as best they might."[244]While the phrase was not widely embraced by Americans, many would embrace "the same conception," as Brodie notes in another footnote citing Admiral Robert B. Carney, U.S. Chief of Naval Operations, in a February 21, 1955 Cincinnati speech: "Presumably massive blows would continue as long as either side retained the capability. . . . With the passing of that initial phase, and if the issue is still unresolved, tough people would carry on across the radioactive ashes and water, with what weapons are left. Sea control will be an elemental consideration in accomplishing either the follow-through phase of atomic war or the better appreciated chores of a prolonged nonatomic war."[245] And while "the conception of 'broken-backed war' appeared to be entirely abandoned in the *Defence White Paper* for 1955, which tended instead to rest everything on 'deterrence,' it has nevertheless continued to underlie and to confuse the basic structure of American and Allied defense planning,"[246] and Brodie questions the probability that a thermonuclear war would resemble the broken-back concept. Brodie agrees that one may "easily conceive of conditions in both contending camps so chaotic, following the opening reciprocal onslaughts, that the war issue will not be immediately resolved and hostilities not formally concluded," and that one may also "picture surviving military units, including some possessing thermonuclear weapons and means of delivering them, continuing to hurl blows at the enemy to the utmost of their remaining though fast-ebbing capacity."[247] "But," Brodie adds, "it is difficult to imagine such intensive continuing support from the home front as would enable 'conventional' military operations to be conducted on a large scale and over a long enough time to effect any such large and positive purpose as 'imposing the national will on the enemy.'"[248] As Brodie explains, "The major premise of the 'broken-backed war' conception was that the result of the initial mutual nuclear violence would be something like a draw. Otherwise it could not fail to be decisive. The second premise (we cannot call it a minor one) was that the level of damage on both sides following the strategic nuclear bombing phase would be limited enough to permit each to equip and sustain air, ground, and naval forces of sufficient dimensions to be able to execute noteworthy military operations. These would, presumably, be conducted at some distance from home, and would therefore require facilities, such as ports and associated railway terminals, which are generally found only in those larger coastal cities which would certainly be among the first targets hit in the nuclear phase! Implicit also was the further dubious assumption that somehow the nuclear phase would end cleanly, or diminish to a trivial magnitude, early in the hostilities, and at about the same time for both sides!"[249] But Brodie adds that "[a]nother and perhaps more practical reason for questioning the 'broken-backed war' conception is that no one seems to know how to plan for such a war," and notes "[t]here are special psychological reasons why official war planners have always in times past found it almost impossibly difficult to predicate a war plan on the assumption of national disaster at the outset. But in this case, even if the spirit was willing, the data and the imagination would be much too weak."[250]

In a passage reminiscent of Herman Kahn's later ultrarealist discussion of total war in the H-bomb era in his best-selling and controversial 1960 tome *On Thermonuclear War*, Brodie considers "The Problem of Survival," and writes that: "There are, of course, numerous examples in recent history of magnificent improvisation following upon disaster, or rather upon what used to be called disaster. But in each of those cases the means of making war, including such vital intangibles as established governmental authority operating through accustomed channels of communication, remained intact. A few battleships sunk, a few armies defeated and lost, even large territories yielded, do not spell the kind of over-all disaster we have to think about for the future. There are limits to the burden that can be placed on improvisation. The improvisation which the survivors of thermonuclear attack may find it within their capacities to come up with will surely have to be largely occupied with restoring the bare means of life."[251]

By means of historical analogy, Brodie explains that the "differences in circumstance that accounted on the one hand for the French resistance in 1914 and, on the other, for the collapse in 1940 were of trivial magnitude compared with the differences between pre-atomic and present-day strategic bombing.[252] An illustrative description of this new thermonuclear reality is presented by Marshal of the Royal Air Force, Sir John Slessor, whom Brodie cites in other works including his forthcoming *Strategy in the Missile Age*, who in his 1954 *Strategy for the West* observed that he had "the perhaps somewhat unenviable advantage of an experience, which fortunately has been denied to most people, of being in a city which was literally wiped out, with most of its inhabitants, in fifty-five seconds by the great earthquake in Baluchistan in 1935, a far more effective blitz than anything laid on by either side in the late war, except Hiroshima and Nagasaki. When people talk light-heartedly about that sort of thing on a widespread scale not being decisive, I have to tell them with respect that they do not know what they are talking about. No country could survive a month of Quetta earthquakes on all its main centres of population and remain capable of organized resistance."[253] And this, Brodie notes, describes "a catastrophe that is free of the additional terrible menace of lingering radioactivity," which makes thermonuclear warfare even more *unthinkable*.[254]

Sounding much like Herman Kahn would sound a few years later, and not entirely unlike the Dr. Strangelove character in the movie of the same name, Brodie writes, "from a sober appreciation of the possibilities in this field of dismal speculation, it seems quite safe to assume that the number of people and the kind and quantity of capital that may survive strategic attack will be important far more for determining the character and degree of national recovery following the hostilities than for controlling the subsequent course of the hostilities themselves," but diverging from the caricatured callousness of Strangelove (and the infamous ultrarealism of Herman Kahn), Brodie would conclude that the "minimum destruction and disorganization that one can reasonably expect from any unrestricted thermonuclear attack in the future must almost inevitably be too high to permit further meaningful mobilization of war-making capabilities, certainly over the short term, and may well prevent effective use of most surviving military units already in being."[255] Adds Brodie, "It should also be recognized once and for all that so far as predicting human casualties is concerned, we are talking about a catastrophe for which it is essentially impossible to set upper limits appreciably short of the entire population of a state. It is not only those in cities and in towns who will be exposed to risk, but, in view of the fallout effect, practically all. . . . What we are in effect saying is that although the uninjured survivors of attack may indeed be many, it is also all too easily conceivable that they may be relatively few. The latter contingency is the more likely one in the absence of large-scale protective measures such as neither we nor any other people have yet shown ourselves prepared to mount. But whether the survivors by many or few, in the midst of a land scarred and ruined beyond all present comprehension, they should not be expected to show much concern for the further pursuit of political-military objectives."[256]

Brodie confronts what he describes as "Ambiguity in Policies," noting that there is a monumental ambiguity in public policy, which reflects in part the ambiguity in the public pronouncements of relevant officials of the highest rank. Even those who preach the catastrophic decisiveness of nuclear strategic bombing seem to find it almost impossibly difficult to grasp the full significance of what they preach," an ambiguity that he sees in the often contradictory remarks of Sir John Slessor, who had so vividly described the horrific calamity of thermonuclear destruction but who "could also be abundantly quoted on the other side of the 'decisiveness' question from the very same book—a book that has a special importance as perhaps the most lucid and comprehensive presentation of the 'massive retaliation' doctrine to be found anywhere."[257] Brodie takes Slessor to task for in essence ignoring his own warnings on the unique and unprecedented catastrophe that thermonuclear warfare would bring, and instead turning to the World War II experience for guidance, where Slessor came to realize: "When things are really bad the people's morale is greatly sustained by the knowledge that we are giving back as good as we are getting, and it engenders a sort of combatant pride, like that of the charlady in a government office who was asked during the London blitz where her husband was—'he's in the Middle East, the bloody coward!' We must ensure that defence, as adequate as we can reasonably make it, is afforded to those areas or installations which are really vital to our survival at the outset of a war, or to our ability to nourish our essential fighting strength."[258] Brodie responds that "[t]here is only one thing to be said about such language and imagery: it fits World War II, but it has nothing to do with thermonuclear bombs."[259]

Brodie is reassured to note that Slessor's view would rapidly evolve, so in just two years he would be "seeing things in a quite different light," as evident in his May 1956 article in *The Bulletin of the Atomic Scientists*, "The Great Deterrent and Its Limitations," for which Brodie wants to "give due credit to Sir John for a flexibility of mind that is no doubt among his special distinctions."[260] And with some sympathy, perhaps as a result of Brodie's own editorship and contribution to *The Absolute Weapon* in 1946, which presented views that sharply contrasted with Brodie's current thinking as a result of the thermonuclear revolution, Brodie suggests that "[p]erhaps there is also something about the experience of being an author, especially the author of a book, that brings one intimately into the rough-and-tumble of the marketplace so far as ideas are concerned" and credits Slessor for a "kind of drastic conversion that Sir John underwent within two years regarding some of his fundamental beliefs," which "is not a common occurrence among his professional colleagues, especially among those still on active duty. As Sir John observes in the aforementioned article: 'Not many people, even in the fighting services themselves, have really grasped the full tactical implications of an age in which nuclear power is the dominant strategic factor in war. There is a tendency almost subconsciously to shy away from those implications, which should not be ascribed merely to the influence of vested interest.'"[261]

Brodie closes his discussion of the new, pressing and dangerous thermonuclear realities and their challenge to strategy with a call for "The Need for Consistency," noting "[t]he sense of Emerson's famous remark about consistency being the hobgoblin of little minds has on the whole enjoyed remarkable verification in military history. Trite historical examples of unintelligent rejection of the novel need not detain us, except possibly to note that the catalog is long."[262] Brodie is more concerned herein with "the instances where eager acceptance of the new is coupled, not only within the same organizations but often within the same persons, with stubborn insistence upon retaining also much of the old. These are the people who on the whole have come off best when the scores were in. For their very inconsistency has often provided a hedge against wrong predictions."[263] Brodie has found that "[t]he intensely conservative or reactionary are always proved wrong" as "changes in armaments over the past century have been much too rapid and drastic to offer any cover to those who will not adjust," and yet, as Brodie himself would find over and again, "the occasional brilliant seers who have the courage of their convictions and the analytical skill to recognize and expose inconsistency when they see it have all too often been tripped up by one or more critical assumptions which turned out to be in error, and then their own consistency worked only to make their whole logical construction dangerously wrong, as was certainly the case with Douhet" and, one might argue, the early Brodie in 1946 who saw the atomic bomb as an *absolute* weapon that made war irrational, if not yet obsolete, and which severed the fundamental Clausewitzian linkage connecting war to politics and with it any hope for rationality.[264] Brodie suggests that, "No doubt a proper intuitive feeling for the hazards of prediction and for the terrible forfeits involved, in the military sphere, in finding oneself overcommitted to a wrong guess, is one of the reasons why military men at a group tend to put a rather modest value on analytical brilliance as an alternative to mature military judgment."[265] But he concludes, "Nevertheless, there is a limit to the amount of inconsistency that is reasonable, especially since in the world of nuclear armaments it may become, to say the least, exceedingly expensive. And if any one thing is clear from all the foregoing, it is that the strategy of 'massive retaliation', as commonly understood, is, like the headman's axe, rather too sharp a cure for ordinary ailments."[266]

Toward a Strategic Balance: Strategy Meets the 'Missile Age'

According to many students of strategy, Brodie's seminal work is his 1959 treatise on the thermonuclear era, *Strategy in the Missile Age*, and which has been described without exaggeration by Colonels William P. Snyder and John A. MacIntyre, Jr., in their 1981 article in *Parameters*, "Bernard Brodie: America's Prophetic Strategic Thinker," as "a landmark study that synthesized the central ideas on deterrence and limited war that had emerged during the 1950s," and which "provided an expanded and analytical examination of the themes discussed in his earlier book, incorporating many of the strategic concepts developed by his colleagues at RAND. Thus, *Strategy in the Missile Age* was a synthesis of the major strategic ideas that had emerged since the beginning of the atomic age."[267] They noted that that this book "was directed equally to military officers and to political leaders; Brodie especially hoped to bridge the intellectual no man's land between those who 'decide how to wage war' and those who 'decide when and to what purpose' wars should be waged."[268] They add that *Strategy in the Missile Age* "was the most important book on American national strategy to appear in the decade of the 1950s" and "provided the first detailed explanation of the advantages, indeed the necessity, of a deterrence strategy and an equally thoughtful analysis of the forces required to achieve deterrence."[269]

As Ken Booth noted in his chapter on Brodie in *Makers of Nuclear Strategy*, *Strategy in the Missile Age* "was a big book which brought together a discussion of many of the problems that had been troubling Brodie over the previous few years," and "[i]n particular, he grappled with the interplay between old and new forces, when the latter were truly revolutionary."[270] The origins of Brodie's widely read and lauded book are discussed by Marc Trachtenberg in his article, "Strategic Thought in America: 1952–1966," which appeared in the Summer 1989 edition of *Political Science Quarterly* as well as in the final volume, "Retrospectives," of Trachtenberg's six-volume anthology, *Writings on Strategy: The Development of American Strategic Thought* published that same year. Once the atomic monopoly ended, and robust nuclear forces became an undeniable fixture on both sides of the Iron Curtain, providing a strategic foundation for the emergence of a bipolar world system, strategy became more complex, less predictable, and more difficult to safely navigate. As Marc Trachtenberg describes in his article, the "question of deterrence could not be divorced from the question of use" and thus the "problem of target selection was, therefore, of fundamental importance."[271] As Trachtenberg observes, "These problems were all very new, but already in 1952 one thing was clear: the targeting philosophy that had developed before and during World War II was becoming increasingly problematic. Indeed, the basic point about the absurdity of all-out war when each side had developed the means of utterly devastating the other must have been tremendously disorienting for professional military officers."[272]

He adds that it had become "clear, to the more discerning officers at any rate, that there were very basic and difficult problems here and that no one as yet had any really satisfactory answers," and General John A. Samford, the U.S. Air Force's director of intelligence, "wrote in 1952 that existing ideas on air power were inadequate and rested on 'too narrow a base'" and "he therefore asked the president of RAND to allow Brodie, whose work he liked and with whom he had been in contact, to 'produce a basic treatise on air power in war.' Since RAND was under contract to the air force, this was in effect the authorization that enabled Brodie to do the work that culminated in his important 1959 book, *Strategy in the Missile Age*."[273] The book, while seminal and enjoying international translations and multiple printings that have continued into the post-Cold War era, was really little more than an anthology of Brodie's papers, speeches, and articles during the decade that had passed since America lost its atomic monopoly, when the strategic environment Brodie had famously analyzed in 1946 in his contributions to *The Absolute Weapon* underwent a profound transformation to a true nuclear-strategic balance the effectively bifurcated the world system. *Strategy in the Missile Age* was thus a treatise on the new bipolar world and how to survive its unprecedented dangers.

While the book was widely praised, Trachtenberg fairly criticizes Brodie for his lack of a clear prescription: "By 1959, when *Strategy in the Missile Age* was published, Brodie had been thinking about these issues full-time for many years. But again he failed to take a clear line. If all we sought was to maximize the pre-war deterrent effect, he wrote, we should 'assign the hardcore elements in our retaliatory force to the enemy's major cities, provide for the maximum automaticity as well as certainty of response, and lose no opportunity to let the enemy know that we have done these things.' The problem was that 'what looks like the most rational deterrence policy involves commitment to a strategy of response which, if we ever had to execute it, might then look very foolish.' 'For the sake of deterrence before hostilities,' he argued, 'the enemy must expect us to be vindictive and irrational if he attacks us'—even if his attack took care to spare our populations and successfully destroyed much of our retaliatory force; but 'a reasonable opposing view' was 'that no matter how difficult it may be to retain control of events in nuclear total war, one should never deliberately abandon control.' "[274]

Trachtenberg notes Brodie "understood that the basic issue in nuclear strategy was target selection," and that "the central problem here was whether the attack should focus on destroying the enemy's retaliatory force, sparing to the maximum extent possible the enemy's population, in order to preserve its hostage value—or whether the enemy's strategic forces should not be targeted at all, since the ability to destroy them might lead the enemy to preempt and thus be destabilizing."[275] But much to Trachtenberg's disappointment, "Brodie simply laid out both sets of arguments and made no serious attempt to resolve the issue. He had 'given relatively little space,' he said in his conclusion, 'to the matter of how to fight a general war if it should come,' because 'the strategy of a total war is like an earthquake in that all the forces which determine its occurrence and its character have been building up over time, as have almost all the factors which determine how it runs its course.' The implication here was that rational analysis could make no real difference. And similarly, on the basic issue of limited war strategy—the question of tactical nuclear weapons—Brodie again simply laid out the pros and cons and drew back in this book from taking a position on the issue himself."[276]

Brodie's ambition for *Strategy in the Missile Age* was to not only imagine the interaction of strategy and the new, and terribly destructive technologies of war—which thanks to the proliferation of intercontinental missiles tipped with thermonuclear weapons that handily reached beyond continents and oceans, now threatened the interior heartlands that had been long insulated from the full trauma of modern war—but to also christen this new and uniquely dangerous era. Having already authored a widely read and highly regarded text on the role of sea power in what he had dubbed, for posterity, "Machine Age," Brodie hoped to not only comment on the new era of intercontinental missiles and their deadly thermonuclear payloads, but to define the new era as a distinct "age" on par with the "machine age." In his numerous papers, articles and speeches written as these new weapons arrived, Brodie refers to the thermonuclear era as distinct from the atomic era, but he concludes that while the H-bomb magnified the destructive power and thereby rendered strategic bombing more efficient, its arrival did not mark as fundamental transformation in war as that which was introduced by the A-bomb itself. And so Brodie looked for a better title to name this new era.

Much is revealed in Brodie's correspondence with his editor at Princeton University Press as this new work gestated, and as its final title was determined, with much persistence from Brodie in his insistence that the term "Missile Age" define his work, and remain part of its title. But in the end, his preferred phrase did not stick, though his work was nonetheless warmly received, positively reviewed, and widely influential—as other phrases jockeyed for position, with the term "Nuclear Age" becoming more commonly applied to the post-Hiroshima period generally. On January 29, 1958, his editor at Princeton, Herbert S. Bailey, wrote to Brodie to discuss a new edition of Brodie's best-selling *Guide to Naval Strategy*, and informing Brodie that Captain J. J. Vaughan, who served as Head of the Correspondence Courses Department at the Naval War College, might be interested in "purchasing 2000 or perhaps more copies of a revised edition of *A Guide to Naval Strategy*, for use in Navy correspondence courses," with "an additional chapter on the lessons of the Korean War," and with an updated chapter on "Tools of Sea Power."[277] Bailey suggested various courses of action were open: doing both, writing the new Korea chapter and welcoming revisions by them of the Tools of Sea Power chapter; welcoming from them both the Korea chapter and a revised Tools of Sea Power chapter; or telling them Brodie was too busy to do a revision but they could "simply have to take the book as it stands, supplying material on the Korean War and on the new weapons and ships by some other means."[278] He added: "I hope that some method can be found to satisfy the Navy without interfering too much with your own work, which is obviously more important currently. I had hoped that your book on *Air*

Strategy would be finished by now, though I suppose these things always take more time than one expects, and I imagine also that the recent advances in rocketry and the like have made some changes necessary."[279] These advances in rocketry in fact transformed the work at its very core, so much so that the book would not be solely about air strategy, but would more broadly explore the strategic implications of a host of new technologies including the increased destructive yield of nuclear weapons as thermonuclear devices entered the arsenals of the superpowers, vastly augmenting the yields of the original atomic bombs; the advent of intercontinental rockets capable of efficiently and rapidly delivering thermonuclear payloads anywhere worldwide without viable defensive countermeasures; and the increasing complexity of the nuclear force structure as the land-air-sea triad took shape, including the emergence of largely invulnerable strategic submarines. These technologies would overshadow traditional air forces, which achieved prominence during the early nuclear era, which relied on large fleets of relatively vulnerable strategic bomber aircraft to less efficiently deliver their atomic payloads deep within enemy territory, bringing us into what Brodie hoped we would call the "Missile Age."

On February 6, 1958, Brodie replied to Bailey, noting that his initial reaction to Captain Vaughan's plans for a rewrite of *Guide to Naval Strategy*—referred to as GNS—for use in naval courses was "negative," since he "had the feeling that there was too much conservatism and orthodoxy in the course's approach for me to want to have anything to do with providing the literature for it. Besides, I have for years looked upon GNS as a book which has served its purpose, nobly so far as my own interests were concerned, and that it should now be permitted to rest in peace. In libraries it could be useful for informing the young on what naval war was like in the days before the H-bomb."[280] But he added that upon further "reconsideration, I think for favorably about the project. First of all, I think I could put some vital new stuff in the book without a great deal of additional writing. I am thinking of the first of the four alternative courses you suggested, secondly, if a correspondence course in naval strategy is going to be given at the Naval War College, one should really not expect that it would or could be anything very daring or imaginative. Where would they get the instructors for it if they were? Thirdly, if there is a reasonably nice piece of cash in it for me, I have a very good use for it."[281]

With that, he turned to his work in progress, which would become *Strategy in the Missile Age*. "Now, about my present work. I too was hoping it would be finished by now. The problem is simply that I have been suffering from, and desperately fighting, certain inhibitions amounting to what people loosely call 'writer's block.' But I have been making progress despite it all. I am sending you separately a long chapter which you have not yet seen (nor have you yet seen the chapter called 'Is There a Defense?', which for the time being is classified but which I am sure we can easily get declassified at the appropriate time. It has been quite favorably received by those who have read it, including, I might say, the Gaither Committee.) I am at work on the latest chapter, and allowing for rewriting and all the rest. I think it is not altogether foolish to talk in terms of another two months of work."[282] In addition to "Is There a Defense"—which became Chapter 6 of *Strategy in the Missile Age* with the same title—Brodie would note in the preface to his July 23, 1958 RAND Research Memorandum (RM-2218), "The Anatomy of Deterrence" (which would become, incidentally, Chapter 8 in *Strategy in the Missile Age* as well as an article of the same title in the January 1959 edition of *World Politics*), that "this paper is one in a series in preparation by the author on the general theory of air strategy in the nuclear age. Although each of these papers is intended as a chapter in the larger study, a few are being released as separate publications in view of their particular relevance to current problems."[283]

The papers listed were—in addition to "The Anatomy of Deterrence" and the aforementioned "Is There a Defense?" which was published as a RAND Research Memorandum (RM-1781) on August 16, 1956 but classified as "Confidential"—his unclassified December 31, 1952 RAND Research Memorandum (RM-1013), "The Heritage of Douhet," which became Chapter 3 of *Strategy in the Missile Age* with the same title; his unclassified "The Implications of Nuclear Weapons in Total War," RAND Research Memorandum, RM-1842, from December 17, 1956, which became Chapter 5, "The Advent of Nuclear Weapons; and his unclassified "The Meaning of Limited War," RAND Research Memorandum, RM-2224, from July 30, 1958, which would become Chapter 9, "Limited War."[284] As well, much of Brodie's May 14, 1957 speech to the Institute of World Affairs at the University of Utah, published by RAND on the same date as RAND Paper P-1111, "Some Strategic Implications of the Nuclear Revolution," would also appear in Chapter 5, with other portions appearing as well as in Chapter 1, "Introduction" (namely, where Brodie discusses the metaphorical implications of the War in Heaven as presented in book VI of Milton's *Paradise Lost*, as he earlier did in his first book, *Sea Power in the Machine Age*). Additionally, much of his June 11, 1953 RAND working paper, "A Commentary on the Preventive War Doctrine," appeared in Chapter 7, "The Wish for Total Solutions: Preventive War, Pre-Emptive Attack, and Massive Retaliation;" and much of his November 18, 1958 public Berkeley lecture, "Unlimited Weapons Choices and Limited Budgets," appeared in Chapter 10, "Strategy Wears a Dollar Sign." *Strategy in the Missile Age* would become, in large measure, an anthology of Brodie's strategic and theoretical reflections on the new thermonuclear weapon and its global delivery systems as reflected in his papers, articles, and lectures during the years that preceded its publication as a single work, and would described in his preface to the Princeton edition as a "one-man enterprise in which I was accorded full freedom to develop my thesis as I saw fit," though he would acknowledge being "especially indebted" to ten of his RAND colleagues, among whom can be found Herman Kahn, Thomas Schelling, Hans Speier, and Albert Wohlstetter, and thankful for the feedback from thirteen several others who had read the manuscript in whole or in part.[285]

As Brodie explained to Bailey in his February 6, 1958 letter, "I expect none of the internal problems in rewriting the naval strategy book that I have mentioned above, probably because the material is less novel and daring."[286] He noted that he had done some encyclopedia work during the past two years, and thus could safely promise to deliver a revised edition by the end of June. Brodie asked Bailey, "are you ready to do a new edition amounting physically to a new book, involving throwing away the present plates (if they exist) for what is after all going to be a pretty limited sale? If that question can be answered in the affirmative, the next question is whether the Navy will agree to a fee for my work which will make it all worth while. I am thinking in terms of a fee of at least $1,000 to $2,000 plus royalties."[287] On March 6, 1958, Bailey wrote to Captain Vaughan, presenting the path he and Brodie had outlined for the revision of GNS: "Presumably Chapters II and II on 'The Tools of Sea Power' will have to be completely rewritten. Dr. Brodie is prepared to do this. He feels strongly that Chapter IX on the 'Tactics of Fleet Action' is the most outdated chapter in the book, and will have to be either entirely eliminated or replaced. In addition, it would probably be desirable to add a chapter on the lessons of the Korean War and later developments. Dr. Brodie has already written a good deal on this subject, and would be prepared to write a special new chapter for the *Guide to Naval Strategy*."[288] Bailey said Princeton University Press could guarantee "2000 copies for $8500 f.o.b. New York, a discount from the $6.00 cover price," adding, "In view of the amount of work to be done, I think this is a very fair price, and I hope it will be possible to for you to get the necessary appropriations."[289] This was agreed to by Captain Vaughan, who phoned Bailey with the news, and on March 22, 1958, Bailey informed Brodie by letter of this: "I just had a telephone call from Captain Vaughan with the good news that they have been able to get the necessary appropriations immediately, so they are drawing up a contract which they will be sending me soon. In other words, we are all clear to go ahead with the revised edition of the *Guide to Naval Strategy*."[290] Brodie was pleased with the news and on March 28, 1958, he replied in writing to Bailey: "I am glad it is all arranged with the Navy. I expect to have no trouble at all writing the required new pages, and will give up my weekends if necessary to do the job without interfering with the new book. . . . The problem is utterly different from and easier than the new book."[291] Brodie added: "If what we were doing for the Navy was a new book, and they wanted to have a look at the manuscript before drawing a contract, I would tell them to go to Hell—as I am sure you would, too. Under the circumstances, however, I do not mind in the slightest."[292]

Brodie informed Bailey that he had nearly completed his new book, and on March 31, 1958, Bailey replied to Brodie, writing: "What wonderful news that you have really come to the end of your new book on Strategy, except for a short summary! I am so glad that you finally got through the problems that were stumping you and got it finished. I shall be looking forward to seeing it."[293] Brodie had asked Bailey about re-using his recent presentation delivered to the University of Utah's Institute of World Affairs, and a lengthy quotation from *Paradise Lost* that had appeared in the front matter of his first book. Bailey assented, writing "by all means go ahead and use them. The quotation in *Sea Power in the Machine Age* is very unobtrusive, not even in the text, and I am sure that virtually no one will notice that you are using the same quotation again. Even if they do, the quotation is so obviously apt for the use to which you put it, that it wouldn't be questioned. And it is so good that it would be a shame not to use it."[294] Over the next few weeks, Brodie would juggle his revisions to GNS with his effort to complete *Strategy in the Missile Age*, and one result was a delay on the printing of GNS. As noted in a letter for Brodie from Bailey on July 17, 1958, required revisions from Captain Vaughan required bumping GNS' printing to August: "I know that it has been hard for you to get the revision of GNS done when your heart is really in your new book, but I think it is worth while and I appreciate the efforts you have made to get it through quickly."[295]

And finally, on December 8, 1958, Bailey wrote to Brodie, "The new edition of GNS is in at last, and two copies are on their way to you separately. I have just been looking through it, and I think it came out quite well. I hope you will be pleased with it."[296] Bailey added: "I have been hoping to hear from RAND that your new manuscript is on the way, but I haven't heard anything yet. I shall be very glad to get it whenever they are ready to release it."[297] On December 16, 1958, Bailey again wrote to Brodie, telling him: "I was of course excited to hear that the new book is at last nearly finished. I am looking forward to reading that copy of the manuscript you are going to smuggle to me. And I certainly hope you won't have any trouble with Hans Speier about the selection of a publisher; I think Speier is favorably inclined toward us. . . . I do want to assure you that we are prepared to put the book through quickly."[298] On December 29, 1958, Brodie replied to Bailey, reassuring him that Hans Speier and James (Jim) C. DeHaven would respect the author's choice for a publisher, and as such, "That means P.U.P."[299] He added, "Of course, when you see the MS you may change your mind about wanting to publish it. However, I am really not worried. Excuse me for it."[300] As a P. S., Brodie added: "If the Navy has paid my fee for the revision of GNS, I can use the $1,500.00 as soon after the New Year as you can send it."[301] On January 2, 1959, Bailey wrote to Brodie, noting the Navy had not yet paid Princeton University Press, "but as soon as they do I shall send you our check for the special $1500 fee, and the regular royalties will be due and will be paid as usual in March."[302]

On January 26, 1959, DeHaven wrote to Bailey "regarding Bernard Brodie's manuscript on 'Air Strategy in the Missile Age,'" reaffirming RAND's support of the author's preference for a publisher, adding RAND was also "influenced by the interest and enthusiasm of a competent publisher for a particular manuscript," so "[b]y both of these criteria, the choice of a publisher in this case seems to converge rapidly on Princeton. We will therefore submit the final manuscript to you."[303] He added, "Some words of caution may be in order at this point. As you know, we can't agree to publication until clearance has been obtained. There is no reason to believe that clearance will be withheld; on the other hand, it may be delayed, or, some changes in the text may be requested."[304] DeHaven concluded his letter by assuring, "You may be sure that we are all looking forward to this continued opportunity for association with Princeton University Press and Herb Bailey."[305]

On January 30, 1959, Brodie wrote to Bailey, in which he discussed the tentative working title to his new work, which he originally dubbed *Air Strategy Meets the Missile Age*. Brodie wrote, "I have no particular commitment to the title I chose, other than the fact that titles are difficult for me to think up. I do think it would be improved by the omission of the word 'Air,' which would leave it simply 'Strategy Meets the Missile Age.' I like the word 'Meets,' because, unlike the word 'Enters,' it suggests that what has gone before it not really appropriate to the situation that now confronts us. By the way I had thought also of the word 'Confronts.' "[306] Brodie added, "I had thought also of having some other word qualifying 'Strategy,' like 'Ancient' or 'Classic.' However, the connotation in these words is not good. Anyway, let's think about 'Strategy Meets the Missile Age' until we think of something better."[307] On February 3, 1959, Bailey replied to Brodie, "I just received your note of the 30th, about the title. I agree that the word 'Air' in the title is not necessary. Let's use 'Strategy Meets the Missile Age' as a working title, but let's also see if we can think of something equally descriptive and more striking."[308] And on February 10, 1959, Bailey again wrote to Brodie, explaining, "I have been thinking over the title, because I am not entirely satisfied with 'Strategy Meets the Missile Age.' We have had too many books about the atomic age, the missile age, the nuclear age, and other kinds of 'ages.' It seems to me that your book is a fundamental development of the whole basis of strategy, and ought to have a title that is simple and imposing. What would you think of simply 'Modern Military Strategy' or 'Strategy for Peace and War'? I don't think it's presumptuous to remember that Clausewitz wrote *On War*—not a bad title."[309] Such a Clausewitzian aspiration would re-assert itself with Brodie's 1973 work, *War and Politics*, and incidentally, Bailey's thoughts mirrored those of Herman Kahn's editors, who had similarly suggested a similarly Clausewitzian title for Kahn's voluminous and controversial lectures on thermonuclear warfare, resulting in its neo-Clausewitzian title, *On Thermonuclear War*.

On February 16, 1959, Brodie wrote to Bailey, continuing their discussion of the title to his latest work: "About the title, I agree about the over use of the word 'Age.' However, one of my former books is, as you know, *Sea Power in the Machine Age*, so I have a certain proprietary commitment in that area. I should like to bring in something about missiles in order to show the newness of the thing, and I also want to have the word 'strategy' in the title. However, I am afraid I am not yet ready to go as far as you suggest in your own tentative recommendations. I want to hold on the few traces of modesty I still have left."[310] Brodie added, "By the way, the two paragraphs of my quotations from Milton on the first page contain a number of wonderful book titles, provided one is not too concerned with communication information. Almost every phrase makes a good title, e.g., 'More Valid Armes,' 'Weapons More Violent,' 'When Next We Meet,' 'And Worse Our Foes,' etc. Milton seems just naturally to have breathed out titles."[311] On February 16, 1959, Bailey replied to Jim DeHaven at RAND, lauding Brodie's newest work: "I am absolutely sincere when I say that I think the book is going to be the most important book of its kind in the decade. I would love to be the editor for the book and put it through the press myself, but I have so many other duties that I know I can't do it. It's going to be in good hands, though. Gordon Hubel, who I think did a wonderful job on *The Berlin Blockade*, will begin to edit the book this week."[312] He added that Princeton University Press planned to put Brodie's new book "on an express production schedule, and I hope to have finished books in May for publication in June. At least that's what I'm shooting at, and if we can get clearance soon, I don't see why we can't do it."[313] Bailey estimated the new book would be 432 pages long, and priced at $6.50. The first print run was expected to be 5,000, but Oxford University Press pre-ordered 1,000 copies so the first print order was increased to 6,000, a sizeable run for an academic work.

While there was much hope for Brodie's newest work, its title remain unsettled, and on March 13, 1959, Bailey wrote to Brodie, noting, "We've been struggling among ourselves over the title of your book, though of course in the long run you will have to decide. To me, and to several others here, 'Strategy Meets the Missile Age' is somehow flat, perhaps because it is a sentence by itself and needs a period after it. Finally, I decided to take a poll of our publishing staff."[314] He added that his "own preferences are, in order, *Strategy for Survival, The New Strategy, New Strategy for New Weapons*. The more I think about it, the more I believe *Strategy for Survival* indicates and implies some of the chief points of the book—that you can't win a thermonuclear war, but that you can hope to survive if your strategy is right. Also, that the best way of surviving is by devising a strategy to prevent war. The word 'survival' clearly implies thermonuclear weapons, since there has been so much talk about their devastating effect. Moreover, *Strategy for Survival* is brief and to the point, would look well on the cover of the book and in ads, and is easily memorable. Again, I think everybody knows only too well that a big war would mean missiles with thermonuclear warheads, so that doesn't need to be said."[315] But he added, "If you don't like *Strategy for Survival*, may I plead for *The New Strategy*? The word 'new' implies a radical change from earlier strategy, and also implies the new weapon. Also, it is short and memorable." Bailey noted that Princeton University Press' advertising department "apparently discussed the problem and settled together on *Strategy for the Missile Age*. Their judgment should be good, but I personally still don't like 'The Missile Age.' It is not an accepted term like 'the machine age,' nor does it pervade the entire civilization in quite the same way. Still, it got four good votes."[316] Bailey closed by adding, "I hope we can settle on a title pretty soon. What do you think of all this?"[317] On March 20, 1959, Brodie replied to Bailey, responding to his suggestions and concerns. "Now, about the title, which I too feel we ought to sew up. I have tried hard not to be stubborn or excessively-in-love-with-own-words. Still, I like mine best."[318] As Brodie explained: "Also, the word 'Survive' or 'Survival' has been used rather too much in titles about war, including, as I recall, the first and widely-read book on the atomic bomb, and the military would be allergic to it. They would consider it 'pushing the panic button.' 'The New Strategy' is much too pretentious for a relatively modest guy like me. . . . I rather like your third choice, 'New Strategy for New Weapons,' but, like the one which comes closest to my own, i.e., 'Strategy for the Missile Age,' it sounds like a prescription for a specific strategy, which my book does not offer, and also ignores the contribution of Part I of my book. I like the word 'Meets' rather than 'for' because it is much more dynamic, and also a closer approximation to what my book is about, which is the *confrontation* of the strategy inherited from the past by a completely new situation in which, by implication, the old ideas don't fit. Also my title is easy to remember and to say. Your comment that the 'Missile Age' is not an accepted term like 'Machine Age' does not sound to me like a demerit. The term 'Absolute Weapon' was not an accepted term either until my colleagues and I used it in that book edited by me."[319] Brodie added: "Naturally, I did not entirely trust my own judgment and tried out the title question on a few people here. It is certainly not possible to get consensus, but what does it matter? Two people liked my title very much, and no one came up with an alternative that anyone else liked."[320]

On the same day, Brodie wrote to Gordon Hubel, an editor at Princeton University Press, noting some problems with the clearance from the State Department for release of his new book: "You have by now heard the unfortunate news about the holdup on my clearance. It seems the people concerned in State simply cannot find the time to finish it. Moreover, I am still hopeful that we will get back in the swing of the original schedule."[321] He turned to the topic of the book's title, adding, "I notice you are using the title 'Strategy for Survival.' Unfortunately, it cannot be that, the reason chiefly being that the military would be allergic to it. Also, the word 'survival' has been used too much in titles concerning matters of this sort. I am writing Herb a separate letter today in which I am explaining why I had to resolve on my original title

'Strategy Meets the Missile Age.'"[322] Brodie referred to Hubel's earlier comment on how Brodie's draft manuscript had proved very useful in helping Hubel understand Herman Kahn's lectures, which would very soon become *On Thermonuclear War*: "I think your comments on how my manuscript enabled you to understand Herman Kahn's lectures is both very complimentary and very important. This is the kind of function I want that book to fulfill."[323] Ironically, Kahn's sprawling lectures would deeply penetrate the American psyche, bringing Kahn fame and notoriety, even inspiring the conception of the Dr. Strangelove character and shaping his apocalyptic vocabulary. Hubel had written to Brodie on March 17, 1959, presenting a proposed advertising schedule for the book he was still calling "Strategy for Survival," and in a P.S. he wrote, "Herb and I attended Herman Kahn's lecturers (sic) at the Center of International Studies Friday and Saturday last, and we were both tremendously impressed with the sweep of his knowledge in this area and his ability to communicate, but without having read your manuscript, I would not have been able to follow him at all."[324] Ironically, Brodie's role, fostering greater understanding of the complex strategic issues of the *Missile Age*, contributed in his publisher's ability to comprehend, and assess the market potential of, Kahn's lectures—which would soon become the voluminous tome, *On Thermonuclear War*, a much less elegant and theoretically less robust work of strategic analysis than *Strategy in the Missile Age*. But in terms of social influence and prestige, *On Thermonuclear War* would become a best-seller, and catapult Kahn to national prominence—so much so that Kahn would become a celebrity in his own time, in contrast to Brodie whose orbit remained peripheral to mainstream society, even as his intellectual influence peaked, no doubt a frustration that would enable Brodie to empathize with a similar frustration felt by Clausewitz in his own time, which itself mirrored the famously frustrating fall of Niccolo Machiavelli, who was not only exiled but was arrested and tortured as well.

On March 25, 1959, Bailey again wrote to Brodie on the topic of the title to what would at last be finalized as *Strategy in the Missile Age*. "We have been talking here again about the title, and much as we want to respect your wishes, we still aren't happy with 'Strategy Meets the Missile Age.' It seems awkward to me, and several people have pointed out that the sense of 'confronts' didn't come through to them immediately. They took 'meets' in the sense of 'how-do-you-do.' This seems absurd, and of course it *is*, but there is something illogical about first impressions, and the first impression a title makes is important."[325] Bailey suggested meeting Brodie half-way: "But can't we compromise on 'Strategy *in* the Missile Age'? This doesn't get across the idea of 'confronts,' but we can work on that ideas in our advertising blurbs. You can't get everything into the title, and perhaps we have been trying too hard. I would be happy to settle for 'Strategy in the Missile Age' if you would. How about it? I hate to keep bringing this up, but the title is important to all of us."[326] Bailey closed by adding, "I hope we hear from the State Department before you get this letter."[327] On April 8, 1959, Brodie wrote to Hubel, updating him on the slow-going clearance review at the State Department, noting "the State Department reader is (all too slowly) approaching the close, and has so far not challenged anything he has seen. I suppose it would be better if I waited until I receive final word, but my impatience needs some outlet, so I am sending you now the second round of galley-proof corrections."[328]

Brodie ultimately accepted Bailey's compromise wording on the title, which was published soon thereafter as *Strategy in the Missile Age*. Bailey continued to radiate optimism as the first copies came off the press, and on August 21, 1959, he wrote to Brodie, reaffirming his belief that the book was destined for success: "I really think the book is going to be a hit. Everybody who has seen it likes it. Yesterday Charles Scribner, who receives a copy as President of our Board, called me up just to tell me how excited he was about it. You can be sure that we are going to do everything we can to make it go."[329] A few days later, on August 25, 1959, Brodie replied to Bailey, writing, "The copies of the book arrived Thursday and I am delighted with their appearance. Everybody comments on how good the pages look, and the cover and dust jacket too. . . . I am going to keep one copy aside for entering minimum necessary changes, in case there is a second printing. Thus I will be able to shoot you such changes as soon as you indicate the need for them."[330] Brodie asked Bailey, when new dust jackets get printed, to swap in a new quote to replace one provided from a *Herald Tribune* review of GNS that was underwhelming in its support of Brodie: "I have always disliked that phrase 'a really adequate guide.' We have so many glowing comments to quote for that book. Excuse this one braying note when I am so pleased with everything else (including your spiel about the new book in your Fall Books announcement), but it has operational value."[331]

But very soon after *Strategy in the Missile Age*'s release, controversy erupted over the publisher's press release and its incendiary tone. In a September 15, 1959 letter to Brodie, Bailey discussed this unexpected situation: "Frankly, I was quite surprised that the people at RAND kicked up such a fuss, since the release was written [right] out of the book, and every sentence in it could be documented."[332] Brodie himself had thought the writer, John Criscitiello, Princeton University Press' advertising manager, "did a good job," and Bailey explained that "apparently the release, in emphasizing the controversial points of the book, put everything together in a way that flustered the authorities, and I agree with you that they are justifiably concerned."[333] Bailey agreed that "we wouldn't send out any release at all. The book will attract plenty of attention anyway, and the reviewers will say what they think about it, no matter what we or the RAND Corporation say or do. I am looking forward eagerly to the reviews, and I am sure you are too."[334] Sales of the book were strong, and on January 20, 1960, Bailey wrote to Brodie, informing him that "about 13,000 copies of the book have already been distributed. I think this is pretty good. Incidentally, I happen to know that it is considerably more copies than Random House has managed to sell of Oscar Morgenstern's book which came out at the same time. Since Oscar runs pretty wild and since I am convinced your book is the best on its subject, I am quite happy about that. Moreover, I am sure that your book will go on selling when Oscar's is forgotten."[335] Bailey invited Brodie to become Princeton University Press' "special advisor on books on military affairs"[336] as part of a new editorial advisory committee. He also discussed Brodie's concerns over some rejections of requests to send out free review copies; Bailey defended Princeton University Press' policy, noting: "I want to defend our practice of not acceding to all requests for review copies. We do distribute review copies very generously, but I don't think you realize how many journals and magazines there are, or how many requests we get from media of very limited circulation."[337] On February 4, 1960, Brodie wrote to Bailey, proposing publication of *Strategy in the Missile Age* in Japan, and noting his surprise that the UK publication of this work was not until February 4, "which happens to be this date. No wonder I have not seen British reviews of it!"[338] Bailey liked the idea of a Japanese edition, and on February 11, 1960 wrote to Brodie, telling him: "I would indeed be keenly interested in arranging for a Japanese edition of your book."[339] He also noted, "I was disturbed also at the delay in British publication," and that it "appears that the book got caught in the end of the printers' strike, and therefore was delayed."[340]

The book quickly went into a second printing, and Brodie sought to make some corrections to the manuscript. On February 18, 1960, he sent a telegram to Bailey noting with concern that a "major batch of corrections sent you October seventh was entirely ignored."[341] On February 22, 1960, Bailey wrote back, acknowledging Princeton University Press' "failure to make some of the corrections requested in the second printing of *Strategy in the Missile Age*" and adding "my personal apologies," noting "the only thing we can say is that something slipped. We were just as astonished as you were."[342] He promised to include them in the next printing. Bailey also noted approvingly Thomas Schelling's positive review of *Strategy in the Missile Age* in the February 19th edition of *Science*. On February 22, 1960, Hubel also wrote to Brodie apologetically, noting after his initial disbelief, he checked the reprinted version and "found that you are entirely correct," and offered up his "sincere apology."[343] The next day, on February 23, Bailey again wrote to Brodie, affirming his "embarrassment and chagrin again," and reiterating his "profound apologies."[344]

Despite this minor setback, *Strategy in the Missile Age* enjoyed a very healthy run, with multiple editions and numerous milestones—after its first hard cover printing in 1959, it would enjoy a second printing in 1960, international editions released in several languages including a Russian language edition published by Moscow's Soviet Ministry of Defense in 1961; a Spanish language edition published that same year by Argentina's Escuela de Guerra Naval in Spanish; and a Polish language edition published by Warsaw's Ministry of National Defense in 1963; a fourth hard cover printing in 1963; a first paperback edition in 1965 with a new preface by Brodie; and a second soft cover printing in 1967 with subsequent paperback printings in 1970 and 1972, the latter with a new preface by Brodie; a fifth hard cover printing in 1971, with subsequent printings by Princeton in 1984 and 1991, and more recently, a September 2007 release by RAND nearly fifty years after its first printing at the dawn of the "missile age." As of this writing, over half a century since it was published, Worldcat.org shows *Strategy in the Missile Age* to be available in 1,116 libraries worldwide, in 27 distinct editions. On August 29, 1969, Princeton University Press' Reprint Editor, Roy E. Thomas, wrote to Brodie, telling him, "It is a pleasure to tell you that we have had to rush into a third printing of the paperback edition of *Strategy in the Missile Age*. As of July 31 1969 this book has sold 6,340 copies in paperback. We have scheduled a reprinting of 3,000 copies, an estimated 2 ½ years' supply. The price of the paperback remains $2.95."[345] He added, "I am sure you must be gratified, as we are, by the continuing success of *Strategy in the Missile Age*."[346]

Strategy's New Beginning: Philosophical Foundations

The frontispiece to Princeton University Press' editions of Brodie's seminal *Strategy in the Missile Age* cites two key influences on his work—the latter from the start of his academic career and the former much more recent: Clausewitz, the philosopher of war; and Plato, an early architect of the modern state, and Socrates' top pupil and chief biographer who has profoundly shaped our understanding of his teacher, and thus preserved his teachings for us through his interpretation. From Clausewitz's *On War*, Brodie cites the following: "In these windings [of special interest] the logical conclusion is caught fast, and man, who in great things as well as in small usually acts more on particular prevailing ideas and emotions than according to strictly logical conclusions, is hardly conscious of his confusion, one-sidedness, and inconsistency." And from Plato's *Republic,* Brodie cites: "And is anything more important than that the work of the soldier should be well done?" From philosophy, Brodie quickly migrates to epic poetry.

When reading the introduction to Brodie's *Strategy in the Missile Age*, it is poetry that greets the reader, not math or science or even history—just as we saw in his opening sentences of his 1947 article, "The Atomic Dilemma" and again in his 1957 RAND Paper (P-1111), "Some Strategic Implications of the Nuclear Revolution," which was the text of a speech Brodie presented to the Institute of World Affairs at the University of Utah on May 14, 1957—with passages from Book VI of *Paradise Lost* cited, with Angle Raphael recounting to Adam the story of the epic war in Heaven that led to Satan's fall, an allegory for the new nuclear age. As Brodie writes, "[a]fter the first day of fighting, Raphael relates, the issue was still in doubt, although the rebellious angels had received the more horrid injury. . . . Satan is persuaded that their inferiority is one of weapons alone, and he suggests: 'perhaps more valid Armes, Weapons more violent, when next we meet, May serve to better us, and worse our foes, Or equal what between us made the odds, In Nature none,'" to which Nisroc, his lieutenant, enthusiastically agrees: "He who therefore can invent/ With what more forcible we may offend/ Our yet unwounded Enemies, or arme/ Ourselves with like defence, to mee deserve/ No less then for deliverance what we owe."[347] Satan announces the invention of a new and transformative weapon, a field gun that will alter the balance of power, which the next day is deployed with "dreadful execution," but "the loyal angels, not to be surpassed in the application of science to war, in the fury of the moment seize upon the 'absolute weapon'" and "[t]earing the seated hills of Heaven from their roots, they lift them by their shaggy tops and hurl them upon the rebel hosts. Those among the latter who are not immediately overwhelmed do likewise. In a moment the battle has become an exchange of hurtling hills, creating in their flight a dismal shade and infernal noise," and "Heaven is threatened with imminent ruin."[348]

In case the point is missed, Brodie writes "The war in Heaven dramatizes the chief dilemma which confronts modern man, especially since the coming of the atom bomb, the dilemma of ever-widening disparity in accomplishment between man's military inventions and his social adaptation to them."[349] Adds Brodie: "Until recently the deadliest weapon known to man represented only a modest refinement of the field gun which Milton describes in his poem. Now, however, we can come much closer to matching, in kinetic-energy equivalents, the hills hurtling through space; we have thermonuclear weapons and the planes and ballistic missiles to carry them." Add to man's newfound destructive power was a worrisome trend in the nature of war itself, which until the twentieth century had managed to retain a "well-recognized function in diplomacy" with an "institutionalized quality" and an "overlay of antique customs, traditions, and observances" that "tended to limit further a destructiveness already bounded by a primitive military technology."[350] Modern war was now at risk of becoming "uncontrolled and purposeless," with a "near-collapse of the factors previously serving to limit war."[351]

As Brodie described, "Today, however, with truly cosmic forces harnessed to the machines of war, we have a situation for the first time in history where the opening event by which a great nation enters a war—an event which must reflect the preparations it has made or failed to make beforehand—can decide irretrievably whether or not it will continue to exist," and this unprecedented fact demands that the pre-atomic world's willingness to let decisions pertaining to the conduct of war be made "in a fairly undefiled world of 'strictly military considerations'" no longer be tolerated: "Obviously, therefore, we cannot go on blithely letting one group of specialists decide how to wage war and another decide when and to what purpose, with only the most casual and spasmodic communication between them." Brodie himself sought to intermediate this conversation between political leaders and the military commanders whose job it would be to fight the next great war, and found his efforts thwarted by those who resisted civilian interference in what had been traditionally military decisions on how to conduct war once hostilities commenced, or by those civilians who questioned his philosophical and historical interpretations. At RAND he found himself at a nexus where the two worlds more comfortably intertwined, but the problem nonetheless persisted, enough so that he felt compelled in 1959, nearly a decade after he was tossed by the Air Staff out of the Pentagon, to address the "Intellectual No-Man's Land," and to describe how "[t]here exists in America no tradition of intellectual concern with that border area where military problems and political ones meet," noting that even the "civilian official in the State Department will rarely know much about current military problems and will therefore have no feeling for their relevance to the issues in his own jurisdiction," and that even the "National Security Council is for that and other reasons mostly a monument to an aspiration," and suggesting "whether any real enrichment of strategic thinking has proceeded from it is another question."[352] Thus, Brodie concludes, "Any real expansion of strategic thought to embrace the wholly new circumstances which nuclear weapons have produced will therefore have to be developed largely within the military guild itself," as it is only "the professional military officer" that is "dedicated to a career that requires him to brood on the problems of war, in which activity he finds himself with very little civilian company."[353]

But Brodie finds "the soldier has been handed a problem that extends far beyond the *expertise* of his own profession," and though "[h]e had learned to collaborate well enough with the physical scientist, to the mutual profit of both and to the advantage of their nation," this has not proven to be the case with regard to "military questions involving political environment, national objectives, and the vast array of value-oriented propositions that might be made about national defense."[354] One reason why, Brodie learned from earlier experience, is "the barrier of secrecy," which he finds now "conceals far more, relatively, than it ever has before,"[355] but he argues that "we must not put too much blame on the security barrier for the general ignorance of defense problems," since "[t]he amount of information available to the public on military and strategy affairs is very much greater than the casual observer would guess," and Brodie believes that the real culprit is thus a lack of understanding of and appreciation for "the stakes involved and also the opportunities available to them to contribute their special insights and skills to a great common problem," a challenge that Brodie takes upon himself to counter, with *Strategy in the Missile Age* "in part intended to help them make that contribution."[356] Once properly motivated to contribute to this common problem, however, Brodie acknowledges that the next challenge is getting through to the "military audience" and overcoming what he describes as the "Traditional Military Depreciation of Strategy," and what we might describe as an inherently Jominian problem (in the reductionist tendency to reduce strategy to stratagem in military circles), or as Brodie himself described as "the general conviction, implicit throughout the whole working structure and training program of the military system, that strategy poses no great problems which cannot be handled by the application of some well-known rules or 'principles', and that compared with the complexity of tactical problems and the skills needed to deal with them, the whole field of strategy is relatively unimportant."[357]

His view is inherently Clausewitzian, and reflects the continuity of a problem Clausewitz himself encountered, and which even he had sought to insulate himself from by shunning publicity, going so far as to publish anonymously and keeping his magnum opus locked away until after he had died, in contrast to Jomini's enduring self-promotion, prolific publishing, and constant effort to generate fame and notoriety. It is in the colorful personage of Herman Kahn, who would emerge to be Brodie's principal rival in many ways, that we find our modern Jomini—not for any wanting absence in his intellect or any shortfall in his strategic thinking, but in his showmanship and self-promotion, his willingness not to just think about the unthinkable as Brodie had been doing from the moment Hiroshima lay in smoldering ruins, but to aspire to become known as the man who *dared* to think about the unthinkable (as if this was something Brodie had somehow neglected!) Kahn's bravado contrasted greatly with Brodie's more mild-mannered approach to publicity, though both did publish widely, and both did seek to break down barriers in communication, Brodie hoping to break down barriers between civilian scholars and defense intellectuals and military professionals, and Kahn hoping to directly engage the public in the great nuclear doctrinal debates of the age, and Kahn would gain great notoriety, achieving a rare level of celebrity and entering into the consciousness of American pop-culture, for his effort—while Brodie would in many ways fade into the background of the very field that he can be credited for founding.

Learning from History

Brodie raises in his introduction to *Strategy in the Missile Age* the still recent strategic bombing campaigns of World War II, noting that it was "rarely criticized on tactical grounds," and that there has been "no serious dissent from the general consensus that, for a new type of operation, the whole job was magnificently handled,"[358] but rather that "[a]ll the important and voluminous criticisms of the effort center upon questions that are essentially strategic," such as: "Were the basic military resources absorbed by strategic bombing too great in view of the returns? Could not these resources have been better used, even in the form of air power, for other military purposes? Were not the wrong target systems selected?"[359] Pulling back somewhat from his earlier critical assessment of these issues, which led to his exile from the Pentagon to the distant think tank of the RAND Corporation, Brodie asserts: "Whatever views one may have about the answers to these questions, or to the spirit behind the questioning, the questions themselves are neither irrelevant nor unimportant."[360]

But Brodie concedes that the reality of war limits commanders' exposure to independent strategic analysis, overwhelmed as they are by their daily need, especially in wartime, to respond to tactical and administrative demands. As Brodie explained: "There is no doubt that tactics and administration are the areas in which the soldier is most completely professional. The handling of battles by land, sea, or air, the maneuvering of large forces, the leadership of men in the face of horror and death, and the development and administration of the organizations that effect these purposes are clearly not jobs for amateurs. In these tasks there is no substitute for the hard training and the experience which the services alone provide."[361] Brodie adds that, "During war the tests of command become far more exacting than in peacetime, and some officers turn out to be more talented than others . . . But unless the officer attains some independent and important command, he may never in his career have to make a decision that tests his insight as a strategist. Small wonder, then, that the services on the whole have paid relatively scant attention to the development of strategic theory," particularly since "[t]oday the basic conditions of war seem to change almost from month to month. It is therefore hard for the professional soldier to avoid being preoccupied with means rather than ends. Also, his usefulness to his superior hangs upon his skill and devotion in the performance of his assigned duties, rather than upon any broader outlook, and if there is one thing that distinguishes the military profession from any other it is that the soldier always has a direct superior."[362]

Brodie turns to history to provide us with the tools required to develop an independent capacity for strategic analysis and to break free from the constraints of dogma and maxims, so that we may respond to the challenges of the nuclear age not with incremental tactical innovation but forward thinking strategic insight. Hence when he asks, "Why Look Back?" he has a ready answer: "if we examine the history of ideas" behind current strategic convictions, "we usually find that they have evolved in a definitely traceable way, often as the result of the contributions of gifted persons who addressed themselves to the needs of their own times on the basis of the experience available to them,"[363] much the way Clausewitz threw himself into a lifelong process of digesting the Napoleonic experience, saving his conclusions for posterity to consider, and to apply to their ages. "Our own needs and our experience being different, we are enabled by our study to glimpse the arbitrariness of views which we previously regarded as laws of nature, and our freedom to alter our thinking is thereby expanded."[364] Brodie notes some might think in our "age of missiles, thermonuclear warheads, atomic powered submarines capable of strategic bombing, and other comparably fantastic systems, it may seem atavistic to look back to strategic views which antedate World War I," but he posits that "ideas about war and how to fight it are not," to which he adds that "we should not deceive ourselves that we have the ability to start from scratch with completely fresh ideas and, guided merely by logic, to fashion a strategy according to the needs of our time," as this is "too much to expect of human beings. For better or worse, we shall be applying our intellects, as presently furnished, to new and baffling problems."[365]

Hence the purpose of Strategy in the Missile Age, to "scan the earlier development of strategic theory . . . and then consider some of the strategic policy choices confronting us today."[366] And so Brodie engages in a dialogue with earlier strategic thinkers, including Clausewitz, who himself engaged in his own dialogue as did so many earlier theorists, many of which have defined what political theorists and scholars of international relations call the *realist tradition*, and which unifies the study of politics with the study of war, hoping to find balance in not just means and ends, but to establish a firewall between order and chaos, maximizing the former while containing the spread of the former, or perhaps more accurately, maximizing the prevalence of order at home while either minimizing the intrusion of chaos across one's frontiers, or when necessary exporting one's own vision of order to pacify those chaotic border lands, or when desperate to impose chaos upon a competing vision of order as would be accomplished by a nuclear retaliatory strike. Brodie thus looks back and joins a conversation that has carried forth since Herodotus first sought to decipher the events that transpired when Greece withstood the onslaught of their militarily superior Persian opponent, and Thucydides sought to grapple with the challenges faced by the Athenians as they clashed with their non-democratic opponents, the Spartans, losing in spite of their faith in the superiority of their democratic system, perhaps because of their ideological presumption of superiority which led then to commit international excesses, violating their democratic principles by committing atrocities abroad, and the students of Socrates sought to avenge his death by the manipulated demos, and to create a more enduring system that would at once enrich the world without imploding upon itself, through variations upon the philosopher-king model, ultimately unleashing Alexander upon the world, and who paved the way for Roman equilibrium to govern for a millennium, a period that Machiavelli would later seek to resurrect, and later realists would attempt to modernize, giving birth to Hobbes' Leviathan, a theoretical blueprint that others would seek to construct, from Napoleon and his interpreters to the wizards of Armageddon, where Bernard Brodie would reconnect with this long tradition, taking from it what guidance he could, as he struggled to prepare his world for the legacy of Hiroshima and the rise of the nuclear Leviathan.

In Brodie's segue to his discussion of air power, at the start of his second chapter, "Prologue to Air Strategy," he again addresses the challenge of strategic theory, and why it so often surrenders to the tide of simplification, emerging as maxims and stratagems: "Military strategy, while one of the most ancient of the human sciences, is at the same time one of the least developed. One could hardly expect it to be otherwise. Military leaders must be men of decision and action rather than of theory. Victory is the payoff, and therefore the confirmation of correct decision. There is no other science where judgments are tested in blood and answered in the servitude of the defeated, where the acknowledged authority is the leader who has won or who instills confidence that he will win."[367] Brodie adds: "Some modicum of theory there always had to be. But like much other military equipment, it had to be light in weight and easily packaged to be carried into the field. Thus, the ideas about strategy which have evolved from time to time no sooner gained acceptance than they were stripped to their barest essentials and converted into maxims or, as they have latterly come to be called, 'principles.' The baggage that was stripped normally contained the justifications, the qualifications, and the instances of historical application or mis-application."[368]

Brodie notes that the "'principles of war' derive from the work of a handful of theorists, most of them long since dead," and that "[t]heir specific contributions to living doctrine are not widely known, because their works are seldom read."[369] He adds that the "richness of their ideas is but poorly reflected in the axioms which have stemmed from those ideas,"[370] tilting his hat toward the likes of Clausewitz, and not Jomini. When it comes to the new field of air power, Brodie adds there has been only time enough for "one distinguished name" to emerge, that of Douhet, whose "essential, correct, and enduring contribution lay in his turning upside down the old, trite military axiom, derived from Jomini, that 'methods change but principles are unchanging,'" instead insisting "that a change in method so drastic as that forced by the airplane must revolutionize the whole strategy of war."[371] Brodie thus directly rebukes Jomini and the Jominian influence, and in his praise of Douhet carves out a function for strategic theory that more properly mimics the complex but insightful tradition of Clausewitz, who in so many ways is the true inspiration for Brodie. Before leaping into his discussion of air power and the legacy of Douhet, which reiterates his December 31, 1952 RAND research memorandum, RM-1013, "The Heritage of Douhet," RM-1013, Brodie presents a quick introduction to the field of "modern strategic thought," including an examination of the dual (and dueling) influences of Clausewitz and Jomini.

Brodie notes the emergence of some half dozen to a dozen enduring "principles of war" that are "supposed to be unchanging despite the fantastic changes that have occurred and continue to occur in almost all the factors with which they deal,"[372] and points out that "[i]n a world of ideas such durability is usually characteristic either of divine revelation or of a level of generality too broad to be operationally interesting,"[373] making these "hallowed 'principles' . . . essentially common sense propositions,"[374] and though they contain obvious "utility,"[375] "unreasoning devotion" to them can also prove to be "unfortunate" as happened when Admiral Halsey refused to divide his fleet in dogmatic obedience to "an antique slogan" only to "throw the whole of the great Third Fleet against a puny decoy force under Admiral Ozawa."[376]

Brodie, much more the Clausewitzian than the Jominian, argues that "[i]f we wish to avail ourselves of whatever light the wisdom of the past can throw upon our present problems, we must go beyond the maxims which are its present abbreviated expression," and while "[t]he maxim may be the final distillate of profound thought," by the time "it becomes common currency it is likely to be counterfeit."[377] And so Brodie turns to a proper understanding of strategic thought, rejecting maxims and stratagems in favor of a more fundamental understanding of the essence of war and strategy. Brodie thus turns to Clausewitz, noting with curiosity that his famous maxim that "'war is a continuation of policy by other means' happens never to be included in the lists of 'basic principles'—an omission that is both curious and significant."[378] Brodie notes "how small is the number of general treatises on strategy even over the span of centuries," in contrast to the bountiful "richness of writings in military history" which "does not prepare us for the poverty in theoretical writings on the strategy of war," with only a "few theorists (that) have enjoyed an exceptional scarcity value," first and foremost among them being Clausewitz, whom Brodie calls "the first great creative figure in modern strategy" on a level comparable to Adam Smith in economics, but who in contrast to Smith, who turned out to mark the "headwaters of a large and still expanding river of thought to which many great talents have contributed," poor Clausewitz "stands almost alone in his eminence," and while "[o]thers may be worthy of honor, especially his contemporary Antoine Henri Jomini," none "challenge his preeminence," and only some "two-thirds of a century later" does there appear a figure of "comparable stature," with the emergence of the naval strategist Mahan, and even later, the air power theorist Douhet.[379] Brodie acknowledges "skipping over the names of some distinguished theorists," but asserts "only a small number of men have left written judgments and precepts that influenced the thinking of soldiers in their own, and subsequent generations."[380] One reason for Clausewitz's endurance, revival, and relevance to the contemporary world has to do with the transformation of war by Napoleon. While "we may have little to learn from the purely military strategy of pre-Napoleonic wars," Brodie suggests that "we may have something to learn from the eighteenth century concerning the use of war in pursuit of political purposes," and this is one of the centerpieces of Clausewitz's analysis and the focus of his most well-known dictum.[381]

Brodie credits Napoleon for introducing us to the "era of modern war on land,"[382] noting his "genius lay less in novel tactical and strategic combinations than in his ability to see basic changes in strategic conditions . . . and to exploit them."[383] Further, "[w]ith national armies raised by conscription and supported by the whole people," an able commander "could do what was not possible with mercenary forces maintained by the prince for strictly dynastic purposes," and so armed, Napoleon was able to "bring superior forces to bear on successive portions of the opposing forces before the latter had a chance to unite," applying "a dense mass of troops, without regard to losses," against the opponent. Brodie was impressed with Napoleon's recognition of the importance of history, writing: "Napoleon's attitude towards the intellectual basis of his art is reflected in a number of his famous maxims, of which the following is representative: 'Read over and over again the campaigns of Alexander, Hannibal, Gustavus Turenne, Eugene, and Frederick. Make them your models. This is the only way to become a great general and to master the secrets of war.' What he was urging was a creative reading of history, not a sterile review of rules and principles, which then scarcely existed in any systematic form. Such also must have been the prescription of his great predecessors. Frederick wrote his own treatises on strategy, but in his active years in the field there had been little of the sort for him to read."[384] Napoleon's influence reached beyond the battlefield, into the very study of war, as his "startling innovations and even more startling achievements inspired the work of Clausewitz and Jomini," of whom the former is elevated as "clearly the greater," even though the latter "was much the more influential." In this observation we find a similar parallel to the nuclear era strategists, Brodie included; after all, it was Herman Kahn whose influence reached beyond the insular world of strategic thinkers, permeating the public consciousness and even engaging pop culture to the degree that it generated parody in the darkly comedic response of *Dr. Strangelove*, suggesting in our own time as during Clausewitz's that the more immediately influential strategic theorist is not necessarily the better theorist, which by most accounts remains none other than Brodie himself, as Nobel laureate Schelling affirmed in his post-mortem tribute to his colleague.

Adding to Jomini's influence was the fact his rival's "major work" was not published until after Clausewitz's death whereas "Jomini enjoyed a remarkably full literary career through a very long life," and that he also "wrote in French, a much more international language than the German of Clausewitz."[385] Further, Jomini's writings were "easier to comprehend" than his rival's and also "more concrete and 'practical,' and more determined to provide guidance for action and to arrive at 'fundamental principles,'"[386] all giving Jomini an edge (and also mirrored by the more successfully marketed work of Herman Kahn, who also aimed more squarely at the world of action than the halls of higher thought and reflection. And so, observed Brodie, "Clausewitz's appeal is limited, for he is much more given than Jomini to 'undogmatic elasticity' in his opinions, and he is more metaphysical in his approach," and though "an active professional soldier, he wrote with competence on philosophical problems pertaining to the theory of knowledge," and "his insights, like those of all great thinkers, can be fully appreciated only by readers who have already reflected independently on the same problems."[387] And so Brodie naturally felt a greater affinity for the famed philosopher of war than his contemporary. Of course, Clausewitz's influence among Prussian and German military professionals grew dramatically as the nineteenth century ended and the twentieth began, so by the time Schlieffen became chief of the General Staff, Clausewitz's star had begun to shine brightly, so much so that he "had become a shade rather than a living spirit, quoted abundantly but not studied in any comprehending fashion," and thus widely misunderstood, a situation the persisted well into the nuclear age, necessitating Brodie's contribution to the 1976 translation of *On War* by means of a guide to understanding the intent of the master strategist, clarifying and explaining Clausewitz in order to prevent continued misperception.

Brodie attributes the continued endurance of Clausewitz and Jomini into our era, making "large portions of their work come alive today, especially that of Clausewitz," not to the "elucidation of principles but rather the wisdom which they brought to their discussion of them," and "[i]n the case of Clausewitz this wisdom is reflected in a breadth of comprehension which makes him dwell as tellingly on the qualifications and exceptions to the basic ideas he is expounding as he does on those ideas themselves."[388] Brodie is further impressed by Clausewitz's "not merely distinctive but very nearly unique" contribution to the study of war: that is, "[n]o other theorizer on military strategy has penetrated so incisively to the nature of the relationship between war and national policy."[389] But at the same time Brodie finds Clausewitz to be much misunderstood, in part because "the fruits of his brooding thought are transmitted by capsular quotations taken out of context," such as his discussion of "total or 'absolute' war,"[390] for which he is wrongly presumed to be an apostle when in fact he believed war to be constrained by political objectives and obscured by many elements of fog. As Brodie observes, Clausewitz's "method," borrowing reverently from Hegel's thesis and antithesis, combined with his "natural inclination of a searching mind to work all around a subject," makes him "quotable on whichever side of an issue one desires," and on top of this, "he is of all the noteworthy writers on strategy the one least susceptible to condensation."[391] But in spite of Clausewitz's best efforts, and the promise his sophistication offered the field of strategic theory, "what developed from the groundwork which Clausewitz and Jomini so brilliantly laid down at the beginning of the century preceding the first World War" was an unfortunate "Decline of Strategic Theory," as his next section is so labeled, and as such, "the study of strategy, which is in part historical but in larger part also analytical and speculative, has tended to fall between two stools, being neglected by the professions of arms and of scholarship alike."[392] While military values "are not incompatible with scholarly values," Brodie has found that the "pursuit of normal duties" doesn't "leave much time" for scholarly pursuits.[393] He noted prior to the atomic age, most "writings in strategy were usually built upon critical study of the military history available to their authors," often "incomplete," sometimes "inaccurate," and always "vicarious" to actual military experience.[394] When the calamity of World War I came to pass, Brodie believes the cause can be at least in part assigned to the failure of strategists to heed Clausewitz's most famous point, that asserting the interconnected nature of policy and war.

In the killing fields of World War I, total war erupted in a conflict that was ultimately about limited objectives. "Thus a war that was clearly not being fought for total objectives, such as the political extirpation of the enemy state, was allowed to become total in its methods and intensity,"[395] and citing the wisdom of Clausewitz, he adds: "Policy is the intelligent faculty, war only the instrument, and not the reverse. The subordination of the military point of view to the political is, therefore, the only thing that is rationally possible."[396] But as things unfolded across Europe, World War I was a "purposeless war, which no one seemed to know how to prevent and which, once begun, no one seemed to know how to stop," as Brodie explained,[397] and was "also a war which, because of technological changes of much lesser degree than those which are new to us now, completely baffled the military leaders who had to fight it. They were not incompetent men, but they had been reared under a regime of maxims and precepts which bore no relation to the situation in which they found themselves," and this "bafflement and confusion contributed enormously to the tragedy."[398] Ominously, Brodie suggested that "if the total war of the future is fated to be the one where victory is pursued blindly, and therefore at wholly incommensurate costs which destroy its meaning, it will be more akin to the first than to the second of the two world wars."[399] Again citing Clausewitz, this time in response to the frenzied release of popular passions during the French Revolution, Brodie provides us with an explanation for the purposeless lethality that erupted in World War I: "The means available—the efforts which might be called forth—had no longer any definite limits; the energy with which the war itself could be conducted had no longer any counterpoise and consequently the danger for the adversary had risen to the extreme."[400]

Nuclear Weapons and Total War

This unlimited "purposeless lethality" as experienced during World War I serves as a compelling prelude to Brodie's exploration of nuclear weapons, and their impact on war. His early conclusions, about the revolutionary impact of atomic weapons, as articulated in *The Absolute Weapon* and in his early articles, are only reinforced by the next leap in destructive power when atomic weapons became dwarfed by thermonuclear weapons. Brodie recounts, in his 1959 work, the remarkable changes that had taken place since *The Absolute Weapon*, finding none challenged the "immediate and almost universal consensus" that formed after Hiroshima that "the atomic bomb was different and epochal."[401] Added Brodie, "On the contrary, the first decade of the atomic age saw the collapse of the American monopoly, of the myth of inevitable scarcity, and of reasonable hopes for international atomic disarmament. It saw the development of the thermonuclear weapon in both major camps. If at the end of that decade one looked back at the opinions expressed so voluminously at the beginning of it, one found almost none that had proved too extravagant."[402]

Brodie suggests, a decade into the atomic era, "we may first ask what difference, if any, the thermonuclear or fusion or hydrogen bomb must make for our strategic predictions," and suggests, hypothetically, "We have been living with the fission bomb for more than a decade, and it may well be that the fusion type of introduces nothing essentially new other than a greater economy of destruction along patterns already established. Unfortunately, that is not the case."[403] With fusion bombs, we find an even greater split with the past than that caused by the advent of fission bombs. At least "fission bombs were sufficiently limited in power to make it appear necessary that a substantial number would have to be used to achieve decisive and certain results," and this "made it possible to visualize a meaningful and even if not wholly satisfactory air defense," thus sustaining our need "to think in terms of a struggle for command of the air in the old Douhet sense," and to "apply, though in much modified form, the lore so painfully acquired in World War II concerning target selection for a strategic-bombing campaign," as it was still "possible also to distinguish between attacks on population and attacks on the economy," and lastly, "ground and naval forces, though clearly and markedly affected by the new weapons, still appeared vital."[404] All this changed with thermonuclear weapons, though Brodie acknowledges that it was possible that "the feeling that the H-bomb was distinctively new and significantly different from the A-bomb argued in part an under-estimation of the A-bomb."[405] But with the destructive power of fusion weapons so much greater than fission bombs, Brodie noted "[o]ne immediate result of the new development was the realization that questions inherited from World War II concerning appropriate selection among industrial target systems were now irrelevant."[406] Brodie adds: "It is idle to talk about our strategies being counter-force strategies, as distinct from counter-economy or counter-population strategies, *unless* planners were actually to take deliberate restrictive measures to refrain from injuring cities." [407]

But Brodie takes care to emphasize the new scale of destructiveness, to dispel any illusions that we may comprehend the scale of destruction in a future thermonuclear exchange, as "never, even when the British-American strategic bombing forces were at the height of their power, were they able to inflict in six months or even a year of bombing the scale of destruction that would lie easily within the capability of the United States or the Soviet long-range bombing forces on Day One or even Hour One of a new war."[408] And Brodie firmly believes that "No one can specify how many bombs it would take to 'knock out' . . . a country as large as the Soviet Union or the United States, since analytical studies of the problem can do little more than suggest broad limits to the reasonable range of figures," and "cannot even touch the imponderables, such as popular panic and administrative disorganization, which might easily govern the end result."[409] Brodie adds that such "people who do such analyses are as a rule interested in the results from the offensive or targeting point of view," so "therefore consider it a virtue to be conservative in their estimates of damage," and even to "dismiss the imponderables as unmeasurable."[410] Brodie notes that "the fantastic degree to which the coming of the A-bomb gave a lead to the offense over the defense," and adds that "subsequent developments in nuclear weapons have tended to further that advantage."[411] Indeed, in even the best case scenario imagined by Brodie, the "*minimum* destruction and disorganization that one should expect from an unrestricted thermonuclear attack in the future is likely to be too high to permit further meaningful mobilization of war-making capabilities over the short term," and "whether the survivors be many or few, in the midst of a land scarred and ruined beyond all present comprehension they should not be expected to show much concern for the further pursuit of political-military objectives."[412]

In many ways the analytical heart of *Strategy in the Missile Age* is Brodie's eighth chapter, "Anatomy of Deterrence"—which first appeared the year before as a RAND paper conceived from the outset as part of his ongoing project on strategy in the aviation age that took book form at *Strategy in the Missile Age*, and which was also published as an article with the same title in *World Politics* in January 1959—where Brodie reasserts his fundamental belief in the strategy of deterrence, which has held steady since his first formal articulation of the theory earlier in the atomic era, and which presupposes America's unlikelihood to "ever deliberately initiate a total war for the sake of securing to ourselves the military advantage of the first blow'"[413] as he had argued in his prior chapter where he reiterated his rejection of preventive war, and "the complementary principle of limiting to tolerable proportions whatever conflicts become inevitable"[414] as he had long argued and which would form the heart of his next chapter on limited war; as a consequence, America settled upon a strategy of deterrence largely by default, rooted ultimately in the "rejection of the idea of 'preventive war.' "[415] This leads inevitably to a serious consideration of such concepts as limited war, flexible response, and the dynamics of intra-war escalation, which are considered by Brodie along with the entire brotherhood of nuclear wizards for the remainder of the Cold War era, sometimes quite fractiously.

Brodie noted deterrence had long been part of both "national strategy or diplomacy" and in and of itself was "nothing new,"[416] and even speculates that deterrence may have played a more active role in the unfolding of history than historians recognize. As Brodie observed, deterrence is as old as the art of war and that "the threat of war, open or implied, has always been an instrument of diplomacy," but that since the advent of nuclear weapons, "the term has acquired not only a special emphasis but also a distinctive connotation."[417] Indeed, the recurrent outbreak of war suggests that "the threat to use force, even what sometimes looked like superior force, has often failed to deter," suggesting the need for there to be "credibility inherent in any threat," and for deterrence to be dynamic, acquiring "relevance and strength from its failures as well as its successes."[418] Brodie suggests that deterrence may be something of a recurring hidden secret, an untold story underlying much of human history, hidden behind all those battles that were never fought—"because avoidance not only of wars but even of crises hardly makes good copy for historians, we may infer that past successes of some nations deterring unwanted action by other nations add up to much more than one would ever gather from a casual reading of history."[419]

But prior to the nuclear age, deterrence could afford to be "dynamic" as it "acquired relevance and strength from its failures as well as its successes," whereas post-Hiroshima the risks of failure had become too great, using "a kind of threat which we feel must be *absolutely* effective, allowing for no breakdowns ever."[420] A feature of deterrence that strikes Brodie as "unreal" is our hope and expectation that "the retaliatory instrument upon which it relies will not be called upon to function at all," and yet must "be maintained at a high pitch of efficiency and readiness and constantly improved . . . at high cost to the community."[421] Or as Brodie similarly described in his *World Politics* article that served as the foundation of this chapter, deterrence in the nuclear age is different in that "it uses a kind of threat which we feel must be *absolutely* effective, allowing no breakdowns whatsoever," since one failure would be "fatally too many."[422] This reveals an underlying contradiction inherent in this so-called absolute weapon: "We thus have the anomaly that deterrence is meaningful as a strategic policy only when we are fairly confident that the retaliatory instrument upon which it relies will not be called upon to function at all," and as a consequence, we will be continuously "expecting the system to be constantly perfected while going permanently unused."[423] As Brodie suggests, "Surely, we must concede that there is something unreal about it all."[424]

Such an unreality can be seen in the doctrine of "Massive Retaliation" that was adopted by the Eisenhower administration after the frustrating and strategically ambiguous conclusion to the Korean War, in spite of the fact that it had remained a non-nuclear conflict, and thus was waged in a manner that was definitively limited. Consider the strategic enunciations of John Foster Dulles, who presented the new doctrine of Massive Retaliation in 1954, a doctrine that appears cut from the same philosophical cloth as Brodie's very first theoretical impulses when articulating the principles of nuclear deterrence in 1945.[425] The logic of massive retaliation or what has been called "assured destruction" clashes with its emotional credibility. Would a massive escalatory response follow a limited attack? Would the center risk its own existence to secure an ally on its distant periphery, or might this violate the essential wisdom of Clausewitz, and those who came before him, for balanced reciprocity? The economic logic, and political logic in the wake of the Korean War, was indeed attractive. But the emotional unreality of massive retaliation became its Achilles heel: since deterrence was designed to preserve the security of the West and to protect its basic liberties, that it at once seemed unreal raised some troubling questions that the warfighters later sought to correct: not trusting in the system to correct itself by self-balancing, and fearing that a failure in credibility would undermine the viability of the system, the warfighters were prepared to take things into their own hands. In a way, their efforts were a reflection of the system's need to correct itself, as the strategists and targeters were part of the system, rooted in the Waltzian first image, raised and nurtured in the bosom of its second to conduct foreign and defense policy, all in an effort to augment the weakness they perceived in the third. This interconnectedness of all three "levels of analysis" or "Waltzian images," at once suggests the continued relevance of classical realism, the overriding imperatives of neorealism, and the intermediating impacts of what some observers would later call neoclassical realism. Adding to the muddle of labels, the individual actors on Level 1 sought to construct weapons systems and decision-making structures at Level 2 in the hope of increasing order at Level 3, and as such suggest that the constructivists, who emphasize the primacy of social construction to both theory and action in international affairs, may also be correct. That is why I prefer to use the unifying concept of "strategic realism" to describe this body of literature, inclusive of political philosophers, historians, strategic theorists, international relations theorists, and practitioners of the art of war, all who share, to one degree, a realist philosophy, regardless of their language, style of theorizing, or level of causality.

Brodie tackles this thorny problem of credibility, and argues that for "basic deterrence," credibility is a non-issue since "the enemy has little reason to doubt that if he strikes us, we will certainly try to hit back."[426] But to back up the threat with deeds, Brodie says we must meet the challenge of "fitting this power into a reasonable conception of its utility," placing a "considerable strain" upon us as we seek to harness that "almost embarrassing availability of huge power," leading us, during our early nuclear adolescence, to espouse the doctrine of massive retaliation, which we later "rejected in theory but not entirely in practice," even while it lacked credibility as a response to "less than massive aggression."[427] To close the gap, Brodie chronicles the evolution of "win-the-war strategies" along "the sliding scale of deterrence," which follows an asymptotic curve of declining deterrent effect as the nuclear force multiplies: just crossing the nuclear chasm contributes the maximum effect, hence the race by so many states to join the nuclear club, particularly now when nuclearization is one of only two known methods to avoid pre-emptive strike by the newly assertive United States, the other being nuclear disarmament or, to some, surrendering without a fight to the West—as witnessed at the Cold War's end by poor nuclear states Ukraine, Kazakhstan, Uzbekistan, and South Africa, each surrendering their nuclear status for a combination of incentives including money and diplomatic recognition by the victorious post-Cold War West.[428] For the bankrupt states of the former Soviet Union, this was a no-brainer since they lacked the indigenous technological capability and financial resources necessary to sustain their nuclear arsenals, which were developed with Soviet intellectual property; and for South Africa, the absolute weapon had been developed as a doomsday weapon to prevent the ouster of the Apartheid oligarchs by the black African majority, but with the peaceful resolution of South Africa's internal, ethno-political dialectic and the constitutional integration of black and white into the newly democratic South Africa, there was no need for an internal deterrent to create a firewall between the races any longer, and the Apartheid scientists hardly desired to see the bomb transforming the military power of sub-Saharan Africa, giving their former enemies an absolute weapon to wield.

Brodie considers the requirements for deterrence to succeed in the nuclear age—and points out that what matters more than "the size and efficiency of one's striking force before it is hit as the size and condition to which the enemy thinks he can reduce it by a surprise attack—as well as his confidence in the correctness of his predictions," a kind of logic Brodie finds traditional military planners uncomfortable embracing, being "unused to thinking in terms of the enemy having the initiative" and inclined by reasons of "training, tradition, and often temperament" to be "interested only in strategies that can win," which is often more than needed for successful deterrence.[429] Brodie concludes that "diversification for the hard-core survival forces" will improve the probability of surviving a surprise attack, and this leads Brodie to prescribe a triad of ballistic submarines, land-based missiles and strategic bombers, each with its various pros and cons, that together helps to offset the others' weaknesses.[430] But having a survivable force structure capable of unleashing God's fury is just the beginning; the end is having a targeting strategy that contributes to the deterrent effect: Brodie argues that we must have, as primary retaliatory targets, targets dear to the heart of the enemy—his cities: "The rub comes from the fact that what appears like the most rational deterrence policy involves commitment to a strategy of response which, if we ever had to execute it, might then look very foolish. And the strategy of deterrence ought always to envisage the possibility of deterrence failing."[431] Because, presumably, the enemy "cares intrinsically more [for] those cities than he does for his airfields, especially after the latter have already done their offensive work," we have little choice but to focus our retaliatory wrath upon them. But what if the enemy, in his surprise attack, takes great caution to protect our cities, and leaves us with "a severely truncated retaliatory force while his force remained relatively intact?"[432] Won't such a counter-city retaliation be an act of "suicidal vindictiveness?"[433]

As such, Brodie deduces that "it is easy to imagine a situation where it is useless to attack the enemy's airfields and disastrous as well as futile to attack his cities."[434] Would our capacity "in our rage and helplessness" to "strike blindly at enemy cities" thus deter him from attacking us in the first place?[435] Just as Clausewitz sought to tame the Napoleonic genie, Brodie seeks to tame the nuclear genie, and suggests that perhaps, "for the sake of maximizing deterrence it is wise deliberately to reject the Napoleonic maxim, 'On s'engage, puis on voit.'"[436] Brodie thus concludes that for deterrence to succeed, a retaliatory response "ought to be not only automatic but sensibly so."[437] Yet contradictorily, Brodie also realizes that "a reasonable opposing view is that, however difficult it may be to retain control of events in nuclear total war, one ought never to abandon control deliberately," and as such, we must be prepared to cope with "an enemy offensive which exercised the kind of discriminating restraint" as he described, since it is plausible that "men who have been reared in the tradition which holds that extra damage from a delivered bomb is always a 'bonus'—a tradition which is probably as strong on the Soviet side of the military fence as it is on our own" would be inclined to think that way.[438] Indeed, Brodie contemplates the benefits of developing a "clean" bomb with minimal nuclear fallout to prevent radioactive blowback on neutral or friendly soil "and even to drift back to the territories of the users of the bomb," which would satisfy most nuclear warfighters; and at the same time, he contemplates the opposite, the development of a "super-dirty" weapon capable of releasing "a much greater amount of radioactive fallout"—which, "when we consider the special requirements of deterrence in the minimal or basic sense of deterring a direct attack upon oneself, it is possible that one can see some utility in the super-dirty bomb," as deterrence demands that the "emphasis has to be on making certain that the enemy fears even the smallest number of bombs that might be sent in retaliation," and consequently, "one wants these bombs to be . . . as horrendous as possible."[439] Thus the logic of deterrence nudges us to make "super-dirty, as well as large" bombs that don't require accurate delivery due to their powerful (and messy) effect.[440]

Thus the goals of successfully waging nuclear war and preventing war through successful nuclear deterrence dictate the development of opposing tools, the warfighter seeking cleaner weapons than the deterrer. As such, would the deployment of super-dirty weapons be, of itself, a less credible deterrent? Does preparing to deter, as opposed to preparing for a fightable, winnable nuclear war, create a greater risk, because it erodes the credibility of use? Brodie expands his reasoning, briefly, from basic deterrence to a "somewhat bolder" manifestation of deterrence that came to define the showdown between West and East, extending deterrence to "territories beyond our shores," and he speculates that perhaps, if we protect our mainland population with shelters, this might make us bolder, and possibly reckless in our willingness to entertain the thought of retaliation if an ally is attacked.[441] However, Brodie suggests that "an adequate civil defense program may prove an indispensable factor in keeping wars limited," by fostering in the enemy "the necessary credibility" that comes with having "some cover for our population."[442] But *some cover* is not necessarily the same secure cover required to preserve a "secure retaliatory force," which is for Brodie the "*sine qua non* of deterrence" and the "one instrument which could conceivably make all other instruments designed for defense unnecessary."[443] Prudence suggests the need to go beyond this basic sine qua non, and to develop "some backstops" such as "a well-designed shelter program for civil defense."[444] And beyond that, Brodie notes some believe it prudent to also protect "the tools and materials required for national economic recovery within a reasonable period after the war," suggesting that "a nuclear war is not necessarily the end of the world for us, let alone humanity," hence the notion of preparing "caves and unused mines" for the "storage or actual operation of essential production capital," so that there can indeed be a day after.[445]

Thus Brodie's preliminary thoughts on nuclear deterrence lead him down the road of nuclear ambiguity, as he comes to grips with the contradictions inherent in a nuclear warfighting posture and a deterrent posture. The most menacing of threats, such as a thermonuclear super-dirty bomb, may not be a practical weapon of warfighting, and as such, raises the question: could deterrence remain credible without pursuing clean nuclear weapons? Obviously it would not; nor would deterrence remain credible if the population was not provided with some cover, and a recovery capability to kick-start the economy after nuclear war not developed. Thus, for deterrence to work, for the system to remain credible, it must evolve beyond the simple, basic threat of a horrific massive retaliation, to a more graduated, calibrated series of potential strategic responses. Deterrence compels us to consider nuclear warfighting, simply for the sake of deterrence. And that's music to the ears of the nuclear warfighters, who did not like being left with only super-dirty bombs to wage a shooting war.

One essential requirement of deterrence is that the threats upon which its successful operation depends must remain *credible*, an issue less pertinent for *basic deterrence* of the American homeland, but which begin to lose credibility when applied to less vital interests, as Brodie's discussion of massive retaliation suggested. Brodie's discussion of credibility and in particular the credible survival of the retaliatory force leads him to contemplate a "sliding scale of protection" that enables a portion of each component of America's second strike arsenal remains intact and capable of striking back, such as through keeping some portion of the strategic bomber fleet "at a very advanced state of readiness"[446] or even airborne, while keeping another portion onboard nuclear submarines, and yet another portion in hardened ballistic missile silos, with each component enjoying relative and varying strengths and weaknesses and the overall mix ensuring the survival of the deterrent force. Thus Brodie concludes that it is "unavoidable that for some time in the future the ideal strategic bombing force will be a mixed missile and manned-aircraft force," though Brodie expects that "the missile would be favored over the aircraft" for the second strike force.[447] As for the targeting of the second strike force, Brodie believes that for the purpose of maximizing the deterrent effect prior to hostilities, we should "assign the hard-core elements in our retaliatory force to the enemy's major cities, provide for the maximum automaticity as well as certainty of response, and lose no opportunity to let the enemy know that we have done these things"[448] so they know, even in the event of a surprise attack, he will pay a high price for his aggression. And yet, as compelling as this logic is, Brodie suggests that in the event deterrence fails, it "might look very foolish" to execute.[449] For instance, Brodie supposes, what if the attacker "took scrupulous care to avoid major injury to our cities," and we retaliated against his cities; then, he would retaliate in kind, so "[o]ur hitting at enemy cities would simply force the destruction of our own, and in substantially greater degree."[450] Brodie contemplates this ambiguity, trying to balance the benefits of the Napoleonic maxim, "on s'engage, puis on voit," and thus responding vindictively and emotionally to the primary attack, versus a more moderated and rational response, based upon the notion that "no matter how difficult it may be to retain control of events in nuclear total war, one should never deliberately abandon control."[451] The matter remains unresolved, but Brodie suggests the need for us to recognize that "wartime decisions may be very different from those we presently like to imagine ourselves making,"[452] as has been demonstrated throughout history.

When contemplating the maximization of deterrence, Brodie considers some seemingly fanciful and inherently horrific solutions, such as "super-dirty bombs" that are designed to inflict a maximum of toxicity and radioactivity, and thus become a weapon of terror aimed at inducing fear among the enemy that "even the smallest number of bombs that might be sent in retaliation" would inflict results that are "as horrendous as possible," a weapon of limited battlefield use, in contrast to cleaner weapons designed to limit the lethality of their side effects.[453] Brodie also considers the role of fallout shelters, noting while we may not predict with any accuracy how big a different they will make, and that "[w]e could be supine with shelters and brave, even reckless, without them," he nonetheless believes that "if they existed at the moment of crisis, they would tend to sustain and fortify an attitude in favor of courageous decision."[454] As well, credibility itself is uplifted by the existence of shelters, since the enemy must, as we must, believe we posses "the requisite willingness" to follow through upon the threat of retaliation, even if the sort of crisis that might precipitate a nuclear exchange "may seem to be utterly improbable."[455] With regard to the "billions we are spending on the total-war aspect of national defense," Brodie notes "most" is being spent on "situations which are, we hope, at least equally improbable," and that "[a]ll our efforts are in fact directed . . . towards making such situations still more improbable. That is what national defense is all about in the thermonuclear age."[456] That being the case, the risks are so great and the worst case so frightful that Brodie embraces arms control efforts, but not necessarily because of any sentimental endorsement of disarmament as a goal, as the compelling logic of deterrence makes it "abundantly clear that total nuclear disarmament is not a reasonable objective," and "[v]iolation would be too easy for the Communists, and the risks to the nonviolator would be enormous."[457] But at the same time, Brodie acknowledges it has become "obvious that the kind of bitter, relentless race in nuclear weapons and missiles that has been going on since the end of World War II has its own intrinsic dangers," and in the post-Hiroshima world that became so "abundantly supplied with multi-megaton weapons and therefore destined hence-forward to be living always on the edge of total disaster," Brodie came to believe "military thinking has to move beyond its traditional fixation on immediate advantage."[458] Consequently, Brodie embraces arms control efforts that promise to "seriously reduce on all sides the dangers of surprise attack," and thus to "reduce on all sides the incentives to such attack, an end which is furthered by promoting measures that enhance deterrent rather than aggressive posture."[459] Breaking a cycle of hypothetical and Apocalyptic violence, arms control can, in the words of theorist and eventual Nobel laureate Thomas Schelling (whom Brodie salutes for providing "one of the most incisive contributions to the literature on disarmament"), "'Self-Defense' becomes peculiarly compounded if we have to worry about his striking us to keep us from striking him to keep him from striking us. . . ."[460] As Brodie explains, any "measures which reduce the probability of accidental outbreak of war also reduce the probability of planned or 'preventive' war,"[461] and in the end, that's precisely why Brodie concludes that "Nothing which has any promise of obviating or alleviating the tensions of such situations should be overlooked."[462]

But just as arms control efforts can, by reducing the risk of surprise attack, strengthen deterrence while at the same time mitigating the risk of preventive war—thereby contributing greatly to international stability, and thus being worthy of pursuit not as an end unto itself, but rather a means toward enhancing the viability of deterrence strategy—Brodie also considers the logic of limited war, which likewise becomes more compelling in the era of thermonuclear weapons when the cost of deterrence's failure is so high that any "large-scale mutual exchange of nuclear weapons on cities reduces war to a suicidal absurdity."[463] Thus Brodie becomes a skeptic on the suicidal implications of massive retaliation and its "'all or nothing' attitude to the use of force."[464] Brodie notes "the total-war idea, which seemed so overwhelming in its simplicity, was a fairly novel one historically," and "[f]ollowing World War I it became axiomatic that modern war means total war," which was again "confirmed and reinforced by World War II" and during the subsequent period of America's atomic monopoly, "there was no great incentive for Americans to think otherwise."[465]

Brodie credits the stalemate of the Korean War for reintroducing the concept of limited war, and which "proved anew that great-power rivals occasionally prefer to test each other's strength and resolution with limited rather than unlimited commitments to violence, and it demonstrated also some of the major constraints necessary to keep a war limited. Most important among these was a willingness to settle for goals representing a considerable degree of compromise with the enemy, and thus readiness to keep contact and to enter and maintain negotiations with him."[466] Because "unrestricted thermonuclear war seems to be at once much too destructive and too unpredictable to be invoked in any but the most dire straits," this can "explain why serious thinking about limited war had to await the coming of the large thermonuclear bomb—besides the obvious reason that basic patterns of thinking, and certainly of political and diplomatic behavior, always change slowly."[467] In contrast to total war, limited war "involves an important kind and degree of restraint—deliberate restraint,"[468] and though great powers are involved, sometimes directly, more often it is waged "through proxies on one or both sides," as would continue to be the case until the Cold War's own conclusion forty years later.[469] Brodie describes the restraint involved as "massive," in that "strategic bombing of cities with nuclear weapons must be avoided,"[470] and it is the scale of this restraint that differentiates contemporary limited warfare "from anything that has happened in the past."[471] Limited war thus "connotes a deliberate hobbling of a tremendous power that is already mobilized and that must in any case be maintained at a very high pitch of effectiveness for the sake only of inducing the enemy to hobble himself to like degree."[472] As Brodie adds, "No conduct like this has ever been known before."[473]

While total war in the nuclear age would involve massive destruction of urban centers, limited war would be defined by its absence, though "[l]imited war might conceivably include strategic bombing carried on in a selective or otherwise limited manner."[474] Brodie takes to task those who perceive limited warfare to be fought only for "a limited objective," as such a view "diverts attention from the crucial fact that the restraint necessary to keep wars limited is primarily a restraint on means, not ends."[475] It's not that the ends are unimportant; indeed, quite the contrary. The ends could prove to be very important; but we must nonetheless "keep the war limited simply because total war as it would be fought today and in the future against a well-armed enemy is simply too unthinkable, too irrational to be borne."[476] And there we have it: Bernard Brodie, one of the earliest and by far the most analytically sophisticated theorist of deterrence strategy, finds the prospect of fighting a total war in the nuclear age to be *unthinkable*.

While Brodie in fact does think a great deal about the unthinkable, so much so that nuclear warfare is clearly not an unthinkable event, just an unpalatable one, and one that he is convinced is mutually suicidal, and thus not in the interest of any major power, because he suggests, indeed explicitly states, that total war in the nuclear age is "unthinkable," he exposes himself to criticism from those who find this most insightful analyst, and intellectual courageous analyst, is something of a nuclear coward, afraid to peer into the nuclear abyss and thus confront the resultant specter of nuclear horror. Brodie is anything but that. He has peered into the nuclear abyss and emerges somehow changed, his realism intact but his ends-means assessment rebalanced. He is not afraid of war—indeed, in the coming decade he would counsel tactical nuclear warfare in Europe as both logical in the face of Soviet conventional superiority, and de-escalatory in the clarity of resolve tactical nuclear use would signal—he not only fully understands the fundamental role war plays in history, but is not afraid to consider the waging of limited nuclear warfare when necessary. And, Brodie is not at all afraid of embracing the logic of nuclear deterrence, which in fact operates upon a threat so horrible, of total war in an age of unlimited destructive potential, that it dwarfs the very power of the Leviathan as imagined by Thomas Hobbes and would result in a chaos as dark as the very state of nature Hobbes so feared. Brodie thus accepts the efficacy of the nuclear leviathan to impose a peace, and to ensure a steadiness to the international equilibrium, maintained by the very same foundation of fear that Machiavelli and Hobbes embraced, and which both Clausewitz and Jomini struggled to interpret in the wake of Napoleon's brief triumph. Brodie was prepared to tolerate a permanence of fear, so long as it was a stable system maintained by reciprocity, and so long as efforts were made to enhance its stability. So it's not that Brodie is frightened into pacifism; indeed, he sees in limited war our salvation from the suicidal logic of massive retaliation and the all or nothing premise of mutual assured destruction, appropriately known as MAD. Later, theorists like Herman Kahn, who appropriated from Brodie the notion of the unthinkability of nuclear war, authoring his own popular tome, *Thinking About the Unthinkable*, as if a knowing affront to Brodie's timidity, and later his *On Thermonuclear War*, suggesting a Clausewitzian realism binding war and politics for the nuclear age, as much an affront to Brodie who proudly earned the title of being the Clausewitz of the nuclear age. In fact, Kahn might be better thought of as the Jomini of the nuclear age, not in that his work was any less worthy but rather that Kahn was as much a man of action as Jomini, who fought at Napoleon's side, was, and was thus able to maintain the enduring embrace of the military leadership with his unblinking fearlessness and bravado, while Brodie, the veritable intellectual of the bomb, was largely overshadowed by less nuanced men for his thoughtful questioning of the effects of strategic bombing, and his skeptical response to SAC's early war plans that, under the influence of LeMay's pre-nuclear thinking, sought to perpetuate so many of the World War II strategic bombing's falsehoods and to disregard so many of its important lessons.

While thinking about something less *unthinkable*, such as limited war in the era of unlimited weapons, Brodie revisits Clausewitz, and to adapt him for the new era. He does not do so lightly, and proceeds with a deep appreciation of the Prussian's theoretical and philosophical contributions to the study of war. As Brodie writes: "It is of course true and important that we cannot have limited war without settling for limited objectives, which in practice is likely to mean a negotiated peace based on compromise. Clausewitz's classic definition, that the object of war is to impose one's will on the enemy, must be modified, at least for any opponent who has a substantial nuclear capability behind him. Against such an opponent one's terms must be modest enough to permit him to accept them, without his being pushed by desperation into rejecting both those terms and the limitations on the fighting . . . We must be clear, however, that the curtailing of our taste for unequivocal victory is one of the prices we pay to keep the physical violence, and thus the costs and penalties, from going beyond the level of the tolerable. It is not the other way around."[477]

Brodie noted there was "Resistance to Limited War Thinking," and that while "[a]ll of us assume almost without question that peace is better than war," that it was "curious and interesting that we do not have the same consensus that limited war is preferable to total war," and he attributes this in part to the persistence of "some people apparently [who] still entertain fantasies of total war which have the United States doing all the hitting while receiving few if any nuclear bombs in return."[478] Brodie comments with dismay, "How these fantasies can exist is a matter of much wonder," particular in that "we have rejected preventive war."[479] Brodie also attributes what he describes as "fantasies of total war" to an underlying psychological cause related to the "repressed rages harbored in so many breasts," a hint of the Freudian influences on his own personal thinking about life, death, and conflict.[480]

But Brodie quickly moves on to "important institutional reasons as well" which he finds to be "more pertinent to our inquiry."[481] This is epitomized by "General Douglas McArthur's remark following his dismissal," that there "can be no substitute for victory," which Brodie found to be "endemic in all the armed services" and which "works strongly against any restraint upon the use of force in wartime."[482] Brodie again cites Clausewitz, noting the philosopher of war was "ambivalent in this as in many other respects" and thus "can be and has often been quoted out of context to demonstrate his vehement rejection of restraint in war."[483] As for the resistance to restraint, Brodie found it to be uneven across the services, with the Air Force in particular "reared on the doctrine of the predominance of strategic bombing," noting that "Airmen, however, have always felt, with special justice since the atomic bomb arrived, that a total war would be primarily theirs to fight," and that a "limited war, on the contrary, seems to throw the Air Force back into the unpalatable role of providing support to the ground forces."[484]

Also contributing to the resistance to restraint was the "adverse effects of the Korean War on limited-war thinking,"[485] and while Brodie had found the experience of Korea largely positive in that it "made it possible to think of limited war in its peculiarly modern form, and on something other than a trivial scale," that during the war and "for sometime afterward, the spontaneous national reaction to it was generally one of distaste and rejection," as it had been both "costly" and "humbling," and as a direct result, Brodie writes that the "most conspicuous result of the war in the field of American diplomacy was the Dulles' 'Massive Retaliation' speech of January 1954."[486] While Korea was extremely helpful for doctrinal and theoretical development, Brodie concedes that America's "handling of the Korean War does not stand as a model for shrewd limited-war strategies," particular in light of General Omar Bradley's widely shared view that it was "the wrong war, at the wrong place, at the wrong time, and with the wrong enemy."[487]

Brodie argues that it's "precisely *because* the chance for total war is finite and real that we must think earnestly about limited war,"[488] but that we must nonetheless proceed with caution and avoid presuming either that limited wars must inevitably escalate into total ones, which Brodie found "to be the vice of intellectuals," or that total war has somehow "now been abolished," a view held primarily by "practical men," thus enabling all of our military resources to be redirected to the execution of limited wars.[489] Brodie believes the latter is "even more dangerous" than the former danger, as "it encourages a neglect of the basic precautions enjoined by the danger of total war," and could result in a "recklessness about the handling of limited wars that will make it more likely they will erupt into unlimited ones."[490] Indeed, this very eventuality would dominate much of Brodie's attention, as reflected in the large percentage of his writing devoted to this rising danger, throughout the 1960s, especially after the Kennedy–Johnson era commenced and the strategy of Massive Retaliation was firmly rejected in favor a new limited war ethos that Brodie came to believe overemphasized fighting conventional wars in its effort to reduce the chance of stumbling into even more dangerous nuclear wars—but which would, Brodie later came to believe, not only place the security of Western Europe at greater risk, but which would lead to unnecessary conventional wars—such as that which ultimately took place in Vietnam.

Brodie's penultimate chapter addresses economic matters, and is titled "Strategy Wears a Dollar Sign," which reiterates his argument presented at a public lecture at Berkeley on November 18, 1954 with the title, "Unlimited Weapons Choices and Limited Budgets," and examines the parallels between economics and strategy, which both "are concerned with the most efficient use of limited resources to achieve certain ends set by society," and whose propositions would be familiar to practitioners of either craft.[491] In Brodie's economic discussion, he notes it "is obviously true that national military security over the long term requires a healthy economy, for the economy must carry the burden,"[492] and how such military leaders as post-World War II army chief of staff Eisenhower, and his successor Bradley, both were concerned that military spending remain at a level that could be economically sustained.[493] He also observes how for most of America's history, it enjoyed great security for a markedly low cost, but now, for the first time, its peacetime military expenditures must be sufficient to sustain the nuclear peace. Nonetheless, Brodie argues while "[i]f there is no end to our insecurity, there does have to be an end to our military expenditures,"[494] but even so, with only a modest increase in defense expenditure, he felt "we could provide an impressive amount of useful passive defense over a few years, both for our retaliatory force and for civil defense, and also a strong force specialized for non-nuclear limited war."[495] And while there remained much uncertainty, Brodie noted that we did know with certainty that "we can afford to do much more for our security without giving up much more than a certain rate of growth in our very high standard of living; that a great deal remains to be done; that if it is done the horrors which a general war would bring would be much alleviated; and that the chances of general war would be to some real even if unmeasurable extent diminished by our doing it."[496] To help assess our defense needs, Brodie notes, the fields of systems analysis and war gaming have emerged, but he cautions that despite being "marvelous ways of bringing informed, scientifically-trained minds intensively to bear on baffling problems,"[497] they each present "imperfections and limitations,"[498] including the fact they are both based upon "assumptions" derived "with great care" and with the "use all kinds of special knowledge" that are "nevertheless estimates untested in war,"[499] and "use not one but many such factors, compounding the chances the model will show significant departures from reality."[500] Further while "[t]he element of chance is recognized and provided for," the "turns of the dice which often govern the war game may not give us a good clue to that one turn which will govern the real thing."[501] As well, sounding again Clausewitzian, but without mentioning the philosopher of war, Brodie notes: "[m]any considerations which we know to be extremely important in real life often cannot be introduced into an analysis because we lack a means for measurement. These involve especially psychological and other imponderable factors."[502] Ultimately, Brodie concludes that "The truth, unfortunately, is that the profound issues in strategy, those likely to affect most deeply the fates of nations and even of mankind, are precisely those which do not lend themselves to scientific analysis, usually because they are so laden with value judgments.

They therefore tend to escape any kind of searching thought altogether. They are the issues on which official judgments usually reflect simply traditional service thinking."[503]

Brodie's discussion of the relationship of economics to strategy, and of the parallels found between economic and strategic thinking, reinforce Brodie's adherence to Clausewitz's most fundamental dictum wedding war to policy (and not just *politics*, as economic policy and broader issues of economic security are important contextually to both the formulation of strategic policy, as well as to the pre-war preparations through weapons development and deployment programs). As well, Brodie's intuitive interconnection of strategy and economics proved in some ways prophetic. As Brodie died in 1978, he did not live to see the widely unexpected collapse of the Soviet Union—not under the pressing duress of a preventive or retaliatory nuclear attack, but more under the cumulative economic strain of its Cold War military expenditures, suggesting the strategy of deterrence, while never tested by force of arms with the exception of several limited wars fought entirely with conventional weapons, delivered its fatal blow through the slow motion but inexorably economic impact of the arms race itself. So the Soviet Union was not crushed by an external blow, but fell to a combination of internal economic collapse and consequent popular uprising, whose end result was the complete collapse of the Soviet Union as a sovereign entity, and the subsequent re-emergence of the nation-states that had been incorporated into the Soviet entity, often by force.

Thus the relationship of economics and strategy, framed broadly by the Clausewitzian ecosystem of war and policy, experienced what was likely thought of by most war planners as an unintended consequence, though from Brodie's discussion of the economic context as well as consequences of strategic planning, one can deduce that he would not have been entirely surprised by the Soviet Union's ultimate end. He full well understood that our strategic programs and policies, and the Soviets' own respective programs and policies, each asserted their own economic pressures on the two nations. Our funding levels turned out to have been at a level that proved to be sustainable, much as Brodie himself predicted, whereas the Soviet economy proved less able to sustain such a continuous output, as its GDP was substantially lower while its requirements for military expenditure remained comparable, and its security environment was considerably more complex, with costs associated with maintaining its empire of internal republics and satellite states, and a wide diversity of neighbors ranging from NATO opponents to emerging rivals such as China, in addition to direct contiguity to the restive Islamic world. So in the end, preparations for the long nuclear peace and their sustained economic commitments led to a show-down, but not one defined by direct hostilities, at least not total war. Rather, a series of limited wars, proxy engagements, and continued economic commitments to the complex systems required for maintaining deterrence—with the final strain that many consider to be the decisive blow emanating from the move, rhetorical if not entirely strategical, away from the logic of assured destruction and toward strategic defense, as the very expensive Strategic Defense Initiative, really from the moment of inception and long before any substantial investment had been required, ultimately bankrupted the Soviet economy, resulting in its internal collapse and fracture into constituent nation-states. Brodie's reflections are especially interesting in light of this final chapter of the Cold War, and how in the end it was not escalation to total war that brought America's principle opponent to its end, but the quiet economic collapse of the Soviet Union, its economy strained to the breaking point by its strategic competition with the United States. Brodie would have been proud to see the complex, and potentially lethal, system of deterrence held steady right up until the end, right to the very eve of the Soviet collapse, proving more stable than the underlying political and economic fabric of the USSR.

Brodie's concluding thoughts in *Strategy in the Missile Age* resonate his fundamentally Clausewitzian outlook on war in the nuclear age, and are reminiscent of the ideas that permeated the philosopher of war's famous work. Just as Clausewitz had struggled with his interpretation of Napoleon's impact on war, learning how to mimic Napoleonic methods in his effort to slow and then reverse his march across the continent, and in the process grappled with complexity, and contradiction, finding dualities and asserting causal linkages such as those connecting war and policy, Brodie similarly grapples with the complexities and contradictions of the nuclear age, accepting ambiguities where they arise and repeatedly rebuking those whose quest for certainty and simplicity, as he found in the military services, led them away from the very complicated truths of the nuclear era. Brodie's journey really starts with a close look at the theorists of airpower, but quickly moves on to a consideration of "the utility of these ideas in a world shaken by the tremendous revolutionary impact of nuclear weapons, now combined with various novel vehicles of delivery including intercontinental ballistic missiles."[504] He further "probed the complexities of the present strategic situation, for which our historical experience with war offers so little guidance," joining Clausewitz in a similarly complex undertaking.[505] Having found the path of preventive war rejected with "quite remarkable unanimity,"[506] and concluding that "it is something approaching idiocy to invite total war on any other basis" since *we no longer have assurance of getting in the first blow,*"[507] there emerges "a special 'it-must-not-fail' urgency about deterrence," even though history presents "little in the experience of our own or any other nation" to shape a "purposeful strategy of deterrence."[508] And yet "the fact is that deterrence can fail," especially so long as there is "great advantage of striking first,"[509] thus America must "devote much of its military energies to cutting down drastically" this advantage, which "means above all guaranteeing through various forms of protection the survival of the retaliatory force under attack,"[510] through its "hardening," something "especially true for the missile age now dawning,"[511] though in the "not so distant future, mobility may have to replace hardening as the main prop of security to the retaliatory force," whether utilizing America's vast and underused rail system or its internal water ways.[512] Brodie identifies as the "second principle of action" the provision of "a real and substantial capability for coping with limited and local aggression by local application of force," which will require a spirit of compromise, including the "possible abjuration of nuclear weapons in limited war."[513] His third principle of deterrence emerges "simply from taking *seriously* the fact that the danger of total war is real and finite," which dictates to us that "[p]rovision must be made for the saving of live on a vast scale," and that "[a]t minimum there is a need for a considerable program of fallout shelters outside cities" in order to offset the long neglected "military risks we seem daily willing to take."[514]

Brodie also considers the "Problem of Stability" that is unique to deterrence, including the seemingly paradoxical "need to limit or control the unsettling effects of our deterrent posture."[515] On this, Brodie elaborates: "Deterrence after all depends on a subjective feeling which we are trying to create in the opponent's mind, a feeling compounded of respect and fear, and we have to ask ourselves whether it is not possible to overshoot the mark. It is possible to make him fear us too much, especially if what we make him fear is our over-readiness to react, whether or not he translates it into clear evidence of our aggressive intent. The effective operation of deterrence over the long term requires that the other party be willing to live with our possession of the capability upon which it rests."[516] This subjective dimension of deterrence is one aspect of Brodie's strategic theorizing that brings him closest to Clausewitz, since Clausewitz embraced the "moral" and intangible dimensions of warfare, and all the ambiguities that entailed. Brodie explains that "we can hardly be too strong for our security, but we can easily be too forward and menacing in our manipulation of that strength," so he cautions that we must no longer be so "lacking in awareness that deterrence is supposed to last a very long time."[517] Compounding our challenge, and further imbuing deterrence with ambiguity, is the probabilistic murkiness of the endeavor, as if it were cloaked in an impenetrable Clausewitzian fog. As Brodie explains, "These considerations would have no merit if we knew that the probability of total war was in any case infinitesimal, or if on the contrary we had reason to regard it as being . . . almost inevitable."[518]

But "because we have no basis for placing the probability in either the very low or the very high category," Brodie concludes that "we have to take earnest account of the fact that our behavior with the new armaments may critically affect it."[519]

Brodie notes both sides in the deterrence relationship have "reasons for being careful," and he dismisses the "almost paranoiac fears which have often been voiced in this country of an 'atomic blackmail' before which we would be bound to retreat because of our presumed greater sense of responsibility or caution."[520] Instead Brodie believes "we have got too accustomed to an attitude which has become increasingly discordant with the facts—the attitude that our government, trusting in the continuity of its superior strength, is really prepared to use our nuclear total-war capability aggressively over a wide array of issues," and that "[t]his is the kind of 'bluff' which results from a failure of self-examination."[521] And while the "complex relationships between military power and foreign policy have by no means been adequately explored," Brodie believes "what we have learned or could learn from history on the subject needs to be reappraised in the light of the totally new circumstances produced by the new armaments."[522] As easy as this sounds, Brodie notes: "experience has nevertheless indicated how difficult it is" to in essence change paradigms, as "they appear to run counter to most of the standard axioms inherited from an earlier day concerning the attitudes as well as the methods by which we should fight."[523] Before the nuclear age, there was some logic to military aggressiveness since that was "an age when it was the same force which took the offensive or stayed on the defensive," and when "an offensive failed, an impromptu redeployment usually achieved a defensive posture."[524] In such a world, Brodie writes, "[t]he accent was therefore appropriately on boldness," because "[e]ven when boldness proved improvident and costly, it rarely sacrificed the life of the nation." After Hiroshima, this was no longer the case, so if deterrence failed, it could be "nearly impossible to avoid total war,"[525] and this might mean ultimately sacrificing the life of the very nation itself.

Brodie acknowledges that he has "given relatively little space to the matter of how to fight a general war,"[526] something his colleague Herman Kahn would later redress with his own work exploring in graphic detail just such a matter. Brodie's reasons for this omission is his belief that "the strategy of a total war is like an earthquake in that all the forces which determine its occurrence and its character have been building up over time, as have almost all the factors which determine how it runs its course."[527] In one manner, Brodie expects the strategy of total war to be simpler than that of World War II, namely the "dominance of strategic air power," and the primacy of the "opponent's strategic bombardment power" as a target. And, Brodie adds: "[t]he strategic air ascendancy which determines the outcome is itself decided by" determining who strikes first, with what degree of surprise, and against what protective preparations of the opponent's retaliatory force. Brodie believes what will result will be "an extraordinarily destructive yet quick contest to determine who retains exclusive capability for yet further nuclear destruction," presumably followed rapidly by armistice negotiations, lest the conflict degenerate into "grandiose, wanton destruction."[528] But it is here that Brodie finds simplicity gives way to "difficulty and complexity," as the "unsolved problem of modern total war is that of how to stop it, quickly, once it is decided."[529] And this great "unsolved" challenge makes it ever more likely that "a future total war, if it comes, will be enormously more destructive than it needs to be to fulfill anyone's military purpose."[530]

Brodie introduces the historian and icon of realist thought, Thucydides, in his closing pages as he examines "The Unpredictability of the Outcome," noting the famous historian of ancient Greece once wrote, "Consider the vast influence of accident in war before you are engaged in it. . . . It is a common mistake in going to war to begin at the wrong end, to act first, and wait for disaster to discuss the matter."[531] Brodie finds this wisdom especially relevant to the nuclear age, since "[i]n wars throughout history, events have generally proved the pre-hostilities calculations of both sides, victor as well as loser, to have been seriously wrong," as "[e]ach generation of military planners is certain it will not make the same kinds of mistakes as its forebears, not least because it feels it has profited from their example."[532] On top of this, Brodie notes the current generation is especially confident because it is "more scientific than its predecessors," but even so, he points out that "[t]he universe of data out of which reasonable military decisions have to be made is a vast, chaotic mass of technological, economic, and political facts and predictions," and "[t]o bring order out of the chaos demands the use of scientific method in systematically exploring and comparing alternative courses of action."[533] But Brodie cautions that experience "thus far with scientific preparation for military decision-making warns us to appreciate how imperfect is even the best we can do," and that "[t]hose of us who do this work are beset by all kinds of limitations, including limitations in talent and in available knowledge," with a further complicating factor: "we are dealing always with large admixtures of pure chance."[534] Add to this the ambiguities inherent in determining the opponent's capabilities and intentions, and the ubiquity of human bias, despite "our strong efforts to be objective."[535] Adding fuel to this combustible fire of complexity is "the utterly unprecedented rate of change that has marked the weapons revolution since the coming of the first atomic bomb,"[536] transporting "us far beyond any historical experience with war," and "much too fast to be fully comprehended even by the most agile and fully-informed minds among us."[537] In what one might consider a potential critique of the emergent school of warfighters who waded calmly into a sea of presumed certainty and simplicity, Brodie writes: "[o]nly someone very foolish could believe he had mastered the unknowns and uncertainties which becloud our picture of future war."[538] To these more Jominian thinkers prone to move more quickly from thought to action, and thus avoid becoming ensnared by the doubt that seems to have ensnared Brodie, he cautions that "[w]e know from even the most casual study of military history how fallible man is in matters concerning war and how difficult it has been for him . . . to adjust to new weapons. Yet compared to the changes we have to consider now, those of the past, when measured from one war to the next, were almost trivial. And almost always in the past there was time even after hostilities began for the significance of the technological changes to be learned and appreciated. Such time will not again be available in any unrestricted war of the future."[539]

Brodie tries to emerge through the fog and uncertainty unscathed, knowing from his study of wars past that great commanders overcome systemic chaos, applying their genius as Napoleon did, and in the manner prescribed by Machiavelli, augmenting their *virtu* with the blessing of *fortuna*. And so Brodie observes that, "[d]espite all this uncertainty, decisions have to be made," and the "military establishment has to be provided and equipped, and it must develop and refine plans for its possible commitment to action," but in Brodie's language, his insertion of the qualifier "possible" rendering action into a possibility, not even a probability, he reinforces his hope that military action is forever displaced by the permanence of threat. Thus he counsels: "We have been forced to revise our thinking about weapons; but unfortunately there is not a comparable urgency about rethinking the basic postulates upon which we have erected our current military structure," which remains rooted to "large measure" in an "ongoing commitment to judgments and decisions of the past."[540] Brodie admits he has in the previous pages "tried to do some of that kind of rethinking," but again it seems vague, unsatisfied or incomplete, clinging to hope that his logic, his confrontation with the all but certain abyss that total war represents "must convince us that Thucydides was right, that peace is better than war not only in being more agreeable but also in being very much more predictable." And so Brodie closes his treatise on nuclear strategy with a reaffirmation of hope that his strategy, his plan of war avoidance rather than warfighting, "offers a good promise of deterring war," and as a result is "by orders of magnitude better in every way than one which depreciates the objective of deterrence in order to improve somewhat the chances of winning," since even if it is true that "winning is likely to be less ghastly than losing, whether it be by much or by little we cannot know." And this pressing uncertainty, Brodie hopes, remains forever shrouded by the fog of unfought future war.

He places some hope that limited wars fulfill the "function of keeping the world from getting worse," not unlike the limited wars fought during the balance of power era, enabling a restoration of equilibrium and preventing a descent into the chaos of total war. Oddly, Brodie, a self-admitted adherent of Freudian psychoanalysis, closes his masterful work of strategic theory with a comparison of two distinct portions of the world, the developing world which faces a self-inflicted chain reaction of its own in its runaway population growth, which he believes perpetuates poverty endemic to the region, surrendering to an "almost unrestrained procreation which keeps people desperately poor;" and the developed world, which "seems to have escaped that danger entirely by increasing its productivity much faster than it increases its population," but which now faces "the greatest danger of destruction from nuclear bombs." These two very different parts of our world, Brodie believes, share in "common the fact that the chief menace facing each of them is man-made," and his final words to his readers—who have traveled through the ages, examining the impacts of new technologies on the underlying nature of war, and in particular the affirmation in the nuclear age of the ascendancy of air power as predicted earlier in the century by Douhet, presenting man with the new and haunting riddle of nuclear weaponry, and the risk forever with man that whether through malice, aggressiveness, or accident, a sudden onset of total war could destroy all that he has built—aims to draw a parallel, between the reckless irresponsibility he finds in one, and the potential for wanton self-destruction he is afraid might engulf the other, asking, "Do they also share in common a bemused helplessness before the fate which each of them seems to be facing?"[541] And so he closes, leaving us to mull over his question, and to apply this closing riddle to his earlier treatise on deterrence.

As conclusions go, it seems to be displaced, and discontinuous, with his earlier arguments, that suggest the need for us to keep focused on the dangers and the risks of total war, so that with each decision that we make, each weapons system imagined or deployed, each response or non-response to aggression, no matter how local or peripheral to world affairs, never be divorced from the permanence of danger, and the systematization of risk, inherent in our new nuclear-armed world. The connection between the population bomb, and the nuclear bomb, was more obvious a generation earlier, before the rapid industrialization of the Southern Hemisphere and the global integration of the world's economies narrowed the poverty gap between the developed and developing worlds. But even so, it reads as if an opportunity has been missed, to close his argument artfully, to reassert his central thesis so rigorously developed in earlier pages, by instead introducing a new referent, and to make a fundamentally new argument about the choice we make. Of course, other futurists including his colleague Herman Kahn would address the issue of population growth and Third World poverty, as a compelling strategic threat, and would even in his Jominian approach to nuclear strategy and his more willing embrace of nuclear warfighting at all levels, consider the Malthusian implications of war in the nuclear age; but nonetheless, Brodie's conclusion to *Strategy in the Missile Age* seems to almost miss the point, as if he is trying to shame the architects of the nuclear world order into showing greater control than their counterparts in the developing world, a parochial, indeed condescending, perspective on a part of the world that would, in just a few years, command America's full strategic attention as the next limited war, even more so than the war fought to a standstill in Korea, greatly taxed and ultimately shook the foundations of American military power.

The Critics Respond: The Domestic Audience

In the June 1960 edition of *The American Political Science Review*, Samuel P. Huntington, then a professor at Columbia University but whose latter years were spent at Harvard, wrote that "Bernard Brodie has been a leader among civilian social scientists in exploring the esoteric realms of military strategy and technology," and that "[h]is principal previous works dealt with naval problems" while his "present volume is concerned primarily with airpower," of which the "first third briefly describes the state of strategic thinking at the beginning of the airpower era" while the "remainder of the volume is an informed, balanced, and often highly original discussion of the current issues of a strategy of deterrence."[542] Huntington finds that the "connection between the two parts of the book is more than tenuous but less than necessary," and notes that even Brodie encourages that "those readers who feel so inclined 'can plunge directly into Part II' without missing any essential elements of his argument."[543]

Huntington observes that Brodie, in writing this work, faces a dilemma: "He can focus primarily upon the issues of the day, given the existing state of weapons research and economic capacity, and produce an analysis grounded in the hard facts of the situation, but whose applicability through time is limited because within a few years those hard facts will be replaced by a different set of hard facts," or he may instead "attempt to develop a broad philosophical framework by which to approach specific problems or to analyse continuing political issues (which change often in form but rarely in substance)" and thereby produce "an analysis of greater continuing value if of less immediate relevance."[544] The review points out that in part two of *Strategy in the Missile Age*, "Brodie has opted for the first horn of the dilemma" and "[a]s a result, his book has a practical, down-to-earth quality, which is quite refreshing," with Huntington adding that "perhaps a primary value of the book is the picture it gives of the complexities, ambiguities, and unknowns which confront the strategic planner. Other writers on strategy have argued that our greatest need is to develop a comprehensive, coherent doctrine, such as the Soviets allegedly possess, to enable us to regain the initiative and to guide us in the bewildering choices which must be made,"[545] but that Brodie takes another path, one that I have argued in these pages is at heart Clausewitzian. As Huntington puts it, "Brodie, on the other hand, tends to be skeptical of doctrines," and notes that Brodie's "historical analysis of the first part of his book is one long case study in the dangers of doctrinal absolutism, and the strategic analysis of the second part is a pragmatic and empirical discussion of specific policy problems. Given this approach, the only major limitation upon Brodie's analysis is the temporal one"—in that Douhet, whose ideas Brodie has argued did not survive their reality test of World War II, was "was somewhat ahead of his time" and in the nuclear era, "Douhet's vision has become reality. With thermonuclear weapons, the country whose strategic air power survives the initial exchange of blows unquestionably will be able to destroy its opponent. The struggle for command of the air has become the struggle; each strategic air force is the other's prime target. A nation must either strike first, which Brodie suggests is beyond us both morally and practically, or be prepared to absorb a first-strike from the enemy and still have sufficient retaliatory forces to strike back."[546] Brodie thus "stresses again and again the prime necessity of adequate defenses for the Strategic Air Command," and the "development and maintenance of this second-strike capability is, as he points out, neither cheap nor easy. Brodie's analysis is thus directed primarily to the current situation in which strategic air forces are the principal targets."[547] While it's "not difficult to foresee in the reasonably near future, how-ever, a new phase in which the retaliatory forces of both powers become virtually invulnerable to attack," Huntington notes that Brodie instead "emphasizes the need to protect now the presently vulnerable air-atomic forces" but "does not to the same extent emphasize the need to develop future strategic forces with high built-in invulnerabilities from mobility and concealment, such as ballistic missile submarines (whose present limitations he very properly stresses)."[548] But as Huntington observes: "Once such relatively invulnerable strategic forces are achieved, however, neither side will be able to deny the other 'command of the air' through offensive measures. The great premium will be on defense, active and passive, to protect the cities and population, which will again become the prime targets of strategic attack. The side which first develops a reasonably effective defense will then have all the advantages which would now go to the side which developed a sure-fire counterforce capability. Brodie recognizes the tendencies in this direction and deplores our neglect of civil defense measures."[549] But, "[d]espite its title," Huntington finds that Brodie's "book is really about strategy in the age of aircraft, and he emphasizes that planes are going to be important for a long while to come. The full implications of the missile age will only be felt with the emergence of mutually invulnerable retaliatory forces. What will a strategy of deterrence require then? Hopefully Brodie has another volume in the works."[550]

In his July 1960 review in the *Annals of the American Academy of Political and Social Science*, University of Illinois history professor Norman A. Graebner writes that Brodie's *Strategy in the Missile Age* "is a critical and disturbing evaluation of current American military practices by one of the nation's most distinguished naval historians," who "substantiates what many military experts have been writing for years" and whose "search for meaning in both the past conduct of war and the strategic concepts which determined it has led him to the conclusion that nations have generally failed less in battlefield tactics than in strategy or the search for broad objectives."[551] To wit, Graebner added: "The Japanese attack on Pearl Harbor, he stresses, was tactically perfect but strategically stupid."[552] Graebner notes that "[o]f the great strategists of the past Mr. Brodie prefers Clausewitz and Schlieffen, for they acknowledged the close relationship between war strategy and national policy," in contrast to the approach taken by leaders on both sides of World War II for whom "war became an end in itself," and "[i]n this context of rational policy the author analyzes the impact of nuclear weapons"—recognizing that "the new destructiveness of weapons has revolutionized the strategy of war" as it "removes the need of traditional modes of fighting and renders both air superiority and the precise definition of targets almost unnecessary."[553]

Graebner writes that Brodie "discounts the current theory of a 'broken-back' war which suggests that after initial bombings on each side the war would resume along conventional lines," since "[w]hen nations in the past improvised successfully after suffering heavy blows, they always had both the time and the incentive to organize such measures—factors that would not be present after a general thermonuclear attack."[554] Adds Graebner: "Never before have weapons placed the advantage so completely in the hands of the nation that strikes first," and Brodie thus "concludes, as have others, that the only answer to the challenge of nuclear weapons is the re-establishment of traditional concepts of limited war which demand both limited means and limited ends. He finds the great danger in the antithetical arguments that war cannot be limited and that war has been eliminated and, therefore, ceases to be a danger at all. Both concepts result in the neglect of conventional forces."[555] But Brodie "criticizes as well the neglect of diplomacy, pointing out that there is no mathematical equivalence between military strength and the ability to bargain successfully," though Graebner regrets that Brodie "never explains fully the significance of this meaningful observation in terms of precise political settlements of cold war issues. If such matters were beyond the scope of this study, Mr. Brodie makes it clear that the only genuine solution to the dilemma of thousands of missiles accurately pointed to enemy targets lies in the diplomatic alteration of the present world environment."[556]

And in the December 1960 edition of *The Journal of Modern History*, University of Chicago professor Robert E. Osgood observes that Brodie, "the first scholar to analyze the real strategic and political significance of nuclear weapons in the aftermath of World War II, has fused into a unified whole, with some new emphasis, the trenchant ideas that he has propounded in public and classified writings over the course of more than a decade," and the "result is a brilliant account, in the first part of the book, of the evolution of the strategic doctrine of airpower through World War II, followed by a masterful commentary, in the second part, on the unprecedented strategic issues that have accompanied the fantastic technological fulfillment of that doctrine since World War II."[557] Osgood comments that "Brodie's book is distinguished throughout by a keen awareness of the role that 'romanticism,' 'myth,' and convention, national ethos, and the professional perspective of military men have played in strategic thinking, and of the role they continue to play in the application of presumed axioms and lessons of the past to the thoroughly revolutionary conditions of the present."[558]

Osgood finds that Brodie is "also sensitive to the significant limitations that democratic governments impose upon defense policies for non-military and often pseudo-economic reasons" but nonetheless, "while recognizing that military strategy is, necessarily, far more than a rational, technical exercise, he does not despair of bringing reason and order to strategic planning" and "[i]n fact, some of his most original passages discuss the applicability of marginal utility theory and 'systems analysis' to the allocation of scarce resources among almost unlimited choices of weapons."[559] Osgood lauds Brodie's "views on contemporary strategic issues" as "well-informed, sober, lucid, and never trite"—and while Brodie "agrees with the great majority of the students of postwar defense policies in deploring the increasing dependence of American security upon nuclear responses, which threaten to precipitate total war, at the expense of adequate and diversified non-nuclear responses, which are appropriate to deterring and countering the less catastrophic and more likely contingencies," Osgood finds that Brodie's "less sanguine than many about the ease of maintaining a 'nuclear stalemate' through a balance of strategic striking power."[560] Osgood observes that, "Never before has so much depended upon military policies devised on the basis of so little knowledge about the effects of weapons and the shape of warfare," and "[n]ever has the interaction between strategy, warfare, and foreign policy been so crucial, yet so speculative. Partly for this reason, wise military policies have never before depended so much upon the insights of social scientists. Brodie's book, like his career, is a heartening demonstration that it is possible to bridge the gap between academic learning and military expertise."[561]

From Moscow with (Tough) Love: An Enemy's Response

Strategy in the Missile Age would command the attention of strategic thinkers and practitioners on both sides of the Iron Curtain, and be translated into Russian in 1961 and published in the Soviet Union by the Ministry of Defense with a critical introduction authored by (then) Major Vladimir Mochalov, who would later rise to the position of Major General and head the post-Soviet Russian Border Control Service, the Federal Agency for the State Border of Russia (*Rosgranitsa*). In his foreword to the Russian edition, Major Mochalov noted: "Contemporary weapons themselves, in the opinion of Brodie, compel military leaders to concern themselves more with strategy than with tactics. In the past military theoreticians worked out tactics for the most part. This situation, the author maintains, has been maintained to this time. Civilian leaders, he complains, also study strategy little."[562] Mochalov notes Brodie's rejection of the Jominian tradition, explaining the "reason the author sees for such a deplorable situation is that the theoreticians and military leaders of the past dogmatically followed the 'eternal' principles of conducting war, considered that these principles were given once and for all, and because of this it was not necessary to occupy themselves with working out problems of strategy."[563] Thus, Brodie "criticizes Jomini and his principles of military art, the blind worship of which gave rise, in the opinion of the author, to errors in the direction of military operations."[564] Mochalov further explains Brodie's rejection of the more simplified style of Jominian thought in favor of the more nuanced and complex style of Clausewitz: "Brodie came to the conclusion that these principles are too abstract and too general to be useful for the directing of war. The author shows by historical examples how some military leaders were too uncritical in their views toward the 'eternal' principles and underestimated the new military technology. They directed their operations the old war and, as a result, they suffered defeat. At present such underestimation of weapons is inadmissible. Brodie thinks that Clausewitz's theory of war should get more attention than the views of Jomini because the first shows the interdependence between military strategy and state policy. Brodie makes a strong point that one must not entrust war only to military men . . . Brodie calls upon the military theoreticians of the United States to consider state policy and not to conduct war just for the sake of war. At present, when the first battle may unconditionally decide the question of existence of a state, says Brodie, 'we must not as before carelessly permit one group of specialists to decide how to conduct war and another group where to conduct it and with what goal.'[565]

Mochalov turns his attention to the second part of Brodie's work, which "examines problems of the use of nuclear weapons, strategic bombing, preventive and limited wars, the strategy of threats, active and passive defense, and other questions dealing with the appearance of atomic and thermonuclear bombs," and notes that Brodie "comes out as a supporter of the necessary use of nuclear weapons in war."[566] As Mochalov describes, "He gives one to understand that 'the stability of the free world' can rest only on the nuclear bomb. Brodie writes that in the United States they consider the use of nuclear weapons 'as a completely normal, realistic and just act.' (p. 339) 'We are not in a position to conduct even small wars without the use of nuclear weapons,' he adds. (p. 348) The use of nuclear reserves, in his opinion, is more advantageous also from the economic point of view: 'The annihilation of a large quantity of population will not cost much.' (p. 183) One cannot think of a more cynical statement. The fact that nuclear weapons will bring terrible destruction for all mankind does not at all touch the author, who is a spokesman for the plans of the reactionary circles. Just so that it is advantageous! Such is the logic of the militarist."[567]

While Mochalov challenges Brodie on doctrine, and rebukes him for his exaggeration of the first strike's importance, he notes that Brodie's approach to strategy, and to the broad goal of containing Soviet power, is distinct from his peers in its rejection of passivity, though as the nuclear brotherhood would grow, Brodie's advocacy of deterrence and rejection of more assertive variants of warfighting doctrine would in fact place him on the more passive end of the strategic spectrum, with more vocal proponents of warfighting like Herman Kahn representing the more active end. But Mochalov's observation is insightful nonetheless, as it is Brodie who, in his groundbreaking effort to modernize strategic theory for the nuclear era, defines this very spectrum upon which he and Kahn come to symbolize the opposing poles. When compared to other philosophical traditions—such as the neorealist school of international relations theory which came to view the bipolar structure of international politics as a permanent state, a dynamic system held in equilibrium by the nuclear arsenals of the superpowers—Brodie's thought does indeed appear to be very much more action-oriented: "Brodie writes about strategy and containment in a completely different way from all the other American theoreticians. If some of them, only as a pretense, ascertain that this strategy pursues the purpose to prevent war, Brodie says straightforwardly that this type of policy us unrealistic. The strategy of containment does not satisfy Brodie for it condemns the United States to passivity. He speaks out for the active preparation for war, uncovers this strategy and demands that the United States maintain a course toward a forestalling blow. The author sees this strategy as a Damocles sword that must hang over the Soviet Union and other socialist countries and fall at the moment when American imperialism finds it necessary. But to threaten the Soviet Union at the time when it has first class weapons in sufficient quantity is clearly hopeless."[568] Mochalov further notes that "Brodie understands that this strategy hides in itself danger for the United States and because of this he asks that besides developing missile-nuclear weapons and strategic aviation the American government should pay more active attention to the question of passive defense. In connection with this, the author insists on the absolute necessity of creating a wide net of covers and shelters for different purposes . . . All of these measures in the opinion of the author will lower the advantages that a surprise attack might have. But here the author is grossly mistaken. No one is even thinking of attacking the United States."[569]

Mochalov examines Brodie's thought on limited war, which "represents at the present time a large part of the official military doctrine of the United States."[570] As Mochalov explains, "Being afraid of the results of a general nuclear war in which the American imperialists could not escape retaliation their ideologists pay much attention to the development and propaganda of the strategy of so-called limited war by which they could save the United States from a nuclear counter blow and at the same time use war as the instrument of their policy," as the "imperialists are convinced that such wars could be conducted against individual socialist countries. With the help of such wars they are thinking of suppressing the national liberation movements in colonial and dependent countries and re-establishing the colonial oppression in these countries that have acquired national independence."[571] Mochalov notes that Brodie "maintains that in the present situation limited war is a lesser evil than a total war," and consequently "the main problem in any limited war will not be how better to conduct it and to achieve victory but how to limit it so that it will not become a total war."[572] He adds that: "In this proposal one can clearly see the intention of the American reactionaries to transfer military operation to the territory of their satellites. When Brodie sheds light on the theory of limited war, he clearly contradicts himself. He ascertains that in order to conduct a war on a limited scale it is necessary to limit not the goals but the means by which the goals could be achieved. Of course the limited means that are used may influence the scope and range of the war. But this is not the main thing. The range of the war depends on the political goals and they are determined by the policy of the warring state. It is evident from history that when far-reaching goals were established huge forces and means were used to achieve them. For achieving their aggressive goals the United States imperialists are already preparing the most destructive means for conducting wars. The author himself fighting for limited war demands the development of strategic means of struggle, nuclear weapons, the strategic aviation and missiles of long range and average action which in essence are intended for conducting total war."[573]

Mochalov concludes his introduction by suggesting Brodie's work provides a window into the mind of one of America's most influential war planners, which would no doubt have surprised Brodie, who found himself locked out of the inner circles of power by men more certain than he, and less willing to embrace both ambiguity and complexity. As Mochalov describes, Brodie's work has "certain interest for it uncovers the true character of the military preparations of the United States, the views of the militaristic circles on the type of modern war, and buildup of armed forces and the methods of waging armed battle under modern conditions. At the same time one should mention that Brodie's views on political and military problems in many respects correspond to the statements of some leaders of the armed forces and political leaders of the United States. The book reminds us that in the camp of imperialism the forces which push the people toward a missile nuclear war do not stop their activities. Because of this and contemporary conditions high vigilance and combat preparedness is demand[ed] as never before from the Soviet people and their armed forces in order to make an adequate rebuff to the imperialistic aggressors should they try to start a war."[574]

Missile Age Revisited: Reflections Five Years On

Brodie's continued thinking about limited war would be reflected in the new preface he authored in December 1964 for the paperback edition of *Strategy in the Missile Age* that was published in 1965. That occasion, he writes, served as a reminder that "some time has elapsed since the original publication" in 1959, "and that in the field of modern strategy time tends to deal severely with concepts as well as facts."[575] Brodie found that "[o]n the whole this book has fared very well," but nonetheless the passage of a half decade did "warrant a statement about what one would do differently if one were writing the book today," and first among these was the coming to power in 1960 of President Kennedy, and his—and his successor, President Johnson's—administrations "pursued an ideology in defense matters markedly different from that which infused the previous administration," while Brodie's 1959 treatise "turned out to be a projection of the intellectual structure within which the defense doctrines and distinctive military postures of the Kennedy administration were to take shape," albeit in a "descriptive rather than a causative sense."[576] Brodie thus qualifies his "later criticisms of certain administration defense policies that seemed superficially to be entirely in line with ideas advocated in the original volume."[577] Brodie thus hopes this explains how he could have, in his May 23, 1963 article in *The Reporter*, "What Price Conventional Capabilities in Europe?", "systematically criticized what I held to be excessive devotion to the idea of resisting possible Soviet aggression in Europe mostly by conventional means" after he "had apparently advocated comparable ideas" in Chapter 9 of *Strategy in the Missile Age*.[578] Brodie explains that "[o]ne relevant fact and partial explanation is that when the book was written (some parts of it were first composed long before 1959), those sections that deal with limited war, and especially with conventional capabilities for fighting a limited war, had to be advanced against much intellectual opposition"—so much so that Brodie's "own writings, then classified, urging that more study and resources be devoted to limited-war capabilities date from the beginning of 1952 (when I first heard of the thermonuclear weapon to be tested the following November), and at that time the views I was expressing met in some quarters not only opposition but amazed disbelief."[579]

Brodie adds that it was "difficult to recall now that at that time it was a completely accepted axiom—despite the ongoing Korean experience, which was regarded as entirely aberrational—that all modern war must be total war. This idea had been by no means completely dissipated at the time of the publication of the book in 1959."[580] And it is in "that respect the situation" Brodie found as 1964 drew to a close "today is vastly different," and that the "present frame of mind on relevant issues within the defense community . . . would make unnecessary today the tone of advocacy sometimes manifested in the book," and had it been written a half-decade later, "it would be more appropriate to point out (as I tried to do in the above-mentioned article and other papers) the limitations and drawbacks attending possible over-emphasis of what is basically a good and necessary idea."[581]

In the five years since *Strategy in the Missile Age* first came to press, Brodie notes with much approval the "revolution in the degree of security built into the strategic retaliatory forces of the two major nuclear powers, especially those in the United States," and while Brodie did "indeed stress in the book the importance of such a chance" in 1959, he found that the "degree to which it has in fact taken place has outrun my expectations," thanks in large measure to the commitments made by Defense Secretary McNamara and his colleagues in the Kennedy and Johnson administrations, who "were quick to recognize the importance of this vulnerability problem, and to push programs designed to cope with it," among the most important of which were the Polaris submarine and Minuteman missile programs, and whose development meant that in a crisis, "the pressure for 'going first' with our strategic forces is not only reduced but well-nigh eliminated," bringing "immeasurably more stability into any crisis situation," as a result of which " 'escalation' to general war is far less to be feared from any commitment to limited war than was formerly the case—even, I would hold, if nuclear weapons should be used."[582]

Brodie also considers the lessons of the October 1962 Cuban crisis, noting that "its most successful resolution for the United States" resulted from the fortuitous fact that Moscow's leaders proved to be "determined to avoid hostilities with the United States—perhaps due in part to the fact that they were less given than our own leaders to distinguishing between local and general war and less ready to think of the possibility of keeping the former from graduating to the latter."[583] And he briefly notes the virtually nil progress made in the area of civil defense since 1959, suggesting that the "reason seems mainly to be that while offensive missiles and devices for their protection promise to *deter* war, fallout shelters and the like appear to have minimum utility for deterrence and are urged mostly for the sake of saving lives if general war does in fact occur," though he found it was "not really surprising that many people derive an additional sense of security from attacking what could be of use only if the unthinkable happens."[584]

Ultimately, Brodie attributes the endurance of his book, and its relevance, across such a tumultuous and fast-changing half decade, to the "considerable orientation of the book towards developing the historical origins of contemporary situations" as much as to his "lucky guesses concerning the future."[585]

Notes

[1-7] Fred Kaplan, *Wizards of Armageddon* (Stanford: Stanford University Press, 1991), 33; 34; 34; 34; 37; 38; 38, respectively.

[8-33] Bernard Brodie, "Strategic Bombing: What It Can Do," *The Reporter*, August 15, 1950, 28; 28; 28; 28; 28; 28; 28; 29; 29; 29; 29; 29; 29; 29; 29–30; 30; 30; 30; 30; 30; 30–1; 31; 31; 31; 31; 31, respectively.

[34-82] Bernard Brodie, "Must We Shoot from the Hip?" RAND Working Paper, September 4, 1951, 1–2; 2; 14; 14; 14; 14–15; 15; 15; 15; 16; 16; 16; 17; 16; 17–18 (These are: First, if we remember our constant (though possibly unrealistic) assumption that the enemy will initiate the war, will his defenses not be well mobilized from the beginning?; Second, may not our early attacks weaken his defensive capabilities, especially if they are directed toward that end?; Third, will we not also learn a few things from the results of our strikes? Is the learning which results from the early combat so one-sidedly in favor of the defensive?; Fourth, is there not a great difference between the learning accorded the defense by continuous raids (which are what is usually envisioned (and that which results from individual strikes widely spaced in time and using different methods of approach? The lessons which the defense derived from the 90-day German V-l attack on England (to mention the classic example) would have come much more slowly from a series of individually concentrated but widely spaced attacks; Fifth, insofar as our urgency stems from a fear of losing advance bases, such concern might suggest other sources of action besides that of dropping all our bombs simply for the sake of getting them dropped. What can be done to make those bases more secure? How can we organize our forces and plan our strikes to reduce the penalty suffered by loss of advance bases? In any case, let us by all means calculate the risks before deciding not to take them."); 18–19; 19; 19–20; 20; 20; 20; 21; 21; 22; 23; 23; 23; 23; 24; 24; 24; 25; 25; 25–6; 26; 26; 26; 26–7; 27; 27; 27–8; 28; 28; 28; 29; 29; 29; 29–30; 30, respectively.

[83-119] Bernard Brodie, "Characteristics of a Sound Strategy," Lecture Delivered to the Naval War College, March 17, 1952, 1; 2; 2; 2; 3; 4; 4–5; 5; 5–6; 6; 6; 7; 9; 9–10; 10–11; 11; 11; 12; 13; 13–14; 14; 14; 15; 16; 16; 17; 17; 17–18; 18; 19; 19–20; 20; 20–1; 21; 21–2; 22; 22–4, respectively.

[120-56] Bernard Brodie, "Changing Capabilities and War Objectives," Lecture to the Air War College, April 17, 1952, 2; 2; 3; 3; 3; 3–4; 4; 4; 4; 5; 5; 5; 5; 9; 10; 10; 10; 11; 11; 15; 17; 17; 18; 19; 19; 19; 20; 20 (Brodie's original wording, in the typed draft of his lecture, was: "One thing this might do, if you're interested, is to make large nuclear resources and the delivery capabilities available for tactical use. Notice that if we're going to have this thing, when we have it we will also have a much large number of the conventional A-bombs than we have today." It was later amended by hand for presentation to read as quoted above.); 20 (Originally he started this sentence with "You" but crossed it out by hand and replaced it with "We" as quoted above); 21 (In the original typed draft, "if you accomplish it" was originally "if you can do it".); 21 (In the original typed draft, "bombing business" was "bombing effect"); 21; 28; 28 (Brodie scratched out the word "prowess" here in his original lecture and replaced it with "successes."); 28; 28; 28–9 (Brodie further elaborates upon his No Cities proposal in his January 23, 1953 RAND working paper, "A Slightly Revised Proposal for the Underemployment of SAC in an H-Bomb Era"), respectively.

[157] Brodie, "A Slightly Revised Proposal for the Underemployment of SAC in an H-Bomb Era," RAND Working Paper, January 23, 1953, 12.

158-72 Bernard Brodie, "Nuclear Weapons: Strategic or Tactical?" *Foreign Affairs* 32, No. 2 (January 1954), 217; 217; 218; 226; 227; 227; 227; 227; 228; 228; 228; 228; 229; 229; 229, respectively.

173-222 Bernard Brodie, "Unlimited Weapons and Limited War," *The Reporter*, November 18, 1954, 16; 16; 16; 16–17; 17; 17; 17; 17; 17; 17; 18; 18; 18; 18; 18; 18; 18; 18; 18; 18–19; 19; 19; 19; 19; 19 (In a 1957 memo to Max Ascoli, the publisher of *The Reporter*, Brodie would reflect on how many of the issues that came to prominence in the 1960s, when limited war became a top issue in strategic studies circles, were anticipated by Brodie many years earlier in this article, his first published discussion of limited war—his earlier RAND papers were classified, limiting their audience—and he would observe with much disappointment that Henry Kissinger did not even include Brodie's article in the bibliography of his best-selling 1957 book on the topic, *Nuclear Weapons and Foreign Policy*—which Brodie would perceive as an intentional sleight, and an effort to erase Brodie's important contribution to the limited war literature from history); 19–20; 19; 19; 19; 19; 19; 19; 20; 20; 20; 20; 20; 20; 20; 20; 20; 21; 21; 21; 21; 21; 21, respectively.

223-4 Bernard Brodie, "Strategy Hits a Dead End," *Harper's Magazine*, October 1955, 33, 33, respectively.

225 Marc Trachtenberg, *History and Strategy* (Princeton: Princeton University Press, 1991), 261. Citing Brodie, "Strategy Hits a Dead End," *Harper's Magazine,* October 1955, 33–7. Many of Brodie's arguments would be reiterated the next year in "Implications of Nuclear Weapons in Total War," RAND Paper (P-1118), July 8, 1957.

226-31 Brodie, "Strategy Hits a Dead End," 33; 33; 33; 33; 37; 37, respectively.

232-5 Bevan M. French, "Brodie Discusses 'Limited' Conflicts, Says All-Out War is 'Meaningless'," *The Dartmouth* CXV, No. 126 (March 20, 1956), 1; 1; 1; 1, respectively.

236-66 Bernard Brodie, "Implications of Nuclear Weapons in Total War," RAND Paper (P-1118), July 8, 1957, ii, www.dtic.mil/cgi-bin/GetTRDoc?AD=AD606443&Location=U2&doc=GetTRDoc.pdf. (This paper is a slightly revised version of RAND Research Memorandum RM-1842 of the same title, "which differs from the original mainly in the deletion of some footnotes," as Brodie noted in an introductory "Note" on page ii), 9; 9; 9–10; 10; 11; 11; 16; 16 (n.3, citing *Statement on Defence, 1954, Presented by the Minister of Defence to Parliament*, February 1954 (London: Her Majesty's Stationery Office, Command Paper No. 9075), 5); 16 (n.4, citing Admiral Robert B. Carney, U.S. Chief of Naval Operations, in a Cincinnati speech on February 21, 1955, as reported in the *Washington Post* and *Times Herald* on February 22, 1955.); 17; 17; 17; 18; 18–19; 19; 20; 21 (n.6, citing Sir John Slessor, *Strategy for the West* (New York: William Morrow, 1954), 111); 21; 26; 27; 27–8; 29; 30; 31; 31; 31; 31–2; 32; 32; 33, respectively.

267-9 William P. Snyder and John A. MacIntyre, Jr., "Bernard Brodie: America's Prophetic Strategic Thinker," *Parameters* Vol XI, No. 4, 2; 2; 2, respectively.

270 Ken Booth, "Bernard Brodie," in John Baylis and John Garnett, eds., *Makers of Nuclear Strategy* (London: Pinter Publishers, 1991), 33.

271-6 Marc Trachtenberg, "Strategic Thought in America, 1952–1966," *Political Science Quarterly* 104, No. 2 (Summer 1989), 307; 307; 307; 324; 324; 324, respectively.

277-9 Herbert S. Bailey, Letter to Bernard Brodie, January 29, 1958, Bernard Brodie Papers (Collection 1223), Department of Special Collections, Charles E. Young. Research Library, UCLA.

280-2 Brodie, Letter to Bailey, February 6, 1958, Bernard Brodie Papers (Collection 1223), Department of Special Collections, Charles E. Young. Research Library, UCLA.

283-4 Bernard Brodie, "The Anatomy of Deterrence," RAND Research Memorandum RM-2218, July 23, 1958, iii; iii, respectively.

285 Bernard Brodie, "Preface," *Strategy in the Missile Age* (Princeton: Princeton University Press, 1959), vi.

286-7 Brodie, Letter to Bailey, February 6, 1958, Bernard Brodie Papers (Collection 1223), Department of Special Collections, Charles E. Young. Research Library, UCLA.

288-9 Bailey, Letter to Vaughan, March 6, 1958, Bernard Brodie Papers (Collection 1223), Department of Special Collections, Charles E. Young. Research Library, UCLA.

290 Bailey, Letter to Brodie, March 22, 1958, Bernard Brodie Papers (Collection 1223), Department of Special Collections, Charles E. Young. Research Library, UCLA.

291-2 Brodie, Letter to Bailey, March 28, 1958, Bernard Brodie Papers (Collection 1223), Department of Special Collections, Charles E. Young. Research Library, UCLA.

293-4 Bailey, Letter to Brodie, March 31, 1958, Bernard Brodie Papers (Collection 1223), Department of Special Collections, Charles E. Young. Research Library, UCLA.

[295] Brodie, Letter to Bailey, July 17, 1958, Bernard Brodie Papers (Collection 1223), Department of Special Collections, Charles E. Young. Research Library, UCLA.

[296-7] Bailey, Letter to Brodie, December 8, 1958, Bernard Brodie Papers (Collection 1223), Department of Special Collections, Charles E. Young. Research Library, UCLA.

[298] Bailey, Letter to Brodie, December 16, 1958, Bernard Brodie Papers (Collection 1223), Department of Special Collections, Charles E. Young. Research Library, UCLA.

[299-301] Brodie, Letter to Bailey, December 29, 1958, Bernard Brodie Papers (Collection 1223), Department of Special Collections, Charles E. Young. Research Library, UCLA.

[302] Bailey, Letter to Brodie, January 2, 1959, Bernard Brodie Papers (Collection 1223), Department of Special Collections, Charles E. Young. Research Library, UCLA.

[303] James C. DeHaven, Letter to Bailey, January 2, 1959, Bernard Brodie Papers (Collection 1223), Department of Special Collections, Charles E. Young. Research Library, UCLA.

[304-5] DeHaven, Letter to Bailey, January 26, 1959, Bernard Brodie Papers (Collection 1223), Department of Special Collections, Charles E. Young. Research Library, UCLA.

[306-7] Brodie, Letter to Bailey, January 30, 1959, Bernard Brodie Papers (Collection 1223), Department of Special Collections, Charles E. Young. Research Library, UCLA.

[308] Bailey, Letter to Brodie, February 3, 1959, Bernard Brodie Papers (Collection 1223), Department of Special Collections, Charles E. Young. Research Library, UCLA.

[309] Bailey, Letter to Brodie, February 10, 1959, Bernard Brodie Papers (Collection 1223), Department of Special Collections, Charles E. Young. Research Library, UCLA.

[310-11] Brodie, Letter to Bailey, February 16, 1959, Bernard Brodie Papers (Collection 1223), Department of Special Collections, Charles E. Young. Research Library, UCLA.

[312-13] Bailey, Letter to DeHaven, February 16, 1959, Bernard Brodie Papers (Collection 1223), Department of Special Collections, Charles E. Young. Research Library, UCLA.

[314-17] Bailey, Letter to Brodie, March 13, 1959, Bernard Brodie Papers (Collection 1223), Department of Special Collections, Charles E. Young. Research Library, UCLA.

[318-20] Brodie, Letter to Bailey, March 20, 1959, Bernard Brodie Papers (Collection 1223), Department of Special Collections, Charles E. Young. Research Library, UCLA.

[321-3] Brodie, Letter to Gordon Hubel, March 20, 1959, Bernard Brodie Papers (Collection 1223), Department of Special Collections, Charles E. Young. Research Library, UCLA.

[324] Hubel, Letter to Brodie, March 25, 1959, Bernard Brodie Papers (Collection 1223), Department of Special Collections, Charles E. Young. Research Library, UCLA.

[325-7] Bailey, Letter to Brodie, March 25, 1959, Bernard Brodie Papers (Collection 1223), Department of Special Collections, Charles E. Young. Research Library, UCLA.

[328] Brodie, Letter to Hubel, April 8, 1959, Bernard Brodie Papers (Collection 1223), Department of Special Collections, Charles E. Young. Research Library, UCLA.

[329] Bailey, Letter to Brodie, August 21, 1959, Bernard Brodie Papers (Collection 1223), Department of Special Collections, Charles E. Young. Research Library, UCLA.

[330-1] Brodie, Letter to Bailey, August 25, 1959, Bernard Brodie Papers (Collection 1223), Department of Special Collections, Charles E. Young. Research Library, UCLA.

[332-4] Bailey, Letter to Brodie, September 15, 1959, Bernard Brodie Papers (Collection 1223), Department of Special Collections, Charles E. Young. Research Library, UCLA.

[335-7] Bailey, Letter to Brodie, January 20, 1960, Bernard Brodie Papers (Collection 1223), Department of Special Collections, Charles E. Young. Research Library, UCLA.

[338] Brodie, Letter to Bailey, February 4, 1960, Bernard Brodie Papers (Collection 1223), Department of Special Collections, Charles E. Young. Research Library, UCLA.

[339-40] Bailey, Letter to Brodie, February 11, 1960, Bernard Brodie Papers (Collection 1223), Department of Special Collections, Charles E. Young. Research Library, UCLA.

[341] Brodie, Letter to Bailey, February 18, 1960, Bernard Brodie Papers (Collection 1223), Department of Special Collections, Charles E. Young. Research Library, UCLA.

[342] Bailey, Letter to Brodie, February 22, 1960, Bernard Brodie Papers (Collection 1223), Department of Special Collections, Charles E. Young. Research Library, UCLA.

[343] Hubel, Letter to Brodie, February 22, 1960, Bernard Brodie Papers (Collection 1223), Department of Special Collections, Charles E. Young. Research Library, UCLA.

³⁴⁴ Bailey, Letter to Brodie, February 23, 1960, Bernard Brodie Papers (Collection 1223), Department of Special Collections, Charles E. Young. Research Library, UCLA.

³⁴⁵ Roy E. Thomas, Letter to Brodie, August 29, 1969, Bernard Brodie Papers (Collection 1223), Department of Special Collections, Charles E. Young. Research Library, UCLA.

³⁴⁶ Thomas, Letter to Brodie, August 29, 1969, Bernard Brodie Papers (Collection 1223), Department of Special Collections, Charles E. Young. Research Library, UCLA.

³⁴⁷⁻⁶⁶ Bernard Brodie, "Introduction," *Strategy in the Missile Age*. Santa Monica: RAND Corporation Report R-335, January 15, 1959, 3 (an electronic copy of the RAND Report is available at the RAND Corporation website. The book's first cloth edition was published by Princeton University Press in multiple editions, with its first paperback in 1965. Much of *Strategy in the Missile Age* appeared in earlier RAND working papers, articles and speeches by Brodie, and while the work is largely perceived to be a stand-alone publication, it is to a remarkable degree really an anthology of Brodie's writings during the decade that followed publication of *The Absolute Weapon*); 4; 4; 5; 6; 7–8; 9; 10; 10; 11; 11; 14; 14–15; 15; 19 (Brodie continues, "Some conception of ends there has to be, but its formulation is not the stuff of day-to-day work. Presumably it is the province of a few in exalted rank, who have been prepared for their high responsibilities by passing slowly through the tactics-oriented lower ranks and whose advancement has been based primarily on their success in posts of command, that is to say on their qualities of leadership. The inevitable tendency is to accept as given the ends handed down by traditional doctrine, usually in the form of maxims or slogans. . . . Today we are talking not about machine guns and barbed wire but about a weapon that may in a single unit destroy all of Manhattan Island and leave some of it a water-filled crater. We may as well admit that the strictly tactical problem of destroying Manhattan is already absurdly easy, and time promises to make it no less easy. That is only to say that its protection, if it can be protected, is henceforward a strategic and political problem rather than a tactical one"); 19; 19; 19; 19–20; 20, respectively.

³⁶⁷⁻⁴⁰⁰ Brodie, "Prologue to Air Strategy," *Strategy in the Missile Age*, Santa Monica: RAND Corporation Report R-335, January 15, 1959, 21; 21; 21; 21; 22; 23; 23; 24; 24; 25; 27; 28; 28–9; 29; 29; 31; 31; 33; 34; 34; 34; 36; 37; 37; 38; 38–9; 39; 67; 67; 55; 56; 55; 68, respectively.

⁴⁰¹⁻¹² Brodie, "The Advent of Nuclear Weapons," *Strategy in the Missile Age*, Santa Monica: RAND Corporation Report R-335, January 15, 1959, 151 (Brodie made this same point, *verbatim*, in "Some Strategic Implications of the Nuclear Revolution," RAND Working Paper, P-1111, May 14, 1957); 151–2 (also "Some Strategic Implications of the Nuclear Revolution," 8); 152 (see also "Some Strategic Implications of the Nuclear Revolution," 8); 153 (also "Some Strategic Implications of the Nuclear Revolution," 8, with the exception of the phrase, "still "possible also to distinguish between attacks on population and attacks on the economy," which Brodie added to his 1959 book); 153 (see also "Some Strategic Implications of the Nuclear Revolution," 8); 155; 156; 163; 164; 164; 165 (also argued *verbatim* in "Some Strategic Implications of the Nuclear Revolution," 12); 167, respectively.

⁴¹³⁻²⁴ Brodie, "The Anatomy of Deterrence," *Strategy in the Missile Age*, Santa Monica: RAND Corporation Report R-335, January 15, 1959, 271; 268; 268; 271 (also *World Politics* 11, no. 2 (January 1959), 174 and RAND Research Memorandum (RM-2218), July 23, 1958, 3); 271 (*World Politics*, 174; RAND (RM-2218), 3); 272 (*World Politics*, 174; RAND (RM-2218), 4); 271 (*World Politics*, 174–5; RAND (RM-2218), 4); 272 (RAND (RM-2218), 4–5); 272–3 (RAND (RM-2218), 5); 268; 268; 273 (*World Politics*, 175; RAND (RM-2218), 5), in *Strategy in the Missile Age*, Brodie modifies this slightly to read: "Surely, there is something almost unreal about all this," 273.

⁴²⁵ John Foster Dulles, "The Evolution of Foreign Policy," Department of State Bulletin 30 (January 25, 1962): 107–10. As Dulles proclaimed: "We need allies and collective security. Our purpose is to make these relations more effective, less costly. This can be done by placing more reliance on deterrent power and less dependence on local defensive power. This is accepted practice so far as local communities are concerned. We keep locks on our doors, but we do not have an armed guard in every home. We rely principally on a community security system so well equipped to punish any who break in and steal that, in fact, would be aggressors are generally deterred. That is the modern way of getting maximum protection at a bearable cost. What the Eisenhower administration seeks is a similar international security system. We want, for ourselves and the other free nations, a maximum deterrent at a bearable cost. Local defense will always be important. But there is no local defense which alone will contain the mighty landpower of the Communist world. Local defenses must be reinforced by the further deterrent of massive retaliatory power. A potential aggressor must know that he cannot always prescribe battle conditions that suit him. Otherwise, for

example, a potential aggressor, who is glutted with manpower, might be tempted to attack in confidence that resistance would be confined to manpower. He might be tempted to attack in places where his superiority was decisive. The way to deter aggression is for the free community to be willing and able to respond vigorously at places and with means of its own choosing."

[426–62] Brodie, "The Anatomy of Deterrence," *World Politics*, 175–6; RAND (RM-2218), 5 (in *Strategy in the Missile Age*, Brodie puts it nearly the same way: "the enemy has little reason to doubt that if he strikes us, we will try to hit back," 273), 6 (in *Strategy in the Missile Age*, Brodie uses the words "linking this power to" in lieu of "fitting this power into," 273); *Strategy in the Missile Age*, 274 (*World Politics*, 176; RAND (RM-2218), 7); 281 (*World Politics*, 180; RAND (RM-2218), 14); 285 (*World Politics*, 182; RAND (RM-2218), 17), 292 (*World Politics*, 185; RAND (RM-2218), 22); 293 (*World Politics*, 185; RAND (RM-2218), 23); 293 (*World Politics*, 185; RAND (RM-2218), 23); *World Politics*, 185 (RAND (RM-2218), 23 (in *Strategy in the Missile Age*, Brodie adjusts "useless to attack the enemy's airfields" to "of little use to hit the enemy's airfields," 293)); 185 (RAND (RM-2218), 23 (in *Strategy in the Missile Age*, Brodie writes "in our rage and recklessness" instead of "in our rage and helplessness," and instead of "strike blindly at enemy cities" he clarifies this to "strike at something," 293)); *Strategy in the Missile Age*, 293; *World Politics*, 185 (RAND (RM-2218), 23; in the PUP book Brodie starts the phrase with, "One view might be that," while in his article and RAND research memorandum he starts with just the word, "Perhaps"); *World Politics*, 186 (RAND (RM-2218), 24. Brodie rewrites the end of this paragraph entirely in the book, though this author's views is that it was elegantly stated in the article and in the RAND research memorandum. In *Strategy in the Missile Age*, he writes: "For the sake of deterrence before hostilities, the enemy must expect us to be vindictive and irrational if he attacks us. We must give him every reason to feel that that portion of our retaliatory force which survives his attack will surely be directed against his major centers of population," 293); *World Politics*, 186 (RAND (RM-2218), 24, in the book, Brodie tweaks the first sentence and its word order, but the meaning is nearly identical: "A reasonable opposing view, however, is that no matter how difficult it may be to retain control of events in nuclear total war, one should never deliberately abandon control," 293); *World Politics*, 186–7 (RAND (RM-2218), 25–6. Again, the wording in *Strategy in the Missile Age* is modified but the meaning remains the same, with a slight change in tone toward greater pessimism with Brodie writing, "we may find a need even for super-dirty bombs," 295, from the more hypothetical original wording, "it is possible that one can see some utility in the super-dirty bomb"); *World Politics*, 187 (RAND (RM-2218), 26, in *Strategy in the Missile Age*, the wording is changed to: "very large and also intensively contaminating," 295), *World Politics*, 187–8 (RAND (RM-2218), 27, in *Strategy in the Missile Age*, Brodie drops the words "somewhat bolder" when discussing extended deterrence, but replaces the words "all-important: with the word "critical" when describing the need to protect the populace, 296); *Strategy in the Missile Age*, 297 (*World Politics*, 188; RAND (RM-2218), 28); *Strategy in the Missile Age*, 298 (*World Politics*, 188; RAND (RM-2218), 29); *Strategy in the Missile Age*, 298 (*World Politics*, 189; RAND (RM-2218), 29); *Strategy in the Missile Age*, 298 (*World Politics*, 189; RAND (RM-2218), 29); *Strategy in the Missile Age*, 284 (RAND (RM-2218), 16); *Strategy in the Missile Age*, 288 (RAND (RM-2218), 19); *Strategy in the Missile Age*, 291–2 (RAND (RM-2218), 22), 292 (RAND (RM-2218), 22); *Strategy in the Missile Age*, 293 (the second sentence is not in the original RAND research memorandum or article, but was added to the paragraph in the book); *Strategy in the Missile Age*, 293 (the second phrase is slightly reworded in the earlier RAND research memorandum and article but retains the original meaning); *Strategy in the Missile Age*, 294 (This sentence is a substantial rewrite from the earlier paper and article which stated more clearly Brodie's concern with the ability to recognize "discriminating restraint," and to react appropriately: "The question is whether men who have been reared on the tradition which holds that extra damage from a delivered bomb is always a 'bonus' . . . are likely to approach the problem in so dangerously fresh a manner," RAND RM-2218, 24); *Strategy in the Missile Age*, 295 (While using different wording, the point is nearly identical in RAND RM-2218, 26. The word "some" replaces "even the smallest number of," but "as horrendous as possible" remains the same); *Strategy in the Missile Age*, 297 (Brodie again adjusts his language but the point remains the same as argued in RM-2218, 27–8: "We could be cowardly with shelters and bold (or reckless?) without them; but surely if they existed at the moment of crisis, their effect would tend to favor courageous rather than craven decision"); *Strategy in the Missile Age*, 297 (RAND RM-2218, 28), 298 (RAND RM-2218, 28–9); *Strategy in the Missile Age*, 300 (RAND RM-2218, 31); *Strategy in the Missile Age*, 300 (the first quoted phrase is nearly identical with the wording in RM-2218, 31 with slightly different word order, but the second phrase appears to have been added by Brodie to the 1959 manuscript); *Strategy in the Missile Age*, 300–1 (This same point is made in RM-2218, but with slightly different wording, 31–2); *Strategy in the Missile Age*, 301 (the wording here differs from RM-2218); *Strategy in the Missile Age*, 302 (the wording here differs from RM-2218), 304 (RM-2218, 33), respectively.

[463–90] Brodie, "Limited War," *Strategy in the Missile Age*, 305; 307; 307; 308; 309; 309; 310; 310; 311; 311; 311; 310; 312; 312; 314; 314; 314–15; 315; 315; 315; 315; 316; 316; 317; 317; 356; 357, respectively.

[491–503] Brodie, "Strategy Wears a Dollar Sign," *Strategy in the Missile Age*, 361 (also see Brodie's "Unlimited Weapons Choices and Limited Budgets," Public Lecture at Berkeley, November 18, 1954, 1–31); 367; 366 ("Unlimited Weapons Choices and Limited Budgets," 12); 376–7 (a similar point is argued in "Unlimited Weapons Choices and Limited Budgets," 3 and 11); 377; 380; 386; 386; 386; 387; 387; 388, respectively.

[504–41] Brodie, "Recapitulation and Conclusions," *Strategy in the Missile Age*, 390; 390; 392; 393; 393; 393; 394; 395; 396; 396; 397; 397; 397; 398; 398; 399; 399; 399; 400; 400; 401; 401; 401; 402; 403; 404; 404; 405; 406; 406; 407; 407; 407; 407; 407–8; 408; 408; 409, respectively.

[542–50] Samuel P. Huntington, "Review: Strategy in the Missile Age by Bernard Brodie," *The American Political Science Review* 54, No. 2 (June 1960), 505–6; 506; 506; 506; 506; 506; 506. 506–7; 507, respectively.

[551–6] Norman A. Graebner, "Review: Strategy in the Missile Age by Bernard Brodie," 156; 156; 156; 156; 156; 156–7, respectively.

[557–61] Robert E. Osgood, "Review: Strategy in the Missile Age by Bernard Brodie," *The Journal of Modern History* 32, No. 4 (December 1960), 426; 426; 426; 426; 426, respectively.

[562–74] Vladimir Mochalov, Introduction to the Russian Edition, *Strategy in the Missile Age* (Moscow: Soviet Ministry of Defense, 1961; English translation of Russian introduction as preserved in the Bernard Brodie Papers at the UCLA special collections. Note 567 further notes that Mochalov further observes that: "Brodie rather extensively proves that the country making the first blow will have the possibility of undermining the enemy's capability for an answering blow or lower this capability to such an extent that the remaining forces and means that have been put into action as a counterblow will be destroyed without difficulty by means of an active defense. 'Such an outcome suggests a complete victory to that one who attacks first.' (p. 225) "We must be prepared to make the first blow both in the moral and military sense," Brodie maintains (p. 291). As the author notes this is especially important because after the first blow by nuclear weapons on different objects no matter where they be located war would be conducted "with a broken back." Such cynical propaganda for a forestalling blow as a method of beginning war might only help to strengthen the international tension but it is a direct call for an aggressive war. It's impossible not to note that the author exaggerates the meaning of the first blow. It is known that a rather strong state in the economic sense that has a large territory could widely disperse and hide the forces and means that are necessary for a counter attack. 'If some forces should be put out of action, which had been designated for making a counter attack, it's always possible to bring into the operation duplicate means and hit the target from reserve positions,' says N. S. Khrushchev." Note 573 further notes that Mochalov further argues: "In his opinion the capability to conduct a limited war presents in itself just as important an element of the forces for containment as the capability to make a counter attack with the use of nuclear weapons. The main problem of limited war in Brodie's opinion consists in excluding the possibility of the use by both sides of the most effective and destructive means of battle. It would seem that after such words must follow a proposal for banning nuclear weapons but the author of the book is silent about this. To some of the views of Brodie on strategy in the missile age we can note that the American military thought tried to take into account new consequences that modern means of combat have introduced to military art. At the same time Brodie was not able to make serious theoretical generalizations. One can see this from the fact that the author doesn't even try to determine the essence of military strategy in subject or content, its laws, principles of strategy, types and character of stragetical operations. The author also does not determine the essence of war and the condition of its appearance, the factors and the decisive outcome of armed combat. This is quite natural for a bourgeois theoretician. To tell the truth about the essence of war and its origin means to uncover the class character of the policy of his government and not one of the armor bearers of imperialism is interested in this. In order for the theory to answer fully all the demands of modern war an account of old [sic] factors influencing armed struggle, social, political, economic and technical, is necessary. Meanwhile the bourgeois military theoreticians make technology their stronghold and because of this their conclusions, as Brodie's book shows, always carries a one-sided character. In order to ensure victory in a modern war, it is not enough only to have the technical means. As never before the meaning and role of man in future war has grown. It is necessary to have beneficial goals which would answer the interests of all the people. This the imperialists do not have; their goals go against modern historical development. Brodie's book is constructed on a false and dangerous conception of fatalistic inevitability of war between the Soviet Union and the United States, on the negation of the policy of peaceful coexistence which is the only sensible way of developing international relations in our time."

[575-85] Bernard Brodie, "New Preface for Paperback Edition of 'Strategy in the Missile Age'," December 30, 1964, 1; 1–2; 2; 2; 2; 2–3; 3; 4; 5; 6; 6, respectively.

CHAPTER FOUR

Rethinking the Unthinkable: New Thinking on Escalation and Limited War

Just a year after Brodie's *Strategy and the Missile Age* came to press with consistently positive reviews from civilian scholars and military practitioners alike, his long time colleague Herman Kahn would publish his very own treatise on the new dangerous era—a massive tome titled *On Thermonuclear War* that was also published by Princeton University Press but which would breakout as a runaway best-seller, generating widespread criticism for its callous insensitivities and ruthless realism while at the same time, perhaps because of the whiff of controversy and consequent curiosity thereby generated, would make its author a household name. Brodie would later reflect on Kahn's 1960 treatise, noting that thus far in the nuclear age, "we have had some experiences that were entirely predictable and some that would have been previously unbeliev-able," and that there has been "much additional thinking about nuclear weapons and about what they would mean in war and therefore in the basic affairs of mankind"—some of which "has taken strange twists and turns and led down weird byways."[1] And while it "would not be cor-rect to say that today our confusion is worse confounded," there has nonetheless "been a good deal of confusion along the way."[2] Brodie reflects on how, in "the minds of the great majority of people, nuclear weapons are objects of unmitigated horror, and so they are—in use."[3] But not all nuclear strategists had accepted this—and perhaps most famous among these doubters was Herman Kahn, who rose to fame for his seeming rejection of the inevitability of such "terrible potentialities," much as Henry Kissinger had gained notoriety for his willingness to consider in detail the potentiality for tactical nuclear warfare a few years earlier.

Brodie discusses—and rebuts—Kahn's thesis as put forth in *On Thermonuclear War*, which struck Brodie as particularly un-Clausewitzian, and which seems to more closely align with the Jominian school in its linearity and purely mathematical logic in discussing escalation toward total war than to the more philosophically complex and less self-consciously scientific inquiry of Clausewitz. As Brodie writes: "Herman Kahn, in the book that made his name a byword, set out to prove that, *provided* certain precautions were taken . . . the United States could survive a strategic thermonuclear war. By that he meant that the fatalities and other casualties, though very large, could be kept within limits that he considered tolerable, and that within a term of years that others might consider astonishingly short, say five to ten years, the country could be back to the GNP that it had enjoyed before the war. The special condition to which he attached such supreme importance was the provision in good time of adequate fallout shelters and other forms of civil defense . . . and also the storage in caves or man-made shelters of certain well-selected machine tools, the preserva-tion of which would greatly assist in the reconstruction."[4] Brodie noted Kahn had commented in a footnote that, "It is the hallmark of the expert professional that he doesn't care where he is going as long as he proceeds competently," and that Kahn had felt this was "a reasonable charge against his book," something with which Brodie "fully agrees, especially concerning the competence."[5] Brodie seems to salute Kahn for his unique "courage to explore as thoroughly as his exceptional ability and knowledge permitted the character of a 'general war' with thermonuclear weapons," something that distinguished Kahn from "other writers in the field of strategy, including myself."[6] And yet, Brodie added, "having expressed this tribute I must take part of it back by declaring that while Kahn cared well enough where he was going, he was helped along by an optimism that has in some critical respects turned out to be unwarranted."[7] Brodie noted that "the precautions that Kahn deemed absolutely essential before his somewhat roseate conclusions could be warranted have not been taken and it is now abundantly clear that they will not be," as America had "reacted violently against the fallout shelter program studied and proposed by Kahn," and that program had thus "collapsed and was never thereafter revived."[8] Further, Kahn "assumed a situation in nuclear weapons that was fast changing for the worse," and he himself conceded his arguments "would no longer be valid a decade hence" without "significant and far-reaching" disarmament; but "that decade has passed, and with MIRV and other developments," the "great increase in the sheer quantity of destructiveness" rendered his assumptions obsolete."[9]

Brodie also chastised Kahn for "being neither by training nor temperament sensitive to the vast psychological and emotional damage that a society like ours would suffer along with the physical devastation of a thermonuclear war," and as such believed Kahn had "undoubtedly underestimated the problems of recovery even from a war taking place under the premises he postulated."[10] Brodie noted: "[p]ast wars and other disasters have proved the human being and his societal structure remarkably resilient, but there are limits," and one pitfall of thinking about the unthinkable is that "one cannot find any real parallels in history."[11] Brodie speculated that we could "intuit with some assurance . . . that democracy as we know it could hardly survive."[12] Ultimately, Brodie rebukes Kahn for not being properly Clausewitzian, observing while "Kahn could see reasons why this unspeakable sum of destruction might nevertheless have to be accepted rather than yield one's position on an important political dispute," Brodie himself could "imagine no such issue that is at all likely to arise."[13] As Brodie further explains: "On the simple Clausewitzian premise that we have repeated throughout this book—that a war must have a reasonable political objective with which the military operations must be reasonably consonant—we have to work back from the assumption that 'general war' with thermonuclear weapons must never be permitted to begin, however much we find it necessary to make physical preparations as though it might begin."[14] So while Kahn "was obsessed with the notion that nations might habitually play the game of 'chicken,' which is to keep rigidly to collision course waiting for the other side to yield," Brodie believes while this may sometimes be true, we must nonetheless "not give up the search for all possible preventives that might be effective against such collision," and furthermore, that the "leaders of no nation will wish to risk the total destruction of their country, and one of the things we have been learning over the past twenty-five years is that there are indeed many stopping points between friction, even some measure of combat, and all-out war."[15]

Brodie remains confident that "we have ample reason to feel now that nuclear weapons do act critically to deter wars between the major powers, and not nuclear wars alone but any wars," and he finds this to be "really a very great gain," one "we should no doubt be hesitant about relinquishing."[16] And, Brodie adds: "We should not complain too much because the guarantee is not ironclad," since it's "the curious paradox of our time that one of the foremost factors making deterrence really work and work well is the lurking fear that in some massive confrontation crisis it might fail. Under these circumstances one does not tempt fate."[17]

Escalation: Some Preliminary Observations

In a September 1962 working paper prepared for U.S. Army Major General Harold K. Johnson, who was "chairman of a special study group on the staff of the Joint Chiefs,"[18] Brodie incisively outlines many of the salient issues associated with "escalation"—one of the new terms that Brodie would later describe as being in "wide use of late," part of a new wave of "fashionable jargon" that emerged once deterrence had stabilized with the unprecedented "degree of security built into the strategic retaliatory forces of the two major nuclear powers" in the early 1960s.[19] While in later years Brodie would lament being perceived as something of an opponent to the "limited war" school, he was in fact one of the first to recognize the need for limited war in thermonuclear era when his earlier description of atomic weapons as *absolute* weapons proved premature, just as the dangers of general war increased so dramatically that the tactical use of nuclear weapons, even the new superbombs, became a necessary tool to prevent escalation to general war and to signal the West's determination to defend its interests from the specter of Soviet attack. This was evident in his entire chapter devoted to the subject of limited war (titled appropriately, "Limited War") in *Strategy in the Missile Age*, not to mention the many papers, articles and speeches that he authored in the years preceding that work's publication that reflected this self-same recognition of necessity to fight limited wars. The topic of escalation was thus a topic of interest to Brodie early on; and while his published monograph on the topic would follow that of his colleague and rival Herman Kahn by several months, and his lengthy internal RAND report on the same topic (and with nearly the same identical content) would appear the same year as Kahn's widely read work, Brodie actually first put pen to paper several years earlier with his introductory paper dated September 13, 1962 that outlined his thoughts and which to a large degree mapped out his argument that would be elaborated in the longer report, and ultimately published as a book four years later under Princeton University Press' imprint.

Like many classic works of strategy, dating as far back as Sun Tzu's famous thirteen chapters, Brodie's preliminary work on escalation was tidy and succinct, just fourteen pages long and presented into twenty-three specific points. These digestible, bite-sized points were tailor-made for the professional military audience, and its pressing need to boil down complex analyses into actionable maxims suitable for the demanding realities of war. A marked departure for Brodie, whose style of theorizing tended to reflect the bulkier literary style of philosophers of war like Clausewitz more than the precisely calibrated style of theorists like Jomini who boiled down the principles of war into similarly bite-sized units as Brodie now presented "Some Preliminary Observations on Escalation," which demonstrated that behind the veil of secrecy that obscured his classified work from public sight, Brodie was nonetheless able to digest war's awesome complexity and boiled down its complicated essence for practitioners of the art of war to handily apply. While not as well known for this art, and quite the critic of those whose works favored boiling down over elaboration, it is intriguing that in the contest to define the challenges of escalation and its solutions, Brodie was among the very first out of the gate, even if in the end he was not recognized for firing the first—and potentially most succinct—shot fired in the escalation battles. Moreover, while later critics would overemphasize Brodie's early belief that the bomb was so absolute that it could only be used to deter war and not to fight one (lest it court national suicide and thus break ranks with Clausewitz's impassioned prescription that war remain linked to its political objectives and that the means thereby remain consistent with the ends sought), and some would thus attack Brodie for emphasizing one Clausewitzian dictum while ignoring another, the confounding importance of the frictional dimensions of war, which prevented war from attaining its absolute potential, Brodie explores in great detail the many frictional components of escalation, including the emotional dynamics as well as the inherent uncertainties and relativisms of intuition. So while later, theorists like Herman Kahn would elucidate the many granular levels of escalation ladders, Brodie would instead shine a light on all the frictional dynamics unleashed that would obscure, and thereby invalidate, the simple, machine-like, mathematically deterministic elegance of linear, logical, rational steps up or down that ladder, when in realist all escalations would be shrouded in many layers of obscuring fog.

In his first point, Brodie observes that the "subject of escalation has been much talked about, but very little thought about," and that a "quick survey of the relevant literature reveals little systematic exploration of the meaning of escalation and of the factors bearing upon it" with "many stated assumptions concerning probabilities of escalation under particular contingencies, but the relevant factual or logical bases for these assumptions are rarely made explicit."[20] Moreover, Brodie notes that "[m]ost of the meagre writing on escalation is concerned with one factor bearing on the subject—the use or non-use of tactical nuclear weapons" while "many other factors are ignored." He aims to remedy this shortfall.[21] His second point is that "[a]ssertions concerning the chances of escalation under particular contingencies are usually derived from intuition," a danger of which is the inescapable fact that "one man's intuition is not another's . . . who brings a different body of experience and different sets of conscious premises and unconscious biases to bear."[22] Brodie ties this relativism of intuition to the recent debate on the use of tactical nuclear weapons in Europe, noting that "it seems to some perfectly clear that even in Europe the introduction of tactical nuclear weapons would be a much more shocking and disequilibrating event in a limited war than, say, the outbreak of hostilities in the first place or the sharp increase of the level of conflict from a few battalions to something comprising the whole of the ground forces on both sides" while others instead may "remember vividly the shock effect of numerous events in World War II besides the introduction of nuclear weapons such as the German breakthrough in France in May, 1940, the German attack on the Soviet Union in June, 1941, or the Pearl Harbor attack" and thus "question the above-mentioned assumption."[23] And while it would certainly "be difficult to .prove either point of view" Brodie nonetheless concludes that it "would help if on the major issues we could make all grounds for holding certain beliefs as explicit as possible."[24] And so he thus proceeds; first by elaborating upon "The Difficulty of Quantifying Probability Estimates," noting in his fourth point that, "Even a great deal of thought and examination is unlikely to produce usable formulations expressed in specific values of probability," with only a few scenarios so high or low in likelihood that they can be presented a either a "virtual certainty" or a probability that's "almost zero," while the rest find themselves along a "great range where we are obliged to use terms no more specific than 'highly probable,' 'rather probable,' or 'rather improbable,' "[25] and thus offering little practical value. His fifth point adds that "[t] oo many available adjectives are worn out from overuse, and there is therefore a common tendency to use terms more extreme than one might be willing to defend," so much so that "when a distinguished writer of more than usual insight and reliability (who has also contributed more than anyone else to our understanding of escalation)," and who is revealed in a footnote to be none other than Thomas Schelling, "asserts that the tactical use of nuclear weapons in limited war increases the chances of escalation to general war 'by an order of magnitude,' he is using that phrase in a rhetorical sense and not at all in the mathematical sense signifying 'by a factor of ten.' He is merely stating forcefully that, in his intuitive judgment, introducing nuclear weapons . . . greatly increases the chances of escalation."[26] Brodie adds in the footnote revealing this "distinguished writer" to be Schelling that he did "not present this remark as a reason for being opposed to the introduction of tactical nuclear weapons in a limited war" but instead "argues, on the contrary, that the demonstration might be necessary, so long as we know what we are doing, which in his opinion is threatening the imminence of general war."[27]

Brodie next turns to "The Emotionally Charged Environment of Limited War," similarly embedding his analysis in an important element of Clausewitzian friction. In his sixth point, Brodie points out how the "usual discussion of escalation ignores the fact that not only nuclear weapons but war itself invariably and deeply involves the emotions, especially those emotions loosely described as anger and fear,"[28] and this recognition of the importance of the emotional reality of escalation (and war more generally) is made a full three years before Herman Kahn's *On Escalation: Metaphors and Scenarios* helped to strip escalation of its emotional core (contributing, as part of a broader literature that sanitized escalation into a mathematical exercise divorced from emotional and political realities that included works of such pre-eminent theorists as Thomas Schelling, to the blind logic that fueled the Vietnam War's continual but ultimately fruitless, but ever so lethal, escalations which somehow turned a series of battlefield victories into a tragic political and strategic failure). Brodie explains that "[w]ars simply cannot be fought without such involvement" and while "[s]trong emotion does not negate rationality" he points out that "it powerfully affects it."[29] Foreshadowing the tragedy of Vietnam, Brodie noted that the emotional dimensions of escalation are reflected in the "difficulty of ending wars, because the losing side usually postpones as long as possible acceptance of the fact of defeat."[30] In his seventh point, Brodie further notes that, "when one asserts that in a postulated limited war the Russians would not do thus-and-so (e.g., use nuclear weapons if we did not) because it would be 'contrary to their interests,' one seems to overlook the fact that the very outbreak of hostilities generally argues some strong irrationality somewhere," and that the "Russians are bound to see their interests and to appraise the factors which bear upon the military and political situation in a quite different way from us. Certainly the Japanese did so at the time of Pearl Harbor."[31] Brodie cautions that we must therefore "try to understand the opponent's views of his interests, because we have to be ready to bargain with him both by act and by word. But in the highly charged atmosphere of conflict we should be ready for surprises, including some surprises concerning our own reactions."[32] Emotional reactions are part of the political and strategic landscape and must not be overlooked; Brodie notes in his eighth point that "[w]hen President Truman made the decision to resist by force communist aggression in Korea in June, 1950, his response was an emotional one" but "it was also, so far as we could see then or now a highly rational one."[33] And while "[t]here were probably several quite different kinds of rational action conceivable," Brodie observes that "the particular one chosen was largely determined by emotion."[34] Other emotions came into play, as America's Korean "involvement was later to engender dismay, alarm, and anger over our defeats at the hands of the Communist Chinese, and present from the first was fear that the Russians were using Korea as a diversion while preparing an attack in Europe."[35] Brodie's next point adds that this "latter fear, which turned out to be entirely unwarranted, was felt strongly even on the level of the Joint Chiefs, and it exercised a predisposing force on policy decision" and "helped us keep under tight control the emotions aroused by the Korean involvement," which contributed to America's ability to "demonstrate in that conflict several historically unprecedented restraints"[36] and demonstrate both the military and emotional viability of keeping wars limited.

Brodie next considers the many "Meanings of the Term 'Escalation,'" noting that the term's "most common use . . . refers to a change from limited to general war," and that "the term itself connotes the idea that the progress from—one condition to the other can be by—stages, which may, however, be traversed rapidly."[37] Brodie adds that "[s]ome further refinement has lately crept into the discussion and the term may now refer to changes: (a) in yields (from non-nuclear weapons to small nuclear weapons, and from small nuclear weapons to large ones), (b) in types of target (with a regressing order of relevance respecting army operations; or one may speak of tactical targets with minimum civilian damage as against tactical targets with large civilian damage), and (c) in zones of targetting (leading from the theater where contact exists between the opposing armies to the ZIs of both sides, which is general war). Another kind of escalation, which might be fitted under (b) or (c) above but which is also somewhat distinctive, is the change from observance to non-observance of certain tacitly accepted sanctuaries."[38] And, point eleven, Brodie suggests that "another and most important kind of change. which is rarely considered as escalation but which clearly ought to be so considered, is that of *rapid increase in the sizes of the tactical forces committed to action*, even if they confine themselves to using conventional weapons,"[39] a point Brodie had been arguing for the better part of a decade against an increasing chorus of conventional war in Europe (CWE) advocates (known to some as firebreak theorists), as he pointed out, "It is interesting that the standard argument in favor of larger conventional forces in Europe not only tends to assume considerable ease of escalation in the size of forces committed but, even more, seems on examination to be willing to make it easy for this kind of escalation to take place . . . by attempting to suppress the threat that increase in scale of commit-ment will trip use of nuclear weapons."[40] History suggests caution when increasing conventional force levels in Europe, and Brodie speculates that "[i]f escalation in size of forces is in fact (espe-cially in Europe) a very dangerous as well as intrinsically destructive kind of escalation, it might be well to seek means for inhibiting rather than encouraging it; one way to discourage it would be to threaten to bring in nuclear weapons relatively early, or actually to do so. In this respect the threat or actual use of tactical nuclear weapons may be counter-escalatory."[41]

Ultimately, escalation is at heart part of a process that calibrates the amount of, type of, and location of force used with the political objectives in an inherently Clausewitzian fashion, and so Brodie turns his attention next to "A Contest of Will over Political Objectives" that defines and contextualized escalation. In his twelfth point, Brodie observes that a "limited war between powerful opponents is not merely a matter of military capabilities" but is in fact "a contest of will over political objectives which is influenced by existing military action and the threat of introducing additional force."[42] Brodie explains that "[t]his follows from the fact that the sources of military strength of both major opponents are not immediately at risk in a limited war; both have important, even dominant, military capabilities that are not yet committed to the local struggle," and as a consequence, "military capabilities can be used to *demonstrate* that one has the political resolution and determination to exact a high price of the opponent for his actions, and to test the latter's willingness to pay it," and this "may serve to keep a local war from growing rapidly and perhaps unnecessarily."[43] In his thirteenth point, Brodie introduces two propositions "concerning escalation" that "can be accorded very high probability," the first being a "new and higher level of violence introduced by one side in a conflict is highly likely to be *at least met* by the other side, so long as the latter possesses the appropriate capabilities and is not ready to relin-quish its position,"[44] and the second that "[i]n war, levels of violence tend almost always to move upwards, rarely downward, until the actual ending of the conflict by armistice or capitulation."[45] Both are highly probably because "they show a high degree of historical persistence" and "the psychological and other reasons for that persistence are relatively easily observed or intuited."[46]

Brodie next looks to "What Constraints Do We Have on the Russians?" in which his four-teenth point is presented, in which Brodie notes while "we can assume that if we use tactical nuclear weapons in a European limited war, it is highly likely the Russians will do likewise" but it remains unclear if the opposite is true—that is, "whether the Russians will be likely to refrain from using them if we refrain and have promised in advance to do so."[47] While Brodie suspects that "[s]ome constraint in that direction we would undoubtedly be exercising," he asks, "but is it a strong constraint?"[48] The answer depends in large measure on "the Russian view of what is 'natural' or 'bizarre' with respect to the use in the field of modern weapons."[49] Brodie notes how, "[u]ntil very recently a proposal to avoid use of nuclear weapons in any substantial hostilities with the Soviet Union, especially hostilities taking place in Europe, would have struck most informed Americans as bizarre" but "now it seems to strike some Americans as quite natural," but it still remains quite unclear whether there is "good reason for supposing that the Russians have made a similar transition in their thinking, or that they are highly likely to do so."[50] While Brodie cannot determine with any measurable degree of probability whether the Russians would "conceive it to be in their interest to launch an aggression with conventional weapons alone if we convinced them we were (1) committed not to accept a significant loss of territory and (2) had nuclear weapons available for tactical support of our forces, even if these were reserved to the control of higher command levels," Brodie does believe it to be probable that the Russians would "(as has been true thus far) choose to refrain from aggression under those circumstances, but if so the thanks are due to something other than our promises to refrain for a while from using nuclear weapons"[51] and can be attributed more likely to the workings of deterrence and the implicit threat of escalation by means of retaliation should they pursue aggression Europe.

Brodie's final section considers possible "Methods of Investigation" and thus outlines the research agenda necessary to address the many unmeasured probabilities associated with escalation that currently rest only on imperfect intuition. As Brodie describes in his fifteenth point, "Most of the above observations indicate the value of investigating problems of escalation through the examination of numerous scenarios, positing circumstances as varied as the disciplined imaginations of the participants can make them," but despite this appeal Brodie notes that the "pursuit of scenarios is not a panacea," and even though "unplanned or accidental issues which can dominate the outbreak of political and military crises are indeed frequently inserted into scenarios," Brodie points out that "accidents are by definition atypical, and the whole range of significantly different possible accidents is beyond imagination."[52] Moreover, just as accident is by nature an unpredictable element, "the constraint imposed by emotion in a diplomatic or military crisis is hard to capture under scenario writing or gaming conditions,"[53] leaving its impact as much to chance and fortune as earlier theorists like Clausewitz and Machiavelli posited long ago. And, Brodie adds, "it is easier to vary accidental events than basic assumptions about the behavior of the enemy and even ourselves, and these can easily be too rigid. All this being said, it remains to add that any *single* scenario which tends to become standard and all too familiar is almost bound to be wrong as an approximation of future reality" as the "significant variations that reality may take in the future are too abundant for that."[54] While several years before Herman Kahn's widely read *On Escalation: Metaphors and Scenarios* would be published, Brodie not only anticipates the approach that will continue to gain traction in the emergent field of escalation studies, but soundly deflates what would become the principal approach to the problem.

As for the specific issue of accidental war, dramatically portrayed in the Sidney Lumet's 1962 novel *Fail Safe*, the very year of Brodie's first effort to flesh out his thoughts on escalation, Brodie writes in his sixteenth point that that "we should distinguish sharply between accidents of circumstance by which and within which crises are developed, and the so-called *accidental war*, which connotes an outbreak of conflict that neither side has desired or really wants to press" such as "local bluffs being unexpectedly called."[55] Thus, "To say that accidental war is a possibility worth a good deal of thought is not the same as saying that a conflict breaking out in Europe is more likely than not to be of the accidental variety. The latter proposition, which is made frequently, deserves to be very carefully examined, because the whole concept of limitation and escalation is greatly affected by it."[56]

In his seventeenth point, Brodie addresses the most likely scenarios of escalation, writing that it "seems clear that under many different kinds of scenario conditions, two general considerations will dominate the probabilities of total escalation to general war," the first being "the importance of the outcome of the local action on the global position of each contestant," and the second being "the relative vulnerability or invulnerability of the major strategic striking forces."[57] He further develops these considerations in his eighteenth point, noting that the relative importance "of the outcome of the local action on the global position" of the superpowers has "long been felt intuitively, accounting for the fact that limited war has generally been considered a more practical and likely contingency for the Far East and the Middle East than for Europe"[58] where extended deterrence has sought to closely bind the fate of America to that of its European allies, raising the stakes and the risks of escalation to general war more so than in peripheral areas where America more freely engaged in conventional combat with an intuitive expectation of a lower risk of general war. Though Brodie observes "[o]nly recently have there been proposals for confining wars in Europe to limited wars, and to large-scale though conventional limited wars at that,[59]" proposals that Brodie has strenuously opposed in his many papers, articles and speeches. As for the "relative vulnerability or invulnerability of the major strategic striking forces," Brodie notes "the prevalence of a feeling that if there does not yet exist a mutual standoff with respect to nuclear strategic striking forces, there will be such a condition soon,"[60] a situation that in fact emerged with the relentless modernization of the nuclear forces of both superpowers and their concerted efforts to secure their retaliatory forces; with the then current asymmetry, with American retaliatory forces more secure than their Soviet counterparts, Brodie notes that "it is sometimes argued that the Russians could probably reply devastatingly against targets in Western Europe even if they would not reply in comparable degree to a strategic first strike by us" and Brodie suggests that the "deterrence value for us in this kind of position— which presents us with a clear advantage and which has already lasted much longer than anyone would have predicted—needs to be examined anew, or rather continuously."[61] Brodie finds that it "remarkable how far we have gone, and how quickly, in discarding a stance (i.e., massive retaliation) upon which until recently (and, no doubt, mistakenly) we were ready to hang everything" but as "we still have an unquestioned strategic superiority," Brodie adds, "issues of escalation are directly affected. Some of these same effects will hold good even in that long-promised but not-yet-arrived situation when the standoff in strategic nuclear response between the two major contestants is really mutual."[62] It is the dynamics of a more balanced, mutual nuclear-strategic standoff that Brodie next addresses in his nineteenth point, noting in such "a standoff situation we can see some marked inhibitions operating against the escalation from limited war to general war," leading Brodie to wonder, "how would such a situation affect escalation of violence within the framework of limited war? Do strong mutually-shared inhibitions against going to general war inhibit also the introduction of nuclear weapons in limited war?"[63] Brodie observes that "[w]e can see one constraint operating in that direction, namely the conviction, or at least strong feeling, that use of nuclear weapons may prompt escalation even to a mutually disastrous general war" while "[o]n the other hand, insofar as the standoff were genuinely and deeply felt to be such, it could easily have the opposite effect with respect to escalation from non-nuclear to nuclear weapons on the tactical level" as Brodie had long argued in response to the CWE advocates: "In other words, if one side or the other deems itself to be advantaged by the introduction of tactical nuclear weapons, it has the bracing assurance that both sides recognize it to be clearly and deeply in their interests to refrain from going to strategic nuclears. In short, stability at the top works to some extent against stability at lower and intermediate levels."[64]

As Brodie approaches the conclusion of his preliminary sketch on escalation, he notes in his twentieth point that his "above remarks . . . deliberately avoided certain important issues that are tangential to the question of escalation," including "the feasibility of tactical nuclear war, that is, whether troops as presently trained and equipped could really live in a nuclear environment, or, if not, whether they could be so trained and equipped;" and in addition "the question whether the incorporation of small nuclear weapons in the armament of forward echelons makes the ultimate escalation to high levels of violence more likely than keeping tactical nuclear weapons to larger sizes which can be controlled by the most senior commanders."[65] Brodie suggests that for "a region like Europe, the most dangerous eruption is probably the one that commits the first battalion, and any deployment that helps to deter that kind of eruption—if it really does so—has much in its favor," and thus re-asserts his confidence that deterrence remains not only the best policy but the wisest strategy, threatening escalation in order to dissuade one's opponent, by deterrence, from taking the sorts of risks that would court escalation.[66]

Thus Brodie questions the currently in-vogue CWE strategy, and argues in his twenty-first point that such a "view holds that forward troops armed with small nuclear weapons are more vulnerable than troops not so armed because they invite nuclear attack, and hence have lower *net* fighting power," while Brodie suggests that "it might be equally plausible to say that a force so armed has a greater effect in deterring attack—since its implicit threat to use (or to prompt surviving units to use) nuclear weapons at tactical levels fairly promptly, hardly strains credibility."[67] And credibility is the sine qua non required for deterrence to succeed; as Brodie observes, "It was after all the credibility issue on which the 'massive retaliation' doctrine was most effectively attacked, though it is worth recalling that credibility was considered especially in question for *areas outside Europe*."[68]

Brodie reiterates his earlier argument that "while our use of nuclears may guarantee enemy use, our non-use of these weapons falls far short of comparably guaranteeing enemy non-use."[69] Because enemy non-use is far from certain, Brodie reminds us that we have to be prepared to in essence think about the unthinkable, a point that would later help make Herman Kahn famous even though Brodie made this very same argument; in his twenty-second point he thus asks the hard question: "are we advantaged by a mutual use of nuclear weapons as compared with a mutual non-use? Surely the primary answer would have to be: 'Not necessarily.' It might even be: 'Usually not.' But surely too the answer would depend on circumstances and places, and perhaps an overriding consideration is that the choice may not be ours to make. A searching inquiry would perhaps come up with something like the following answer: unless we could have high confidence that non-use by us tactically would enjoin non-use on the enemy, we have to be both prepared physically to use them and also accustomed to the idea of using them."[70] In short, we have to be prepared to not only *think about the unthinkable*, but to also, as Peter Lavoy, Scott Sagan, and James Wirtz would argue four decades later, *plan the unthinkable*. In a footnote, Brodie adds: "The question whether one can and should distinguish between nuclear and non-nuclear weapons is, however, quite distinct from the question whether or not they should be used," and noting that at the time he published *Strategy in the Missile Age* in 1959, "the tide of military opinion was flowing overwhelmingly in the direction of advocating free and easy use of tactical nuclears," and so Brodie was "therefore inclined to sound cautionary notes. The situation is quite different today."[71] Brodie closes his preliminary reflections on escalation with an eye on future conflicts, perhaps engaged in succession, each one affected by its predecessor: "Another thought requiring mention is that so long as we are thinking about limited war, we are thinking not about a single conflict (which is all we do think about with general war) but possibly a succession of conflicts. Thus, it should be borne in mind that each case will have a great effect on expectations concerning the next outbreak of hostilities. One cannot expect to play each military episode as though it were historically unique."[72]

Technology and Escalation: 'From Crossbow to H-bomb'

In a strategic partnership that is reminiscent of Marie von Clausewitz's dedicated effort to bring her late husband's strategic theory to publication posthumously, in 1962, just a few short years after Brodie's *Strategy in the Missile Age* was published, and even sooner after Kahn's *On Thermonuclear War* came out, Bernard Brodie and his wife Fawn—herself a leading historian and best-selling author who pioneered the field of psychohistory—co-authored *From Crossbow to H-Bomb*, an historical discussion of the role of technology in war, with a subtitle "The evolution of the weapons and tactics of warfare." As recounted by Newell G. Bringhurst in his biography of Brodie's wife Fawn, in 1960, Bernard had been "awarded a Carnegie Corporation Reflective Year Fellowship, to commence in July," under whose terms he would "live abroad while engaged in what was termed 'reflective scholarship'" and would thereby "free him from the pressures of research and writing at RAND." He and the family thus headed to France; he, Fawn, and their two youngest children, Bruce and Pamela, would be in Paris and their older son Dick headed to the University of Grenoble. To "help cover the costs, Bernard signed a contract with Dell, a paperback publisher, to produce a history of the impact of science on military technology," which was "intended for the college market, specifically for courses in military science and related disciplines. Although Bernard assumed primary responsibility for the authorship of this volume, clearly within his own area of expertise, he enlisted Fawn's help in doing the research. In the end, Fawn would do most of the actual writing as well." Prior to the family's departure, "Fawn completed research for *From Crossbow to H-Bomb*," and "had assumed primary responsibility for the manuscript, even though Bernard had been the one to sign the book contract with Dell." After the Brodies completed *From Crossbow to H-Bomb*, Bernard "eagerly looked forward to the year away from RAND, where he had become increasingly dissatisfied. The experience in Paris, he hoped, would regenerate his spirits and enable him to return to California with renewed enthusiasm."[73]

Their introduction explains their book is "about the history of the application of science to war," and though their book suggests the starting point will be with the "crossbow" with its medieval origins, in fact they gaze further back in time to the "giant crossbow or 'ballista' of antiquity," though the precise point of origin for their discussion they believe is largely "an arbitrary matter." Interesting, however, to me, is the linguistic connection from the ancient "ballista" to the contemporary "ballistic missile," which define a technological arc spanning from the ancient world to our modern one, where we have grappled with the challenges and riddles of security. Their book, in contrast to Brodie's other heady works, is not a theoretical or philosophical discussion, but rather an historical account of technology evolution and innovation and at times revolution. In the portions dealing with the nuclear era, however, we do find some snapshots of Brodie's thinking of interest to our discussion here. As well, their comparative historical perspective suggests some broad theoretical insights on the nature of historical and doctrinal change, and from their comments we can see how Brodie found the contemporary period, and the tremendous impact of technology on war, to reflect an accelerated impact that was not evident in earlier times, when technology's impact on war was less dramatic and less celeritous.

As the Brodies note, "a single chapter takes him through antiquity and into the Middle Ages," as "[i]n contrast to our own times, the equipment of war changed very slowly in those days, and what changes occurred usually had little to do with science."[74] Indeed, because science as we know it is of itself new, they explain "we must say that the application of science to war is new."[75] But even broadly defined to include the role of "craftsmen, or intuitive inventors, who were able to accomplish wonderful things,"[76] the Brodies nonetheless observe a "slowness of weapons progress prior to the nineteenth and especially the twentieth centuries," and conclude that "[w]hat science there was, and what talent there was for invention, seem often to have been dedicated to other pursuits than new weapons, and in fact to have avoided that field."[77] Even in the contemporary era, the Brodies note having "seen certain nuclear scientists staring appalled at the weapons which their own talents had spawned, and striving to control and then to dissociate themselves from their creations." They cite Scottish mathematician, John Napier, who "was induced to turn his mind to the invention of war machines at the time the Spanish Armada was threatening to invade England," but "once the Spanish threat collapsed, he did his best to keep his various inventions secret," and on his deathbed explained his reasoning: "for the ruin and overthrow of man, there were too many devices already framed, which if he could make to be fewer, he would with all his might endeavor to do so."[78]

Such thinking pertains to the nuclear age, in particular the emergence of limited war theory from the shadow of total war cast by the first generation of nuclear strategy, when the threat of massive retaliation or assured destruction was the principal mechanism for ensuring the nuclear peace. Toward the end of *From Crossbow to H-Bomb*, the Brodies discuss the "Strategic Consequences of the Nuclear Revolution," noting how after Hiroshima ushered forth the atomic era, "reasonable people at the outset conceded" that the bomb's strategic impact would be "enormous for any future wars in which it might be used," even if its direct causal impact on Tokyo's surrender cannot be conclusively determined. The Brodies suggest that "[p]erhaps the most significant thing about their use against Japan was that the world was thereby granted a demonstration of their awesome power in the most arresting and sobering way possible,"[79] as "[n]uclear bombs made it clear first of all that there could be no question among reasonable people and objective men about the decisiveness of strategic bombing in future wars,"[80] even if the results of strategic bombing in World War II remained subject to debate, which "made the problem more ambiguous"[81] prior to the advent of the bomb, which the Brodies believe "quashed the question after a relatively brief flurry of argument," upon which "the dominance of nuclear strategic bombing in any war in which it is used is hardly any longer in question," as "the effective range of strategic bombing was now enormously extended."[82] That's because with nuclear weapons, "any bomber was an effective instrument at whatever range it could reach," even if only carrying a single bomb. And "[w]ith the bombers available from the end of World War II onward, this meant that all great nations, and specifically the United States and the Soviet Union, were within effective bombing range of each other."[83] Further, the "coming of nuclear weapons also put a premium on developing new types of carriers," driven by the unprecedented "effectiveness" of atomic weapons. But this same rise in effectiveness "also made defense against strategic bombing enormously more difficult and disheartening to the defender." So effective were these new weapons in their destructive capabilities that the Brodies invoke Clausewitz and his famous dictum uniting war as the means with policy as the ends. As they reflect: "Finally, the atomic age has seen the first widespread questioning of the basic utility of war as an instrument of national policy. Clausewitz consistently preached that war makes no sense unless fought for a specific political objective, and that this objective should be allowed to determine the whole character of the fighting. This was an ideal approach that was sometimes catastrophically lost sight of, as in World War I, but the most imprudent nation, pursuing a conflict blindly and needlessly, could nevertheless rise from the ashes. With atomic weapons, the possibility of recovery in a reasonably short time has become dubious. Between opponents who possess substantial stores of atomic weapons and the means of delivering them there can no longer be positive objectives in war, only negative ones, like avoiding being overrun and overwhelmed."[84]

Later, with the emergence of thermonuclear weapons, there were few or no real changes "of basic consequence" from the A-bomb era, as "the A-bomb revolution was so drastic that no mere multiplication of the bomb's power, even by a thousand times, could compare with its significance," but the emergence of the H-bomb "forced home some conclusions that were insufficiently absorbed before," and the "revolution is now unambiguous and unchallengeable."[85] The increased destructive power of H-bomb was soon joined by the arrival of "long-range, intercontinental, and the intermediate-range missiles" that "followed hard upon the development of thermonuclear weapons," and the Brodies believe that "[t]he combination of the thermonuclear bomb and ballistic has given a further excruciating twist to the problem of defense against strategic bombing," adding that one could be "tempted to say that it has made really hopeless what was formerly only apparently so, but one must avoid saying this because there are always some defensive devices which are better than others and maybe even intrinsically worth pursuing," even though "long-range missiles with thermonuclear warheads . . . greatly reduce the efficacy of radar screens and other detecting devices, and also that of the 'active defenses,' which depend upon shooting down the attacking carriers," and thus "enhance the importance of 'passive defenses,' which depend on concealment, dispersion, armoring, mobility, and the like," and also "enhance the importance of concentrating attention on defending the retaliatory force, especially since such defenses can hardly be applied to cities, and to only a limited extent to the populations within cities."[86] As the Brodies explained, "In defenses against thermonuclear weapons and missiles it is essential to concentrate on what is feasible and worthwhile and let the other things go," and as such the "retaliatory force must be defended at all cost; otherwise one has no defense at all, no dissuasion for the aggressive impulses or designs of the enemy." Additionally, while "this force can be defended," it may only be done using "measures which are novel, and neither inexpensive nor easy to acquire," and which "must put a minimum dependence upon warning, and an equally minimum dependence upon shooting down or otherwise destroying the attacking enemy forces," but instead "[w] e must depend upon passive defenses which are always in operation."[87] The Brodies cite "the Polaris-firing nuclear submarine" as "[o]ne of the most significant new developments in this regard," as "[t]here has never before been an instrument of such potential power which was also so invulnerable to detection," and its "relative invulnerability relieves us of much of the pressure in a crisis to 'hit while the hitting is good.' "[88]

The Brodies reassert that in the era of H-bombs, "the most important force that a great nation can have, the one indispensable force it *must* have, is its striking force, which is wholly offensive and not at all defensive except insofar as it succeeds in deterring war," or in the event deterrence collapses, "in destroying the enemy before he can retaliate."[89] But the latter is possible "only if one side has not made his retaliatory force secure," which renders a system designed for deterrence "highly unstable militarily."[90] The Brodies consider the high cost of failure of deterrence, and observe that as atomic weapons gave way to their thermonuclear offspring, it became necessary to revised Bernard Brodie's original theory on the "absolute weapon," finding room for a more relative, or limited, kind of warfare beneath the ominous thermonuclear shadow. The Brodies neatly summarize this new thermonuclear logic (which in Bernard Brodie's later *Escalation and the Nuclear Option* would ramble on, without the same elegance or precision) into two brief paragraphs:

> Finally, the recent developments in thermonuclear weapons and missiles have given new impetus to the necessity of limiting war. If contests cannot be avoided in some areas, it might be possible to limit them to a military action which is not all-destructive, and therefore absurd. The idea has developed that wars can be fought which avoid strategic bombing, and perhaps nuclear weapons, altogether. The old axiom that modern war is total war is now receiving some serious and long due consideration.
>
> This problem is too complex to be discussed in any detail here, but we should repeat that much depends on whether or not the retaliatory forces of both sides are adequately defended. If they are, it is possible to fight limited wars, and in fact senseless to resort to any other kind. If they are not, the reverse is true. Then limited wars of any duration or magnitude become impossible to contain, because it is too dangerous to withhold that great striking force which is terribly powerful but also terribly vulnerable. The importance of protecting adequately the main retaliatory striking force of the nation is at this writing second to no other security question.[91]

While technology has made war itself now deadlier than ever, introducing a new and seemingly contradictory logic that suggests protecting the very means of Apocalyptic destruction must be the top priority, and that the continued vulnerability of cities is also a necessity to sustain a stable system of mutual deterrence, the Brodies find that technology offers up new hope and not just fear, and that comes not from new machines of war but rather from new modes of thought. In their chapter on "Operations and Systems Analysis: The Science of Strategic Choice," they explore this new manner of thinking, a scientific style of thinking that tips the scale away from that other Clausewitzian theme, of strategy being an art (contrary to Jominian thinking, which believed it to be more a craft, with elements that mirrored science and mathematics and in particular geometry, itself a tradition that inspired Hobbes to construct his mighty Leviathan). While Brodie is widely considered to be America's Clausewitz, or the Clausewitz of the nuclear age, he breaks from his philosophical mentor by embracing science and rejecting art, though to be fair, Clausewitz did not enjoy such tools as operations or systems analysis, which may well have enabled him to counter Jominian simplicity with a more mathematical, more scientific embrace of complexity. But Clausewitz was born at a time when only philosophy provided him with the tools required to probe complexity, and explore the inner folds and creases of war.

Noting the rapid advances in ballistic missile accuracy and range recently made, the Brodies observe that in "this development, incidentally, involving as it does the simultaneous perfecting of guidance and of propulsion, we see illustrated the importance of the fact that science and technology have been advancing along a multiplicity of fronts,"[92] and that "[e]ach weapons system is likely to become so complex that it must call on many separate fields of knowledge,"[93] and "[i]n recent years the stimulation and mutual assistance across fields has been enormous, and this accounts for much of the acceleration in the advance of science generally."[94] The result has been "the application of the scientific method not simply to the hardware designed for military purposes, but to the whole field of military strategy and tactics itself," which the Brodies believe "is the most novel and possibly the most hopeful development of all."[95] Citing B. H. Liddell Hart, who back in 1935 had made a "prophetic observation that the military problem had developed in complexity beyond the competence of the military profession," and in the nuclear age, the Brodies assert, this very problem was now "not only beyond the competence of any one person or group of persons but beyond the competence of any one profession."[96] That's because: "When the military officer was first plunged into involvement with nuclear weapons, he found himself obliged to master a new kind of scientific lore. It was not too troublesome at first, but as nuclear techniques rapidly developed, the problems of choice became serious and difficult. The new promise of missiles added to his difficulties. It was clear that the soldier needed assistance from people . . . trained in the appropriate sciences and able to act as advisors on critical issues of choice between systems."[97] With help from new research and analysis organizations like the RAND Corporation, where Bernard Brodie spent many years, military planners could benefit from "operations analysis," including the application of the newly emergent field of game theory, and later "systems analysis," for their decision-making with regard first to tactical weapons systems, and later "strategic issues of broad import."[98] The experience has not been without some bumps. For instance, the Brodies noted that the "services have naturally looked upon this development with mixed feelings, glad for the assistance but alarmed at some of the conclusions reached—and withal aware of the fact that their status as unique possessors of an esoteric kind of knowledge is increasingly challenged."[99] Additionally, systems analysis itself proved to be "far from infallible," since it was "dealing with so many uncertainties," depended on a limited pool of talent, and the realities of funding limitations as well as other factors that could result in even good analyses being ultimately rejected by the military decision-makers. As well, the Brodies realize, in a manner that would make Clausewitz—who was inspired by art and philosophy to compose both a broad and a deep canvas—proud, that "above all, scientific analysis is applicable to important problems, but usually not the most important. The profound issues of strategy and certainly of politics, those likely to affect most deeply the fates of nations and even of mankind, are precisely those which do not lend themselves to scientific analysis, usually because they are so laden with value judgments. Therefore they tend altogether to escape any kind of searching thought. It is also true that the complexity and difficulty of the problems with which we have had to deal have far outrun the development of our techniques for analyzing them."[100] Adds Brodie, "There are some grounds for satisfaction, on the other hand, that the same kind of ruminating and objective thinking and research that produced the nuclear weapons and missiles which add so much to our own cares is now being directed to the consideration of what we do with them. It is the second best thing to not having those cares at all, but in this imperfect world it should not on that account be disdained."[101]

In a new chapter added to the later (1973) edition of their work, "Recent Weaponry Changes (1962–1972)," the Brodies revisit the topic of limited war, and the re-intensified focus on conventional warfighting, which they described as a "notable development in strategic thinking during the past decade," describing it as "that modification in strategic thought which has resulted in renewed emphasis on the 'conventional' weapons of war, inevitably at some cost to the emphasis that would otherwise have been placed on nuclear weapons and associated instruments."[102] They thus address "The New School of Conventional War Thinking," and note even though "[n]uclear weapons are certainly far more efficient engines of destruction than any other kind, and in previous eras that would have been enough to guarantee that they would displace all competing types," that "they are perhaps *too* efficient—and therefore hardly the weapons for all seasons."[103] They again cite Liddell Hart, noting he "had cautioned against too great a preoccupation with total or unlimited war," but that "these complaints by him and others did not get much attention," and after Hiroshima, "the coming of nuclear weapons absorbed the attention of those who by inclination and self-training were competent to think about and to discuss *strategy*, as distinct from tactics and weaponry."[104]

But when the H-bomb came along in 1952, the Brodies note, "all that was changed,"[105] as its greatly increased destructive capacity "began to stimulate thinking among a few about the need to limit war," as evidenced by American military behavior in Korea, which demonstrated "the kind of restraint needed" in this new and dangerous era.[106] When Dulles reasserted massive retaliation as policy after Korea, which reflected Eisenhower's economic concerns about America's ability to "maintain both a large nuclear capability and a large conventional capability." By relying on nuclear weapons, a "substantial conventional capability was superfluous." But "critics of this view argued that this was unrealistic thinking" in light of Korea, and that "aggressions like that . . . would not necessarily be deterred, inasmuch as the potential aggressors would doubt the American readiness to resort to nuclear weapons in small-scale affairs."[107] When President Kennedy came to power, he would bring "into power with him an entirely different philosophy," one shared by his defense secretary Robert McNamara as well as his military advisor, General Maxwell Taylor. As the Brodies recount: "Secretary McNamara at once appointed to his staff a group of civilians, mostly young, to assist in his reforms. These included a contingent from the RAND Corporation who were skilled mostly in systems analysis but who had also developed to a novel degree the idea that the best way to avoid nuclear war was to build up large conventional capabilities. McNamara quickly made these ideas his own."[108]

But the Brodies were skeptical of the idea that a conventional build-up would further deter Soviet aggression, noting "we had on the basis of experience every reason to believe, contrary to the assumptions of the new school, that nuclear weapons in our possession, including over 7,000 tactical nuclear weapons situated in Europe, deterred not only a nuclear attack but *any* deliberate attack on the part of the Soviet Union against the NATO powers," a view shared by our allies in Europe who refused to implement America's ideas on bolstering their conventional armies, though America did proceed with its conventional build-up, something that "probably had much to do with our involvement in Vietnam," given that combat forces "were in fact available" when President Johnson considered their deployment to Indochina.[109]

A Clean Break: Countering the Firebreak Theorists

In his May 23, 1963 article in *The Reporter*—"What Price Conventional Capabilities in Europe?"—Brodie presents a synthesis of his ideas developed in a series of recent RAND working papers that rebuke the policies embraced by Defense Secretary Robert McNamara in his zeal to redirect America's strategic policy from Massive Retaliation toward a more credible limited war strategy—one that Brodie found had gone too far in its emphasis of conventional warfare in Europe (CWE), noting while the "administration's authentic views on the subject have not been readily available to the public," that there was "some reference to them in Secretary of Defense Robert S. McNamara's Ann Arbor speech of June 16, 1962" and a "later and much better source is his book-length statement before the House Armed Services Committee on January 30, 1963" whose "relevant comments" may have been "characteristically lean, but their significance is clear."[110] As Brodie writes: "After point-ing out that '... we must continue to strengthen and modernize our tactical nuclear capabilities to deal with an attack where the opponent employs such weapons first, or any attack by conventional forces which puts Europe in danger of being overrun,' Mr. McNamara went on to say: 'But we must also substantially increase our non-nuclear capabilities to foreclose to our opponent the freedom of action he would otherwise have, or believe he would have, in lesser military provocations. We must be in position to confront him at any level of provocation with an appropriate military response. The decision to employ tactical nuclear weapons should not be forced upon us simply because we have no other way to cope with a particular situation.' "[111]

While "somewhat ambiguous concerning the maximum level of Soviet non-nuclear attack that Mr. McNamara would like to see us able to oppose successfully with non-nuclear means," Brodie notes "additional clarification is provided later in the statement," and in "Section IV on 'General Purpose Forces,' he added the following: 'Although we are still a long way from achiev-ing the non-nuclear capabilities we hope to create in Europe, we are much better off in this regard than we were two years ago. Today the NATO forces can deal with a much greater range of Soviet actions, without resorting to the use of nuclear weapons. Certainly, they can deal with any major incursion or probe. But we must continue to do everything in our power to persuade our Allies to meet their NATO force goals so that we will possess alternative capabilities for dealing with even larger Soviet attacks. And until these capabilities are achieved, the defense of Europe against an all-out Soviet attack, even if such an attack were limited to non-nuclear means, would require the use of tactical nuclear weapons on our part.' "[112]

Brodie notes that it remains "clear that Mr. McNamara would like to be able to meet even an 'all out' Soviet non-nuclear attack by non-nuclear means," but as he had argued in his earlier critique of CWE, "on this issue as well as on several others, our major allies have for some time shown themselves markedly resistant to our persuasion," particularly the French, who not only rejected "Britain's admission to the Common Market" but likewise whose "rejection of American leadership in military and other matters has been violent and extreme," which Brodie explains is partly "because President de Gaulle does not like to be led, but it is also in part a reaction against specific U.S. policies. And however much the French behavior is regretted by our other allies, the latter are not about to respond with a larger conventional effort."[113] As Brodie further explains, "In trying to understand this attitude, one must first remember that the view our government is now advancing as the only reasonable one is the reverse of the idea that our leaders were preaching only a few years ago" and that it was "also well known abroad that the new view is by no means accepted by the majority of senior American military officers, including the recently retired Supreme Allied Commander Europe, General Lauris Norstad."[114] Brodie adds that it was the "Germans especially who distrust the future implications of that peculiarly intense conviction—as though we had achieved a 'breakthrough' in thought—and who distrust also so extraordinary a goal as having a capability for stopping by conventional means any non-nuclear attack that could be mounted even by the full field strength of the Communist bloc," particularly as "[n]o answer is given to the ques-tion of how much territory in Europe we should be ready to give up before deciding that we can no longer withhold nuclear weapons."[115] After reiterating much of what he argued in his September 24, 1962 paper, "A Critique of the Doctrine of Conventional War in Europe (CWE)," Brodie recalls the incisive words of Winston Churchill, who, as Brodie recounts, "once wrote, concerning the planning for a particularly ill-starred offensive: 'However absorbed a commander may be in the elaboration of his own thoughts, it is necessary sometimes to take the enemy into consideration.' In the spinning of military theories, it is really remarkable how seldom that is done."[116]

And, in a new conclusion that strengthens the argument put forth the previous fall, Brodie injects some Clausewitzian analysis, noting that the "real issues are much more political than technical,"[117] and it is an understanding of not only the political dynamic but the political context that has long informed Brodie's understanding of strategy—and which undergirds his continuing critique of CWE, which he feels conflicts with nuclear deterrence and ignores to all of our peril its successful implementation thus far in the Cold War. And so, Brodie reflects, "Our experience with the Russians, crowned by the Cuban episode of last October, tells us that the Soviet opponent is not ten feet tall in the moral intangibles of power—as he would have to be to do some of the bold things he does in war games. Even in the Berlin 'blockade' of 1948–1949, when we failed altogether to test the Soviets' resolve to deny us access on the ground, they did not attempt to interfere with our airlift, as they could easily have done simply by jamming our Ground Controlled Approach radar system. Why should we go on postulating a kind of behavior that is radically different from what they have demonstrated over a long time? After all, the Soviet leaders have now openly broken with the Marxist-Leninist philosophy of inevitable war, avowedly on the ground that nuclear weapons do matter."[118]

Brodie closes his article by reaffirming that it was nuclear weapons that "have vastly affected the expectation of major war in Europe, and it is absurd not to make the most of that change" and "illogical to propose that the NATO powers should add substantially to their defense burdens in order to exploit a probably slim chance for moderating a possible future European war—which, however, the present dispositions make highly improbable."[119] As Brodie explains, "It is one thing to exhort our allies to see that their contributions of forces maintain reasonable standards of efficiency, which certainly ought not to exclude a capability for limited conventional operations. It is quite another to invoke fantasies of great modern armies locked in desperate combat in Europe with never a nuclear warhead going off between them. The one attitude invites credit for our political sense as well as for our strategic thinking; the other merely discredits us in both respects."[120]

Morality and Escalation

While Brodie does not often directly engage idealists and their language of morals and moralism, preferring instead to communicate in a language of realism better-suited to the hard choices of the nuclear age, he did consider the intersection of morality and strategy and what can be thought of as the moral dimensions of escalation, in a September 1964 article, "Morals and Strategy: Distinguishing Virtue from Ignorance in Problems of National Defense," in the September 1964 edition of *Worldview* magazine, published by the Carnegie Council for Ethics in International Relations. It is telling that Brodie, never afraid to speak truth to power, was as prepared to speak (the realities of) power to (the presumption) truth.[121] Brodie started how his article by noting that the "community of intellectual and moral leaders of the nation have tended to treat with an aloofness that certainly reflects a feeling of moral opprobrium those who labor in the field of national defense, especially those who contribute to the intellectual content of that field. They frequently speak or write as if those professionally involved with national defense have somehow betrayed their intellectual heritage."[122]

Brodie cites a recent review of John Strachey's *The Prevention of War*—a topic dear to Brodie's heart dating back at least to 1938 when as a student of Quincy Wright he first probed the moral complexity of "peaceful change," which later became conflated with appeasement as peaceful change led the best-intentioned of Western powers down the path to total war—by Peter Ritner in *The New Leader*, quoting a lengthy paragraph that takes aim at Brodie and his colleagues at RAND: "With urbane competence Strachey expounds the developing views on retaliatory capability, credibility, first strikes, second strikes, equations of deterrence, etc., of the American Clausewitzes: Messrs. Kahn, Morgenstern, Brodie, Kissinger, and others. And as anyone who tries to keep up with it knows, the intellectual refinement of this literature has reached a point of such byzantine preciosity that one wonders whether there has ever existed in the history of the world a politician or military commander capable of comprehending it, or acting upon it."[123]

Brodie believes that "the answer to the implied question of the last sentence is 'No,' which is a bit irrelevant. I offer the passage not because of what the reviewer says but because of the feeling that pervades it, which is one of distaste. He doesn't say that these people (Kahn, Morgenstern, Brodie, Kissinger) are immoral, but he implies that there is something a little unspeakable about their work."[124] Brodie points out that despite Ritner's criticisms, he was nonetheless "unavoidably involved in the activity which he dislikes," and as "his taxes help pay for it," then his effort "to protest against it only by this kind of statement . . . is extraordinarily weak" and "he is by default of real opposition a collaborator, and by much more than his monetary contribution. For there are certain benefits in this system which he is not only enjoying, but which he probably insists upon—I mean those things which we generally imply when we talk about national security."[125] In contrast to what he views as a collaborator's compromise—a morally tenuous half measure—Brodie observes that he has "always felt respect for the thoroughgoing pacifist, though obviously I cannot share his values," finding a less hypocritical philosophy in "the person who is totally opposed to violence in all its forms and who is willing to accept the necessary consequences for being so opposed—which of course would mean the acceptance and the spread abroad of all kinds of tyranny, as well as the strong possibility of his personal subjugation to it" since the pacifist is "at least consistent, and the moral tenet which he has raised to an absolute— the avoidance of violence—is hardly a contemptible one."[126]

But Brodie notes "this kind of complete pacifist is very rare," as "the vast majority of those people who habitually express feelings like Mr. Ritner's are not that kind of pacifist. They do wish to resist injustice and tyranny and especially to oppose its spread where it threatens to do so by violence, and they are therefore willing to support the only instrument of force which is both available to us and capable of doing the job, and that is the national military power."[127] And, Brodie adds, "Because that power is national, the interests for which we appropriately use it can only be national interests."[128] The moral dimensions inherent in the use of national military power are certainly less black and white, but are nonetheless very much real: "Once the decision is made that one is interested in maintaining certain national interests by force of arms if necessary, or at least by the provision of arms, then it is difficult to establish the exact limits that morality imposes in the way we go about it. The end we have accepted certainly entails also the acceptance of certain well-established means. Nevertheless, the intellectual and moral community often finds itself looking back nostalgically at its lost innocence. One frequently encounters, therefore, controversies in which there is a wilful confusion between virtue and ignorance."[129]

The first example considered by Brodie is that of preventive war—an issue he had addressed in several RAND working papers in the early 1950s and which reappeared in chapter form in his 1959 *Strategy in the Missile Age*, when many of Brodie's earlier thoughts presented within the confidential world of RAND would enjoy their first wide public viewing. Brodie writes that he knows of "only one outstanding issue since World War II when it seemed to me that a moral issue was genuinely involved in a debate on national security," and that "happened not to be a politically important debate, not only because it was mostly hidden from public view but mostly because there was never a chance that the decision would be different from what it was."[130] Brodie explains that "[t]his was the debate in the early days of the atomic era—in the late '40's, that is— concerning the question of 'preventive war'."[131] As Brodie recalls, "A small group of people, who were to be found mostly though not exclusively within the military, thought that the time to wipe out the menace of the Soviet Union was now. 'Now, while we have monopoly of the Atom Bomb, and before they get it. We can't afford to let them get this instrument. Our bombers ought to be on the way—the sooner the better.' This in general was the voice of that school, which had a number of rather prominent adherents. One of them, Major General Orvil Anderson, then Commandant of the Air War College, achieved public notice in the autumn of 1950 for advocating this idea publicly, and for getting fired from his War College job as a result."[132]

Despite its strong adherents in the air services, Brodie notes that "[i]n political terms this view was absolutely unimportant" as "[c]ertainly the great majority of people in this country, including the Administration of the day, were totally opposed to it," as was Brodie himself, who had strongly rebuked the policy from the get go: "And I believe it was essentially an immoral proposition. Why? Because it called for our carrying out a tremendous destruction of innocent lives for the sake not of saving ourselves from impending attack but simply of sparing ourselves fear, a vague fear of ultimate danger."[133]

And here Brodie coins an eloquent phrase, one so compelling it seems odd that it has not been often repeated—perhaps because the venue, *Worldview*, for the article was along the periphery and not smack dab in the center of the strategic studies universe. *Simply sparing ourselves fear, a vague fear of ultimate danger.* This vague fear would surface throughout the Cold War, and carry over into the post-Cold War era when the vague fear would manifest in the pre-occupation by many with failed states, rogue states, and stateless terror, leading to a war that would be waged for over a decade against terror itself.

Brodie also considered the more morally ambiguous decision at the end of World War II to drop the atomic bomb—and thereby "use the two atomic bombs over Japan, the only two in our arsenal at the time they were used."[134] Brodie explained that he found "that most relevant comments on that issue concern the imputed necessity of dropping the bombs," noting that the actual "immorality of doing so was somewhat overshadowed by the fact that shortly before the Hiroshima and Nagasaki bombs were dropped, there were 1,000,000 deaths from the great fire-raid on Tokyo with conventional incendiaries and high explosives."[135] Brodie admits, perhaps for the first time, "to believe that it was unnecessary to drop those bombs when we did because (1) our invasion was not scheduled until November, and we had the months from August to November to see whether or not the Japanese would yield, and (2) we were suffering very few casualties during that period, so that we could have afforded to wait."[136] But he adds that "if dropping those bombs was militarily unnecessary, which was not clear at the time, was it also for that reason immoral? In a contest in which the Tokyo forms of attack were not regarded as immoral, it is not clear to me that it was immoral to use the atom bombs."[137]

Brodie draws from this an important lesson: that it's "always desirable before we strike a moral pose to be clear about the state of our relevant knowledge,"[138] And one might add, *relative* knowledge, with which one can interpolate through the inherent ambiguity of the situation, and find a better measure of moral clarity.

Another example presented by Brodie on the moral essence and inherent ambiguity of the strategic realm is that of civil defense, and what he described as the "great shelter scandal of two or three years ago"—and he calls it a great scandal "because I believe the intellectual community behaved scandalously."[139] He recalled that "[o]ne image, totally irrelevant and trivial, was repeated ad nauseum. It pictured a man at the door of his shelter keeping his neighbors out with a gun. 'Isn't this what we are inviting?' the argument ran; 'Isn't this what is going to happen?' "[140] Rather than surrender to emotional arguments, Brodie prefers a more sober assessment of the facts: "So far as a government program was concerned, the first question to be asked was: 'Would a particular shelter program help to protect life in the event of war?' That is a statistical question, and it requires knowledge to answer it, not feelings. It is a problem one can study, and incidentally it has been studied—by some of the unspeakable RAND people. But people who had given it no study at all were confident they had all the answers."[141] Brodie adds that a "second question to ask about a shelter program is, 'Would it have any effect on deterrence of war?' " and he recalls that "[o]ne of the arguments frequently made at the time was that it would weaken deterrence. If true, that would be both pertinent and important," asking: But on what basis was the truth of that assertion established? On no basis at all, except strong distaste for the idea. I consider as simply preposterous the argument that people and their governments will be readier to resort to total war with nuclear weapons merely because there are shelters scattered around the countryside."[142] As for the financial cost, also much criticized, Brodie noted that "we are already spending about 51 billion dollars annually on national defense, which includes buying offensive weapons like long-range missiles, why not spend say one per cent of that amount on so purely defensive a medium as shelters? How could shelters be more 'provocative' than missiles?"[143]

Like many great theorists of war including Sun Tzu, Napoleon, Clausewitz, and Mao, Brodie finds that an essential dimension to strategy is knowledge—of the environment, of the opponent, and of oneself. It is knowledge that enables to commander to make the right decisions, and the rightness of a decision, as Clausewitz had often noted, included the moral as well as the physical. Brodie writes, "This is one of the numerous instances where the answers to all the pertinent questions can be, if not established, at least explored—but only by a diligent search for the facts. Perhaps the relevant research carries us only a small part of the way that we would like to go, but it's the best we can do. Systematic and disciplined speculation is a lot better than random, emotionally motivated impressions."[144]

Brodie examines more recent conflicts, including the Korean War and the decision, which Brodie at the time agreed with but later came to question, not to use nuclear weapons, as well as the decision, which Brodie had faulted in numerous other papers, articles, chapters, and lectures, to reduce offensive pressure on the opponent during the peace negotiations, which "was done for the sake of making a gesture—a sort of goodwill gesture" of the sort "[w]e tend to feel . . . is morally good to make"—but which Brodie came to believe prolonged the war unnecessarily, and in the end disadvantaged the American position. On the decision not to use nuclear weapons in Korea, Brodie recalls that at the time, "we only had only a small stockpile, which we wished to hold in reserve for what our leaders thought was the more threatening situation in Europe," and that commanders in the field "did not at that time think that nuclear weapons had much tactical utility."[145] Brodie writes how he had "thought at the time that it was the better part of wisdom that we did not use them," but has since revisited the decision, finding "[m]y present attitude is that I'm not so sure," as the "Chinese Communists intervened in that war after we had been fighting for about five months and after we had suffered defeats without being provoked to use nuclear weapons," leading Brodie to forever wonder, "Would they have intervened if we had used them? The answer is not clear, but it is worth considering."[146] As for "[o]ur relaxation of the pressure" during the armistice negotiations, Brodie believes this "gave them the chance to save themselves, to restore their army from a condition of absolute demoralization," and "of course also relieved the pressure on the Communist negotiators," whose "result was that war dragged on for something over two years," while Brodie remains convinced "that had we continued that offensive until an armistice was actually signed—as nations at war have always done in the past—the negotiations would have lasted a few days to a week rather than over two years, and the terms would have been much more favorable to us," and Beijing "would not now be calling the United States a 'paper tiger,'" a label Brodie fears "does us harm in a way that may ultimately cost lives."[147]

Brodie next examines the Berlin crisis, which he notes has been a "continuing crisis," and which presents us with "another opportunity for examining certain presumably 'moral' attitudes," finding that as with the Korean armistice negotiations, moral sensitivities can inadvertently contribute to even greater moral challenges as a direct consequence. As evident in the festering Berlin crisis, the very same moral hazards revealed by the pre-World War II peaceful change advocates who tried in vain to appease aggression before recognizing the danger of their misplaced moralism, Brodie observed that "[t]hose words 'negotiation' and 'compromise' have in our times certain moral overtones," but he "must ask simply . . . negotiate what? compromise what? It seems quite clear from even a casual study of the record that every change that has been made since the end of World War II . . . has been a change in the Russian favor, without exception. Often these changes have been brought about illegally through a *fait accompli*, which we did not thereafter challenge,"[148] but which Brodie believes—had we shown greater determination and leveraged our considerable knowledge of the opponent—may have been prevented. As Brodie writes, "It is in this area particularly that sophisticated knowledge about Russian behavior is extremely pertinent. We find that these minor aggressions are in fact probes, many of which are trivial—pin-pricks, affronts against our dignity rather than anything else"—such as the many seemingly minor violations of the agreement of occupation, such as Russian insistence that American officials "show their papers at checkpoints" or that American troops "dismount when the caravan is stopped for checking on the autobahn."[149]

As Brodie observes, the "tendency of the uninformed is to say that a person of wisdom grants these things, which are obviously not important. But a person of wisdom does not grant these things, because they *are* important. They are important because they are intended by the Russians as probes to see how much we will tolerate, and to achieve gradually accumulating gains through steady erosion of our resistance. Informed people are generally convinced that we should resist vigorously the most minor aggressions; that it is not wise to ignore pin-pricks; and that initial resistance will save us from more serious confrontations later on."[150]

This became especially apparent to Brodie during the Cuban missile crisis of 1962, which he has examined at length in many of his writings, and which he observes "seems to bear this out. One of the important questions to ask about the Cuban crisis is *why* did the Russians put missiles and bomber aircraft into Cuba only to show themselves ready to take them out the moment they were confronted with our readiness to use force?"[151] Brodie believes that it was "clear that they put the missiles in not because they were willing to take great risks, which clearly they were not, but because they thought from our preceding behavior that we would let them get away with it."[152] Brodie believes instead that "we must have flashed them the wrong signals in the year and a half preceding that week of crisis," and that we "could have been spared the confrontation that finally did take place in October 1962 if we had previously convinced the Russians that we would not in fact tolerate missiles and bomber aircraft in Cuba. Was it really so hard to do so?"[153]

Brodie's notes "one of the things the Cuba episode proved, at least to me, is the benefit in terms of wear and tear on the nerves of being strong. When the crisis broke, I personally lost no sleep over it. I felt utterly confident that this crisis would not deteriorate into war."[154] In this confidence, Brodie revealed his faith in the stability of the bipolar order that had taken root in the post-Hiroshima world—and that it would hold throughout the diplomatic crisis. As Brodie explains, "This confidence separated me from some of my friends, and I am sure it annoyed them. I felt this confidence simply because I had information which convinced me that we were enormously superior in every important branch of arms to the Russians, and that *they knew it*. And knowing a few other things about the Russians, I was about as confident as one can possibly be under those circumstances that no conflict would come of it. I was sure that when they realized we meant what we said, they would yield. They would and could take no other course."[155] Brodie is thus skeptical of those, like "Walter Lippmann and Joseph Alsop, among others" who "rushed forward with a round burst of applause for our government for its 'wisdom' and 'statesmanship' in granting the opponent a broad avenue of gracious retreat, thus sparing him excessive humiliation," a view Brodie presents as "another example of emotion suffused by sweet moral feeling getting the better of our knowledge." Indeed, he found that "[t]hroughout the Cuban crisis, Khrushchev acted absolutely in the classic Bolshevik pattern," which "demands, whenever retreats are necessary, disdain for the fear of suffering 'humiliation.' "[156]

From these experiences—Korea, Berlin, and Cuba—Brodie draws enduring lessons on not just morals but also *moralism* in the realm of strategy, finding that excessive moralism can contribute to a perception of weakness that ultimately fuels aggression, as learned so tragically during the interwar years when idealism sought to constrain the darker ambitions of an expansionist aggressor through the earnest but in the end misguided effort to appease him. This leads him to reaffirm his belief in realism, which if properly exercised, yields many moral dividends. As he explains, on the matter of negotiating with an opponent, particularly the Soviet opponent, "it is obvious that they should always be calculated to serve the national interest. If this is disputed, I would ask: What other interests should they serve? After all, we enter these negotiations as a national entity. The persons empowered to carry out negotiations for us are empowered to do so for the country by the national Administration. World peace is also a national interest of the United States, and the charge cannot stand that the Administration is likely to be forgetful of that."[157] Importantly, "before making any far-reaching decisions of national policy, whether for negotiations or for any-thing else," Brodie counsels that "we must take full account of the nature of the situation and the nature of our opponent. In many important instances there is far more relevant knowledge avail-able to us than non-specialists are in a position to understand. The entire burden of my argument is that this knowledge should be further cultivated, and it should be applied. This brings us back to the ultimate and traditional morality of politics as well as strategy—the obligation to acquire and to apply the relevant knowledge, and to do so courageously. The injunction to avoid what is dangerous and evil is superfluous. Knowledge tells us what is or is not unduly dangerous, and in issues of war and peace only moral monsters have the wrong values."[158]

Some Further Thoughts on Escalation

Brodie would soon revisit escalation in longer form authoring a book-length treatise on the subject whose first appearance came in a June 1965 RAND Research Memorandum, and which with minor changes was published the next year in book form by Princeton University Press. As Brodie had noted in his preliminary 1962 discussion of escalation, attitudes in the United States continue to change with regard to limited war, and the climate of fear and anxiety that had contributed to what Brodie felt to be a dangerous persistence of massive retaliation as strategic doctrine continued to soften as deterrence continued to hold along the central front, and as the principal Cold War adversaries continued to grow accustomed to each other's destructive capa-bilities, separating those to some degree from their intentions and from that separation forging ahead with new relationships designed to last.

With this continuing reduction of anxiety, Brodie found that the earlier resistance to limited war thinking in official circles also began to soften; and so in this context, in June 1965 he would author a lengthy RAND Research Memorandum (RM-4544-PR), *Escalation and the Nuclear Option*, that became the next year an uncharacteristically thin volume for Brodie—whose earlier works were considerably more voluminous, from his 786-page doctoral thesis to his 432-page *Strategy in the Missile Age*—bearing Princeton University Press' imprint, just over 150 pages in length including its index, with the same title as his RAND report. While Brodie's classic text *Strategy in the Missile Age*, authored in 1959, was followed quickly the next year by Herman Kahn's *On Thermonuclear War*, which took a then-contrarian view on nuclear warfighting and directly challenged Brodie's impassioned advocacy of deterrence and more cautionary approach to the dangers of escalation, Brodie's later volume on escalation came to press the year after Kahn's own *relatively* thin work—at 300 pages, less than half the length of *On Thermonuclear War* but still twice the length of Brodie's treatment of this subject—on escalation, published in 1965: *On Escalation: Metaphors and Scenarios.*

But this publishing sequence does not suggest Brodie's volume was a direct response to Kahn's, since as he notes in his introduction to the published version of his treatise on escalation, "I should mention Mr. Kahn's most recent work," but it "unfortunately, was published too late to be of assistance to me in writing the essay which follows, especially since the latter had to spend some time in going through clearance. Otherwise I should have had more than one occasion to mention it."[159] That his RAND report was published midway through 1965 also contributed to the absence of full discussion of Kahn's work, since a juxtaposition of the text of the two versions of this work shows only minor, cosmetic changes to the RAND report by the editors at Princeton, who elected to leave its content alone (with the exception of the appendix added to the work, a very brief September 1964 RAND paper by Brodie, *The Intractability of States*).

As Schelling would later observe in his tribute to Brodie upon his death: "By the middle 1960s he had to change sides on a number of policies to oppose 'carrying an intrinsically good idea so much too far,' publishing the brief and slightly polemical *Escalation and the Nuclear Option*," which paid a revisit to the question of nuclear use during limited war, and his earlier reluctance to cross the nuclear threshold, and thereby risk the danger of uncontrolled escalation. With deterrence showing signs of both stability and endurance, Brodie felt compelled to reconsider some of his earlier ideas that were formulated during times of greater international anxiety and see if they had withstood not just the passage of time but the increased survivability of the great powers' nuclear arsenals.

Brodie starts out the published edition of his treatise on escalation with something of a confession: first, that he had expected to further "develop and expand" his manuscript prior to publication so it would be "a substantially larger book," but it took so long to gain the necessary clearances that he ended up only adding the "present Introduction" to the work, and including as an appendix the paper he presented to a panel at the 1964 American Psychological Association conference on "Pacifism, Martyrdom, and Appeasement: Dealing with Intractable State by Non-Violent Means," which provided Brodie with a chance to rebuke the pacifist's perspective and at the same time reinforce his belief that psychology and strategy are somehow bound, perhaps by the same intangible threat that Clausewitz noted joined the physical and moral in war.[160] While the "reader is perhaps advantaged thereby," as the "book has less weight, can be read faster, and is cheaper to buy," it does seem that Brodie himself was disappointed by the book's relatively light nature, even though he acknowledged that "[t]o expand is not always to improve."[161]

His preface to the RAND Memorandum of the same title issued the year before (and largely the same substance, less the introduction crafted for the Princeton edition), Brodie further notes that his effort "represents a tentative effort to introduce some fresh thoughts into the discussion of escalation and its relation to the use of tactical nuclear weapons," and "stresses the importance, in making any choice of strategies, including the decision to use or refrain from using nuclear weapons, of gauging the *intent* behind the opponent's military moves," which Brodie contends "should not be difficult," particularly when it comes to differentiating between "a probe or a determined aggression."[162] Brodie's study "also suggests that the use or threat of use of tactical nuclear weapons may often be counterescalatory" and thus "may check rather than promote the expansion of hostilities."[163] As in the Princeton volume, in his RAND Memorandum, Brodie seems self-conscious with regard to the light nature of the work, and explains that in his belief that "the study of escalation needs more systematic study than it has yet received," he thus "hopes to develop a larger and more comprehensive analysis" of the topic as well as "an intensive survey of the literature."[164]

In his "Introduction" crafted for the 1966 Princeton edition of *Escalation and the Nuclear Option*, Brodie also starts off apologetically, noting he "presents an argument," albeit one he hopes is "respectably analytical and even objective," as he has "tried to be fair to opposing arguments."[165] His opponents, he admits, "had has an astonishing success both among students of strategic affairs and among those responsible for determining . . . official defense policies," and with publication of this work, Brodie expresses his hope "to take my leave" of the debate, though he expects "the subject is bound to continue to be important for a long time to come." Brodie sounds a regretful tone in writing "[m]y in this controversy can hardly be one to give me great satisfaction," as he had found himself "obliged to defend the idea of using or threatening to use tactically what J. Robert Oppenheimer has recently called 'that miserable bomb.' Who can enjoy finding himself in a position which, besides being somewhat lonely intellectually, seems by contrast with that of the opposition to be more than a little insensitive, heartless, and even wicked?"[166] Add to this the "irony" that "I have been opposing a position which—as the record shows—I played a special part in helping to create,"[167] and since the dawn of the thermonuclear era, he "began to urge . . . we must seek means of limiting war, even between the superpowers, and also of avoiding too exclusive a dependence on nuclear means of fighting," a view that may even have seemed "trite" at the time of *Escalation and the Nuclear Option* but which at the time he first articulated it required "the fortitude to be willing to appear something of a crackpot—even within the RAND organization itself."[168] Indeed, he recalls that "[e]ven as late as the Quemoy crisis of 1958, few of our combat aircraft had bomb-racks suitable for carrying 'conventional' or non-nuclear bombs,"[169] so any armed intervention would have required "nuclear means" owing to our seeming "insufficient conventional capability."[170] Brodie recalls being "consistently critical of the official views and policies of the time, which I held to be excessively obsessed with general nuclear war."[171] But now, midway through the 1960s, Brodie found that "times have changed," with "ideas of limited war and of non-nuclear fighting . . . very much in the air."[172]

While Brodie credits the "nuclear genie" with "some useful service," namely by "critically reducing the probability of war" between the superpowers, he understands why "all civilized persons must share in greater or less degree a desire to put the nuclear genie back in the bottle," but he nonetheless feels compelled to "plead for keeping and indeed expanding the benefits that have come to us from that same 'miserable bomb',," and thereby avoiding "the cost and possibly even danger of carrying an intrinsically good idea much too far, and with so much excess of fervor and religiosity, that it becomes a crippling obsession," and thus allow for the continued "self-denial" of a limited, tactical nuclear option. Brodie thus hopes to counter those views, official and otherwise, that "inhibit unduly our capacity to use—or much more important, our capacity effectively to threaten to use—nuclear weapons on the tactical level."[173] He thus takes aim at the "allegedly self-propelling escalatory effect of any use of nuclear weapons,"[174] a fear he had once held during the prior era of heightened nuclear risk.

Though Brodie had admitted from the outset of his introductory chapter that he had "been engaged in this debate,"[175] he later modified this somewhat by explaining it was only a "debate" in the academic sense of the word, "as a sort of intellectual courtesy," but that in fact he found there has "in fact been a conspicuous lack of any real debate," in part because only a "very small"[176] number of people were "responsible for developing the leading ideas in the strategic thinking of our time,"[177] making it easy for an idea to "win what looks like overwhelming acceptance" and thus for the small brotherhood of strategic thinkers to come to "apparent consensus," as "has certainly been the case with the 'conventional war' idea," leaving important questions on the use of tactical weapons "hardly at all discussed publicly,"[178] presumably reflecting "a lack of real rumination . . . within classified studies."[179]

While Brodie's work was written concurrently with Kahn's *On Escalation* and thus does not address his contemporary's current thoughts on escalation, he does reference Kahn's earlier *On Thermonuclear War*, mildly rebuking Kahn for what could describe as strategic shallowness, or perhaps not thinking hard enough about the unthinkable. Brodie cites the way Kahn described "when an engineer puts up a structure designed to last twenty years or so, 'he does not ask, 'Will it stand up on a pleasant June day?' He asks how it performs under stress, under hurricane, earthquake, snow load, fire, flood, thieves, fools, and vandals.' "[180] To this Brodie adds, "One should add, however, that the warranted strength of the structure also depends on its purpose, on the anticipation of the *probability* of some of the catastrophes above mentioned during the use span envisioned, and in many cases on the choice between having a structure able to cope with the worst possible catastrophes and not having one at all. Few dwellings are built to withstand tornadoes, and few architects would suggest that they should be. All but a minute fraction of these structures last out their natural lives without suffering such visitations or various other of the catastrophes that Kahn mentions."[181] And these probabilities, when specifically applied to the risk of nuclear war and not to the metaphorical examples of catastrophes mentioned by Kahn, have considerably declined, and Brodie notes "one of the striking changes in the climate of the times since Kahn published the above-quoted lines," is that "the same bomb that caused the fears of fifties to which Kahn was giving expression at the end of that decade has caused also the more relaxed attitude of the sixties," and thus a "remarkable change" in the "prevailing climate of expectation concerning the probability of future catastrophe."[182]

Brodie closes his introductory chapter with one further apology, noting he has "been taxed by some of my colleagues with the reminder that I had in the past asserted in print that there was no essential difference between tactical and strategic nuclear weapons to warrant the distinction in terminology," to which he admits, adding his view has now changed "on the grounds that technology has indeed moved on to the point where there are already very marked distinctions and where there could be even sharper ones if we exploited more of the possibilities for specialized bombs."[183] So in addition to his admitted "past error," Brodie notes the emergence of a "large family of weapons which are specifically intended for possible tactical use and would rarely if ever be considered for strategic use."[184] But when it comes to the "much more important point of criticism" that Brodie has put himself "in the position of arguing for the use or threat of use, when appropriate, of specific types of weapons in a limited and essentially tightly controlled manner, even though existing arrangements may make it quite difficult or even impossible to exercise such control," Brodie concedes the latter point "is probably true," but he finds this "criticism irrelevant over the long term," since "whatever tactical nuclear doctrine we have is obsolete and ought to be altered," and that the neglect of "small-scale, controlled use" of tactical nuclear weapons "should be corrected, and with some urgency," so that they may play their role "primarily as a deterrent and, if they fail in that function, as a de-escalating device." Hence Brodie's determination to counter the belief that tactical weapons are "in fact the opposite," a tool not of de-escalation but of escalation itself.[185] There becomes his thesis, which he presents in greater detail in subsequent chapters of his work.

In his next chapter, "Escalatory Fears and the Effectiveness of Local Resistance," which marked the first chapter of his RAND Memorandum on escalation, Brodie revisits his observation on the profound shift in international anxiety, and how "[n]ot long ago it was only the sudden surprise onset" of nuclear war "that was considered a real possibility," with an "overwhelming" temptation to strike first in the event hostilities commence. But by the mid-1960s, "the conviction has spread and deepened that in the future, so long as we keep something like our present posture, general war can hardly occur except through escalation from lesser conflicts."[186] Now, added Brodie, "the constraints to refrain from strategic nuclear attack . . . have become great and also obvious,"[187] driven by both physical and psychological changes, the former being "the enormous and continuing improvement in the security of our retaliatory forces . . . against attack through the well-known devices of hardening, concealment, and mobility," and the latter because "[o]ur confidence is further increased by the fact that this physical change has served to buttress a comparably profound psychological change" borne of "improved understanding . . . of the motivations and psychology of the opponent."[188] Recalling Dulles' speech on massive retaliation, Brodie writes "[t]he time for insisting mainly on such strategies, or rather threats, is clearly past," and American policy had "for some time been committing us to the principle that local aggressions on the part of our major opponents must at least initially be resisted locally," and this means, Brodie unhesitatingly affirms, "[t]he possibility of further escalation will, to be sure, be unavoidably but also usefully present," as it will "tend to induce caution on both sides" and "more especially tend to dissuade the aggressor from testing very far the efficacy of a *resolute* local defense."[189]

An irony of the strategic relaxation Brodie has observed is that the "very easement of the danger of surprise strategic attack has stimulated a special fear of what in quite recent times has come to be called escalation," which now appears to be "the only way, or at any rate much the least unlikely way, in which general war can occur."[190] In earlier years when the fear was that "any outbreak of unambiguous hostilities . . . would escalate almost immediately to general war," Brodie explains, strategic thinkers "therefore concentrated our concern on avoiding the outbreak of war, rather than on the escalation that we feared must surely follow such an outbreak."[191] Once the prospect of limit war was imagined, "escalation, which is to say the erosion or collapse of limitations, became quite appropriately the object of special attention," and Brodie found that "the abhorrence that most civilized people feel towards nuclear weapons" shifted to "the *tactical* use of such weapons in limited war," driven in part by a widely held presumption "that use of them in limited war would be *critical in tripping off uncontrolled escalation*."[192]

And while avoidance of any use of nuclear weapons might be politically desirable, Brodie questions the automaticity, even if he cannot disprove the possibility, that "resort to such weapons could be the critical factor in provoking uncontrolled escalation," he suggests the opposite may also be true, that "a weapon which is feared and abhorred is so much the less likely to be use *automatically* in response to any kind of signal."[193] But even this fundamental ambiguity cannot change the fact that "views attributing a powerful and automatic escalatory stimulus to nuclear weapons—views not the less firmly advanced for being based entirely on intuition—have been of critical importance in molding attitudes toward appropriate strategies in the event of limited war," and "thereby greatly affected force postures" and the "whole gamut of national defense policies."[194]

Brodie next considers "The Methodological Problem" (he changed the title of this chapter to "The Analytical Problem" in his next year's Princeton release), a very brief chapter of just five pages that considers the challenges inherent in realistically estimating "the risks of escalation," in which he explains that "we are dealing . . . with issues of human behavior under great emotional stress in circumstances that have never been experienced,"[195] and as a consequence, "the appropriate degree of fear or dread on both sides is thus only dimly imagined."[196] He argues that there are thus "no special tools, devices, or gimmicks by which we may drastically improve our predictions concerning the chances of escalation in any crisis," and while using "such techniques as war or crisis gaming helps importantly to enlarge the perspectives of the players . . . it does not provide them, or those who read their reports, with answers to the crucial questions," nor with "the kind and degree of emotional tension and feeling of high responsibility bound to be present among decision-makers in real life crises in the nuclear era."[197] War gaming and crisis simulation may nonetheless provide us with a useful analytical tool, albeit one which, Brodie notes, for "present purposes the improvement of the players' 'conceptions and understandings' of the world they live in is much more essential to our ends than the use of the game technique itself."[198]

Brodie next considers "The Relevant Image of the Opponent," since "[e]stimating probabilities of escalation is essentially an exercise in predicting the behavior" of both our opponent's and our own leaders "under various kinds of crisis situations."[199] Brodie believes that Soviet leaders, as well as those in Communist China, were fully aware of the "terrible hazards of general nuclear war,"[200] as evidenced by not only the statements of Soviet leaders but also their relatively restrained behavior during various crises including the 1948 and 1961 Berlin crises, and during the 1962 Cuban Missile Crisis, where Khrushchev's ultimate decision to remove the missiles must "surely modify one's estimate of his boldness in putting the missiles in," leading Brodie to comment: "Khrushchev may have been foolish, but was he really being foolhardy?"[201] (In the Princeton volume published the next year, Brodie adds the following sentence, further clarifying his view on Khrushchev's relatively moderate behavior: "Clearly he not only did not want war, but he thought he was taking no real risk of it."[202]) Brodie in fact chides the United States for "having made a bad prediction" about Soviet behavior, adding this "does not itself justify our calling the Russian 'unpredictable.' "[203] Indeed, Brodie finds Soviet behavior during the Cold War period to have been impressively restrained, with "no infringement of frontiers and not the slightest skirmish between their troops and ours,"[204] suggesting that arguments made by the United States to justify a buildup of NATO's conventional forces fostered "an image of the Soviet Union which inflates Soviet military aggressiveness" (in Brodie's Princeton revision the next year, he changed "inflates" to "grossly inflated.") [205]

Brodie's reading of history suggests that concerns about accidental escalation are also overblown, with events ranging from Hitler's invasion of Poland to China's intervention in the Korean War, upon closer analysis appear not to be evidence of "accidental" wars, even if there was indeed some "miscalculation" involved in the decision-making; indeed, Brodie sees in Korea evidence not of the dangers of accidental escalation but "the degree to which escalation was in fact controlled and stopped."[206] As earlier discussed in our philosophical examination of realism, which has at times been juxtaposed to idealism when in fact the two philosophies have more in common than many appreciate, the core difference in world views can be attributed to contrary dispositions, one toward optimism and the other toward pessimism. Those alarmed by the prospects of uncontrolled escalation can be described as pessimists, in contrast to Brodie who looks to history and concludes such concerns are overstated, finding in history enough solace to emerge an optimist on this matter.

Thus Brodie asks, "What should now cause accidental war . . . to become more probable in a nuclear age than it has been in the past?"[207] He considers and dismisses "the possibility of gadgetry malfunctioning," noting "extensive and elaborate precautionary measures" have been taken; and he also considers and dismisses the likelihood that unintended clashes between opposing units would tend to escalate, not finding evidence of the necessary "limitless concern with saving face" nor the sufficient "ground-in automaticity of response and counterresponse" to ensure "a swiftly accelerating ascent in scale of violence."[208]

Brodie admits that it "would be foolish and irresponsible to insist that accidental war is impossible" or even that "efforts to picture its occurrence in scenarios," which is part of the subtitle of Kahn's own work on the topic, "are misguided," and adds that "No doubt the capability for dreaming up 'far out' events is to be cultivated and cherished, but so is the capability for applying a disciplined judgment about the probability of those events."[209] Indeed, grappling with the interplay of chance and probability, Brodie acknowledges that "important things happen that few had previously thought probable—occasionally things that no one had conceived of."[210] But he adds "[t]hat does not, however, establish that we must consequently abandon the notion that some things are very much more probable than others, and that with appropriate study we can have a good deal to say about which is which."[211] It is Brodie's belief that "[t]hough it is good to be imaginative and important to keep an open mind, it is imperative to avoid basing far-reaching policy decisions on contingencies which can be called conceivable only because someone has conceived of them."[212]

Brodie's next chapter, also very brief at just over four pages, addresses "The Attenuation of Incentives For 'Going First'," in which he further develops his view that the "rapidly diminishing . . . advantage and thus incentive of going first in any *strategic* exchange" . . . "must have a great and possibly decisive influence in reducing the danger of uncontrolled escalation following from any local outbreak."[213] Brodie cites a 1963 statement from Defense Secretary McNamara that illustrates American recognition that "the degree of advantage that was until recently thought to accrue to the side making a surprise strategic attack—where it could hope to wipe out the retaliatory force of the opponent with near impunity—is gone and not likely to return."[214] Or, as Brodie explained in a new paragraph added to the end of this chapter in the Princeton release the next year, "the opportunities for a 'first strike' are rapidly diminishing if not already gone."[215]

In "What Is the Enemy Up To?" Brodie starts off by commenting that "much of the public discussion concerning the appropriate time for introducing nuclear weapons in tactical operations has neglected to consider the enemy's intention," and instead has concerned the "mechanical phenomena, like the scale of hostilities reached or the rate at which territory is being yielded," rather than what Brodie believes "the first consideration" should be: "What is the enemy up to?"[216] (In the revised edition released by Princeton the next year, Brodie strengthens his opening remark to: "It is amazing but true that practically all public discussion," from "much of the public discussion."[217]) Brodie is confident that "upon the outbreak of any real hostilities," our opponent's intentions are "likely . . . to be fairly obvious," and no longer cloaked by such a "probable obscurity."[218] Indeed, Brodie points out that a "deliberate major aggression will look very different from a probing action," and in his 1966 revision augmented this by adding to this, "out of which 'accidental' wars are supposed to grow."[219] This means, Brodie contends, that "[f]or the sake of deterrence, and also to reassure our allies, it would seem appropriate to relate flexibility of response mainly *to discrimination of enemy intent.* That would make more sense than saying, as we have in effect said in the past: 'We will use conventional weapons until we find ourselves losing.' "[220] Brodie suggests instead that since "the possibility of a deliberate massive Soviet attack against western Europe is exceedingly remote, so much the more reason for avoiding ambiguity concerning our response to it."[221]

Brodie observes that even as "the idea that sudden general or strategic war between the great nuclear powers has become extremely improbable," many observers "seem to find unsettling the effects of that conclusion upon their estimate of the probabilities of war on any lesser scale," and "seem to be tacitly . . . assuming that the probability of *some* kind of war occurring has remained basically fixed," implying that with the risk of general war lessened, "that limited war (including quite large-scale limited war) has become more so!"[222] Brodie considers the risk of general war in Europe, finding it to be highly implausible; he notes a Soviet attack upon Western Europe "would be the kind of operation that would come closest to triggering the general war that they are, with good reason, desperately anxious to avoid," leading him to speculate that if it does occur, it "must come about through escalation from Soviet probing actions," or barring that, from "an attack by us upon them," as Soviet ideology long expected to be the more likely scenario.[223] Brodie believes that "the most fruitful question we could ask about the use of nuclear weapons in tactical operations . . . would be: How could their use, or non-use, or threat of use affect the prospects for the occurrence of escalation from small-scale to large-scale combat."[224] Added Brodie: "We should not to be talking, at least not initially, about using a great many nuclear weapons; that is a possibility that occurs only after a conflict has already graduated to large proportions. We are interested mainly in seeing how it can be prevented from ever reaching such proportions. We are interested, in other words, in the deterrence of escalation—though not for a moment are we less interested in the deterrence of initial hostilities."[225]

Brodie found that "the phrase 'if deterrence fails' rolls rather too readily off the tongue among those many defense specialists whose work requires them to think about what happens in actual combat," but he believes we should also ponder "some all-important intermediate questions, like: Why should deterrence fail? How could it fail? How can we keep it from failing?"[226] With the exception of facing "utter madmen," Brodie believes "there is no conceivable reason why in any showdown with the Soviet Union, appropriate manipulations of force and threats of force . . . cannot prevent deterrence from failing."[227]

Brodie next turns to "The Status Quo as a Standard," in which he argues avoiding "major war without politically disastrous retreats implies . . . that we have preferably a commanding superiority in our overall force posture" or "at least a position that we cannot be induced to recognize as inferior" and "that there be some standard in the world by which both sides can . . . simultaneously distinguish acceptable behavior from the intolerably deviant kind."[228] On the former, Brodie recalls from history that assessing superiority "has always had more complications than appeared on the surface," but that "[i]n our own time the problem has become enormously more complicated as a result of the special intolerability of nuclear devastation."[229] Brodie places great import on maintaining the status quo, since "things-as-they-happen-to-be," in strategic affairs, are "conspicuously inseparable from peace,"[230] with an added plus being its maintenance is "usually also supported by international law."[231] Even in Europe, with its division into East and West and the formal division of Germany into two states, however temporary that arrangement was envisioned to be, Brodie observed that the "territorial status quo has gained markedly in sanctity in the nuclear era,"[232] as "both sides . . . definitely prefer a not too unhappy peace to any kind of war," and thus "appear reconciled to continuing indefinitely what was once recognized by both to be a temporary state of affairs," an "indispensable consensus" that "does not exclude what we used to call 'peaceful change'."[233] Even those who advocated German reunification came to believe such change had to occur "*ohne Krieg*—without war."[234]

It is within this context, of preserving the status quo, and thus maintaining the peace, that Brodie puts forth his argument for the tactical use of nuclear weapons. They no longer become a tool of escalation so much as the means by which aggression can be withstood. His intention is to thus restore to the discussion a proper balancing of ends and means, which had become disentangled as opponents of nuclear use, in their horror at the thought of risking escalation, in effect deflated aggression, even massive aggression, from its proper scale. As Brodie explains: "However, the debate on nuclear versus conventional strategies or 'options' has so sharply focused men's minds on the dread consequences of using nuclear weapons tactically that the very act of aggression that might invoke these possibilities has been excessively deflated by comparison. In many discussions of the issue, the fact of aggression is given about the emotional loading of an enemy prank. It is supposed to be contained in a manner that is effective but at the same time tolerant and wise. The argument . . . that we should be unambiguous at least about opposing with nuclear arms any deliberate and massive Soviet attack in Europe is in one sense only a plea to resume treating such aggression with the seriousness it deserves."[235]

In his next chapter, "On Enemy Capabilities Versus Intentions," Brodie takes up the riddle of "whether our defense preparations and planning must be responsive to enemy capabilities or to enemy intentions," and concludes the "answer has to be, and is inevitably, to 'both'."[236] The former presents a necessary measure for comparing "their strength and ours,"[237] but it's only one factor to keep in mind. The latter helps us to determine "not only the magnitude but also the character of our preparations," even though such assessments are "generally considered to be more subjective, tenuous, and faulty" than measurements of capabilities.[238] When contemplating the potential response by an opponent to a crisis, Brodie finds, "[i]n our spontaneous, entirely intuited, ambivalent, and highly uncertain answers . . . are wrapped up all our fears and doubts about escalation," and he thus concludes that "*The control of escalation is an exercise in deterrence,*" and that means, at "inducing the enemy to confine his actions to levels far below those delimited by his capabilities."[239] In a parenthetical note Brodie added just before press time to the close of his next chapter, "The New and Different Europe," in the 1966 Princeton release of *Escalation and the Nuclear Option* on this very dynamic nature of deterrence, which requires efforts to induce restraint by pushing back against the probing efforts of the opponent in an effort to hold violence to sustainably low levels, Brodie lauds the efforts and the courage displayed by President Kennedy during the Cuban Missile Crisis, and rebukes the critical remarks of reviewer I. F. Stone in his review of Elie Abel's 1966 *The Missile Crisis* for suggesting that Kennedy's audacity was of itself dangerous, with Stone placing his fears of escalation before what Brodie believes to be the greater risk of Soviet aggression. As Brodie explains: "with respect to the Cuban missile crisis . . . when this book first went to press I thought it quite unnecessary to point out that against an opponent given to probing an occasional *confrontation* was an essential ingredient of deterrence. However, a review-article by I. F. Stone . . . was one long expression of horror that President Kennedy had had the audacity to make this confrontation. Mr. Stone did not hesitate to attribute the late President's action to his vanity. In view of the extremely favorable outcome of that confrontation, one would have thought it incumbent upon Mr. Stone at least to speculate on what might have been the consequences had Kennedy lacked the courage to make it."[240]

In the next chapter, "How Big an Attack?," Brodie again takes up his earlier proposition that a massive Soviet attack against NATO across the central front "ought to be put among the lowest levels of probability," despite the fact it "happens to be the kind of war outbreak in Europe that has been most discussed in official circles."[241] (In his 1966 revision for Princeton, Brodie notes this need not be "necessarily paradoxical" since "it is the existence of NATO that makes, or helps to make, the probability of Soviet attack so low."[242]) But while such massive attacks defined modern European warfare prior to the nuclear era, Brodie believes the splitting of the atom forever changed things, and in the post-Hiroshima world, "it is virtually impossible to discover in the real world the considerations that could make the Soviet leaders undertake to do such a thing in the face of minimum gains and the enormous risks they would be incurring."[243] This leads him to "assign a far higher probability to the breaking out of conflicts on a small scale initially rather than on a grand scale," and to predict that "neither side will be able seriously and convincingly to use for political ends threats of strategic nuclear attack, or anything that in scale is even close to it."[244] Instead, Brodie asserts, "What one can threaten are lesser actions that *could* start events moving in that direction," and as the "opponent cannot at any stage be deprived of the choice . . . of making the situation more dangerous or less so; but we can reasonably hope and expect to influence his choices appropriately. This is what we must henceforth mean by containing aggression militarily."[245] (In his 1966 revision, Brodie added the word deterrence to this sentence for clarity: "what we must henceforth mean by deterrence, or by containing aggression militarily."[246]) In Brodie's formulation, deterrence itself becomes a more dynamic enterprise, whose aim shifts in emphasis from preventing total war to containing escalation by restraining the military aggression of the opponent, which of itself means by threatening, and engaging in, limited wars to prevent aggression from increasing toward totality. Brodie presents his new thinking as follows, explaining that "[o]ur military measures ought, so far as possible, (a) to be effective enough initially to prevent extensive deterioration of the military situation, especially such deterioration as basically alters the character of that situation; (b) to be limited enough to leave unused, at least temporarily, such higher levels of violence as are not likely to be immediately necessary to accomplish the objective stated under (a)—levels which must be most unattractive for the enemy to enter; and (c) to be determined enough to show that we are not more unwilling than he to move toward those higher levels."[247]

Brodie further points out that "(b) simply defines limited war" while "(c) establishes what *is* essential to effective containment through limited means,"[248] and thus "[w]ithout (c) we either lose outright, or we encourage the enemy to move to higher levels of violence in which we avoid losing only by following him,"[249] hence Brodie's support of Kennedy's courage during the Cuban Missile Crisis showdown, and his determination to persuade the Soviet Union that he was certainly no more unwilling than they to move higher on what would later become popularly known as the escalation ladder.

Brodie next continues his exploration of the nuclear threshold, or what he calls "The 'Firebreak' Theory," with the "firebreak" signifying "at the tactical level the distinction between the use and non-use of nuclear weapons," a term he attributes to Alain C. Enthoven that had come to prominence, usurping Brodie's own less elegant phrase, "vast *watershed* of difference" between nuclear and non-nuclear weapons.[250] The notion of such a firebreak had gained so wide a following that Brodie found "almost everyone must now subscribe to the firebreak idea," even if the "notion that the atomic bomb is 'just another weapon' was . . . not wholly illogical," even if it was "insensitive to the importance of a distinction, however arbitrary, that most of the world was obviously going to insist upon."[251] (In his 1966 revisions, Brodie strengthened his comment on the near universal acceptance of the firebreak theory to: "almost every thinking person must now subscribe to the firebreak idea."[252]) While America's non-use of atomic weapons in Korea reflected that war's "certain special circumstances not likely to be repeated in the future,"[253] Brodie does find relevant to the future the high level of anxiety "mere mention of nuclear weapons by the President" generated in British Prime Minister Atlee, which illustrated how "since the beginning of the nuclear era there has been in the minds of men a strong tendency to distinguish between nuclear and non-nuclear weapons, combined with a widespread fear of and aversion to the former" which has grown "stronger with time rather than weaker."[254] While Brodie takes care to differentiate between "[r]ecognition of that important fact" and its advocacy, he does note that as of his writing in the mid-1960s and in contrast to the previous decade that "a nearly universal consensus exists within the ranks of professional military people that small military operations are simply out of bounds so far as concerns the use of nuclear weapons,"[255] and that this "consensus unquestionably extends over a fairly considerable and quite important zone of contingencies."[256] Further, Brodie notes the United States now "possesses a substantial non-nuclear capability" sufficient to redress a "quasi-accidental outbreak of fighting or small foray" of the sort that confronted America during the 1958 Quemoy crisis, so much so that it was now "most doubtful that any voices would be raised, as some then were, to insist that we ought to intervene with nuclear weapons or not at all."[257] (Indeed, in Brodie's 1966 revisions, he added that America's "large conventional commitment to Vietnam" was "proof of that."[258]) And while the "more enthusiastic advocates" of firebreak theory advocate "building up our conventional capabilities" to enable postponing "introducing nuclear weapons until a very high level of military operations is reached," Brodie cautions that their logic may be flawed, as "the standard argument for rejecting as a useful firebreak any discrimination according to *size* of nuclear weapons is that it gives the enemy too much opportunity to mistake or deliberately exaggerate the size of the bombs one has used, and thus to proceed to larger ones. One never senses in connection with this argument any inclination to question whether the enemy will *want* to do so, an issue that would surely predominate over the question of his capacity to discriminate."[259] (In his 1966 revisions, Brodie adds to this, "He might very well want to do the opposite."[260])

Further, Brodie suspects the formal introduction of a firebreak would contribute to an unhesitating escalation up to that level of violence so determined, and his analysis of the Cuban Missile Crisis suggests to him that the United States was likely the beneficiary of the absence of such a notion, as the Soviets "clearly wanted no fighting at all" given their fear that "*any* fighting was extremely dangerous," a viewpoint they may not have had if a firebreak had been established or asserted.[261] Brodie suspects it was the absence of a firebreak that resulted in "the immediate amelioration in the tension over Berlin"[262] that followed the crisis in Cuba, even though "the Russians enjoy local conventional superiority."[263] Brodie finds that the "firebreak proponents seem to feel that the present anti-firebreak Soviet attitude *may* help deterrence but is much more dangerous to us if deterrence fails. For that reason they want to speed up Soviet acceptance of the idea, which they regard as anyway inevitable. One might in passing notice in this reasoning the interesting differentiation between what are alleged to be deterrence interests and what are alleged to be war-fighting interests."[264] It is this bifurcation of deterrence and warfighting interests that came to define a major cleavage within the field of strategic theory, and which carried over to doctrinal and policy debates through to the end of the Cold War, without ever truly being resolved. Partly why, of course, is the artificial nature of this bifurcation, when the fundamental ambiguity inherent in deterrence suggests the absence of a clear boundary separating deterrence from warfighting, which thrives in the absence of such clarity. Hence clear assertions of nuclear non-use, whether the firebreak concept discussed by Brodie in this chapter, or the later notion of no-first-use that became popular toward the end of the Cold War period, may in fact increase the likelihood of war, which of itself could increase the probability of escalation to nuclear war, thus clashing with the original intent of the declarations.

Brodie notes that when the Chinese intervened in the Korean war it came only after "five months of watching us fight, sometimes desperately, without nuclear weapons —a fact which could be relevant," a view supported by the work of Allen S. Whiting in his 1960 *China Crosses the Yalu: The Decision to Enter the Korean War.*[265] (Brodie strengthened this speculation in his

1966 revisions with more affirmative wording: "a fact which was unquestionably relevant and could have been important."[266]) Brodie suggests that quite contrary to the firebreak theorists, it may in fact be more in America's interest to "soften" and not "promote further . . . those distinctions between nuclear and non-nuclear weapons," as had been done by many American officials in their efforts, largely unsuccessful, to "induce our European allies to build up their conventional forces."[267] At the very least, Brodie believes "we cannot avoid debating on its merit a question as important as this one,"[268] and hence turns in his next and final chapter to "Predicting the Probabilities of Escalation: Some Sample Cases," which at twenty-seven pages (twenty-two as the pages were laid out in the 1966 revision published by Princeton University Press) is one of the longest in his book. Brodie starts out be reiterating his belief that "wherever deterrence-of-war objectives diverge from either war-fighting or anti-escalation objectives, as they inevitably do in important ways, it would be seriously wrong to sell the former short."[269]

While he finds most defense experts then believed America's system of deterrence, in particular its "powerful and low-vulnerability strategic bombing system," faced "little danger, at least in the near-term, of being challenged," Brodie remained concerned with the consequences of deterrence failing, and believed we must "consider what to do militarily if it does," and this means "considering how and under what circumstances it will have failed."[270] He thus considers a scenario relating to a show-down over a Berlin convoy that risks escalating toward accidental war, which leads Brodie to ponder "the circumstances that can really make such a situation . . . go out of control,"[271] which he finds "boil down basically to two categories of factors,"[272]: "the prevalence of rigid mechanisms of military response such as do tend or at least have tended in the past to pervade war-initiation concepts and also to get written into war plans," and "that bundle of psychological factors summed up by (a) concern with loss of face and (b) tendencies to yield to feelings of hatred and rage."[273] He noted with both interest and alarm that after the Cuban Missile Crisis, there was a "tendency to think or at least to talk in such simplistic but absolute terms" as conveyed by such "common expressions about 'pushing the button' or 'the balloon going up,'" in spite of the "sophistication they had presumably been accumulating in the preceding months concerning the appropriateness of flexible response and the feasibility of limited operations."[274] But on the other hand, Brodie, ever the deterrence theorist, finds such a "crisis-induced regression to older patterns of thinking about war and peace" to be complementary to deterrence objectives since "the fear of precisely such semi-automatic escalatory reactions on the part of the opponent acts as a powerful deterrent to both sides,"[275] and the "present intensity of such fears among all the major powers" shows how much Europe in the Cold War differed from "what it was before 1914 or even 1939."[276] Brodie finds these fears to be "counterescalatory at lower levels of violence, and that the levels at which automatic or spontaneous escalation may tend to take over are being pushed critically higher," strengthening deterrence by "moving towards much higher levels of tolerance for types of behavior that previously would have been considered impossibly offensive."[277]

As for saving face, Brodie suggests "[a]n imputed universal preoccupation with saving face" undergirds "why most people so readily assume that resort to nuclear weapons must make for spontaneous escalation."[278] But history shows when it comes to choosing between saving face, or saving your country from destruction, nations, even superpowers, will choose the latter, hence the reason "the Soviet Union backed down in Cuba," and why the United States "to a considerable degree back down in Korea . . . when it quite clearly modified its objectives as a result of Chinese intervention."[279] Whether it's rage or humiliation, Brodie found that "governments, even Communist dictatorships, tend today to be corporate entities in which emotional feelings of individuals, regardless of how highly placed, are likely to be moderated and contained by the counsels of their advisers."[280] When turning back to his scenario of an escalating conflict over the convoy supplying Berlin, Brodie argues that "one of the great drawbacks of following the so-called firebreak theory is that the more that confidence is built up in the firebreak, the less is each side restrained from committing larger and larger conventional forces within the limits of its capabilities. In other words, the effect is to stimulate escalation on the conventional side of the barrier."[281] If for any reason NATO forces had not achieved conventional parity with the Soviet side, Brodie explains, this would leave NATO with an uncomfortable choice between a conventional rout, or to escalate with a nuclear threat to counter the strategic imbalance on the ground.

Brodie fully expects such a nuclear threat would de-escalate the crisis, rather than contribute to an escalatory cycle past the nuclear threshold, since in this scenario the conflict has been largely accidental, and not reflective of the desire of either party for war. Hence the Soviet Union, when faced with a nuclear risk, would have no reason to counter, much as it had no reason to challenge the American threat in Cuba. And even if the Russians do not back down, and show an uncharacteristic recklessness, Brodie believes American resolve, if demonstrated "by using the weapons rather more abruptly than the Russians seem to have bargained for," might well be "the best way, perhaps the only way, for us to avert not only defeat but unnecessary escalation."[282] Of course, Brodie recognizes it remains an open question "whether our own leaders could marshal the necessary psychological resources to introduce the use of nuclear weapon and to outbid any Soviet use," but while "it is one thing to say we could not," he finds that it's "quite another to say we should not,"[283] which advocates of both a conventional build-up in Europe and of the firebreak theory were strongly suggesting if not outright counseling. Brodie notes his speculative scenarios "encompassed only cases in which a relatively small number of nuclear weapons are used more or less in demonstrations"[284] (and in his 1966 revisions adds that he recognizes "[t]here could be variations on this theme, including fairly wide use of small and highly specialized weapons—but the essential issue is maintaining tight control.")[285] Lacking that, Brodie explains, would mean that it would no longer be the case that "both sides share a common determination to avoid going into an exchange that is many, many times more costly than any imaginable political goal could be justify," and this would mean "we are inevitably back in the world of massive retaliation."[286]

Brodie considers the situation in Asia, noting our prior non-use of nuclear weapons in the Korean War, and he speculates that for various reasons, whether "some romantic . . . spirit of fair play" or our being "restrained by the firebreak idea," it remained "quite possible that we could fight another war in the Far East as large as the Korean War without using nuclear weapons."[287] But this would mean "going about the job in the hard way," while at the same time causing "repercussions for the future that would in the net be not to our liking," as "we will have fixed for [our opponent] a pattern" of our non-use of nuclear weapons that "they have every further incentive to exploit."[288] America's "gigantic nuclear capabilities" had "already been appreciably cut down in their effectiveness for deterring aggression by what might be called established world opinion opposed to their use,"[289] and Brodie cautions that "it behooves us to examine much more carefully than we have thus far some of the main propositions and arguments commonly made in support of our own drive to push even further toward what is in effect the psychological self-neutralization of our nuclear capabilities."[290] Brodie counter charges that "we have not really faced up to the awful risks inherent in miscalculation" by arguing that such "risks are something that we have to measure as best we can," and his discussion of escalation in the above pages reflected his "effort to contribute to such measurement," on his realist assessment that "[w]e cannot forfeit the task simply by allowing in advance such gross exaggeration of the risks as to 'play it safe'" particularly as a 'second look quickly tells us that we do not really add to our safety by doing so."[291]

Psychology and Escalation: The Intractability of States

In the 1966 Princeton University Press edition of *Escalation and the Nuclear Option*, Brodie includes as an appendix his September 1964 RAND Paper (P-2970), "The Intractability of

States: A Distinctive Problem," which he had prepared for delivery on a panel on "Pacifism, Martyrdom, and Appeasement: Dealing with Intractable States by Non-Violent Means" at the 1964 American Psychological Association conference, one of the rare revisits that he makes to the topic he probed as a student of Wright in 1938, appeasement—then widely called *peaceful change*.[292] His inclusion of this paper is intriguing, reinforcing his belief in the need for considering the psychological dimensions of escalation that are all-too often overlooked by more mechanistic and metaphorical discussions of the subject, notably by Herman Kahn and his detailed but largely emotionally antiseptic escalation ladder (colorfully described in 1970 by Raymond Aron as surreal and the strategic equivalent of science fiction in his chapter, "Modern Strategic Thought" in his Praeger volume *Problems of Modern Strategy*. As Aron writes, Kahn "imagines, invents, and describes with minuteness bordering on unreality, dozens of situations of conflict reduced to simplified schemes, and the decisions that suit these situations. Failing science fiction, what other name but strategic fiction could one give to this form of literature?"[293])

Brodie starts his paper by humbly noting as "an outsider who seeks to advise psychologists how they should think about war and peace, or rather about 'pacifism, martyrdom, and appeasement,' " that he was "suddenly aware of [his] ignorance how in fact they do think about these matters."[294] He added that he did have "more than the usual number of psychoanalysts" among his "friends and acquaintances,"[295] and was known to have been an open and outspoken advocate of psychoanalysis at RAND. In this paper, he considers the role of psychology in statecraft, and the relevance of applying psychology to deterrence and escalation; but he dismisses drawing direct parallels between the psychology of the individual and the behavior of national governments, noting a limit to the relevance of psychoanalysis when analyzing aggregates of human beings beyond the singular individual. In what seems like a mild rebuke of his hosts, he notes that within the context of treating a "deeply disturbed" individual patient, "it is a mark of competence in such a physician that he is able to do so by non-violent means."[296] With regard to the title of his panel, Brodie notes the words selected to convey nonviolence—pacifism, martyrdom, and appeasement—suggest "something not merely non-violent, but definitely passive and even masochistic," and are thus "not a triumph over violence but rather a surrender to it."[297] Brodie thus addresses "the imagery provoked" by these words, which he finds to "reflect individual and personal rather than state behavior."[298]

Brodie believes that "[i]f we speak about influencing an 'intractable' adversary, it makes an enormous difference whether we are speaking about a person or about a government of a great nation," even though governments "are of course made up of persons, and we have reason for feeling that we have by now learned a great deal about the behavior of persons. Especially in our own century, with its deep exploration of the realm of the unconscious."[299] But Brodie, despite his own faith in the probing and revelatory powers of psychoanalysis, and its ability to extract insight from the hidden chaos of human thought itself, cautions that "it is important to realize that we know very little about the influence of personal psychology on the behavior of states," despite the best efforts of pioneering political psychologists like "Howard D. Lasswell and others, who attempted to bring to the study of politics, including international politics, the then relatively novel and revolutionary insights of psychoanalysis."[300] Even knowing state behavior is ultimately "a direct result"[301] of individual decision-making, and even though Brodie has faith that democratic governance "works pretty well" in generating leaders who are "generally healthy psychically rather than the reverse," and even if "we could materially improve by appropriate selective and also therapeutic processes the psychic and emotional equipment of those who govern us," Brodie remains firm in his belief that "we would have moved on the whole a relatively little distance towards curing or even materially improving the situation we have in mind when we speak of problems of war and peace."[302] This is partly because political decision-making involves "many factors that greatly modify the emotional and other psychological elements which so directly influence individual behavior," and state behavior results more from "decisions reached by groups rather than by individuals," with a longer "time factor between stimulus and response," though exceptions to these general trends do happen.[303]

An historical examination of two recent crises, the 1950 decision to intervene in Korea, and the 1962 decision to respond assertively in Cuba, suggests "another enormous difference between the behavior of states and that of individuals," namely that our adversary was in both cases "an abstraction," and thus our confrontations in both Korea and Cuba "were not of the face-to-face character so often characteristic of personal relations and so important a factor in those relations."[304] Brodie finds it "most important of all" that "governmental behavior is modified not only by the cultural milieus but also by the national traditions and by the distinctive political precepts which may characterize each of the several parties to the confrontation."[305] In both cases considered, Brodie found we were facing "an adversary whose avowed political precepts, goals, and modes of behavior were quite different from ours."[306] This does not mean "the psychological make-up of our own policy-makers . . . is unimportant," just that "we must beware of generalizing too easily from the area of personal behavior to that of government."[307] Brodie believes that when it comes to "learning how to deal with states led by difficult or hostile governments, clinical experience with intractable patients is not only unlikely to be of help" but also "to be deceptive,"[308] as "the intractability of states is sure to be a totally different phenomenon from that of individuals."[309] Because of inherent differences in the political traditions, cultures, and systems of governance of states, it is natural for there to be mutual misunderstandings and misapprehensions, but these "derive from something other psychopathology," and with competing ideologies, Brodie adds: "[w]e are bound to be opposed to their goals, and also have special problems in interpreting what is after all a system extraordinarily different from our own." Thus, Brodie concludes, any "resulting misperception and misjudgment are obviously completely compatible with having men in power on both sides who are about as healthy psychically as anyone could reasonably expect them to be."[310]

This does not mean that Brodie rejects the utility of psychology as a tool "to contribute in improving our understanding of the relations between states, and especially of the optimum means of avoiding violence between states," as he believes "it has a very great deal to offer," but not primarily for "relations between states."[311] Rather, Brodie expects psychology can yield more useful insights for examining "the relations of individuals within each state," since psychology can better explain "those areas I which human beings interact as persons rather than as corporate and abstract entities called governments."[312] To understand interstate behavior, and in particular "how wars may be avoided," Brodie suggests we can gain more from "understanding the character of state power, meaning primarily military power, and how it is developed and used in order to effect the major ends of state power."[313]

Brodie thus reaches back to the very origins of realism in political theory, right to the heart of Thucydides' realism, and his effort to fathom the underlying causal currents of the Peloponnesian War, and echoes a hint of Machiavelli who grounded his political philosophy in a realist assessment of political power as the primary means of imposing order on a chaotic and dangerous world. Brodie's underlying philosophy, the backdrop to his nuclear strategic theorizing, and his effort to somehow tame the nuclear genie and render its destructive power a means for inducing peace, is thus classically realist, tied to his understanding of history and its somber lessons. As a realist, Brodie believes that one of the ends of state power "is certainly the maintenance of peace without the sacrifice of important values or without accepting any ultimate degradation of our position."[314] This contrasts with the pacifist, who "turns his back on power in a world which governments hostile to our own use power to pursue what even he, the pacifist, considers inimical goals."[315] Brodie concludes, "I think that is why the pacifist has been generally ineffective in our time," as he "refuses to have anything to do with that power, which, when correctly developed and well handled can account for the favorable resolution of a crisis,"[316] as demonstrated in Cuba. Thus it becomes "important to know what kind of confrontation to make and how to appraise its results," even though "[t]he answers to such questions are certainly not obvious."[317]

In addition to understanding state power, Brodie believes we can also greatly benefit from a "thorough knowledge of the special idiosyncrasies of [our] adversary," and not "as a human being or group of human beings but as a complex of people organized as a state with distinctive political institutions," so that we may gain some insight into "the interpretations that an opponent widely removed from us in culture and in political doctrine will put upon our actions."[318] These insights will require broad expertise in the nature of our opponent, which means even if our experts are in possession of "considerable psychological insight," that this knowledge, "while real," will not be "necessarily commanding."[319] Instead, Brodie believes, our experts should employ "other kinds of equipment," and in particular analytical tools that help to form a complete "image of the opposing head of state as a part of a highly idiosyncratic political apparatus rather than as a representative human being."[320]

Escalation and the Nuclear Option was favorably reviewed, with one sympathetic review authored by fellow RANDite and Soviet military strategist Thomas W. Wolfe in the January 12, 1967 issue of *The Reporter*, "The Levels of Nuclear Strategy."[321] As Wolfe writes: "Most people believe that it would be a fine thing if the nuclear genie could be put back in the bottle. However, in a world where technology and politics together have given the nuclear age a seemingly irreversible character, men must learn to live with the genie in their midst."[322] And while "[n]o one can predict how this awesome and enormously complex learning process will ultimately turn out," he notes that "[i]n the meantime, there are obviously wide differences of view concerning the lessons to be drawn from the world's nuclear experience to date, including those lessons pertinent to the place of nuclear weapons in the U.S. defense policy," and "[t]his is brought home anew by the latest of Bernard Brodie's many contributions to nuclear-age strategic thought. In an earlier influential work, *Strategy in the Missile Age*, Brodie—once a member of the RAND Corporation and now a professor at the University of California at Los Angeles—had cautioned against overdependence on strategic nuclear power at a time when the doctrine of massive retaliation still dominated American strategic planning."[323] Now, adds Wolfe, "In his new book, *Escalation and the Nuclear Option*, he again swims against the stream of prevailing opinion, now questioning the wisdom of building up NATO's conventional forces in Europe as a substitute for reliance on tactical nuclear weapons."[324] As Wolfe describes:

> As Professor Brodie sees it, deterrence on the strategic level has worked and is likely to keep on working, particularly since the greatly reduced vulnerability of strategic retaliatory forces has largely removed any incentive to strike first. But deterrence must also operate at lower levels of possible conflict in order to ensure against escalation to major dimensions of warfare. It is here, and especially in the case of Europe, to which his essay is mainly devoted, that Professor Brodie finds cause for concern.
>
> His argument—a great deal of which touches upon familiar issues in the running controversy of the past few years over a suitable position for NATO—can be summarized thus: The effort to enlarge NATO's conventional forces substantially in order to broaden the available options, up to that of dealing if necessary with a deliberate large-scale Soviet aggression, has been both redundant and bad for deterrence, besides having unwelcome political effects upon the alliance: redundant because the strategic stalemate and Soviet prudence make a blatant Soviet assault on Europe highly unlikely; bad for deterrence because raising the tactical nuclear threshold may encourage the idea that it is safe to allow minor military conflict to grow to considerable scale without danger of nuclear escalation. Hence, in Professor Brodie's

view, the best policy to ensure against escalation of possible low-scale conflict or to deter hostilities in the first place would be to retain an unambiguous tactical nuclear option. By the same token, what should be avoided is a policy that might give the Soviet Union unambiguous assurance that nuclear risks no longer apply.[325]

Wolfe notes that in "a sense, Brodie's position has been partly overtaken by events and the passage of time, as he himself recognizes by noting that U.S. preoccupation with NATO's conventional forces has given way somewhat to 'stressing the rapid growth of our store of tactical nuclear weapons in Europe, coupled with renewed affirmation that they would be used if necessary,' " adding this "narrows the argument essentially to this question: Under what circumstances would NATO's resort to tactical nuclear weapons be judged 'necessary'; and unless ambiguity about this is removed in advance, is deterrence likely to suffer seriously?"[326] Wolfe contends that "[o]ne may say that there has never been much ambiguity at the extreme but unlikely ends of the spectrum," and "[s]hort of deep and dramatic change in the political situation, for instance, it is clearly unlikely that a no-use commitment would be given, so as not to create temptation, destabilize the delicate military balance, and so on. And, as President Kennedy once put it, referring to the other and equally unlikely extreme, 'In some circumstances we must be prepared to use the nuclear weapon at the start, come what may—a clear attack on Western Europe, for example.' "[327] But "[a]s for the indeterminate zone in between these extremes, and this is where the search for broader 'options' has been carried on," Wolfe observes, "decision makers have been manifestly reluctant to be pinned down to precise definition of the circumstances that would call for a nuclear decision. Although this has doubtless lent ambiguity to the nuclear response that might follow some forms of aggression, deterrence thus far has not failed, despite the existence of uncertainty, or perhaps even because of it. Recognizing the tendency of governments to resolve their choices in favor of what seems to be working, one may therefore suspect that there will be no official stampede to heed Professor Brodie's plea for less ambiguity."[328]

Another positive review of Brodie's *Escalation and the Nuclear Option* was sent to Brodie on January 6, 1966 by John W. Chapman of the University of Pittsburgh, the associate editor of *NOMOS: Yearbook of the American Society for Political and Legal Philosophy (ASPLP)*. Chapman's comments are especially interesting in that he makes an explicit connection linking Brodie's theoretical and philosophical response to the bomb with Hobbes' own efforts in an earlier time, and would in two years author an article in the January–February 1967 edition of *Air University Review*, "American Strategic Thinking," comparing the strategic thinking of Brodie, Kahn, and Schelling that considers their respective efforts with reference to Hobbes' earlier endeavor to forge order during a time of great chaos: "Dear Mr. Brodie, I thank you for your kindness in sending me your articles. I am delighted to have them, and they could not have arrived more opportunely as I am just starting off on my seminar on strategy. May I say that I thought "Escalation and the Nuclear Option" immensely cogent and impressive. Surely it cannot help but alter thinking appropriately! You may wish to know that I have been trying to interest the ASPLP in holding a meeting and producing a *NOMOS* volume on the subject of strategy, or more broadly, security. It seems to be that you and your colleagues have done and continue to do the job that Hobbes did in another time of troubles, namely, logically to formulate the conditions of security, and I should like to add, with equal success. Many have been saying that political theory is dead. I think not. It just goes on, as it always has, on the frontiers!"[329]

A June 1967 review in *Choice* described the work as an "extension of many articles and two books" by Brodie, calling it a "useful addition to books such as: *On Escalation: Metaphors and Scenarios*" by Herman Kahn, and noting "Brodie contends that American reluctance to use tactical nuclear weapons is leading to the neutralization of that kind of capability, both in terms of deterrence, and the ability to use such weapons," and "calls for reexamination of the reasons given in support of the non-use philosophy, i.e. fear of war, fear of escalation after war has begun, fear of nuclear proliferation. In an appendix Brodie criticizes attempts to understand the behavior of intractable nations by studying the clinical experiences of intractable individuals."[330] The Spring 1967 edition of *The Key Reporter* writes that "a former RAND expert fears that by overstressing the need to keep wars limited and arguing that the use of tactical nuclear weapons will inevitably escalate to total war, we have come close to depriving ourselves of a valuable option should the need to employ it arise."[331] And in the Summer 1967 *Current Thought on Peace and War*, editor L. Larry Leonard from the Department of Political Science at Wisconsin State University writes: "In choosing strategies for the future, the importance of avoiding exclusion of the option to threaten use of tactical nuclear weapons should be stressed. Considering the need to fix on the intent behind an opponent's military moves, the deterrent effects of America's gigantic nuclear capabilities have already been diminished by our own repeated statements of reluctance to use them. Assuming that extreme nuclear restraint in our strategic planning will help us to avoid war or to reduce the probability of escalation is an error. This erroneous assumption and others like it are generally derived from an intuition which is at odds with our historical, psychological, and political knowledge. This volume includes chapters on: escalatory fears and the effectiveness of local resistance; the relevant image of the opponent; the attenuation of incentives for 'going first;' what the enemy is up to; the status quo as a standard; on enemy capabilities versus intentions; the new and different Europe; how big an attack; the 'firebreak' theory; predicting the probabilities of escalation: some sample cases."[332]

In a longer review in the May 1967 edition of London's Royal United Service Institution *RUSI Journal*, sent to Brodie "With the Compliments of the Editor" on June 16, 1967, it is recalled that: "When John Kennedy succeeded General Eisenhower as President of the United States in January 1961, strategic policy turned, largely due to his influence, from reliance on the nuclear deterrent and re-oriented itself on the idea of limited war and of non-nuclear fighting. Kennedy's pronounced aim was to put 'the nuclear genie back in the bottle,' and to build up conventional forces. Professor Brodie, who until recently was a member of the Rand Corporation, is concerned with the use of 'tactical nuclear weapons primarily as a deterrent, and, if they fail in that function, as a de-escalating device'. In particular he urges that immediate attention should be paid to the development of specialized tactical nuclear weapons to be used on a strictly controlled and small scale basis.. . . This is a small volume packed with thought-provoking material, as one might expect from the author of *Strategy in the Missile Age*."[333]

How Not to Lead an Alliance: Brodie vs. McNamara

After his year in France, Brodie "returned to his duties at RAND as a thoroughgoing Francophile," which Newell Bringhurst notes "added a new dimension to ongoing difficulties with various RAND colleagues, a significant number of whom were strong Anglophiles who looked upon the flamboyant, independent Charles de Gaulle with suspicion and disdain for having pulled France out of NATO, seeming to abandon the United States and other cold war allies. Bernard, by contrast, admired France for asserting itself as an independent third force between the United States and the Soviet Union, and this pro-French position accentuated his loner status at RAND." Brodie was "disappointed at not having been asked to join the New Frontier defense analysts in Washington following John F. Kennedy's 1960 election. His expectations had been raised as the new secretary of defense, Robert S. McNamara, recruited a number of Brodie's colleagues at RAND. Brodie himself seemed destined for appointment, given his well-known Democratic leanings–and the fact that John F. Kennedy himself had personally expressed his favorable reaction to Bernard's recently published Strategy in the Missile Age." But working against this ambition, "Brodie's views on tactical nuclear warfare were at variance with those of important officials in the Kennedy administration. His reputation as a loner–not a team player– also worked against his appointment. He was, according to at least two close RAND associates, outspoken and unwilling to 'adapt his views to . . . conventional wisdom.' Brodie himself blamed his longtime nemesis at RAND, Albert Wohlstetter" who "had been able to 'gather round him- self a veritable court' of individuals at RAND . . . who, according to Brodie, were 'not quite of the first rank intellectually, but nevertheless very able.' Yet Wohlstetter had an inside track that enabled to get his people appointed. 'All of the so-called "whiz kids" around McNamara were either members of [Wohlstetter's] original RAND following . . . or people who were intellec- tually beholden to them,' Brodie claimed, whereas he himself, not being one of Wohlstetter's favored persons, was passed over." Brodie nonetheless remained "active in his own research and writing" and "continued to be outspoken and blunt regarding American foreign policy, and his views reflected the deep division of opinion among RAND people." His May 1963 article in The Reporter ("What Price Conventional Capabilities in Europe") "further isolated him from various RAND colleagues. According to one observer, Bernard 'occasionally displayed a savage temper and a bristling ego, especially if he thought others were robbing his ideas.'"[334]

One of Brodie's most critical—and public—assaults on McNamara's CWE strategy and his approach to relations with the Atlantic Alliance would be made in his March 9, 1967 article in The Reporter, "How Not to Lead an Alliance," whose title captured in six harsh words how little con- fidence Brodie had in the administration and its defense chief, particularly in light of De Gaulle's decision in 1966—after years of discord with NATO—to ask all non-French NATO troops to quit French soil. As recounted by Edward Cody in the Washington Post, "President Charles de Gaulle infuriated the United States when he suddenly pulled France out of NATO's military command in 1966, arguing he had to preserve French independence in world affairs."[335] NATO's internal tensions had been swirling since De Gaulle ascended to the French presidency in January 1959; he had opposed American dominance of the alliance and its close relationship with England, and had sought a mire equitable tri-partite directorate to run the alliance; as early as March 11, 1959 France withdrew its Mediterranean Fleet from NATO's command, and later that year he banned foreign nuclear weapons from French soil. By 1966, all French forces were removed from NATO's military command, and when all non-French troops were asked to depart, it necessitated the relo- cation of Supreme Headquarters Allied Powers Europe (SHAPE) from France to Belgium, though France remained a member of the alliance, albeit an independent-minded one.

Brodie lamented sharp tensions between France and the alliance, writing that the "North Atlantic Treaty Organization has now lost one of its two major continental powers, and is clearly diminished by more than that very substantial loss," and was as a consequence "presently mov- ing its most meaningful organ, SHAPE . . . from the western outskirts of Paris to a corner of Belgium called Casteau, references to which are usually amplified with the information that it is 'near Mons,' which some of us last heard of as a place the British Army retreated from in the early days of the First World War."[336] At the same time, the North Atlantic Council was moving from Paris to Brussels. Brodie suggested that NATO was perhaps nearing its demise, and "[a]lthough one hesitates to call an international body dead to which many good and some quite able people are still devoting considerable energies, we know from long experience that organizations may go through the motions of being alive while being in fact spent. NATO seems to be in or approach- ing that condition."[337] As the "United States has been the acknowledged leader of NATO," Brodie writes that "we really have to ask, first, how much did our actions contribute to or provoke de Gaulle's behavior, and second, what did we do independently to supplement or amplify the nega- tive consequences of his actions?"[338] Brodie believes that the "key U.S. decision in this respect . . . was the rejection of de Gaulle's proposal to President Eisenhower in the autumn of 1958 that a sort of directorate be formed comprising France, Britain, and the United States," and Brodie believes that "among the real reasons" for America's rejection of France's effort "was that the United States did not wish the intrusion of French advice concerning its foreign policies, especially in areas outside Europe, such as Africa—or Vietnam."[339] Brodie adds that "the United States by this rejection asserted its unwillingness to water down or share its extraordinarily dominant role in the Organization" while "[i]n French eyes it was seeking to keep France on a level with Luxembourg."[340] Brodie also notes the harm caused in 1961 by the "hortatory and scornful public comments that Secretary of Defense Robert S. McNamara directed toward the French nuclear program, which we wanted to see abandoned," and which, Brodie adds, was "incredibly clumsy diplomacy on our part, because it should have been obvious that de Gaulle would not in the slightest degree be deflected from his course by our castigations."[341] Brodie adds that "we should not have expected Frenchmen to appreciate the reasons for our overtly differentiating between the British nuclear effort, which we regretted but found excusable, and the French effort, which we condemned."[342]

But Brodie suspects these "irritations we thereby inflicted on our ally were probably secondary in importance to the support our remarks gave to some already deeply embedded French and German suspicions . . . that American insistence on maintaining monopoly control within the alliance of its nuclear power reflected a diminishing reliability of that power, and "[t]his apprehension was strongly enhanced by our concurrent pressure upon our allies to build up their conventional forces for a strictly conventional role," a policy Brodie had long—and vehemently—opposed.[343] As Brodie explains, "Our repeated insistence that the United States was absolutely to be trusted in these vital nuclear matters, and that American views concerning them were not at all subject to change into the indefinite future, could of course not be taken seriously by any reasonable European with some sense for history—least of all a Frenchman who has a tradition of skepticism about political morality and who should hardly be asked to attribute to the United States a sharply higher degree of morality and fidelity than he can possibly accord his own country. Must we ask him to believe that Frenchmen and Britons but not Americans are capable of a Munich-type sellout? And especially in the nuclear age?"[344]

Brodie proceeds to lambast the Americans for their arrogance in their relations with Europe, recalling how "[s]ince its beginning. American officials having anything to do with NATO have usually been sure that they understood far better than the Europeans the problems of European defense and their solution, and they did little or nothing to avoid projecting that conviction," though Brodie notes "[m]ost Europeans long accepted this claim as probably correct, partly because of the American near monopoly of nuclear weapons but more especially because of the initially impressive and peculiarly American efflorescence of strategic thinking and writing, especially on the part of highly intellectual civilians" from "institutions like the RAND Corporation which attracted to themselves not merely respect but mystique."[345] But "[i]n recent years," Brodie observes, "the Europeans have become increasingly disenchanted," partly in response to the "sudden and drastic changes in American strategic doctrine," which shifted from its earlier emphasis "on tactical as well as strategic nuclear weapons" to "the McNamara conception" favoring CWE, which reflected "a complete reversal" of the earlier American strategy.[346] While "[f]ive years may seem like a long enough time to warrant a basic change in thinking," Brodie points out that "each strategy was supposed to look indefinitely into the future."[347] Brodie recounts how his "[c]onversations with senior officials in European defense ministries or NATO delegations have tended increasingly in the last few years to expose complaints of American 'doctrinalism' and 'pushing,' to use the words of one of them," and "[f]rom being a highly respected figure, Secretary McNamara has for many, especially in Germany but by no means exclusively there, turned into the personification of all that is wrong with American leadership in NATO."[348]

As had become the case for much of Brodie's writing in this period, such as his 1965 review of William Kaufmann's 1964 book on McNamara, *The McNamara Strategy*, Brodie took the opportunity to again critique the firebreak theory, devoting the better part of a whole page of his seven-page article to the issue of the conventional buildup, noting this single issue "has perhaps caused more trouble in NATO and more disenchantment with American leadership than all the other issues put together."[349] He adds that the "ramifications of this idea have pervaded every aspect of our NATO relations," and while Brodie agreed "no sane person wants to see nuclear weapons exploding in anger either strategically or tactically, especially in densely populated Europe," he noted "[m]oreover, no one wants to see any kind of serious war breaking out in Europe, whether nuclear or non-nuclear" and that "the Europeans would rather see war avoided by the threat of using nuclear weapons than take the risks which might stem from letting that threat become ambiguous."[350] As Brodie explains, "Let us first be clear that we are talking not about skirmishes resulting from 'pinpricks' but about real war, usually conceived of as resulting from massive, deliberate, but somehow non-nuclear attack by the Soviet Union. No one questions the need for suitable conventional forces to deal with accidental outbreaks of violence along the frontiers or the Berlin autobahns. But one does not have to *build up* for these purposes."[351] But under the new strategic precepts embraced by McNamara, Brodie observes: "[a]ll our copious advice to the European countries about how they should arm themselves has stressed the importance of their preparing themselves for conventional combat."[352] But, Brodie points out, "[f]rom the European point of view, the objections to the American antinuclear doctrine may be summed up under two points—apart from the obvious one that the Russians could always match in kind a western conventional buildup," the first being that the "deterrence of large-scale war has been at least as important as attempting to avoid the use of nuclear weapons in such a war, the more so as deterrence appeared nearly certain of accomplishment," and the second being that the "European leaders felt, in common with many of our own specialists in Kremlinology that the conventional-war arguments completely distorted the image of the opponent."[353] As Brodie explains, "It would in fact take an extraordinarily bold enemy to possess what the advocates of the doctrine imputed to him: not only a readiness to commit large-scale military aggression against the West, but a readiness to assault our nuclear-armed forces with conventional arms alone! The doctrine thus asserted that the Russians could be willing to enter a duel to the death while leaving to us the choice of weapons."[354] Some Europeans, particularly the Germans, were starting to show a preference for the French assessment of their mutual opponent, and "although de Gaulle's nuclear power is only a fraction that of the American, he at least knows how to use the advantage that power gives him."[355]

Further straining American relations with the Europeans, and also a reflection of the myopic view taken by McNamara on the matter of conventional forces, Brodie feels the need for "mentioning the American involvement in Vietnam, concerning which the Europeans were not consulted and in which the United States appears to have become increasingly absorbed to the growing exclusion of other concerns," and observes that "[p]ractically every European official or leader of opinion interviewed by this writer last fall expressed dismay at and inability to comprehend that involvement," most especially De Gaulle, who "filled with the sense of France's historic role in that area until only yesterday, a role which in fact continues in the French air patrolling of the Demilitarized Zone under its Geneva commitments," for whom "the absence of consultation was especially rankling."[356] Brodie reflects on how De Gaulle's "1958 proposal apparently asked for this kind of consultation, and in view of the situation we have got ourselves into in Vietnam, hindsight tells us we could have done worse than consult with him beforehand."[357]

Brodie recalls how the previous year, on March 30, 1966, "Senator Wayne Morse asked Secretary McNamara whether his Ann Arbor speech of four years earlier still held, and McNamara answered thus: 'I think that that speech, plus others that have been made by military and civilian officials of the Department, and other government representatives over the years, is gradually introducing some sense of realism in the thinking about nuclear forces. More and more

Frenchmen are beginning to realize that the force de frappe is not a true deterrent force in any sense of the word. It is a myth as far as deterrent force is concerned.' " Brodie responds to these remarks by noting, "If this kind of immobilism really reflects the views of the Secretary and his colleagues in the government, then the future of our efforts in Europe is not promising."[358] With the prospect of warming relations between the superpowers, Brodie believes it is more important than ever to consider the European perspective on issues of strategy: "What the French seem to fear most is that we will seek a detente with the Soviet Union in which they are left out. They are far from being opposed to such a detente, but they are determined to; be partners in it, and partners of the first rank. The British seem not to have the same fears of betrayal by us, and they still cherish their special relationship with the United States. But their eyes are turning increasingly toward Europe. They have long sought improved relations with the Soviet Union, and in this respect their policy seems to bear a close kinship to that of France—as well as to that of West Germany, whose new leaders appear to have concluded that the only hope for eventual reunification is by opening doors to the East. For all of them, the North Atlantic Treaty is an important backstop that can enable them to pursue openings to the East with steady eyes and without fear."[359] Brodie thus argues that it was now "time we let things loosen up, and doing so would win a new kind of respect for our leadership, which ought as much as possible to acknowledge the role of partnership. Such respect will certainly not be gained by our continuing to insist that nothing fundamental has changed."[360]

Dueling Views on Escalation

Just as John W. Chapman looked comparatively at Brodie and Kahn (along with Schelling) in his 1967 *Air University Review* article, "American Strategic Thinking," Fred Iklé would review the works of Brodie and Kahn, juxtaposing their ideas in an interesting side-by-side comparison of their two nearly simultaneous treatises on escalation: Kahn's 1965 *On Escalation: Metaphors and Scenarios* published by Frederick A. Praeger, and Brodie's 1966 *Escalation and the Nuclear Option*, published by Princeton University Press, which had published his 1959 *Strategy in the Missile Age*. In his July 1967 review in *World Politics,* Iklé observes that what became known as escalation since 1950, when the era of limited war began in earnest on the Korean peninsula, was really just a new label to describe an old process, one dating back to at least the Middle Ages, in which "one or both of the belligerents could have done significantly more to fight his enemy but chose not to do so" and instead limited the escalatory dynamic of war, preventing it from becoming total.[361] He notes that there are "many ways in which a limited war can become less limited and many reasons why, during a war, governments change the level of effort that they devote to bargaining, fighting, and deterrence," and each of these is "tucked under the label 'escalation' " today.[362] Iklé adds that the word escalation "makes us think of stepwise increments, each of which confronts the enemy with a noticeable challenge" and "suggests that such steps succeed each other up or down a 'ladder'."[363] It's precisely this image of a ladder that absorbs the attention of Herman Kahn, who Iklé notes was "aware that the metaphor of an 'escalation ladder' has serious shortcomings (to which he devotes a full chapter)" and "that the level of military effort (or violence) need not change in discrete steps"; Kahn thus "invented his forty-four steps precisely to remind us 'that there are many relatively continuous paths between a low-level crisis and an all-out war," and that in the fog of battle, "Both the distinct quality of a rung [on the ladder] and the distance between rungs can be blurred, particularly if a participant in the escalation wishes to blur them," and Iklé adds that "Kahn also makes the important point that the participants in a war will have different perceptions of these various levels or intensities of military power."[364]

Iklé suggests that "if we think in terms of a single ladder descending from here to hell, we are likely to overlook important trade-offs between an increment in one dimension and a decrement in another,"[365] but he notes "a sophisticated author like Kahn would be the first to recognize these trade-offs, and he begins his book by stressing that there are several ways to 'escalate' a conflict," whether heading vertically up or down the ladder or expanding geographically at the same rung (whether to an adjacent theater or to an altogether different region, in what he dubs "compound escalation.")[366] Kahn's taxonomy of escalatory steps include not just increments of hard power, but includes "economic sanctions and verbal or symbolic acts (hostile propaganda, declarations of war, and such).[367] While Kahn's book is "largely analytical in that it deals with a wide range of possibilities and takes up many aspects of escalation," Brodie's book is instead "essentially a plea for a change in U.S. policy, a plea that the United States give tactical nuclear weapons a greater role in NATO (to deter large-scale aggression) and cease to press for stronger conventional forces."[368] Iklé finds that what makes Brodie's book "somewhat frustrating to an exacting reader" is that the "various motives for and against nuclear escalation are inextricably intermingled in his easy-flowing prose."[369] As Iklé further describes: "On the one hand, he seems to argue that our use (or threatened use) of nuclear weapons would give us an advantage on the battlefield (or would threaten to do so)," while "[o]n the other hand, he seems to be uninterested in affecting the local military situation and instead wants to use tactical nuclear weapons merely to introduce 'the threat that leaves something to chance.' What we can threaten, Brodie argues, is some action that 'could escalate,' but we 'have to leave to the opponent in his next move the choice of making the situation more dangerous or less so . . .' In the event of large-scale Russian aggression, Brodie writes, 'the best way, perhaps the only way, for us to avert not only defeat but unnecessary escalation is to demonstrate clearly that our readiness to take risks is not less than theirs. How can we do that except by using [nuclear] weapons—demonstratively, few rather than many, and in as controlled a manner as possible, but nevertheless rather more abruptly than the Russians seem to have bargained for in launching their aggression?' But if it is Brodie's objective to increase the shared risk of nuclear war and to demonstrate our willingness to compete in this risk-taking, it is not at all clear why we need 'tactical' nuclear weapons. A single 'strategic' bomb against a military target might be just as effective, perhaps more controllable, and would certainly belong to a less vulnerable category of weapons."[370]

Iklé speculates that "[p]erhaps the fairest interpretation of Brodie's book is that he wants us to rely more on tactical nuclear weapons for both reasons: the better to defeat aggression locally, and to scare the enemy into retreat by raising the risk of further escalation. After the mid-1950's, the possibility of such a dual effect of our tactical nuclear weapons might indeed have helped to deter the Russians from military aggression against NATO or against Berlin, assuming the Russians had to be deterred at all. But the proposal that, in the future, NATO should rely more rather than less on this effect is a bit like walking over thin ice and then saying, 'Let's do it again—it was so nice and smooth!'[371] Iklé cautions that to "demonstrate our 'readiness to take risks' by exploding nuclear weapons that we call 'tactical' is not an appealing strategy for an alliance, particularly if this demonstration is to occur so close to our allies' heartland."[372]

Iklé is concerned that "once fighting has started and we then do introduce tactical nuclears, will the enemy know when the fighting has to stop? That is, will he know that he should stop instantly? Brodie's point is well taken, that the enemy would have a strong incentive to recognize our controlled, small-scale use of nuclears as such and that he would contemplate his option of responding in kind with utter dismay. But Brodie skips over the difficulties of war termination in suggesting that the enemy would be less 'willing to accept defeat (or even stalemate) in a battle that has remained conventional than in one that has gone nuclear,'"[373] and this raises for Iklé an important element in escalation overlooked by both Brodie and Kahn: that of the time dimension. "Even if the enemy did not respond in kind to our introduction of nuclears, he need not stop the advance of his conventional forces. His superior conventional forces might overcome our 'demonstration' use of tactical nuclears, if—as Brodie seems to recommend—our conventional forces were kept small relative to his and our use of nuclear weapons remained very limited. Should we then step up the use of nuclear weapons? Doing so might finally bring us success on the battlefield (assuming the enemy still withheld his nuclears), but it would confront us with the 'tactical' vulnerability problem: the fact that in the realm of 'tactical' nuclears, a large-scale first strike does pay. And if we therefore decided on a 'tactical preemption' instead of leaving this option to the enemy, could we rely on the firebreak between tactical and strategic weapons? Or should we go all the way? My point here is that we cannot separate the introduction of tactical nuclears from a certain willingness to threaten strategic nuclear war, or at least a willingness to move into some of Herman Kahn's 'bizarre' crises of 'limited strategic war.' "[374]

And while we "have some idea about how conventional wars are fought, what havoc they might cause, how they might become larger, and how the fighting can be stopped," Iklé is concerned that "[o]ur image of nuclear wars is a house of cards with one untested hypothesis piled upon another. The only thing we know fairly certainly are the physical effects of nuclear detonations. It is one of Brodie's themes that since conventional war can be so awful (and conventional preparations so costly), we should bring the nuclear deterrent up closer on the heels of conventional fighting."[375] Iklé agrees that "[t]his is a valid motive," but cautions that "we must not become smug about the reliability of nuclear deterrence. Deterrence, in the long run, is dangerous."[376] But despite the inherent dangers of deterrence, Iklé concedes that "[a]gainst the threat of strategic nuclear attack we may have no other choice-for decades to come—but to rely on deterrence."[377] But he disagrees with Brodie's recommendation that we counter Soviet conventional superiority with our tactical nuclear edge; "in view of the long-term danger just alluded to, it would seem prudent to choose strategies that will help to curtail the implements and role of nuclear deterrence."[378]

Iklé is aware that Brodie and Kahn are, in essence, debating, and that their dueling treatises are point and counterpoint in this debate; but he observes that "we cannot have a useful debate—much less intellectual progress—unless we make it clear where we agree and disagree,"[379] and he finds that this has been the case in these two works. "I would have found it useful if Bernard Brodie had related his themes more to the existing body of thought. He never mentions Schelling's 'threat that leaves something to chance,' and yet this is what he primarily seems to have in mind (if he does not, all the more important to say so). And, in a footnote, Brodie writes that Kahn's present book came too late for him to consider. Yet one wishes Brodie had added some linkages with Kahn's work (after all, he did have time to add an appendix after Kahn's book had come off the press). For instance, some of the points that seem to be missing in Brodie's criticism of the 'firebreak theory' can be found in Kahn's rich chapter on the nuclear threshold."[380] On the other hand, Iklé acknowledges that "Brodie meant to write one coherent essay, not a lexicon of cross-references."[381] In contrast, Kahn "is less willing to make sacrifices for the harmony of his prose" and "enjoys sticking in little asides" even if that affects his narrative flow, though at times his lucidity shines through, particularly, Iklé believes, in Kahn's Appendix, "Relevant Concepts and Language for the Discussion of Escalation," which he describes as "a masterpiece in comprehensiveness and lucid categorization" and which can serve as the foundation that "could become a truly definitive synopsis of the subject" with additional refinement, and believes that "one of the merits of Kahn's book that it deals with so many aspects of escalation," including important observations on the often-overlooked topic of war termination and de-escalation, as well as the complicated question of escalation dominance.[382]

Setback in Vietnam: How Not to Fight a Limited War

In his December 3, 1967 *Los Angeles Times* article, "Learning to Fight a Limited War," Brodie recalls how in December 1951, he joined a small committee at RAND of three with Dr. Ernest Plessett, chief of RAND's physics division, and the head of its economic division, Charles J. Hitch—later to become the president of the University of California. The committee was formed to "devise over the next two or three months individual briefings, for presentation to the Air Force and the secretary of defense, which would combine communication of the news that thermonuclear weapons were now feasible"—the first would be tested that coming November, but experts anticipated it would likely be successful—"with suggestions about the implications of those new weapons."[383] Brodie notes that his briefing "amounted to a plea for the study of a new kind of limited war, one wholly different in motivation and character from the 18th century variety, where the limitations were usually due to unwillingness or inability to mobilize the full resources of state."[384] (In a March 5, 1959 speech to the State College of Washington in Pullman, Brodie discussed the topic of limited war, recounting that this "subject happens to have been my intellectual specialty for the last seven years," and as he had been contemplating since the end of 1951 as the H-bomb era fast approached, he reiterated that "the possibility of total war should make us look very soberly on the importance not so much of winning limited wars cheaply and conveniently but rather of keeping them limited."[385] He advocated—seemingly contradicting his view as articulated through the 1960s as he faced off against McNamara and the firebreak theorists advocating a conventional war strategy for the defense of Europe that Brodie came to oppose—that "[w]e certainly ought to reexamine the notion that we must use nuclear weapons in limited wars, with the implication that it is always to our advantage do so," adding in a hand-written note to his typed speech the following: "We also should reexamine the program which has resulted in the great reduction of those forces especially adapted to fighting non-nuclear limited war."[386] While Brodie would become an early and outspoken critic of the Vietnam War, that it was fought conventionally from start to finish, fully consistent with the strategic reexamination that he proposed in his 1959 speech.)

With the Vietnam War escalating dramatically, Brodie observed that was necessary in the thermonuclear era "to withhold in war a force *already* mobilized and alert, and far the most powerful such force ever available to any state—our nuclear strategic bombing force. With thermonuclear weapons mutual strategic attacks by two great nations would consume in their devastation any conceivable political objectives. Thus, the problem was, insofar as there must be confrontation or actual hostilities, to 'bring war back to the battlefield.' "[387] Brodie came to realize that, "Above all we must avoid the mutual destruction of cities"—something Brodie had "already urged . . . in a special report prepared for the chief of staff of the Air Force, General Hoyt Vandenberg, a year earlier, but the thermonuclear weapon not only gave added pointedness to the argument but required the complete withholding of strategic nuclear bombing except as a very last resort."[388] Brodie concedes that "[a]t that time these ideas were regarded as somewhat crackpot," owing to the depth of the entrenchment of the famous axiom then in vogue, "all modern war is total war," as he had argued now for a number of years.[389] After John Foster Dulles' famous massive retaliation speech on January 12, 1954, the strategy of limited war in Korea was now "officially" recognized to be "a mistake, never again to be repeated," and as a consequence, the "response of the services, especially the Air Force, to the limited-war views of myself and later of others remained not only resistant but hostile for years afterward."[390]

But there was a "strong reaction the Dulles speech," which "provoked new writings urging the dangers of massive-retaliation strategy," so "[b]y the time of the publication of Henry A Kissinger's *Nuclear Weapons and Foreign Policy* in 1957, the tide was running strongly the

other way," and since then, "those civilian intellectuals who theorize about military operations of the future have been almost uniformly committed to the limited-war concept, including even that hardy and unique soul, Herman Kahn, whose first book, *On Thermonuclear War*
(1960), was about the unlimited variety."[391] With the ascension of the Kennedy administration
and his defense secretary McNamara, "the shift to limited-war thinking" was now "official,"
with both Kennedy and his defense chief "enamored of the idea" and committed to "reorient-
ing our national strategy not only towards limited war . . . but also toward conventional rather
than nuclear weapons on the tactical level," with the aim, as colorfully described by Richard E.
Neustadt, of putting "the nuclear genie back in the bottle."[392]

Brodie noted that "[s]everal dedicated advocates of the conventional-war-only school entered
the Administration, especially in the Department of Defense," who directed the armed services
to "adapt to the new thinking," a shift that Brodie had vociferously criticized throughout the
early 1960s.[393] But now Brodie showed a moderated view, commenting, "Though it had its own
excesses, this trend was unquestionably necessary" since the "world cannot now support what
is officially called 'general' (i.e., total) war, and we have to be clear about that," just as we cannot
"guarantee, or expect, uninterrupted peace free of confrontations."[394] But Brodie argues that "we
have to concede that the kind of limited war thinking that came into fashion in the Kennedy
Administration played some causative effect in getting us involved in Vietnam," and which "also
accounts in large part for our failure in Vietnam," of which Brodie believes, writing in 1967, it
was "now possible to speak definitively of a failure there."[395] Brodie concludes Vietnam was a
failure, a full eight years before hostilities would end, both for the "political and social costs to
ourselves, as well as to the Vietnamese," which "it will be difficult historically to justify," as well
as the "question of the morality of our intervention."[396] Brodie asks a question many had not yet
had the courage to ask: "How did this happen?"—especially in light of the fact "that this miserable and obviously unfortunate interventions was largely stimulated by the ideas of a group that
included some very enlightened and talented people."[397]

Brodie attributes the failure to "the neglect or abandonment of the political dimension of the
limited-war thinking of the last dozen years," even though the architects of the failed intervention would argue their advocacy of "an extreme kind of conventional-war doctrine" reflected
a "special sensitivity to political considerations," but Brodie believes such considerations "were
often biased, always inadequate, and usually naïve."[398] Brodie observes how he had "read scores
of 'scenarios' which purported to describe some possible limited war of the future, and the one
thing they have in common is their total irrelevance to what we have encountered in Vietnam—
and also at home as a result of our involvement in Vietnam."[399] Brodie adds that "[t]here was
also in the theorizing about limited war little questioning of U.S. political capabilities to fight a
prolonged and thus apparently stalemated limited war," and "[n]ext to our lack of understanding
of the enemy we were fighting and of the regime we were supporting, we must place the crucial
absence of political understanding of the home scene."[400] Additionally, while "[s]cenarios on
limited war have almost universally assumed that the United States would be free to escalate,
or de-escalate, or make whatever other adjustments in policy that the President and his advisers might think desirable," the reality has been that "since we reached the level of about half a
million troops in Vietnam, we have been essentially locked in," and even with the occasional
addition of "air targets now and then," Brodie finds that "what we do cannot really be called
meaningful escalation," particularly with the ever present risk, albeit small, of triggering "the
intervention of China."[401] Brodie also notes how "[t]here was in our projections little concern,
and certainly no objective reasoning, about how the people and governments of our allies and
other countries might regard our involvement in such a war," which turned out to have "been
almost everywhere unfavorable and sometimes intensely so," a tragic irony since this was "the
world we are trying to impress with our resolve!"[402] One further lesson from the painful reality

check of Vietnam was "the nearly total irrelevance of 'cost-effectiveness' analysis," which many of the war's architects "assumed to be coterminous with the whole realm of strategy" but which turned out not to be the case in Vietnam.[403] Ultimately, Brodie finds the Vietnam experience has painfully demonstrated that limited "war is difficult to fight partly because it is difficult for the people who support it to understand why the fighting that must be limited need to be engaged at all," and "[t]his question naturally grows with the prolongation of the conflict."[404] But as negative as the experience has been, Brodie cautions that the "military, if left to their own devices, would almost certainly have done a good deal worse," since the "fact that all wars are fought for political purposes and must be guided by political ends, though stressed by Clausewitz, is an idea to which they have proved enormously resistant."[405] And perhaps one silver lining to an otherwise tragic series of events: "At least we can be grateful that thus far nuclear weapons have been kept out of a business that is unfortunate enough already."[406]

In June 1968, Brodie participated in the Studies in Violence Symposium, held at UCLA on June 1 and 2, where he presented a paper titled "Changing Attitudes Towards War," also published later that year in UCLA Security Studies Paper Number 17, *Bureaucracy, Politics, and Strategy*, an anthology that included one paper by Henry Kissinger and four by Brodie.[407] The period in which he wrote coincided with the intensification of the anti-war movement on college campuses across the United States, as draft-age youth came to increasingly oppose to the American war in Indochina, and vehemently against the involuntary conscription of their generation to fight such a limited war so far from home and against an opponent that did not appear to present a military threat to the United States. While Brodie's peer, Herman Kahn, would famously court members of the anti-war and hippie movement in an effort to come to understand their generational perspective, Brodie sought instead to inform and educate them on the broader historical context of the war his nation was engaged in—and while sensitive to popular opposition to that war, he hoped to inform his audience on the broader historical trends, in particular the emergence after World War I of a strong revulsion from war itself, and especially wars of aggression, and that war was no longer viewed to be the noble and celebrated activity it had been perceived to be before the enormous and seemingly pointless bloodshed of that conflict. Brodie recalled how "World War I far exceeded all previous wars in magnitude and intensity. The war was also fought on both sides with extraordinary ineptitude, so that we had a succession of great offensives or 'pushes' which accomplished absolutely nothing but vast shedding of blood," and which "tell a story of unutterable grimness and slaughter—as well as of the professional incompetence of the military leaders which contrasted most incongruously with their pretensions."[408] He adds that "perhaps the most significant result of the war, with respect at least to the subject I have chosen for this paper, was the mood which quickly followed it—a mood of profound disillusionment with the acts and ideas of the political leaders who had triggered the conflict and who had attempted to conduct it. World War I, unlike World War II, could not be found after the event to have had a purpose remotely warranting for any one of the powers truly engaged in it the great sacrifices it had been forced to make."[409]

When Hitler's excesses pushed the world to war again in 1939, Brodie noted in contrast to the nationalist fervor and euphoria that greeted the start of World War I, "All the nations, including the Germans, went to war with feelings of dismay and glumness, obviously fearing for what the future might bring,"[410] and in its wake, there was no "special glorification of the war; it had been too costly and bitter for that."[411] Brodie observes that "[o]ne of the important changes that World War I began and World War II completed was the liquidation from positions of power, if not from existence altogether, of that aristocratic and monarchial caste that had previously ruled affairs in most of Europe and in Japan. This caste had derived many of its moral and political values, including attitudes towards war, from the Middle Ages. The virtual wiping out of this formerly powerful caste in those nations which it previously controlled is a change of enormous consequences for the behavior of governments which I think we too frequently overlook."[412] As Brodie has found, "certain attitudes towards war which national governments used to be able to count upon, or feel obligated to take into account, have gone out of fashion or even out of existence since 1945, and even more markedly since 1914. The kind of mindless fervor which brought people out on the streets when their national government declared war seems quite definitely a thing of the past."[413]

In the years since World War II, Brodie observed, "[t]he United States has been mainly involved in the Korean War of 1950–53, and in the Vietnam war that still goes on today. In the case of Korea, we backed into a kind of war tha[t] ran counter to one of our axioms of the time that 'all modern wars must be total wars,' and we did so out of a kind of helpless feeling that our position of world leadership left us little choice to do anything else."[414] Brodie describes the Korean War as "the first example of modern limited war, about which there has since been a good deal of theorizing," and "[b]y modern limited war—as distinct from earlier types—we mean a kind of war in which at least one of the powers involved is a major power and is deliberately refraining from using the most powerful and terrible military capabilities under its control, especially nuclear weapons."[415] The Vietnam War, Brodie noted, has "had similar yet distinctive characteristics," as the United States "got involved the way we did mostly out of the feeling that after the French defeat and departure, there was again no one else to do what we thought needed doing, which was to carry out what we called containment.... In both wars we have shown ourselves willing to settle for a negotiated compromise peace while exercising massive restraint against the militarily inferior enemy. In the Korean War we never bombed beyond the Yalu River, although the major enemy was China. In the case of Vietnam, we refrained not only from the use of nuclear weapons, which we now had in enormous numbers, but from any attempt at invasion of North Vietnam. The bombing in the North, at this writing suspended, has always been of a controlled and relatively constricted kind, and we have also exercised great restraint on the [shipping] lanes leading to Haiphong."[416]

Brodie explains he "mentions these points not to attempt in the least degree to justify our political and military intervention either in Korea or Vietnam, but rather to point out that the United States, which is a very great power, is practicing a kind of behavior marked by conspicuous military and political restraint such as would have been totally unthinkable prior to 1914."[417] Adds Brodie, "Some of course hold that we have been too restrained, and have thus made ourselves militarily ineffective," Brodie has found "the tide of opinion is all in the opposite direction. Any future president of the United States, at least in the next decade or so, is likely to view the personal disaster of President Johnson in Vietnam as a compelling reason for not intervening in like manner somewhere else, rather than as a good reason for throwing off restraint. And surely if there has been any degree of enthusiasm for the war in Vietnam or elsewhere, it has not been particularly noticeable. The same was true of Korea."[418]

Brodie's thoughts on Vietnam would appear in various speeches, articles and presentations throughout the long conflict—including his presentation to the Tenth Annual Conference of the Institute for Strategic Studies at St. Catherine's College in Oxford on September 19–22, 1968. His paper, titled "Technology, Politics, and Strategy," included several references to Vietnam, where America's technological superiority failed to deliver a strategic victory. Brodie started out by noting how the "whole impressive development of systems analysis and of related techniques, especially in the United States, has fostered the notion that selection of future weapons systems for appropriate development and deployment represents most of what there is to modern military strategy. I suspect that the former American Secretary of Defense, Mr. Robert S. McNamara, tended automatically to think in such terms."[419] As a consequence, Brodie has found "[m]ilitary history, which used to be the main acknowledged source of strategic insight—Clausewitz and Mahan are examples—has been enormously downgraded in favor of the new analytical techniques."[420] But as Vietnam would demonstrate, the new systems analytical tools proved inadequate when tested by fire in Vietnam, where perhaps more proper historical analysis might have gone further to prepare America for the confrontation.[421]

But it was not just America's technological edge that proved a let down in Indochina; America's strategic doctrine, shaped by the many pressures of the nuclear age into a doctrine of limited war that proved successful in Korea, would also take a bruising. Brodie noted that by the "end of this first decade" of the nuclear age, "the ideas were already developing that were subsequently to constitute a theory of limited war, the existence of which has in itself had enormous political consequences—including on the negative side, I regret to say, helping to get the United States involved in the Vietnam war."[422] As Brodie explained, what made the Vietnam War "especially germane to our discussion today is that a vast American technological superiority in practically every department has turned out to be of much lesser value than we had expected and sometimes even dysfunctional" in "that we sometimes fix our attention on ways for utilizing our technological superiority rather than on methods of solving the tactical problem. One result is that the Air Force and the Navy's air arm compete with each other to produce high sortie rates. When we begin to put an emphasis on sortie rates and on weight of bombs and shells dropped, we are not only tearing up real estate needlessly but also requiring additional services of supply to maintain those rates of expenditure."[423] Brodie adds that the "problem seems to be intensified . . . by the fact that there is no front line to bring both sides into common agreement on how they are doing" so that "both sides know who at the moment is winning or losing," while instead "the kind of war we have been fighting in Vietnam is one in which our 'winning' is demonstrated by the use of charts containing data. These data may or may not be accurate and they may or may not be terribly relevant. The enemy is probably using a very different kind of criteria for determining gain or loss from what we are using. This is something beyond what is generally meant by a non-zero sum game."[424] The war would continue to its tragic end for another eight years, six with America militarily involved and two more as its abandoned ally in the south fought on, alone and without American assistance, until the Republic of Vietnam collapsed in a decisive defeat. But Brodie believed it was none too soon to assess the strategic failure that was unfolding and to consider its lessons: "Although the fighting still continues, we cannot wait for its end to being organizing our thinking about what has gone wrong in Vietnam. The effects of our enormous frustration in that land will long influence United States military and diplomatic policies elsewhere. Some of these effects will no doubt be beneficial. A more realistic appraisal of our true capabilities is always to the good; but we have probably experienced a real constriction of those capabilities rather than merely a clarification of them. The political disunity within the United States which is so largely attributable to the war in Vietnam, and the disaster which has overtaken President Johnson as a result of his personal commitment and involvement, will not soon be forgotten by his successors."[425]

Brodie acknowledged that he "cannot presume to know all the important things that have gone wrong in Vietnam," but he had little "doubt we can group most of them under the heading of 'political misjudgment,' " and turning to the great Prussian strategic theorist for guidance, Brodie added: "Clausewitz did his best to warn us against neglecting the political dimension in strategy, but that was a long time ago."[426] And while "[i]t may not be fair to blame this neglect of political considerations upon our preoccupation with technology and with the various analytical skills we have developed," he found it "remarkable how few of the pitfalls we have encountered in Vietnam were taken into account in the kinds of war games, scenarios, and cost-effectiveness analyses done at places like RAND over the past twenty years."[427]

Added Brodie: "Nobody engaged in these pursuits warned us of the pitfalls involved in attempting to support through military action a regime or series of regimes which show a high common denominator of corruption and ineptitude and which have in an case failed utterly to attract the allegiance of the people. Certainly no one ever warned us about the possibility of getting into a bind where we could neither escalate, nor deescalate, nor extricate ourselves from an impossible situation; war games always assumed in these matters wide latitudes of choice. Nor do I remember that we ever took into account what frustration from denial of victory or at least of clearly visible progress might mean with respect to the attitudes of the American people in supporting such a war, and also the attitudes of other people who were simply witnessing hat was going on. We had in fact had some warning in the Korean experiences."[428] Brodie found "[o]ne of the great weaknesses of our Vietnamese military policy is that it has been based on the draft," and that as "both a parent and a teacher I have seen at first hand how insidiously the draft affects the plans and outlooks of the young men who are subject to it. It does not depreciate them to surmise that most of their moral indignation over our Vietnamese adventure has been connected with the draft. There are, indeed, other reasons for being concerned with real moral issues in Vietnam, one certainly being the effects upon the Vietnamese people of this prolonga- tion, however, is to some degree draft-connected, for the draft accounts for the one-year rotation system, which has been extremely costly to our military effectiveness." Brodie believed that the United States would be better served, and could "surely afford a professional army where the incentive to enlist is higher pay."[429] By his estimation, "We are now spending about thirty billion dollars per year in Vietnam, which amounts to about $60,000 for each military person we have in that country. That leaves a good deal of room for increased pay, especially if we get direct and disproportionate increases in efficiency as a result of being able to lengthen periods of rotation or to dispense with rotation altogether."[430] In short, Brodie explained, "This is really a cost- effectiveness issue."[431] He added that the annual $30 billion cost of the war "amounts to some $100,000 for each North Vietnamese or Viet Cong fighting man engaged in the war. I am not speaking here of enemy casualties, which cost astronomical figures each to produce, but simply of soldiers in the field. War seems always to confine us to the costliest possible way of producing (or failing to produce) a desired result."[432]

While avoiding a direct discussion of "whether it was or was not a correct policy to become too committed in the first place," a complex issue that would require more time than Brodie had for his presentation, and one that "would in any case be a digression," he observed that he had "a strong allegiance to the idea that failures of the kind we have experienced thus far should be predictable. Some persons did in fact predict failure, and for approximately the right reasons. Before committing U.S. combat troops we had rich opportunities for informing our- selves about the situation in Vietnam, and actually since that time we have had few surprises from the environment."[433] Indeed, Brodie added: "The major surprise is that the environment has changed so little. Naturally, to avoid predictable failure means either to avoid the commit- ment altogether or to change the methods normally used for fulfilling such a commitment. Our experience in shaking bureaucratic structures in order to bring about a change in methods does not warrant optimism about the results of such attempts. It is also relevant that our declining to invade North Vietnam—in line with the concept of 'sanctuary' which is so conspicuous a part of modern limited-war theory—affected the conditions of the war in a most fundamental way, and inasmuch as we were making that choice we should have some awareness of the probable penal- ties. The restraint was, surely, a correct one; what was incorrect was our failing to appreciate the military burden it entailed."[434] Brodie commented on how Vietnam was at once the most closely watched and more actively reported military event in history, and yet suffered from a debilitat- ing "information gap" that not only "flies in the face of a marked advance in the technology of communications,"[435] but which also contributed to America's strategic failure.[436]

Brodie closed his discussion of the Vietnam War and its lessons by reiterating what he has "called 'the political dimension' is remarkably visible in Vietnam. So is the fact that a virtually complete monopoly of air power and a great preponderance of every other form of war material have brought us only the conviction that we cannot escape the quagmire through military defeat, as the French did. Also, if pride goeth before a fall, members of the American strategic fraternity have had both their pride and their fall. Let us hope we recognize the fall for what it is and do not rationalize away its benefits."[437] As for technology's contribution to American strategy, and its impact on the unfolding of military history, Brodie comments that "we learn from history that while battles and campaigns have sometimes been won largely with the help of clever technological devices, others have been quite unaffected by considerable technological superiority. We should learn that although technology amounts to very much indeed—it after all is what separates the rich and the powerful from those who are neither—it falls very short of being the name of the game which is strategy."[438]

Brodie discussed the strategic implication of America's Vietnam War experience in an op-ed published later that month in the October 17, 1968 edition of *The Los Angeles Times*, titled "Paying in Full for a Limited War," but which in an earlier draft bore the proposed title, "Ending a War: Is the Korean Lesson Valid for Vietnam?" but which retained this original title when published as part of UCLA's aforementioned Security Studies Paper Number 17, *Bureaucracy, Politics, and Strategy,* published in 1968. In this article, Brodie recalled the loss of America's military momentum when, with China's Red Army in retreat and its morale collapsing under pressure from the U.N. forces, negotiations were begun, enabling America's opponent to re-arm, refresh, and regain momentum. "In the spring of 1951 U.N. forces launched an offensive against the combined Red Chinese and North Korean armies, jumping off from the line deep into South Korea to which the Chinese had driven us following their massive intervention in the previous November. The new U.N. offensive made good progress from the start. The Red armies fell back as the U.N. forces gathered momentum, until the battleline was once again in the area of the 38th Parallel which had originally divided North and South Korea. At this point a few words by Soviet U.N. Ambassador Jacob Malik had an effect which was beyond the power of the retreating Red armies. Malik suggested that the North Koreans and their Chinese allies might now be prepared to negotiate. President Truman, urged by many around him and also by our British ally, Prime Minister Clement Attlee, immediately gave orders to halt the U.N. offensive. This was to be a gesture to make it easier for the other side to negotiate."[439]

But around this time, Brodie writes, "Dr. Herbert Goldhamer of the RAND Corp., who had been involved in POW interrogation, sent a memorandum to his chief which vividly described the deep morale crisis that had developed among the Red armies during our offensive," and "[p]risoners confirmed our observation of efforts at defection, and painted a picture of advanced desperation." The memo "was forwarded to the Tokyo headquarters of Gen. Matthew B. Ridgway where it apparently created a sensation," as "[i]t had not been known that the enemy was so badly off. However, the orders to stop the offensive had already taken effect. Although there were some limited U.N. attacks afterward, the pressure was never fully reapplied."[440] As Brodie has described in *Strategy in the Missile Age*, "We paid bitterly for that error in the great prolongation of negotiations, in the unsatisfactory terms of settlement, and above all in the disillusionment and distaste which the American people developed as the main emotional residue of their experience with limited war," adding that "during negotiations, which dragged on for more than two years, we lost more American lives to enemy fire than we had lost in the hostilities preceding the negotiations."[441] Brodie noted that what the United States "did in Korea was a radical departure from previous practice—and the new experiment proved disastrous. Relieved of pressure the Chinese armies quickly recovered, and their political leaders were freed of any inducement to come to terms. Only a slightly veiled threat in mid-1953 by the newly installed President Eisenhower that he might be forced to use nuclear weapons in a renewed U.N. offensive moved the Communists finally to agree to an armistice on what was essentially the status quo ante bellum."[442]

With this as prelude, Brodie asked, "What does this experience with Korea suggest to us concerning the termination of war in Vietnam?"—and noted that like the communist forces in Korea, Brodie was confident that in Vietnam America's new opponent "must be hurting," with significant enemy losses and "[r]eports in recent months have consistently pointed out the much reduced role of the Viet Cong as compared with North Vietnamese troops. There has also been a marked rise in the rate of defections, both from the Viet Cong and especially from the North Vietnamese. People who defect usually believe that their side is losing. This would seem to be the time for Americans to increase their pressure rather than to relax it."[443] "But," Brodie wondered, "whether we are in a position to increase it effectively is another matter. And here we see surfacing the contrasts with the Korean situation of 17 years ago."[444] Brodie also notes several differences in the Vietnam situation. "First, there has never been in Vietnam, as there was in Korea, a front line, the movement of which backwards or forwards tends to signal the same message to both sides about who is at the moment winning or losing," so while "[w]e have multiple criteria for estimating our gains or losses, and the enemy is probably preoccupied with quite other criteria—certainly including what is happening within the United States. Both sides may be right in thinking they are winning according to their respective criteria, but the opponent may have the better set."[445]

In addition, Brodie has found that "we have ourselves from the beginning imposed such a marked restraint upon our military action that the initiative has perforce been left to the enemy."[446] For instance, he noted "we have never even threatened to invade North Vietnam. For two years we conducted a restrained and selective bombing in the north but that has now been stopped. All that is left is some strictly interdiction bombing in and just north of the 'demilitarized zone.' "[447] The upshot is that the entire "territory of North Vietnam is a total 'sanctuary,' and much of South Vietnam is effectively so. This means that the North Vietnamese forces largely make the judgment when and where to fight, and if they have too rough a time of it they can retire. We can impose heavy casualties on them, but probably not enough to destroy their staying power."[448] As well, Brodie observes, "Nor is there much likelihood today that we can go back up the escalation ladder to levels of fighting intensity not previously approached in this war. Of the various presidential and vice-presidential candidates in the field today, probably only Gen. Curtis LeMay would have sufficient insensitivity to public opinion at home and abroad to make the really savage ripostes that could make the North Vietnamese sue for peace."[449] Brodie described, "Gen. LeMay is a complete prisoner of the traditional Air Force view that air power overwhelms, and on the cheap. He probably would favor a rapidly ascending rate of bombing, perhaps intended to give the opponent reason to fear our use of nuclear weapons if he did not opt for peace on our terms. There is reason to suppose that such a strategy would work if we could bring ourselves to apply it, and there is relatively little likelihood that the Chinese or the Russians would intervene against us in a war that had suddenly become so dangerous. However, the main trouble, apart from the absence of guarantees, is that all possible remaining political motives for fighting this war would go down the drain."[450] And it is "the political constraints that have been operative all along and have become critical," especially as it "has become abundantly clear that an overwhelming majority of Americans are now fed up with our continuing entanglement in Vietnam, and most consider our intervention to have been a mistake from the start—which is not to say they are yet ready to see a simple abandonment of our commitment."[451]

But with the "persistent and intense opposition of two special classes," the "young people, whose idealism may well be qualified by a dislike for the draft but who nevertheless have in large numbers been moved to a state of open rebellion," and "the intellectuals, largely associated with universities, whose alienation has grown over the last two years"—and while the latter "are relatively small in numbers compared with the rest of the population," Brodie notes "their influence gains weight by their articulateness."[452] Brodie has found that "[t]hese groups especially, and now the majority of the American public, have proved unable to accept the Administration's justification of its war policy," and Brodie believes that "[u]nquestionably, it is mostly frustration that is at the root of the public's rejection of the government's war aims and war policies. Frustration, which is to say military failure, also accounts for the great growth of the feeling that the war is basically immoral. Actually, failure does contribute to creating a real moral issue, simply by the fact that it results in the prolongation of the war and thus the suffering of the Vietnamese people."[453] But he adds that "[t]his leads us to what is perhaps the basic difference between the situation today and that of 1951 or even 1953," which is that [w]e are very much farther down the course now than we were then. The great military power of the United States has been applied to the coercion of a third-rate power and, under the special circumstances, has been found wanting."[454]

After Vietnam: Reuniting War and Politics

In May 1968, Brodie and five of his colleagues completed a UCLA Security Studies Project on *The Future of Deterrence in U.S. Strategy*—prepared for the United States Air Force Directorate of Doctrine, Concepts and Objectives under contract AF-49(638)-1772. It presents a unique anthology of essays on the international and strategic implications and dynamics of deterrence whose narrative structure enunciates, implicitly, a systemic theory of international politics with the mutuality of deterrence and its endurance the very superstructure that defines the bipolar international system. Published midway between the 1959 publication of Kenneth Waltz's *Man, the State, and War* and Waltz's 1979 *Theory of International Politics*, this work straddles the fields of strategic studies and international relations theory—and had it been more widely read may well have worked its way into the curricula of courses in both fields. But it seems to have only been read by a limited audience of strategic studies scholars and today is listed in Worldcat. org at six libraries worldwide, University of Pittsburgh, U.S. Army War College, Marine Corps Research Library, Joint Forces Staff College, Indiana University, and Air University Library—only two of which are at civilian institutions, with a downloadable copy at the Defense Tech Information Center (DTIC Online) at Fort Belvoir, Virginia. In his preface written on May 20, 1968, Brodie salutes the hands-off approach to the research project taken by the Air Force in his foreword, noting the service "limited its control to specifying the subject matter for the research study," but "allowed us complete freedom to organize the project according to our own lights, and pursue our research and writing without restriction."[455] Brodie, on behalf his fellow project participants—which included Klaus Knorr, Arnold Horelick, Richard Rosecrance, Daniel Weiler, and Arnold Kramish, in addition to Brodie—expressed "gratitude to that service, and specifically the officers concerned, for their generosity in supporting in a fashion so appropriate to scholarship a project of direct interest not only to them but also to all students of international security. The publication starts with an introduction on "Concepts of Deterrence Since 1945," followed by five main chapters: "The Alliance Environment," by Knorr; "The Opponent Environment," by Horelick; "The Systemic Environment," by Rosecrance; "Deterrence and Military Capabilities," by Weiler; "Technology and Deterrence," by Kramish; followed by a conclusion authored by Brodie. Its conceptual layout thereby explores the strategic landscape in which deterrence operated.

Brodie's contribution to the anthology is the work's conclusion, in which he lays out his thoughts on the challenges inherent in predicting the future of deterrence—issues he would develop further in a 1971 monograph published by the National Strategy Information Center, *Strategy and National Interests: Reflections for the Future*. In "The Future of Deterrence," he observes that "[i]n discussing the future of deterrence, as in the future of almost anything else dealing with human affairs, we are dealing with precarious predictions rendered doubly precarious because of the wide range of relevant issues," but despite its precarious nature, "prediction is not only necessary but inevitable—at least to a degree," though Brodie admits he prefers "avoiding unnecessary projections into remote futures."[456] Brodie adds that the "number of specific decisions we have to make now to cover contingencies twenty years hence or more is minimal, and we should take advantage of that" and thus "should seek wherever possible to keep our choices open concerning more remote futures and to limit our hard and fast decisions to contingencies closer in time," much as he would reiterate in 1971.[457] He explains that "when we speak of predictions being inevitable over the shorter term, we mean simply that every policy decision implies a prediction or a pattern of predictions" and that the "decision for one kind of policy implies a prediction that the consequences of that policy will prove superior to the consequences of available alternative policies, or at least—wherever we feel oppressed with uncertainty—that the policy chosen serves better than other available policies to cover a wide array of possible contingencies."[458]

That being said, Brodie notes this "does not mean that we presume to predict particular events," and like the science of quantum mechanics where inherent uncertainty defines the micro-landscape, strategy and policy more generally operates in a probabilistic universe much like that described by Clausewitz where a shroud of fog introduced a variety of incalculable uncertainties known as friction, a concept some critics of Brodie would argue he overlooked but which is clear upon a close look at his reasoning and his understanding about deterrence played a key though at times understated role. As Brodie describes, "Policy decisions concerning deterrence must take into account our prevailing uncertainty about particular events, and may indeed underline that uncertainty. Nevertheless, it is clear that some categories of contingencies are more probable than others; also, other kinds of contingencies must be provided against even when the probability of their occurring is deemed very low."[459] New disciplines like game theory had, Brodie noted, "made us familiar with the 'mini-max principle,' which is analogous to the older idea of choosing that policy which will turn out least bad if the relevant predictions go awry,"[460] but he would ultimately conclude that game theory and systems analysis would prove dangerous if decision makers depended upon them at the exclusion of more fundamental political analysis weighing means to ends, deferring to a scientific form while neglecting the underlying scientific method of objective analysis. As the structure of the publication on the future of deterrence (and international relations more generally) reveals, the complex and dynamic environment in which deterrence operates must be closely examined; as Brodie writes, "In deterrent policy particularly, we must remember also the reactive aspects of our policy decisions. Not only our opponents but also our allies will respond to what we do, and the ability to predict these responses correctly—or at least to avoid egregious blunders—takes wisdom as well as ample and accurate knowledge."[461]

As well, given the high costs associated with the strategic weapons systems required for deterrence, a realistic appreciation of the economic factors is also of great value: "It should by now be unnecessary to add that especially with respect to anything as expensive as deterrence measures are likely to be, we are always confronted by limitations of resources. This factor affects not only our systems choices within the budgets allocated for the purpose, but on a higher level it determines what that budget should be," as "[o]ur deterrence efforts, like our military policies generally, are made within a society which has other goals beyond military security" and "[e]xcessive military costs will also be a drain on both economic and social-resource growth potentialities. It is not only the economic power but also the social and political cohesion of the U.S. that make for its present greatness and its superiority over its rivals, and these elements are not to be taken lightly in preparing for the future."[462] Ultimately, deterrence requires rational decisions, and that means moving past axiomatic thinking to a more thoughtful analysis, in short to continue moving in the direction of Clausewitzian thought and away from the more doctrinaire style of the Swissman Jomini, who in Brodie's interpretation lacked the depth of analysis as his Prussian counterpart. As Brodie observes, "In all these matters we have undoubtedly, by means of the various axioms to which we have become addicted since World War II, grossly overlooked the fact that on most relevant issues we have rather wide areas of choice. We are familiar with the methods and advantages of making intelligent choices among weapons systems, and to a lesser degree among strategies, but choice figures also in the national policies which dominate those strategies."[463]

As Brodie would examine three years later in his 1971 National Strategy Information Center monograph *Strategy and National Interests*, America had come a long way in a short time, rising from a marginal to dominant world power: "As a result of World War II, stimulated also by the advent of nuclear weapons, this nation shifted from a pattern of foreign policy generally known as isolationism to something which has been to a radical degree the direct reverse," and as the Vietnam crisis intensified and America's global reach became increasingly controversial, Brodie adds that "[t]he question is already being asked, with increasing intensity, whether we have gone too far—whether we have in fact been too prodigal in our commitments. The current debate over our involvement in Vietnam is a crucial case in point."[464] Writing in 1968, five years before America's strategic withdrawal from Vietnam, Brodie already senses a connection of the tragic events unfolding in Indochina to America's effort to implement the complex challenges of deterrence, and Brodie reiterates his view—made even more stridently in his 1973 *War and Politics*—that the guiding hand of military policy must remain on the civilian side, with the military implementing the policies embraced by the civilian political leadership: "From the point of view of the military community, the important thing to remember about the Vietnam debate is that its outcome will be mainly determined by others" and the "the provident military leader has to be aware of deep currents of change affecting our national policy, where his own role is perforce largely passive. Whenever one hears anyone expressing strongly the view that 'the public needs to be educated' to something or other, one can usually set that person down as having limited political sensitivity. The many forces acting to educate the public speak with conflicting voices, and most of them are generated within the public itself. They are subject to some influence but certainly nothing resembling control from the defense community. Out of Congress and out of the electorate are presently emanating statements concerning Vietnam which indicate a very deep disenchantment with the policy that committed our forces there, and this disenchantment is not markedly less characteristic of the so-called hawks than it is of the doves. These views naturally reflect in large degree the views of the wider public."[465] As for the lessons Vietnam offered the political leadership, Brodie expects that "President Johnson's successors for some time to come will be impressed by what Vietnam did to his presidency," a point he would make again in the coming years—and he predicts quite accurately that "[a] ny future president will, at least for a time, be more limited in his responses, and also more closely watched by the Congress," and "this adds up simply to the fact that whether we like it or not, the authoritative determination of what constitutes the nation's vital interests—always a flexible and ambiguous concept" and one he would explore in greater detail in his 1971 NSIC monograph—"is clearly undergoing change in a manner that will profoundly affect our whole national security policy."[466]

While thinking about the political risks associated with military action, Brodie looks next "to the subject of deterrence more narrowly considered," that of nuclear deterrence, and presents a quick recap of the history of American nuclear strategy, noting how atomic weapons were "at once recognized to be a strong deterrent" though "there was nevertheless a notable lack of confidence in its reliability" that "reflected the fact that for the first time in the history of warfare we were demanding a kind of deterrence that would work 100 per cent of the time," but in time America's confidence grew, in response to "a number of changes, which included the mere passage of time without war but which more importantly involved other factors including a clearer perception of the nature of the major opponent," the result of which was that "we tended to become much more confident about the capability of our nuclear weapons to deter a general war, or at least one which would start full blown as a general war."[467] But "[a]t the same time we became less confident in our ability to deter lesser aggressions through our nuclear threat" and "tended, to a degree that was certainly not matched in the Soviet Union, to distinguish sharply between general war and limited war," and thus "developed increasing confidence that we knew how to keep wars limited, but the idea became dominant in Administration circles that keeping war limited depended above all on avoidance or rejection of nuclear weapons," as advocated by the architects of the CWE doctrine, now known as the *firebreak* theorists."[468]

Brodie takes a more even-handed approach to the impact of the firebreak theorists here than in his more polemic treatises, noting "we can see that this kind of thinking helped produce a conspicuous success, that of the Cuban Missile Crisis of 1962" in which it became "clear that the fact that President Kennedy and his entourage had by that time become accustomed to differentiating fairly sharply between general and limited war enabled them to 'keep their cool' in their manipulation of this crisis" and whose "outcome would prove as favorable as it in fact turned out to be—over a whole range of issues, including Soviet behavior concerning Berlin."[469] But he also notes this kind of thinking would produce only a few years later a conspicuous failure, Vietnam—and Brodie concludes that "there can be no doubt that our limited war thinking which enabled us to envisage fighting a war against the Viet Cong and possibly also Hanoi without necessarily becoming involved with China and the Soviet Union, also played a very considerable part in our letting ourselves become involved in Vietnam. But now we were treated to an unpleasant surprise: our forces, operating in a conventional manner and restrained by the considerations considered to be necessary to keep the war limited, are not nearly as effective as we had hoped."[470] The restraint required in limited war contributed to a hobbling of military power that left the war unwinnable: "We must notice the pattern that is involved in Vietnam: first, in order to refrain from provoking the intervention of China, we have refrained from invading North Vietnam, which has meant leaving the military initiative almost entirely to the opponent; second, we have refrained from using nuclear weapons of any kind, which in that terrain might not be particularly useful anyway; third, partly because we have already thus limited our options, the number of troops committed is not readily permitted to go much above half a million—which is already far above the level that must have been anticipated two and three years earlier."[471] This "combination seems on the whole to be without profit, at least in this terrain," and while it was not yet sure if the primary lessons learned would be that "wars of this sort must be fought differently or that they must not be engaged in at all" or perhaps even more "likely, that the answer may fall somewhere between these divergent possibilities" as America becomes "much less ready to commit . . . to actions in distant lands where the payoff to be expected, even with the most optimistic prognosis of success, is on the whole small," even as America remains "quite ready to use our power to a much fuller extent in those areas where commitment seems to our national leaders to be inescapable."[472]

As for "[w]hether using our power to a fuller extent will include the use of the threat of nuclear weapons, at least against tactical targets, is a question for which the answer is far from being fully determined," and despite Brodie's enduring criticism of the CWE doctrine, he notes while the "fervent expression of and adherence to the firebreak principle has been largely an act of faith" that "despite the logical fallacies inherent in so much of the argumentation for it, it has certain self-fulfilling properties," one of which was Schelling's famous "tradition of non-use."[473]

Interestingly, Brodie omits mention of Schelling, the originator of this popular phrase, writing only:" For one thing, what someone was called the 'tradition of non-use' of nuclear weapons tends to become increasingly strong as a guiding operational principle the more it is adhered to over time."[474] In Brodie's 1971 NSIC monograph further developing many of the ideas presented in this 1968 report, he would formally attribute this popular phrase to its originator Schelling but the reason excluding attribution here is a curious offense—particularly since in the preceding sentence, Brodie does reference his own *Escalation and the Nuclear Option*, and, incidentally, in so doing wrongly dating his book as a 1967 publication, when it was actually published by Princeton University Press in 1966, and released internally by RAND as a research monograph the year before.[475] Brodie notes that "the United States has engaged in two wars" since the Cold War began, and each "resulted in relatively heavy casualties and other costs," yet it "has nevertheless refrained from using nuclear weapons. In the first of these wars, in Korea we suffered some heavy defeats in the process. In the latter of these wars, still going on, we have not had the restraining factor of very limited nuclear stockpiles, which certainly helped restrain us in the earlier war. Nevertheless we have continued to refrain from using the bomb."[476] The tradition of non-use has thus been strengthened, and along the way Brodie notes "[t]here can be no question that the threshold of crisis above which use of nuclear weapons seems appropriate has moved gradually upward over the last score of years."[477]

But even as the tradition of non-use is extended and the trigger point for nuclear use has risen higher, Brodie points out there is "equally no question that the nuclear weapon remains forever in the background, an object of felt presence even when unused, and that given sufficient motivation we will in fact use it" and it is this hidden nuclear hand that ensures deterrence continues to operate, and Brodie counsels that whether "the threshold will be between use and non-use, or between non-use and threat of use, is something upon which dogmatism is not warranted," but he paradoxically argues, somewhat dogmatically as his critics and even friends would suggest during his long crusade against the firebreak theorists, that "it must be added that it is difficult to see any advantage to the national interest by a constant reiteration of the promise that we will not use nuclear weapons even under a wide variety of quite serious circumstances," and Brodie anticipates, with some relief, that "the retirement of Mr. Robert S. McNamara as Secretary of Defense and his replacement by Mr. Clark Clifford will have a very substantial effect in this regard."[478]

Brodie observes that "[o]ne of the most significant yet little noticed revolutions in defense strategy and policies since the end of World War II has been the development of techniques, including the submarine launcher and the underground silo, for giving a high degree of security to the retaliatory forces," an issue he similarly noted in his new preface to the paperback edition of *Strategy in the Missile Age* just a few years earlier. As Brodie described, "The specter of surprise attack wiping out such forces appears far less grim than it did a decade ago, when Mr. Albert Wohlstetter, for example, published his well-known article 'The Delicate Balance of Terror,' " and "the fact that retaliatory forces can be made secure, at least under present technologies, has had a profound effect on both our strategies and the national policies which interact with those strategies," and "[a]n even more revolutionary result is that it enormously diminishes the advantage, and thus the incentive, of going first in any strategic exchange,"[479] a situation that had lingered into the mid-1960s before finally being remedied (by policies embraced by the very same Defense Secretary McNamara Brodie has so vociferously criticized for the CWE doctrine). As Brodie recalls, "Until the early or middle '60s the advantage of striking first in such an exchange promised to be so huge and so obviously decisive that it was probably the chief factor that would have made for rapid escalation to general war following the outbreak of hostilities between the two major superpowers."[480] But one "important side-effect of this change has been to create a targeting dilemma for our strategic retaliatory forces," with "[t]he general consensus approving the no-cities targeting philosophy" becoming "overlaid with disbelief in counterforce targets, simply because destruction of a sufficient proportion of the latter to achieve significant 'damage limiting' cannot be relied upon," with one implication being that the "strong moral and political inhibitions that Americans have consistently felt in the nuclear era against hitting first with nuclear weapons will now be supported on the strategic level by cold calculations which will impress one with the lack of urgency for doing so," to which Brodie adds, perhaps with some hope, that the "same disincentives will be even more obvious on the Soviet side."[481] It was then not clear if "this change promises to be permanent, or whether on the contrary it may be overturned by some change in missile technology" such as the MIRVing of nuclear forces or the development of ABM technologies, Brodie remained confident that at least for "the next fifteen years or so, it seems in the net fairly safe to predict that the advantages once thought to be inherent in a strategic first strike—where the side launching it could hope to wipe out the retaliatory force of the opponent with near impunity—is gone, and is most unlikely to return."[482] And even with the emergence of such countermeasures, Brodie points out that "with time the number of missiles and other vehicles on both sides capable of retaliation tends to increase, and this increase itself appears to diminish the chances of achieving an acceptable first-strike coup."[483]

Brodie closes with a quick discussion of nonproliferation, a topic that Brodie has only infrequently addressed given his enduring advocacy of nuclear deterrence and his implicit neorealist faith, ever since his early discussions in early 1946 with his former professor Jacob Viner, that nuclear weapons would tend to bring order to the international arena and restrain the behavior of states, a view that would be enshrined in the neorealist theory of Kenneth Waltz. Brodie notes that "the non-proliferation treaty initial [sic] between the United States and the Soviet Union has aroused a good deal of resentment among our allies and third parties, some of whom are likely not to sign it in its present form," and Brodie adds that "[i]n any case, the legal obligation to refrain from building nuclear weapons must, in order to be effective, be strongly buttressed by the existence of disincentives to build such weapons."[484] What is interesting and often ignored by experts in the field of nonproliferation is that many states that would eventually sign onto the NPT may very well have decided on their own not to pursue nuclear weapons programs owing to their high cost and limited utility (primarily deterring great power aggression), and as such many of the NPT success stories are in fact non-stories. As Brodie points out, "It is well-known that several countries could easily produce nuclear weapons if their governments elected to, but that thus far they have chosen not to do so," and while "the number of nations capable of building nuclear weapons will inevitably increase," the salient question of "[w]hether or not the disinclination to convert capability into reality will continue depends on a number of circumstances and will certainly vary among individual nations," as a state like Israel "will no doubt have a considerably higher incentive than Switzerland" to cross the nuclear chasm owing to the hostility of its general neighborhood.[485] Brodie identified "three major disincentives for building nuclear weapons for nations that have a capability to do so are: (a) cost of the entire system; (b) provocativeness of such a capability; and (c) lack of a felt need," and he notes "[t]he cost is not likely to diminish with time for any nation, especially when we are considering whole systems, but we should bear in mind that it is easy to exaggerate the costliness of nuclear retaliatory capabilities" when in fact for "an Israeli defense minister, a few nuclear weapons capable of being carried with the same aircraft that are now available for carrying conventional weapons would seem to be an important capability for deterrence of the hostile Arab states."[486] Additionally, the "tendency to withhold the development of nuclear weapons on the grounds that they might be provocative could decay if a movement towards the building of such capabilities suddenly became widespread" after which it "would then appear to be the normal rather than the special and provocative thing to do."[487] Brodie suggests that "[p]erhaps the best reason for the United States avoiding the use of nuclear weapons as much as possible in the future is in order to continue, for the purpose chiefly of avoiding incentives to proliferation, the so-called *tradition of non-use*."[488]

Brodie closes his conclusion by taking one more swipe at the firebreak theory—long the target of Brodie's critical analysis—noting that "careful avoidance of the use of nuclear weapons is not by any means summed up in the usual firebreak theories," which instead "tolerate unnecessary commitments to unnecessary wars, so long as they are conventional" and thereby fostering instead of preventing the outbreak of wars, and Brodie reaffirms his enduring faith that nuclear deterrence is by far the better option: "Stressing readiness to rely on nuclear deterrence wherever commitments are important and unavoidable might be at least as effective in avoiding the actual use of nuclear weapons in military action by the United States. Thus far, the articulation of the case for non-threat as well as non-use has been overwhelmingly one-sided. However, new opportunities are unquestionably arising for redressing that situation."[489]

Restoring a Clausewitzian Balance: Strategy and the National Interest

Brodie's critical writings on firebreak theory and his continuing belief in the necessity to continue to understand (and support) deterrence strategy and refrain from diluting its credibility by embracing strategies that risked undermining its logic and thereby jeopardizing the stability that it brought, and his later reflections on Vietnam (which grew, he believed, out of the myopic commitment to CWE and the mistaken belief that escalation could be divorced from the same political context that defined war, its objectives, and ultimately made peace possible) are generally viewed to have come to something of a symphonic climax with Brodie's 1973 tribute to Clausewitz, *War and Politics*, but many of Brodie's climactic observations appeared two years earlier with his much shorter 1971 *Strategy and National Interests: Reflections for the Future*, a forty-page booklet published by the National Strategy Information Center (NSIC). It is more closely connected to Brodie's series of papers written in the 1950s and 1960s grappling with escalation, rebutting the firebreak theorists, and dissecting the lessons (often well ahead of his peers) of Vietnam, presenting a synthesis of these works and like Clausewitz recognizing an inherent complexity and uncertainty in the strategic landscape that helped to elevate strategy to a high art.

Brodie's 1971 NSIC monograph was one of many papers by him addressing the question of national interests and the importance of national objectives in defining the aims of strategy as counseled by Clausewitz in an earlier time, and an issue which consumed much of his attention as a member of the Strategic Objectives Committee (SOC) at RAND since 1952. As described by Alex Abella in *Soldiers of Reason: The RAND Corporation and the Rise of the American Empire*, "Beginning in the fall of 1952, Brodie, Andrew Marshall, [Charles] Hitch, and others formed an informal group they called the Strategic Objectives Committee. Meeting at lunchtime and after hours, they argued about the best way to deploy the enormous nuclear arsenal the United States was accumulating."[490] Brodie's 1971 discussion of strategy and national interests starts off with—and revisits throughout—the complex challenge of not only defining the national interest, but applying military means in order to achieve the objectives thereby defined. In his brief, two-page introduction, he notes that the "aspect of United States foreign policy that relates to the uses of military power is one we can traverse blindfold, if we wish, with the help of innumerable clichés ready at hand to guide us," a tempting approach as "we are dealing here with problems that become extraordinarily perplexing the moment we reject the commonly accepted answers; that may demand difficult, costly, and even dangerous commitments; and concerning which there is often the requirement of a high degree of national consensus."[491] For instance, the commonly held view that Brodie has long cherished, "that our foreign and military policies must be completely geared to each other," is open to wide interpretation, from the view that "foreign and military policies must be finely attuned to each other" to that which believes "there can be substantial latitude in each field without reference to the other," with some fearing "too much boldness" and yet others concerned more with "the possible reemergence of isolationism," and the complex mix of policies and objectives leads Brodie to recognize the need to "find a common language with which these various views can be rationally discussed," his primary concern in "this present essay."[492]

Brodie observes that policymaking, just as policy recommending or criticizing, "is inevitably a predictive process because it always involves a projection into the future. We choose the policy that we expect will prove more feasible, or more successful, or at least disagreeable in its consequences than one or more suggested alternatives. Shrewd prediction requires first of all an insightful awareness of the dimensions of uncertainty. We should know, in other words, what we are justified in trying to predict."[493] And, Brodie adds, it "also requires a full awareness of the dimensions of uncertainty. We should know, in other words, what we are justified in trying to predict, and also what we cannot predict with any significant degrees of confidence. For policy can and should adjust to uncertainty as well as to legitimate projections."[494] And "while prediction always benefits from good intuition," Brodie notes it "benefits also, and strikingly, from good training. One *learns* how to gather and appraise relevant information, and also how to discipline oneself to accept uncertainty."[495]

Brodie dives next into his long second chapter, "Major Determinants of United States Strategic Policies," noting America's "contemporary strategic policies . . . derive first of all from the very great power of this country," rooted in "its inherent strength in industrial, technological, and manpower resources," a reservoir so deep that Brodie presumes that we can safely predict the United States "is destined to remain for a long time to come—certainly for that rather limited time period in the future for which to makes sense to project military problems and policies—the most powerful industrial nation of the world," with its undiminished "ability to marshal the greatest resources for war."[496] And while its "will or resolve to do so may vary," Brodie notes that "resolve is largely influenced by events, and not least by what our opponents do."[497] As of Brodie's writing, America's resolve was ebbing, its commitment to Vietnam nearing its end and American military confidence at an historic low; but fully cognizant of America's great and undiminished potential rooted in its vast reservoir of latent power, an "intrinsic power" tied to America's long tradition of being "extraordinarily successful as a nation," Brodie observes that in its "long career, the United States has surmounted far greater crises than it faces today, especially that of secession and the Civil War, followed by its bitter aftermath" and the still "vivid memory" of the Great Depression "not to mention the less divisive crises such as the second of the two world wars—which was, in fact, a triumph of unity and national achievement."[498] Despite the optimism of his backward glances, Brodie explains they are "by no means" meant "to depreciate the seriousness of present divisions in the country" nor "the importance of taking their causes into account in determining the real capabilities of the country," but despite the doldrums faced during the final years of the Vietnam War, Brodie insists on pointing out "[o]ur past successes transcend our present frustrations," and "[r]ecalling them may give us faith in our abilities to surmount present difficulties."[499] And beyond faith, Brodie adds we can identify one recurrent pattern that connects these past successes overcoming adversity: "the leaders who carried us forward in the past were those who were fully aware that nothing is static in the affairs of the world and the nation."[500] Indeed, Brodie runs briefly through some of this dynamic flux in world affairs and America's response, from its early commitment to "no entangling alliances" as counseled by founding president George Washington in his farewell address, to its ascendancy as "leader of the free world" with a "considerable packet" of alliance commitments and international obligations, not to mention a global military presence responsible for the security of a good portion of the globe, recently divided at the end of World War II into a new, and global, bipolar order.[501] Brodie comments that "[f]or these among other reasons, United States strategic moves, and even its strategic ideas, are inevitably of great importance to the rest of the world. Where power and ideas for the use of that power have changed so much in so short a period of time, we may be confident that they are subject to further change, a likelihood that some of our allies appear to be more aware of than we are."[502]

And it was not just American ideas and policy prescriptions that would rapidly shift; the new ideological split between East and West that defined the bipolar world itself evolved into a more complex system as time went by: "The simplicity of this bifurcation has been greatly modified and qualified over the years by fractures in both the Communist world and what by contrast we call the 'free world,' " even as "much of American diplomacy and strategy" remained "dynamically affected by the goal, or rather the felt necessity, of opposing the spread of communism" through the broad policy known as containment, first described by George Kennan and which "as a major goal of policy" was "almost exactly coeval with our advance to world military leadership" and thus "of very recent origin" and "historically novel," thereby "subject to a good deal of debate as to its applicability in particular cases, and as to the methods of so doing,"[503] This would account in part for the contentious nature of foreign policy debates during the Vietnam War period, when containment was applied to a peripheral conflict zone that many would later judge to be of little consequence to the bipolar order America sought to preserve—with its adversary, the Vietnamese Communists, proxies neither of the Chinese or the Soviets. Before the trauma of Vietnam, Brodie recalled his own trauma watching as the Kennedy Administration in 1961 sought to "reject, or at least seal off, nuclear weapons as the basic element in our military power—a move which contrasted markedly with that adopted under President Eisenhower and then known as the 'new look,' sometimes identified with the phrase 'massive retaliation.' "[504] Brodie still expresses shock when he recalls, "It is remarkable that the nation which led the world in nuclear power should also have led the attempt to dispense with the use of that power, seeking even to reduce its significance as a latent threat," and regret when he adds that "[t]here is no question, however, that the choice registered in the eight years of the Kennedy-Johnson Administration has profoundly affected the world of today and the future,"[505] notably in the lingering trauma experienced in the conventionally fought, and soon to be lost, war in Vietnam.

As Brodie had been arguing for years, nuclear weapons—despite the prior administration's seeming disdain for their overwhelming power—"do and will remain in being as a keenly sensed pedal tone in all those aspects of our foreign policy that have military implications," and thus all "[t]alk about nuclear weapons being 'decoupled' from diplomacy, or 'neutralized' by the comparable weapons of the opponent, is decidedly farfetched. Barring true miracles of diplomacy in the field of disarmament, we shall continue to live in a world in which nuclear weapons of all types exist in large numbers, and where our major opponents possess them as well as ourselves. It is important, too, that those opponents have given every indication of being just as alive to the special and awful nature of nuclear war as we are," and "very much less important that a sophisticated few are now also becoming accustomed to thinking that nuclear war itself may take varying forms with different degrees of intensity and ferocity."[506] Indeed, Brodie finds some solace in observing that throughout America's two limited wars and its many other confrontations on the brink of war since the nuclear era began, decision makers remained "greatly affected by the knowledge that the collapse of limitations must lead to nuclear war."[507]

Fueling America's rise as a military power, and thus an underlying determinant of American strategic policy, is "the technological revolution throughout the whole range of weaponry" from the conventional to the thermonuclear.[508] As Brodie observed, "Since World War II, however, we have experienced such a revolution in the degree of complexity and speed of development of weaponry as to constitute a basic change in the character of change," with new weapons defined by not only their unprecedented lethality and global reach, but also their "hugely ascending costs" and their need to be "selected well before they exist—and developed according to predictive and sometimes speculative specifications" in marked contrast to the "old method" of "buying weapons off the shelf after they had been developed and proved."[509] Related to the impact of technological change on American military power are new "revolutionary methods of choice for dealing with the revolutionary rates of change in technology," whose "hallmark" is "modern 'systems analysis,' " which "are identified with such relatively new and themselves revolutionary institutions as The RAND Corporation" where they put to practice the new, post-World War II and "almost entirely" American innovation—one that would prove to be tragically over-emphasized during the war in Vietnam, obscuring more fundamental political calculations that should have revealed a fatal disconnect between the objectives sought, and the means applied.[510]

Another determinant of American strategic policy has been the evolving "fund of relevant experiences" of the United States since the end of World War II, including its two limited wars and its many crises from Berlin to Cuba: "These and other experiences, as reconstructed in the interpretations that have gained ascendancy, greatly influence strategic policy today, and will continue to do so in the future," albeit "subject to modification by further experience and further interpretation."[511] Perhaps foremost among these experiences in war and peace has been "having lived for almost a quarter of a century with the Soviet Union and China in a nuclear world without anything really approaching catastrophe, and, as a result, with much less general uneasiness today than at the beginning of the period," and "[c]onsidering also that our intervention in both the Korean and Vietnam wars was a matter of fairly free choice," Brodie points out that the "world since 1945 could have been very much more tranquil for us than it has been in fact."[512] Brodie suggests that if this is indeed the case, then "there may be in these contrasting events some lessons in how best to contain, and where."[513]

In closing this chapter, Brodie invokes his spirit guide and philosophical mentor, Carl von Clausewitz, that kindred spirit from another time of great consequence and danger; Brodie notes he has "tried to outline what are simply the more important factors going to make up the strategic capabilities of the United States," revealing a complex and evolving mosaic. Brodie comments, "just as the term 'strategy' is usually too narrowly interpreted as applying only to strictly military objectives, like defeating an enemy army (an error which Clausewitz, the greatest of the strategic theorists, repeatedly warned against in his famous but neglected book *On War*), so we tend to normally confine our conceptions of strategic capabilities to forces-in-being," and while forces-in-being should never be underappreciated, Brodie argues in Clausewitzian fashion that "just as strategy and strategic policies are always directed towards achieving *political* ends, with respect to which military objectives are only way-stations, so must strategic capabilities be reckoned in terms of the capacities of the state, first, for selecting reasonable ends to be pursued abroad, and second, for efficiently organizing its resources—intellectual and emotional as well as material—to accomplish those ends."[514]

While Brodie's next chapter is a lengthy discussion of vital interests titled "Vital Interests: By Whom and How Determined," it forms the core of a similarly titled chapter, the eighth in Brodie's 1973 *War and Politics*, "Vital Interests: What Are They, and Who Says So?" which further develops elements of the chapter but also repeats nearly all of its paragraphs, many verbatim or nearly so. In it, Brodie notes that it "is obvious that prevailing conceptions of American vital interests, which are effectively those held by the Administration in power, have changed drastically with time, especially over the three decades since we entered World War II," and on "closer scrutiny, we can see them continue to change before our very eyes."[515] Brodie points out that a "superpower like the United States does have unique (though far from unlimited) capacities to influence events throughout the world, and its leaders would be remiss in their duties if they did not regularly seek to exercise that influence in a manner calculated to enhance the nation's long-term interests, meaning above all its security interests."[516] But doing so can be a lot harder in practice, where 20–20 hindsight is of little value. Brodie recounts how in 1950, Secretary of State Dean Acheson omitted South Korea from America's defense perimeter, five months before the North Korean invasion, upon which President Truman "promptly committed the United States to military intervention" with Acheson being "one of those who most strongly urged him to do so."[517] Asks Brodie: "Were we fulfilling a vital interest?"—and if so, "why had it been not merely unrecognized but actually disavowed before the attack?"[518] And the same can be asked of President Johnson's decision to escalate America's Vietnam commitment from an advisory to a combat role, as it can of President's Nixon to not only withdraw those very same forces from South Vietnam (and thereby dooming that republic), but to publicly disavow the availability of a comparable level of military support for America's neighboring ally, Thailand— leading Brodie to ask, "Here was a sharply changing approach to the description of our vital interests—or was it in the estimation of our military capabilities?"[519]

With the definition of vital interests so dynamic, so rapidly evolving, and seemingly so contradictory, one can see how America's iron-clad nuclear commitments might come to be questioned. As Brodie recounts, "with the rapid growth of Soviet nuclear capability, the notion was gaining some currency among our European allies that the United States nuclear guarantee could no longer be relied upon," something the American government would deny "vehemently," and in Brodie's eyes, rightly so.[520] But as he reflects, "Still, in these matters how can one be truly convincing? It is difficult because the post-World War II nuclear world is totally different from any we have known before," and despite the heart-felt reassurances of our leaders, "doubts cannot be stilled—possibly including their own."[521] And "[e]veryone recognizes that total nuclear war would be an infinitely more fearsome thing than the greatest wars of the past" and "that much may hang on the identity of the President of the day, and no one can predict who will occupy that office some four years hence."[522] Nonetheless, Brodie points out—as he has done before—that "the question of 'nuclear reliability,' while not quite irrelevant, does not really deserve the kind of priority that the doubters automatically give it," and as demonstrated during the 1962 Cuban crisis, where "American moves and postures were adopted without any specific reference to nuclear weapons, although with an acute awareness of their contextual existence," there is a persistent nuclear effect caused by the bomb's mere existence, and even as the American monopoly gave way to a decisive American strategic superiority which in turn gave way to strategic parity with the Soviet Union, the "Soviet Union can hardly be more desirous of war with a nuclear equal than with a nuclear superior, certainly so long as parity is measured in large capabilities."[523] Brodie adds that "one argument against skepticism with respect to American nuclear reliability is that it reflects a gross exaggeration of the adversary's proclivity for going to the nuclear brink," and as "long as the Soviet Union has no ironclad guarantee that the United States will not use nuclear weapons, she has much to be careful about."[524]

Brodie concludes his discussion of vital interests by observing they "are not to be found in objective reality but rather in the minds of men," but they are nonetheless not "something insubstantial, but rather about what we will *fight* for," and America "at any one time does have a distinctive set of strategic policies, visible and quite firm, tied to equally visible foreign policies with their core of 'vital interests,' also relatively firm," often "rather easily identified by certain slogans" whether containing communism or resisting aggression or defending liberty or securing the free world.[525] But despite the simplicity and clarity of such slogans, Brodie points out that "future crises when they come may breed their own patterns of responses, and these are certainly more difficult to predict than superficial pronouncements would have us believe,"[526] leaving much to prediction and to the complex challenge of assessing probabilities of outcomes during events that may not only be unforeseen, but which might unfold along trajectories that bear little resemblance to past conflicts. It is the challenge of making such predictions, and calculating the probabilities of such future strategic challenges, that Brodie turns to in his fourth and final chapter, "Possible Modifications in United States Strategic Policies."

Brodie proceeds to "consider future determinants in United States strategy," noting the necessity in a world of limited resources to "avoid not only the much-warned-against error of preoccupation with any single contingency, but also the opposite error of attempting to embrace every conceivable contingency" since "inasmuch as every hedge against a possible untoward event is a bet requiring that large sums of money be put on the line, we must think automatically (even if roughly) in terms of degree of probability."[527] Brodie notes "[w]e may well find ourselves legitimately spending large sums to cope with quite low-order probabilities" if by doing so the probability becomes even lower "and if the event guarded against would be devastatingly costly," as evident in "the sum of our preparations against thermonuclear strategic war," an investment well worth making—in contrast to the substantial expenses dedicated in recent years to "contingencies that are at best wildly improbable," as Brodie saw "our national dedication to the proposition that the Soviet Union might attack Western Europe massively with conventional weapons in the hope *and expectation* that the ensuing hostilities would stay non-nuclear," an idea that "provoked a large and costly buildup of our own conventional forces, and an intensive but futile effort to get our European allies to do likewise"[528]—a topic that consumed much of Brodie's attention during the preceding decade.

Brodie observes that conventional buildup "reflected a philosophy which at this writing, mostly as a result of our experience in Vietnam, has lost much of the favor it once enjoyed" and Defense Secretary McNamara's "constant advocacy of maintaining a wide range of options, especially non-nuclear options, no longer appears so obviously prudent" and the scenarios upon which McNamara's vision was predicated "appeared less impressive" to his "successors than they did to him," fueled in part by NATO's determined "refusal . . . to respond to those scenarios" and to the decreasing attention paid to the "prospect of the Soviet Union and its Warsaw Pact allies making a massive conventional attack on Western Europe."[529] With this fog now lifting, Brodie rejoices that "[w]e are again capable of realizing that when the Russians look westward, they see enormous numbers of tactical nuclear weapons, including well over seven thousand in Europe. One does not need to threaten their use. The fact that they are there is what matters."[530]

With Vietnam winding down and with it the long preoccupation with a conventional build-up and to conventional conceptions of limited war also now greatly "dimmed," Brodie observes an emergent unwillingness to sustain large military expenditures, not only in America but among its allies—and presumably across the Iron Curtain as well.[531] While members of the defense community have long been "well aware that defense resources are always limited enough to require certain hard choices in military allocation," with America's unique wealth one of the defining ingredients of its latent power, "expenditures that might otherwise have been regarded as unnecessary or even wasteful were sometimes recommended on the ground that they imposed comparable or presumably less tolerable expenditures on the opponent,"[532] a situation that would recur a decade later with President Reagan's enthusiastic commitment to ballistic missile defense, his famous Star Wars plan, which many lauded for the intense economic pressure it placed on the near-bankrupt Soviet economy, which within a few years collapsed completely. A mixture of the bitter aftertaste of the Vietnam debacle (and its high material and human cost) and a series of well publicized and egregious cost-overruns such as the Lockheed

C-5A air transport combined with inflation pressures combined to sap the appetite America long had for sustaining its level of military expenditures. Brodie surmises that "[w]e may expect that, in the future as in the past, the willingness of our elected representatives to spend large sums of money on defense will respond fairly elastically to the kinds of perturbations abroad that have usually stimulated defense spending," even if at the moment of Brodie's writing with the Vietnam crisis at its peak, "we may be entering a period in which a desire for retrenchment in military expenditures will coincide with a desire for the reduction of our foreign security commitments," and during which "the intensity and fervor which we have hitherto brought to our major alliance commitments is likely to undergo some cooling, again barring conspicuous enemy-initiated provocations."[533] But despite this cooling, Brodie notes there remains "no doubt that the West European countries want to maintain the American alliance," even if their assessment of the risk of Soviet attack remains low," but he suggests that the North Atlantic treaty "will prosper better in the future if Americans take a lower-keyed approach to it than they have in the past."[534]

Brodie concedes that the "chance of a general thermonuclear war as a result of a surprise attack by either of the superpowers upon the other is about nil, and commonly recognized to be so," meaning that a "major nuclear war can occur only if a lesser-war escalates out of control, and the mere possibility that it may do so is what makes nuclear weapons a deterrent even to local wars between powers mutually possessing them."[535] So the salient "question become, What are the issues and places over which there may be confrontations that may lead to what, initially at least, is local conflict?"[536] And it is here that the Vietnam experience must be considered. Brodie notes in contrast to Korea, where the commitment to the defense of South Korea was precipitated by the "open arrogance and brusqueness of the Communist attack," Vietnam came about more gradually over the course of a decade after the French withdrawal in 1954 before making a combat commitment in 1965, affording "plenty of time to examine the situation and to ruminate on appropriate goals and the possibilities of success," although Brodie concedes "[s]uch rumination seems not to have gone very deep."[537] Perhaps fueled in part by America's underestimation of "the extent of Hanoi's independence from Peking," America misapplied its containment strategy, waging limited war against a peripheral power that was not the Soviet or Communist Chinese proxy it was perceived to be; moreover, Brodie notes "Americans do well in situations where military operations are easily isolated from political constraints, and where the fighting is of such a unique nature as to require the abundant use of military commodities"[538]—neither of which was presented by Vietnam. But Brodie finds some comfort from the expectation that the "Vietnam experience should help to clarify in our minds which are the most important decisions in strategic policy," and that "[t]hese are the decisions that are deeply involved with political imponderables and that are taken up with the reevaluation of national purposes, partly on the basis of new insights into feasibility," and as Brodie would reiterate later in 1971 in his *Foreign Policy* article on the tragic strategic failure of Vietnam, these turn out to be "the decisions that obviously do not lend themselves to characteristic forms of systems analysis and related techniques," and while systems analysis and associated methods "remain not simply invaluable, but actually indispensable, tools" for "pertinent" decisions such as between competing weapons systems, Brodie points out that for "more basic decisions . . . obviously do not lend themselves to the accepted patterns of scientism," even though he still hopes they will be "treated a good deal more scientifically" by which he means "more objectively and more systematically."[539] Nonetheless, he concedes that "[i]t would be foolish to predict that they will be so treated," even though "it is a consummation devoutly to be wished."[540]

Brodie writes that the "technological revolution in weaponry, we are assured by those who know best, will not only not pause; it will not even slow down," and were it "not for development lead times and desperately ascending costs, changes in weaponry would go on accelerating at an ever dizzying rate."[541] But "[a]dvancing technology is both a servant and a master," the former "because it usually molds military tactics into patterns," albeit ones that "suit the United States better than they do any other country;" and the latter because "it obliges us to pour huge sums into projects which change nothing basically, but which if neglected would adversely affect our ever-varying position vis-à-vis our major opponent."[542] And while technology continues its advance, "the new methods of weapons systems analysis" will see much less of an acceleration caused by the "deflation in the enormous prestige which its practitioners enjoyed in the McNamara period," during which the Defense Secretary appeared to have been "persuaded that they were coterminus with the while field of strategy and strategic policy,"[543] resulting in his overdependence on these new methods, neglecting to first resolve more basic political questions relating to the objective sought, its probability of success, and whether a vital interest was at stake.

Looking one last time at the unique role for nuclear weapons, which—as he has long argued—find their greatest utility in their non-use, Brodie observes that the "fact that nuclear weapons have not been used since Nagasaki no doubt helps to confirm what Professor Thomas C. Schelling has called the 'tradition of non-use,'" and adds that the "horror of nuclear weapons has certainly not diminished as a result of this uninterrupted period of non-use" even if "the issues over which we have actually engaged in military operations during this period were not of a kind to warrant the use of nuclear weapons."[544] Brodie reiterates his long-standing critique of the CWE advocates and their firebreak theories that postulated the strategic benefits of keeping a European war conventional, and thereby reducing the escalatory risk to general war, which Brodie long held to be illogical and preposterous, since holding back on nuclear use would not only undermine deterrence but would risk the loss of Europe to a massive Soviet conventional attack—and in the face of such a loss, nuclear use would not only be logical, but necessary to prevent such a major strategic setback. In short, Brodie saw no benefit for the effort, and only an increase in risk. And yet the CWE "philosophy that reached its zenith under President Kennedy and continued to dominate American strategic thinking" was rooted, in Brodie's mind, in "notions that governments of other countries . . . considered untenable and even ludicrous."[545] And so, "[d]espite lip service, our European allies disregarded our repeated requests that they build up their conventional forces," and in the end "[o]ur own leaders came to realize there was really no way to defend Western Europe against a massive Soviet attack except by the relatively early use of nuclear weapons," a realization that "is saved from being a horrible thought by the fact that nuclear weapons provide the decisive (but surely not the only) reason why the Soviet Union shows not the slightest disposition to make such an attack. If there must be war, it is no doubt better to have it non-nuclear than nuclear; but if nuclear weapons help critically in avoiding a third world war, there begins to be some reason to value rather than deplore their existence."[546]

Taking a cue from the terminology of the Kennedy era, whose policies Brodie challenged from start to finish, he recalls earlier placing "a special premium on *insightful awareness* of the indicators for the future which are already visible in the present scene," adding that what is "[a]lso needed, one might add, is a 'flexible response' in one's perceptions, that is, a readiness to stand apart from one's preconceptions, for these are not simple derived from the past but overcommitted to the past."[547] While our first priority is to plan for the near term and not remote future, when "we are obliged in some instances to deal with the more remote future, the first requirement is to understand and become reconciled to the character and dimensions of uncertainty," and that means instead of "preparing for the worst," we should instead aim for "understanding what things we cannot predict," since one "can waste much effort and money attempting to provide against the 'worst possible' case, which is both unlikely to occur and, in a nuclear era, probably impossible to provide against."[548] And thus, "for nations as well as individuals, there is often merit as well as comfort in keeping one's cool."[549]

Restating the Case for Tactical Nuclear Weapons

Brodie would make one last concerted effort to make the case for tactical nuclear weapons in the defense of Europe, in his introduction to a July 1976 National Strategy Information Center (NSIC) Agenda Paper, *Toward a New Defense for NATO: The Case for Tactical Nuclear Weapons.* In his preface to the paper, Frank R. Barnett writes that the NSIC had "convened a private conference in Washington, D.C., on January 23–24, 1976, to consider the role of tactical nuclear weapons in modern war, and especially in the defense of Western Europe against a possible attack by the Soviet Union and its Warsaw Pact allies," noting that this topic had been "much neglected in the literature of nuclear strategy and tactics, although the option of a new generation of 'clean,' precision-guided tactical nuclear weapons offers a logical means to blunt the thrust of a massive Soviet armored offensive into Germany and Yugoslavia."[550] Barnett added parenthetically, "Since we do not match the new Czars in sheer weight of numbers, or ruthless disregard for casualties, or deception and surprise, we ought to ensure that high technology is always on the side of the Western democracies."[551] The NSIC found the "deliberations of the conference . . . were so stimulating and productive that we have considered it worthwhile to make a summary of them, together with supporting documentation, available to a larger audience as part of NSIC's Agenda Papers series," with "an Introduction to the subject by Bernard Brodie, the military historian and analyst."[552] In his introduction to the work, Brodie would reiterate his opposition to the firebreak theorists and their advocacy of conventional strategies for defending Europe, reasserting his confidence in tactical nuclear weapons as effective deterrents to Soviet aggression. He recounts how at the start of the atomic era, "there was naturally much confusion—but hardly any doubt—that nuclear weapons would be used in any war that they failed to deter," and at that time there was "little distinction between strategic and tactical use, but the prevailing preoccupation was with the former. Nor was there much thought of 'brushfire' wars before Korea. The accepted wisdom of the time was frequently voiced in the phrase: 'Modern war is total war.' "[553]

Brodie noted that the "first important change of thinking in this area came toward the end of the Korean War" but explained "it was not in the first instance stimulated by that war" but instead "resulted from the knowledge within a limited circle that a thermonuclear weapon was soon to be tested and that success was virtually certain," leading Brodie and his colleagues Charles J. Hitch and Ernst Plessett to form a "small group at the RAND Corporation" after they had "acquired this information near the end of 1951," to "prepare briefings that would suggest to senior Air Force officers some of the implications of the new weapon"[554]—a series of briefings, Brodie added in a footnote, that were "highly classified, never published, and have probably been lost."[555] Brodie observed that "[t]here developed from this exercise the idea that the thermonuclear weapon, which the Soviet Union could be expected soon to duplicate, made a strategic bombing exchange far too costly to bear and too devoid of opportunity for either side to gain significant advantage—without which, as Clausewitz had argued 120 years earlier, war can have no meaning."[556] Instead, the "alternative recommended was that war be returned to the battlefield (with nuclear weapons, of course), and that on the strategic level everything be concentrated on deterrence," though while the Korean War "was now seen to disprove the view that modern war was inevitably total war," it was fought below the nuclear firebreak; and as Brodie described, "To be sure, nuclear weapons were not used tactically in Korea; but there were special reasons for that, the most important being the conviction prevalent in the Pentagon during 1950–51 that the Soviet Union was using Korea simply as a blind behind which it was preparing to launch, very soon, a massive attack in Europe. The small existing stockpile had to be saved for the main event."[557] Korea's enduring lesson was nonetheless that war "could be sculpted meaningfully, omitting strategic bombing where that seemed indicated"[558]—demonstrating that war could be kept limited in the nuclear age, consistent with limited objectives.

Ironically, the successful experience of waging limited war in Korea was followed by the announcement, the year after that conflict was concluded, of the new " 'massive retaliation' idea, to which Secretary of State Dulles gave expression in his speech of January 12, 1954," a doctrinal shift that "owed nothing to the prior thinking just described" but which was enunciated by those who "viewed Korea in retrospect as simply the wrong way to fight a war, certainly for any country that possessed nuclear weapons under near-monopoly conditions. Besides, President Eisenhower felt deeply that· the country could not afford both a strong nuclear and a strong conventional capability. Inasmuch as the choice had to be made, it was obvious how it must go."[559] For Brodie, the "main significance to our story of the 'massive retaliation' idea is that it stimulated a widespread reaction which, for the first time in the nuclear age, evoked arguments stressing the need for conventional forces," and these new arguments would gain greater credence, becoming policy during the Kennedy administration that would follow Eisenhower's. As Brodie explained, "Many now realized that nuclear weapons could not be used in all cases of military challenge, and certainly not in the small conflicts called 'brushfire' wars. The United States was indeed able to afford both kinds of capability, or so the general argument went, and it must therefore provide for both."[560] It was this "next major mutation in nuclear age thinking" which "brings us to the controversy which is the subject of the present Agenda Paper," Brodie noted, as during "the dying days of the Eisenhower Administration and the bright new dawn of the Kennedy Presidency, another group—again comprised mostly of analysts at RAND—were now determined to make the world safe against all nuclear explosions."[561] And this group, Brodie adds, was led by Albert Wohlstetter, "although Alain C. Enthoven has been the most frequent spokesman in print for their position," and he was joined by "Malcolm Hoag, W. W. Kaufmann, and Henry Rowen," all of whom Brodie would challenge internally in various RAND working papers and presentations before he left for UCLA toward the end of the Kennedy–Johnson era.[562] As Brodie describes, the "idea of returning war to the battlefield and mutually deterring any strategic nuclear exchange was all well and good, these men held; but nuclear weapons must be done away with on the battlefield, too. In fact, they warned, it was essential to do so in order to avoid a strategic nuclear exchange, because nothing was more certain to trigger such an exchange than any use of any nuclear weapons anywhere,"[563] a view Brodie did not share given his enduring faith in deterrence as sound strategy, and in nuclear weapons as potential de-escalatory tools.

Brodie explains that according to the firebreak theorists, this would "be accomplished in any major war, especially one in Europe . . . simply by building up US and NATO conventional ground and air forces to something like parity with those of the Warsaw Pact—which, these advocates insisted, did not really require much extra effort," in marked contrast to the views on this matter by the Europeans with whom Brodie felt greater accord [564] According to the CWE advocates, as they were sometimes referred, "Doing so would raise the 'nuclear threshold' to so high a level as virtually to eliminate the chances of its being breached. It did not matter that the universally accepted premise on our side of the Iron Curtain was that if there were a major war in Europe, it would be a Soviet attack that initiated it. Inasmuch as everyone on both sides would understand that our European allies would be much more willing to resist Soviet aggression if they had confidence that the resulting battle would remain nonnuclear (the determination of the United States at that time being above all doubt, at least among Americans), the proposed posture would greatly enhance real deterrence."[565]

But Brodie suggests that "[w]hether such high confidence could ever be achieved, or ought under any circumstances to be entertained, was one of several embarrassing questions that the new school thought best not to scrutinize too closely," and "[t]hey apparently believed that the logic of the new idea was so compelling it would quickly be accepted by Soviet military leaders as well as our own."[566] Brodie noted that, "[t]o be sure, our people were determined not to lose a war in Europe," so consequently "there would be no first use unless we found ourselves losing."[567] Brodie added that the "Russians were somehow expected to accommodate to this rigidity on our part, which they would no doubt regard as slightly peculiar"[568]—and perhaps not all that credible. Brodie recalls that "the original protagonists of this view harbored a sufficiently high expectation of a Soviet attack in Europe to advocate with some urgency a considerable improvement of NATO forces there, although they also seemed to find it forensically necessary to insist that NATO forces were already very nearly equal to those of the Warsaw Pact in military manpower," and as Brodie further described in a footnote, "Dr. Enthoven has consistently argued this point in several publications, the most recent being his article, 'U.S. Forces in Europe: How Many? Doing What?' " in the April 1975 edition of *Foreign Affairs*, in which "Enthoven holds that Warsaw Pact forces on M-Day plus 60 would be 1,241,000 (as compared with NATO's 1,105,000)," leading Brodie to wonder "what happened to the Soviet Union which, without allies, suffered the loss of five to six million troops during the first five and a half months of war in 1941, and then went on to win"?[569] Despite Brodie's skepticism that there was anything close to practical parity between NATO and Soviet conventional forces in Europe, he found that this "theory was attractive enough to win ready converts in the highest reaches of the Kennedy Administration, including the President himself, his vigorous Secretary of Defense, Robert S. McNamara, and the President's military advisor, General Maxwell Taylor," who "had already been moving somewhat in that direction anyway, mostly out of repugnance for the cuts in the size of the Army that went with Eisenhower's adherence to 'massive retaliation.' "[570] But countering this enthusiasm as the highest levels of American power, it "was, however, entirely predictable that our NATO allies would not go along with the new American idea, despite the fervor with which our government urged them to strengthen their conventional forces, and also urged the France of Charles de Gaulle to desist from developing its own nuclear weapons"— indeed, Brodie notes he himself had predicted European resistance to CWE in his May 23, 1963 article in *The Reporter*, "What Price Conventional Capabilities in Europe," an article that was later "included, with a note of approval by the editor, in Henry A. Kissinger's anthology, *Problems of National Strategy* (1965)."[571] Not only did Europeans not want to increase the size of their standing armies or invest in a conventional build-up, they also came to believe that "the Soviet threat seemed to be receding rather than the reverse. Why, therefore, spend more money?"—or, moreover, why do "anything that seemed to undercut the grand nuclear deterrent," leading NATO to elect to "cushion themselves somewhat from American pressures simply by giving lip service to the notion of 'graduated response' " while being "less than ever inclined to expand or flesh out their conventional forces since they were in fact clearly disposed in the opposite direction."[572] So despite the enthusiastic embrace of CWE by the highest levels of the Kennedy administration, European reluctance ensured that "the physical prerequisite to the idea of fighting a large conventional land battle in Europe never came into existence."[573] Added Brodie: "Simple facts, do not normally impede messianic vision,"[574] but on several fronts, these facts provided the apostles of CWE with a stiff reality check: "What was a novel and radical doctrine 15 years ago has now, in the mid-1970s, become the conventional wisdom of the interested public and of most of the defense community," although "military officers tend today to be ambivalent on the matter" and "usually are prepared in principle to use tactical nuclear weapons if the other side uses them first—or, as something of an afterthought, in case we find ourselves losing without them. But their thinking shows the results of 15 years of propagandizing by those bright and persuasive civilians who had the backing of strong Secretaries of Defense, including most recently Dr. James R. Schlesinger. They have, by the frank admission of some of them, simply not been thinking very much about it."[575]

Brodie concedes that the "theory that the use of theater nuclear weapons can be avoided even in a major conflict in Europe simply by organizing forces for their nonuse is a seductive one" and that "[o]ne wants to believe it, especially if one can be persuaded that forces so organized make for more rather than less deterrence," and while "[s]trategic nuclear weapons are generally accepted as necessary, even in large numbers, because they deter at the same time as they threaten the ultimate holocaust," the advocates of CWE argue that, "inasmuch as the mutuality of that ultimate destruction is so completely assured, no one will dare trip any nuclear trigger that might set it off."[576] But Brodie finds this is where "we see the dubious keystone of the argument: the insistence that the vast difference or 'firebreak' between use and nonuse of any kind of nuclear weapon of whatever size totally diminishes and obscures all other 'firebreaks' or discontinuities, such as that between battlefield fighting on the one hand and a strategic holocaust on the other, or even between war and nonwar. War, especially major war, used to be considered serious. Now its seriousness seems to be secondary to, and decidedly less than, the choice among weapons to fight with on the battlefield."[577] As memories of the total destruction of World War II continued to fade, so apparently did the perception of conventional warfare in Europe as total war. And while Brodie agrees that it was "no doubt right at one time to challenge the 'just another weapon' attitude with which some Army officers pondered the nuclear stockpile," that time was now past, and "after years of drastic change in the whole strategic environment" it was now "time for another look. The threat of the ultimate holocaust does indeed powerfully add to the already considerable inhibitions against any kind of war between the two superpowers, who are thus far almost alone in possessing the means for making it possible. But what is so forbidding a sanction against the outbreak of war must also be a powerful inhibition against escalation from all lesser forms of warfare to its own dread self."[578]

Another wild card to consider is the perspective of the opponent, the Russians, whose "public discussion of that contingency always projects a mirror image" of America's strategic presumption – that the next war will necessarily be started by Moscow—and instead presumes "any war in Europe is initiated by us! To be sure, this is not an unhealthy state of affairs; but in any event, we must stick to our own premise and let them worry about theirs. One must then ask, Can anyone believe, with confidence, that the Soviet Union would challenge us to so deadly a duel and yet leave the choice of weapons entirely to us? Can anyone seriously think that if the Russians launched such an attack, they would not be determined to win it as quickly as possible by offensive action, with whatever weapons were necessary to accomplish that victory?"[579] Brodie is confident "that they would indeed be so determined," as is suggested by "their public discussion of strategic affairs."[580]

Brodie also notes that many of the escalation theorists "have told us, over and over again, that we have to take account of accidents, of conflagrations starting without anyone wishing them to start, and then rapidly escalating to levels that are even more dismaying to those who were only trying a little probe," and that this fear of unintended escalation "is one of the chief reasons why the nuclear weapon must not be used too soon," a scenario that Brodie finds to be historically without precedent in modern times, and thus finds "it is astonishing that accidental war—something that has never happened before in at least the last three centuries—should be considered so dangerous a possibility in a world that knows nuclear weapons, where it is even less likely."[581] Brodie includes in his tally of wars that were not accidentally triggered both World Wars, the American civil war, and all European wars dating as far back as the Thirty Years War, though one could challenge his perception of World War I, where a rigid alliance structure seemed to escalate to total war without rationality upon the most minor of provocations, contradicting Brodie's conclusion of the implausibility of such a scenario. Though Brodie does concede that wars "may be, and often have been, the result of foolishness. But they are never the result of accident."[582]

Brodie also questions "the assumption that the same forces that are organized, equipped, and trained to fight a nonnuclear war are capable of shifting at a moment's notice to a nuclear posture,"[583] an essential precondition for firebreak theory to work—since the capacity to escalate across the nuclear threshold in the event defeat is imminent by conventional defense is necessary for deterrence to hold. Brodie draws on his knowledge of naval warfare to illustrate what is "[p] erhaps the most extreme example of nonadaptability," that of "combat naval forces organized primarily around huge aircraft carriers of the so-called *attack* variety, anyone of which can be utterly destroyed and largely vaporized by a single quite small nuclear weapon which can be discharged against it from an aircraft, a surface vessel, a submarine, or even a shore-based missile launcher," and he cautions that "[w]e might do well to remember that Admiral S.G. Gorshkov, chief of the Soviet Navy since 1955, explicitly and publicly rejected the development of large attack carriers for the Soviet Navy in 1967 on the specific ground that they were too vulnerable to nuclear weapons,"[584] though Brodie adds in a footnote that Moscow was instead "apparently building six smaller carriers of a type which we usually call ASW carriers" that "are capable of operating helicopters and V/STOL aircraft" and which "are much smaller than our huge attack carriers" and perhaps better suited to the current strategic environment; but Brodie adds that "one must not expect Soviet admirals to be any more consistent than our own" and suggests that "[o]ur carriers must exert a considerable prestige pressure."[585]

Brodie turns, in closing, to the eternal wisdom of Winston Churchill who "once wrote: 'However absorbed a commander may be in the elaboration of his own thoughts, it is necessary sometimes to take the enemy into consideration,' " borrowing the phrase from his earlier 1959 text of *Strategy in the Missile Age*.[586] No matter how imminent or great the threat to Europe by Soviet forces might be, Brodie points out that "to defend against the threat, whether exaggerated or not, is what NATO and its force structure is all about"—and as a result, "whatever resources are devoted to securing Europe (and ourselves) against military attack should be organized and spent in the best way that our deeply considered judgment permits us to do so."[587] And for Brodie that continues to mean fully leveraging the tactical utility of nuclear weapons in war to offset Soviet conventional strength—and its historic potential to augment that strength with an even deeper reserve force, as it did when it reversed the Nazi onslaught, and ultimately triumphed at such great human and material cost.

Notes

[1–17] Bernard Brodie, *War and Politics* (New York: Macmillan, 1973), 381; 382; 407; 419; 419; 419–20; 420; 420; 420; 421; 421; 421; 421; 421; 430; 430; 431, respectively.

[18–72] Bernard Brodie, Preface, "Some Preliminary Observations on Escalation," RAND Working Paper, September 13, 1962, ii; 4 (New Preface S/M); 1; 1; 1; 1–2; 2; 2; 2–3; 3; 3; 3; 3; 4; 4; 4; 4; 5; 5; 5–6; 6; 6; 6; 6; 7; 7; 8; 8; 8; 8; 8; 8; 9; 9; 9; 9; 10; 10; 10; 10; 11; 11; 11; 12; 12; 12; 12–13; 13; 13; 13; 13–14; 13 (n.5); 14, respectively.

[73–109] Bernard Brodie and Fawn Brodie, *From Crossbow to H-Bomb*, Revised Edition. Bloomington: Indiana University Press, 1973, 7 (originally published by New York: Dell Books, 1962 without the chapter, "Recent Weaponry Changes (1962–1972),"which was added to the 1973 edition); 7; 8; 8; 11; 261; 261–2; 262; 262; 263; 264; 264; 266; 266; 266; 266; 266; 267; 268; 268; 269; 269; 269; 270; 272–3; 277; 278; 280; 281; 281; 281–2; 282; 282; 284; 285, respectively. As recounted by Newell G. Bringhurst in his biography of Brodie's wife Fawn, in 1960, Bernard had been "awarded a Carnegie Corporation Reflective Year Fellowship, to commence in July," under whose terms he would "live abroad while engaged in what was termed 'reflective scholarship'" and would thereby "free him from the pressures of research and writing at RAND." He and the family thus headed to France; he, Fawn, and their two youngest children, Bruce and Pamela, would be in Paris and their older son Dick headed to the University of Grenoble. To "help cover the costs, Bernard signed a contract with Dell, a paperback publisher, to produce a history of the impact of science on military technology," *From Crossbow to H-Bomb*, which was "intended for the college market, specifically for courses in military science and related disciplines. Although Bernard assumed primary responsibility for the authorship of this volume, clearly within his own area of expertise, he enlisted Fawn's help in doing the research. In the end, Fawn would do most of the actual writing as well." Prior to the family's departure, "Fawn completed research for *From Crossbow to H-Bomb*," and "had assumed primary responsibility for the manuscript, even though Bernard had been the one to sign the book contract with Dell." After the Brodies completed *From Crossbow to H-Bomb*, Bernard "eagerly looked forward to the year away from RAND, where he had become increasingly dissatisfied. The experience in Paris, he hoped, would regenerate his spirits and enable him to return to California with renewed enthusiasm." See: Newell G. Bringhurst, *Fawn McKay Brodie: A Biographer's Life* (Norman: University of Oklahoma Press, 1999), 153; 154; 158; 158; 162; 162; 163; and 168 respectively.

[110-120] Bernard Brodie, "What Price Conventional Capabilities in Europe?" *The Reporter*, May 23, 1963, 25; 26; 26; 26; 26; 26; 28; 33; 33; 33; 33, respectively.

[121-58] Bernard Brodie, "Morals and Strategy: Distinguishing Virtue from Ignorance in Problems of National Defense," *Worldview*, Washington, DC: Carnegie Council for Ethics in International Affairs, September 1964, 4 (it is interesting to note that three years later, amid the social upheaval of the Vietnam War, Brodie took a similar approach to protesting students in an op-ed published in the UCLA *Daily Bruin* on December 1, 1967, "Students and the Military-Industrial Complex," as reprinted in William P. Gerberding and Bernard Brodie, eds, *The Political Dimension in National Strategy: Five Papers*, Security Studies Paper No. 13 (Los Angeles: UCLA Security Studies Project, 1968), 33–5, in which he challenged the moral presumptions of student protesters opposed to Dow Chemical's recruitment efforts on campus because of its role manufacturing napalm, then in wide use in Vietnam. Brodie points out that the decision to use napalm rests with the government, and thus reflects the popular will—so student efforts to reverse the decision reflect the effort "for a minority to use whatever pressure it can at whatever critical point it chooses in order to intrude its will upon the majority." (p. 34) Brodie's experience suggests that contrary to the students' belief, there was no "evidence of any intervention of industry with respect to such high policy decisions as those determining our interventions," (p. 35) from Korea to Vietnam, nor "of their guiding other policy decisions in any significant respect, such as those involving the use of—or non-use—of napalm," leading Brodie to ask: "Is that what we wish to change?" (p. 35) Brodie recalls that napalm during World War II was used successfully as "an instrument that helped to reduce drastically casualties of American forces landing on the islands of the Pacific," (p. 34) at which time Brodie recalled there was "absolutely no protest" (p. 35) against such use against such "deeply dug in" (p. 34) Japanese forces. Brodie further observed that war is "inherently destructive and murderous, and the difference between one weapon and another is usually a matter of efficiency in particular uses," (p. 34) and while "being burned is a horrible way of dying . . . so is being torn apart by shell fragments." (p. 35)); 4; 4 (citing Peter Ritner's review John Strachey's *The Prevention of War* in *The New Leader*); 4; 4; 4; 4; 4–5; 5; 5; 5; 5; 5; 5; 5; 5; 5; 5; 5; 5; 5; 5; 5–6; 6; 6; 6; 6; 6; 6–7; 7; 7; 7; 7; 7; 7; 8; 8; 8, respectively.

[159-291] Bernard Brodie, *Escalation and the Nuclear Option* (Princeton: Princeton University Press, 1966), 21. n. 14; (PUP 1966), preface (i); (PUP 1966), preface (i); RAND Memorandum RM-4544-PR (Santa Monica: RAND Corporation, June 1965), Preface, iii; (RAND RM-4544-PR, 1965), Preface, iii; (RAND RM-4544-PR, 1965), Preface, iii; (PUP 1966), 3; (PUP 1966), 3; (PUP 1966), 3–4; (PUP 1966), 4; (PUP 1966), 4); (PUP 1966), 5; (PUP 1966), 5; (PUP 1966), 6; (PUP 1966), 7; (PUP 1966), 8; (PUP 1966), 3; (PUP 1966), 9; (PUP 1966), 8–9; (PUP 1966), 9; (PUP 1966), 10; (PUP 1966), 20; (PUP 1966), 20; (PUP 1966), 21; (PUP 1966), 22; (PUP 1966), 22; (PUP 1966), 23; (RAND RM-4544-PR, 1965), 1; (RAND RM-4544-PR, 1965), 1; (RAND RM-4544-PR, 1965), 2; (RAND RM-4544-PR, 1965), 3–4; (RAND RM-4544-PR, 1965), 7–8; (RAND RM-4544-PR, 1965), 8; (RAND RM-4544-PR, 1965), 8–9; (RAND RM-4544-PR, 1965), 9; (RAND RM-4544-PR, 1965), 9–10; (RAND RM-4544-PR, 1965), 11; (RAND RM-4544-PR, 1965), 11–12; (RAND RM-4544-PR, 1965), 12; (RAND RM-4544-PR, 1965), 13 ; (RAND RM-4544-PR, 1965), 15; (RAND RM-4544-PR, 1965), 15; (RAND RM-4544-PR, 1965), 19; (PUP 1966), 45–47; (RAND RM-4544-PR, 1965), 20; (RAND RM-4544-PR, 1965), 21; (RAND RM-4544-PR, 1965), 21; (RAND RM-4544-PR, 1965), 23; (RAND RM-4544-PR, 1965), 25; (RAND RM-4544-PR, 1965), 25–6; (RAND RM-4544-PR, 1965), 27–8; (RAND RM-4544-PR, 1965), 29; (RAND RM-4544-PR, 1965), 29; (RAND RM-4544-PR, 1965), 29; (RAND RM-4544-PR, 1965), 29; (RAND RM-4544-PR, 1965), 31; (RAND RM-4544-PR, 1965), 32–3; (PUP 1966), 66; (RAND RM-4544-PR, 1965), 34; (RAND RM-4544-PR, 1965), 35–6; (RAND RM-4544-PR, 1965),

36–7; (RAND RM-4544-PR, 1965), 37; (RAND RM-4544-PR, 1965), 37; (RAND RM-4544-PR, 1965), 38; (RAND RM-4544-PR, 1965), 38; (RAND RM-4544-PR, 1965), 39; (RAND RM-4544-PR, 1965), 39–40; (RAND RM-4544-PR, 1965), 40–1; (RAND RM-4544-PR, 1965), 41; (RAND RM-4544-PR, 1965), 41; (RAND RM-4544-PR, 1965), 43; (RAND RM-4544-PR, 1965), 43; (RAND RM-4544-PR, 1965), 44; (RAND RM-4544-PR, 1965), 46; (RAND RM-4544-PR, 1965), 47; (RAND RM-4544-PR, 1965), 47; (RAND RM-4544-PR, 1965), 47; (RAND RM-4544-PR, 1965), 49; (PUP 1966), 96; (RAND RM-4544-PR, 1965), 56; (PUP 1966(), 97; (RAND RM-4544-PR, 1965), 56; (RAND RM-4544-PR, 1965), 59; (RAND RM-4544-PR, 1965), 59–60; (PUP 1966), 101; (RAND RM-4544-PR, 1965), 60; (RAND RM-4544-PR, 1965), 60; (RAND RM-4544-PR, 1965), 60–1; (RAND RM-4544-PR, 1965), 62; (RAND RM-4544-PR, 1965), 63; (PUP 1966), 104; (RAND RM-4544-PR, 1965), 63; (RAND RM-4544-PR, 1965), 64; (RAND RM-4544-PR, 1965), 64; (RAND RM-4544-PR, 1965), 64; (RAND RM-4544-PR, 1965), 65; (PUP 1966), 106; (RAND RM-4544-PR, 1965), 65–6; (PUP 1966), 107; (RAND RM-4544-PR, 1965), 67–8; (RAND RM-4544-PR, 1965), 68; (RAND RM-4544-PR, 1965), 68; (RAND RM-4544-PR, 1965), 69; (RAND RM-4544-PR, 1965), 69; (PUP 1966), 111; (RAND RM-4544-PR, 1965), 69; (RAND RM-4544-PR, 1965), 70; (RAND RM-4544-PR, 1965), 71; (RAND RM-4544-PR, 1965), 72; (RAND RM-4544-PR, 1965), 75; (RAND RM-4544-PR, 1965), 75; (RAND RM-4544-PR, 1965), 75; (RAND RM-4544-PR, 1965), 75–6; (RAND RM-4544-PR, 1965), 76; (RAND RM-4544-PR, 1965), 76; (RAND RM-4544-PR, 1965), 76–7; (RAND RM-4544-PR, 1965), 77; (RAND RM-4544-PR, 1965), 78; (RAND RM-4544-PR, 1965), 79; (RAND RM-4544-PR, 1965), 79–80; (RAND RM-4544-PR, 1965), 83; (RAND RM-4544-PR, 1965), 85; (RAND RM-4544-PR, 1965), 85; (PUP 19566), 131; (RAND RM-4544-PR, 1965), 86; (RAND RM-4544-PR, 1965), 86–7; (RAND RM-4544-PR, 1965), 87; (RAND RM-4544-PR, 1965), 87; (RAND RM-4544-PR, 1965), 88; (RAND RM-4544-PR, 1965), 88, respectively.

[292] Brodie, *The Intractability of States: A Distinctive Problem*, RAND Paper P-2970(Santa Monica: RAND Corporation, September 1964); also reproduced as "Appendix: The Intractability of States: A Distinctive Problem," in *Escalation and the Nuclear Option*, 135–48 with only minor cosmetic and grammatical modifications, including several sentence rewrites marked by either the addition, subtraction or rewording of words or phrases and only the occasional sentence restructuring (mostly to strengthen the formality of the writing.)

[293] Raymond Aron, "Modern Strategic Thought," tr. J. E. Gabriel, *Problems of Modern Strategy* (New York: Praeger, 1970), 31. As cited by Barry D. Watts, *The Foundations of U.S. Air Doctrine: The Problem of Friction in War* (Maxwell AFB, Alabama: Air University Press, December 1984), 103, n. 91.

[294-320] Brodie, *The Intractability of States: A Distinctive Problem*, RAND Paper P-2970 (Santa Monica: RAND Corporation, September 1964), 1; 2; 2; 2; 2; 3; 3; 3; 4; 4–5; 7–8; 8; 8; 9; 9; 9; 10; 11; 11; 11; 11–12; 12; 12; 12; 12–13; 13; 13, respectively.

[321-8] Thomas W. Wolfe, "The Levels of Nuclear Strategy," *The Reporter*, January 12, 1967, 63; 63; 63; 63—note 249 further states: As Wolfe further notes, "The book has exposed several abrasive issues, some of which are of great moment. Perhaps the most fundamental of these turns on the essentially moral question: Are there any circumstances in which the use or threat of use of nuclear weapons is justified? If the answer is 'No,' and some persons will so answer as a matter of conscience or for other reasons, then there is obviously no place for books like Professor Brodie's, which rests on the premise that nuclear weapons may serve condign purposes, such as to maintain the peace, through deterrence, or for self-defense against unprovoked aggression. Since this premise seems to be widely shared by men and their governments, including our own and that of the Soviet Union, Professor Brodie may at least be deemed to have secular sanction for his inquiry, which happens to focus upon the wisdom of certain military arrangements and concepts in NATO that he thinks may dilute the effectiveness of nuclear deterrence. Exception may of course be taken in one measure or another to Professor Brodie's specific analysis and recommendations. At the same time, it is hard to quarrel with the general proposition from which he begins, namely, that if the existence of nuclear arms has reduced the chances of war between the United States and the Soviet Union, as the nuclear-age record thus far indicates, then it behooves one to inquire closely into how things can best be kept that way;" 63; 63; 63–4; 64—note 253 further states: Wolfe had engaged in an earlier exchange of letters with Brodie on his earlier RAND paper on the same topic but with regard to an earlier draft of Brodie's treatise in escalation that he had read while Brodie was still at RAND. In a memo dated March 16, 1965 titled "Comments on "Escalation and the Nuclear Option,'" Wolfe described to Brodie that he was "greatly impressed" by Brodie's

draft paper and that it demonstrated an "admirable degree your surgical skill in dissecting the stereotypes into which strategic thinking seems so often to fall. Something like this is needed periodically to strip away the fatty tissue and expose the fundamentals underneath." He added it was his hope to see it "serve as the basis for a larger piece later on that would do for the late sixties what *Strategy in the Missile Age* did for us several years ago. But that can wait. Here I want only to comment briefly on the portions of the paper mentioned in your note." Referring to "Section III, Relevant Image of the Opponent," Wolfe wrote that "[i]n general, your appreciation accords with my own image of the opponent we are dealing with, and puts stress on the points that merit stressing—such as the combination of political aggressiveness and probing with extreme military caution. My comments are either in the nature of a further excurses on points you have made, or minor quibbles, rather than reflective of any substantial disagreement." He proceeded to discuss several of these "quibbles," and then on Brodie's discussion of accidental war and unauthorized" actions lending to war, Wolfe says he was "in agreement with your argument, and would only add the point that even what are generally called 'accidental' war outbreak situations do not seem likely to occur automatically or spontaneously from an 'accident' or some isolated act of mischief, but from some responsibly authority's decision to set the engines of war into motion after an accident or an act of mischief has occurred. Given what we know of the Soviet command and control setup . . . a decision is more likely to be subjected to careful and painful deliberation at the highest authority level than to be the hasty product of automaticity at lower levels of command." And with regard to Brodie's discussion in "Section IX, How Big an Attack?," he adds "[t]his section gives me no trouble, except perhaps that the title itself doesn't quite convey what the section is about. As I read it, the question dealt with is: what are the prospects that the Soviet view of the risks of war in Europe (little and big war) may change? I don't know how to put this question (if it is the right one) in a nice concise heading." And lastly, "One other point that might be introduced, and which you have touched on elsewhere in differentiating between deterrence of escalation and deterrence of initial outbreak of war," and that is, "Up to the present, the Soviets have tended to regard outbreak itself as the most critical threshold to be avoided. Over time, if both the strategic dialogue and practice should suggest that it is possible for the Soviet Union to ease into conflict with the United States without subsequent severe escalation (the demonstration might occur in some part of the world other than Europe), one should probably not rule out the possibility that the Soviets may come round to believing that they can safely put aside the outbreak threshold and get away with the game of escalate-a-bit in Europe. This, I take it, is what you are concerned to forestall." On March 24, 1965, Brodie responds to Wolfe's memo, writing "I deeply appreciate your generous views on my ['Escalation and the Nuclear Option'], D-13302-PR, and especially your taking the time and trouble to read it with such care and to offer me the benefit of your valuable comments. The latter will of course be most useful in the RM draft on which I am now working." Brodie added that he had "read, with customary admiration and benefit so far as papers by you are concerned, the excellent classified papers you prepared for Jerry Page's special study," as well as "your superb statement before the Sub-committee on the Far East and the Pacific of March 11, 1965, 'The Soviet Union and the Sino-Soviet Dispute.' The latter is by far the best paper relating to that subject I have seen anywhere. I am trying to get extra copies so that I can make them required reading for my seminar at UCLA." Brodie further commented, "I hope you do not think from my above and other recent remarks on your work that it is a habit of mine to gush. It is simply that T. W. Wolfe has become one of my very favorite authors, and I am grateful for the fact that he seems to be able to write prodigiously as well as brilliantly." Bernard Brodie Papers (Collection 1223), Department of Special Collections, Charles E. Young Research Library, UCLA.),

³²⁹ Letter from John W. Chapman, University of Pittsburgh, to Brodie, January 6, 1966, Bernard Brodie Papers (Collection 1223), Department of Special Collections, Charles E. Young Research Library, UCLA.

³³⁰ *Choice*, June 1967, Bernard Brodie Papers (Collection 1223), Department of Special Collections, Charles E. Young Research Library, UCLA.

³³¹ *The Key Reporter*, Spring 1967, Bernard Brodie Papers (Collection 1223), Department of Special Collections, Charles E. Young Research Library, UCLA.

³³² L. Larry Leonard, *Current Thought on Peace and War*, Summer 1967, Bernard Brodie Papers (Collection 1223), Department of Special Collections, Charles E. Young Research Library, UCLA.

³³³ Royal United Service Institution, *RUSI Journal*, May 1967, Bernard Brodie Papers (Collection 1223), Department of Special Collections, Charles E. Young Research Library, UCLA. The review also writes: "His arguments appear to rest on the assumptions that the deterrent effects of America's formidable armoury of

strategic nuclear weapons has been diminished by her repeated statements of reluctance to use them; that in any case the risk of general nuclear war is now negligible; but that the risk of local hostile incidents which might lead to escalation is still present. To support this thesis he examines hypothetical local incidents between American and Soviet forces around Berlin and assumes that they escalate into conventional warfare between Russia and NATO partners. At this stage, he asserts, the threat to use tactical nuclear weapons or even the actual employment of two or three of them would be justified, and far from causing escalation, such action might well act as a deterrent and lead to a negotiated peace. This may well be the case, particularly where the confrontation is with the Soviets and in Western Europe. But what about China? Professor Brodie feels that there is even more justification for the use of tactical nuclear weapons in the event of open conflict between U.S.A. and China, since failure to do so would only encourage Peking to further aggression. As an appendix, the author has added a paper entitled 'The intractability of states', the purpose of which is to point out the danger of drawing analogies between the behavior of individual heads of stage and governments under conditions of stress. In foreign affairs the expert study of foreign administrations is of paramount importance, as witnessed in the case of Korea and Cuba."

[334] Newell G. Bringhurst, *Fawn McKay Brodie: A Biographer's Life* (Norman: University of Oklahoma Press, 1999), 162; 162; 163; and 168 respectively.

[335] Edward Cody, "After 43 Years, France to Rejoin NATO as Full Member," *Washington Post*, March 12, 2009.

[336-60] Bernard Brodie, "How Not to Lead an Alliance," *The Reporter*, March 9, 1967, 18; 18; 18; 18; 18; 18; 19; 19; 19; 19; 19; 19; 20; 23; 33; 33; 33; 34; 34; 34; 34; 34; 34; 34; 34

[361-82] Fred Charles Iklé, "When the Fighting Has to Stop: The Arguments about Escalation," *World Politics* 19, No. 4 (July 1967), 692; 692; 692; 692; 693; 693; 693; 694; 697; 697-9; 699; 699; 703; 703; 703-5; 705; 705; 705; 705; 707; 707, respectively.

[383-4] Bernard Brodie, "Learning to Fight a Limited War," originally published in the *Los Angeles Times*, December 3, 1967, reprinted in *The Political Dimension in National Strategy: Five Papers*, eds. William P. Geberding and Bernard Brodie, Security Studies Paper No. 13 (Los Angeles: University of California Security Studies Project, 1968), 26, 26, respectively.

[385-6] Bernard Brodie, "Disarmament Goals and National Security Needs," Speech to State College of Washington, Pullman, WA, March 5, 1959, 28; 28 respectively.

[387-406] Brodie, "Learning to Fight a Limited War," 26; 26-7; 27; 27; 27; 27; 28; 28; 28; 28; 28; 28; 28-9; 30; 30; 30; 31; 31; 32; 32, respectively.

[407-18] Bernard Brodie, "Changing Attitudes Towards War," Paper Presented at the Studies in Violence Symposium, UCLA, June 1-2, 1968, 1 (also included in Henry A. Kissinger and Bernard Brodie, eds., *Bureaucracy, Politics, and Strategy*, Security Studies Paper Number 17 (Los Angeles: UCLA Security Studies Project, 1968), 15-26. A chapter of the same title appeared as Chapter 6 in Brodie's 1973 *War and Politics*), 7; 7-8; 8; this was footnoted by Brodie as: Chapter VII; 9; 12; 10; 11; 11; 11-12; 12, respectively.

[419-38] Bernard Brodie, "Technology, Politics, and Strategy," Paper Presented to the Tenth Annual Conference of the Institute for Strategic Studies at St. Catherine's College in Oxford, September 19-22, 1968, 2 (also included in Henry A. Kissinger and Bernard Brodie, eds, *Bureaucracy, Politics, and Strategy*, Security Studies Paper Number 17 (Los Angeles: UCLA Security Studies Project, 1968), 27-40 and published separately as an Adelphi Paper: Bernard Brodie, "Technology, Politics, and Strategy," Adelphi Papers 9, No.:55 (1969), 21-9); 2; 2 (as Brodie observed, "I shall be emphasizing mainly the limitations of technology in strategy, and also the limitations of the study of technological trends as a means of acquiring strategic insights. The time is indeed overripe for considering these limitations. Vietnam is almost too conspicuous an example of technological superiority having inadequate payoff and of the modern techniques to which I have referred proving irrelevant. Over the past year, incidentally, I have witnessed two instances where a remark like the one I have just made provoked in each case the retort that systems analysis could not have been proved inapplicable in Vietnam because it has not been tried—the implication being that an appropriate trial might produce some very far-reaching results. In each case the person making that retort was a distinguished member of the strategic intellectual fraternity. I feel that such a reply reflects either a profound misunderstanding of what has been happening in Vietnam, or a stubborn refusal to distinguish between the areas of consideration where systems analysis is applicable and indeed invaluable and those in which it has little or no relevance. I suspect it reflects both."); 4; 13; 13; 13-14; 14-15; 15; 15; 15-16 (Brodie

added: "The Vietnam war is reported daily on the television screens of America, with more than enough views, in color, of the fighting, the killing, and the destruction. It is surely the first war in history that has been so reported. Yet it is a war in which the public, including that part of it which is usually highly informed, seems to be at a loss not only about the issues but about the facts of the situation. The government, with its own monumental but bureaucratic sources of information, which tend to overwhelm or at least displace outside and contradictory sources, is probably differently confused rather than less confused. The books, articles, and shorter news reports on the war are by now voluminous, but to get some detached view of what is really going on is extraordinarily difficult, even among the few who try. The question of stopping the remaining bombing in North Vietnam has now become a hot election issue, yet probably not one in a thousand voters has any idea what kind of bombing is involved, or where it takes place."); 16; 16; 16; 16; 17; 17; 17; 18, respectively.

[439-54] Bernard Brodie, "Paying in Full for a Limited War," *L.A. Times*, Part II, October 17, 1968 (also included in Henry A. Kissinger and Bernard Brodie, eds., *Bureaucracy, Politics, and Strategy*, Security Studies Paper Number 17 (Los Angeles: UCLA Security Studies Project, 1968), 41–5 under the original title of "Ending a War: Is the Korean Lesson Valid for Vietnam?") Note 453 adds: As Brodie explained: That the failure stems largely from a policy of restraint does not mean that that policy can now be reversed. In view of our often expounded war aims, restraint was in any case essential from the beginning. The choice was between non-intervention and intervention with restraint, not between the acceptance or rejection of restraint. In any case the people of the country are bewildered and deeply divided, and they want out. We may be told that the government of Syngman Rhee in Korea was just as corrupt and as oppressive as the successive regimes which have ruled South Vietnam, including the present one under Gen. Thieu. The fact is that by 1968 we have had plenty of time to smell and to contemplate that corruption and ineptitude, which we had not had by 1951. Besides, the government of Rhee was hardly so inept as the successive regimes which we have called governments in South Vietnam. Some may not know it, but it is much more difficult for anyone to threaten the use of nuclear weapons in 1968 than it was in 1953, especially where there is no real threat to the existence of ourselves or our major allies. If Richard Nixon is elected President, as it now appears he will be, he will enter office with far less prestige than Gen. Eisenhower had in 1953. Mr. Nixon will understand fully that he must terminate the war rapidly, but he will also understand, I expect and trust, that he cannot do it by any threat of massive re-escalation opening toward anything so horrible as the possibility of using nuclear weapons on North Vietnamese cities. We do indeed have something to bargain with, above all the continuing American presence in Vietnam, which Hanoi and also much of South Vietnam would gladly do without. But in terms of what our original war aims were, it is probably not enough. If that is so, these aims much be drastically reduced.

[455] Bernard Brodie, ed., *The Future of Deterrence in U. S. Strategy*, UCLA Security Studies Project (Los Angeles: UCLA, 1968), i.

[456-89] Bernard Brodie, "Conclusion: The Future of Deterrence," in Bernard Brodie, ed., *The Future of Deterrence in U. S. Strategy*, UCLA Security Studies Project (Los Angeles: UCLA, 1968), 126; 126; 126; 126; 126; 126; 127; 127; 127–8; 128; 128; 129; 129; 129; 129–30; 130; 130; 130; 130; 130 (n.71); 130; 130–1; 131; 131; 131; 131–2; 132; 132; 133; 133; 133–4; 134; 134; 134, respectively.

[490] Alex Abella, *Soldiers of Reason: The RAND Corporation and the Rise of the American Empire* (New York: Houghton Mifflin Harcourt, 2008), 91.

[491-549] Bernard Brodie, *Strategy and National Interests: Reflections for the Future* (New York: National Strategy Information Center, January 1971, 1; 1–2; 2; 2; 2; 3; 3; 4; 4; 4; 5; 6; 6–7; 7; 7; 7–8; 8; 8; 8; 8–9; 9; 9; 10; 10; 11; 13; 21; 21; 22; 22; 22; 22–3; 23; 23; 23; 24; 25; 26; 27; 27; 27–8; 28; 29–30; 31; 32; 32; 32; 33; 34–5; 35; 34; 34; 34; 33; 33; 34; 35; 35–6; 36, respectively.

[550-52] Frank R Barnett, "Preface," *Toward a New Defense for NATO: The Case for Tactical Nuclear Weapons*, NSIC Agenda Paper No.5 (New York: National Strategy Information Center, July 1976), vii, vii, vii–viii, respectively.

[553-87] Bernard Brodie, "Introduction," *Toward a New Defense for NATO: The Case for Tactical Nuclear Weapons*, NSIC Agenda Paper No.5 (New York: National Strategy Information Center, July 1976), 1; 1; 1 (n.1); 1–2; 2; 2; 2; 2–3; 3 (n.2); 3; 3; 3; 3–4; 4; 4; 4 (n.3); 4; 4–5 (and also n.5); 5; 5; 5; 5; 5–6; 6; 6; 6–7; 7; 7; 7–8; 8; 8; 8 (n.6); 8 (also see *Strategy in the Missile Age*; op. cit.; 56); 9, respectively.

CHAPTER FIVE

Clausewitz for America: Reuniting War and Politics in the Nuclear Age

It is no coincidence that Brodie, one of the most Clausewitzian of the Cold War strategists, was also a Clausewitz scholar, and a principal member of Princeton's "Clausewitz Project" that sought throughout the 1960s to bring the famed Prussian strategist's works to an Anglo-American audience, newly translated and freshly interpreted by experts that included Peter Paret, Michael Howard, and (briefly) Liddell Hart, and Raymond Aron—in addition to Brodie. Brodie's later works would bear an increasing resemblance to Clausewitz's *On War* in both form and substance, notably his 1959 *Strategy in the Missile Age* that fleshed out the complexities of nuclear deterrence in the thermonuclear era—updating his preliminary (and remarkably prescient) thoughts penned at the very dawn of the nuclear age in the 1946 *The Absolute Weapon*, and his 1973 *War and Politics*, which bears both its strikingly Clausewitzian title and its fundamentally Clausewitzian analysis of war. Brodie's unrivaled embrace of complexity (long before complexity theory became vogue) would, in the end, distinguish Brodie's work from many of his contemporaries, particularly the peer of his that would emerge as something of an alter ego, with a level of influence matching and later exceeding his own, and a level of literary productive output rivaling his own prodigious output—albeit with a distinctly less philosophical and a decidedly more doctrinal approach to thinking about the unthinkable—Herman Kahn.

As noted by Bruce Fleming in his Spring 2004 *Parameters* article, "Can Reading Clausewitz Save Us from Future Mistakes?"—"Perhaps most important among the recent commentators seeing *On War* as a book that, read properly, would have saved us from many mistakes was Bernard Brodie, the 'dean of American civilian strategists'—as he is called in the jacket copy for his magisterial *War and Politics*."[1] Fleming continues: "Brodie takes Clausewitz's most famous assertion as central for *War and Politics*. Its cover gives a visual equivalent of the title, as well as of Brodie's understanding of Clausewitz's famous assertion. The cover shows a soldier's combat helmet side-by-side with a diplomat's silken top hat. Brodie's summary of Clausewitz's concept is that 'war takes place within a political milieu from which it derives all its purposes.' Brodie comments: 'This understanding has never fully got across to the great majority of those people who think or write about war, and even less to those who fight it.' Brodie recommends, as a result, civilian control of the military—more specifically, control by civilians who know something about the capabilities of the military and who themselves have taken to heart Clausewitz's central perception, what Brodie calls 'genuine civilian control.' In arriving at this last notion, Brodie evokes and rejects what he considers the simplistic and wrongheaded view of a relation between civilian control and the military: 'a simple 'stop-go' approach, so that the actual outbreak of war was the occasion for instituting completely new sets of values and objectives, especially the objective of winning the war for the sake simply of winning . . . The disposition towards this attitude is especially a mark of the military profession . . . All the more reason for genuine civilian control.' "[2]

On Clausewitz's most famous dictum, that war is a continuation of policy by other means, Fleming observes that Brodie believes "Clausewitz is offering a statement in the form of 'should' rather than 'is.' War should be the continuation of policy, but all too often is not. All we have to do is pay attention to Clausewitz to save ourselves a lot of trouble. Brodie quotes from the final chapter of *On War*: 'The subordination of the political point of view to the military would be unreasonable, for policy has created the war . . . The subordination of the military point of view to the political is, therefore, the only thing which is possible.' . . . In Brodie's view, a careful reading of Clausewitz can explain our failures in the past; at the same time there is hope that taking our principles to heart can prevent such debacles in the future."[3] As Fleming writes, "We should therefore ask, When Clausewitz offers as a dictum 'war is the continuation of policy by other means,' should we understand this as a definition valid for all time? Or is it a goal to aim for? Perhaps, as a third alternative, a generalization about most situations? Is it an expression of his Kantian side, or his pragmatic one? And this means that we must ask the larger question: What is the relation between theory and practice in this work as a whole?"[4] Fleming notes: "the fact is that *On War* is a deeply ambivalent work as regards the relation it proposes between theory and practice . . . The text itself is a theoretical mess . . . For this reason, commentators should go slowly in claiming that dipping into *On War* helps to 'prove' their particular position. It can be used just as easily to 'prove' the opposite. Brodie's invocation of Kant makes clear some of the pitfalls of any author with one foot in the ideal and one foot in the real, and shows us the difference between an author, Kant, who consciously set up two disparate realms, and another, Clausewitz, who alternated between them and never was able to relate them."[5]

Brodie seems to intuitively grasp Clausewitz's fundamental challenge, the use of philosophy, a practice of the mind, to probe the depths of the reality of war, and to somehow bridge the gap between action and thought, between reality and the philosophical abstractions used to contemplate it. Brodie takes his cue and his inspiration from the master philosopher of war, and in the course of his journey confronts the self-same ambiguities and contradictions. Clausewitz tried to comprehend, and wholly explain, the new contours of total war, and Brodie sought the same of nuclear war, and both struggled with their audiences, particularly the desire in military circles for clarity and certainty, two seeming impossibilities in a world obscured by fog and riddle with inherent ambiguity. In his 1959 lecture on "Strategy as an Art and a Science," Brodie writes that Clausewitz "represents what we might call the 'philosophic interpretation of military history,' and who is certainly the greatest figure in that tradition."[6] As Brodie points out, "Clausewitz has been called 'the prophet of total war,' when in fact he is almost the very opposite: he is almost 'the prophet of limited war.' His deductions on strategy were derived from a close reading of the military history especially of his own times, which embraced the Napoleonic wars, but also the wars of the preceding two centuries. Of the ten volumes into which his posthumous works were gathered, seven are devoted to monographs in history. His treatment of military history is comprehensive, careful, and, above all, objective. This, I submit, is still the key to the good utilization of history and strategic studies."[7] Brodie adds that "the qualities that make Clausewitz great" include "his philosophic penetration and breadth, which make him examine the place of war in the lives of nations and which thus save him from the error which is common to so many lesser figures in the field—the error of considering war as though it were an isolated act, serving no purpose outside itself," as well as "his insistence upon looking at the particular subject he is discussing from all sides. He is just as determined to make clear the exceptions to any rule as he is to set down the rule itself. It is for the latter reason that Clausewitz insists that there are no principles of war; that is, there is no system of rules which, if pursued, will guarantee success. His contemporary Jomini scolded him for that position. Clausewitz has been criticized on the grounds that he left no 'system' of strategy, no method which can be indoctrinated by teachers and learned by students. The observation is true, but I consider it to his great credit rather than a ground for criticism."[8]

Brodie's thoughts on Clausewitz and Jomini and their fundamental differences provide us with a natural segue into an examination of his own contributions to strategic theory. In the nuclear age, we discover a parallel dualism, as nuclear warfighters (largely but not exclusively within the military services) and deterrence theorists (largely civilians, but not exclusively—mostly in academia, government, and the many policy-research organizations with a foot in both worlds) faced off, presenting two distinct visions of order for the nuclear age: one primarily emphasizing action, the other primarily thought, with reality nestled somewhere in between. While they shared much in common, including an appreciation of the destructive magnitude of nuclear weaponry, and like Jomini and Clausewitz possessed great knowledge of the roots of contemporary conflict, their theoretical styles differed much like Jomini's and Clausewitz's did. In the case of Herman Kahn and Bernard Brodie, each wrote about the same phenomena (the impact of the bomb on international security, the dynamics of escalation, the nature of limited war, and the necessity for thinking about the unthinkable), much like both Jomini and Clausewitz wrote about the impact of Napoleon on European security, and how he transformed not just the nature of war but the entire strategic landscape. So similar were Brodie's and Kahn's interests that they twice authored volumes that deeply influenced the strategic debate within a year of each other; first with Brodie's 1959 *Strategy in the Missile Age* and Kahn's 1960 *On Thermonuclear War*, and next with their sequential texts in the mid-1960s on the topic of escalation, with Kahn's 1965 *On Escalation: Metaphors and Scenarios* and Brodie's 1966 *Escalation and the Nuclear Option* written at nearly the same time and thus without reference to the other. And both influential strategic thinkers either coined or became closely associated with prominent terms and phrases of the era, ranging from the *absolute weapon* to *thinking about the unthinkable*.

The "Clausewitz of the Age of Nuclear Deterrence"

Like so many scholars on the Brodie–Clausewitz nexus, Ken Booth argues in his chapter on Brodie in *Makers of Nuclear Strategy* that "[s]trategic history will acclaim Brodie as the Clausewitz of the age of nuclear deterrence," even if, during his lifetime, he was "somewhat overshadowed in fame by more prolific, protagonistic and precocious members of his profession" and thus "failed to have Albert Wohlstetter's direct influence on policy;" "never displayed Herman Kahn's inflated virtuosity;" "did not exhibit Thomas Schelling's formal reasoning;" and "lacked Henry Kissinger's experience in the practice as well as the theory of great power."[9] But despite lacking these qualities associated with his better known colleagues, Brodie's "reputation has been secure in the minds of the most distinguished of his profession," winning praise from these very same peers, with Thomas Schelling, now a Nobel laureate for his contributions to game theory, saluting him upon his passing as being "first—both in time and in distinction" among his peers, and historian Michael Howard having "described him as 'quite the wisest strategic thinker of our generation'."[10]

As John Baylis and John C. Garnett, editors of *Makers of Nuclear Strategy* which, in their introduction, note "Edward Meade Earle's classic *Makers of Modern* provided us with a model," and add that it was "fitting that the first chapter should focus on the work of Bernard Brodie, who edited *The Absolute Weapon*, a "major landmark in the story of thinking about nuclear weapons," and whose contribution argued that the "unique destructiveness of the new weapons meant the avoidance of war was now all-important . . . opened the debate and set down an agenda for deterrence which became the main preoccupation for nuclear strategists for decades ahead."[11] Echoing Booth, they laud Brodie's work as being "outstanding in the way it explained the new and frequently ambiguous interrelationship between war, politics, and strategy," and predict that "[f]uture generations of are likely to acclaim Brodie as 'the Clausewitz of the age of nuclear deterrence.'"[12] They further argue that "Brodie's contribution to strategic studies is profound. Students of the subject, Booth argues, have more to learn from 'a silent dialogue with a major thinker of the past,' like Brodie, than with 'the loudest talkers of the present,'" and according to Booth, "there has been no one to match him since."[13]

Booth recognizes Brodie as "the quintessential strategist of the first generation of the nuclear age," and "[a]bove all he was concerned to nurture the roots of strategic thinking," which Brodie believed "had been most comprehensively expressed by Carl von Clausewitz."[14] And so, "Brodie attempted to develop Clausewitz's legacy for the first nuclear generation," and "explained the novel and frequently paradoxical interrelationships between war, politics, and strategy."[15] Booth remains convinced that "[s]trategic history will acclaim Brodie as the Clausewitz of the age of nuclear deterrence," even if he, during his lifetime, was overshadowed by many of his peers. As Booth noted, Brodie was "somewhat overshadowed in fame by more prolific, protagonistic and precocious members of his profession," and "failed to have Albert Wohlstetter's direct influence on policy," "never displayed Herman Kahn's inflated virtuosity," "did not exhibit Thomas Schelling's formal reasoning," and "lacked Henry Kissinger's experience in the practice as well as the theory of great power," but despite so being overshadowed, his "reputation has been secure in the minds of the most distinguished of his profession," winning praise from his more widely recognized peers, with Michael Howard having "described him as 'quite the wisest strategic thinker of our generation'" and Thomas Schelling, now a Nobel laureate for his contributions to game theory, saluting him upon his passing as being "first—both in time and in distinction" among his peers.[16]

As Marc Trachtenberg has observed, an essential component of Brodie's solution to the fundamental riddles and enduring ambiguities that lay at the heart of the nuclear discourse, would come through his steady application of, and reflection on, Clausewitz's philosophy of war. Clausewitz, renowned for the complexity of his thought and his own legacy of contradiction within his sprawling text, is not well suited to simple solutions of simple maxims that boil down complex realities to pithy sound bites, offered instead a rich mosaic of reflection on history, war, and strategy through the lens of deep analysis, one that is best appreciated over time. Brodie's earliest known writing starts with a quest for understanding the legacy of Socrates, the founder of Western philosophy, revealing a willingness to embrace complexity and ambiguity and accept the dualities inherent in reality; later, as he sought to harness his intellect and apply it to the challenges of strategic thought, he turned to Mahan, America's very own "Clausewitz of sea power," a towering figure in not just naval strategy but in the broader intellectual history of war. But after Hiroshima, Brodie famously recognized that Mahan's insights, so useful for navigating America's emergence as a global maritime and naval power, had reached the limit of their utility. As he gazed into what Joseph Nye has called the "crystal ball" of the nuclear age, recognizing an absoluteness to contemporary war that knew no parallel in the past, Brodie realized that there was at least a template that could guide him forward—and that was provided by the famed Prussian theorist, Carl von Clausewitz, who grappled with the emergence in his time of total war on an historically unprecedented scale. While the "total war" of the Napoleonic era was an order of magnitude (or even more) *less* destructive than that of the atomic era, which was again at least an order of magnitude less destructive than that of the thermonuclear era that soon followed, the theoretical framework provided by Clausewitz offered Brodie a starting point for his own analysis, and in particular to arm him as he challenged the more doctrinaire and partisan solutions offered by his peers and colleagues, civilian and military, as they staked out their own positions in the nuclear debate that took place from 1945 until the Cold War's end nearly a half century later.

Clausewitz became Brodie's constant, and while this never meant a simple or elegant solution to the riddles of the nuclear age, it at least provided a starting point for debate and a reference point to drive forth a dialectic, as thesis was countered by an endless series of antitheses, in the hope that at the end something like a synthesis might emerge. Brodie's contribution to the nuclear debate was often perceived to be advocacy of one thesis or another, and at times he came out stridently for or against a certain policy, but he would adapt and respond to changes in technology and the military balance on the ground, amending his viewpoints as required; as such, his real contribution was in his provision of a framework that offered his colleagues the best hope for attaining synthesis, including the occasional kick by way of antithesis to a popular thesis of the day, thereby helping the pendulum to continue its swing. With both the end of America's atomic monopoly, and the advent of thermonuclear weapons in the arsenals of both superpowers, the already dangerous art of nuclear strategy became ever more lethal. As Trachtenberg described, "Peace would depend, Brodie had argued even in the late 1940s, on a universal conviction 'that war is far too horrible even to be contemplated. And the great dilemma is that the conviction can be sustained only by our making every possible effort to prepare for war and this to engage in it if need be.' The problem of deterrence could therefore not be divorced from the problem of use," but in the thermonuclear era, nuclear war would very likely be "tantamount to national suicide. Brodie had earlier thought that Clausewitz, with his insistence on the close linkage between political objectives and military means, had become obsolete: even the early atomic weapons were too destructive to be harnessed to rational political goals. But he had since come to see that Clausewitz had been 'saying something very profound.' He had been saying that 'war is violence—to be sure, gigantic violence—but it is planned violence and therefore controlled. . . . [T]he procedure and the objective must be in some measure appropriate to each other.' Brodie's views had been moving in this direction even in 1949 and 1950," but once the thermonuclear threshold had been crossed in 1952, now "one had to think about strategies that were not suicidal—that the means of violence had to be controlled and limited."[17]

This measured balancing of ends and means, central to Clausewitzian strategy, would become Brodie's mantra, leading him time and again into combat with his peers. This is evident, as we will see in the pages below, in his theoretical clash with his former RAND colleague Herman Kahn, whose bold advocacy of nuclear warfighting, he felt, blurred the ends-means balance and contributed to a muscular tendency to over-react, much the way Nobel laureate Thomas Schelling more nuanced re-articulation of bargaining theory, whose effect, Trachtenberg has noted, "was to transform strategy once again into tactics writ large—not military tactics this time, but bargaining tactics," as the central "problem of war and peace, was reduced to the problem of behavior during times of crisis and after the outbreak of hostilities. The purely military side of war causation, as Brodie later complained, became the focus of analysis, as though war itself were not in essence a political artifact—as though the basic insight of Clausewitz, whom they all respected, was somehow obsolete."[18] Rumors of Clausewitz's imminent obsolescence in the nuclear age, at least to Brodie, were premature. But Clausewitz was so complex, and contradictory, a writer that his words and thoughts would be welcomed by those more action-oriented than the reflective Brodie, with President Eisenhower, who had led the allied armies to victory over the Nazis a decade earlier, and no stranger to the Prussian philosopher of war, finding in Clausewitz's thoughts some justification for a vigorous thermonuclear attack to a menacing Soviet Union, as he remarked at a July 29, 1954 National Security Council meeting when citing "Clausewitz's principle of 'diminishing as much as possible the first blow of an enemy attack'" and who three years later again referenced the famed Prussian strategist, when noting a Soviet attack on the American homeland would cause some 50 million casualties, that "the only sensible thing for us to do was to put all our resources into our SAC capability and into hydrogen bombs," as Trachtenberg has cited.[19]

Trachtenberg later explains that Eisenhower approached deterrence with skepticism, and that he "was never able to accept the argument about a nuclear stalemate and the possibility that a general war might be fought with only conventional weapons,"[20] rejecting the suggestion by General Ridgway at a December 3, 1954 NSC meeting that the Soviets might refrain from using nuclear weapons if the United States did, retorting that he "did not believe any such thing" and earlier in the year, at a June 24, 154 NSC meeting, said that such expectations of restraint from Moscow were "completely erroneous;" the next August he reiterated his view, explaining that he "cannot see any chance of keeping any war in Europe from becoming a general war" and as a consequence "we must be ready to throw the book at the Russians should they jump us," and that "we would be fooling ourselves and our European friends if we said we could fight such a war without recourse to nuclear weapons."[21] To Ike, "Nuclear weapons dominated all lesser forms of weaponry, and it was obvious to him that in a major conflict they would in the final analysis be used," and Trachtenberg finds "[h]is thinking was right out of the first few pages of Clausewitz: war has an innate tendency to become absolute. It followed that also that no restrictions or limitations could be placed on the way nuclear forces would be used in a general war with the Soviet bloc."[22]

While Eisenhower framed his warfighting logic in Clausewitz terms, it clearly was a selective interpretation of Clausewitz, and not rooted in a fuller or more nuanced interpretation as Brodie would endeavor. Brodie looked at the same challenges, the same transformation of military technology, and the same theorist of war as Eisenhower, but drew far different conclusions. As Trachtenberg observed, "With the coming of the hydrogen bomb, he argued, the strategy of unrestricted warfare had become obsolete; indeed, 'most of the military ideas and axioms of the past' no longer made sense in a world of thermonuclear weapons. But it was not enough to allow these 'old concepts of strategy' to 'die a lingering death from occasional verbal rebukes.' What was needed, he said, was a whole new set of ideas, a comprehensive and radically different framework for thinking about strategic issues. And over the next decade that was exactly what took shape. Strategy as an intellectual discipline came alive in America in the 1950s. A very distinctive, influential and conceptually powerful body of thought emerged."[23]

"An Understandable Abhorrence of Absolute War"

Barry Steiner, in his comprehensive study of Brodie, would flesh out Brodie's contribution to the emergence of contemporary strategic studies, and his challenge to advocates of "[c]ontemporary axiomic strategy" that remained "most confined . . . to doctrines of the offensive use of military forces, particularly the earliest possible use in war of atomic weapons," which would "ensure horrendous casualties without necessarily forcing an end to hostilities."[24] Steiner notes Brodie suggested that it was "perhaps because they were so strongly believed, those doctrines were historically often not clearly related to combat experience," and that he had asked in his 1973 *War and Politics*: "Why had not the most obvious lessons of combat experience been absorbed by commanders who were to send great new armies into battle?" to which he answered, "Because for the most part experience not personal to themselves was not really alive to these commanders, who were not students of history, even of military history, but who had absorbed an intensive indoctrination laced through with religious fervor on the merits of the offensive."[25] And so even if Eisenhower cloaked his reasoning in Clausewitzian terms, his commitment to the offensive was nonetheless rooted in his pre-nuclear thinking—or as Brodie suggested, a pre-nuclear instinct forged more by indoctrination to the cult of the offensive and less to thinking or analysis proper; Brodie would thus aim to hit a strategic reset button, and update Clausewitz for the nuclear age. As Brodie wrote in "The Continuing Relevance of *On War*" in the 1976 edition of *On War* published by Princeton University Press, "Clausewitz is probably as pertinent to our times as most of the literature specifically written about nuclear war."[26]

Steiner has observed that in the course of Brodie's strategic and philosophical evolution during the nuclear era, he would reprise his original rejection of Clausewitz's continued applicability—whose ideas on the political nature of war Brodie initially thought became obsolete after Hiroshima, after which war could no longer serve any rational purpose—returning to the famed theorist of war and finding in his work a place for rational, logical applications of force, even nuclear force. As Steiner writes, Brodie recalled in April 1952 how: "Six months ago, I could and in fact did deny in print that the famous, often-quoted statement of Clausewitz's, 'War is a continuation of policy by other means,' could have any meaning for modern times. I felt that modern war, modern total war, is much too big, much to[o] violent to fit into any concept of a continuation of diplomacy. I felt that war by its very outbreak must create its own objective—in modern times, survival—in comparison with which all other objectives must hide their diminished heads. I have since come to believe that Clausewitz was in fact saying something very profound. What he was saying, it now seems to me, is that war is violence—to be sure, gigantic violence—but it is planned violence and therefore controlled. And since the objective should be rational, the procedure for accomplishing that objective should also be rational, which is to say that the procedure and the objective must be in some measure appropriate to each other."[27]

This underlying rationality led Brodie to reconsider the place of restraint in modern war, thus opening up to his hitherto rejected possibilities for limited nuclear warfighting. Clausewitz thus survived the advent of nuclear weapons, with Brodie, as cited by Steiner, recognizing "the political objective of wars of war cannot be consonant with national suicide—and there is really no use talking about large-scale *reciprocal* use of fission and thermonuclear weapons against cities as being anything other than national suicide for both sides."[28] But Brodie came to believe "we ought at least to begin considering the feasibility and utility of exercising some restraint upon our own capabilities when hostilities begin and obliging the enemy to use a similar restraint."[29] Brodie's connection to Clausewitz was not just a theoretical or philosophical connection; there were deeper, psychological links, as Brodie empathized with Clausewitz's own battle with depression, and senses a mutuality in their frustrations dealing with smaller minds. As Steiner noted, Brodie felt "great frustration at not being called upon to exercise policymaking or policy-advising responsibility at high levels of government," which "helps explain his very critical remarks about the military establishment, first informally and later in his final study, *War and Politics*." Steiner later addresses these "apparent parallels between Brodie's understanding of his later frustrations and those he ascribes to Clausewitz in his psychoanalytic explanations of Clausewitz's career" in a separate chapter toward the end of his biography. Steiner alludes to Brodie's frustrations in his biography, noting in addition to Brodie's frustration arising from his lack of high-level policy advising or policymaking, that he also felt some frustration with his work environment at RAND, which became increasingly evident from his criticisms of them, including rebuttals of Herman Kahn's work on escalation and warfighting, that appeared in his published work. Steiner noted: "Brodie's later belief that his reputation as a RAND analyst was stagnating relative to that of others," and cited a letter Brodie wrote in 1952 on his motivations for moving to RAND and leaving academia: "One may have a lesser audience, measured in number of readers when writing from RAND rather than from a university; but one is likely to be a great deal more influential."[30] Steiner suggests that Brodie's "need for approbation would have required that others at RAND defer to him," but that his "major project at RAND during the 1950s, published as *Strategy in the Missile Age*, was largely one of synthesis and conceptualization, following rather than leading other RAND analysis and apparently not receiving at RAND the great attention it inspired among informed people outside the organization."[31]

Steiner also examined Brodie's efforts to reunite war and politics along a Clausewitzian axis interconnecting the two, and thus address "the political core of strategy and the overvaluation of narrower military and technical approaches to war-making."[32] As Steiner writes, "That politics was central to strategy Brodie had learned from Clausewitz when, following news of the first projected test of fusion weapons, he was persuaded of the political futility of strategic nuclear war. 'We must . . . proceed,' Brodie wrote in January 1954, 'to rethink some of the basic principles (which have become hazy since Clausewitz) connecting the waging of war with the political ends thereof, and to reconsider some of the prevalent axioms governing the conduct of military operations.' In his later works, especially *War and Politics*, he applied war-making to political interests as Clausewitz had done, taking account of contemporary experience."[33] It took the leap in destructive power introduced by thermonuclear weapons to induce Brodie's Clausewitzian evolution, and Steiner notes Brodie "had followed a very different approach from that taken in his *Guide to Naval Strategy* and in his essays in *The Absolute Weapon*," and his new "approach was unorthodox for a strategist in any era, and Brodie pioneered in it as Clausewitz had earlier."[34]

Steiner cites Brodie's introduction to the 1976 translation by Michael Howard and Peter Paret of Clausewitz's *On War*, in his essay titled "The Continuing Relevance of *On War*," in which Brodie wrote: "Clausewitz is probably as pertinent to our times as most of the literature specifically written about nuclear war" among which "we pick up a good deal of useful technological and other lore, but we usually sense also the absence of that depth and scope which are particularly the hallmark of Clausewitz. We miss especially his tough-minded pursuit of the idea that war in all its phases must be rationally guided by meaningful political purposes. That insight is quite lost in most of the contemporary books, including one which bears a title that boldly invites comparison with the earlier classic, Herman Kahn's *On Thermonuclear War*."[35] Steiner notes that "[u]sing Clausewitz to argue for the political irrelevance of attacking with thermonuclear weapons, Brodie, like Clausewitz, understood that war would not invariably serve 'meaningful political purposes."[36] Brodie felt Clausewitz's concept of "absolute war," which was "characterized by the absence of restraint on the pattern of the Napoleonic wars," was particularly applicable to the thermonuclear era, and "shared with Clausewitz an understandable abhorrence of absolute war and the view that guiding warfare by political considerations protected best against the tendency of war to become absolute."[37]

Just as Brodie would come to believe that the destructiveness of thermonuclear weapons made total war incompatible with political objectives and demanded a rebalancing of war and politics, other strategists, notably including Herman Kahn, felt otherwise and in fact believed the opposite: that thermonuclear war was no different from any other kind of war, making planning for such a clash a Clausewitzian necessity rather than a Clausewitzian violation. Citing Kahn, Barry Steiner notes the famed nuclear warfighting theorist recalled how, with a note of criticism, that the "invention of the atomic bomb . . . seemed to end any constructive thinking about strategy and tactics. Nuclear war was simply unthinkable—both literally and figuratively. This phenomenon, known as psychological denial, meant that while one side (ours) did little or no thinking about nuclear weapons, the other side simple regarded them as 'bigger bombs' . . . and also did not undertake any fundamental rethinking of classical and strategic assumptions."[38] Kahn would endeavor to correct this, though critics would conclude he merely mirrored the other side by embracing their bigger-is-better approach to classical strategic concepts. Kahn viewed Brodie's 1955 *Harper's* article "Strategy Hits a Dead End," a relatively rare moment of national prominence for Brodie when his article appeared in a national mass-circulation publication, as symptomatic of this "block in strategic thinking" induced by the new destructive power of nuclear weapons.[39] But Steiner believes Kahn overstated the case, and underappreciated the efforts Brodie had made to in fact think about the unthinkable, noting "Brodie's first work on this subject was hardly characterized by psychological denial."[40]

Nonetheless, there is indeed an emotional tension separating the works of Kahn and Brodie. Brodie feared the destructive powers of total war in the nuclear age, forcing him to question the political utility of general war after Hiroshima. As Steiner observes, "Brodie's major contribution to nuclear strategy and his more mature complacence about the risks of nuclear war stemmed from his confidence about the narrower but equally important area of what the superpowers ought *not* to do with nuclear weapons."[41] Steiner further notes that "by 1952 Brodie's analyses focused more on what not to hit with nuclear bombs, notably American and Soviet homelands, than on potentially attractive targets."[42] If deterrence did fail, Brodie persisted in his belief that restraint was necessary in the new nuclear order. As Steiner observed, "Arguing that nuclear weapons could more efficiently destroy enemy assets than their predecessors, Brodie also warned that capitalizing illogically and passionately upon force efficiency could be suicidal," and "logical planning and decision making became proportionately more important. In at least four instances, he argued in favor of restraining the efficient use of nuclear force: employing a large nuclear arsenal to discourage major attack; using a nuclear arsenal to enforce restraints in limited war; and employing nuclear weapons to serve political objectives commensurate with the cost of war-making."[43]

Brodie's emphasis on restraint did appear to come into some conflict with Clausewitz's emphasis on decisive action, and Steiner cites Brodie's 1959 assessment in *Strategy in the Missile Age*: "It is of course true and important that we cannot have limited war without settling for limited objectives, which in practice is likely to mean a negotiated peace based on compromise. Clausewitz's classic definition, that the object of war is to impose one's will on the enemy, must be modified, at least for any opponent who has a substantial nuclear capability behind him."[44] Steiner notes: "Brodie was mainly interested in doing in war and in crisis what the superpowers were doing prior to those eventualities—that is, maintaining controls on the use of force," and his "horror at any strategic bombing that employed fusion weapons appears to have prevented him from studying the consequences of such bombing and the political developments conducive to it."[45] Steiner observes: "the most important continuity in his thinking was his advocacy of using nuclear weapons to deter general war," and as a consequence "he was much less worried than others that giving primacy to deterrence would impair the search for unilateral advantage in nuclear war."[46]

Hence Brodie's tribute to Thucydides in *Strategy in the Missile Age*: "What we have done must convince us Thucydides was right, that peace is better than war not only in being more agreeable but also in being very much more predictable. A plan and policy which offers a good promise of deterring war is therefore by orders of magnitude better in every way than one which depreciates the objective of deterrence in order to improve somewhat the chances of winning."[47] Steiner believes that "Brodie was at his best as a strategic analyst when seeking alternatives to scenarios in which the unlimited killing power of nuclear weapons was likely to be displayed,"[48] such as the scenarios that came to define Kahn's prolific canon of work from *On Thermonuclear War* to *On Escalation: Metaphors and Scenarios*. Added Steiner: "If Brodie's analyses of the physical use of nuclear weapons were generally weaker than his discussion of their coercive use, it may have been because he invariably assumed weapons yields that were uniform, large, and too unwieldy for any strategy apart from the coercive. War-winning scenarios that depended upon attacks by a diverse arsenal against a diverse array of targets would have required detailed, problematic, and elaborate studies less suited to Brodie's prevailing approach to nuclear strategy. But Brodie did not neglect war-winning strategies altogether; he merely associated them with the coercive use of nuclear weapons, in which visible restraint in force employment was the key ingredient."[49] Brodie thus came to distinguish the "deterrence of general war" from "deterrence *in* war," the latter made possible only by differentiating the efforts for "strengthening deterrence of general war" from "strengthening deterrence of hostilities at other levels."[50] So, Steiner reasoned, "Brodie did sharply distinguish, by 1949 but not in 1946, coercive use of nuclear weapons from purely physical employment of them, a refinement critical for military restraint in a major war and for applying nuclear warfare to political objectives."[51] But that left the issue of and challenges inherent in the physical employment of nuclear weapons largely unexplored, and thus Brodie "had little to say about strategic targets."[52] This sharply contrasted with the *warfighting* tradition that would come to be exemplified in the popular imagination by Herman Kahn, as illustrated by his many works as well as the unique and pervasive permeation of Kahn's thinking, and its decidedly bold style, into popular culture—most famously from Peter Sellers' portrayal of the (at least partly) Kahn-inspired Dr. Strangelove character in the popular film of the same name, which drew heavily upon Kahn's writing, borrowing his most colorful expressions and scenarios for use in this smartly written and brilliantly acted parody of the nuclear era.

In his ninth chapter, "On Strategy and Strategists," Steiner considers the "Psychological and Psychoanalytical Interpretations of Clausewitz," noting Brodie was influenced by the 1971 biography of Clausewitz authored by Roger Parkinson, titled *Clausewitz*, that suggested Clausewitz, "who had never held a senior command position, had been ambitious but later in life saw himself as a failure, had frequently been melancholy and depressed, and had broken his melancholia only when anticipating war and participation in battle."[53] Steiner added that "Brodie seemed attracted to Parkinson's presentation by his own deeply intuitional understanding," and in a later to his colleague Peter Paret in 1973 noted Parkinson "came up with some remarkable letters or statements that certainly ring some kind of bell,"[54] and that Brodie went on to make "a series of deductions about Clausewitz's character from statements in *On War*, each echoing Parkinson's findings," and that "[w]hen he went beyond assertions about character traits to more boldly probe Clausewitz's unconscious motivations, Brodie depended even more upon Parkinson's materials."[55]

Interestingly, Brodie "conjectured that Clausewitz's neurotic passions produced the first draft of *On War*, since 'the first draft is "from the heart," or from wherever it is that emotions reside.' That draft, Brodie pointed out, deals mostly with winning wars, in contrast to the final version, which had been revised to highlight war as policy by other means."[56] Clausewitz expert and translator Peter Paret disagreed with Brodie, and in a 1973 letter wrote that "Almost to the last day of his life, Clausewitz was active, productive, and self-confident, and . . . we have no reason to believe he was a depressed human being," and cited many positive dimensions of Clausewitz's life and career including his being "very happily married," possessing "very close and long-lasting friendships," and thoroughly enjoying his life as a soldier, theorist, and writer, whose "creative life was characterized by steady, constant productivity."[57] Steiner suggests that "[a]s to why Brodie should have focused so tenaciously on Clausewitz's depression, it may be conjectured that because he so much admired Clausewitz as a writer on war, he probably focused upon parallels he saw between himself and Clausewitz in this and other areas," and having himself suffered from depression during "his last years," Brodie "may well have presumed that Clausewitz's character was in this respect similar to his own."[58]

Steiner also noted that Brodie and Clausewitz each endeavored to prevent war from becoming absolute, and thereby losing any rationality of purpose: "Brodie, like Clausewitz, understood that war would not invariably serve 'meaningful political purposes',", and Brodie strived to prevent the very cataclysm that Clausewitz witnessed during Napoleon's retreat from Moscow; "reacting to the Clausewitzian concept of absolute war," Brodie observed how "Clausewitz insists and reiterates that war is always *an instrument of policy* because he knew, and we know today, that the usual practice is rather to let war take over national policy."[59] Steiner finds that "Brodie's assertion in the 1950s that war once begun had an inherent tendency to become 'orgiastic,' the starting point for his effort to strengthen war limitations, is especially compelling from this same perspective. Brodie also shared with Clausewitz an understandable abhorrence of absolute war and the view that guiding warfare by political considerations protected best against the tendency of war to become absolute."[60] Thus Brodie reasoned, in his 1959 classic work, *Strategy in the Missile Age*, that "Clausewitz's classic definition, that the object of war is to impose one's will on the enemy, must be modified, at least for any opponent who has a substantial nuclear capability behind him."[61]

Steiner believes that "Brodie's interest in Clausewitz was more abstract than practical," and "used him to caution against tolerating extremes, distinguishing as did Clausewitz between total and less than total war-making efforts for a given purpose," since Clausewitz described, in total war "all proportion between action and political demands would be lost," and in order to "discover how much of our resources must be mobilized for war, we must first examine our own political aim and that of the enemy. We must gauge the strength and situation of the opposing state. We must gauge the character and abilities of its government and people and do the same in regard to our own. Finally, we must evaluate the political sympathies of other states and the effect the war may have on them."[62] As Steiner notes, Brodie "accepted Clausewitz's rational equation between war-making and political objectives because he was as committed as Clausewitz was to logical strategy and to combating axiomatic views."[63] But he also keenly appreciated Clausewitz's recognition of the emotional side of war, and even sympathized with Clausewitz's own apparent struggle with melancholy or depression, sensing a kindred spirit; as Steiner suggests, Brodie "so much admired Clausewitz as a writer on war, he probably focused upon the parallels he saw between himself and Clausewitz," which included "their distinctive roles as critics of the conventional wisdom and recognized authority" as well as "their major but unsuccessful efforts to gain larger recognition for their ideas and contributions, and their interest in the impact of emotions upon war-making. Inasmuch as Brodie is known to have been aware of these parallels and is known, furthermore, to have been depressed in his last years, he may well have presumed that Clausewitz's character was in this respect similar to his own."[64]

Thus when Brodie set his mind to untangle the riddles of thermonuclear warfare, he came up with a decidedly different response from Eisenhower. Steiner cites a letter Brodie wrote to Schelling that recalls how, "At the beginning of 1952, when some of us here at RAND heard that a thermonuclear weapon would be tested the following November and would probably work . . . I proposed that strategic bombing be interdicted altogether. . . . I was not going to have them bomb any targets . . . within the homeland of the Soviet Union, but sought to confine targets strictly to battlefield zones, and to disallow the larger cities even there."[65] Brodie explained to Schelling that he "thought then, and still think[s], that it would be easier to preserve a limitation founded on gross distinctions of geography than to distinguish between military and civilian targets within enemy territory, especially since the two types might in many instances be in very close juxtaposition to each other."[66] Brodie wrestled with the many uncertainties associated with limiting war in the nuclear age and as Steiner recalls, "Much of Brodie's work during the 1950s was to expose what he believed to be insufficient attention given, especially by military staffs, to these uncertainties, which were both military and political."[67]

Bringing Clausewitz to America: The Clausewitz Project

Brodie came to realize that one earlier theorist of war had shared with him the very same objective—that of bringing wisdom, in the form of philosophical inquiry, to the study of war, its nature, and its conduct, and that was the great Prussian strategic theorist, Carl von Clausewitz. In the early 1960s, Brodie commenced participation in a long-term project associated with

Princeton University Press known as the "Clausewitz Project," a collaboration with renowned Clausewitz scholars Peter Paret and Michael Howard, which continued for more than a decade that aimed to bring to the Anglo-American audience many of Clausewitz's works, including some never before translated into English. As originally envisioned, the project would have yielded several volumes to be published over several years. But various issues including problems with translation and ongoing delays eventually caused the project to be cancelled, but not before it produced an important contribution to the Clausewitz literature with Princeton's seminal 1976 translation of *On War*.

By the spring of 1963, the idea of the Clausewitz Project headed up in part by Paret had taken root, and Paret mentioned this idea to Brodie. In a follow-up letter the next fall, written on Princeton University Center of International Studies letterhead on November 7, 1963 while he was a visiting scholar there, Paret wrote to Brodie: "You may recall our conversation last spring about the possibilities of preparing a scholarly edition of Clausewitz's writings in English. This project has now reached the final stage of planning. We are thinking of a number of volumes— perhaps as many as six—presenting a reliably translated text together with very substantial introductions and analyses. Some members of the editorial board are Gordon Craig, Klaus Knorr, Michael Howard, and myself."[68] Paret added, "Klaus and I wonder whether we could persuade you to join us. Specifically we would like you to undertake the interpretation of On War. We recognize that this is the most important and most difficult task of all, and we know that is no-one as well qualified as to handle it. The analysis should, of course, not only place the work in its historical context, but also speculate on the meaning Clausewitz's approach may have for contemporary problems of war and strategy. At present our time-table is flexible, and—needless to say—there is no expectation that such a major piece of work could be done quickly. Please let me know how you feel about this. I look forward to your reactions with great interest."[69] Paret wrote again on January 13, 1964, providing some "early information about the organization of the Clausewitz project," and noting: "Gordon Craig and I will act as the general editors of the series, which will probably consist of six volumes," and the other editors would include Basil Liddell Hart, Michael Howard, Klaus Knorr, John Shy, Karl Dietrich Erdmann, and Werner Hahlweg.[70] A meeting was planned for Europe, and Paret asked Brodie if he had any suggestions for a meeting place. He also noted he was seeking translators "who can turn Clausewitz's prose into clear and—I hope—reasonably elegant English."[71] Noting he and Craig had met with the other editors already, they asked Brodie if they could get together "for a thorough exploration of the editorial and interpretive problems of your volume before the general meeting in June," perhaps out in the Bay Area closer to Brodie's Santa Monica location, since Paret was only in Princeton until the end of that month.[72] On January 17, 1964 Brodie replied to Paret, noting he was "delighted to have further news about the Clausewitz project, especially the news that it is to include also people like Liddell Hart and Michael Howard."[73] With regard to a possible meeting place, Brodie felt "somewhere in Germany seems appropriate," and noted he had visited the Fuerungsakademie in Hamburg, and that he had been "greatly impressed with the attractive person and exceptional intelligence of the commandant, with the fine military library run by an unusually dedicated and knowledgeable director, and with the attractive physical plant located on the outskirts of the city near a very fine natural park. I am sure the group would be most welcome there and would find the environment a congenial one for the meeting. The German Defense Ministry would also be pleased with such a choice and would probably find ways of being helpful."[74] He also suggested "an even more pleasant locale for a meeting in the middle of June would be somewhere in southern France like Arles or Aix-en-Provence," and added: "Our British colleagues would probably appreciate a chance to warm up."[75] Brodie also suggested two translators for the project: Ewald Schnitzer, a former RANDite then at UCLA, and Freda Mendershausen. And noting he promised his family a ski trip to Mammoth or Yosemite during Easter week, he suggested dropping in to Davis after for the meeting.

On January 22, 1964, Brodie authored a memo sent to C. A. H. Thomson, J. M. Goldsen, and R. McDermott, titled "Participation in Clausewitz Project," noting he was invited by Paret to "participate in a project to be led by Paret and by Professor Gordon Craig of Princeton, which has as its purpose the preparation of a new edition of all the writings by Clausewitz," much of which "has never been translated into English, and this will now be done. Also a new translation will be prepared of his famous work, *On War*."[76] Brodie's "responsibility would be for editing *On War*, and that others in the project would be responsible for other portions of the work."[77] Brodie noted he had "accepted Paret's invitation (in a longhand letter written from home, of which I did not retain a copy) subject to the proviso that I could not begin work on it for another six months," which was accepted, so "I am now committed to the task."[78] Brodie added: "My understanding is that there will be no fees or royalties of any kind; at least nothing of the sort has been mentioned. It is strictly a scholarly enterprise, obviously a worthy one, and my association with it will, I trust, reflect credit on RAND."[79] Brodie expected "to do the work on my own time, although I may wish at some future time to raise the question whether the project is not relevant enough to RAND to warrant my attending meetings of the project members on work time rather than on leave."[80]

Klaus Knorr, of Princeton, wrote to Brodie on January 22, 1964 on the Clausewitz Project: "I am also delighted with the Clausewitz project, the way it is going, and your participation in it."[81] And on January 24, 1964 Brodie replied to Knorr, praising Knorr's recent article, in "Memorandum No. 28," saying he had "done quite a superb job, your arguments being right in every detail and also exceedingly well expressed."[82] But he also added, "I must rebuke you, however, for bowdlerizing (p. 26) the quotation of a former teacher of yours (and mine) in the late '30s. My recollection is that Viner said 'Pacifism is *like manure*, a fine thing if evenly spread.' Of course, it is somewhat dangerous to use the simile, because some people might think you mean to draw the correspondence between the two commodities even closer." Brodie added: "I am delighted that we are now going to be on the Clausewitz project together . . ."[83] A February 26, 1964 letter to Knorr raised some logistical issues including Brodie's desire to get hold of a "formal announcement of the new project from the Princeton University Press" to submit to RAND for consideration as "a legitimate part of what we call 'RAND-sponsored research," which would thus "make it possible for me to charge travel time on the project to RAND, and probably get some help on the travel expenses."[84] Knorr replied on March 2, noting the formal announcement was in the works, and would send a copy as soon as it became available. He added that "John Shy has procured finance from some other source," so Brodie should attend the June meeting as "it will be financed one way or other."[85] He added that "If RAND should decide against a contribution I should be able to find the money somewhere."[86]

On March 17, 1964 Brodie wrote to Paret with detailed information on available flights to Sacramento for their meeting with Craig. The next day, on March 18, 1964, Brodie wrote to Gordon Hubel, noting "I am eagerly awaiting that announcement you are preparing for the Clausewitz project. In fact, more than eagerly. So is Peter Paret for similar reasons. We both need it in our business. We shall appreciate your sending it as soon as you can."[87] The very next day, on March 19, Brodie wrote again, somewhat apologetically explaining, "I feel I owe you an explanation for my perhaps too-vehement request of yesterday," and explaining his need to document his request for "RAND-sponsored research," and adding he had been told by Herb Bailey that "the thing was in your hands."[88] Brodie also noted "since I pledged myself to the project some time last November or December, I am embarrassed that I still don't have in my hands the kind of descriptive statement I need. It is, of course, not your fault; but, at any rate, you are the one we are now looking to produce the required words."[89] On March 27, 1964, Brodie updated Knorr on the results of his meeting in Davis with Paret, noting the trip "turned out to be most fruitful. We talked in the main about the sorts of things that ought to be covered in my introduction to *Vom Kriege*; also about the possibilities of expanding the committee, perhaps by including one or two Frenchmen."[90] As Brodie has not yet secured approval from RAND for the project, he "had to make the trip as part of my annual leave" and was "obliged also to send you the airlines receipt, for reimbursement of my travel expenses," which included $43.79 for the return airfare and $5 for ground transport including parking.[91] Brodie reiterated he was still awaiting the formal announcement from Princeton University Press' Hubel and thus could not yet submit the project to RAND for consideration, so did not yet know whether they would support the project.

At last, on April 10, 1964, Princeton University's Department of Public Information announced: "A critical edition in English of the writings and correspondence of the 19th century political and military theorist, Carl von Clausewitz, is being prepared under the auspices of the Center for International Studies at Princeton University, Professor Klaus Knorr, Director of the Center, announced today," which was expected "to consist of six volumes" that "will require several years to complete."[92] The announcement presented a brief synopsis of Clausewitz's contribution to the study of war, and noted "Not more than one-tenth of Clausewitz's writings have been in print at one time since his death in 1831. The new Princeton series will contain material that has never been published, and much that has been out of print even in Germany since the 19th century."[93] On May 1, 1964, Brodie wrote to Knorr, commiserating with him on his back treatment in hospital, as he was himself on the mend from back surgery earlier in the year. He also sought clarity on the timing and location of the June meeting. On April 25, 1964, Paret wrote to Brodie, confirming the press release had been sent to RAND, and incidentally noting that in his recent clearance investigation for a Top-Secret clearance, the issue of having "once been under psychiatric care" came up, when Paret had noted he had undergone analysis while in England and had even provided the name of his analyst to RAND security with "full authorization to question him," and that the RAF had in fact interviewed him. Paret told the Air Force investigators that "they had been misinformed, that I had never in my life seen a psychiatrist professionally, that I had been analyzed when I lived in England, and that I hoped they understood the difference between analysis and psychiatry. They nodded—but rather doubtfully, I'm afraid . . . It is pointless, I am sure, to be irritated by the clearance process; but this episode did strike me as both inefficient and naïve."[94]

On May 7, 1964, J. M. Goldsen sent a RAND Memo to George Clement on the subject of "RSR Grant for Bernard Brodie." It noted Brodie had been invited to participate in the Clausewitz Project, and to "edit the translation of *On War*, the most famous and the most important of Clausewitz's writings, and to provide an introductory essay."[95] Brodie had "accepted while he was still on sick leave last Fall" and that "It did not appear to him that he would have to cut into any RAND time, or seek any RAND support for his participation," and that he had "expected that the expenses for the few conferences planned with members of the project would be reimbursed by the project and that he could carry on his own participation via annual leave. It now appears that the amount of time required will be somewhat greater than Bernard originally estimated. Moreover, Princeton did not allocate travel funds, and whatever funds for travel Klaus Knorr has available he groans to allocate to this purpose."[96] The Social Science Department reviewed with Brodie the amount of time he would need to spend on the project, and asked for funds to enable him to spend no more than 15 days on the project in each of the years 1964 and 1965 plus $1,000 in travel funds in each of those years.

On May 15, 1964 Brodie wrote to Knorr, upbeat about the upcoming Berlin meeting in June and noting that Joe Goldsen had submitted a request for funding to RAND, but that he had not yet heard the result and could not predict the outcome due to "special problems within

RAND at this time."[97] Brodie budgeted his flight to Berlin at $874.20 in economy class, with additional expenses to be no more than $50 to $75. He added he would "not wait to see you compare notes about broken backs. I will send you a letter on the subject next week."[98] On May 22, 1964, Brodie wrote to Paret, noting he "will see you at the Hotel Am Zoo on Friday,"[99] near to the Tiergarten. After the meeting Brodie intended to fly to Paris for a nine- or ten-day tour of Burgundy, Provence, and Languedoc, and asked: "Would you like to come along?" and adding, "I am looking forward to our meeting in Berlin, which is now really quite close."[100] On May 28, 1964, Brodie wrote to Paret, asking for clarity on Berlin meeting date and whether it was scheduled for 13–14 June, or 12–13 June; he also noted he had found a good translator in Washington whose "writing style in English is quite elegant," in addition to the two persons he had mentioned earlier. Not having more details on the terms of employment he suggested waiting until Berlin before taking any further initiatives on this matter.[101] On May 31, 1964, Paret wrote to Brodie, noting he too was looking forward to the Berlin meeting "and to Europe generally," and adding his thanks for the travel invitation, "It is just what I should like to do, and I wish I could join you; but I am giving a lecture in Hamburg on the 22nd—just the wrong time." Noted Craig had "invited some interesting people from the University, RIAS, etc., to join us for dinner on Saturday. It should be very pleasant."[102]

On July 29, 1964, Gordon Hubel, the executive assistant at Princeton University Press, wrote to Brodie, noting he had received the minutes of the editorial board meeting on the Clausewitz project, "as well as a note from Peter Paret. Everything seems to be going along well, which gives me great pleasure. This is going to be a really important publishing event, and I am glad you are so closely connected with it."[103] The minutes of the "13–14 June 1964 Meeting of the Editorial Board" noted the project "intends to make available to the Anglo-American reader the significant historical, political, and theoretical works of a writer whose pioneering role in the development of modern military and political thought is not yet fully understood," and which would include multiple volumes including volumes on military history, the Prussian Reform era combing history and strategic theory, political writings and letters, and one volume containing *On War*.[104] The organization of each to include "a carefully translated text, based on the best German original, whether published or unpublished, accompanied by a critical apparatus and an extensive analytic introduction," as well as a "brief general introduction that describes the edition as a whole and places the particular volume within it." [105] Gordon Craig had begun work on his political writings; John Shy on the campaign of 1796; Peter Paret on the Prussian Reform era; and the "special and diverse problems posed by *On War* can be most effectively managed by two editors, and Bernard Brodie and Michael Howard have agreed to share responsibility for this volume—each writing a separate essay."[106] Possibly expanding the project was discussed, such as including the later Napoleonic campaigns, such as the 1799 and the 1812–1815 campaigns; translation, and additional editorial problems such as footnotes and bibliographies were also discussed. Administrative and financial matters "are in the hands of Klaus Knorr," as CIS at Princeton "sponsors the project," and the first two or three volumes were expected to be ready in 1965.[107]

But reality set in, and it was not until April 23, 1967 that Paret wrote to Brodie, at long last, that: "Enclosed is a revised translation of ch. 1 of *On War*. I'd be very glad to have your comments on I, particularly since it is one the most important theoretical parts of the whole work. I would have sent it to you much earlier, but in going over the typescript of the translation before sending it to the printer, the P.U.P. editor and I discovered so many misspellings, deletions, and plain mistakes (on the part of the translator as well as of the various typists) that we have had to go very carefully over the entire ms once more. It has been a very time-consuming process, but a necessary one, and I believe the result is worth the effort."[108] Paret added: "Michael Howard, who was in Princeton for a few days, discussed the outline of his introduction with me. Klaus unfortunately was in the hospital, and could not share in our talk. Michael believes, and I agree with him, that a historical introduction would be meaningless without some analysis of the text. This would relieve you of the need to analyze ON WAR in detail, and instead give you the opportunity of using the work as a basis for a discussion of the possibilities and methodological problems, and limitations of systematic analyses of conflict in general. In this connection I would again be very glad to have your views on the enclosed chapter. We are returning to California around the middle of June, and I hope it will be possible for, you and me to get together during the summer. Until then, with all good wishes."[109] On May 11, 1967, Brodie wrote to Paret, noting receipt of the revised translations of Chapter 1 of *On War* on April 23, 1967:

> The translation looks to me to be superb. Knowing of your own considerable intervention, I am naturally assured of its complete accuracy, and it reads exceedingly well. Simply on the merits of the translation it will obviously be a great advance over the Modern Library version by Jolles. Klaus Knorr was here in the latter part of last week and told me of the great amount of work you had to do on it personally after it had left the hands of the translator. It is too bad you had to spend so much time on it, but I hope you will feel that the results are rewarding enough to justify your effort. I get a positively electric effect out of reading this chapter. It is the stimulation one gets from witnessing a really great mind at work. It leaves me in no doubt that there will be much to say concerning the present utility of Clausewitz—a question about which I wondered. I agree in principle that Michael Howard should in his historical introduction be free to make some analysis of the content. But I would like to have a better idea just how far in that direction he plans to go. I am not concerned with having my own thoughts pre-empted, but I do worry about how many pages devoted to introduction the book can stand. Two long essays would probably be too much. Michael was down here a couple of weeks ago; but when I raised the subject of the Clausewitz project, he brushed it aside by saying his conversation with you had led him to feel that the task still lay much in the future. I was therefore surprised to get your letter and its enclosure so soon after that discussion. Perhaps when the piece is farther along, he and I can get together again and do some real planning. I might say the two issues which interest me the most at present are: a) Clausewitz's great and ubiquitous emphasis on the dominance of the political aim (which is what makes his work so modern and alive), and b) the contrast of his methodology with the types presently in vogue.[110]

Brodie also raised the question of Paret's planned departure from U.C. Davis' faculty: "Let me now ask you a few questions about yourself. I hear you are thinking of going to England, and that you might accept an academic appointment at LSE. If you are interested in leaving Davis, would you consider UCLA a sufficient improvement? . . . The history department here clearly needs building up, and getting you here would be the best way I know for starting that process. The university itself has very much to commend it, and the area ought to be congenial to both you and especially your wife, with her special interest in psychoanalysis."[111]

Brodie's concern—expressed in his May 1, 1967 letter to Paret—that Howard's comments had left him with the impression that apart from their progress on the translation of *On War*, the bulk of the multi-volume Clausewitz project "lay much in the future," would prove to be well placed; while the translation of *On War* would resume and successfully march toward completion over the coming years, the rest of the Clausewitz Project would not. The fate of the project would be described by PUP editor Herb Bailey in a latter to Brodie on January 12, 1973: "I want to come back to the eight-volume edition of Clausewitz that we once agreed to do, and that we finally and regretfully felt that we couldn't sustain as a continuing commitment. I don't know what happened to that, but I want to say again that our decision not to carry the project as a continuing commitment did not mean that we felt that we could never do it. In particular, if and when the new translation of ON WAR is completed and ready for publication, we would like very much to consider it. Perhaps other volumes too, if one could project them on a reasonably sure schedule. How does the matter stand? I hope you will keep our interest in mind."[112]

Clausewitz's Passion for the Study of War

In January 1973—the year Brodie would publish his own Clausewitzian treatise on war, *War and Politics*—Brodie penned a book review of Roger Parkinson's 1971 *Clausewitz: A Biography* in *World Politics*, where he goes well beyond reviewing Parkinson's work, presenting his own thoughts on Clausewitz, which would be further developed in *War and Politics* as well as in his contributions to the 1976 Princeton edition of *On War*.[113] Brodie writes that we are "especially indebted to the author of this book because of the extraordinary paucity of biographies of the great man who is its subject," who, as the author's mentor, Michael Howard, noted in the foreword, "remains almost completely unknown."[114] Brodie recognizes the book's "notable virtue" but also points out that its author had "within a rather short span of years published two books prior to this one and already another one since, and none of the others bears any relation in period, and very little in locale or field of interest, to the matter of this book. To slip in and out of a subject like Carl von Clausewitz betrays to any thorough historical scholar an undue note of bravura. Clearly the author is not a specialist on the period of the Prussian military reforms, and one should not expect from him the kind of primary scholarship in the field that one gets from a Peter Paret, or, for a later date, from Howard himself."[115]

But to the author's credit, Brodie adds that his vocation "seems to be that of a war correspondent (there have indeed been enough wars to keep a man going between scholarly pursuits), in which respect he stands in some excellent historical and contemporary company—beginning, I suppose, with Friedrich Engels. . . . Parkinson belongs with the best of this breed, and his vocation has no doubt assisted him in developing a talent which would in itself make him a worthy pupil of Howard's: he writes extremely well. The present book is a pleasure to read, and if the author is not as insightful about the challenging psychological aspects of Clausewitz's nature as he ought to be—one should be able to recognize deep depression as a morbid symptom—he does at least as well in that area as the great majority of scholarly specialists in the field could do."[116] Brodie finds that Parkinson "has done what might be called a 'sufficiency' of research, to which I will try to give meaning by suggesting that he could profitably have done more, but for the present it will do. . . . and while he may have skipped an item or two, what he has read he has read perceptively, and he has been deft in weaving the resulting insights into his narrative," marred only by the occasional "dubious conjecture or evidence of carelessness or outright error" that "pops up."[117] Among such doubtful elements of Parkinson's work is his "observation (derived from Karl Schwarz, Clausewitz's chief German biographer) that it was Kant who should be or at least has been 'held responsible for the logical methods and dialectical sharpness in Clausewitz's own work'" when it is Brodie's firm belief that "the one he obviously followed with the most respect and whose dialectical method he unfortunately adopted, however superficially, was clearly Hegel, who is not mentioned in Parkinson's book at all."[118] Brodie adds that "Hegel's philosophy of history and of the state was certainly more congenial to Clausewitz than the entire teaching of Kant, who was after all the author of the tract on Perpetual Peace (1795), where in his moral scheme of things war has no place—an idea that Hegel explicitly and emphatically rejected."[119] He further notes the "well-known Hegelian troika of thesis, antithesis, and synthesis is apparent in Clausewitz's presentation, especially in the 'finished' first chapter of On War." [120]

Brodie seizes upon Parkinson's sensitive description of Clausewitz—with his "high fore-head; the large, intelligent, rather mournful eyes; the sensitive and faintly humorous mouth: this might be a poet or composer of the early Romantic period rather than a man who had first put on uniform at the age of twelve and who served as a professional soldier from beginning to end of the Revolutionary Wars of 1792–1815"—writing "one should add, as the man who wrote Vom Kriege, not simply the greatest book on war but the one truly great book on that subject yet written. The fact that he looked intelligent should not surprise us, because he was in truth a genius."[121] Brodie describes this projection onto Clausewitz's soft appearance of an almost Kantian belief in his sensitivity as not inaccurate, but incomplete, writing: "Looks in these matters are notoriously deceiving, but we do know . . . that tenderness and compassion were truly in him, but, as we shall see, they were in conflict with something else. It is this conflict, mostly shut out of his awareness but resulting in melancholy and depression, that becomes an important key to understanding Clausewitz the man."[122] Noting Clausewitz's "unfortunate admiration and imitation of the Hegelian style," which "committed him to statements which, especially when read out of context, have him breathing words of fire as though he felt a perverse love for them," Brodie concedes "there is no doubt that there was something about war which Clausewitz found deeply exciting, and it may well have been not the glory in it but the violence. He may indeed have had a perverse love for those fiery words and the thoughts they conjured up."[123] But importantly, Clausewitz proceeds throughout On War to "introduce modifying principles, and he continues to do so throughout the book," but as Brodie describes, "By his own conscious choice of formal logic there is no inconsistency in his doing so. For he points out that it is only in 'the abstract realm of pure conception' (that is, in the 'idealistic' realm of Plato and his too numerous followers, including Hegel) that war permits of no modifying principles; in the real world, in which war is a political act to achieve a valid political purpose or else quite meaningless in an altogether abhorrent fashion, we are dealing with a quite different brew. It is still a devil's brew, but that is neither Clausewitz's fault nor his intellectual concern. He lived, like the rest of us, in a world he never made; but unlike many living today, he could not really imagine an alternative world and likely did not want to."[124]

While Brodie identifies a closer affinity between Clausewitz and Hegel than with Kant, in contrast to Parkinson (among others including his more recent biographer of our generation, Hew Strachan), he also notes the Prussian's unique respect for Machiavelli, "who had written, besides his more famous Il Principe, the Arte delta Guerra and the Discorsi, the first being obviously and the second quite largely on the art of war. Clausewitz treated Machiavelli with respect because, like him," citing the words of Felix Gilbert's chapter in Makers of Modern Strategy, "he was convinced that the validity of any special analysis of military problems depended on a general perception, on a correct concept of the nature of war."[125] Brodie marvels on how Clausewitz, "whose whole life from boyhood on was spent in military service and who as a scholar and philosopher was totally self-taught, was able to grasp the essence of the issue, the nexus between politics and strategy, so much more clearly than virtually all of his contemporaries and successors," which Brodie attributes primarily to "his native intellectual prowess, the extraordinary power and reach of his mind" but that as a catalyst, Clausewitz "also had some bitter personal experiences to help him along the way," as "[h]is entry into the Prussian army coincided with the beginning, in France, of the Terror" and "[h]e was to be deeply immersed in the whole vast Napoleonic cataclysm" and "soon came to look upon Napoleon (whom he always referred to as 'Bonaparte') about as our own generation looked upon Hitler—the enemy of Europe and of mankind."[126] Brodie notes with approval that Clausewitz "was nevertheless objective enough always to credit this detested man with being a superlative general."[127]

It was the "searing experiences" at war against Napoleon that "burnt the idea of the necessary unity of war with its objective deeply into the consciousness of this sensitive, retiring, and deeply emotional man," and which illuminated his theoretical endeavors during the "sixteen years of life remaining to him," which "were externally uneventful—no doubt a good thing for his literary production—but left him ever more deeply dissatisfied."[128] He was soon "promoted to Major-General in 1818, at the age of 38, and made director of the Allegmeine Kriegsschule in Berlin," where "his duties excluded teaching and were confined to administration," which "gave him more time for his writing but heightened his gloom. . . . He was again made military tutor to the Crown Prince, which certainly showed some mark of royal favor, and in 1827 his noble status and that of his brothers was at last fully authorized. But Clausewitz still felt not sufficiently noticed. And he was always sad."[129] But his melancholy did not impede his theoretical and analytical output, and Clausewitz "had already written and privately circulated a substantial amount and even published some of it; almost all of it was well received. Within the next decade he would write much more, all of it obviously having high value in his own eyes and those of the few others who saw it."[130]

Brodie speculates that Clausewitz's depression was fueled in part by the relative ennui of peace and notes that in 1830, "events occurred that caused Clausewitz to spring to animated life and, for a while, to become almost deliriously happy. The troubles that broke out all over Europe in that year, and especially the new revolution in France . . . seemed to bring the likelihood of a new war. His father-in-law reported Clausewitz as being positively cheerful at the thought of war, which was expected to break out with his own old enemy, France."[131] But in the end, "there were no military operations, and 'Clausewitz's depression returned far deeper than ever before.'"[132] Brodie writes, "We must confront the fact that this man, who had seen so much of the worst horrors of war, whose face still bore the marks of the frostbite he had acquired in the Russian campaign, had been brought from chronic depression into positive exultation at the thought of going to war again, especially against the French. When he found this was not to be, that there was going to be no war at all, he was plunged back into the deepest gloom."[133]

Brodie looks inward to a psychological explanation to explain Clausewitz's depressed response to the continuation of peace: "Why this relapse? To a chief of staff aged fifty, who must have known in his heart that he was cut out to be a staff officer and not a commander, a new war could bring no special honors. Did he really have a passion for glory, or did he feel that as a soldier his real fulfillment in life could only be found in campaigning? Or did he simply love war? If the latter, we must again ask, why? Someone who loves war must love, among other things, aggression and violence, terrible violence, which he can both witness and partake of. Such a taste is common enough, but is by no means to be considered normal. It argues some inner rage-repressed, unconscious, but alive. We can no longer hide our thoughts and questions behind 'thesis' and 'antithesis.' The bloody phrases so often quoted out of context from his great posthumous work burn with their own fierce fire. They are kindled by something within."[134] Brodie notes that this "inner rage" is "indeed countered and, on intellectual balance, overcome with other words in which the intellect is at work rather than passion; and the intellect in this case is tremendously strong," but concludes that: "We are dealing here with a deep internal conflict, and there can be no doubt that this conflict is directly linked to his growing depression. That is about all we can say on the basis of what we know, and it is really not very much. Let those who take fright at the thought of 'analyzing' the dead notice that our speculative thrust has not penetrated very deep, and that it is based on tell-tale signs of the most unquestionable singularity and importance. Chronic depression as Clausewitz knew it, only fitfully interrupted by rather odd stimuli, does not suggest a state of emotional health."[135] Brodie adds: "One wonders also how a man in the throes of such conflict and depression could produce as much writing as Clausewitz did. He did speak about feeling 'paralyzed,' and such a feeling and also the connected behavior are the common consequence of attempting to cope with strong unconscious conflicts. But he was not paralyzed in actuality."[136] Indeed, Brodie suggests that "[p]erhaps the fact that the writing was always about war gave him the needed release. Just as Machiavelli's great work was inevitably a projection of himself acting as a prince, and as a prince who knows when and how to refrain from mercy (which is just about always), so Clausewitz's was a projection of himself acting not as chief of staff but as a field marshal, and the occupation contemplated was not statecraft but war. In his case, however, the slaughter and destructiveness inherent in war were made good by the fact that a superb intelligence was guiding everything towards a politically wise end. Slaughter can at least be dedicated to statecraft, and the use of intelligence can achieve economies in the necessary acts of destruction."[137]

When Clausewitz succumbed to cholera in 1831, at 51, just nine hours after showing his first symptoms, Brodie observes that his "doctors said he had died because he lacked the will to live, and Marie agreed with this. Cholera can take the lives also of those who want to live, and can do so very fast; but it is significant that the doctors and Marie could entertain their own special convictions on the matter."[138] Brodie shares Parkinson's observation, that: "Marie knew very well the reason for her husband's death. 'Life for him was a nearly uninterrupted succession of disappointments, of suffering, of mortification. . . . Oh yes, on the whole, he had achieved much more than he could expect when it started. He was well aware of that, and grateful. But nevertheless, he never reached the summit. And every satisfaction always had a thorn in it, to add pain to the pleasure. He had friendship, to a rare degree, with the excellent men of his period. But not recognition.'"[139] While sympathetic with Marie's sentiment, Brodie notes "Clausewitz had indeed 'achieved much more than he could expect when it started,' and if that left him with a feeling of 'a nearly uninterrupted succession of disappointments,' then, as one would put it today, he had a problem—one that was internal to himself and not external. And how characteristic of such a problem that 'every satisfaction always had a thorn in it.' It is most certainly not true that he lacked recognition."[140] Indeed, Brodie adds: "The King and the Crown Prince, incidentally, did not omit to express their condolences publicly as well as privately to Marie on her husband's death. And why, in heaven's name, should he have expected to reach 'the summit'? As Clausewitz had said over and over again, she, Marie, would publish his work after his death. Back in Berlin she had packets of papers, his Hinterlassene Werke (posthumous works), which would ultimately reach ten volumes, the first three of which would be On War. In the scarcely more than four years remaining to her, Marie would herself prepare and edit eight of these ten volumes. At the time of Clausewitz's death, few if any had read this great bulk of writing. He did in fact reach the summit, in the only way possible to a man whose gifts are mainly if not exclusively intellectual, but he was bound to reach it posthumously."[141]

Brodie closes his discussion of Clausewitz—and to a lesser degree, of Parkinson's work—with an examination of Clausewitz's most famous dictum, that war is a continuation of policy by other means, which in the years that immediately followed Clausewitz's death seems to have been lost on military practitioners, the result, in part, of the unfinished state of Clausewitz's writing, which obscured this central thesis from all but the first and final books of his multi-volume opus. As Brodie writes, the "most important single idea in On War, the one that suffuses so much of it and makes it great, is the idea that war must never be an act of blind violence but must be dedicated to achieving the supreme goals of statecraft and must therefore be controlled by that dedication. Parkinson shares the view that this is Clausewitz's basic contribution, and he cites some appropriate passages from the work to underline it."[142] Brodie writes that "[w]e have long known that Clausewitz too shared the view that this was his most important contribution," and recalls that "Marie's brother, Heinrich von Brühl, in helping his sister to edit her late husband's work, came upon a note written by Clausewitz in 1827 that read as follows: 'I regard the first six books, of which a fair copy has now been made, as only a rather formless mass which will be thoroughly revised once more.' Clausewitz stressed in this note the primary importance he attached to the conception according to which war is regarded as 'nothing but the continuation of state policy with other means'" but "then added: 'This point of view, everywhere maintained, will bring much more unity into our investigation, and everything will be easier to disentangle. Although this point of view will chiefly find its application in Book VIII, nevertheless it must be fully explained in Book I and also contribute to the revision of the first six Books. By such a revision the first six Books will be freed from many a piece of dross; many a fissure and gap will be closed; and many a generality can be converted into more definite thoughts and forms.'"[143] Brodie notes that Clausewitz later wrote that, "If by the revision of Book VIII [where his ideas on political control of military action are mainly developed] I have cleared up my ideas, and the main features of war will be properly established, it will then be the easier for me to infuse the same spirit into the first six Books, and there, too, to make those features everywhere visible."[144] But Brodie adds: "All this Clausewitz failed to do before his death; however, the first chapter of the first book, which is the only chapter he considered completed, does bring in very prominently and almost at once the idea mentioned above as his basic conception, and in the later pages of that same chapter it is developed considerably. It is then virtually lost to view until the last part, Book VIII, where it comes to the fore again and is developed much further. We know now that he would have suffused the relevant ideas through the remainder of the book, where it would have been much less easy to lose sight of them—and much less easy also for later editors deliberately to blur or delete them."[145]

But because Clausewitz died before completing his revisions, the "bulk of the work in its present state is devoted to describing how to win wars," and Brodie wonders, "What would have been the results if he had accomplished his goal? We know that the military profession has always been, at least until quite recently, allergic to the idea which Clausewitz considered his most important one. The elder von Moltke, who had been a student officer at the Berlin War Academy while Clausewitz was director of it and who subsequently read *On War* fervently, was nevertheless able, as a field marshal, to declare: 'The politician should fall silent the moment that mobilization begins.' That was certainly the idea of the generals who prepared for and who fought World War I."[146] Thus, "In the various condensations of *On War* that were published under military auspices in the nineteenth century and down to World War II, the sections which contain Clausewitz's thoughts on the primacy of the political objective—the basic idea that war is too important to be left to the generals—are either obscured, corrupted, or entirely eliminated."[147]

And the price of this would prove high. As Brodie concludes: "Well, one might say, what can one expect of the military, who, among other things, don't like to have control taken away from them? But the fact is that even so distinguished a German military scholar as the late Dr. Herbert Rosinski was able to make substantially the same error. He asserts that the basic teaching of Clausewitz (as he puts it: it was only when 'he turned back to seek his foundations in the inner logic of his subject that he found himself on firm ground at last') is—what? That the aim of war is 'the overthrow of the enemy's power of resistance.' That is what Rosinski calls Clausewitz's 'unique achievement.' Achievement it may be, unique it certainly is not. And if is not unique, it is hardly much of an achievement, although it makes more sense than 'winning ground' or gaining 'the honor of the battlefield.' Rosinski certainly saw a great deal more in Clausewitz than these few words of his indicate, but the basic message passed him by. Clausewitz, had he lived to finish his work, would at least have caught the Rosinskis of this world. And even the military would have found it more difficult to escape. His book would also be more alive today for scholars."[148]

War and Politics: A Tribute to Clausewitzian Theory

In his January 12, 1973 letter to Brodie reaffirming his interest in publishing the new translation of *On War* if and when it was completed, Bailey also congratulated Brodie on his recently

254 STATE OF DOOM

published review article, "Review: On Clausewitz: A Passion for War," in the January 1973 edition of *World Politics*. As Bailey described, "I have just finished reading your review-article on Clausewitz in the current issue of *World Politics*, with great pleasure and interest, and it brings on a flood of thoughts. First, the article is written with such clarity and force that it makes me again most regretful that we aren't publishing your new book,"[149] Brodie's 1973 *War and Politics*, his effort to apply Clausewitz's most famous dictum linking war and politics to the historical experience of modern warfare. Bailey continued, "It also suggests other things, the first being that you yourself ought to write the book on Clausewitz that Parkinson didn't write. Your article is full of knowledge of Clausewitz in depth and detail, combined with the kind of feeling for the man and the situation that would yield the kind of book on Clausewitz that is needed. Why don't you do it? It would be a big project, but an absorbing one, and obviously the subject appeals to you."[150] But if taking on another big Clausewitz project, so soon after the last one had collapsed, did not appeal, Bailey offered that "[t]here is another possibility that comes to mind, a shorter book on Clausewitz, not a biography but an appreciation of his intellectual contribution, relating it to twentieth-century experience. You refer in your article to the preparations for World War I, and there is a brief reference to Hitler, but in reading it I couldn't help thinking about the experience of Korea and Viet Nam. It is possible that, in terms of putting knowledge to work, an interpretative work of this kind might be more effective, and it could also be done in briefer compass."[151] Ironically, that was precisely Brodie's objective in *War and Politics*, which indeed reflected upon the Korean and Vietnam experiences from a Clausewitzian perspective, from which Brodie would attribute the Vietnam war's ultimate strategic failure. Perhaps unaware that Brodie's forthcoming *War and Politics* was already at heart a tribute to Clausewitz, Bailey suggested, "I would love to hear how all this strikes you. In any case, congratulations on an excellent article."[152]

Brodie's thinking about Clausewitz was not limited to his role introducing the new translation of *On War* but would also serve to frame a separate volume on strategy that is indebted to Clausewitz's most famous dictum on the interconnection of war and policy and which came to press several years before the much anticipated translation of *On War*. Indeed, Brodie's 1973 *War and Politics* showed how deep an inspiration Clausewitz was to Brodie, inspiring not only the title, but permeating its very essence, in which he sought to apply this most fundamental component of Clausewitz's theory of war to his own era, and more so than in *Strategy in the Missile Age*, and to explain the interconnection of war and politics, not just nuclear war, but all the wars of the nuclear age, through an historical analysis of World War II and in particular its strategic bombing, which transformed in that war's closing days into the world's first and so far only nuclear war; Korea; and Vietnam (and its failure), and a theoretical discussion about war not only in the nuclear era but the humbled, post-Vietnam era.

While *War and Politics* is at heart a tribute to Clausewitz, Brodie also pays tribute to two of his most influential professors who had recently died. Brodie is said to have been Quincy Wright's protégé, as reported by Kaplan in *Wizards of Armageddon*, among others, but he was also greatly influenced by the economist Jacob Viner, as Kaplan has also noted. But in Brodie's preface to *War and Politics* in 1973, he credits Viner first and foremost, saluting him for his enduring intellectual influence, writing "I would like to pay my grateful respects to the memory of my greatest teacher, Jacob Viner, who at the time I was his student in graduate school over thirty years ago was Professor of Economics at the University of Chicago. Whatever is good in my work owes something to him, and I was especially conscious of his eyes over my shoulder in writing chapter 7."[153] This glowing attribution of a lifelong influence is in marked contrast to his tribute to Wright: "I also offer my respects to another dedicated and scholarly teacher of whom I was very fond, Quincy Wright, formerly Professor of International Law and Political Science at the University of Chicago. Both were friends and colleagues as well as former teachers."[154]

From the language Brodie uses to present these two tributes, it is clear he is acknowledging a deep intellectual debt to Viner, and merely a close fondness for Wright, quite a distinction. That Viner is said to have helped Brodie come to the important realization that nuclear weapons were a stabilizing force in the world, and from this derived an enduring faith in the strategy of deterrence—putting him at odds with colleagues who would question their faith along the Cold War's half-century long turbulent journey, but providing a consistency to his work as he repeatedly chastized doubters on the underlying mechanisms of deterrence when they lost sight of them—helping to thereby direct Brodie along a trajectory he would follow for another three decades, and providing the intellectual seed that was perhaps the ultimate foundation for Brodie of his formulation of deterrence, something that was yet fully developed to any degree of certainty when he first addressed the new weapon in 1945, but which was firmly resolved by 1946 and remained resolved in Brodie's mind for the rest of his life.

It is interesting to note that Chapter 7 is the only chapter that Brodie attributes in his preface to a prior publication even though *War and Politics* is not unlike *Strategy in the Missile Age* in being largely an anthology of Brodie's works, with a substantial portion of his chapters having appeared earlier as papers, articles, or lectures—sometimes with whole passages verbatim, while others are updated with additional information. A quick glance reveals chapters (and there subsections) sharing titles with past work, and a closer look reveals identical paragraphs flowing at times in identical sequence with other identical paragraphs, having been largely pasted from past work into the present work—but not universally, as often new paragraphs are inserted, and at other times, new sentences are added to pre-existing paragraphs. But Brodie only acknowledges in his preface that, "An earlier version of Chapter 7, 'Some Theories of the Causes of War,'" appeared in the two-volume *Festschrift* published in Paris in 1971 in honor of a friend and a great contributor to insight on matters of war and peace," Raymond Aron; "I have, however, entirely rewritten it and greatly expanded it for this book. The rest is almost entirely new."[155] While it is true that Brodie has "greatly expanded" and largely rewritten his earlier chapter, it is hard to argue that it was "entirely rewritten"—nor, moreover, to overlook that he published in Security Studies Paper No. 17, *Bureaucracy, Politics, and Strategy* co-edited by Brodie and Henry Kissinger (with one chapter from Kissinger and four from Brodie), a chapter (more aptly a paper, since the Security Studies Papers were collections of shorter works that included newspaper articles, lectures and speeches, conference papers, and other brief works) with the title "Theories on the Causes of War," differing only in the absence of the word "Some" from the chapter in *War and Politics*.[156]

Because Brodie was the series editor as well as the paper author, it seems curious that its origins were overlooked, and for the sake of historical accuracy—of the origins of that 1973 chapter within the very structure and substance of the earlier 1968 paper, which covers much similar ground—recognition of this fact by Brodie would have been helpful to later scholars. But Brodie's claim that the rest of *War and Politics* "is almost entirely new" rings somewhat hollow upon realization that not just Chapter 7, to which he gratefully credits Viner for his seemingly watchful and protective eye looking over Brodie's shoulder from the great beyond, but many other chapters had their origins elsewhere—including Chapter 8, "Vital Interests: What Are They and Who Says So?" which is derived in large part (though not entirely), and with much verbatim (including many paragraphs in identical sequence, albeit not all), from his 1971 booklet, *Strategy and National Interests: Reflections for the Future*—which we discussed at the end of chapter five of this work—published by the National Strategy Information Center, whose third chapter is "Vital Interests: By Whom and How Determined?" on pages 11–24. Further, in Chapter 10, "Strategic Thinkers, Planners, Decision-Makers," in *War and Politics*, one sees many echoes of his earlier work, including a section on the "Scientific Strategists" that bears much in common with his chapter of the same name in Robert Gilpin and Christopher Wright, eds, *Scientists and National Policy-Making* published by Columbia University Press in 1964 and the longer version of that chapter with the slightly elongated title, "The American Scientific Strategists" that appeared as a RAND working paper in October 1964 but which also includes elements that bear a similarity to his discussion in his 1971 *Foreign Policy* article, "Why Were We So (Strategically) Wrong?" as well as his discussion of systems theory and the *scientization* of national security decision-making and over-dependence on systems theory, causing a tragic neglect of more fundamental political issues in his 1971 *Strategy and National Interests: Reflections for the Future.*[157]

Brodie does credit Michael Howard for his assistance with Brodie's first chapter ("De quoi s'agit-il?") on the meaning of Clausewitz's notion that war has its own language but not its own logic, which is defined by the political objective (boiled down into the more famous Clausewitzian dictum, *war is a continuation of policy by other means*), though the ideas presented therein can be traced back to numerous articles, papers, chapters, and reviews by Brodie on and about Clausewitz including reviews of Howard's work on Clausewitz and their joint collaboration with Peter Paret on the decade-long Clausewitz Project that yielded the seminal Princeton translation of *On War* in 1976; and similarly, among the six scholars Brodie credits for their assistance on his chapters on Vietnam is William Gerberding, with whom he co-edited and jointly contributed chapters to their 1968 UCLA Security Studies Paper No. 13, *The Political Dimension in National Strategy: Five Papers*—whose title is at heart Clausewitzian—and which included Brodie's article, "Learning to Fight a Limited War," which discussed Vietnam in critical detail, paving the way forward to Brodie's later 1971 article in *Foreign Policy.*

So while there is much that is new and certainly updated in *War and Politics*, there are so many connective threads to his earlier work that one can define the book as less a *new* contribution to Brodie's vast canon, and *more* a synthesis of his work since *Escalation and the Nuclear Option* and an effort to reframe his work that followed *Strategy in the Missile Age*, reasserting the importance of (and challenges inherent to) limiting war and reflecting on the dangers of divorcing the dynamic of escalation from its important, Clausewitzian political context. Brodie dueled with Kahn on the nature of escalation, and sought to embed escalation in its political context—but his voice of restraint was overshadowed by the towering voices of his colleagues, including Kahn (and also the highly influential Schelling), whose ideas on a separate logic of escalation appealed to the architects of American defense policy during the Kennedy and Johnson administrations and whose legacy was the humbling, and Brodie believes, preventable debacle, of Vietnam. But as tragic as Vietnam was, as Brodie had noted in his December 3, 1967 article in the *Los Angeles Times*, "Learning to Fight a Limited War," "At least we can be grateful that thus far nuclear weapons have been kept out of a business that is unfortunate enough already."[158] And even with the tragic inevitability of the Vietnam defeat approaching its final act, Brodie, as noted in *War and Politics*, finds reassuring that the underlying global stability predicated upon mutual nuclear deterrence held firm, suggesting "one argument against skepticism with respect to American nuclear reliability is that it reflects a gross exaggeration of the adversary's proclivity for going to the nuclear brink," and adding: "Thus far, there has been none of that reckless playing of 'chicken,' of swift resort to brinksmanship, that filled so many of the fantasies of Herman Kahn and others in the 1960s."[159] At least with regard to nuclear war, a Clausewitzian balance held, and with it the recognition that war must remain rational.

This is perhaps why Brodie feels so passionate about revisiting Clausewitz's tragically ignored counsel; Brodie thus starts off *War and Politics* with Clausewitz's profound but often overlooked insight that war "has its own language but not its own logic,"[160] something the escalation theorists as well as the firebreak theorists who advocated CWE failed to grasp as they logically proceeded up the escalation ladder, seeking to convey a language of war without being cognizant of the foundational political logic—and fighting an unnecessary and costly (albeit limited) war, not only to a conventional stalemate fought well below the nuclear firebreak, but ultimately to a self-imposed defeat, leaving the field of battle to its opponent without really having ever been defeated at the tactical level. Vietnam, in its tragedy and wasted effort, would prove Brodie correct—that the firebreak theorists who advocated CWE had completely misunderstood how deterrence worked, and the all-important, intimate connection of war to politics (and the supremacy of the political objective), which Brodie sought to reassert in *War and Politics*, his final synthesis of the many smaller pieces he had written to a very wide audience, from classified military briefings to college lectures and conference panels; from esoteric academic journals and small student-run university newspapers to major urban dailies. Brodie knew war and politics were connected, and so he spoke to all of its pillars, from the civilian to the military, from the lay public to the highest levels of strategic command. With Vietnam on his mind but the final defeat still yet to come, Brodie would conclude his 1973 work with an allusion to the Clausewitzian principle that he started with some 496 pages earlier, writing in his final sentence: "Yet the civil hand must never relax, and it must without one hint of apology hold the control that has always belonged to it by right."[161]

War and Politics also reflects something a synthesis for Brodie of his very first reflections on Socrates as a young student in 1932 and Socrates' best known student and biographer, Plato, with his later philosophical mentor, Clausewitz; whom he noted in 1945 but would not fully embrace for another half-decade, when the advent of thermonuclear weapons forced a reassessment of the Prussian's relevance. Plato in many ways turned Brodie on to knowledge and its strategic importance (as well as the challenge of its ambiguities)—while Clausewitz taught him to use that knowledge to understand, as much as possible, the causes and dynamics of war, to better prevent war and, if prevention was no longer possible, restrain war from its own absolute and terrible logic. Brodie recalls how there was "a tradition among scholars going back at least to Plato that considered it a corruption of the best fruits of the human mind to try to put them to practical use," and that the "glory of knowledge for *its own sake* perhaps explains why Plato was so intent on having the rulers of states study geometry, which might be of use to an engineer or an architect but hardly to a king."[162] Brodie would turns to both Plato and Clausewitz to understand the failure of Vietnam; first, Clausewitz showed how to extract meaningful lessons from history: "We have, after all, in all these pages been lauding the modernity of Clausewitz," but "[i]t is, however, the kind of modernity that will not give us the answers to our contemporary problems but which, at its best, will sharpen our receptivity to appropriate insights about those problems."[163] Thus, Brodie writes, "We noted Clausewitz's explanation why Napoleon, to defeat Russia, had to go to Moscow. As it happens, the same reasoning goes far to explain the motivation for the North Vietnamese Tet offensive of 1968. But it is a similarity with enormous differences."[164] While "Clausewitz would have had a lively appreciation for both the similarities and the differences" of these two events that span a century and a half, Brodie observes: "We do not, of course, have to read Clausewitz to understand the latter campaign. It may be that the recognition that his comments do in fact bear upon that campaign provides us little more than a titillation of scholarly delight, just as reading in Plato some sharp insight into human nature gives us today, some 2,400 years later, a twinge of delight that is really one solely of recognition that he saw things as we do. It is not that Plato adds to our understanding; we can feel the pleasure only because that understanding already exists."[165] In contrast, "We do in fact *learn* something from Clausewitz—a good deal more, I think, than we ever learn from Plato. Yet, without some measure of sensibility to begin with, the reading of Clausewitz or of Plato, will confer neither delight nor advantage. Still, what we get from Clausewitz is a deepening of sensibility or insight rather than a body of rules, because insofar as he does offer us rules he is at once avid to show us all the qualifications and historical exceptions to them."[166]

As he explained in his preface, Brodie pays ultimate tribute to Clausewitz, the guiding inspiration throughout *War and Politics* from its first page to its last: "The central idea of this book I have borrowed from Clausewitz who, as a seventeenth-century writer said of Machiavelli, 'hath been too often taxed for his impieties.' It is a simple idea, and the novice would justly imagine it to be commonplace—that the question of *why* we fight must dominate any consideration of means. Yet this absurdly simple theme has been mostly ignored, and when not ignored usually denied."[167] Brodie wrote that Clausewitz's effort to develop his thesis contextualizing war in policy was "an accomplishment against perennial resistance, indicated by the fact that this understanding has never fully got across to the great majority of those people who think or write about war, and even less to those who fight it."[168] Brodie believes when Clausewitz argued his "often quoted but constantly misrepresented dictum" positing war's interconnection with policy that the theorist was "very far from intending this remark cynically, as is often supposed," and in fact "intended to make, had he lived" it "the central organizing thesis of the whole."[169] Brodie in *War and Politics* seeks to present much the same central thesis, applying it to the world that was twice embroiled in world war, and was now confronting not only "the advent of nuclear weapons" but also America's "particularly perplexing and tragic involvement in a distant and hitherto obscure peninsula in Southeast Asia," which revealed a global scale of conflict that greatly eclipsed the nineteenth-century warfare that Clausewitz had intuited totality from, but which did not achieve true totality until Brodie's era.

The Clausewitz Project Concludes

On February 22, 1973, Princeton University Press editor Bailey again wrote to Brodie, starting off with a word of encouraging clarification on the new letterhead used by the press: "Dear Bernard, I want to assure you that I am still here at dear old PUP. The names at the top of the letterhead list are our Board of Trustees, and Harold W. McGraw, Jr. (whose full-time job is being president of McGraw-Hill) is the president of our Trustees. I go by the title of director—a fine distinction."[170] And so, Bailey had not defected to McGraw-Hill; instead, its president was serving as president of the board at PUP. Bailey thanked Brodie "for telling me about Peter Paret's and Michael Howard's reaction to my letter on the Clausewitz project," explaining, "I'm not sure how well informed you were, since our dealings were through Cy Black in his capacity as director of the Center of International Studies here. The Clausewitz project ran far beyond the deadlines originally agreed to, and constituted a heavy financial commitment at a time when publishing is difficult. Therefore we informed Cy that in accordance with the provisions in the contract we could no longer consider ourselves bound, though we would be willing to reconsider the project if and when manuscripts could be presented. I guess I'll have to straighten it out with Paret and Howard, so that there won't be any misunderstanding."[171]

On May 19, 1973, Brodie wrote to Bailey, providing him with an update of the soon to be completed translation of *On War*, on the hope that PUP would still be interested in publishing it despite the collapse of the more ambitious multi-volume project that the press had given up on, writing that "Peter Paret and Michael Howard, having now completed their translation of Clausewitz's ON WAR, have authorized me to write you to inquire whether you are still interested in securing its publication for Princeton University Press."[172] Brodie added: "I sincerely hope you are, and I say that with no proprietary interest in the matter," and explained that "[t]his is the first complete translation into English of this great work from the original uncorrupted text, and the extraordinary competence of this team of translators would guarantee its being a superb translation. Both men are distinguished historians, both are thoroughly at home in German, especially Paret, and both write extremely well in English, especially Howard, whom

I would nominate as perhaps the best stylist among historians writing today in the English language."[173] Brodie noted, with prescience that would anticipate the high regard and enduring reputation of what generations of students would come to know as the seminal translation of *On War*, that it "will not be improved upon as a translation" and "reads extremely well in English," and "incidentally reads quite differently from the next best translation—that produced by Jolles in the Modern Library Edition of 1943, which has been long out of print. The version which Penguin Books is currently circulating is a truncated edition of the old Graham translation, with a perfectly awful introduction by Anatole Rappaport. Thus, the competition in the field is strikingly surpassed."[174] Added Brodie, "I need not go into the reasons why I think you should publish it. You have shown yourself quite well aware of those reasons, especially in your letter to me following my review-article on Clausewitz in World Politics last January, in which I called Clausewitz's work the only truly great book on war ever written. In your letter you expressed a keen desire to have a chance to bid again on this particular work when it was completed."[175]

Describing the status of the translation project, Brodie noted he had in his "possession Xerox copies of only a few chapters of the work, though enough to give me a feeling for the quality of the translation. Peter Paret has what I believe is the only copy of the whole translation, and because the money in the original grant has long since run out, it would be up to the publisher to produce one or more Xerox copies for the threepersons—the two translators and myself—who are committed to writing introductory essays."[176] He added that it was "of course a very long book, about as long as the Jolles translation, which runs to 631 pages sans index in the Modern Library edition, each page having at least half again as many words as any of the books of mine published by PUP. The plan is to have in addition three introductory essays, probably of unequal length, by Paret, Howard, and myself, dealing respectively with (a) a note on the present transla-tion and on the person of Clausewitz, (b) the place of *On War* in the history of strategic thought, and (c) the value of the book to the modern reader. Plans for these essays have not proceeded very far, and our thought was that if you undertake to publish it, we should be most interested in your views about how much space to devote to the three essays."[177] Brodie concluded that, "In sum, this translation represents a scholarly accomplishment of the first importance by an international team which also commands an exceptional degree of prestige. Paret is well known for his writings on Prussian military reforms at the time of Clausewitz, and of Howard one can justly use the word 'famous' for his work on the *Franco-Prussian War*. He has also just won a much coveted prize in Britain—the Wolfson Prize I believe it is called—for his writing of *Grand Strategy*, which is Vol. 4 of the official British history of World War II," and humbly added, "I expect to derive more glory from being associated with this production than I could possibly lend to it with my own name."[178] Brodie closed his letter with a discussion of communication protocols, on the expectation the project would be embraced once again by PUP: "Peter Paret suggests that I should communicate to him your reply, but if I am right in assuming that that reply will be favorable, I propose instead that you write directly to him at Stanford—with a copy to me and also one to Michael Howard at All Souls, Oxford. It will be Peter who signs whatever contract is concluded, on behalf of himself and Michael Howard. My own contribution will not be even remotely sufficient to warrant my being a party to the contract. I am here functioning simply as a special friend of this one publisher and also of the translators. The latter agree with me that Princeton University Press would be unquestionably the best American publisher to handle it, bearing in mind also PUP's affiliation with Oxford University Press."[179] In a P. S., Brodie added that he had "finally got some extra copies of my own new book, War and Politics, and I am putting one in the mails for you this very day."[180]

Just three days later, on May 22, 1973, Bailey wrote directly to Peter Paret as Brodie had suggested, explaining the demise of the multi-year, multi-volume Clausewitz Project, while reaffirming his interest in bringing to press the new translation of *On War*. He referenced the

May 19 letter from Brodie that he enclosed with his letter to Paret, and observed, "Bernard is certainly right; we would like very much to see the manuscript of the translation of Clausewitz's ON WAR that you and Professor Howard have prepared. If it lives up to Bernard's advance billing, which I don't doubt, it will surely be a book we want to do."[181] He added that "of course you know that we have been interested in this project since it was started at the Center for International Studies at Princeton, and we canceled the overall contract for the Clausewitz volumes only long after the deadline had been passed and when we felt that circumstances did not permit us carry that series as a continuing commitment. Thus I am particularly pleased that the translation of ON WAR can be made available to us, and I hope that you will send it at the first opportunity. Then, assuming that after examination we are able to proceed, we shall be glad to provide the Xerox copies required for the three editors. We shall also perhaps have some ideas about the introductory essays."[182]

Bailey noted that Princeton's "long-standing relationship to Oxford University Press will be discontinued after August 1 of this year, and we are making independent arrangements to sell our books in the British Commonwealth," and while "[t]his will include, where appropriate, selling editions or rights to individual British publishers, including in some instances Oxford," he explained that "there will no longer be the automatic flow of Princeton books through Oxford."[183] Bailey concluded that "the main thing is the book itself, and I shall hope to be receiving the manuscript from you. Many thanks for remembering our interest."[184] In a letter dated the same day, Bailey wrote to Brodie, enclosing a copy of his letter to Paret, noting "As you can see from the enclosed copy to Peter, I was delighted to receive your letter about the translation of Clausewitz's ON WAR. Your comments on the translation are most helpful, and I trust that we shall be able to go ahead with it. Many thanks for keeping us in touch."[185] He added, "I was glad to hear that a copy of your new book WAR AND POLITICS is on its way to me, and I shall look forward to reading it. Many thanks in advance. I just wish it were on our list."[186]

With PUP and the original team of translators and contributors re-engaged, a smaller version of the once massive Clausewitz Project would continue, involving the new translation by Howard and Paret of *On War* with commentary and analysis by Brodie. In a brief letter from September 14, 1973, PUP associate director and editor R. Miriam Brokaw wrote to Brodie, noting that Bailey had passed along to her Brodie's "letter of September 7, with the description of what you plan to do in your introduction to the Clausewitz. This is fine, and I want to thank you for it. As soon as we have all of the outlines, we will give the manuscript to a reader."[187] And just two days later, Bailey wrote to Brodie, noting he had that day "received both your general introduction entitled 'Why Read On War Today?' and the detailed chapter-by-chapter analysis," and while "[o]bviously I haven't had a chance to read any of the material yet, though I will as soon as I can," he explained that the "purpose of this letter is mainly to acknowledge receipt."[188] Bailey added: "From a quick look, it seems to me desirable to separate the general introduction from the detailed analysis, with the detailed analysis as an appendix," which is in fact how they were ultimately presented; and while Bailey had not "yet received the introductions from Peter Paret and Michael Howard," he was "expecting them by the end of the month. Then we'll start the book into the editorial process and production, and it will be good to have it under way here at last."[189] As for Brodie's *War and Politics*, Bailey added, "Did I tell you that I am enjoying your book WAR AND POLITICS, which I didn't quite finish before returning to the Press from my summer's leave. I am a great admirer of the Brody (sic) style, and I keep wishing that the book had a Princeton imprint."[190] All the elements for the new translation of *On War* ultimately arrived, and the project was put under contract by PUP on February 24, 1974; when finally published two years later, complete with supplemental analysis by Howard, Paret, and Brodie, it would contribute greatly to the resurgence in Clausewitz studies, gaining a wide and enduring readership among scholars, strategic analysts, and professional soldiers.

Prior to publication, the project participants considered the best manner for dividing book royalties, and a draft contract for a three-way split between Paret, Howard, and Brodie struck Brodie as being overly generous to him given the substantial amount of time and effort that Paret and Howard devoted to the project, and to the challenge of their translation effort. As Brodie explained in a letter to Paret written on January 21, 1974, "I am sorry to be flagging down a train which seems at last to be moving so smoothly, but I am returning the contract forms because I cannot sign them in their present form."[191] As he explained, "Of course I appreciate your generosity, but that is exactly what is wrong with the present contract. I have always felt that I ought not even be a party to the contract, if for no other reason than that it tends to bind you to accepting my contribution, which you have not yet seen and may not approve of."[192] Brodie added: "I have no idea how many copies will be sold, but I don't doubt that neither you nor Herb expects it to be a run-away bestseller. Under the present terms, if the total royalties come to $1500 or thereabouts, I share equally with you and Michael. In view of the tremendous work that you and he have done on the translation, in addition to which you both are also going to write introductory essays, I consider that quite unfair and something I cannot accept."[193] Indeed, Brodie suggests he "should be happy to be included simply for the glory of the thing, but if you feel happier with my getting remuneration, I suggest the following: 10 per cent of the royalties to go to me from the beginning, the other 90 per cent to be divided equally between you and Michael. That still seems generous to me. I will not make an issue of whether or not I am a signatory to the contract but I repeat that I consider it unnecessary that I should be."[194] The final terms of the contract, titled "Princeton Press Contract for Clausewitz" and dated February 28, 1974, included among its many details item number "5. Delivery of Manuscript," with a commitment that the authors will "agree to deliver the complete manuscript, together with all illustrations, maps, charts, drawings, or other material (except index) to be included in the work, not later than June 1, 1974," and item number "10. Royalties," which committed to the following royalty stream, "On regular hardback book sales within the United States (except for the special cases listed below), the following stipulated percentage of the list price: 10% on the first 5,000 copies sold; 12-1/2% on the next 5,000 copies sold; and 15% thereafter," with item number "14. Additional Provisions" identifying a royalty split along the lines proposed by Brodie to Paret: "The royalties shall be divided as follows: 10% to Professor Brodie, 45% each to Professors Howard and Paret."[195] All three signed the contract, bringing the long-gestating project one step closer to fruition. In the coming months, the project participants would discuss their respective introductory materials.

On May 30, 1974, Brodie wrote to Paret and enclosed some samples from his evolving "Guide" to reading *On War*. "I am sending you herewith another portion, where some of the examples I give in the commentary to individual chapters are drawn from quite recent events. I don't know whether this is good or bad."[196] Brodie continued, "Let me explain how I got to where I am. When I first began my essay, I had (as is usually the case with me when I begin writing a piece) only a very vague and tentative idea of where I wanted to go. I knew I wanted to make the point that ON WAR deserves reading for what it conveys of perennial importance about war. I also had a somewhat banal but very pragmatic objective, which was that of trying to help the person reading ON WAR for the first time to understand it."[197] Brodie added that the "latter objective was sparked by a number of things, but mainly by my two visits to the Naval War College at Newport, R. I. during the last year. There, as you know, they truncated and in the horrible Graham translation. It also has the useless and obnoxious introduction by Anatole Rapoport. It was clear [the] student officers were quite restive under the obligation to read the book, and simply weren't getting anything out of it. They could not see that it was saying anything of value to them. This struck me as a waste and a pity. Naturally, a good number of those people are probably not bright enough to appreciate Clausewitz on any terms, but some among them are."[198]

Brodie explained that he "did not intend to get into a detailed commentary, but after finishing my general remarks in thirteen pages, I felt that someone had to help the reader get into and understand that marvelous first chapter. Some of the commentaries I have seen by experts do the very opposite. So many writers talk about how esoteric and metaphysical is the Clausewitzian approach. What the reader needs to have pointed out to him is that the metaphysical touch is quite superficial and confined mostly to the first chapter, and that he should not let himself be bugged by it. [It] is profound, but the profundity is entirely pragmatic, and that's what I try to bring out."[199] As Brodie noted, "Naturally, after finishing the first chapter and then the rest of Book I, the mold seemed set for going on. I recalled vaguely that you or Michael was going to include something of a synopsis with his contribution, and I certainly did not want to compete. But I do want to be sure that the task of helping the novice reader to understand what is in this book does not fall between those three stools. However, I am not psychologically or emotionally committed to anything. It is clear to me that I must finish going through the book again, which for me will be the fourth or fifth time, and the commentary I am writing is really a set of notes on what I am reading. Then, if you think it best, I can use the material which is now in book-by-book commentary to flesh out what is now in the first thirteen pages, so that I will finish with an essay of perhaps forty to fifty pages. That would also mean shortening my entire piece."[200] So while Brodie agreed with Paret that "the original scheme continues to make sense," he added. "I also submit that a synopsis is not integral to any of the three headings you list under Paret, Howard, and Brodie, and also that a simple synopsis is not of much value"—and "[b]y 'simple synopsis'" he meant "something that is essentially an outline without commentary"—Brodie informed Paret: "I shall proceed as I am going until I hear further from you, but I am quite prepared for a drastic change in course."[201]

On August 23, 1974, Michael Howard wrote to Brodie, enclosing "both the draft of my Clausewitz introduction and a copy of my review of *War and Politics*. The latter may be quite extensively revised in proof, but as it may be some little time before it appears I thought you would like to see at least my preliminary reflections. They are not, as you will observe, entirely unfavourable!"[202] As Howard explained, "We seem to disagree only about Churchill's strategy. In almost the only book I have written to which you have not made a flattering reference, *The Mediterranean Strategy in the Second World War*, I tried to show that Churchill's strategy did not, except on one or two exceptional occasions and at the very end of the war, have any 'power political' considerations in mind, and in so far as it had they were concerned to assert British independence and prestige quite as much against the United States as against the Soviet Union. Still, this is a very minor difference: on the whole I thought the book quite splendid, and full of marvelously quotable quotes."[203] Howard noted he had reduced his introductory essay on Clausewitz from around 9000 to 6000 words, and explained that he "would not like to see the edition expand to two volumes," since "[i]n so doing, I think it would lose much of its point. But I would like to explore the possibility of including your comments in small print at the beginning of each book. This should not take up a great deal of space and would give us the best of both worlds. I agree that serving officers do need some guide through the jungle, especially in Book V!"[204] Howard closed by welcoming Brodie's comments on his enclosed draft. Brodie replied on September 1, 1974 with a long list of notes and suggestions, including numerous typographical and grammatical comments. Upon further reflection, Howard decided against breaking apart Brodie's "Guide," coming to the very same conclusion that Paret and Brodie came to.

Brodie also wrote to Howard on September 1, 1974, following up on his earlier letter "containing my general (not unfavorable) comments on your Clausewitz piece," with this new letter containing "the specific notes I promised you," adding "I have considered nothing that crossed my mind too trivial to mention."[205] On the trivial, Brodie suggested, for consistency's sake that perhaps Howard will not "want to use the 'von' before Clausewitz if you do not use his first name," as that "seems not to accord with recent usage—or be consistent with Peter's or mine in the same book."[206] On a matter of substance from a footnote on page three, Brodie mentions that "Neither you nor, I think, Peter anywhere mentions why Count von Bruhl made changes in the wording between the first and second editions. Were they printer's errors? Was Cl.'s handwriting difficult to read? Or was von Bruhl being simply arbitrary? You might not have the answer, but if you do it should certainly be included."[207] On a matter of historical interpretation, Brodie noted that on page four, "in exact middle of page, you have the following sentence: 'In France General Foch, who was in other respects the most outstanding follower of Clausewitz, wrote in 1903 in his principles of war . . . etc.'"[208] Brodie challenges Howard on this point: "Now, it has been a long time since I read Foch, though I have the book in my possession and will look through it again the first chance I get. However, my strong recollection about his book leads me to feel that what you say about him in the portion I have quoted above is unjustified. My strong conviction is that his book stands in the most striking contrast to just about everything Clausewitz said he stood for, your own immediately following quotation from him being but one example. He is unreflective, full of dogmatic principles, given to extraordinary errors in his historical examples, etc. I know that Foch paid lip service to Cl., but he was in no sense a follower, deriving much more from the tradition of Jomini via du Picq and adding his own arrogant, unthinking, boastful machismo. If I may say so, I wrote an essay on Foch right after reading his book, and you will find it in my *Strategy in the Missile Age*, pp. 40–55."[209] Back to the trivial, Brodie adds: "Incidentally, you don't have a comma where I put one above after 'Clausewitz' (your words are run together at that point)," and on a matter of historical accuracy, Brodie adds: "and in 1903 he was not a general but a colonel (I think)."[210]

Brodie engages Howard in a debate on who best interprets the strategic environment on the eve of World War I, noting: "Same page, a few lines further down, you speak of Col. Colin's book ranking as 'the outstanding summary of the military situation in Europe on the eve of the Great War.' Are you not forgetting Ivan Block? To be sure, Block wrote in the 1890s, but he certainly predicted the character of W.W.I infinitely better than the Foch's and the Colin's. Colin's book I read very long ago and Block's I reread only recently, but I do not remember being at all impressed with Colin."[211] Brodie added: "In general, I think you let Foch and Colin get away with too much. True, they were children of their time, as in some respects Clausewitz was a child of his, but in the respect that matters here Cl. went counter to his own time and thus became timeless, where Foch and Colin reject the idea that the strategy of a war must conform to the political aim they were doing their part to making, capped by an empty victory. The only one I can see on the eve of World War I who was truly Clausewitzian is Schlieffen—the concept of the plan is lifted bodily out of the last chapter of Book VIII—and I think Schlieffen is on record as writing that if the Plan fails, Germany must at once seek a negotiated peace."[212] Brodie concludes this point by adding, "As you know, I speak briefly about Foch in my piece, and I plan to say something about Schlieffen too in the revision, and while I am not worried at all about you and me overlapping, I do think we need to be concerned about gross inconsistency between us. I shall therefore appreciate your letting me know what modifications if any you make in your remarks—and I shall of course send you a copy of my revised version."[213] Brodie engages Howard in further debate over Clausewitzian doctrine, noting: "Page 6, second Paragraph. You speak of Cl.'s 'doctrine of the two kinds of war' and ask whether one did not 'imply a valid alternative objective in the *attrition* of the enemy.' I suspect that Cl.'s answer would be a resounding 'no,' if by attrition you mean what happened in W.W.I. That attrition was after all *Vernichtungsstrategie* in slow motion, and was clearly different from what Cl. was talking about in Par. 2 of the 'Notice' and throughout *On War*. You translate Delbruck's *Ermattungsstrategie* as 'strategy of exhaustion' and find that it characterized the warfare of the 18th C. 'and the campaigns of Frederick the Great.' My German dictionary translates *Ermattung* as 'exhaustion,' but also as 'lassitude,' and the verb form as 'growing weary'. It is in this latter sense, it seems to me, that Cl. speaks of 18th C. warfare and of Frederick's enemies. Frederick himself was willing enough to fight desperately to achieve his end, but he clearly counted (according to Cl.) on his enemies *not* doing so. Clausewitz may condemn Austrian generals for not showing enough enterprise, but he never criticizes Austrian governments for dispensing with ultimate strategies."[214]

On page seven, at the end of the first paragraph, Brodie comments, "You are quite right in saying that Cl. was 'intensely parochial' in the sense that he paid not the slightest attention to sea power, despite the role it played in the Peninsular War," but counters that "it seems too much to charge him with bequeathing this 'most disastrous legacy' to the German Army. After all, the Prussia of his time did not have the High Seas Fleet that Germany had in 1914, and one would expect 20th C. Germans to do some thinking for themselves. And to mention a war with which you have more than passing acquaintance, the Franco-Prussian war was affected not at all by the fact that France had absolute naval superiority."[215]

Brodie continues the debate on Foch, commenting on page eight, paragraph two, that: "This continues a point I have made above. Your first sentence ends with the words 'perhaps a little misleading,' which I think is a considerable short-fall from what needs saying. I agree with your comment about Liddell Hart putting it well (about Foch) but disagree strongly with your sentence that Foch 'borrows heavily' from Cl.'s ideas. What you quote is not substantial enough to warrant such a remark, and, incidentally, I would not castigate Foch for failing to make attribution for an idea that has entered the domain. We all frequently use ideas the source of which we have forgotten."[216] Also on page eight, in the final full paragraph on that page, Brodie challenges Howard's interpretation of the influence of Clausewitz on French doctrine: "Your quote from the French F.S.R. of 1895 does not seem to me to bear out your remark that 'the French Army had become as totally imbued with Clausewitzian ideas as had its German adversaries.' It seems to me you account for this quote in your own excellent statement which begins at the bottom of your page 1 with the words: '. . . many of the ideas which we now think of as peculiarly Clausewitzian. . . etc.' A short quote like that on your page 8 really proves nothing except that a certain catch phrase has caught on, like that concerning 'imposing one's will on the enemy.' You and I have heard many people use that expression who didn't have the slightest idea what Clausewitz was all about. The sense of what you quote could just as well have come from Jomini, and I refer again to your statement beginning at the bottom of your page 1."[217]

Brodie comments on page ten, at the end of paragraph three, noting to Howard: "You quote Liddell Hart's 'Not one reader in a hundred' statement and follow it with your own: 'The reader will have to judge for himself as to the correctness of this verdict.'"[218] Brodie concludes: "I come down on the side of L. H., which is why I think my Baedecker's guide is so necessary. It was particularly that first chapter that made me embark on it. It certainly confused me the first time I read it, and I had studied philosophy as an undergraduate, which the great majority of readers will not have done."[219] On the next page, Brodie corrects Howard for exaggerating Clausewitz, noting on page eleven, paragraph two, "You very aptly cite L. H.'s critique of Clausewitz with approval, and include the phrase 'the contempt for manoevre.' (sic) I do not see a 'contempt for manoeuvre' in Cl. He certainly condemned 18th C. fascination with it, but he also at every opportunity warned against direct frontal attacks, and talked about the necessity for outflanking or enveloping the opposing army, and how one can do that without 'manoeuver' (sic.) I don't know. One could perhaps speak of 'a seeming contempt for manoeuvre.'"[220] Brodie added, in a note on the inconsistency of spelling of the word maneouvre, "By the way, one way in which British spelling differs from American is in that word which you call 'manoeuvre' and which modern American dictionaries call 'maneuver,'" though this does not account for the wide range of spelling employed by Brodie in his letter. Brodie's final comment is from page twelve, paragraph two, noting "where you quote the U.S. Army F.S.R. for 1923. My comment is the same as that of the top paragraph on this sheet, relative to the French F.S.R. of 1895, only more so."[221] He closes by writing, "Zu Ende. Despite my above comments, I still think yours is a magnificent essay."[222] As a P.S. he added a further compliment, noting "I very much enjoyed your review of the Hoopes book on Palles in the TLS," the *Time Literary Supplement*.[223]

Paret wrote to Brodie on September 11, 1974, noting "I talked with Herb [Bailey], and before I had a chance to suggest the solution you and I had discussed" with regard to placement of Brodie's "Guide," Bailey himself had "suggested it on his own. He thinks that it would be a shame to cut up your detailed analytic commentary, and feels that the proper way of handling it would be to print it as a block at the back of the volume."[224] Howard described this solution in his own words in a letter on September 18, 1974 to Brodie, beginning his letter as per his usual manner with "My Dear Bernard," noting receipt of both Brodie's August 31 and his more thorough and critical September 1 letters as well as Brodie's "final draft of your introduction and guide to ON WAR."[225] He added: "Also today a letter from Peter with his comments on my introduction and his proposed solution to your bulk problem—i.e. printing your guide at the end of the volume. To this I am entirely agreeable. I also think that your introduction would be printed first."[226] (Brodie's introduction was ultimately placed third after Paret's and Howard's.)

Howard next addressed the issue of his review of Brodie's *War and Politics* in the *Time Literary Supplement*, noting, "First, the TLS rushed my review of *War and Politics* into print while I was away and before I could even correct the proofs. I hope that you have by now seen it in the issue of September 4th, with a very good photograph of yourself to grace it. In the light of this I won't take up any of the points you made except to say that my Mediterranean Strategy in the Second World War is not the same as Vol IV in Grand Strategy. It was a short book I wrote earlier, specifically dealing with the (in my view mistaken) belief that Churchill's strategy was 'politically' inspired. I am putting a copy in the post to you."[227] Next, Howard took up a point by point response to Brodie's many critical responses to his introductory essay, both the trivial and the substantive—agreeing with many but not all of Brodie's points. "As for my Clausewitz introduction, I shall deal with your points seriatim," after which he addressed just a single issue of substance in Brodie's "excellent introduction."[228] Howard agreed with Brodie on the issue of the 'von', conceding, "All right: not 'von' Clausewitz."[229] On the matter of "Von Bruhl's corrections. Having waded through the first edition one can see why they were necessary. There are innumerable misprints and obscurities which frequently defeated even Peter. Since the original manuscripts have disappeared one cannot now say whether this was due to illegible handwriting or clumsy phraseology. But you are right: the point must be clear."[230] As for "Foch: again you are right. To describe him as 'a disciple of Clausewitz' tout court is very misleading, and I shall omit the phrase entirely."[231] On the matter of Jean Lambert Alphonse Colin, author of the 1912 *The Transformations of War*: "Our first disagreement. A lot happened between 1899 when Block wrote and 1912, when Colin did, and Colin gave the last general conspectus of what armies were like and what their doctrines were before war broke out in 1914. He certainly did not attempt the kind of forecasting which made Block so outstanding, but he gave a very sound and thorough summary of 'the conventional wisdom' of his time. I don't think it is a matter of 'letting him get away' with anything. He wrote what he wrote: I try to explain why he wrote it, rather than make the rather obvious point that he, in common with nearly every one else, got it wrong. NB my quotation of what I consider to be one of Clausewitz's wisest remarks at the bottom of page 4. Clausewitz was a timeless genius: Colin and Foch were not—they were in different ways very typical of their generation. I don't think that there is any difference to resolve between us over this."[232] As for "'The two kinds of war.' The controversy in the periodicals was over precisely the point that you make. I could have a long footnote describing it but, as I said in my text, it did not bear at all on contemporary military thinking and so I have spared the reader. Gordon Craig deals with it very well in his essay on Delbruck in Makers of Modern Strategy."[233] On

"Clausewitz and sea power. Yes: it is worth making the point that Clausewitz wrote in and for a land-locked Prussia. Incidentally French command of the sea did have a noticeable effect on the second half of the Franco-Prussian War. Gambetta was able to re-equip the French forces very largely because of foreign arms importations and the continuation of trade kept French credit high."[234] Howard noted: "I am prepared to modify what I say about Foch's debt to Clausewitz by saying this his borrowings were extremely selective, but the passages I quote are pure Clausewitz. Even if they were by then idées reçues that makes them none the less Clausewitzian. I suspect that Foch got them from his Ecole de Guerre lecture notes rather than from reading the text; but since these are virtually the only general ideas (apart from his obsession with the offensive) that are to be found in his Principles of War, and since one finds really nothing comparable in Jomini, I am afraid that I see no reason to change my mind over this. The same applies to the French FSRs—and I could find you many such quotations. The concept of war as a clash of wills and its object being to impose ones will on the enemy which ultimately could be done only by taking the offensive—one does not find this kind of thing in Jomini and his followers. They are not perhaps the passages in *On War* which do Clausewitz the greatest credit, but they are certainly those which had the greatest influence at the time."[235] As for "Liddell Hart on Clausewitz's obscurity. I think he exaggerates this but, as I say, the reader must decide for himself."[236] Howard proceeded to British versus American spelling conventions, noting: "For 'contempt for manoeuvre' read 'apparent downgrading of manoeuvre'. The English spelling of this and other words will no doubt be picked up by the copy editor."[237] And on "US Army FSR. Again, I could back this up by many quotations from Marshall's directives and Eisenhower's correspondence about the need to break the enemy will to fight by defeating his main forces in battle. Perhaps I should expand this paragraph."[238]

Howard next turned Brodie's introduction, writing: "About your own excellent introduction I have only one quibble: your giving Schlieffen the accolade of being a true disciple of Clausewitz on the strength of one reported statement (tu quoque!) that, if the Schlieffen plan failed, Germany should make peace. Now I accept that he was a follower of Clausewitz in the sense that I have described on page 5 of my text, but so far as politics was concerned he was, according to Gerhard Ritter, an agnostic in that he just didn't want to know: he did his job and the politicians did theirs. He would no doubt have scrapped the plan if his Kriegsherr had told him it was politically unacceptable, but he did not see it as his job to worry about such things. This was not really a Clausewitzian attitude. In any case it is not really enough to say that Schlieffen was 'on record' with such a statement. When did he make it, how often, and under what circumstances? It certainly does not come through as an intrinsic part of his military doctrines, and I have not come across it myself."[239] Howard closed by noting "that is literally my only criticism" and adding, "You will pick up the mistypings for yourself. All best wishes to you both, Michael."[240]

Howard sent Brodie an additional, but undated letter, written by hand and in response to an earlier letter from Brodie dated September 23, 1974, addressing additional issues of substance and historical interpretation, and after a kind salute to "My dear Bernard," explained, "I have not replied sooner to your kind and useful letter of September 23rd since I have been ploughing through the proofs of the text before getting to your appendix, in the hope that I could repay you in kind. All I can offer, apart from some obvious misprints which you will certainly have picked up, is a. a contradiction between the introduction, when you give Clausewitz's age on first seeing service as 12, and the appendix, when you give it as 13 (the latter I think is right); b. a slight inaccuracy in your introduction when you suggest that Clausewitz died on the Polish Frontier rather than after his return to take up his new post vide. Paret's introduction. Your comment on galleys 41–2 about Clausewitz's limited experience of mountain warfare is of course correct, but one must bear in mind that his first experience of war was in the Vosges in Alsace, and he had three years of it at rather a formative period of his life."[241] He added: "Incidentally I cannot agree with you that the low German casualty figures on the Western Front in World War I compared with those of the Allies indicated that they had absorbed the Clausewitzian doctrine of the defensive. The whole of German military literature from about 1890 until 1915 argues the contrary, as does their record in the war itself. After the failure of the Schlieffen Plan they launched three major offensives in the West, all at heavy cost: 1st Ypres in November 1914, 2nd Ypres in spring 1915, and Verdun in 1916. It was then very largely the ascendancy of the "Easterners," Hindenture and Ludendorf, in OHL, which led to the decision to stand on the defensive in the West, but only in order to take the offensive in the East. Once the Eastern Front was liquidated they resumed the offensive in the West in March 1918. I.E. you were to look at comparative casualty figures August 1914 until June 1916 I think you get a fairer picture; and even then one must take into account such variables as tactical doctrine, training levels and feed back from experience. Still, we can argue this one out privately!"[242]

On October 3, 1974, Brodie wrote to Howard, presenting "Comments on new draft (2nd version) of 'The Influence of Clausewitz,'" noting "All are picayune except the last."[243] While trivial, they are nonetheless of interest to historians of Clausewitz as well as of Brodie and his generation of strategic thinkers. On page one, Brodie comments: "The very long first paragraph can be divided into two or three. My own suggestion would to be to put paragraph markings at lines 12 and 22. You might go through the MS and check the length of all paragraphs."[244] Also on page one, with regard to the second line from the bottom, Brodie writes the "[w]ord 'Jominian' is all right if my essay comes first, because I mention Jomini by full name and say something about who he was. I should nevertheless prefer to see: 'with the dogmatism of a Jomini.' "[245]

As for page two, the second full paragraph, Brodie comments: "The third sentence bothers me slightly. What you are saying may have been true when Cl. wrote the notice of 1827. But as I read *On War* now, the contrast between books 7 and 8 is quite marked. Bk. 7 is very clearly still a rough draft, but Bk. 8 looks to be very much more finished. Chapters 6 and 9 are among the greatest in the whole work. I suspect he did a good deal of work on Bk VIII after writing the 1827 document, though there are still evidences of its being other than completely finished." Of a more picayune nature, in the same paragraph Brodie writes: "You mention a 'first theme' and a 'second theme,' but in the following paragraph you refer to 'the above three elements.' So I went back looking for the third theme, which I finally found in the very last clause of the par. It should be clearly marked as 'third theme.' "[246]

On page four, line four, Brodie comments substantively, "I think that word 'only' is a little extreme and perhaps unjustified. 'Almost exclusively' would be better. It is true that Bk. I, Ch. 1 and Bk. VIII, Ch. 6 bear almost the whole burden of the argument, but my recollection is that he at least speaks of it several times elsewhere. For example, in describing the necessary qualifications of the commander-in-chief he says that he also has to be something of a statesman, to understand the political objective of the war and conform to them."[247] On page six, line ten, Brodie reverts to the trivial: "Title *Nation in Arms* should be underlined. (In general I believe in not reposing any confidence in the copy editor, at least until you know who the creature is going to be and how competent he or she is. The one I had for *War and Politics* was unbelievably bad)."[248] In a similar vein, he writes of the second to last line in this same paragraph on page six, "The word 'fewer' seems to me to be slightly better than 'less.' It's like the difference between 'paucity' and 'dearth': one refers to numbers and the other to quantities other than numerical."[249] And on historical interpretation, Brodie comments on page eight, paragraph two, line six: "I suggest changing the date '1870' to '1815.' There were a great may developments along the lines you mention between 1815 and 1870."[250] And on page eleven, on the line in the middle of that page with the word "presciently," that the "remark you quote of Schlieffen's strikes me as being the very reverse of prescient. What happened in W.W.I is that it did prove possible to conduct a strategy of attrition 'when the support of millions of combatants runs into milliards of marks.'

Schlieffen, like so many others, was entirely off the mark on that argument. Bloch, incidentally, was one of the very, very few who understood what resources the state could mobilize."[251] And, on the trivial, on "Same page, seventh line from bottom: Word 'his' strikes me as slightly better than 'its.' "[252] Similarly picayune, "Page 12, line second from end of first par. A dash should be substituted for the semicolon."[253]

This brings Brodie to what he describes as "the one truly substantive comment, which I hesitate to make because I made it on your first draft. After one intervention one should be prepared to agree to disagree. However, the point is an important one and what you say about it bothers me very much, especially because I consider the 'strategy' of W.W.I., if it can be called that, so blind, so stupid, and so loathsome."[254] As Brodie describes: "It first comes up at the bottom of your page 10, which is, I think, close to or identical with what you had before. All I will say about it now is that the word "valid" (4th line from bottom) is at the very least ambiguous. The real issue arises with what you say at the bottom of p. 14 and the top of p. 15. The two points I object to are 1. That there is any significant similarity between the attrition strategies of W.W.I and what could be called (with considerable license) the attrition strategies of the 18th century, and 2. That one can find in Clausewitz any significant justification for the kind of prolonged insane slugging that went on, especially on the western front, for over four long years."[255] After presenting such detailed feedback on Howard's interpretation of Clausewitz's applicability to World War I, Brodie closes with a positively upbeat general assessment of Howard's introductory essay: "Having said all this I must assure you again that my admiration for your paper is (with the sole exception of the point made just above) absolutely unbounded."[256]

On October 10, 1974, Herb Bailey wrote to Brodie, enclosing a copy of a letter to Paret that he authored on the same date, addressing Brodie's lengthy "Guide" for the reading of Clausewitz's *On War*. Bailey noted that the "enclosed copy of a letter to Peter is self-explanatory. It answers some of the questions in your letter of October 5," and explaining that "Much as I like your Reading Guide, I think it is just too much to add to the introductions before the reader gets to the text. I hope you will like the solution I have proposed. The paragraph referring to the Guide is obviously only a draft, and you may want to rewrite it entirely."[257] Bailey also mentioned his intervention in a dispute between Brodie's wife Fawn and her publisher, regretting his involvement in the matter: "Finally, a last word on the Julian Boyd-Fawn M. Brodie dispute. I wish I had never gotten into it, since I don't think I accomplished much and I succeeded only in alienating both parties. Although I think I was right in my general perception of the situation, I did not take enough care with the letters I wrote, and so it would have been better if they had not been written at all. Really I should have left the whole thing to Julian and Fawn, and stayed out of it myself altogether."[258] He closed his letter by reaffirming his admiration for Brodie's "Guide," writing: "To get back to ON WAR, I think that I have not sufficiently expressed my admiration for your Reading Guide. I think it is a superb contribution, and it will surely help to make our edition the one that is the most widely used."[259] He included as an attachment a draft paragraph for insertion at the end of the three introductory essays, alerting readers to the "Guide" in the book's back matter, with the note, "Insert at end of Brodie introduction, p. 23."[260] The proposed text stated: "It may seem odd at the end of these three introductions, dealing with the genesis of ON WAR, its influence, and its relevance today, to refer the reader to the Appendix: A Guide to the Reading of ON WAR. Thinking that we have already interposed perhaps more than enough comment between the title page and the text, we have placed this guide at the end of the book. We do not want to direct attention away from Clausewitz's text, but we suggest that the use of the Guide, before, during, or after reading, will enable most readers to gain more from Clausewitz's rich and profound work."[261] In the end, this text would be boiled down to a more concise "Thinking that we have interposed enough comment between the title and the text, we have placed at the end of the book

'A Guide to the Reading of *On War*.' Eds."[262] This abbreviated note appears on page 58 of the published edition.

In Bailey's letter to Paret, also penned on October 10, 1974, he noted that he had "now read the three introductions, and I want to say first of all that I am most enthusiastic about them. Although there are some repetitions, and perhaps cross-references should be inserted as you suggest, they fit together very nicely. I happened to read Bernard's introduction first, and I liked it so much that I immediately felt it should be the first in order. But now, having read the other two introductions, I think it would be better to go back to the original order: Paret, Howard, Brodie. They provide a logical sequence, and it would be hard to choose among them on any other basis."[263] As well, Bailey noted he had "also read Bernard's Guide, which I think is very illuminating and helpful, and I am delighted that it is going to be in the book. However I'm concerned about putting too much material before the beginning of the Clausewitz text, and so I come back to the idea that the Guide should be put at the end of the book, as an appendix. I don't want it to be overlooked, though, so in addition to listing it in the contents, I have prepared a paragraph to be added at the end of Bernard's essay (after the asterisks), calling the reader's attention to the Guide. Bernard may want to say it differently, but this draft at least suggests a direction. A copy is enclosed."[264] Bailey presented some feedback on the introductory essays, noting, "It would be false and misleading to give the impression that Clausewitz had said the last word on all types of warfare, but one gets the strong feeling from the Howard and Paret essays and from the first part of the Brodie essay that Clausewitz really is very relevant today."[265]

On September 22, 1975, Paret wrote to Brodie, noting although Howard and he had "agreed that he would do the proofreading of the entire opus," that "[n]ow that we have galleys I have of course gone over my introduction (and found quite a few errors in the process) and have also read the other two introductions and your guide. I am sending Michael my corrections and suggestions for his piece, and am doing the same with yours. Enclosed are those galleys that I have marked—as you see, there are only a few."[266] Paret added: "Let me also suggest that you check your quotations with the final text. It would be embarrassing if any discrepancies slip through."[267] Paret concluded: "Having read the three introductions and your guide I feel certain that we have produced a useful piece of work. Readers will take different things from our various analyses, but everything dovetails nicely, and I do think the total effect is enlightening rather than obscurantist."[268] Brodie and Howard traded several letters offering corrections to each other's work. Final proofs of the manuscript became available in December, during which Brodie and Lewis Bateman, the editor assigned to the project, clashed over the presentation of Brodie's "Guide," whose placement in the back matter of the book seems to have caused Brodie some offense, a condition worsened by the editor's decision not to provide *special typographical recognition in the contents*, which Brodie had sought. As Bateman wrote in a letter to Brodie on December 19, 1975, "While I agree with you that your 'guide' is more than an appendix, its quality alone will indicate this. Thus, I do not think that it needs special typographical recognition in the contents. In any case, as you know, the display of this element in the contents is a question for the designer who, while considering your request, will make the final decision."[269] Brodie responded by bringing the matter to Bailey's attention, and in his Christmas day letter to Bailey wrote, "I feel it is time for me to go direct (sic.) to the boss, for which I trust Mr. Bateman will forgive me. I am sending him a copy of this letter anyway."[270] Noting Bateman's response to the presentation in the contents of Brodie's "Guide," he explained to Bailey that: "This was in reply to a letter of mine pointing out that with my Guide now at the back of the book, the mousy way in which it is indicated in the "Contents" permits it to be quite lost to view. This concern is doubly warranted by the fact that the title page as presently structured, a copy of which was enclosed with Bateman's letter, makes no mention of the Guide—unless it is submitted under 'with commentaries by' Peter, Michael, and myself. It seems to me that that promise is quite fulfilled by the three introductory essays. In other words, I am not worried about the reader's thoughts on the Guide when he reads it (i.e., concerning Bateman's reference to "its quality"), nor am I worried about the careful reader missing it."[271]

Brodie raised a second concern, which while "of much less importance" was "nevertheless not trivial."[272] Brodie had asked Bateman "to consult with you [Bailey] on whether I could have my contribution bound separately (that is, introductory commentary and guide) for presentation to friends and colleagues," and "got back an answer that seemed rather arbitrary. I was told I could buy the whole book, which of course I knew in advance. Now it happens that for most of the persons I have in mind, it would not only be too costly but inappropriate. I don't know what it says about them, but I actually have friends who are more interested in Brodie than in Clausewitz."[273] Brodie added that "Unfortunately, I do not normally make copies of my own letters when I type them myself, so I don't know just how I put the matter originally. Anyway, no one asked me whether I was prepared for thirty to fifty copies, which, if for the price were within reason, I would. By the way, I do not know yet what the whole book will cost. And am I wrong in assuming that you are not intending to put it out in paperback?"[274] Bailey responded to Brodie on December 31, 1975, noting "I have your letter of December 25," and commenting, "Let me say immediately that I have confidence in Mr. Bateman as an editor, and I think you should too," while at the same time agreeing with Brodie that "there is a real problem of emphasis here, and some changes should be made in the direction that you suggest."[275]

Bailey further agreed that "it is also significant, especially from a publishing point of view, that commentaries have been provided by three such well-known scholars," and also "that a Guide by Bernard Brodie is included. These are things that readers will want to know, and that we as publishers want to convey to readers in order to sell the book."[276] And so, Bailey noted: "I am again alerting our sales department to the fact that the presence of the commentaries and Guide will sell the book as much as the existence of a new and improved translation. And this of course should be reflected in the typography of both the jacket and the book itself. I have been over the proofs with Mr. Bateman, and we have agreed on some changes. The title page will be properly descriptive, stating that the translation is by Paret and Howard, the commentaries are by Paret, Howard, and Brodie, and the Guide is by Brodie. Mr. Bateman is sending a draft title page to Peter for his approval, since he has handled all the arrangements. I am also sending Peter a copy of this letter."[277] Bailey added that "In the text of the book, the commentaries and the Guide will each be set off by a separate half title, and appropriate changes of emphasis will be made in the table of contents. The exact typography will of course be worked out by the designer, but Mr. Bateman as editor will oversee the work to make sure that the typographical emphasis is appropriate."[278] Bailey added: "I'm glad that you brought this matter to my attention, because I really think that we were not sufficiently emphasizing some of the most attractive aspects of this volume. It will be relatively easy at this point to make the necessary changes. I hope that you and the other editors will be pleased."[279] As for the pricing, Bailey noted "we are planning a list price of $17.50," and that "Promotion plans are already under way, the book is included among the leading titles in our spring catalogue, and at about the time of publication we will let you know in detail what advertisements will appear, etc."[280] With regard to Brodie's desire for printed excerpts of his contributions to the work, Bailey wrote: "Mr. Bateman asked me earlier about the idea of providing separates of the Guide, and I told him (as he wrote to you) that we would greatly prefer not to provide them, even at cost. The reasons he gave are genuine, and in addition it does cost a good deal of disruption in the production process to have to provide separates of sections of a book."[281] Bailey added: "I hope you won't think that this is an arbitrary decision; indeed there would be no reason to make such a decision arbitrarily when we would much prefer to please you and the other editors. I know that it is common to provide separates of journal articles, where the routines are set up for it, but it is a different matter with books."[282]

In the final production of the long-awaited translation of *On War*, Bailey's described changes were made largely as described with only minor modifications. The front cover started with "CARL VON CLAUSEWITZ," in bold type followed by "ON WAR" in larger bold type sandwiched between two horizontal lines, underneath which appeared "*Edited and Translated by*" in non-bold italicized type, beneath which came in three lines "MICHAEL HOWARD *and* PETER PARET," followed in turn by "*Introductory Essays by* PETER PARET, MICHAEL HOWARD, *and* BERNARD BRODIE; *with a Commentary by* BERNARD BRODIE" in smaller type. (A 1984 edition was published with an index added, that resulted in a modification to the front cover, with the words "*Indexed Edition*" added in non-bold, italicized text of an even smaller type. The inside cover was presented much the same, but instead of "*Indexed Edition*" up top, at the very bottom of the page appear "*Index by* ROSALIE WEST," in the same sized type as the three lines describing the introductory essays and commentary.) In the table of contents, "A Commentary" is presented after Book Eight, "War Plans" in the same sized type, and the title to Brodie's "Guide," officially "A Guide to the Reading of *On War*," is in the same sized type as the sections of each of Clausewitz's chapters. And so, after over a decade, the Clausewitz Project, in a greatly reduced and far less ambitious form, came to press.

On July 29, 1976, with the new translation of *On War* ready to be release, PUP's publicity and promotions coordinator, Marcia Brubeck, wrote to Brodie on the matter of promotional copies: "Now that ON WAR is almost out, we are completing the lists of people to receive complimentary copies. We are asking you, Mr. Howard, and Professor Paret each to suggest three individuals to receive promotional copies. Mr. Bateman has given me your letter of March 19 suggesting Admiral Turner and Major Winton. Would you like to add the name and address of a political scientist?"[283] Brubeck again wrote on October 6, 1976, confirming that PUP had "sent a copy of *On War* to International Security" and that the requested "copy of *The Role of Providence in the Social Order* will be sent to you as soon as it is available. Unfortunately, I must report that your 40% author's discount does not apply to the *Papers of Thomas Jefferson*, but you may of course buy copies at the list price of $22.50"[284] per copy, adding, "I hope this is helpful."[285]

With the much truncated Clausewitz Project now finally completed with the publication of the Princeton edition of *On War*, Bailey wrote to Brodie on October 14, 1976, observing that "ON WAR is off to a good start, I think, and I trust that you are pleased with the appearance of the book, even after all the discussion of the arrangement of materials, the title page, etc. It's hard to please everyone, but I think we came out with a reasonable solution. Certainly I think your own contribution to the book is going to be recognized as invaluable."[286] Bailey planted the seed for a new Brodie project on strategy, noting that the "problem of nuclear proliferation is on everyone's mind these days, along with the special problems of new types of war heads and missiles. Ed Tenner, our science editor, and I have been wondering whether it isn't time for a new book to put these subjects in perspective from several points of view—military strategy, economic implications, technology exchange, the problem of intelligence, and so forth."[287] Bailey added: "Perhaps the principles haven't changed much since your STRATEGY IN THE MISSILE AGE, but the circumstances certainly have. We also now have behind us the experience of Vietnam, greater knowledge of biological warfare, etc. In short, perhaps it is time for a reassessment of the broad question of strategy today, or at least the question is worth asking? What do you think? Is it something that you yourself would want to undertake, or would you suggest someone else? At any rate I'd be grateful to have your thoughts on the subject."[288]

Brodie responded favorably to Bailey's suggestion, and on October 29, 1976 Bailey again wrote to Brodie, in which he observed being "delighted that my letter suggesting that the time is ripe for a new overall look at the general question of military strategy, which of course relates to international politics (vide Clausewitz), caught you at the right time. There aren't many people who have been immersed in this subject as long as you have, or have made such contributions to it, and a new book from you now is a most pleasing prospect."[289] Bailey added that he "shall be looking forward to hearing how your ideas progress and how the work goes along. Obviously something like this is going to take time, but you will be drawing on years of thinking about the problems."[290] Bailey closed his letter by reiterating, "I really am glad that my letter struck the right note with you."[291]

The Continuing Relevance of On War

Brodie had first heard of Princeton's effort to bring forth a modern translation of Clausewitz's work for the Anglo-American world in a conversation with Peter Paret in the spring of 1963, and participated in the project for the better part of a decade before the project would be cancelled owing to its many challenges. But one major portion of the project, the translation of Clausewitz's classic tome, *On War*, was completed and came to press, at last, in 1976, with both a brief, fourteen-page introductory essay ("The Continuing Relevance of *On War*"), and a lengthier, seventy-page commentary presented as a commentary in the book's back matter ("A Guide to the Reading of *On War*"). As the editors finally agreed, the "Guide" was presented immediately following Brodie's introductory essay with these brief words: "Thinking that we have interpreted enough comment between the title page and the text, we have placed at the end of the book, 'A Guide to the Reading of *On War*.'"[292]

In "The Continuing Relevance of *On War*," Brodie contemplated Clausewitz's seminal tome's relevance to the world after Hiroshima. Not only might the reader wonder if "a book written a century and a half ago, and on war of all things, is really worth his time? That question would arise even if nuclear weapons had never been invented, but those weapons do indeed seem to make a totally new universe. Or do they?"[293] While this question would percolate beneath Brodie's words for many more years, and would in fact define his efforts as a theorist stretching from the dawn of the nuclear age to the immediate post-Vietnam era, he attempts to address it head on in this introductory essay to *On War*: "There has been a good deal of fighting without nuclear weapons since the two were used on Japan in 1945, including wars which for some of the participants represented total commitment. Still, if it is not yet an established fact it is at minimum a strong possibility that, at least between the great powers who possess nuclear weapons, the whole character of war as a means of settling differences has been transformed beyond recognition. Why then read Clausewitz?"[294] Brodie contends that "Clausewitz's work stands out among those very few older books which have presented profound and original insights that have *not* been adequately absorbed in later literature," and while "there are other books including some dealing with contemporary and especially nuclear weapons issues," he believes that "none can equal it in importance or displace it in its timeliness."[295] Indeed, Clausewitz's work stands in marked contrast to such important military theorists as Foch and Douhet, whose influence was widespread in their own time, but whose longevity proved much more limited, without, in Brodie's estimation, any lasting utility. Clausewitz, Brodie believes, "is probably as pertinent to our times as most of the literature specifically written about nuclear war," and while the latter present "a good deal of useful technological and other lore," they also suffer from "the absence of that depth and scope which are particularly the hallmark of Clausewitz. We miss especially his tough-minded pursuit of the idea that war in all its phases must be rationally guided by meaningful political purposes."[296]

Brodie specifically castigates his increasingly popular colleague Herman Kahn for this very reason: "That insight is quite lost in most of the contemporary books, including one which bears a title that boldly invites comparison with the earlier classic, Herman Kahn's *On Thermonuclear War*. Kahn incidentally based his main argument—that the United States could survive and therefore ought not too much fear a thermonuclear war with its chief rival—on technical premises that are certainly obsolete today, whether or not they were realistic when his book was published in the not-so-distant year of 1960. Also, Kahn's book does not, as Clausewitz's does, have much to say of relevance to the Vietnam War which has intervened since and which caused the United States so much soul-searching and agony, though far less of the latter than that borne by the nation it set out to save. Kahn may still usefully supplement Clausewitz, but only in a limited sense is he more timely, and he does not in any way help to supplant him."[297] This goal, perhaps, was Brodie's very own inner aspiration, as he pursued a path toward philosophical greatness much like the enigmatic Socrates that he explored as a young student in 1932, and Kahn's failure to supplant Clausewitz may well have kept this prize unclaimed for Brodie to pursue with his fullest vigor.

Brodie reflects on Clausewitz's undogmatic style, noting he was "often intent upon demonstrating the pitfalls of such axioms, which is the quality chiefly in distinguishing him from Jomini, as well as from virtually all his successors. That is one of the chief reasons why military people are so often disappointed with Clausewitz, for they are particularly accustomed in their training to absorbing against a tight schedule of time specific rules for conduct, a practice reflected in their broad use of the term "indoctrination." Clausewitz, on the contrary, invites his readers to ruminate with him on the complex nature of war, where any rule that admits of no exceptions is usually too obvious to be worth much discourse."[298] As for the post-World War I efforts to "encapsulate centuries of experience and volumes of reflection into a few tersely worded and usually numbered 'principles of war,'" as reflected in the proliferation of field manuals, very much in the Jominian tradition, Brodie believes "Clausewitz would have been appalled," and no doubt "not surprised at some of the terrible blunders that have been perpetrated in the name of those 'principles,'" much like those contemporaries of his whom Clausewitz described as "'the scribblers of systems and compendia.'"[299] However, Brodie is aware (and later came to personally experience) that the "price of admission to the Clausewitzian alternative of intense rumination, sometimes in pages most densely packed with sharp insights, is a commitment to be responsive. This requires a different kind of reading from what we are normally accustomed to," and in contrast to the speed reading suitable to "the great masses of stuff" facing most professionals: "With Clausewitz, however, one should be prepared to tarry, to pause frequently for reflection."[300]

Final Thoughts on Clausewitz

Brodie revisited Clausewitz during his final year in a review of Peter Paret's 1976 Oxford University Press book, *Clausewitz and the State*, in the Winter 1978 edition of the *Journal of Interdisciplinary History*, one of Brodie's very final publications, and incidentally, his second review of Paret's book—his first appearing a year earlier in the Winter 1977 edition of *International Security*, "In Quest of the Unknown Clausewitz: A review of Paret's Clausewitz and the State."[301] Brodie and Paret had engaged in a long dialogue on Clausewitz dating back many years, and while they did not always agree on all things Clausewitz, Brodie's review found Paret's contribution to the literature to be "distinguished" and that it "would be a magnificent example of the historian's art at its best even if its subject were a person of less significance than Carl von Clausewitz."[302] Brodie observes that Paret's work "gives us access, in English, to the mind and work of one whose name is a byword but whose life and thought are virtually unknown to all but a small handful of scholars, most of them German or of German origin. And for these few Clausewitzian scholars, in whatever language they write, it is an original contribution of first importance."[303] Brodie notes that "Paret not only analyzes and clarifies Clausewitz's philosophy in its final bloom but also traces its development from early adult-hood," and that he is "keenly attuned to the influences upon Clausewitz's development of the philosophical thought and the military and political events of the frenzied and volatile period in which Clausewitz lived his two lives, the active military one and the scholarly one."[304] Brodie adds that "[i]t might also be relevant in this age of psychohistory to point to something not altogether evident from the book itself," and that is "Paret comes from a family of psychoanalysts, and his wife is one," and Paret "himself has devoted a good deal of study to the work of Freud and his followers, and he is clearly sympathetic to that work."[305]

Brodie notes Paret "acknowledges that he has deliberately 'understated' those aspects of his subject's inner life that might have occurred to him as he read Clausewitz's voluminous personal documents, such as his letters to his wife and others," adding that "[p]erhaps he does so excessively, and he admits as much. But in his last chapter, where he makes a calm assessment of Clausewitz's character and personality, mostly to refute what he regards as unfounded assertions by others, he explains his caution. It is a brief chapter, but unusually important, even apart from its centering on Clausewitz. Paret apparently believes, with Freud, that the door to the unconscious does not open easily."[306] As Brodie elaborates: " 'Historians,' he says, 'may consider it useful to attempt interpretations of the psychological elements and dynamics of their subjects. But unless they and their readers are content with purely subjective speculations, their interpretations will . . . have to deal critically with all the evidence, and be prepared to admit ignorance when necessary evidence is lacking' Paret, in short, though with no less knowledge of the relevant discipline, is at the opposite end of the spectrum from a Mazlish, who in a recent 'psycho-biography' of Henry Kissinger, based entirely on open sources and one pro-forma interview, declared that he knew Kissinger better than Kissinger knew himself."[307] Brodie finds that the "reputation of Clausewitz is great enough to warrant his being the subject of Paret's largest and finest work thus far," and he notes its publication "has come just prior to that of the new and superior translation of *On War* by Paret and Michael Howard," published by Princeton University Press, that Brodie contributed to by means of both a foreword and an afterword, and which "happens also to coincide with the publication in Paris of the two-volume work on Clausewitz by Aron."[308]

Brodie describes the challenge of Clausewitz's endurance, owing to his complexity of thinking and the inability to boil his philosophy down to simple maxims, noting: "Yet what a strangely ambiguous thing is the Clausewitzian reputation, resting on a base that is solid in merit but projected through a century and a half mostly on the strength of hearsay. As one who sedulously avoided the propounding of precepts or 'principles' in the manner of his contemporary Antoine Henri Jomini, or of later writers such as Alfred Thayer Mahan, Ferdinand Foch, or Giulio Douhet, Clausewitz is not likely to have had any indirect influence. The basic ideas of each among the others could be summed up more or less adequately in relatively few words and transmitted, usually with an aura of revealed truth, to many who have never read him or possibly have never heard of him. That could not be done with Clausewitz. He could influence only those who carefully and thoughtfully read at least his major work, first published posthumously in 1832. To do this was long impossible to anyone not at home in the German language."[309] Brodie rhetorically asks: "If his influence was so clearly limited outside Germany and somewhat questionable even inside that country, why does he, at this late date, merit so much attention?"[310]

The answer to this question of Clausewitz's long influence is: "Simply because his has been the one truly great mind throughout man's warring history to have committed itself to developing a comprehensive theory of the essential character and purposes of war and of the means of studying it," and that Clausewitz "succeeded sufficiently to produce a profound work with strong claims to timelessness. In short, one reads Clausewitz today not because of his real or alleged influence in the past or because certain modern ideas about war are supposed to be traceable mainly to him, but because of his continuing intrinsic value."[311]

And it was this realization, ultimately, that Brodie would embrace with every fiber of his being—catapulting him from the very frustrating present-day context of declining influence on the actual making of strategic policy, into the annals of posterity, where his work would join that pantheon of great and celebrated strategic thinkers whose wisdom would resonate across the ages. Indeed, as noted in the introduction to this work, Ken Booth, in his biographical chapter on Brodie in *Makers of Nuclear Strategy*, observed of Brodie's declining influence on the making of strategic policy precisely what Brodie had observed of Clausewitz: "Who now worries whether Clausewitz had any influence? What counts is the enduring worth of what he wrote."[312] Booth recounts that Brodie wrote of Clausewitz that "the startling insights that leap up at us from so many pages of his great work are still often directly applicable to our own times. There has been no one to match him since."[313] To this Booth aptly adds: "Among the first generation of nuclear strategists, these words could be Brodie's own epitaph." [314]

*   *   *

Final Thoughts on Brodie: The Rise of the Civilian Strategists

To help us live with the new dangers of the nuclear age—and to hopefully avoid the very sorts of strategic blunders that led, both ironically and tragically, to America's Vietnam debacle—a new corps of civilian strategists would emerge who dedicated themselves to the new and in so many ways unprecedented challenges of the post-Hiroshima world—an era created by the very wizardry of civilian scientists serving the higher purpose of a nation at war, and one that would require a new wizardry of civilian strategic theorists to ensure there would be a lasting peace. And Brodie can be found its very forefront, some might say its very founder.

Among his peers of Cold War nuclear strategists, Brodie was unique among in that he was equally adept as a *theorist* and *strategist* and was as aware of the historical uniqueness and importance of the new field that he was pioneering as he was of the particular strategic challenges it was grappling with. In this vein, he was more like Carl von Clausewitz, the great philosopher of war who was himself a sophisticated philosopher of knowledge, and something of a pioneer in the still non-existent field of complexity theory, anticipating a method of analysis that would not emerge until the next century. Brodie would ask, over the years, whether strategy was more art or science, concluding as the years passed that it should contain elements of both. But early on in his work, he intuited the profound need for strategic theory to become more properly scientific, and in so doing to gain an analytical capacity that had generally been eluded in the long march of time since Clausewitz. Brodie would in fact be celebrated later on as the father of civilian-scientific strategy. In his graduate work, Brodie had looked primarily to America's "Clausewitz of the Sea," the naval theorist Alfred Thayer Mahan, for inspiration, but before long he was expanding his historical lens to include the more recent theorist of air power, Giulio Douhet, as well as the famed theorist of war from the Napoleonic era, Carl von Clausewitz. Brodie would put pen to paper on multiple occasions as he probed the lessons these past thinkers could bring to the challenges of the nuclear age.

One of his most illuminating efforts was in his July 1949 *World Politics* article, "Strategy as a Science," which appeared just one month before the Soviet Union joined the nuclear club with its first successful atomic test on August 29, 1949. Brodie started off this article by noting a series of resignations from high-ranking positions in the U.S. government by top military officials, which he thought, with relief, would "no doubt allay somewhat the suspicions current a year or more ago that the military were 'moving in' where they did not belong," though he noted that their "original appointment to civil posts . . . was hardly due to design on the part of the armed services, being quite easily and plausibly explained on other and quite innocuous grounds."[315] Nonetheless, Brodie pointed out that "the military departments unquestionably do have a greater influence upon high policy decisions than was true before the recent war" and that it was "therefore time to express concern not so much that that military will move in where they do not belong, but rather that in the process of moving in where in part, at least, they do belong, their advice will reflect their imperfections not as diplomatists but as soldiers."[316] Brodie therefore reiterated his view, oft-made, that we must never forget the "immortal expression in the famous apothegm of Clemenceau that war was too important to be left to the generals" and that "the waging of war or the preparation for it requires many skills to which the soldier makes no pretensions," including, Brodie contends, "the skill which is peculiarly his own" which "is in all but the rarest instances incomplete with respect to one of its fundamentals—a genuine understanding of military strategy."[317]

Yes, Brodie has come to believe that strategy itself, the very science of generalship, has become too complex and requires too much theoretical rigor for the military man to fully grasp; as he explains, it "is hardly surprising, since the understanding would have to follow the development of a theoretical framework which as yet can scarcely be said to exist" and "[c]reating the mere foundations of such a framework would require a huge enterprise of scholarship, and the military profession is not a scholarly calling—as its members would be the first to insist,"[318] and even the "scholar who on rare occasions appears within its ranks can expect but scant reward for the special talents he demonstrates," something Brodie experienced firsthand. Brodie notes that it's "for quite different accomplishments that the silver stars which are the final accolade of success are bestowed," and that the "soldier's rejection of the contemplative life would be of no concern to him or to us if the universally enduring maxims of war—the so-called *classical principles of strategy*—which are quite simply elucidated and easily understood, really did provide an adequate foundation upon which to erect precise strategic plans," as soldiers have "been trained to believe."[319] But Brodie believes otherwise and in his article he aims "to demonstrate that on the contrary the theory contained in those maxims is far too insubstantial to enable one even to begin organizing the pressing problems in the field, that the bare core of theory which they do embody is capable of and demands meaningful elaboration, and that that elaboration and the mastery of it by military practitioners must require intensive, rigorous, and therefore prolonged intellectual application."[320] In short, Brodie's conception of strategy bears a greater similarity to Clausewitz's complex, at time convoluted, and intellectually rigorous conception of the military art, than it does to Clausewitz's counterpart and in many ways antithesis, Jomini, who clearly elucidated maxims warmly embraced by military practitioners in the wake of Napoleon's revolutionary transformation of war, including American civil war generals on both sides of that bloody conflict.

Brodie's effort, if successful, will thereby "demonstrat[e] that strategy is not receiving the scientific treatment it deserves either in the armed services or, certainly, outside of them" and also "show that our failure to train our military leaders in the scientific study of strategy has been costly in war, and is therefore presumptively—perhaps even demonstrably—being costly also in our present security efforts."[321] Brodie considers the endurance of "certain basic ideas about fighting a war which over the centuries have been proved valid" and which "have been exalted by various writers to the status of 'principles,' and have been distinguished from other elements in the art of generalship chiefly by their presumptive character of being unchanging," such as Jomini himself had argued in his famed and "often-quoted dictum," in which he argued "Methods change, but principles are unchanging," but while unchanging Brodie notes they're "certainly not esoteric" and thus "many generals, from Napoleon to Eisenhower, have stressed their essential simplicity."[322] Brodie further noted that these so-called principles "are skeletal in the extreme" and "not only contain within themselves no hints on how they may be implemented in practice, but their very expression is usually in terms which are either ambiguous or question-begging in their implications—a trait which has grown more marked since Jomini's day under the effort to preserve for them the characteristic of being un-changing."[323] Case in point, the principle of "Economy of Force," or as dubbed by the Canadians, "Economy of Effort," an idea that is "thus reduced to a truism" but whose very "violation has often been advocated during war and sometimes practiced."[324] Brodie finds similar fault with related conceptions like "Principle of Concentration" and "Principle of Aim," whose most noted commonality, to Brodie, is the "barrenness of the concepts."[325] Unchanging principles may have had their use in "a day when the techniques of war changed but little from one generation to the next," a time when "they were more than adequate," but a time that as of the nuclear era had clearly passed.[326] Brodie is more sympathetic to Napoleon, who embraced a simplicity of precepts but who rightly cautioned those who would try to follow too literally in his footsteps: "Napoleon, who often mentioned the simplicity of the principles by which he was guided, nevertheless admonished those who would emulate him: 'Read over and over again the campaigns of Alexander, Hannibal, Caesar, Gustavus, Turenne, Eugene, and Frederick. Make them your models. This is the only way to become a great general and to master the secrets of war.' It is still a good rule. . . . In the present day, with the techniques of war changing radically not only from generation to generation but from decade to decade, a list of theorems inherited almost intact from the early nineteenth century, however much embroidered by examples even from recent military history, can hardly serve the function generally reposed upon it."[327]

As Brodie concludes, "Principles may still survive those changes intact, but if they do it will be because they have little applicability or meaning for the questions that really matter. The rules fathered by Jomini and Clausewitz may still be fundamental, but they will not tell one how to prepare for or fight a war."[328] The only reason these "'enduring principles' have endured so long as a substitution for a body of live and flexible theory is due mainly to their exceptional convenience," and that they "lend themselves so readily to 'indoctrination,'" making them "peculiarly well adapted to the traditional patterns of military education."[329] Brodie is as dismissive of the value of these enduring principles as he is of military slogans and maxims, noting that the "maxim may indeed be the supreme distillate of profound thought, but only at its first use—that is, when it is still an apt expression and not yet a slogan. No sooner does it become currency than it is counterfeit."[330] Brodie points out that the "function of a slogan is to induce rigidity of thought and behavior in a particular direction," and that the "progress of strategy as a science will be roughly measurable by the degree to which it frees itself from addiction to the slogan."[331] Noting Eisenhower's effort after World War II to "set up a commission under General L. T. Gerow to study the lessons of the European theatre in World War II," Brodie suggests that "[w]ith their traditional reverence for what they term the 'practical,' the military are inclined to dignify by the name of 'battle experience' what is in fact an excessively narrow pragmatism," and while "[t]here is of course no substitute for the test of battle or experience in war," Brodie suggests that "there are at least three reasons why such experience is of limited usefulness and may even be positively misleading."[332] The first is that "since great changes occur from one war to the next, military planners are obliged to make far-reaching decisions on issues concerning which there is little or no directly applicable experience."[333] The second is no matter what the merits or detractions of a particular decision made in war, "since the enemy's responses have a good deal to do with" the end results, those very "results often fail to provide a basis for judgment upon those decisions," making it all but impossible to know with any certainty whether "a decision which turned out well rather than ill [was] a good decision."[334] And, the third is that "even within the scope of what our experience does illuminate, the lessons it affords are rarely obvious in the sense of being self-evident," and we must therefore remain "on the alert for rigidities of thought and action in the actors which vitiated the results of even repeated experiment" and at the same time "look for the hidden jokers in a situation, the vagaries of circumstance which profoundly affected the outcome, and . . . clearly distinguish between the unique and the representative. In short, [we] must engage in a refined analytical operation involving a large element of disciplined speculation. The task requires a mind trained for analysis and for the rigorous scrutiny of evidence."[335]

Brodie notes, in contrast to the field of economics, which "has produced a tremendous body of literature of impressive quality," the "far older profession of arms, content with mere reiteration of its wholly elementary postulates, which change not with the changing years, has yet to round out a five-foot book-shelf of significant works on strategy. The purpose of soldiers is obviously not to produce books, but one must assume that any real ferment of thought could not have so completely avoided breaking into print."[336] In a footnote that follows, Brodie observes, "I am trying desperately here to restrain the bias of the academician that the effort of writing is an almost indispensable catalyst to the production of original thoughts. On the other hand, too many people have found that it is so to enable us quite to reject the idea."[337] The upshot, to Brodie, is the dearth of truly worthy strategic theoretical literature when compared to the younger but more bountiful field of economics: "The comparison drawn above between economics and strategy is especially telling in view of the similarity of objectives between the two fields. Although the economist sometimes disclaims responsibility for those community values which determine economic objectives, it is quite clear that historically he has been devoted mainly to discovering how the resources of a nation, material and human, can be developed and utilized for the end of maximizing the total real wealth of the nation. . . . Strategy, by comparison, is devoted to discovering how the resources of the nation, material and human, can be developed and utilized for the end of maximizing the total effectiveness of the nation in war."[338]

In both cases, Brodie notes: "we are dealing primarily with problems of efficiency in the allocation of limited resources and with measuring means against policies and vice versa."[339] Therefore, Brodie observes, "One might expect to find, therefore, that a substantial part of classical economic theory is directly applicable to the analysis of problems in military strategy. One might further expect that if the highly developed conceptual framework which lies ready at hand in the field of economics were in fact so applied, or at least examined for the suggestive analogies which it offers, some very positive results would follow."[340] It is interesting to note that this is precisely what theorists of international politics endeavored to do with their application of systems theory to the problems of war and peace, starting with Morton Kaplan, then refined by Kenneth Waltz; as they likewise did with the application of game and bargaining theory to these very same thorny problems, as illustrated by the work of Nobel laureate Thomas Schelling, who interestingly won his Nobel for Economics, and not for Peace, even though the end goal of his theoretical effort was peace, and not economics. As Brodie reflects, "It might of course be aesthetically abhorrent to discover gallant admirals and airmen discussing their common problems, or the occasional amiable debates between them, in terms like 'marginal utility,' 'diminishing returns,' or 'opportunity costs.' It happens, incidentally, to be quite abhorrent to this writer to find himself inadvertently pleading for a jargon in any discipline, though in this instance there is no danger of corrupting the pure; the military already have a quite substantial jargon of their own. But the advantage of using symbols which are tied to well-thought-out formulations has at least two advantages besides the obvious one of providing a short-hand for intra-discipline communication: first, it may help to assure that the fundamentals of a problem will not be overlooked, and secondly, it may offer economies in the process of thinking the problem through."[341]

Brodie concedes there remains a "great hurdle between clear understanding of the principles applicable to a problem and the practical resolution of that problem," but he firmly believes there's "a great practical difference between that rule of thumb which is recognized to be the optimum feasible realization of correct theory and that much more common species of rule of thumb which simply replaces the effort of theorizing."[342] He adds that "some of the more glaring errors of our recent military history could not have been perpetrated by intelligent men who were equipped with even a modicum of theory,"[343] so many in fact that "examples could be piled on indefinitely."[344] And "[w]hether this or that concept can be applied with profit is something which interests us only in passing," Brodie's main point and one he reiterates in later works is that it's "in the field of methodology that a science like economics has most to contribute, and the point which it is the whole purpose of this article to bring home is that what is needed in the approach to strategic problems is genuine analytical method."[345] Especially after Hiroshima, as Brodie notes, "Formerly the need for it was not great, but, apart from the rapidly increasing complexity of the problem, the magnitude of disaster which might result from military error today bears no relation to situations of the past."[346]

From the prenuclear world, Brodie takes inspiration from Mahan, who despite representing "evidence of the primitive development of strategic theory,"[347] nonetheless wielded great influence, filling; Brodie notes Mahan most "[c]ertainly . . . could not be called systematic,"[348] and, with his backward-looking naval observations, was "in some essential respects behind his own times."[349] Despite such faults of analysis, and evidence of the primitive state of strategic theory in the prior century, Brodie observes that Mahan nonetheless "stood before his colleagues as one who seemed to know the purpose for which warships were built, and he carried all before him," and while his contribution sets him apart, Brodie notes that "Mahan has remained, for the United States Navy at least, an isolated phenomenon" and any "groundwork which he laid for what might have become a science of naval strategy was never systematically developed by the profession," and in the decades that followed, "years of overwhelming technological and political change—the service from which he sprang has not produced his successor."[350] A similar absence of strategic and analytical achievement, Brodie notes, was not unique to the Navy: "Air power is still young, but it is certainly not new. Yet it is not possible to find in any language a treatise which explores in discerning and relatively objective fashion the role of air power in war, the factors governing its potentialities and limitations, its relation to other arms, and the chief considerations affecting its mode of operation. Sea power has at least had its Mahan; the literature of air power is all fragments and polemics."[351]

Brodie struggles to identify "available remedies," explaining that the problem is that we're "dealing fundamentally with a conflict in value systems," as the "profession of arms requires inevitably a subordination of rational to romantic value," and where "[a]ction, decisiveness, and boldness are idealized," resulting, unfortunately, in an "anti-theoretical bias which is in fact anti-intellectual" and where the "emphasis is on the so-called *practical*"—and "in his eagerness to be doing, he does throughout his career a fantastically large amount of work of a sort which contributes nothing to his greater understanding of his art even on the technical level."[352] Even the "training at one of the various war colleges—which he reaches at about the age of thirty-five to forty—is looked upon as an interlude in the more active phases of his career," and Brodie argues that we "need to make of our war colleges genuine graduate schools in method and duration of training," and that "military staffs should be chosen for the special attainments of their members in the several fields of strategic analysis" and that students at the war colleges "should be selected according to standards which give due weight to the intellectual purpose of the institution."[353] Brodie expects that the "military will object that it is not their purpose to train scholars, that there are other besides intellectual qualities necessary in a military leader, and that their needs in strategic planners are after all very limited. They are of course right."[354]

He concedes that a "successful military leader must have something besides a good mind and a good education in strategy" but explains that this means only that "the military calling is more exacting than others," and that it carries a unique burden: "In what other profession does the individual affect or control directly not only the lives of thousands of his fellow citizens but also the destiny of the national community and perhaps also of western civilization as we know it? Analytical acumen need not be emphasized to the exclusion of those other qualities (i.e., 'leadership,' et al.), but it has a long way to go to gain consideration even comparable to the latter."[355] Brodie believed that no matter "how limited was the actual need in such special skills as strategic analysis, we should have to have a respectably broad base for selecting those called to the task and an adequate means of training them."[356] In a short time, as the dangers of the nuclear-armed world spiraled upward, first on August 29, 1949 with the Soviet ascension to the nuclear club, and then, only three years later with the first successful thermonuclear test on November 1, 1952 during Operation Ivy Mike at Enewetak Atoll, the burden of command would increase in tandem, and with it the need for capable strategic analysis to ensure that war and policy maintained their inherently, and in Brodie's mind *normatively*, Clausewitzian balance.

Crossing the Civil-Military Chasm

In an internal debate at RAND over Brodie's views on the strategic theoretical capabilities of the military versus the rising corpus of civilian defense intellectuals, Brodie is taken to task for articulating with too little subtlety a condescending outlook on his military counterparts, during which Brodie clarifies his views on the fundamental differences in strategic thinking of these two distinct groups of strategic realists. The squabble emerged in late 1954 after Brodie sent his young colleague Nathan Leites some glowing feedback on Leites' latest article, "If War Were to Break Out Tomorrow," in which he made comments perceived by RAND's then-director Hans Speier as dismissive of their military colleagues and, importantly, funders, whose continued largesse RAND depended upon. On November 5, 1954, Brodie wrote to Leites, lauding his article, describing it as "brilliantly incisive, sensitive, and novel. This is the sort of analysis we need, but I have seen nothing like it before."[357] Brodie noted he had made a "very small number" of critical remarks in the margins and in his letter to Leites said these were "of much too trivial a nature to be mentioned here."[358] As for the "general organization" of Leites' article, Brodie made some recommendations, writing: "I have a feeling that your leading points or ideas could be made to stand out more clearly and crisply than they do. Your writing in this paper tends sometimes to give one the feeling that you are musing out loud, rather than that you are communicating some ideas which are already well developed in your mind. This is an intangible sort of thing, and it is hard for me to put my finger on it. But I do believe it is organizational rather than stylistic."[359] What got Brodie into trouble were his remarks concerning the military, and Leites' obligations to present his entire article to them: "Of course much depends on what you plan to do with this paper. I do not expect that our Pentagon friends will be able to make anything of it, so its being put into an 'R' or 'RM' would be largely a matter of form and of courtesy. On the other hand, a simplified summary which more or less outlined the basic points might indeed be useful. But I am thinking more about publication for scholars."[360] Brodie suggested "it has the substance now for an excellent *World Politics* article," though in need of some abbreviation.[361]

On November 19, 1954, in a personal memo to Brodie, Hans Speier made reference to these comments from Brodie: "I do not think the impression of entertaining, the opinion that the people who are intelligent enough to finance RAND lack the ability to understand its research results; or that we fulfill our obligation toward RAND and the Air Force if we publish something in scholarly or popular magazines. I believe your letter to Nathan can easily be misunderstood to the effect that you regard the RAND audience as less important than other audiences which RAND and the Air Force permit us to reach. *World Politics* would indeed be a suitable place for publishing Nathan's excellent piece, but it will be desirable first to put it into a form which might raise your hope that our governmental readers will understand it."³⁶²

A few days later, on November 23, 1954, Brodie responded to Speier's memo with his own lengthy and detailed personal memo, in which he noted that he had been "erroneously of the opinion that I was commenting on some RAND-sponsored research, in which the Air Force presumably has no proprietary interest," but adding that "Victor Hunt corrected me on that."³⁶³ Brodie also explained: "I grant you that contemptuous feelings where they exist are in danger of being ultimately betrayed to the object of those feelings, and are therefore legitimately a matter of concern with respect to the relationship between RAND and its clients. On the other hand, in this instance I feel that 'contemptuous feelings' are not involved but that simple realism is. I earnestly believe that the substance of the remark of mine to Nathan which you quoted is something with which you yourself, upon reflection, would fully concur."³⁶⁴ Brodie further defends his remark, explaining: "More important in your own mind, I think, was your statement: 'I do not think we should permit ourselves ever to develop, or give the impression of entertaining, the opinion that the people who are intelligent enough to finance RAND lack the ability to understand its research results. . . ' I do not see how it is possible for you to mean that literally."³⁶⁵ Brodie observed "RAND hires, among other things, nuclear physicists, mathematicians, and social scientists whose training includes a measure of psychoanalysis," adding "I certainly would not expect Air Force officers to feel, and it would be extremely naïve of them to feel, that all the written products of such specialists should be interesting or intelligible to them . . . Neither the statement I have just made nor the one I made to Nathan carries the implication that our clients are unintelligent—only that they are not intellectuals trained in our special brand of intellectualism. Nathan's paper as I read it would not make much sense to any Air Force officer I have met, some of whom I regard as having high intelligence, but I do think, as I said to Nathan, that 'a simplified summary which more or less outlined the basic points might indeed be useful.' If this is a contemptuous or ungracious thought, then you and I must either have read different versions of Nathan's paper or have known entirely different kinds of military officers."³⁶⁶ Brodie further explained: "This would not be worth going into at such length if we were dealing with an isolated incident. But you have several times chided me gently on my attitude on the intellectual endowment of the military, and I think there is a possibly important misunderstanding between us on that score. Let me first of all point out that my own best and most careful work has always been done for military audiences, including the recent *Reporter* article, which was originally worked up as a lecture to the Army War College . . . Also, if my remarks or bearing really exuded contempt for the intelligence of the military generally, I should hardly have been welcomed over many years at the various war colleges, to which I have devoted a great deal of earnest and careful work; and I should hardly number, as I do, so many military officers among my close friends."³⁶⁷ Brodie conceded that it was "certainly true that [some]³⁶⁸ of the things I have written and said have called attention to the conceptual and intellectual shortcomings of the military guild. I have hear you privately do likewise, as for example when you were describing to me a year or so ago a conversation or briefing you had with a group of general officers which included General Doolittle. You were at that time profoundly shocked, as I think you had every right to be. Now, we ought to be clear, is this question generally a forbidden area, even for private discussion (e.g., a fairly personal letter to Nathan), or do you simply feel I am wrong and am exaggerating? Maybe the difference between us is that you feel the Doolittle episode you described was atypical, whereas I would regard it as typical."³⁶⁹

Brodie listed his views "about the intelligence of the military," noting "They compare favorably in average I.Q., and in the range of intelligence of individual members, with any profession I know of other than those specifically involved with learning. In other words, they compare favorably (i.e., about on par) with MD's, but not with scientists or university professors at leading universities. How could they, since the latter are selected for their intellectual attainments, while the military are and must be selected for quite different skills and talents."[370] Further, Brodie notes: "Their training, by and large, is certainly not comparable in intensity or in manipulation of abstract ideas with that of the usual Ph.D. candidate at one of our graduate schools. They are not 'intellectuals,' and certainly don't regard themselves as such."[371] And, he added: "There is also a certain endemic anti-intellectualism in the gild, which I regard as entirely natural to a profession which must stress action rather than subtleties of thought in according both deference and preferment. The degree of anti-intellectualism varies considerably, however, from person to person within the profession."[372] Brodie also observes that "Each military service tends to be a closed corporation, and also a tightly-knit hierarchical one. These conditions further a traditionalism and conservatism which is already fostered by the conditions of non- or anti-intellectualism referred to above."[373] Brodie finds that "The record show unequivocally that in the past, with technological changes of far lesser moment and degree than those we are witnessing now, the military have usually proved themselves conceptually behind-handed at the onset of each major war. Because of the nature of the enterprise, the national cost has often been hideous and tremendous. These thoughts are so far hardly novel, being shared and more or less forcefully argued by almost all major students of war, including the professional officers among them."[374] And lastly, Brodie adds that "Because of the nature of the technological changes occurring today, the lag between concept and reality is bound to be both far greater in degree and far costlier in effects than any similar lag in the past."[375]

While noting he "could go on," Brodie closes his memo by stating "these are in general the ideas that inform so much of my work. Naturally one must always exercise due tact in expressing them. I am grateful for correction where I slip from due tact or from avoidance of gratuitous references to military shortcomings. But that is another matter entirely from saying either that this comprises a forbidden area of discourse, or that in certain specific respects my views are wholly wrong. I should very much appreciate your remarks on these points, which are obviously of great importance to me."[376]

On November 30, 1954, Speier sends Brodie another long personal memo quibbling over whether Leites' paper was "Rand-sponsored rather than Project RAND," the former not requiring presentation to the government and the latter being required to in "a more detailed fashion."[377] Speier notes Brodie still believes he had given Leites "good advice," while Speier counters, "I still think you did not," and that the memo Brodie sent to Leites on this matter "embarrasses me in two ways," the first being Speier believes Leites "should not follow your advice, but I find it is difficult to tell him so myself, because your advice was given to him in a personal letter. Next, I think in your reply to me you built up a straw man that suffered the fate awaiting all straw men."[378] Speier believes strongly that Leites' study "should be given a form suitable for presentation to our sponsors," and while Brodie views "a simplified summary to be a matter of courtesy to our sponsors," Speier regards "the preparation of the whole study in suitable form as an obligation on our part."[379] He adds Brodie is "less interested in the preparation of a simplified summary than in the publication of the study in *World Politics*. I think, in the case of Project RAND studies, that Nathan's study will eventually reach wider audiences as well," or to "put it differently, there is no reason why Nathan's brilliant study, 'If War Were to Break Out Tomorrow,' should be regarded as intellectually less intelligible to our sponsors than his Study of Bolshevism. The new small study needs the kind of rewriting and editing from which the earlier and fuller work profited. You were helpful to Nathan and to RAND at the time by suggesting ways of improving the form of the larger study. Why do you think that the smaller one cannot be understood by our sponsors if it is suitably revised?"[380]

Recalling remarks Speier had made regarding the issue of the "intellectual endowment of the military profession," Speier explained he had told Brodie, "'I do not think we should permit ourselves ever to develop, or give the impression of entertaining, the opinion that people who are intelligent enough to finance RAND lack the ability to understand its research results.' You gave me the impression, perhaps inadvertently, of entertaining just such an opinion in the quoted passage of your letter ... This impression has in part been corrected by your declaration that you do not consider our clients to be unintelligent."[381] Speier further explained, "I do not advocate that you suppress any of your thoughts on the ability of the military, either in general or specifically with regard to their ability, to understand a given RAND study. I do suggest that in case of an unfavorable opinion in this regard you should ask yourself whether such inability is our fault or theirs. If ours, I think we should try to correct it, instead of saying let's be quick and courteous with our sponsors and think of publication elsewhere."[382] He added that the "larger question at issue in this correspondence, however, is not what you and I think of the intellectual endowment of the military. We are free to think what we like as long as we believe that they are able to stick to the good and change toward the better, and as long as we, on our part, are able to meet our obligations in RAND without compromising truthfulness and accuracy in our work for the sake of popularization."[383] He further reflected, "I am not sure that the major question is really one of tact ... Possibly the real question has to do less with tact than with stylistic predilection. In the past I have tried whenever an occasion arose to convey my impression to you that you delight in pejorative statements about men of power. In your condemnations I hear faint echoes of the Jewish Prophets or the Puritan preachers: like them you speak with the righteousness of your cause and you are harsh if others don't serve it. I am glad to acknowledge that you are keeping good company, as it were, but is it the company you, as a scientist, really want to keep?"[384] Speier concluded: "I suspect that these predilections sometimes distract you from an effort to render your studies scientifically even more rewarding than they are. I know that I can learn much from you. You disappoint me whenever I seem to learn less than expected merely because you are engrossed in scolding some uninteresting people with well-known names. It is only natural, I suppose, that I should expect your influence on your military audience as well to be even greater than it is if you chided them less often. The response to stern and frequent chiding by an outsider will depend not only upon their intelligence but also upon their pride."[385]

Speier proposed a memo to Leites reaffirming the need to "first consider revising the study for distribution as a RAND publication to our government sponsors," and also explaining that Brodie was not aware the study was "undertaken for Project RAND."[386] This put the matter to rest, while allowing for an illuminating discussion about the strategic thinking of the military and the unique role of RANDites in probing military complexities, often with such detailed expertise that their analysis might prove of limited understanding and potentially limited practicable utility to the men of arms who created RAND, helping to thus give birth to a new generation of nuclear wizards to grapple with the world's unprecedented strategic challenges.

Military Strategy: "Most Ancient and Least Developed"

Brodie revisits his discussion of the need for a more scientific and analytically rigorous approach to strategy, further extending his observations on sea power to the equally analytically challenged field of air power, in his April 1955 *World Politics* article, "Some Notes on the Evolution of Air Doctrine,"[387] where, he reiterates his views that military strategy is "of all the human sciences at once the most ancient and the least developed," adding, "It could hardly be otherwise. Its votaries must be men of decision and action rather than of theory. Victory is the payoff, and is regarded as the most telling confirmation of correct judgment. There is no other science where judgments are tested in blood and answered in the servitude of the defeated, where the supreme authority is the leader who has won or can instill confidence that he will win."[388]

But that notwithstanding, Brodie points out that "[s]ome modicum of theory there always had to be. But like much other military equipment, it had to be light in weight and easily pack-aged to be carried into the field. Thus, the strategic ideas which have from time to time evolved have no sooner gained acceptance than they have been stripped to their barest essentials and converted into maxims. Because the baggage that was stripped normally contained the justifica-tions, the qualifications, and the instances of historical application or misapplication, the sur-viving maxim had to be accorded a substitute dignity and authority by treating it as an axiom, or, in latter-day parlance, a 'principle.'"[389] As Brodie had noted six years earlier, the "so-called 'principles of war' have been derived from the work of a handful of theorists, most of them long since dead," and "[t]heir specific contributions to living doctrine may not be widely known, because their works are seldom read, and the dimensions of the original thought may find but the dimmest reflection in the axiom which has stemmed from it. Nevertheless, by their ideas, however much those ideas have suffered in the transmission, these theorists have enjoyed in the most pragmatic and 'practical' of professions a profound and awful authority."[390]

But that's not the case with air power, since it was still "too young to have among the theorists of its strategy more than one distinguished name, and he has carried all before him"[391] much the way Mahan did for sea power, as he discussed in his 1949 article: "The views of General Giulio Douhet would be worth study today even if air force thinking had progressed consider-ably beyond him and away from him, because he would still remain the first to have presented an integrated, coherent philosophy for the employment of air power," Brodie observed,[392] adding that "the fact is that air strategists have moved very little beyond or away from him. American air strategists today may or may not acknowledge in Douhet's philosophy the origin of their present doctrine, but there can be no doubt about the resemblance between the two."[393] Brodie, who would go on to discuss Douhet again in much detail in a his 1959 *Strategy in the Missile Age*, argues that the "contribution of Douhet which commands greatest respect is that he turned upside down the old trite military axiom, derived from Jomini, that 'methods change but princi-ples are unchanging,'" and "insisted instead that a change in method so drastic as that forced by the introduction of the airplane must revolutionize all the so-called principles of war."[394] Brodie suggests that it "took a bold and original mind to conceive that the sacrosanct principles might be outmoded, and a strong and independent will to assert it,"[395] a comment that we in hindsight can apply to Brodie as well, who very likely was of the same opinion. Brodie noted that Douhet "not only asserted it but supported his arguments with remarkably firm and consistent logic," adding that it "would be well if we were capable today of the same kind of originality and bold-ness with respect to the new nuclear weapons."[396] Like Brodie: "Douhet himself refused to justify his ideas according to whether they did or did not accord with some inherited gospel. He was much more interested in whether they accorded with the facts of life as he saw them," and was "too proud of his intellectual independence to appeal to the authority of the old principles where they happened to implement his own views."[397] Nonetheless, despite Douhet's own best efforts and intentions, Brodie observes "the controversy over the proper role of air power has often, on its more intellectual fringes, revolved around the question whether the Douhet thesis, or, more loosely, the emphasis on strategic bombing, does or does not conform to the tried-and-true, 'enduring' principles of war,"[398] so much so that air power theorists have turned to such "vener-ated authorities like Clausewitz, who after all has been dead for a century and a quarter," such as Captain Robert H. McDonnell, who in his article, "Clausewitz and Strategic Bombing," in the *Air University Quarterly Review*[399] is cited by Brodie for countering critics of strategic bomb-ing who believed it was a violation of Clausewitzian principles, suggesting "what is needed is 'a closer examination of Clausewitz' principles!'"[400]

And so Brodie turns his attention to Clausewitz, the grand master of strategic theory, who asserts an enduring, and compelling, presence throughout Brodie's career. Brodie asks, "What then are these ancient teachings to which appeals are so constantly made," and even "[m]ore important, from whence do they derive such commanding authority?"[401] Brodie expects much from these so-called principles of war, since they are "a body of ideas or axioms to which in our own time literally millions of lives have been sacrificed, and on the basis of which within the last decade great battles have been organized and fought. More to the point, we are concerned with a heritage of thought which even today dominates decisions on which the life or death of our nation may well hinge."[402] He finds that, "[i]n the main, the maxims or axioms which we call 'principles of war' are simply common-sense propositions, most of which apply to all sorts of pursuits besides war," and sounding much like Ovid, the master Roman strategist who turned his attention to the challenges of courtship and seduction, "If a man wants to win a fair and virtuous maiden, he must first make up his mind what he wants of the girl, that is, the principle of the objective, and must then practice the principles of concentration, of pursuit, of economy of force, and certainly of deception."[403] Brodie agrees that "common-sense principles are valuable precisely because they represent common sense, and are valuable only so long as they are compatible with common sense," but unfortunately he's found "too many examples in recent war of a slavish devotion to the so-called principles of war offending against common sense," which he attributes to a "slavish devotion" and a "low intellectual estate to which these maxims have fallen today" that obscures their more noble and intellectually enlightened origins. Brodie recalls that Clausewitz was "the first great figure in what might be called modern strategy, just as Adam Smith is the first great figure in modern economics," which—continuing his line of thought articulated in his aforementioned 1949 article; indeed in note 7, he cites his earlier article, writing, "For a more extended discussion of the relevance and irrelevance of strategic principles, see my 'Strategy as a Science,'" article—reflects a "science which is in many respects remarkably analogous. But unlike Smith, whose *Wealth of Nations* proved to be only the headwaters of a mighty and still expanding river of thought to which many great talents have contributed, Clausewitz is also, except for his lesser though impressive contemporary, Antoine Henri Jomini, almost the last great figure in his field,"[404] and while "[o]thers may also be worthy of honors and of notice, but they do not challenge his preeminence."[405]

Indeed, Clausewitz stands on so high a pedestal in the pantheon of strategic theorists that "it was very difficult to be original in this field after Clausewitz," and "[n]ot until two-thirds of a century later does anyone appear of anything like comparable stature, and Alfred T. Mahan, by confining himself to naval strategy, put himself into a rather more limited context than did Clausewitz."[406] It is only "[a]fter Mahan [that] we come to the unique name of Douhet, that is, unique in a separate and new field of strategy," though Brodie concedes that he was "of course skipping over the names of some writers, not many, who would have to be considered in any history of strategic thought," some of whom "showed real originality" while others were "more important for their influence on their times than for originality or incisiveness," such as Ferdinand Foch.[407]

Brodie found it "interesting to note that Clausewitz, who was certainly the most profound as well as systematic thinker on war who has yet appeared, specifically rejected the idea that there could be such things as principles or rules," even though we can "find discussed at considerable length in Clausewitz, as in Jomini, most of the basic ideas later to be exalted to the status of principles. But what makes large portions of Jomini and especially of Clausewitz come alive today in the reading is not the elucidation of basic ideas or principles but rather the wisdom that these two thinkers, one profound and the other incisive and eminently practical, brought to their discussion of these ideas. This wisdom is reflected in a flexibility and breadth of comprehension that makes Clausewitz dwell as tellingly on the qualifications and historical exceptions to the basic ideas he is promulgating as he does on those ideas themselves, though of course at lesser length."[408] Adds Brodie: "Another respect in which the wisdom of Clausewitz is manifested concerns a subject in which his contribution is not merely distinctive but unique. No other theorizer on military strategy, with the possible exception of Mahan, has devoted anything like comparable attention and careful thought to the relationship between war strategy and national policy. Clausewitz' contemporaries, notably Jomini, took the dependence of strategy upon policy so completely for granted that they thought it worth little mention, whereas those who are more nearly our own contemporaries, notably Douhet, lost the point entirely or denied it."[409] And so it's in "this regard more than in any other, Clausewitz has had not only the first word, but also practically the last," but it was "in this respect as in all others," Brodie observes, that "the fruits of his brooding intelligence have been not transmitted, but rather catalogued in the form of capsular quotations taken out of context," which Brodie found to be "especially ironical," particularly that "some of the very quotations which are often cited to prove that he was the prophet of total or absolute war are wrenched from a chapter in which he specifically insists that 'war is never an isolated act' and that military aim and method must always defer to the political object."[410]

Brodie himself would be misunderstood during his own time, his earlier thoughts held up against his later re-assessments, with the former often overshadowing the nuances of the latter. As Brodie explains, "Clausewitz is especially subject to such misinterpretation because of his subservience to the method of the contemporary German philosopher Hegel, whom he apparently studied with great reverence. Thus, after vigorously building up a case for war being in theory subject to no limitations of violence, he goes on to develop with equal vigor the point that in practice there must be many qualifications to the theoretical absolute, which of course reflects Hegel's well-known method of presenting the thesis, the antithesis, and then the synthesis. This method, plus the natural inclination of a searching mind to feel all round the subject, makes Clausewitz amenable to being quoted on whatever side of an issue one desires, and he has been amply abused in this fashion. Moreover, he is of all the noteworthy writers on strategy the least susceptible to condensation."[411]

Political Science and Strategic Studies: A Call to Arms

In his December 1957 article in *The Scientific Monthly*, "Scientific Progress and Political Science"—based on his paper presented to the joint session of the National Academy of Economics and Political Science, the American Political Science Association, and Section K (Social and Economic Sciences) of the American Association for the Advancement of Science at the New York meeting of the AAAS in December 1956—Brodie presented something of an update to his 1949 *World Politics* article, "Strategy as a Science," suggesting there was still a long way to go toward completing the bridge he hoped would span the civil and military sides of the strategic community, and thereby stimulate the emergence of a robust and active civilian-scientific strategic community. Part of the problem was resistance within the field of political science to the new discipline of strategic studies, even though it—on the surface—looked to be a natural incubator of civilian-scientific strategists, especially with its long tradition and interest in world affairs and international politics. There were many explanations for this resistance, many inherent to the field of political science and its traditions. In a discussion of "Politico-Military Problems," Brodie observes that "a weakness exists which is not at all necessary and which demands a remedy," a "weakness that is pervasive in American intellectual life" and that is America has "no tradition of intellectual concern with that increasingly wide border area where military problems meet political ones. Political science has a greater obligation in this respect than has any other single discipline. Few scholars consider it their primary business to inquire about the effects that current and projected military developments must have upon politics, and vice versa."[412]

Brodie adds that "[t]his particular poverty in the intellectual life of the country is bound to be reflected in the world of affairs," and even though "the military approach to strategic problems needs to be extended and leavened by the relevant insights of the statesman, such insights are likely to be undeveloped among those real-life civilians with whom the military actually have to deal. There has been much advocacy of closer communion between politicians and soldiers in matters relating to foreign policy. This closer communion, unquestionably desirable, has been much less often urged on the ground that civilians might have a beneficial influence upon military policy—a fact which reflects an almost universal consensus, presumably erroneous, that military affairs are inaccessible to the layman in a way different from that in which foreign affairs are."[413] Brodie explains that the "problem is not simply one of achieving closer communion between two groups of men of markedly different training and orientation. It is, rather, that of developing a real competence on each side to penetrate and comprehend the issues with which the other side is currently seized."[414] He points to the National Security Council as "a monument to an aspiration, and the aspiration is undeniably sound. But whether any real enrichment of strategic thinking has proceeded from it is another question."[415] Brodie suggests it in fact "works much better as a medium by which the military can impress their views on the civilians than the reverse—always excepting the matter of imposing budget ceilings on military expenditures, where arbitrariness generally rules."[416] Brodie believes "[t]here cannot be a real enrichment of strategic thinking unless and until considerable numbers of scholars in germane fields begin to concern themselves with the relevant issues."[417] Brodie writes that "[t]here are a number of reasons why the contribution of political scientists could be crucial," one being "political scientists, especially that group of them who specialize in international affairs, are concerned with the context of military operations in a way that the military themselves are not," as a "military officer is forced by the heavy professional demands of his craft to be preoccupied with tactical, as against strategic, matters, and to the relatively small degree that he concerns himself with the latter, his interpretation of strategy is likely to be a restricted one."[418]

Brodie recalls how Clausewitz, "himself a general, pointed out 125 years ago that the object of a war, which is always political and therefore appropriately determined by the politicians, must govern the whole conduct of that war; but this idea has never really been absorbed and digested by the military profession. To the military, the means available, rather than the object, are what determine the character of a war, and they have usually resisted any 'interference' from their civilian chiefs with respect to their choice of means."[419] This has become increasingly apparent in the Cold War, and Brodie recounts how "the Korean war uncovered a deep and pervasive confusion on the matter of ends and means. The politicians restrained the soldiers' use of means because they spontaneously recognized that the true objects of American intervention required such restraints. On the other hand, largely because of the novelty of the situation, the political leaders were so inept at formulating and explicating those objectives that they made basic and even elementary errors of direction," as he had noted in earlier critiques of American strategic policy in Korea.[420] Brodie noted that "Americans do not understand a kind of war in which relatively heavy sacrifices are made, yet in which they appear to be committed to something less than a clear victory. Yet 'limited' or 'peripheral' wars are by all odds the kind most likely to engage us within the next decade or two if we become involved in military actions at all," since limited war presents what in fact may be the only viable military option—"[n]oninvolvement may mean surrender of important positions, and certainly the only other alternative, all-out thermonuclear war, is an infinitely more grim and forbidding prospect than any kind of local war."[421] Furthermore, Brodie notes "the posture that deters the enemy from all-out attack does little, if anything, to deter him from making peripheral challenges."[422]

And while less likely, the far graver consequences of general war demand attention be paid to the risks and challenges of nuclear warfare; as Brodie observes, "[o]ne of the most critical changes wrought by the atomic bomb is almost universally overlooked and at great peril," and that is the "extent and character of military capabilities for any future crisis tend to be prede-termined by peacetime preparations made long before the event. . . . Decisions have been made and are being made now which will determine whether limited wars can be pursued at all and, if so, under what circumstances and with what constraints. The manner in which the character of any total war of the future is being predetermined by current preparations is even more strik-ing, though less interesting from a political point of view, both because it is less likely and also because it is potentially annihilative."[423]

Brodie notes how in recent years, the "Soviet retaliatory air capability continues to grow" and with its growth, "the conditions under which we can hint at a possible use of our strategic air force against the U.S.S.R. become vastly more circumscribed" and will likely "be confined to use only against the threat of a direct strategic air attack upon this country, which means that it will cease to be of much significance for a host of lesser contingencies. Yet there is no evidence that there has been any fundamental reorientation of politico-military outlook on the world since the days when America enjoyed undisputed monopoly of the atomic bomb."[424] Brodie turns back to the challenges—and opportunities—facing political science, observing: "Clearly, these are great problems on which political scientists could have much of value to say, if more of them could interest themselves."[425] One inhibiting factor Brodie notes is the need for secrecy and the limitations in access to classified information, though Brodie has come to the conclusion that "the information in the public domain is so immeasurably greater in volume and significance than what is kept secret that the latter may well be ignored except for quite special problems," and that "in most instances, the secrets are of relevance to technicians and not to political policy specialists" and that overall "secrecy is much less important than other factors."[426] A "second inhibiting factor is that the esoteric nature of the military art is commonly exaggerated," and even though "one does not learn how to be a general by reading books," Brodie points out that "no general becomes really outstanding without absorbing a kind of knowledge available in books—and there is nothing to keep civilians from reading the same books. In other words, one can learn from books what is consequential (the strategic as distinct from the tactical) about the military art, though very few people attempt to do so."[427] And a "third factor in this context is that technological change is rampant everywhere in society but nowhere more so than in the military art," but even here the civilian is no more disadvantaged than the military professional, who "tends to develop an inferiority complex toward the scientist and the engineer, though he has good defenses against letting his attitude of deference spread."[428] The last inhibiting factor, Brodie notes, is "that tradition determines, to some degree, scope and method in political sci-ence," where "the favored fixations tend to be too enduring even to be called fads, often lasting for a generation or more," slowing the pace of change and adaptation, and thus far preventing a full embrace of strategic studies as a bona fide subfield: "One of the most enduring attitudes of all has been that which exempts the study of war itself from a field in which scholars are intensely (and quite properly) concerned with the matters that tend to produce or to prevent war," and in addition to the issues he has thus far discussed Brodie observes "there is also some redolence of an attitude that was much more prominent during the interwar period than it is now—namely, that the preoccupation with matters military is somehow immoral in a scholar, or at least not wholly respectable. In the 1920s and 1930s one was expected, instead, to be interested in the finer points of the League of Nations Covenant, which was designed to prevent war. And although that attitude has itself largely disintegrated, its consequences linger on. The military profession is often charged with being unduly staid, but it cannot begin to compete in that respect with the curriculum designers in American colleges."[429] Brodie cautions that "[n]either an indictment nor a justification of political science is called for, but rather an explanation of some of its peculiarities of scope and method," and in particular "the failure of political science to cope with the many political problems associated with the nature of modern war, especially in its more novel aspects, should be emphasized."[430] After all, Brodie writes, "the H-bomb does raise some oppressively important issues."[431]

The American Scientific Strategists

In his October 1964 RAND paper, "The American Scientific Strategists"—which became in shorter form and slightly abbreviated title, "The Scientific Strategists," a chapter in Robert Gilpin and Christopher Wright, eds, *Scientists and National Policy-Making*—Brodie dived headlong back into the discussion he started in his seminal 1949 article, "Strategy as a Science" and which erupted in a series of heated memos a few years later at RAND, and recalled that "[p]ublications on military strategy" had until recently "been rather rare" and that "[m]ost of the few people who wrote them were career military officers."[432] He speculated that this was possibly "one reason why the publications were so few," as the "specific qualifications and virtues required of a military officer have always left little room for what is essentially a scholarly, analytical, and preferably also a literary activity."[433] But all that was now changing; indeed during "the last dozen years the situation has been vastly changed, at least within the United States" and "[a]rticles and books on strategy or strategic problems have become relatively abundant, not as compared with other intellectual fields but certainly as compared with former times.[434]" And, Brodie adds: "the writers of these publications are almost always civilians, and of a particular type. They are highly trained in the formal academic sense, and their training is basically scientific," and particularly "since the coming into office in January, 1961 of the Kennedy–Johnson Administration, they have risen spectacularly in importance."[435] And while the new breed of civilian strategists have "little military experience themselves or occasionally none," with some being "too young to have served in World War II," Brodie notes that "the special abilities of these 'scientific strategists' have been recognized and fully used by the military services, often even with enthusiasm, and the relations between these civilians and the military officers whom they have served is on the whole quite close," Brodie, "The American Scientific Strategists," though as Brodie would discover, this is not always the case. As these new scientific-strategists rose to the complex and dangerous challenges of the nuclear era, Brodie found that it was "no exaggeration to say that all the distinctively modern concepts of military strategy, most of which have been embraced by the military services themselves, have evolved out of their ranks,"[436] including the cornerstone of America's Cold War strategy, deterrence. Brodie added that "[d]espite the still relatively small number of these specialists, the contrast between the situation today and that existing before 1950, or at least before World War II, is spectacular."[437] While the landscape of strategic theory had been punctuated by the occasional prophetic voice, whether a Mahan or Corbett of the sea, or a Douhet or Mitchell of the air, or a Clausewitz or Jomini of the land, but their voices were few and preciously infrequent; with regard to land warfare, Brodie noted: "[t]here had been no really great writer on strategy since the towering Karl von Clausewitz, who died in 1831, and the very influential though lesser figure of the Swiss mercenary, Antoine Henri Jomini, both career staff officers of the Napoleonic period."[438] The approach of these more *classical* strategic theorists, Brodie points out that the "method of these men was mainly the scrutiny of military history to see what abiding lessons could be derived from the experience of the past," and that "[s]ome, like Du Picq and Mahan, had been careful and mostly objective historians" while "others, like Foch, were not averse to distorting history, with which they had little enough familiarity, to serve their pre-existing convictions."[439] But Brodie added that "none of these figures, including the most recent, had been at all interested in applying quantitative measures to their data," adding that "[p]erhaps the modern school of strategists contrasts most sharply with the old in precisely this difference of attitude about numbers."[440]

Before the renaissance in strategic thinking fostered by this new generation of civilian scientific-strategists, Brodie noted that "if we were to include the names of all the lesser figures whose writings on strategy make them worth mentioning at all, the total number in this field in the hundred years preceding 1950 would still be remarkably small," and all said, "the theoretical study of military strategy, has been until now the most sparsely-populated of intellectual pursuits, despite the periodic recurrence of important wars."[441] But despite the small size of the strategic-theoretical community, it was nonetheless an influential group, but not necessarily benign in its influence. As Brodie commented, the "important military decisions were in the past the work of men who, though professional soldiers, were rarely specialists in strategy" and while "[t]he generals or admirals in top command were usually older men who had spent their lives in those varied pursuits that we call military," Brodie notes "much of it had to do with drill and very little of it with the conduct of war."[442] In Brodie's view, "by any pragmatic standard we have to concede that the system worked very badly for those whom it was supposed to serve. The tactical and strategic 'lessons' presented by the experience of successive wars often had to be learned over and over again, always at great cost and frequently at the risk of defeat."[443] Asks Brodie, "Why had not the most obvious lessons of combat experience been absorbed by commanders who were to send great new armies into battle? Because for the most part experience not personal to him was not communicated to the leader of new forces, who was likely to pride himself more on being a man of action than on being a student of history, even of military history."[444] Brodie also cautioned that "[o]ne must remember too—and the military are not the only ones of whom this is true—that people wedded to dogmas will often continue to cherish them undiminished after direct personal experiences which should prove them wrong," and "[i]n a profession where rank means so much, and where promotion is so much at the mercy of one's seniors, who will question or challenge the dogmas of his elders?"[445]

But with the series of sweeping technological transformations of war that took place during World War II, the traditional approach to strategic theorizing came under new pressures, and required "a different and more flexible kind of military leader," and "among the more conspicuous factors of change, two deserve special mention. The first was the introduction at the very end of the conflict of the atomic bomb, which not only presented in itself a basic strategic change of totally unprecedented importance but also signalled the beginning of an era of extremely rapid and also extremely costly technological development. The second was the heavy reliance upon scientists to assist not only top military commanders but even heads of government to reach critical tactical and strategic decisions."[446] as Brodie explained, the "tremendous novelty of the new military conditions was naturally bound to throw some doubt on the pertinence of the professional soldier's military experience," just as the unprecedented "destructiveness of nuclear weapons meant that total or 'general' war (which for the first decade of the atomic age was practically the only kind one thought about) would have to be fought with forces in being at the outset—a change that effectively pushed all the major strategic decisions, including choice of weapon systems, of deployments, and of targets, into the pre-war period, when the military man has not yet 'taken over' from the civilian."[447] Added Brodie: "Furthermore, the rapidity of change that resulted from the development of a wide range of nuclear weapons, combined with the development of fabulous new vehicles for carrying them, diminished greatly the utility of simple professional judgment in selecting the appropriate systems, especially in view of the tremendous sums of money involved in the choices. The military man had all he could do to keep abreast of current technological developments pertinent to his work."[448] While it "was not altogether a new problem for the military to have to think ahead technologically," Brodie observed that "certainly the dimensions and complexity of the problem was totally new," and this meant that the military would increasingly depend upon "technicians who could be counted on to maintain an alert understanding of the evolving 'state of the art' in any one technological field."[449]

Fueled by this growing need, as well as by "the new prestige of scientists as a result of the nuclear developments," Brodie describes how "a development took place in the United States that was to have consequences far beyond those expected by the sponsors. This was the founding of a number of institutions closely associated with but outside the military services, where people with various kinds of scientific training and access to classified information would devote themselves on a full-time basis to the consideration of military problems," organizations like the RAND Corporation, both the "prototype of these organizations and the best known among them."[450] As Brodie recounts, "those who were given the task of organizing RAND included in it almost from the outset divisions of mathematics, economics, and social science, as well as the more-to-be-expected engineering and physics divisions," adding that their "inclusion of an economics division turned out to be of especially critical importance, and the inclusion of a social science division made it possible to undertake, among other things, a thoroughgoing study of the Communist enemy or enemies of a kind that had too long been lacking from the strategic studies."[451] Indeed, Brodie describes numerous "conceptual parallels between strategy and economics," recalling that in his 1949 article, "Strategy as a Science," he "called attention to the remarkable similarities in both method and objectives between the science of economics and what could become a science of strategy."[452]

Indeed, he observed that a "majority of those who have made their mark today as theorists in strategy have been trained as economists, or at least have more than a bowing acquaintance with the concepts and principles in that field," including Herman Kahn, who in addition to being a physicist, "trained himself quite seriously as an economist, and was once even offered a professorial post in economics in a leading American university," as well as Thomas Schelling and Albert Wohlstetter, who "were intensively trained as economists," among many others—including several economists "who were formerly of RAND but now hold important posts in the Department of Defense."[453] So while "[e]arlier generations of strategic writers used practically no tools other than history," Brodie found that "few of the present writers in the field ever trouble to read history"—which would itself become problematic in the years to come as historical insight all but lost out to the new scientific logic.[454] As Brodie observed, "One is sometimes amazed at how little some of the best-known strategic analysts of our times may know about conflicts no more remote in time than World War I, let alone earlier wars (the same is, however, true of professional military officers). It is not that they have no time for history but rather that the devotees of any highly developed science—and economics is clearly the most highly developed of the social sciences—tend to develop a certain disdain and even arrogance concerning other fields. It is a grave intellectual fault, but a very common one."[455] Brodie found that the "modern training of economists, with its heavy emphasis on mathematics and other tools of quantitative analysis, tends to fit one peculiarly well for grappling with certain characteristic problems of strategy, especially in what we call 'cost-effectiveness' analysis."[456] But other analytical tools would be required, as the "importance of being sensitive to the political issues that are omnipresent in strategic questions would be hard to overestimate,"[457] and as "some of the most important factors relevant to determining the performance of a system are not finally reducible to dollar comparisons."[458] Nonetheless, "at every stage decisions are made which are difficult at best and impossible to make wisely without utilizing all the tools that modern concepts of economic and strategic analysis have made available to us. This is a new and now permanent condition, a state of the world undreamed of in 1939."[459] Indeed, Brodie can't understate the complexity of the challenge confronted by strategic analysts: "As we move to a larger context we see that we have hardly begun to measure the complexity of the major issues of strategy. We observe that a nation makes its strategic dispositions not against a more or less predictable state of nature but against an opponent or group of opponents whose present intentions and capabilities have to be analyzed to the best limits of our information and their future course predicted. These opponents are cunning and have objectives in direct conflict with our own. . . . Moreover, one has to adjust to a *range* of possible situations—the single most likely situation does not necessarily have a high degree of likelihood. And, obviously, one's defensive preparations when detected will affect the offensive designs of the opponent and vice versa."[460] But as Brodie observes, "As the 'scientific strategists' have become more at home in their work, their greater maturity has resulted in important changes in basic approach. Where their tendency used to be to try to find the optimum method of dealing with a single most-expected contingency, the realization that the enemy might play the game differently from the way in which we think we ought to play it has prompted us instead to seek that mixture of solutions which does rather well over a complex of contingencies."[461] Brodie discusses both the use and limitations of gaming techniques, noting that game theory "as developed mostly by the late mathematician John von Neumann" was "generally of little importance to the strategist" and that in fact "many strategic analysts do important and excellent work in their field without having much understanding of game theory. What matters is the *spirit* of the gaming principle, the constant reminder that in war we shall be dealing with an opponent who will react to our moves and to whom we must react. It is amazing how little this simple conception has characterized war plans in the past."[462] Brodie explains that "the greatest value of the gaming technique is in conditioning the analyst or decision-maker to ask himself spontaneously: 'How is the enemy likely to respond if I carry out (or refrain from) this proposed action, and what new problems will that response create for me.' "[463]

While the scientific approach to strategy is not without its faults, Brodie found that its "greatest limitation" was that decision makers "often fail to use scientific method when they should or when they pretend to" and in "[s]uch lapses" reveal that "they are human, and thus disposed to sharing the infirmities of humanity."[464] But, he points out, "Even in the areas in which strictly scientific analysis is appropriate, the complexity of the field, the impossibility of really testing conclusively one's suppositions or deductions, and the fact that one is constantly running up against value judgments or simply against the mysteries of the future mean that temptations always exist both to shortcut some of the analytical difficulties and to pretend to analytic objectivity where it has ceased to operate."[465] A more scientific approach was thus "not what we have too much of but what we too often fail to achieve," but despite its faults, Brodie believed that the "great merit of the scientifically trained analyst is that he tries more persistently than others, and he can perhaps be more easily made aware of his lapses when they occur. When we do succeed in using scientific method for the systematic exploration and comparison of alternative courses of action, we are doing simply the best we can do to bring some order into the vast, chaotic mass of technological, economic, and political facts and predictions which form the universe of data in which reasonable military decisions have to be made."[466]

Brodie discussed the relationship between the civilian strategists and their military clients, noting "relations between the civilian scientific strategists and their military clients have in the main been thoroughly good and mutually profitable," and when this "has not been so, it is usually because we are dealing with character weaknesses on one or both sides. Most military officers know their own worth, and their special qualifications for indispensable service, and are content to recognize the limits of their training and experience. Some are not."[467] Brodie added that the "same is true on the side of the analysts. It has always been true that creative abilities are not necessarily combined in the same person with such character endowments as tact and modesty."[468] The relationship had become especially close with the "coming to office with the Kennedy Administration of the extraordinarily able, vigorous, and self-confident Mr. Robert S. McNamara as Secretary of Defense," which "had extraordinary consequences with respect to the relationships we have been discussing," and though "[s]ome of these consequences are likely to be enduring," Brodie cautioned that "others will no doubt be but temporary."[469] Brodie described the "team that entered office with Mr. McNamara" as including "in positions of relatively high responsibility, a small group of persons who had made their mark as strategic analysts of the kind we have been describing," and "[t]his nucleus of experts on the staff were able also to enlist the services, on a part-time consultative basis, of others who had had the same kind of training and experience. With such able and knowledgeable people on his staff or otherwise available to him, and speaking a kind of 'cost effectiveness' language which as a former industrialist he had come to understand and appreciate, Mr. McNamara quickly developed so marked a confidence in his own judgment that he was before long making decisions that ran counter to the unanimous advice of committees of his military advisors."[470] Indeed, McNamara did this with "the now famous TFX airplane controversy, and also in refusing to countenance the construction of more new aircraft carriers (besides the already-built Enterprise) with nuclear propulsion, insisting instead on the cheaper conventional propulsion," but "[e]ven more important was his insistence on planning to fight even large-scale local wars with conventional rather than with tactical nuclear weapons,"[471] a policy that would come to haunt him after the humbling defeat in Vietnam.

But importantly, Brodie commented that "[i]t should be noted that no previous Secretary of Defense had ever made a decision of mostly military significance against a unanimous judgment of the Joint Chiefs. Some of them had reluctantly intervened when the Joint Chiefs were hopelessly split, but only after urging them to come to a meeting of minds if possible. What was new in Mr. McNamara's method was not only that he was willing to place his own judgment against that of his military advisors, but also that the kind of analytical investigations which the separate services had previously conducted on their own initiative and responsibility, which enabled them to reserve to themselves authority to accept or reject the advice they received from the institutions like RAND which they supported, were now being reported directly to the Secretary of Defense. In short, the military to a large extent lost control of the kind of analytical operations which they had themselves sponsored. It probably did not help matters that some of the civilians involved were very young and not inclined to be especially tactful or deferential to the military. The remarkable thing is that relations did not become more critical."[472]

Brodie anticipated that "much of this situation is bound to be impermanent" and saw "little chance for institutionalizing the pervasive and searching kind of civilian control of the whole gamut of important military decisions that a very special kind of Secretary aided by an unusual array of assistants has eagerly undertaken," predicting that "[m]ost future Secretaries will not want to shoulder that kind of responsibility" and as a consequence, we could "thus expect in the future to see the military chieftains or the Joint Chiefs regain much of their formerly unchallenged responsibility and authority for major military decisions and for providing their political superiors with appropriate advice."[473] However, Brodie added that "[o]n the other hand, a number of important trends already existing before the present Administration and brought to fuller fruition under Secretary McNamara represent long-term and largely irreversible changes," including "the new kind of budgeting according to strategic functions rather than to services" as well as "the tendency for the making of decisions on major weapons systems to be brought into the direct purview of the office of the Secretary of Defense."[474] Brodie further expected it would be "probably unlikely that military leaders will quickly forget the salutary shock of being required to present closely reasoned justifications for their recommendations, rather than merely their sovereign judgment," and "since their problems are not getting any simpler, we may expect that they will continue to rely heavily on the kind of intricate systems analysis to which they have by now become entirely accustomed."[475]

The Runaway Theorists: "What RAND Hath Wrought"

And the military would indeed "continue to rely heavily on the kind of intricate systems analysis to which they have by now become entirely accustomed," yielding to the analytical prowess of the new corpus of civilian strategists at RAND and, increasingly, serving at the highest levels of the Pentagon. Only a few years later, such a sea change in how strategy was made would come back to haunt both sides, as the effort at controlled-escalation taking place in Vietnam began to tragically spin out of control.

As Colin Gray recalled in his Autumn 1971 *Foreign Policy*, "What RAND Hath Wrought," the 1950s "saw a renaissance of strategic thought" during which "such civilian theorists as Albert Wohlstetter, Henry Rowen, Bernard Brodie, Thomas Schelling, Herman Kahn, William Kaufmann and Henry Kissinger constructed an edifice of strategic theory that has come to have a profound impact upon all important aspects of U.S. defense policy" and so when President Kennedy came to power at the dawn of the 1960s, "the promise was high"—particularly as the "civilian strategists came to Washington to assume an influential role in a new administration."[476] But a decade later, when Gray was writing in 1971, he felt it was "fair to say that their performance has not lived up to their promise," adding, "[a]nd that's putting it mildly."[477] As Gray observed: "The Vietnam war, the conduct of the strategic arms race and major intra-alliance difficulties suggest that the following charges may be leveled at the strategic scholars whose theories won official acceptance in Washington."[478] The first is that the "methodology of the civilian strategists has been dominated by an 'economic conflict' model" and its "assumption that international conflict can be analyzed in terms of rational 'strategic men' has been vital for the progress of theory-building in strategy, but it has proved fatal to the relevance of theorists who have shifted from model-building to prescription."[479] The second is that "[b]ecause they are essentially men of ideas, the civilian scholars of strategy have been overimpressed with the potential transferability of theory to the world of action."[480] And third, that "[t]he civilian scholars who arose in the 1950's to fill certain obvious holes in strategic understanding succeeded, first, in gaining intellectual access to political and military elements in opposition to the Eisenhower Administration, and, second, gained access in the early 1960's to the actual policy making processes of government. The prophets became courtiers. The consequence has been that since the middle and late 1960's the United States has been living off its strategic theoretical capital."[481] As Gray sees it, "If policy prescription may be described as the advocacy of 'viable solutions,' so scholarship should be viewed as the pursuit of truth. The civilian strategist has fallen between the two extremes. The 'think-tank' world, as exemplified by the RAND Corporation, has been the middle ground between academe and government. Yet because of its dual loyalty—to the needs of problem-oriented officials and to the disinterested or 'policy-neutral' standards of scholarship—it has tended to produce both irrelevant policy advice and poor scholarship."[482]

And this was particularly evident in Vietnam: "It would appear that by most criteria the Vietnam War has been a massive failure for the United States," Gray writes; "Success or failure are not to be measured solely in terms of the objectives attained, but also by the costs incurred."[483] Gray observes that the Vietnam War "has unfortunately been taken to be a test case for the doctrine of flexible response," where the United States had "tried everything short of a 'take-over' of the government in Saigon, the employment of nuclear weapons and an invasion of the sanctuary area of North Vietnam. Nation-building, counterinsurgency, limited war, a controlled escalation of punishment by air-power—all have been attempted and all have failed to produce either the military-political defeat of the Viet Cong/North Vietnamese or the negotiated settlement that was expected."[484] On the other hand, Gray thinks that Vietnam "does not demonstrate the inutility of flexible response."[485] Instead, "What it does demonstrate is that the United States was ill-advised to wage a protracted, semi-conventional war on the Asian mainland against an enemy whose pain threshold for settlement was either non-existent or was unattainable, and in tandem with a local government distinguished by its lack of popular support and by its degree of corruption (these distinctions are, of course, far from unique)."[486] Thus the "failure of America's strategic theorists over Vietnam was not at the level of theoretical understanding. Rather, the theorists failed to insist to their government in strong enough terms that the task was too great. There is good reason to question the mode of employment of American military power in Vietnam (particularly the air war against North Vietnam and the extensive and unrewarding 'search and destroy' operations). But the truth appears to be that, in the 1960s, South Vietnam was not a nation that could be 'built' by massive American intervention. The most that could be accomplished, at frightful cost to the American political system, was the elimination of the possibility of military victory by the Viet-cong, while the victory of North Vietnam in the long term would seem to have been assured."[487]

In the Winter 1971–1972 edition of *Foreign Policy* magazine, Brodie authored an article titled "Why Were We So (Strategically) Wrong?" that responded to Gray's "What RAND Hath Wrought" in the previous edition that "charged that a number of civilian strategists (including this one) fell flat on their faces over the past decade in trying to predict the character and outcome of the Vietnam war."[488] Brodie concedes that "[i]n this he is obviously quite correct, and it is an important and disturbing conclusion. It might be highly instructive to explore why they (or we) have erred, and that is why, at the request of the editors of *Foreign Policy*, I am responding to Mr. Gray's critique."[489] Brodie cites Gray, who wrote that "If policy prescription may be described as the advocacy of 'viable solutions,' so scholarship should be viewed as the pursuit of truth. The civilian strategist has fallen between the two extremes."[490] Brodie notes Gray's attitude "reflects much of the social science thinking of our time, but I find it particularly inopportune in this instance. For strategic thinking, or 'theory' if one prefers, is nothing if not pragmatic. Strategy is a 'how to do it' study, a guide for accomplishing something and doing it efficiently. The question that matters in strategy—as in many other branches of politics—is, will the idea work? More, will it be likely to work under the precise and inevitably special circumstances under which it will next be tested? How much these circumstances are known or knowable depends partly on how close we are to the moment of testing. The failure of the civilian strategists in Vietnam, as Mr. Gray fails to notice, is that that part of their theory he most admires proved utterly irrelevant, and many of their ideas which were not irrelevant proved false."[491] Adds Brodie, "The score as tested against the special reality of Vietnam was much worse than it should have been, and the error is measured in something much more tragic than red-faces. Mr. Gray chides the 'civilian scholars of strategy' with being 'overimpressed with the potential transferability of theory to the world of action.' What, pray, could their theory possibly be for if it were not meant to be transferable to precisely that world? The theory of strategy is a theory for action, or, to turn around Gray's own words, strategy is a field where truth is sought in the pursuit of viable solutions."[492]

Brodie explains that strategic theory "differs from theory in the pure sciences only in that the latter is content to describe and explain rather than to prescribe," but that at heart both face the reality check of the real world.[493] "Social scientists who yearn for the theoretical and methodological elegance of the physical sciences often seem unaware that theorists in physics evaluate their formulations entirely by whether they are ultimately proved or disproved by experiments or other observations, in other words by whether they accord fully and consistently with the real world."[494] Brodie also notes that Gray "accuses these well-meaning but dangerous people of whom he writes of insinuating themselves, especially during the McNamara regime, directly into the policy-making process," suggesting a complicity and perhaps even a malicious intent that mirrors the popular misperception of Machiavelli as the conniving would-be courtier ingratiating himself with the Prince's circle.[495] Brodie cites Gray, who "puts it, 'The prophets became courtiers,' with a consequent loss of their purity and allegedly also a bootless using up of their 'strategic theoretical capital.' "⁴⁹⁶ Brodie rebukes Gray for such a generalization, and also reveals his own frustration having lacked an enduring connection with the decision-making elite: "People like in general to be more, rather than less, useful, and as one who was not invited into the McNamara circle I am bound to say I would not have felt sullied if I had been. My own service at high levels in the Pentagon came much earlier in time, and during a very few months in that place I learned a great deal that was useful to my subsequent thinking. Perhaps the most useful thing I learned was how badly things are done at the strategic level in the 'world of action,' but the shocks that go with the experience help overcome the diffidence which an outsider might otherwise feel."⁴⁹⁷ Brodie thus sympathetically describes the enormous weight on the shoulders of the strategic theorists, and recounts how when he joined RAND in 1951 he was the sole analyst with an interest in, and knowledge of, strategy—and over time, even as the number increased, "the number has always remained small—especially if one limits the count to those who demonstrated a capacity for some originality. Upon this small group there fell by default the job of determining how to think about the atomic bomb, and how to do so under technological and political circumstances that were steadily and rapidly changing."⁴⁹⁸

Brodie retells the story of his lone opposition to the conventional build-up by NATO in the face of Soviet armed strength along the central front, noting that "[o]n the question, for example, whether or not the United States and its NATO allies should build up large conventional forces in Europe, which for several years was the prime issue in American foreign security policy, I believe that mine was the only American voice raised in criticism and opposition, at least as recorded in published statements," and had Brodie "desired to avoid offending leaders of the inner circle," he explains, "the Administration view would have escaped any criticism. Not that it mattered greatly in this instance, because the effective opposition came from the sit-down strike of our NATO allies. Whether I was right or wrong is beside the point; what counts is that the issue, which was certainly important enough, did not present such self-evident answers as to warrant the near-absence of debate."⁴⁹⁹

Brodie discusses his own skepticism for systems analysis, and a widespread over-dependence upon it, noting that "[a]nother great misfortune in the last two decades was the wholly excessive attention and deference paid to systems analysis, a deference which Mr. Gray fully shares."⁵⁰⁰ And while Brodie accedes that, "[c]ertainly the technique of systems analysis is indispensable for the consideration of many important military questions raised in the modern era" such as selecting "appropriate weapons systems among types not yet developed," which "would be a baf-fling and terribly wasteful business without it," Brodie believes while "it is an important tool in making some military decisions, it is not coterminous with strategy, as Mr. Robert McNamara, among others, thought it was."⁵⁰¹

Brodie lays blame for the Vietnam debacle squarely on systems analysis, and the overde-pendence of strategic analysts, especially that of Defense Secretary McNamara, upon this new method. As Brodie explained, "Classical systems analysis, despite the yeoman's work done by Alain Enthoven's office, has had just about zero relevance to everything concerned with Vietnam."⁵⁰² Brodie believes "[o]ur failures there have been at least 95 percent due to our incom-prehension and inability to cope with the political dimensions of the problem, not forgetting that part which is internal to the United States," and that "[i]f we had understood these prob-lems we should certainly not have gone in, and the failure belongs not simply to the 'civilian strategists' but also to the political science profession, at least that part of it which is involved in foreign policy questions and regional studies."⁵⁰³ And "[a]mong those errors that were primarily military," Brodie places "at the top the failure to anticipate properly the importance of giving the opponent a sanctuary which comprises his entire homeland," as "[f]or over three years it was not a sanctuary against bombing (which also failed to deliver the results expected of it—and let us hear no more from Admiral U.S. Grant Sharp about our not having done enough bombing); but it has always been a complete sanctuary against ground force incursion, which meant that the enemy could, to paraphrase Lord Bacon, take as much or as little of the war as he wanted, and could shift his degree of participation whenever he wanted. Our errors here, partly the result of misreading the lessons of Korea, were disastrous."[504] But as Brodie observes, "that disaster pales in comparison with the consequences of our willful blindness in trying to shore up a corrupt, inefficient, and thoroughly unpopular regime. We had no business trying, and we could not succeed."[505] Brodie cites Gray, who wrote, "The failure of America's strategic theorists over Vietnam was not at the level of theoretical understanding. Rather the theorists failed to insist to their government in strong enough terms that the task was too great."[506] Brodie responds, "Well, one would wish that that were so. It is pretty nearly the opposite of the truth."[507] Indeed, as Brodie observes, "At the level of 'theoretical understanding' their error was total."[508]

Brodie considers "the cures," noting that "Gray has some, but I do not fully understand them. They seem to be counsels of perfection—more emphasis on purer theory and on avoiding 'the seductions of power.'"[509] Brodie presents, perhaps in frustration at his own exclusion from that inner circle, "the opposite advice for a man of younger or middle years, provided he were invited to be operational at or near the highest levels," as "[h]e would learn a good deal that is perennial about the military, the politicians, and 'how things are done,' and inasmuch as he would last at most for one administration and probably much less if he were a free spirit with an independent mind, not too much of his life would be taken up in the process."[510] But "[i]f he wants to be a thinker about important issues and make significant contributions in writing, he must of course avoid getting entangled in the bureaucracies, though even they manage to absorb some quite exceptional men without always ruining them," such as "George Kennan, and there are some others."[511]

Ever the realist, Brodie finds much learning taking place from the Vietnam experience, noting that "[w]e are even now learning a great deal from the Vietnam experience precisely because it has been so searing and so prolonged. We are witnessing in various places, including the pages of this journal, what appears to be a searching post-mortem (though at this writing the war is not yet the corpse it ought to be)."[512] Brodie adds that "[w]e are learning to be mistrustful of political dogmas, and less diffident about confronting military dogmas," and that "[w]e certainly need to stress the superior importance of the political side of strategy to the simply technical and technological side," and to "[p]reserve and cherish the systems analysts, but avoid the genuflections."[513] Brodie believes there remains "a long way to go," but points out that "much distance has already been traveled. When we recall how we discussed methods for demonstrating 'our superior resolve' without ever questioning whether we would indeed have or deserve to have superiority in that commodity, we realize how puerile was our whole approach to our art. Well, one learns from hard experience, though in this case we have learned also the importance of depressing the quantity of comparable experience in the future."[514]

Strategic Thinkers, Planners, Decision Makers

Brodie would continue to examine, through to his very last article published in 1978, the rise of the civilian strategists, that group of defense intellectuals Fred Kaplan colorfully dubbed the *Wizards of Armageddon*, a group to which Brodie not only belonged, but for many its most esteemed member. Brodie described this group less colorfully than Kaplan, but perhaps more accurately as the *civilian-scientific strategists*, or as the *new scientific strategists*, and he would close his 1973 book, his tribute to Clausewitz titled *War and Politics*, with a discussion of their rise in his final chapter of this final book, "Strategic Thinkers, Planners, Decision Makers," resuming his quarter-century discussion since his 1949 *World Politics* article of the civilian defense intellectual, and his increasing—though by no means untroubled—contribution to the formulation of strategic-military policies.

In this chapter, he revisits Clausewitz, as well as his predecessor Machiavelli, as well as his generation of military and civilian strategists, bringing to a close his discussion of war, and politics, and the fundamental relationship between the two. He starts out with the insights of the "great Marshal Maurice de Saxe," who "observed in his *Reveries* that most commanding generals displayed on the battlefield the utmost confusion," attributing this to the fact that "very few men occupy themselves with the higher problems of war," and instead "pass their lives drilling troops and believe that this is the only branch of the military art," so "[w]hen they arrive at the command of armies they are totally ignorant, and, in default of knowing what should be done, they do what they know." Brodie seems to find some personal comfort in these observations, and notes while "these words were written over 200 years ago, they have applied perennially to the art of the soldier, and apply about as well now as when they were written."[515] Brodie wonders how the "few military geniuses that time and the passage of many wars throws across our vision" managed to "learn the art of the general," and how those who assumed the highest levels of command "learn *strategy*?" Brodie finds that the "strategic conception is more abstract than the tactical one" and thus less readily learned through "precept and experience," suggesting that there needs to be an "inventiveness, a native cunning, and a tendency to reflect on the enemy's goals as well as the needs and aspirations of his allies."[516]

While Maurice, like Frederick the Great, put pen to paper and authored his "own little book" published posthumously in 1757, Brodie observes that "[l]ike Frederick's *Instructions to His Generals* (1747) and memoranda to his successor, Maurice's book was not intended by its author for publication," and like Frederick, Maurice "dwelt mostly on homely matters concerning the handling and provisioning of armies, and only incidentally and in passing made observations or contributions on what we should now consider fundamental strategy."[517] And when Clausewitz emerged a century later in the wake of Napoleon, penning "the first really adequate treatise on strategy, and still by a wide margin the greatest, he paid little attention to either Maurice de Saxe of Frederick," and instead "pa(id) his respects to the original Renaissance source of wisdom on politics and strategy, Niccolo Machiavelli."[518] As Brodie observed, "Clausewitz, who tended to scorn most other military writers, treated Machiavelli with respect because like him 'he was convinced that the validity of any special analysis of military problems depended on a general perception, on a correct concept of the nature of war."[519] Brodie further reflects that "Machiavelli's large contribution reminds us that there have always been some few civilians to whom the study of warfare was intriguing as something besides history, and of course we know that most military history has been written by civilians, especially in modern times. Soldiers have always cherished the image of themselves as men of action rather than as intellectuals, and they have not been very much given to writing analytical inquiries into their own art."[520] Indeed, Brodie noted that "[p]erhaps as a result of some defensive feeling on the matter, military men have in the past turned a certain degree of obloquy on those of their colleagues who were in their eyes too scholarly about war," much like the later naval strategist Mahan, who "would be called 'a pen-pushing sailor'" and who only truly came into his own when "he was transferred to an essentially civilian pursuit as a faculty member of the new U.S. Naval War College."[521] By and large, however, Brodie has found "civilian writers with something important to say have usually been well received by the professionals, who understand their own needs and also the paucity of contributions by their own brethren," though Brodie notes "[s]ome professional military may in certain moods, inveigh against 'armchair strategists,' by which they mean interlopers on their terrain who are not identifiable by service uniform, but this is usually an attitude of disgruntlement concerning particular views in which they are in disagreement," and concedes "there are an always have been a few primitives who consider the fact of wearing or having worn a uniform the indispensable entitlement to the expression of any views on military affairs; but these are normally the ones who would never read anything of a reflective character anyway even if written by one with the most unchallengeable military credentials."[522]

Brodie explains that the "role of the civilian in contributions to this field, which became so prominent following World War II, is more understandable when we reflect further on what strategy really means and what it embraces," and his definition starts with the concept from Mahan that defined strategy as pertaining to operations prior to contact with the enemy, and upon contact, tactics are employed.[523] Brodie accepts this as a starting point, as it "helps us to get on with the real job of exploring the true meaning of the idea," which he traces back once more to Clausewitz, the intellectual inspiration of *War and Politics* and to whom its title is largely a tribute. "The idea stressed repeatedly in this book, explicitly and implicitly, is that which most makes Clausewitz stand out from those who might otherwise come near to being his peers and which accounted for his being impressed with Machiavelli," and this is "the concern with the fundamental nature of war as a branch of politics."[524] So while the "general has indeed been trained or conditioned to want desperately to win, and will be willing to pay any price possible to do so,"[525] there nonetheless "has to be at the top, certainly in the civilian and preferably also in the military departments o the government, the basic and prevailing conception of what any war existing or impending is really about and what it is attempting to accomplish. This attitude includes necessarily a readiness to reexamine whether under the circumstances existing it is right to continue it or whether it is better to seek some solution or termination other than victory"[526]—as ultimately happened in Vietnam.

Brodie finds in Clausewitz such a sensibility, noting he had "learned from experience very early in his career the importance of 'the correct political bias' for any nation at war,"[527] and notes with interest that "Clausewitz, whose life from boyhood on was spent in military service and who as a scholar and philosopher was totally self-taught, should have grasped the essence of the issue, the nexus between politics and strategy, so much more clearly than virtually all of his peers and successors," and attributes the clarity of his insight to "the extraordinary power and reach of his mind" as well as to "some bitter and extraordinary personal experiences to help him along the war."[528] Among these was Clausewitz's decision (along with "various others of the leading reformist soldiers of Prussia") to resign his commission serving Friedrich Wilhelm, and to cross over to the Russians, "thus becoming nominally the enemy of his own king and that of the king's army, which contained two of his brothers."[529] And, Brodie added, "[w]ith the Russians he fought in the great campaign of 1812, in which the *Grand Armee* went to Moscow and then perished in the retreat," and "witnessed with his own eyes and was torn to the core by the unspeakable horrors of this flight."[530] This would "no doubt accentuate his feelings of that the correct use of thought in the handling of (war) deserved a very high priority." Brodie notes Clausewitz's "real anguish at the horrors he saw" clashed with his strategic logic that a more aggressive blow against the retreating French was needed to consolidate the victory, and he speculates that "the inner conflict between his undoubted compassion and something much fiercer in his nature must have contributed to the depression that seems to have developed steadily throughout his life."[531] Brodie feels a connection with "this sensitive, retiring, and deeply emotional man," and though he "knew very well the worth of his own ideas, such searing experiences, including that of the occupation of Paris afterwards, would burn deeply into his consciousness the necessary unity of war with its object."[532] Brodie notes Clausewitz was especially "appalled by the vindictive behavior and attitudes of his Prussian colleagues," which "undoubtedly confirmed his feelings about the supreme requirement of appropriate political direction during war and its aftermath, which he developed so persistently in his *On War*."[533]

Brodie considers Clausewitz something of a strategic prophet, whose ideas still resonate with relevance today. "Although no single author could be an adequate 'guide' to us in our present problems, and not alone because the world we live in is so different from his, the startling insights that leap up at us from so many pages of his great work are still often directly applicable to our own times. There has been no one to match him since."[534] Brodie notes Clausewitz "specifically rejected the notion that there could be any well-defined body of particular rules or principles that universally dictated one form of behavior rather than another," in contrast to "his contemporary, Antoine Henri Jomini," and Brodie suspects Clausewitz "would have been appalled" at recent efforts by "various army field manuals" that "attempt to encapsulate centuries of experience and volumes of reflection into a few tersely worded and usually numbered 'principles of war.'"[535] While such a "catalog of numbered principles . . . may be necessary to communicate to second-order minds (or minds too busy with the execution of plans to worry much about the specific validity of the ideas behind them)," or "may help the ordinary commander to avoid the most glaring or commonplace errors," Brodie believes a such a "catalog of principles must be recognized for what it is, which is a device intended to circumvent the need for months and years of study of and rumination on a very difficult subject," and notes that in his time, "in the training of the modern officer such study and rumination are not allowed for, either at the staff college level or the war college," as it "takes too much time" and requires "analytical and reflective qualities of mind that are not commonly found either among student officers or among their instructors."[536] On top of this, Brodie observes the "military services have learned very well that what they need most in their commanders is that quality called 'leadership,' and in this they are quite right."[537] As consequence, however, "that talent which is also necessary in the top leadership, that is, strategic insight, may come off a very poor second."[538] In Clausewitz's time, Brodie notes, this was resolved "by distinguishing between the qualities necessary in the commander, who was expected to provide leadership and aggressive drive, and his chief of staff, who was supposed to do much of his tactical and strategic thinking for him," much as Clausewitz himself had served.[539]

Brodie finds "[t]here are some today who yearn to see created a true science or theory of strategy, replete with principles that are both immutable and deeply meaningful, but they only indicate by that desire a basic misunderstanding of their subject," and taking his cue from Clausewitz's generality, recalls how "in these pages" he has "been lauding the modernity of Clausewitz," but that his modernity is not the kind to "give us the answers to our contemporary problems but which, at its best, will sharpen our receptivity to appropriate insights about those problems."[540] Brodie contrasts this strategic insight fostered by Clausewitz with the "twinge of delight" we feel when reading Plato's insights from two millennia ago: "It is not that Plato adds to our understanding; we can feel the pleasure only because that understanding already exists." However, he believes "[w]e do in fact *learn* something from Clausewitz—a good deal more, I think, than we ever learn from Plato," even though in the end "what we get from Clausewitz is a deepening of sensibility or insight rather than a body of rules."[541] Nevertheless, Brodie assures us that strategic thinking is ultimately "pragmatic," and thus aims to generate a "theory for action," one that accepts that "uncertainty is itself a factor to be reckoned with in one's strategic doctrine."[542] Because strategic theory is designed to be "transferable to the world of action," Brodie explains, "it is like other branches of politics and like any of the applied sciences, and not at all like pure science, where the function of theory is to describe, organize, and explain and not to prescribe."[543]

Brodie noted the civilian-scientific strategists belonged to "a group that evolved almost entirely since World War II, mostly in the United States, and usually associated with institutions like the RAND Corporation and a number of other organizations that have sprung up."[544] Brodie noted that the "use of scientists for assistance in making tactical suggestions goes back to at least World War I," but that "employment of scientists for advice in military decisions was carried very much further in World War II, especially in the novel field of strategic bombing," and at that war's end "the nuclear scientists showed what they had been up to all this time in the extremely secret Manhattan District Project," and "the prestige that the accomplishment of the nuclear bomb gave to scientists in general . . . accounted probably more than any other one thing for the conviction of General H. H. Arnold," the chief of staff of the U.S. Army Air Forces "that scientists should be retained on a continuing basis in peacetime," and so RAND was established as an outside, autonomous organization that was "closely associated" with the Air Force.[545]

His conviction on the continued utility of scientists to America's strategic planning was reinforced by the worrisome "fact that the Germans had rather disturbingly beat us in several important technological advances, including a jet engine" that may well "have been enough to stop entirely the Anglo-American air offensive" had it been applied not to bombers as Hitler urged, but instead to fighters.[546] Arnold's decision, Brodie added, was imitated by the other services. Brodie credits RAND for its "outstanding contribution . . . to modern strategic thinking" with systems analysis, which promised "to be far superior to anyone's simple, intuitive judgment,"[547] and to "produce far more reliable results."[548] With the election of John F. Kennedy, and his appointment of Robert S. McNamara as Secretary of Defense, came to the office of the Secretary of Defense "a mind most sympathetically attuned to the charms of systems analysis,"[549] which would come to play a central role in decision-making, resulting in a "struggle to control" the decision-making process with the services. Brodie cites several leading military men, whose opposition to the rise of the defense intellectual appeared uniform. General Thomas D. White, who served as Air Force chief of staff, wrote: "In common with many other military men, active and retired, I am profoundly apprehensive of the pipe-smoking, tree-full-of-owls type of so-called professional 'defense intellectuals' who have been brought into this nation's capitol. I don't believe a lot of these often over-confident, sometimes arrogant young professors, mathematicians and other theorists have sufficient worldliness or motivation to stand up to the kind of enemy we face."[550] And General Curtis LeMay, who headed up SAC and commanded the strategic bombing campaign in Japan, retiring after serving as Air Force chief of staff, echoed this sentiment, writing: "The military profession has been invaded by pundits who set themselves up as popular oracles on military strategy," and "Today's armchair strategists, glibly writing about military matters to a public avid for military news, can do incalculable harm. 'Experts' in a field where they have no experience, they propose strategies based upon hopes and fears rather than upon facts and seasoned judgments."[551] Brodie challenges LeMay, noting "[i]nsofar as he is clearly alluding to the trials of thermonuclear war, he does not explain where in fact the military have got the 'facts' and the 'seasoned judgments' that are denied to the civilians who are also occupying themselves full-time on the same problems."[552] Indeed, Brodie counters LeMay's dismissal of the seeming inexperience of civilian strategists by noting the "much-touted 'experience' that the military so commonly advance in their special claims to superior wisdom in military decisions is in this realm almost always irrelevant," though Brodie does concede, as he earlier did, that "[c]ertainly senior military men possess indispensable skills acquired only through experience," and "[c]hief of these is the ability to command."[553] But "when it comes to choosing major weapons systems for some future state of affairs that may be considerably more different from the present . . . there often exists no military experience whatever that is relevant."[554]

However, Brodie does not overplay his defense of the civilian strategists, noting their own "overvaluation of systems analysis," and he explains how "[t]he best of the systems analysts have most often been trained as economists,"[555] which means they are "normally extremely weak in either diplomatic or military history or even in contemporary politics," and yet are "rarely aware of how important a deficiency this is for strategic insight."[556] Brodie notes in contrast how "the great strategic writers and teachers of the past, with the sole and understandable exception of

Douhet, based the development of their art almost entirely on a broad and perceptive reading of history—in the case of Clausewitz and Jomini mostly recent history but exceptionally rich for their needs," while "the present generation of 'civilian strategists' are with markedly few exceptions singularly devoid of history."[557] And though Brodie admits, "[i]t could be argued that in a world that has to adopt itself to nuclear weapons, the reading of history may be an impediment," he concludes that this is not the case "if we continue to consider strategy what Clausewitz considered it—a branch of politics, a 'continuation of politics by other means.' "[558]

Brodie's efforts to empower the civilian defense intellectual, and to increase his influence over the formulation of strategic doctrine in the nuclear age, was a four-decade endeavor chronicled by his biographer, Barry Steiner, in his 1991 volume, *Bernard Brodie and the Foundations of American Nuclear Strategy.* As Steiner put it, "For forty years, until his death in 1978, Bernard Brodie's career as a strategist coincided with, and spurred on, the dispersion of strategic thinking away from the professionals on active military duty who had long monopolized it."[559] This was driven by "the growing legitimation of the subject of military strategy, by the rising demand within the military establishment for reflection about it, and by the unprecedented change in the conduct of war."[560] Steiner notes that after World War II, "when Brodie became especially prominent in rationalizing and guiding American ideas about strategy—that is, about the shaping of war-making forces to national objectives—the extent of the dispersion has been unparalleled."[561] Indeed, as Steiner credits, "One of Brodie's major postwar accomplishments was to legitimate the study of military strategy for civilians lacking a military background."[562]

Farewell Address: Brodie's Place in the Development of Nuclear Strategy

Brodie's final article would be published just months before his 1978 death in the pages of *International Security*—though it had first appeared two years earlier as a 1976 Advanced Concepts and Information Strategy (ACIS) working paper and later re-appeared posthumously as a chapter in the 1983 anthology *National Security and International Stability* that he co-edited with Michael D. Intriligator and Roman Kolkowicz, and which ensured Brodie had a hand in writing his own epitaph and thus a say in his own legacy. "The Development of Nuclear Strategy," as it was titled, was based on his plenary address at the Inter-University Seminar on Armed Forces and Society National Conference held at University of Chicago that year. It is fitting that this broad theme was the topic of his final article, since Brodie was a pivotal player from the very start of the atomic era when his phraseology would help to define the new era with the publication of *The Absolute Weapon*. His later effort to top this with the formulation of the "Missile Age" as what he hoped would become the defining concept of the next chapter of the nuclear age did not take—though his book by the same title, as earlier discussed, became one of the most highly regarded works on that era, and in many ways it was his failure to so define that next chapter of the nuclear period that would mark the beginning of his decline in influence. Nonetheless, even if he failed to achieve the same level of celebrity as his best-selling and more extroverted colleague Herman Kahn, he remained an active voice with a steady presence in the academic literature throughout the nuclear period right up until his death.

Brodie rightly claims credit for being there right at the starting gate, noting the central concept that "was put forward almost at once at the beginning of the nuclear age" and which was "still the dominant concept of nuclear strategy" was "deterrence," and that "[i]t fell to me—few other civilians at the time were interested in military strategy—to publish the first analytical paper on the military implications of nuclear weapons," his Fall 1945 Occasional Paper at the Yale Institute of International Studies, "The Atomic Bomb and American Security."[563] Adds

Brodie, "[i]n expanded form it was included as two chapters in a book published in the following year under the title *The Absolute Weapon*, which contained also essays on political implications by four of my Yale colleagues."[564] Brodie cited from that work his most famous paragraph, widely cited, with and without his approval, which stated that "the first and most vital step in any American security program for the age of atomic bombs is to take measures to guarantee to ourselves in case of attack the possibility of retaliation in kind," and while "[t]hus far the chief purpose of our military establishment has been to win wars. From now on its chief purpose must be to avert them. It can have almost no other useful purpose."[565] Brodie reflected that "while the idea of deterrence per se was certainly nothing new, being as old as the use of physical force, what was distinctively new was the degree to which it was intolerable that it should fail. On the other hand, one could add that 'in no case is the fear of the consequences of atomic bomb attack likely to be low,' which made it radically different from a past in which governments could, often correctly, anticipate wars that would bring them considerable political benefits while exacting very little in the way of costs."[566]

Brodie observes that since *The Absolute Weapon* was published over thirty years earlier, "there has been much useful rumination and writing on nuclear strategy and especially on the nature of deterrence, but the national debates on the subject have revolved mostly around three questions, all relating directly to the issue of expenditures," which were: "1) What are the changing physical requirements for the continuing success of deterrence? 2) Just what kinds of wars does nuclear deterrence really deter? and 3) What is the role, if any, for tactical nuclear weapons? Far down the course in terms of the public attention accorded it is a fourth question: If deterrence fails, how do we fight a nuclear war and for what objectives? The latter question has been almost totally neglected by civilian scholars, though lately some old ideas have been revived having to do with what are called limited nuclear options. Otherwise most questions about the actual use of nuclear weapons in war, whether strategic or tactical, have been largely left to the military, who had to shoulder responsibility for picking specific targets, especially in the strategic category, and who were expected to give guidance about the kinds and numbers of nuclear weapons required."[567] Brodie points out the unprecedented fact that "[v]irtually all the basic ideas and philosophies about nuclear weapons and their use have been generated by civilians working quite independently of the military, even though some resided in institutions like Rand which were largely supported by one or another of the services," and as a result, when it came to the new art of nuclear strategy, "the military have been, with no significant exceptions, strictly consumers, naturally showing preference for some ideas over others but hardly otherwise affecting the flow of those ideas."[568]

One consequence of the prominent role played by civilian strategists in conceptualizing deterrence was that "to the military man deterrence comes as the by-product, not the central theme, of his strategic structure," and "[a]ny philosophy which puts it at the heart of the matter must be uncongenial to him. One military writer significantly speaks of the deterrence-oriented 'modernist' as dwelling 'in the realm of achieving non-events in a condition where the flow of events is guided, not by his initiatives, but by other minds.' And further: 'The obvious difficulty with deterrent theory . . . is the yielding of the initiative to the adversary.'"[569] Brodie disagreed with the view that initiative was surrendered to the adversary, since "to prepare against all possible crises in the future, it is desirable to minimize that proportion of our retaliatory forces which the opponent can have high confidence of destroying by a surprise blow and to help keep alive in his mind full awareness of the penalties for miscalculation," which provided America with a mission to ensure that deterrence would endure until the political conditions that defined the Cold War stand-off resolved themselves, as they would just a decade after Brodie's death.

Brodie observes that the strategic community is "inhabited by peoples of a wide range of skills and sometimes of considerable imagination," and that as a result, "All sorts of notions and propositions are churned out," but whether they are "worth a second thought, however, is another matter," and "should undergo a good deal of thought before one begins to spend much money" in their development, since on matters of national defense, "sums spent on particular proposals can easily become huge."[570] Brodie cautions that "thinking up of ingenious new possibilities is deceptively cheap and easy, and the burden of proof must be on those who urge the payment of huge additional premiums for putting their particular notions into practice."[571] Brodie's own thoughtful analysis, across nearly half a century of technological and strategic change, instead proffered us a consistent set of ideas firmly embedded in an historical context—one that did not presume simplicity but instead recognized the complexities and ambiguities in the world, and in so doing, endeavored to reduce the grave dangers inherent therein and to combat lesser ideas that were oft-floated, whether in the pages of the popular press, more erudite scholarly journals, or top-secret-stamped memos circulating in the halls of power.

In a March 23, 1978 letter (just eight months before Brodie died from cancer on November 24 that year) from a then very young Dennis Ross—a 1970 graduate of UCLA and former graduate student in its political science department who would leave the academic world for the policy arena, rising to the very highest levels of power as an advisor to three American presidents in both major political parties—writing in praise of Brodie's final article, "The Development of Nuclear Strategy," "Dear Professor Brodie, I just wanted to drop you a note to let you know how much I enjoyed your recent ACIS paper—'The Development of Nuclear Strategy,'" noting Brodie had "reminded us, once again, of the larger questions we should be addressing. While my present surroundings seem to place a premium on narrow operational thinking, your teachings prevent me from straying too far into the realm of strategic fantasy—thanks. Take care, Dennis Ross."[572]

Strategy as an Art: A Classical-Military Response

In an intriguing response to the theorists of deterrence and the limitations of their civilian-scientific orientation is presented by U.S. Army Col. Richard L. Curl in his 1975 *Strategic Review* article, "Strategic Doctrine in the Nuclear Age."[573] Adding to its intrigue, this work—critical as it is—was nonetheless cited by Brodie himself in his Spring 1978 *International Security* article, "The Development of Nuclear Strategy," his final work. We will first examine Brodie's discussion of the article, and then look more closely Curl's critique of deterrence and its theoretical tradition.[574]

Brodie had observed how, "Since 1946 there has been much useful rumination and writing on nuclear strategy and especially on the nature of deterrence, but the national debates on the subject have revolved mostly around three questions, all relating directly to the issue of expenditures . . . 1) What are the changing physical requirements for the continuing success of deterrence? 2) Just what kinds of wars does nuclear deterrence really deter? and 3) What is the role, if any, for tactical nuclear weapons?"[575] But Brodie noted that "[f]ar down the course in terms of the public attention accorded it is a fourth question: If deterrence fails, how do we fight a nuclear war and for what objectives?"[576] Brodie contends that this "latter question has been almost totally neglected by civilian scholars," a view that Herman Kahn would surely disagree with, "though lately some old ideas have been revived having to do with what are called limited nuclear options. Otherwise most questions about the actual use of nuclear weapons in war, whether strategic or tactical, have been largely left to the military, who had to shoulder responsibility for picking specific targets, especially in the strategic category, and who were expected to give guidance about the kinds and numbers of nuclear weapons required. In that connection, one must stress a point which certain young historians who are new to the field have found it difficult to grasp.[577]

Brodie writes that "[v]irtually all the basic ideas and philosophies about nuclear weapons and their use have been generated by civilians working quite independently of the military, even though some resided in institutions like RAND which were largely supported by one or another of the services," and thus "the military have been, with no significant exceptions, strictly consumers, naturally showing preference for some ideas over others but hardly otherwise affecting the flow of those ideas. Whatever the reasons, they must include prominently the fact that to the military man deterrence comes as the by-product, not the central theme, of his strategic structure. Any philosophy which puts it at the heart of the matter must be uncongenial to him."[578] It is here that Brodie cites Curl, noting: "One military writer significantly speaks of the deterrence-oriented 'modernist' as dwelling 'in the realm of achieving non-events in a condition where the flow of events is guided, not by his initiatives, but by other minds.' And further: 'The obvious difficulty with deterrent theory . . . is the yielding of the initiative to the adversary.' In the preceding sentence initiative has already been called the sine qua non of success.[6]"[579] These quotations, as noted in footnote number six, are from Col. Richard L. Curl, "Strategic Doctrine in the Nuclear Age," *Strategic Review* 3 (Winter 1975), 48.

The article itself was derived from Curl's thesis at the U.S. Army War College, which juxtaposes the "classicist" versus "modernist" influences on military strategy, noting the former was "dominated by military-historical influences," but the "advent of the atomic era brought an ascendancy of civilian-scientific influences," and while "classical strategy sought to serve political ends by achieving military victory, the modern strategists have been preoccupied with avoiding war, not with winning it," a preoccupation that Curl argues dates back before the atomic era when "concern for the destructive power of weapons had led some to conclude that war was now impractical and weapons should be limited by agreement," but whose "[e]xpectations of universal peace foundered in an era of great wars."[580] Curl's article starts off with Brodie's famed aphorism, first articulated in 1945 but more widely read in his contributions to the 1946 *The Absolute Weapon*, and to which Curl attributes Brodie's famous words: "Thus far the chief purpose of our military establishment has been to win wars. But from now on, its chief purpose must be to avert them. It can have almost no other useful purpose." As Curl observes, "When Bernard Brodie and his collaborators in the Yale Institute of International Studies penned these lines in 1946, they were giving expression to a philosophy which seemed so apparent, considering the awesome destructive potential of the A-Bomb, so attuned to the American view of war as an unmitigated disaster, and so compatible with America's new position as a satiated superpower, that the philosophy rapidly became dogma," and this "dogma, in turn, became the foundation for the strategy of deterrence which has guided our national military and foreign policy ever since."[581]

It is intriguing that Curl recognizes Brodie's philosophy had reified into dogma, and also ironic in that Brodie was such a passionate critic of doctrinaire thinking and his entire approach to the philosophy of war, with all its complexities, has been to resist dogma and the over-simplification of reality that it courts, as evident in his critique of rules-based military handbooks that seek to boil down war's many complexities into simple, actionable aphorisms. Brodie waged a lifelong battle against dogma, and dueled with those he felt succumbed to its oversimplicity, emulating Clausewitz and rebuking Jomini for failing to embrace complexity with the same fervor as the Prussian he so admired. That his efforts helped foster the emergence of the predominant strategic dogma of the Cold War is truly sardonic. Curl believes Brodie's 1946 book "marked a dramatic change in the character and quantity of American strategic thought," one Curl believes was "dramatic enough to be termed revolutionary" with three parts: first that the "influential thinking was now overwhelmingly 'civilian-scientific' instead of 'military-historical';" secondly, that as a "consequence, the center of gravity of strategic thinking shifted from its traditional European base to America;" and thirdly, that the "'classical' strategist was relegated, if not to an intellectual graveyard, at least to a semi-moribund state of catatonia."[582] In contrast to *classicist* who "devoted his time and talent to determining how wars could be won," the new *modernist* instead "believed that force could be eliminated or at the very least intelligently controlled" and in so doing "took the *threat* of the use of force as a major element in the definition of strategy, and devoted their time to determining how wars could be avoided."[583]

The classicist favors action, while the modernist hopes for inaction, or as Curl describes, in the passage that caught Brodie's eye and was subsequently quoted in his Spring 1978 *International Security* article, his very last article before he passed from this world that very same year: "The classicist can focus on fairly concrete events and outcomes while the modernist must dwell in the realm of achieving non-events in a condition where the flow of events is guided, not by his initiatives, but by other minds. In classical strategic theory, the initiative is considered a *sine qua non*—the key to success."[584] Moreover, Curl argues, the "superior strategist is he who controls his adversary's actions—who causes him to react predictably and to the strategist's advantage. The obvious difficulty with deterrent theory in these terms is the yielding of the initiative to the adversary," and thus it is "scarcely surprising then to find, as one traces the development of deterrent theory to America, a distinct thread of intellectual frustration over this point. Indeed the search for the initiative, though disguised with words such as 'increased options' or 'flexibility,' is the single most prominent evolutionary thread of modern strategic theory."[585]

This thread sought to redress the general neglect by deterrence theorists to offer a road-map forward should deterrence fail; indeed, Brodie, even in his seminal 1959 *Strategy in the Missile Age*, which "essentially codified deterrent theory to that point . . . offered no thought on how, if worst came to worst and deterrence somehow failed, nuclear war should or could be conducted."[586] And so it "was left to one of his RAND colleagues, Herman Kahn, to attempt for the first time in his behemoth effort, *On Thermonuclear War*, a more classical-oriented approach on how to survive and win," and which argued "nuclear war could be ended with a majority of the U.S. population surviving—the proportion of which could be increased by a number of pre-paratory measures," and that there existed "options which might be available within a range of nuclear conflicts," so instead of "assuming a spasm type of war as the only possibility, Kahn suggested a controlled nuclear war-fighting strategy with targets tied to political ends."[587] While Kahn's classical approach to strategy generated a "barrage of criticism ranging from unfriendly to hysterical" from the more modernist deterrence theorists that was "notable more for a sense of moral outrage than for objective or intelligent analysis," Curl lauds Kahn for restoring "some of the key elements of an operational, positive strategy which had been missing for the past ten years."[588] The clash of Brodie's thesis with Kahn's antithesis would yield to a new synthesis of "*enhanced* deterrence" that went beyond "graduated response" to a more "credible response," but as Curl describes, "deterrent theory had seen an increasing search for a strategy more sensitive to the classical concepts but still centered, first and foremost, on the avoidance of war."[589]

Brodie—in contrast to the gregarious Kahn (whose training was as a physicist and whose strength appears to have been in his ability to deliver engaging, often hilarious, and almost always marathon briefings)—was much more the *philosopher* of nuclear war whereas Kahn would be its chief publicist. Their written works addressed many of the very same themes, often at the same time, but whose styles and personalities so differed with a notable impact on the reach and influence of their efforts, Brodie penetrating more deeply into the fundamental, indeed one might say *academic*, essence while Kahn more broadly disseminating ideas to the lay public as well as the policy and warfighting communities. This parallelism strikes an uncanny resemblance to the rivalry between Clausewitz and Jomini during the Napoleonic period, so much so that both Clausewitz and Brodie would die much sooner than their more popular rivals, and as a result,

Kahn and Jomini would not only get the last say, so to speak, but they would be able to lay the institutional foundation for their influence to penetrate deeply into the formulation of military doctrine during their lifetimes and in the years that immediately followed. It would take the passage of much time for Clausewitz to be rediscovered, and for his voice to finally echo well beyond his grave as new generations of theorists found his wisdom reached far into the future, and this is in part one of my reasons for revisiting the works of Brodie, sensing the time may be right for his wisdom to emulate that of his great Prussian mentor and reach across the chasm of time. On the irony of Kahn's greater notoriety, one of his popular works was *Thinking About the Unthinkable*, with a new edition to come out immediately after his death called *Thinking About the Unthinkable in the 1980s*, influencing the debate that was then raging on nuclear strategy even after he had passed on to eternity.

Brodie had sought to label the thermonuclear era as the "Missile Age," inspired by the earlier "Machine Age" that became part of his first book's title, *Sea Power in the Machine Age*, insisting to his publisher that his widely regarded *Strategy in the Missile Age* retain the "Missile Age" in its title. His original title was *Strategy Meets the Missile Age*, which his publisher found awkward on the ear. Even the famous concept of the *absolute weapon*, while the title of the 1946 book on nuclear strategy edited by Brodie, was not his own invention—but that of his colleague and fellow contributor to *The Absolute Weapon*, William T. R. Fox, but it would be forever tied to Brodie because this influential book appeared with his byline, under his editorial leadership.[590]

Brodie's and Kahn's topics were nearly identical, but their styles, their philosophical and theoretical approaches, and their use of language greatly differed—sometimes subtly, sometimes obviously. While the warfighters favored action over inaction and were thus prepared (on the surface) to cross the nuclear threshold, and the deterrers favored inaction over action and thus sought to preserve that threshold forever unbroken, each in his own way thought about, and risked, the unthinkable. The warfighters appeared, on the surface, to be more firmly in the tradition of classical realism (their language was bolder, and more aligned with action), but it was the deterrers who threatened a far more absolute Apocalypse in their effort to hold the line and to prevent the outbreak of nuclear war. What they threatened to unleash was far more destructive than the more limited nuclear use contemplated by the warfighters (at least during the early stages of nuclear war). Which approach was the more dangerous, and which more likely to sustain the peace, remained a riddle throughout the Cold War, and even in these many years since that conflict's quiet end, the ambiguity remains, unresolved.

Brodie famously probed deeply, hoping to penetrate the fog of complexity, in contrast to Kahn, who surveyed broadly, aiming for clarity and in the end achieving celebrity for his efforts. It was Brodie who had the most enduring impact on the evolution of strategic theory, while Kahn's approach found greater favor in the formulation of strategic doctrine—as noted by Jeffrey D. Porro in the June/July 1982 edition of *The Bulletin of the Atomic Scientists*. Porro examined the battle for strategic influence between Brodie and Kahn, one of the few articles to explicitly juxtapose these two prominent theorists within a dialectical framework, with Brodie representing the Clausewitzian perspective, and Kahn representing a decidedly non-Clausewitzian perspective.[591] Porro's article starts out by noting, "The ideas of two men have set the terms of the debate among U.S. policymakers over nuclear strategy. For the moment, the view of one has prevailed," namely Herman Kahn; "But if we are to reduce the risk of nuclear war, we must return to those of the other," none other than Bernard Brodie. As Porro observes, "Throughout his work, Kahn the physicist never asked the questions that bothered Brodie: What possible political goal could justify the loss of a hundred cities or even a 'few' million people? Could the people of a nation which suffered even 'limited' nuclear damage be expected, in Brodie's words, to 'show much concern for the further pursuit of political-military objectives?'"[592] And while not everyone "who rejected Brodie's view of nuclear strategy agreed completely with Kahn," or disagreed with Kahn's rosy optimism on "the prospects of recovery from nuclear war," most came to believe "Brodie's view of deterrence was insufficient, and that it would be more advantageous for us if our forces could fight a nuclear war by attacking the Soviet military."[593] And while "supporters of Brodie's version of deterrence were far from silent," Porro found that "they no longer had their former impact" and by "late 1976, even the 'moderates' writing about nuclear arms accepted the need for increased war fighting capabilities."[594] While "[s]ome in what had become the minority Brodie school placed their hopes in the election of Jimmy Carter," Porro observes that Harold Brown, Carter's defense secretary, "began to sound like the others. In 1978 he said: 'We cannot afford to make a complete distinction between deterrence forces and what are so awkwardly called war-fighting forces.' Over the next two years he elaborated what he called a 'countervailing strategy,' which meant having plans 'to attack the targets which comprise the Soviet military force struc-ture and political power structure, and to hold back a significant reserve.' "[595]

While Brodie had acknowledged, in *War and Politics* in 1973, that it was "not acceptable to all that deterrence is all-important and that 'winning' is a matter of crude and brutal irrelevance," and noted "the military, among others, have consistently refused to accept this notion,"[596] by the end of Brodie's life, what had once been a dialectic pitting Brodie's thesis against Kahn's antithesis had achieved a synthesis of sorts. As the dueling ideas of the *Wizards of Armageddon*, the phrase elegantly coined by Fred Kaplan, inched their way closer to reality, and the debate became entwined by the evolution of doctrine and policy, a passionate and partisan debate that engaged academia, government, and the military for over a generation would find a consen-sual middle ground, aiming for deterrence while preparing for its failure. We thus witnessed a fascinating dialectical interaction between theory and doctrine, as abstract thought interacted with the constant probing of military action (and preparations)—and in this dance of thought influencing action (which in turn influenced thought again), deterrence and warfighting began to converge, forming a nuclear dialectic that guided the pace and composition of the arms race between the Soviet Union and the United States, until the two competing superpowers, locked in their own deadly struggle, experience their own unique, and unexpected, synthesis, bringing to a peaceful end a struggle that had once threatened an Apocalyptic end to civilization itself.

Brodie Remembered: A "Gardener in the Fields of the Mind"

In its obituary marking the passing of Bernard Brodie on November 24, 1978, *Arms Control Today* recalled in its February 1979 issue how five years earlier, in her dedication of *Thomas Jefferson: An Intimate History*, Fawn Brodie wrote, "to Bernard, ever the young gardener," and explained that Brodie, "like Jefferson, took joy in working the soil of his garden," and under his attentive care, the "Brodie hilltop . . . dripped color and fragrance under Bernard's hands."[597] It was "[w]ith the same attentiveness—and the same fecundity" that Brodie "gardened in the fields of the mind," and across his "twenty-years of teaching, writing and lecturing, he left those who think about military history, strategy and arms control a good deal to ponder."[598] Further, the "richness of Bernard Brodie's work came from his sensible bias against lifting problems of strategy from their contexts in human history and human psychology," as he "spent a lifetime cautioning against what he called 'the temptation to throw the past out the window.' "[599]

Noting his foresight, Brodie "wrote *The Absolute Weapon* in 1946, just a year after the use of the first atomic bomb at Hiroshima, when debates were still raging about what exactly *were* the physical effects of an atomic blast," while "[t]oday the paragraphs" of that work "seem extraordi-narily prescient."[600] To Brodie, the "gravest danger . . . would result from a failure of U.S. military and political leaders to adjust to the atomic bomb in their thinking and planning," and was one of the very first to foresee "the nature of mutual deterrence" between the superpowers.[601] He "shaped as well as predicted the U.S. approach to strategy in the atomic age," and was a "technical advisor to the U.S. delegation at the United Nations Conference in 1945, a RAND Corporation thinker, a teacher at Dartmouth, Yale and [the] University of California at Los Angeles, a visiting scholar at Princeton and the Carnegie Endowment, and a frequent lecturer to the military at the National War College in Washington, and elsewhere," and further "supplemented the influence of his writing with the imprint he left upon three generations of students, colleagues, military officers and friends."[602] Importantly, his "word always carried an optimism that through logic and rationality mankind could cut through the darkness of the atomic age." And so, "Many, many generations of students of defense will look to Bernard Brodie's lifetime of thought as a touchstone of reasoned thinking, persuasive argumentation, rich contextuality, and great wisdom."[603] A survey of Brodie's contribution to the strategic literature was presented in the 1981 article in the U.S. Army War College's journal, *Parameters*, by Col. (ret.) William P. Snyder and Col. John A. MacIntyre, Jr., who argue that Brodie "was the most original and thoughtful of the civilian strategists who helped shape American and Western strategic thought in recent decades and deserves ranking with the major classical strategists."[604]

Several months after Brodie's death, Thomas C. Schelling, the famed strategist, game theorist and recent Nobel laureate, published "A Tribute to Bernard Brodie and (Incidentally) to RAND" in the Winter 1978/79 edition of *International Security* 3, No. 3, which was reissued as a RAND paper in July 1979. In it, he noted: "The 1950s were the first time in at least a century that Americans became professionally concerned, in peacetime, with military strategy," and "[a]mong the originators of that academic profession, Bernard Brodie was first—both in time and in distinction," and in addition to his early works on naval strategy, "[a]s editor and one of the chief contributors to *The Absolute Weapon* (1946), he set standards for thinking about nuclear strategy;" and "his articles on limited war, deterrence, and strategy as science . . . culminating in *Strategy in the Missile Age* (1959), were of an analytical and literary distinction that set him apart," making him a "central figure in the RAND 'oral tradition' that gave shape to strategic thinking as it emerged in the 1960s and—it is still about all we have—the 1970s."[605] Schelling wrote that by the mid-1960s, Brodie "had to change sides on a number of policies to oppose 'carrying an intrinsically good idea so much too far,' publishing the brief and slightly polemical *Escalation and the Nuclear Option*,"[606] followed by in 1973 his *War and Politics*, which revisited the very real wars fought in his lifetime "rather than the hypothetical nuclear wars that his own work, I truly believe, has helped us to avoid."

As Schelling saluted his esteemed colleague and close friend: "He, more than anyone else, helped us to learn to think about to survive in a world with nuclear weapons."[607]

Notes

[1-5] Bruce Fleming, "Can Reading Clausewitz Save Us from Future Mistakes?" *Parameters* (Spring 2004): 65–6; 66; 66–7; 68–9; 69, respectively.

[6-8] Bernard Brodie, "Strategy as an Art and a Science," February 1959. Online at: www.maxwell.af.mil/au/awc/awcgate/theorists/brodie1.htm. (Note 6 adds: At this point in his speech, he said the following words that I have edited out for space considerations: "Clausewitz was himself a professional officer and also a profound student not only of war but of the science and philosophy of his times. He was a great admirer, for example, of the philosopher Hegel, who was ten years older than he and who died in the same cholera epidemic of 1831. His admiration caused him, unfortunately, to imitate the characteristic Hegelian dialectic in his own writing. Thus, like Hegel, he presents first the thesis of his argument; then, the antithesis; and, finally, the synthesis. This is the characteristic which makes Hegel so difficult to read, and such is also the case with Clausewitz. We see it, for example, in the first chapter of his book entitled *On War*—the only chapter he edited and considered completed before his death—in which he sets forth, first, the proposition

that war in its pure form scorns any modifications of violence. This is the theme on which the book opens, and it is developed with considerable eloquence. Then, suddenly, after a few pages, he begins to develop the opposite theme: that war, however, never exists in its pure form but is rather a phase in the political activity of states. This brings him to qualify considerably everything he said previously about war being pure violence. Because of his dialectical method, Clausewitz is very difficult to understand by anyone who tries to read him casually. But he is easy enough to quote, and some of the sentences in his opening pages have quite a lot of blood and thunder in them. The authority of his words has therefore been used to underline the absurdity of trying to moderate war when, in fact, the whole tenor of his book is that war is a political act and must therefore be governed by the political objective. He returns to this theme again and again throughout the book.")

9-10 Ken Booth, "Bernard Brodie," in John Baylis and John Garnett, eds, *Makers of Nuclear Strategy* (London: Pinters Press, 1991), 19; 19, respectively.

11-13 John Baylis and John C. Garnett, eds, *Makers of Nuclear Strategy* (London: Pinters Press, 1991), 4; 5; 6, respectively.

14-16 Booth, "Bernard Brodie," 19; 19; 19, respectively.

17-23 Marc Trachtenberg, *History and Strategy* (Princeton: Princeton University Press, 1991), 7; 45; 134 (n. 121); 138; 138 (n. 136); 138; 261, respectively.

24-67 Barry Steiner, *Bernard Brodie and the Foundations of American Nuclear Strategy*, 7; 7; 202 (citing "The Continuing Relevance of *On War*," in Paret and Howard, tr., Carl von Clausewitz, *On War* (Princeton: Princeton University Press, 1976); 51); 15 (citing Bernard Brodie, "Changing Capabilities and War Objectives," Lecture to the Air War College, April 17, 1952, 2); 15; 15; 26; 26; 195; 195; 195; 202–3; 203; 205; 206; 206; 234; 236; 237; 238; 41; 241–2; 242; 246; 246; 249; 249; 249; 217; 217; 218 (Steiner also cites Brodie's January 1973 *World Politics* article, "On Clausewitz: A Passion for War," which delves more deeply into Clausewitz's inner psyche: "The blood phrases so often quotes out of context from Clausewitz's great posthumous work burn with their own fierce fire. They are kindled by something within. They are indeed countered and, on intellectual balance, overcome with other words in which the intellect is at work rather than passion; and the intellect in this case is tremendously strong. This intellect is guided by a firm honesty, so that he will not refrain from going where it directs him and from expressing every thought that it brings to him. But the destructive passion against which that intellect is working is also strong. We are dealing here with a deep internal conflict, and there can be no doubt that this conflict is directly linked to his growing depression." Steiner, *Foundations of American Nuclear Strategy*, 219); 219; 220; 222–3; 203; 203; 238; 212; 213; 222–3; 152; 152; 171, respectively.

68-9 Paret, Letter to Brodie, November 7, 1963, Bernard Brodie Papers (Collection 1223), Department of Special Collections, Charles E. Young Research Library, UCLA.

70-2 Paret, Letter to Brodie, November 13, 1963, Bernard Brodie Papers (Collection 1223), Department of Special Collections, Charles E. Young Research Library, UCLA.

73-5 Brodie, Letter to Paret, Jan 17, 1964, Bernard Brodie Papers (Collection 1223), Department of Special Collections, Charles E. Young Research Library, UCLA.

76-80 Brodie, memo to C. A. H. Thomson, J. M. Goldsen, and R. McDermott , January 22, 1964, Bernard Brodie Papers (Collection 1223), Department of Special Collections, Charles E. Young Research Library, UCLA.

81 Klaus Knorr, Letter to Brodie, January 22, 1964, Bernard Brodie Papers (Collection 1223), Department of Special Collections, Charles E. Young Research Library, UCLA.

82-3 Brodie, Letter to Knorr, January 24, 1964, Bernard Brodie Papers (Collection 1223), Department of Special Collections, Charles E. Young Research Library, UCLA.

84 Brodie, Letter to Knorr, February 26, 1964, Bernard Brodie Papers (Collection 1223), Department of Special Collections, Charles E. Young Research Library, UCLA.

85-6 Knorr, Letter to Brodie, March 2, 1964, Bernard Brodie Papers (Collection 1223), Department of Special Collections, Charles E. Young Research Library, UCLA.

87 Brodie, Letter to Gordon Hubel, March 18, 1964, Bernard Brodie Papers (Collection 1223), Department of Special Collections, Charles E. Young Research Library, UCLA.

88-9 Brodie, Letter to Gordon Hubel, March 19, 1964, Bernard Brodie Papers (Collection 1223), Department of Special Collections, Charles E. Young Research Library, UCLA.

[90-1] Brodie, Letter to Knorr, March 27, 1964, Bernard Brodie Papers (Collection 1223), Department of Special Collections, Charles E. Young Research Library, UCLA.

[92-3] Princeton University Public Announcement, April 10, 1964, Department of Public Information, Princeton University, Bernard Brodie Papers (Collection 1223), Department of Special Collections, Charles E. Young Research Library, UCLA.

[94] Paret, Letter to Brodie, April 25, 1964, Bernard Brodie Papers (Collection 1223), Department of Special Collections, Charles E. Young Research Library, UCLA.

[95-6] J. M. Goldsen, RAND memo to George Clement, May 7, 1964, Bernard Brodie Papers (Collection 1223), Department of Special Collections, Charles E. Young Research Library, UCLA.

[97-8] Brodie, Letter to Knorr, May 15, 1964, Bernard Brodie Papers (Collection 1223), Department of Special Collections, Charles E. Young Research Library, UCLA.

[99-100] Brodie, Letter to Paret, May 22, 1964, Brodie, Letter to Paret, May 22, 1964, Bernard Brodie Papers (Collection 1223), Department of Special Collections, Charles E. Young Research Library, UCLA.

[101] Brodie, Letter to Paret, May 28, 1964, Bernard Brodie Papers (Collection 1223), Department of Special Collections, Charles E. Young. Research Library, UCLA.

[102] Paret, Letter to Brodie, May 31, 1964, Bernard Brodie Papers (Collection 1223), Department of Special Collections, Charles E. Young. Research Library, UCLA.

[103] Gordon Hubel, Letter to Brodie, July 29, 1964, Bernard Brodie Papers (Collection 1223), Department of Special Collections, Charles E. Young. Research Library, UCLA.

[104-7] Minutes from 13–14 June 1964 Meeting of the Editorial Board, Princeton University Press,, Bernard Brodie Papers (Collection 1223), Department of Special Collections, Charles E. Young. Research Library, UCLA.

[108-9] Paret, Letter to Brodie April 23, 1967, Bernard Brodie Papers (Collection 1223), Department of Special Collections, Charles E. Young. Research Library, UCLA.

[110-11] Brodie, Letter to Paret, May 1, 1967, Bernard Brodie Papers (Collection 1223), Department of Special Collections, Charles E. Young. Research Library, UCLA.

[112] Bailey, Letter to Brodie, January 12, 1973, Bernard Brodie Papers (Collection 1223), Department of Special Collections, Charles E. Young. Research Library, UCLA.

[113-48] Bernard Brodie, "Review: On Clausewitz: A Passion for War," *World Politics* 25, No. 2 (January 1973), 288–308; 288; 288; 289; 288; 290; 290–1; 291; 291; 292; 292; 293; 293–4; 299; 299–300; 301; 301; 302; 302; 302; 303; 303–4; 304; 304–5; 305; 305; 305; 306; 306; 306; 306–7; 307; 308; 308, respectively.

[149-52] Bailey, Letter to Brodie, January 12, 1973, Bernard Brodie Papers (Collection 1223), Department of Special Collections, Charles E. Young. Research Library, UCLA.

[153-5] Bernard Brodie, *War and Politics* (New York: Macmillan, 1973), viii; viii; viii, respectively.

[156] See Henry A. Kissinger and Bernard Brodie, eds, *Bureaucracy, Politics, and Strategy*, Security Studies Paper No. 17 (Los Angeles: University of California, Los Angeles, 1968), particularly its fifth chapter/paper, "Theories on the Causes of War," 46–60.

[157] See: Bernard Brodie, "Why Were We So (Strategically) Wrong?" *Foreign Policy* 5 (Winter 1971–1972), 151–61 and Bernard Brodie, *Strategy and National Interests: Reflections for the Future* (New York: National Strategy Information Center, 1971).

[158] Bernard Brodie, "Learning to Fight a Limited War," in *The Political Dimension in National Strategy: Five Papers*, Security Studies Paper No. 13 (Los Angeles: UCLA, 1968), 32.

[159-69] Brodie, *War and Politics*, 364; 1; 496; 240 (What Brodie may have overlooked is that Plato wanted the ruler to comprehend, and sustain, the foundational geometry of state since the just city was a balanced one, and balance required a geometrical understanding. And so geometry, as Thomas Hobbes would later also recognize, became an essential tool of statecraft and governance as rulers sought to maintain a domestic equilibrium while at the same time endeavoring to do the same within the international realm. In more modern times, balance of power politics and geopolitics would reflect a geometrical conception of world politics.); 451; 451; 452; 452; vii; 2; 2, respectively. "Unfortunately," Newell Bringhurst, the biographer of Fawn M. Brodie, observed: "*War and Politics*, which Bernard regarded as his most important work, was not initially well received, although in time it did gain the recognition it deserved. The book's early failure was due, at least in part, to the fact that neither Bernard nor his ideas were attracting the attention of important foreign policy experts. Contributing to Bernard's diminished visibility since the 1940s and 1950s was

his physical condition, as well as the 'writer's block' he had suffered during the 1960s. Removed from the public spotlight, he had lost the prominence he had once enjoyed in the field of American foreign policy." Newell G. Bringhurst, *Fawn McKay Brodie: A Biographer's Life* (Norman: University of Oklahoma Press, 1999), 221.

[170-1] Bailey, Letter to Brodie, February 22, 1973, Bernard Brodie Papers (Collection 1223), Department of Special Collections, Charles E. Young. Research Library, UCLA.

[172-80] Brodie, Letter to Bailey, May 19, 1973, Bernard Brodie Papers (Collection 1223), Department of Special Collections, Charles E. Young. Research Library, UCLA.

[181-4] Bailey, Letter to Paret, May 22, 1973, Bernard Brodie Papers (Collection 1223), Department of Special Collections, Charles E. Young. Research Library, UCLA.

[185-6] Bailey, Letter to Brodie, May 22, 1973, Bernard Brodie Papers (Collection 1223), Department of Special Collections, Charles E. Young. Research Library, UCLA.

[187] R. Miriam Brokaw, Letter to Brodie, September 14, 1973, Bernard Brodie Papers (Collection 1223), Department of Special Collections, Charles E. Young. Research Library, UCLA.

[188-90] Bailey, Letter to Brodie, September 16, 1973, Bernard Brodie Papers (Collection 1223), Department of Special Collections, Charles E. Young. Research Library, UCLA.

[191-4] Brodie, Letter to Paret, Jan 21, 1974, Bernard Brodie Papers (Collection 1223), Department of Special Collections, Charles E. Young. Research Library, UCLA.

[195] "Princeton Press Contract for Clausewitz" and dated February 28, 1974, Bernard Brodie Papers (Collection 1223), Department of Special Collections, Charles E. Young. Research Library, UCLA.

[196-201] Brodie, Letter to Paret, May 30, 1974, Bernard Brodie Papers (Collection 1223), Department of Special Collections, Charles E. Young. Research Library, UCLA.

[202-4] Michael Howard, Letter to Brodie, August 23, 1974, Bernard Brodie Papers (Collection 1223), Department of Special Collections, Charles E. Young. Research Library, UCLA.

[205-23] Brodie, Letter to Howard, September 1, 1974, Bernard Brodie Papers (Collection 1223), Department of Special Collections, Charles E. Young. Research Library, UCLA.

[224] Paret, Letter to Brodie, September 11, 1974, Bernard Brodie Papers (Collection 1223), Department of Special Collections, Charles E. Young. Research Library, UCLA.

[225-40] Howard, Letter to Brodie, September 18, 1974, Bernard Brodie Papers (Collection 1223), Department of Special Collections, Charles E. Young. Research Library, UCLA.

[241-2] Howard, Letter to Brodie, in response to Brodie's September 23, 1974 letter, Bernard Brodie Papers (Collection 1223), Department of Special Collections, Charles E. Young. Research Library, UCLA.

[243-56] Brodie, Letter to Howard, October 3, 1974, Bernard Brodie Papers (Collection 1223), Department of Special Collections, Charles E. Young. Research Library, UCLA. Note 255 continues: Brodie further elaborates on these two points: Concerning point 1: You know much more than I about eighteenth-century warfare, and also about nineteenth- and twentieth-century warfare for that matter. However, I have just finished studying very carefully a fine, new translation of Clausewitz, who throughout his work makes frequent comparisons between eighteenth-century warfare and what he calls the "modern" style, which he identifies with the Napoleonic. His comments are usually to the effect that eighteenth-century warfare was "lacking in energy," and "incoherent," with the campaign of one year bearing little relation to the campaign of the next, etc. I enclose a couple of paragraphs selected almost at random, but these happen to be from Bk. IV, Chapter 12, which I shall be quoting in the essay I am writing for Klaus Knorr. Concerning point 2: The key sentence is what you say at the top of p. 15. Your wording has changed somewhat, but you speak now of Cl.'s alleged "disdain for strategic maneuver." I see no evidence of such disdain in *On War*, and I see plenty of evidence of the opposite. I see evidence of concern with strategic and tactical maneuver. As I think I said previously, he shows over and over again a real hatred of frontal attacks (an attitude he shared with Wellington) which I think to be pretty significant considering his times as compared with World War I and also considering the attitudes he might have been expected to have about the "pushes" of World War I. When you talk about Cl's alleged advocacy of compelling the enemy "to use up his reserves at a greater rate than one is expending one's own," I think that word "compel" is not really justified, but more to the point, Cl. is describing a decisive battle which begins and ends in one day, and where the real victory, meaning the real destructed of the enemy's forces, comes in the pursuit during the night following the battle. He makes quite a point of the fact that during the battle the losses tend to be approximately equivalent on both sides (which is bad but acceptable because of what follows) but it is during the pursuit following the

battle that the enemy's army suffers the great losses and one's own suffers almost none. Naturally, one can say that a one-day battle was out of the question by 1914, but one of the reasons I said in my last letter that Schlieffen comes closest among his contemporaries to being Clausewitzian in his ideas was that he wanted to condense into several days (rather than several months or years) the kind of battle that Clausewitz was specifically describing as taking place within one day. And the kind of maneuver (strategic) that Schlieffen set up for the execution of his plan comes straight out of Bk. VIII, Chapter 9 of *On War*. I think you would be justified in saying that only by the most superficial (hence unwarranted) analogies could the generals of W.W.I claim to find some inspiration in Clausewitz. Concerning Cl's "dogged refusal to be put off by heavy casualties," we simply cannot know from his attitudes concerning Napoleonic-type wars what they would have been for W.W.I. After all, he was the one who insisted that strategy must conform to the political objective, and I wonder whether he would not have found the casualties accepted in W.W.I as being in conflict with that basic principle.

[257–62] Bailey, Letter to Brodie, October 10, 1974, Bernard Brodie Papers (Collection 1223), Department of Special Collections, Charles E. Young. Research Library, UCLA.

[263–5] Bailey, Letter to Paret, October 10, 1974, Bernard Brodie Papers (Collection 1223), Department of Special Collections, Charles E. Young. Research Library, UCLA. Note 265 continues: The full text of Bailey's comments to Paret follows: "On first reading I had the impression that Peter's essay was a little longer than it needed to be, and that there were some unnecessary repetitions. I didn't mark them, and last night I went back through the essay to try to see where it could be easily cut. Frankly I didn't find the sort of cutting that I thought might be possible, so perhaps my first impression was wrong. At any rate I think that the essay might be looked at again in this light, and I'll ask Lewis to keep this in mind also when he goes through it. I thoroughly enjoyed Michael Howard's piece on the influence of ON WAR, but I had a little feeling of letdown at the end, with the brief reference to MacArthur's dismissal during the Korean war. Was there no influence of Clausewitz on the Viet Nam War or on the Arab-Israeli conflict? Bernard refers to Viet Nam on page 12 of his essay. Perhaps it was planned to leave these more modern references to Bernard, but I kept wondering whether there ought not to be at least references to such events as the war of attrition during negotiations in Korea, the concept of limited war in the nuclear age, the development of political control and political officers in the Communist military doctrine, and the emergence of guerilla warfare as a significant modern variety. I would like to see a little more said about these topics either in the Howard essay or in Brodie's. It would be false and misleading to give the impression that Clausewitz had said the last word on all types of warfare, but one gets the strong feeling from the Howard and Paret essays and from the first part of the Brodie essay that Clausewitz really is very relevant today. But on page 15 of Bernard's essay he says, "Nevertheless, we must now really confront this issue of datedness, and consider to what extent this factor detracts from the utility of reading Clausewitz today." Then through page 19 there follows a series of rather weak arguments, with several "fall-back positions," that are almost enough to convince one that reading Clausewitz is hardly worth the trouble. I wonder whether this can't be stated more positively without being false to the material. This concludes my observations on the essays, though I want to finish by saying that I thoroughly enjoyed them and believe they will serve as excellent introductions to the Clausewitz text. I shall look forward to hearing what you think about all this."

[266–8] Paret, Letter to Brodie, September 22, 1975, Bernard Brodie Papers (Collection 1223), Department of Special Collections, Charles E. Young. Research Library, UCLA.

[269] Lewis Bateman, Letter to Brodie, December 19, 1975, Bernard Brodie Papers (Collection 1223), Department of Special Collections, Charles E. Young. Research Library, UCLA.

[270–4] Brodie, Letter to Bailey, December 25, 1975, Bernard Brodie Papers (Collection 1223), Department of Special Collections, Charles E. Young. Research Library, UCLA. Note 271 continues: Brodie continued, "What I am worried about is that its very existence will be overlooked by all sorts of casual reviewers and browsers, yes, all eighty-odd pages of it. I am not putting an exaggerated value on my own work; it is enough that others besides myself thought it worth including in this volume. I am only saying that so long as it is there, its presence ought to be adequately signaled. Let me not be vain about it, but it might even help to sell the book. The type size in which it is presently given is the same as that for the individual chapters of ON WAR, some of which will be only one page long and none over about twenty-five pages. . . . I think that the Guide, and for that matter also the three introductory 'commentaries', should be set off in a type of a size approximating that used for the titles of the eight books of ON WAR, which individually happen to average about the length of my Guide (though I well understand that length is not all there is to it). In any case it seems to me a strange notion, indeed an absurd one, that in a matter of this importance the designer 'will make the final decision.' This is the first time I've encountered that idea. Bateman seems to have anticipated my disappointment with the title pages, because he suggests that any reservations I might have be taken up by Peter Paret. This I shall do by sending Peter a copy of this letter. I do not feel that any special display is indicated but I do feel strongly that a separate mention is necessary—separate, that is, from the reference to the 'commentaries' by M., P., and B."

275–82 Bailey, Letter to Brodie, December 31, 1975, Bernard Brodie Papers (Collection 1223), Department of Special Collections, Charles E. Young. Research Library, UCLA.

283 Marcia Brubeck, Letter to Brodie, July 29, 1976, Bernard Brodie Papers (Collection 1223), Department of Special Collections, Charles E. Young. Research Library, UCLA.

284–5 Brubeck, Letter to Brodie, October 6, 1976, Bernard Brodie Papers (Collection 1223), Department of Special Collections, Charles E. Young. Research Library, UCLA.

286–8 Bailey, Letter to Brodie, October 14, 1976, Bernard Brodie Papers (Collection 1223), Department of Special Collections, Charles E. Young. Research Library, UCLA.

289–91 Bailey, Letter to Brodie, October 29, 1976, Bernard Brodie Papers (Collection 1223), Department of Special Collections, Charles E. Young. Research Library, UCLA.

292 Introduction to Carl von Clausewitz, On War, translated and edited by Michael Howard and Peter Paret (Princeton: Princeton University Press, 1976).

293–300 Brodie, "The Continuing Relevance of On War," Carl von Clausewitz, On War, translated and edited by Michael Howard and Peter Paret (Princeton: Princeton University Press, 1976), 49, 49, 50, 51–2, 52, 57, 58. Note 298 continues: Brodie continued, "This quality is seen especially in his attitude toward such notions as were already beginning to be called 'principles of war.' Though he could hardly avoid establishing certain generalizations, which is inevitably the result and the purpose of analytical study, he specifically and vehemently rejected the notion that the conduct of war can reasonably be guided by a small number of pithy axioms. It was Jomini, not Clausewitz, who has been responsible for the endlessly quoted remark that 'methods change but principles are unchanging,' and it is largely for that reason that Jomini had far greater influence on military thinking in his own and later times, at least among non-Germans. It was Jomini who was looked to for guidance by both sides in the American Civil War, which in his very long life he lived to see concluded. And, as we have seen, it was Jomini whom Mahan called 'my best military friend.'"

301 Bernard Brodie, "In Quest of the Unknown Clausewitz: A review of Paret's Clausewitz and the State," International Security 1, No. 3 (Winter 1977).

302–11 Bernard Brodie, "Review of Clausewitz and the State by Peter Paret," Journal of Interdisciplinary History 8, No. 3 (Winter, 1978), 572; 572; 573; 573; 573–4; 572; 572; 572; 573, respectively. Note 304 continues: Brodie added, "As the title indicates, Clausewitz's changing concept of the state is selected as the central organizing thesis, for it is the basic idea in the Clausewitzian philosophical structure that war has meaning only as it carries out the policy of the state. Fortunately, however, Paret does not permit this theme too exclusive a dominance. Paret has the advantage through birth and rearing of being completely at home in three languages, including German, in which he does most of his research, and English, in which he writes smoothly and with a flawless clarity. To that he adds a capacity for meticulous scholarship, which is marked also by extraordinary breadth and depth. He seems to have read and absorbed everything of even the most modest relevance to his work. The connections he reveals between persons, writings, and events bear witness both to a penetrating insight and to the most fastidious care for the correctness of his factual detail. Such a level of historical scholarship is rarely attained."

312–14 Booth, "Bernard Brodie,"Makers of Nuclear Strategy, 51; 52; 52, respectively.

315–356 Bernard Brodie, "Strategy as a Science," World Politics 1, No. 4 (July 1949), 467; 467; 467; 467–8; 468; 468; 468; 468; 469; 469; 469; 470; 470; 471; 471; 472; 472; 473; 473; 473; 474; 476; 475 (n. 9); 476–7; 477; 478; 480; 483; 483–4; 484; 484; 484; 484; 485; 485; 485; 486; 486; 487; 487–8; 488; 488, respectively.

357–61 Brodie, Letter to Hans Speier, November 5, 1954, Bernard Brodie Papers (Collection 1223), Department of Special Collections, Charles E. Young. Research Library, UCLA.

362 Hans Speier, Letter to Brodie, November 19, 1954, Bernard Brodie Papers (Collection 1223), Department of Special Collections, Charles E. Young. Research Library, UCLA.

[363-7] Brodie, Letter to Speier, November 23, 1954, Bernard Brodie Papers (Collection 1223), Department of Special Collections, Charles E. Young. Research Library, UCLA.

[368] Brodie, letter to Speier, November 23, 1954, Bernard Brodie Papers (Collection 1223), Department of Special Collections, Charles E. Young. Research Library, UCLA.

[369-76] Brodie, Letter to Speier, November 23, 1954, Bernard Brodie Papers (Collection 1223), Department of Special Collections, Charles E. Young. Research Library, UCLA. Note 368 continues: Note that the word "some" is written by hand, scratching out the word "many" that was originally typed.

[377-86] Speier, Letter to Brodie, November 30, 1954, Bernard Brodie Papers (Collection 1223), Department of Special Collections, Charles E. Young. Research Library, UCLA.

[387-411] Bernard Brodie, "Some Notes on the Evolution of Air Doctrine," *World Politics* 7, No. 3 (April 1955), 349–70; 349; 349; 349; 349; 349–50; 350; 352; 352–3; 353; 353; 353; 353 (See: Captain Robert H. McDonnell, "Clausewitz and Strategic Bombing," *Air University Quarterly Review* VI, No. 1 (Spring 1953), 43–54); 353 (n. 6); 354; 354; 354; 354; 354–5; 355; 355; 355; 355–6; 356; 356, respectively.

[412-31] Brodie, "Scientific Progress and Political Science," 317; 317; 317; 317; 317; 317; 317; 317; 318; 318; 318; 318; 318; 318; 318; 318; 319; 319; 319, respectively.

[432-75] Bernard Brodie, "The American Scientific Strategists," RAND Working Paper (P-2979), October 1964, 1; 1; 1–2; 2; 2; 3; 4; 5; 5; 6; 6; 9; 10; 11; 11–12; 13; 13–14; 15; 18; 20; 21; 21; 22; 21–2; 22; 23; 25; 25–6; 28–9; 30; 31; 32; 33; 34; 34; 34; 36; 36–7; 37; 37; 38; 38; 38; respectively.

[476-87] Colin S. Gray, "What RAND Hath Wrought," *Foreign Policy* No. 4 (Autumn 1971), 111; 111; 111; 111; 111; 111–12; 112; 112; 112; 112; 112; 112, respectively.

[488-514] Bernard Brodie, "Why Were We So (Strategically) Wrong?" *Foreign Policy* 5 (Winter 1971–1972): 151; 151; 151; 151–2; 152; 152; 152; 152; 152; 152–3; 153; 153; 153; 154; 156; 156; 156; 156; 157; 157; 157; 160; 160; 160; 160–1; 161; 161, respectively. Note 498 continues: Brodie's entire description is quote compelling to digest in full: "The civilian strategists, as Gray concedes, represented a very thin line upon whom was thrust a tremendous burden. When I joined RAND in 1951, I was the single member of it who appeared to be interested in strategy—certainly the only one who had published anything on strategy, nuclear or pre-nuclear. Albert Wohlstetter and Herman Kahn were already members of that organization (Malcolm Hoag, William Kaufmann, and Thomas Schelling were to show up later) but their thoughts had not yet sortied out into the open reaches of national strategy. They were still working on technical problems of limited scope defined by RAND's sponsor, the U.S. Air Force, and thereby helping to develop systems analysis. Other persons at other places were to appear gradually, but the number has always remained small—especially if one limits the count to those who demonstrated a capacity for some originality. Upon this small group there fell by default the job of determining how to think about the atomic bomb, and how to do so under technological and political circumstances that were steadily and rapidly changing. When I say 'by default' I mean that the professional military, with exceedingly few exceptions, contributed little but resistance—especially resistance to the idea of restraint—and have continued ever since to contribute little or nothing to the understanding of the basic strategic-political problems of our times. That is not to be wondered at, because they have been improperly educated for that part of their job. They have in fact a trained incapacity for dealing with it, and their performance in Vietnam should be all the proof we need. The fact of small numbers of contributors is of acute importance. Among people who are grappling with new and baffling problems, opinions are bound to be expressed which are dubious or false, and the appropriate response or refutation will often not be heard because there are too few or perhaps even none available to make it. Those that formed McNamara's "court" comprised a highly like-minded school which absorbed a large proportion of the available talent, and dissident voices outside were few and easily drowned out." Note 501 continues: As Brodie described in detail, "Secretary McNamara, by training a statistician, was plainly in love with it. He gloried in the graphs, multicolored, in layer upon layer, and rejected the 'poetry' of those who sought to introduce a little political intuition. His 'court' was comprised mostly of systems analysts (Enthoven, Wohlstetter, Rowen, et al.). Nor was Mr. McNamara alone in his infatuation. Within RAND itself there was a quiet but strongly felt status differential between those who knew how to handle graphs and mathematical symbols, especially if they also knew how to manage teams of similarly equipped young men, and those who merely knew how to probe political issues. Elegance of method is indeed marvelously seductive, even when it is irrelevant or inappropriate to the major problems. At RAND it seduced some who were trained to be political analysts

and might have become good ones. The point was made well enough back in 1960 by Charles J. Hitch, now President of the University of California, at a conference of systems and operations analysts in Aix-en-Provence. When one excited participant urged that their special techniques, thoroughly computerized, be immediately adapted to the solution of foreign policy problems, Hitch, himself a pioneer in the field, dryly responded that they really appeared more appropriate to rationalizing traffic over the George Washington Bridge." Brodie, "Why Were We So (Strategically) Wrong?" 155–6. Note 508 continues: Brodie elaborated, "Also, I know no one among the civilian strategists Gray mentions and some others besides who by the end of 1965 had manifested any misgivings about the course that President Johnson had embarked upon. Most assuredly I know of none of the group who seemed to think that the 'task was too great.' On the contrary, for some of them it was precisely the kind of application of their ideas which they could not help but relish—for example, the concept that by granting sanctuary to North Vietnam from our ground forces we could assure China's staying out of the war. This would mean, they thought, that we could keep the war limited and fight it on our own terms. They were probably right about keeping China out, but not about the price. One also painfully remembers all the talk about building up conventional forces not only for Europe but for stamping out 'brush fires'—which by definition included Vietnam—until we began to pour oil on the flames."

515–58 Brodie, *War and Politics*, 434; 435; 436; 436; 436; 436; 437; 437–8; 438; 438; 438; 439; 440; 441; 443; 443; 445; 446; 446; 446; 446; 448; 448; 448; 449; 451; 452; 452; 453; 453; 453; 459; 462; 463; 464; 466; 467; 467; 472; 472; 474; 475; 475; 475, respectively.

559–62 Steiner, *Bernard Brodie and the Foundations of American Nuclear Strategy*, 1, 1, 1, 7, respectively.

563–71 Bernard Brodie, "The Development of Nuclear Strategy," *International Security* 2, No. 4 (Spring, 1978), 65 (published earlier as a 1976 Advanced Concepts and Information Strategy (ACIS) working paper with the same title, and republished posthumously as Chapter 2 in the 1983 anthology *National Security and International Stability* (Cambridge: Oelgeschlager, Gunn & Hain, 1983) that Brodie co-edited with Michael D. Intriligator and Roman Kolkowicz, 5); *International Security* 65 (*National Security and International Stability*, 5); *International Security* 65 (*National Security and International Stability*, 5–6); *International Security* 66 (*National Security and International Stability*, 6); *International Security* 66 (*National Security and International Stability*, 6–7); *International Security* 66 (*National Security and International Stability*, 7); *International Security* 66 (*National Security and International Stability*, 7); *International Security* 83 (and nearly verbatim in *National Security and International Stability*, 21); *International Security* 83 (*National Security and International Stability*, 21), respectively.

572 Letter from Dennis Ross to Brodie, March 23, 1978. Bernard Brodie Papers (Collection 1223). Department of Special Collections, Charles E. Young. Research Library, UCLA. Ross was then working in the Secretary of Defense's Office, and would later serve as Policy Planning Director at the U.S. State Department in the first Bush Administration, later becoming America's special envoy to the Middle East, during the entire two-term presidency of Clinton—returning as a special envoy for the region at the start of the Obama administration in February 2009, where he is now grappling with the complex transformation of the Arab world known as the "Arab Spring."

573 Richard L. Curl, "Strategic Doctrine in the Nuclear Age," *Strategic Review* 3 (Winter 1975), 46–56.

574–9 Bernard Brodie, "The Development of Nuclear Strategy," *International Security* 2, No. 4 (Spring, 1978), 65–83; 66; 66; 66–7; 67; 67, respectively.

580–9 Richard L. Curl, "Strategic Doctrine in the Nuclear Age," *Strategic Review* 3 (Winter 1975), 46; 46; 46–7; 47; 48; 48; 49; 49; 49, 49 respectively.

590 As noted in *The Absolute Weapon Revisited: Nuclear Arms and the Emerging International Order*," William T. R. Fox anticipated the relative versus absolute gains debate when he coined the phrase *the absolute weapon*: 'When dealing with the absolute weapon, arguments based on relative advantage lose their point.' Richard J. Harknett, "State Preferences, Systemic Constraints, and the Absolute Weapon," in T. V. Paul, Richard J. Harknett and James J. Wirtz, eds, *The Absolute Weapon Revisited: Nuclear Arms and the Emerging International Order* (Ann Arbor: University of Michigan Press, 1998), 67, citing William T. R. Fox, "International Control of Atomic Weapons," in Bernard Brodie, ed., *The Absolute Weapon*, 181.

591-5 Jeffrey D. Porro, "The Policy War: Brodie versus Kahn," *The Bulletin of the Atomic Scientists* 38, No. 6 (June/July 1982), 16–20; 17; 17; 19; 19, respectively.

596 Brodie, *War and Politics*, 378.

597-603 "Bernard Brodie 1910–1978," *Arms Control Today*, February 1979, 10; 10; 10; 10; 10; 10; 10, respectively. As Newell G. Bringhurst observed in his biography of Brodie's wife Fawn, for Bernard, "gardening provided an effective counterweight to the atomic bomb—the grim focus of his research and writing activities at Yale." He later noted Brodie found his work at RAND to be "stimulating and fulfilling" but also "intense, high-pressure, and always grim, focused as it was on questions of strategic deterrence of thermonuclear warfare and mass destruction," and to help ease the strain, an "important pastime for Bernard was gardening. He was 'a mad gardener, ... terribly intent on having beautiful surroundings.' He carefully maintained gardens containing all types of flowers around the Brodies' homes; specific varieties were planted to bloom at different times of the year. Another leisure activity for Bernard was classical music. He was not much of a concert goer but enjoyed listening to his music at home, thanks to his state-of-the-art high-fidelity stereo system, which he built himself and continually upgraded in response to technological improvements." Indeed, during his very final days, Brodie's "only consolation seemed to come from directing the planting of daffodil bulbs and lilies in his beloved garden—and from listening to music," which in addition to the study of war were two of his life-long passions. See Newell G. Bringhurst, *Fawn McKay Brodie: A Biographer's Life* (Norman: University of Oklahoma Press, 1999), 120, 148, 237 respectively.

604 William P. Snyder and John A. MacIntyre, Jr., "Bernard Brodie: America's Prophetic Strategic Thinker," *Parameters* Vol XI, No. 4, 2. At the time of publication, Snyder served as Associate Professor of Political Science at Texas A&M University, whose faculty he joined in 1975 upon retirement from the U.S. Army as a Colonel. He was a 1952 West Point graduate who earned his Ph.D. in political science at Princeton University in 1963, and a graduate of the U.S. Army War College in 1971. He is the author of *The Politics of British Defense Policy, 1945–1962* (1964), *Case Studies in Military Systems Analysis* (1967), in addition to numerous articles and reviews. Colonel John A. MacIntyre, Jr. was, at the time of the article's publication, assigned to the Office of the Surgeon General in the Department of the Army. A graduate of Pennsylvania Military College, he earned master's degrees from George Washington University in international business in 1971 and from Trinity University in health care administration in 1975. Colonel MacIntyre graduated from the U.S. Army Command and General Staff College in 1976 and the U.S. Army War College in 1980.

605-7 Schelling, *A Tribute to Bernard Brodie and (Incidentally) to RAND*, RAND, July 1979, 1; 2; 2, respectively.

Bibliography

Abella, Alex. *Soldiers of Reason: The RAND Corporation and the Rise of the American Empire* (New York: Houghton Mifflin Harcourt, 2008).

Alberts David S., and Thomas J. Czerwinski, eds, *Complexity, Global Politics, and National Security*. Washington, DC: National Defense University Press, 1997.

Aldridge, Robert. *Counterforce Syndrome*. Washington, DC: Transnational Institute, 1978.

Aligica, Paul Dragos and Kenneth R. Weinstein, eds, *The Essential Herman Kahn*. Lanham, MD: Lexington Books, 2009.

Arms Control Today (G. D.), "Bernard Brodie 1910–1978," *Arms Control Today* (February 1979), 10.

Aron, Raymond. *Clausewitz: Philosopher of War*, trans. Christine Booker and Norman Stone (Englewood Cliffs, NJ: Prentice Hall, 1985).

Aron, Raymond. "Modern Strategic Thought," trans. J. E. Gabriel, *Problems of Modern Strategy* (New York: Praeger, 1970).

Ashley, Richard K. "The Poverty of Neorealism," *International Organization* 38, No. 2 (Spring 1984), 225–86.

Bailey, Herbert S. Letter to DeHaven, February 16, 1959, Bernard Brodie Papers (Collection 1223), Department of Special Collections, Charles E. Young. Research Library, UCLA.

Bailey, Herbert S. Letter to Vaughan, March 6, 1958, Bernard Brodie Papers (Collection 1223), Department of Special Collections, Charles E. Young. Research Library, UCLA.

Bailey, Herbert S. Letters to Brodie, January 29, 1958; March 22, 1958; March 31, 1958; December 8, 1958; December 16, 1958; January 2, 1959; February 3, 1959; February 10, 1959; March 13, 1959; March 25, 1959; August 21, 1959; September 15, 1959; January 20, 1960; February 11, 1960; February 23, 1960; January 12, 1973; February 22, 1973; May 22, 1973; September 16, 1973; October 10, 1974; December 31, 1975; October 14, 1976; October 29, 1976, Bernard Brodie Papers (Collection 1223), Department of Special Collections, Charles E. Young. Research Library, UCLA.

Bailey, Herbert S. Letters to Paret, May 22, 1973; October 10, 1974, Bernard Brodie Papers (Collection 1223), Department of Special Collections, Charles E. Young. Research Library, UCLA.

Barnett, Frank R. "Preface," *Towards a New Defense for NATO: The Case for Tactical Nuclear Weapons*. New York: National Strategy Information Center, July 1976, vii–viii.

Bassford, Christopher. Clausewitz in English: The Reception of Clausewitz in Britain and America, 1815–1945 (Oxford: Oxford University Press, 1994).

Bassford, Christopher. "Jomini and Clausewitz: Their Interaction," The Clausewitz Homepage, www.clausewitz.com/CWZHOME/Jomini/JOMINIX.htm, an edited version of a paper presented to the 23rd Meeting of the Consortium on Revolutionary Europe at Georgia State University, 26 February 1993.

Bassford, Christopher. "Review Essay: Carl von Clausewitz, *On War* (Berlin, 1832)," posted online at: www.clausewitz.com/readings/Bassford/DefAnReview.htm, originally published in *Defense Analysis*, June 1996.

Bateman, Lewis. Letter to Brodie, December 19, 1975, Bernard Brodie Papers (Collection 1223), Department of Special Collections, Charles E. Young. Research Library, UCLA.

Baylis, John and John C. Garnett, eds, *Makers of Nuclear Strategy* (London: Pinters Press, 1991).

Bayne, M. G., U. S. Navy Vice Admiral and Commandant. Letter to Brodie, August 28, 1974, Bernard Brodie Papers (Collection 1223). Department of Special Collections, Charles E. Young. Research Library, UCLA.

Betts, Richard K. "Should Strategic Studies Survive?", *World Politics*, 50, No. 1, Fiftieth Anniversary Special Issue (October 1997), 7–33.

Beyerchen, Alan D. "Chapter 7: Clausewitz, Nonlinearity, and the Importance of Imagery," in David S. Alberts and Thomas J. Czerwinski, eds, *Complexity, Global Politics, and National Security* (Washington, DC: National Defense University Press, 1997), www.dtic.mil/cgi-bin/GetTRDoc?Location=U2&doc=GetTRDoc.pdf&AD=ADA460550.

Beyerchen, Alan D. Clausewitz, "Nonlinearity and the Unpredictability of War," Appendix 1, in Tom Czerwinski, ed., *Coping with the Bounds: Speculations on Nonlinearity in Military Affairs* (Washington, DC: National Defense University Press, 1998), 151–97, as posted on The Clausewitz Homepage, www.clausewitz.com/readings/Beyerchen/CWZandNonlinearity.htm.

Bobbitt, Philip, Lawrence Freedman, and Gregory F. Treverton. *U. S. Nuclear Strategy: A Reader.* London: Macmillan, 1989.

Bobbitt, Philip. *The Shield of Achilles: War, Peace and the Course of History.* New York: Alfred A. Knopf, 2002.

Bonaparte, Napoleon. *Napoleon's Maxims of War* with notes by General Burnod. Translated from French by Lieut.General Sir. G. C. D'Aguilar, C. B., and published by David McKay of Philadelphia in 1902. Available online: www.pvv.ntnu.no/~madsb/home/war/napoleon/.

Booth, Ken. "Bernard Brodie," in John Baylis and John Garnett, eds, *Makers of Nuclear Strategy* (London: Pinters Press, 1991), 19–54.

Boyd, John R. "Destruction and Creation," Unpublished Paper, September 3, 1976, 6–7. A copy is available online at: www.goalsys.com/books/documents/DESTRUCTION_AND_CREATION.pdf.

Bringhurst, Newell G. *Fawn McKay Brodie: A Biographer's Life.* Norman: University of Oklahoma Press, 1999.

Brodie, Bernard. "A Comment on the Hoag Doctrine," RAND Working Paper, July 17, 1962.

Brodie, Bernard. "A Commentary on the Preventive War Doctrine," RAND Working Paper, June 11, 1953.

Brodie, Bernard. "A Critique of Army and Navy Thinking on the Atomic Bomb," *The Bulletin of the Atomic Scientists*, August 1947, 207–10.

Brodie, Bernard. "A Critique of the Doctrine of Conventional War in Europe (CWE)," RAND Working Paper, September 24, 1962.

Brodie, Bernard. *A Guide to Naval Strategy* (New York: Praeger, 1965), Fifth Edition.

Brodie, Bernard. *A Layman's Guide to Naval Strategy.* Princeton: Princeton University Press, 1942.

Brodie, Bernard. "A Slightly Revised Proposal for the Underemployment of SAC in an H-Bomb Era," RAND Working Paper, January 23, 1953.

Brodie, Bernard and Fawn Brodie, *From Crossbow to H-Bomb*, Revised Edition. Bloomington: Indiana University Press, 1973. Originally published by New York: Dell Books, 1962.

Brodie, Bernard. "Can Peaceful Change Prevent War?" Term Paper Submitted to Political Science 363, Spring 1938, University of Chicago.

Brodie, Bernard. "Changing Attitudes Towards War," Chapter 6, in *War and* Politics (New York: Macmillan, 1973), 223–75.

Brodie, Bernard. "Changing Attitudes Towards War," in Henry A. Kissinger and Bernard Brodie, eds, *Bureaucracy, Politics, and Strategy*, Security Studies Paper Number 17 (Los Angeles: UCLA Security Studies Project, 1968), 15–26.

Brodie, Bernard. "Changing Attitudes Towards War," Paper Presented at the Studies in Violence Symposium, UCLA, June 1–2, 1968, 1–16.

Brodie, Bernard. "Changing Capabilities and War Objectives," Lecture to the Air War College, April 17, 1952, 1–20.

Brodie, Bernard. "Characteristics of a Sound Strategy," Lecture Delivered to the Naval War College, March 17, 1952, 1–24.

Brodie, Bernard, C. J. Hitch, and A. W. Marshall, "The Next Ten Years," RAND Working Paper, December 30, 1954.

Brodie, Bernard, "Conclusion: The Future of Deterrence," in Bernard Brodie, ed., *The Future of Deterrence in U. S. Strategy*, UCLA Security Studies Project (Los Angeles: UCLA, 1968).

Brodie, Bernard. "Defense Policy and the Possibility of Total War." *Daedalus* 91, No. 4, American Foreign Policy: Freedoms and Restraints (Fall 1962), 733–48.

Brodie, Bernard. "Defense Strategy in its Political Context," a paper delivered to the Fifth International Wehrkunde Conference sponsored by the Verlag Europaisch Wehrkunde, Munich, Germany, February

10–11, 1968, in William P. Gerberding and Bernard Brodie, *The Political Dimension in National Strategy*, Security Studies Paper No. 13 (Los Angeles: UCLA, 1968), 36–47.

Brodie, Bernard, ed., *The Absolute Weapon*. New York. Harcourt, Brace and Company. 1946. Especially, Part I: The Weapon, Chapter One, War in the Atomic Age," and Chapter Two, Implications for Military Policy."

Brodie, Bernard, ed., *The Future of Deterrence in U. S. Strategy*, UCLA Security Studies Project (Los Angeles: UCLA, 1968), in particular, "Conclusion: The Future of Deterrence," 126–34.

Brodie, Bernard. "Ending a War: Is the Korean Lesson Valid for Vietnam?" in Henry A. Kissinger and Bernard Brodie, eds, *Bureaucracy, Politics, and Strategy*, Security Studies Paper Number 17 (Los Angeles: UCLA Security Studies Project, 1968), 41–5 under the original title of

Brodie, Bernard. *Escalation and the Nuclear Option* (Princeton: Princeton University Press, 1966).

Brodie, Bernard. *Escalation and the Nuclear Option*, RAND Memorandum RM-4544-PR (Santa Monica: RAND Corporation, June 1965).

Brodie, Bernard et al., "Discussion of the Eastern Europe," in Quincy Wright, ed. *A Foreign Policy for the United States* (Chicago: University of Chicago Press, 1947), 202–23.

Brodie, Bernard et al., "Discussion of the Far East," in Quincy Wright, ed. *A Foreign Policy for the United States* (Chicago: University of Chicago Press, 1947), 139–61.

Brodie, Bernard et al., "Discussion of General Security," in Quincy Wright, ed. *A Foreign Policy for the United States* (Chicago: University of Chicago Press, 1947), 97–125.

Brodie, Bernard et al., "Discussion of Great-Power Relationships," in Quincy Wright, ed. *A Foreign Policy for the United States* (Chicago: University of Chicago Press, 1947), 34–71.

Brodie, Bernard et al., "Discussion of International Economic Policies," in Quincy Wright, ed. *A Foreign Policy for the United States* (Chicago: University of Chicago Press, 1947), 292–310.

Brodie, Bernard et al., "Discussion of International Informational Policies," in Quincy Wright, ed. *A Foreign Policy for the United States* (Chicago: University of Chicago Press, 1947), 349–92.

Brodie, Bernard et al., "Discussion of the Latin America," in Quincy Wright, ed. *A Foreign Policy for the United States* (Chicago: University of Chicago Press, 1947), 234–55.

Brodie, Bernard et al., "Discussion of the Near East," in Quincy Wright, ed. *A Foreign Policy for the United States* (Chicago: University of Chicago Press, 1947), 170–93.

Brodie, Bernard. "How Much Conventional Force Do We Need?" *Foreign Service Journal*, April 1973, 18–22.

Brodie, Bernard. "How Not to Lead an Alliance," *The Reporter*, March 9, 1967, 18–24.

Brodie, Bernard. "How Strong Is Britain?" *Foreign Affairs* 26, No. 3 (April 1948), 432–49.

Brodie, Bernard. "Implications of Nuclear Weapons in Total War," RAND Paper (P-1118), July 8, 1957, www.dtic.mil/cgi-bin/GetTRDoc?AD=AD606443&Location=U2&doc=GetTRDoc.pdf.

Brodie, Bernard. "In Quest of Socrates: Man and Philosopher," Paper Submitted to Course 101, Department of Philosophy, University of Chicago, December 1932. Bernard Brodie Papers (Collection 1223), Department of Special Collections, Charles E. Young. Research Library, UCLA.

Brodie, Bernard. "In Quest of the Unknown Clausewitz." [A review of Paret's Clausewitz and the State.] *International Security* 1, No.3 (Winter 1977), 63–6.

Brodie, Bernard. "Influence of Mass Destruction Weapons on Strategy," Lecture, Naval War College, February 6, 1956.

Brodie, Bernard. "Introduction," *Towards a New Defense for NATO: The Case for Tactical Nuclear Weapons*. New York: National Strategy Information Center, July 1976, 1–9.

Brodie, Bernard. "Introduction," Carl von Clausewitz, *On War*, translated and ed. Michael Howard and Peter Paret (Princeton: Princeton University Press, 1976).

Brodie, Bernard. "Learning to Fight a Limited War," originally published in the *Los Angeles Times*, December 3, 1967, reprinted in *The Political Dimension in National Strategy: Five Papers*, ed. William P. Gerberding and Bernard Brodie, Security Studies Paper No. 13 (Los Angeles: University of California Security Studies Project, 1968), 26–32.

Brodie, Bernard. Letter to Hans Speier, November 23, 1954, Bernard Brodie Papers (Collection 1223), Department of Special Collections, Charles E. Young. Research Library, UCLA.

Brodie, Bernard. Letter to Hans Speier, November 5, 1954, Bernard Brodie Papers (Collection 1223), Department of Special Collections, Charles E. Young. Research Library, UCLA.

Brodie, Bernard. Letter to Klaus Knorr, January 24, 1964; February 26, 1964; March 27, 1964; May 15, 1964, Bernard Brodie Papers (Collection 1223), Department of Special Collections, Charles E. Young Research Library, UCLA.

Brodie, Bernard. Letter to Michael Howard, September 1, 1974; October 3, 1974, Bernard Brodie Papers (Collection 1223), Department of Special Collections, Charles E. Young. Research Library, UCLA.

Brodie, Bernard. Letters to Bailey, February 6, 1958; March 28, 1958; July 17, 1958; December 29, 1958; January 30, 1959; February 16, 1959; March 20, 1959; August 25, 1959; February 4, 1960; February 18, 1960; May 19, 1973; December 25, 1975, Bernard Brodie Papers (Collection 1223), Department of Special Collections, Charles E. Young. Research Library, UCLA.

Brodie, Bernard. Letters to Gordon Hubel, March 20, 1959; April 8, 1959; March 18, 1964; March 19, 1964; Bernard Brodie Papers (Collection 1223), Department of Special Collections, Charles E. Young Research Library, UCLA.

Brodie, Bernard. Letters to Herman Kahn, January 4, 1962; January 12, 1962; January 19, 1962; January 25, 1962; January 31, 1962; February 9, 1962; February 16, 1962; September 18, 1963, Bernard Brodie Papers (Collection 1223), Department of Special Collections, Charles E. Young Research Library, UCLA.

Brodie, Bernard. Letters to Max Singer, November 9, 1963; November 11, 1964, Bernard Brodie Papers (Collection 1223), Department of Special Collections, Charles E. Young Research Library, UCLA.

Brodie, Bernard. Letters to Peter Paret, January 17, 1964; May 22, 1964; May 28, 1964; May 1, 1967; January 21, 1974; May 30, 1974, Bernard Brodie Papers (Collection 1223), Department of Special Collections, Charles E. Young Research Library, UCLA.

Brodie, Bernard, Michael Intriligator, and Roman Kolkowicz, eds. *National Security and International Stability.* Cambridge: Oelgeschlager, Gunn & Hain, 1983.

Brodie, Bernard. "Morals and Strategy: Distinguishing Virtue from Ignorance in Problems of National Defense," *Worldview Magazine*, Carnegie Council for Ethics in International Affairs, September 1964, 4–8.

Brodie, Bernard. "More About Limited War," *World Politics* 10, No. 1 (October 1957), 112–22.

Brodie, Bernard. "Must We Shoot from the Hip?" RAND Working Paper, September 4, 1951.

Brodie, Bernard. "Navy Department Thinking on the Atomic Bomb," *The Bulletin of the Atomic Scientists*, July 1947, 177–80, 198–200.

Brodie, Bernard. "New Preface for Paperback Edition of 'Strategy in the Missile Age'," RAND Paper (P-3033), Santa Monica: RAND, December 30, 1964.

Brodie, Bernard. "New Tactics in Naval Warfare," *Foreign Affairs* 24, no. 2 (January 1946).

Brodie, Bernard. "New Technologies of War and National Policies," *Technology and International Relations* (Chicago: University of Chicago Press, 1949).

Brodie, Bernard. "Nuclear Strategy in its Political Context" Box 20, Bernard Brodie Papers at the UCLA Library Special Collections, reprinted in Marc Trachtenberg's *The Development of American Strategic Thought: Writings on Strategy, 1961–1969* (New York: Garland Press, 1988), 353–68.

Brodie, Bernard. "Nuclear Weapons and Changing Strategic Outlooks," Lecture, U. S. Army War College, Carlisle Barracks, Pennsylvania, February 20, 1956.

Brodie, Bernard. "Nuclear Weapons and Changing Strategic Outlooks," RAND Paper P-811, February 27, 1956.

Brodie, Bernard. "Nuclear Weapons and Changing Strategic Outlooks," February 1957 edition of *The Bulletin of the Atomic Scientists*, 56–61.

Brodie, Bernard. "Nuclear Weapons and Changing Strategic Outlooks," Lecture, Dartmouth College, Great Issues," March 1956.

Brodie, Bernard. "Nuclear Weapons: Strategic or Tactical?" *Foreign Affairs* 32, No. 2 (January 1954).

Brodie, Bernard. "On the Objectives of Arms Control, Bernard Brodie," *International Security* 1, No. 1 (Summer 1976), 17–36.

Brodie, Bernard. "Paying in Full for a Limited War," *L.A. Times*, Part II, October 17, 1968.

Brodie, Bernard. "Political Consequences of the H-bomb," RAND Working Paper, November 7, 1952.

Brodie, Bernard. "Political Impact of U. S. Forces," Air Force Advisory Group (AFAG) Talk, RAND, May 28, 1963.

Brodie, Bernard. "RAND Memo to Thomas W. Wolfe, March 24, 1965, Bernard Brodie Papers (Collection 1223), Department of Special Collections, Charles E. Young Research Library, UCLA.

Brodie, Bernard. "Review of Clausewitz and the State by Peter Paret," *Journal of Interdisciplinary History* 8, No. 3 (Winter, 1978), 572–4.

Brodie, Bernard. "Review: On Clausewitz: A Passion for War," *World Politics* 25, No. 2 (January 1973), 288–308.

Brodie, Bernard. *Sea Power in the Machine Age* (Princeton: Princeton University Press, 1941).

Brodie, Bernard. "Some Notes on the Evolution of Air Doctrine," *World Politics* 7, No. 3 (April 1955), 349–70.

Brodie, Bernard. "Some Preliminary Observations on Escalation," RAND Working Paper, September 13, 1962.

Brodie, Bernard. "Some Strategic Implications of the Nuclear Revolution," RAND Working Paper, P-1111, May 14, 1957.

Brodie, Bernard. "Strategic Bombing: What It Can Do," *The Reporter*, August 15, 1950, 28–31.

Brodie, Bernard. "Strategic Objectives and the Determination of Force Composition," RAND Working Paper, June 9, 1959.

Brodie, Bernard. *Strategy and National Interests: Reflections for the Future* (New York: National Strategy Information Center, January 1971).

Brodie, Bernard. "Strategy as a Science," *World Politics* 1, No. 4 (July 1949), 467–88.

Brodie, Bernard. "Strategy as an Art and a Science," Naval War College Lecture, September 18, 1958, reprinted in the *Naval War College Review*, February 1959. Online at: www.au.af.mil/au/awc/awcgate/theorists/brodie1.htm.

Brodie, Bernard. "Strategy Hits a Dead End," *Harper's*, October 1955, 33–7.

Brodie, Bernard. *Strategy in the Missile Age* (Princeton: Princeton University Press, 1959).

Brodie, Bernard. *Strategy in the Missile Age*. Santa Monica: RAND Corporation Report R-335, January 15, 1959.

Brodie, Bernard. "Tactical Effects of H-Bombs," RAND Working Paper, November 7, 1952.

Brodie, Bernard. "Technology, Politics, and Strategy," Adelphi Papers 9, No.: 55 (1969), 21–29.

Brodie, Bernard. "Technology, Politics, and Strategy," in Henry A. Kissinger and Bernard Brodie, eds, *Bureaucracy, Politics, and Strategy*, Security Studies Paper Number 17 (Los Angeles: UCLA Security Studies Project, 1968), 27–40.

Brodie, Bernard. "Technology, Politics, and Strategy," Paper Presented to the Tenth Annual Conference of the Institute for Strategic Studies at St. Catherine's College in Oxford, September 19–22, 1968, 2.

Brodie, Bernard. "The American Scientific Strategists," RAND Working Paper (P-2979), October 1964.

Brodie, Bernard. "The Anatomy of Deterrence," RAND Research Memorandum (RM–2218), July 23, 1958.

Brodie, Bernard. "The Anatomy of Deterrence" *World Politics* 11, No. 2 (January 1959), 173–191.

Brodie, Bernard. "The Atom Bomb as Policy Maker," *Foreign Affairs* 27, No. 1 (October 1948), 17–33.

Brodie, Bernard. "The Atomic Bomb and American Security," in Philip Bobbitt, Lawrence Freedman, and Gregory F. Treverton, eds, *U.S. Nuclear Strategy: A Reader* (London: Macmillan, 1989).

Brodie, Bernard. "The Atomic Bomb and American Security," Memorandum Number Eighteen, Yale Institute of International Studies, New Haven, Connecticut, November 1, 1945,

Brodie, Bernard. "The Atomic Dilemma," *Annals of the American Academy of Political and Social Science* 249, Social Implications of Modern Science (January 1947), 32–41.

Brodie, Bernard. "The Continuing Relevance of *On War*," in Carl von Clausewitz, *On War*, edited and translated by Michael Howard and Peter Paret. Princeton: Princeton University Press, 1976, 45–58.

Brodie, Bernard. "The Development of Nuclear Strategy," Advanced Concepts and Information Strategy (ACIS) Working Paper, UCLA, 1976.

Brodie, Bernard. "The Development of Nuclear Strategy," Chapter 2 in *National Security and International Stability* (Cambridge: Oelgeschlager, Gunn & Hain, 1983) eds Bernard Brodie, Michael D. Intriligator and Roman Kolkowicz, 5–21.

Brodie, Bernard. "The Development of Nuclear Strategy," *International Security* 2, No. 4 (Spring, 1978), 65–83.

Brodie, Bernard. "The Heritage of Douhet," RAND Research Memorandum (RM–1013), December 31, 1952.

Brodie, Bernard. *The Intractability of States: A Distinctive Problem*, RAND Paper P-2970 (Santa Monica: RAND Corporation, September 1964).

Brodie, Bernard. "The McNamara Phenomenon," *World Politics* 17, No. 4 (July 1965), 672–686, a review article of William W. Kaufmann, *The McNamara Strategy* (New York, Harper & Row, 1964).

Brodie, Bernard. "The Missing Middle—Tactical Nuclear War," RAND Working Paper, May 8, 1964 (a revised version of his April 9, 1964 speech to RAND's Air Force Advisory Group (AFAG) of the same title).

Brodie, Bernard. "The Security Problem in the Light of Atomic Energy," in Quincy Wright, ed. *A Foreign Policy for the United States* (Chicago: University of Chicago Press, 1947), 89–96.

Brodie, Bernard. "Theories on the Causes of War," in Henry A. Kissinger and Bernard Brodie, eds, *Bureaucracy, Politics, and Strategy*, Security Studies Paper Number 17 (Los Angeles: UCLA Security Studies Project, 1968), 46–60.

Brodie, Bernard. "Theories on the Causes of War," Presented at Royce Hall, UCLA, on November 11, 1968 as part of the Faculty Lecture Series on "War and the Human Race," 1–20.

Brodie, Bernard. "U. S. Political Objectives in a Context of Strategic Bombing," RAND Corporation Working Paper, February 19, 1953.

Brodie, Bernard. "Unlimited Weapons and Limited War," *The Reporter*, November 18, 1954, 16–21.

Brodie, Bernard. "Unlimited Weapons Choices and Limited Budgets," Public Lecture at Berkeley, November 18, 1954, 1–31.

Brodie, Bernard. *War and Politics* (New York: Macmillan, 1973).

Brodie, Bernard. "War Department Thinking on the Atomic Bomb," *The Bulletin of the Atomic Scientists*, June 1947, 150–155, 168.

Brodie, Bernard. "What Price Conventional Capabilities in Europe?" *The Reporter*, May 23, 1963, 25–33.

Brodie, Bernard. "Why Were We So (Strategically) Wrong?" *Foreign Policy* 5 (Winter 1971–1972): 151–161.

Brodie, Memo to C. A. H. Thomson, J. M. Goldsen, and R. McDermott , Jan 22, 1964, Bernard Brodie Papers (Collection 1223), Department of Special Collections, Charles E. Young Research Library, UCLA.

Brodie, Memo to Max Ascoli, September 6, 1957, Bernard Brodie Papers (Collection 1223), Department of Special Collections, Charles E. Young Research Library, UCLA.

Brubeck, Marcia. Letter to Brodie, July 29, 1976, Bernard Brodie Papers (Collection 1223), Department of Special Collections, Charles E. Young. Research Library, UCLA.

Brubeck, Marcia. Letter to Brodie, October 6, 1976, Bernard Brodie Papers (Collection 1223), Department of Special Collections, Charles E. Young. Research Library, UCLA.

Bryant, Stewart F. "Review of *Sea Power in the Machine Age*," *Annals of the American Academy of Political and Social Science* 218, Public Policy in a World at War (November 1941), 202.

Buchan, Alastair. "Review: War and Politics," *The American Political Science Review* 69, No. 2 (June 1975), 731.

Calder, Nigel. *Nuclear Nightmares*. New York: Viking Press, 1980.

Calder, Nigel. *Nuclear Nightmares: An Investigation into Possible Wars*. London: British Broadcasting Corporation, 1979.

Cannon, Michael W. "Clausewitz for Beginners," *Air Power Journal* (Summer 1989), 48–57.

Carnesale, Albert, Paul Doty, Stanley Hoffmann, Samuel P. Huntington, Joseph S. Nye, Jr., Scott D. Sagan, Derek Bok (Harvard Nuclear Study Group), *Living with Nuclear Weapons*. Cambridge, MA: Harvard University Press, 1983.

Cavell, R. G. "Review of *The Absolute Weapon*," edited by Bernard Brodie," *Pacific Affairs* 19, No. 4 (December 1946), 450–51.

Chapman, John W. "American Strategic Thinking," *Air University Review* 18, January–February 1967, 25–33, www.airpower.au.af.mil/airchronicles/aureview/1967/jan-feb/chapman.html.

Chapman, John W. Letter to Brodie, January 6, 1966, Bernard Brodie Papers (Collection 1223), Department of Special Collections, Charles E. Young Research Library, UCLA.

Choice. "Review: Escalation and the Nuclear Option," *Choice*, June 1967, Bernard Brodie Papers (Collection 1223), Department of Special Collections, Charles E. Young Research Library, UCLA.

Clausewitz, Carl von. "Chapter 1, Strategy," Book III, Of Strategy in General, *On War* (London: N. Trübner, 1873), tr. Colonel J.J. Graham, posted on the Clausewitz Homepage, www.clausewitz.com/readings/OnWar1873/BK3ch01.html.

Clausewitz, Carl von. *On War*, translated by J.J. Graham, 1873, www.clausewitz.com/readings/OnWar1873/BK2ch01.html.

Clausewitz, Carl von. *On War*. Princeton: Princeton University Press, 1976, edited by Michael Howard and Peter Paret.

Clausewitz, Carl von. *Principles of War* were translated and edited by Hans W. Gatzke, and re-published in 1942 by The Military Service Publishing Company, www.clausewitz.com/CWZHOME/PrincWar/Princwr1.htm.

Clausewitz, Carl von. "The Introduction of the Author," *On War*, translated by Col. James .John Graham. London; N. Trubner, 1873, www.clausewitz.com/readings/OnWar1873/Intro.htm.

Clausewitz, Marie von. "Preface to the First Edition," Carl von Clausewitz, *On War*, translated by Col. J. J. Graham, London, 1873, www.gutenberg.org/files/1946/1946-h/1946-h.htm#2H_4_0004.

Craig, Campbell. Glimmer of a New Leviathan: Total War in the Realism of Niebuhr, Morgenthau, and Waltz. New York: Columbia University Press, 2003.

Curl, Richard L. "Strategic Doctrine in the Nuclear Age," *Strategic Review* 3 (Winter 1975), 46–56.

DeHaven, James C. Letters to Herbert Bailey, January 2, 1959; January 26, 1959, Bernard Brodie Papers (Collection 1223), Department of Special Collections, Charles E. Young. Research Library, UCLA.

Dulles, John Foster. "The Evolution of Foreign Policy," Department of State Bulletin 30 (January 25, 1962): 107–10.

Dunn, F. S. "Law and Peaceful Change," *American Society of International Law Proceedings* 38 (1944).

Dunn, F. S. "Foreword," in Bernard Brodie, The Atomic Bomb and American Security," Memorandum Number Eighteen, Yale Institute of International Studies, New Haven, Connecticut, November 1, 1945.

Edward Cody, "After 43 Years, France to Rejoin NATO as Full Member," *Washington Post*, March 12, 2009.

English, John A. Marching Through Chaos: The descent of armies in theory and practice. Wesport: Praeger 1996.

Fleming, Bruce. "Can Reading Clausewitz Save Us from Future Mistakes?" *Parameters* (Spring 2004): 65–9.

Ford, Daniel. "When Sun-tzu met Clausewitz: John Boyd, the OODA Loop, and the Invasion of Iraq," 2009.

French, Bevan M. "Brodie Discusses 'Limited' Conflicts, Says All-Out War is 'Meaningless'," *The Dartmouth* CXV, No. 126 (March 20, 1956), 1.

Gerberding, William P. and Bernard Brodie, eds *The Political Dimension in National Strategy: Five Papers*. Security Studies Paper Number 13 (Los Angeles: UCLA Security Studies Project, 1968.)

Ghamari-Tabrizi, Sharon. *The Worlds of Herman Kahn*. Cambridge, MA: Harvard University Press, 2005.

Ghamari-Tabrizi, Sharon. Website of Sharon Ghamari-Tabrizi, www.sharonghamari.com/excerpt/GhamariExcerpt.pdf.

Glaser, Charles L. "Realists as Optimists: Cooperation as Self-Help," *International Security* 19, No. 3 (Winter 1994/95), 50–90.

Goldsen, J. M. RAND memo to George Clement, May 7, 1964, Bernard Brodie Papers (Collection 1223), Department of Special Collections, Charles E. Young Research Library, UCLA.

Graebner, Norman A. "Review: Strategy in the Missile Age by Bernard Brodie," *The Annals of the American Academy of Political and Social Science* 330 (July 1960), 156–7.

Gray, Colin S. "What RAND Hath Wrought," *Foreign Policy*, No. 4 (Autumn 1971), 111–2.

Gray, Colin. *Strategic Studies and Public Policy: The American Experience*. Lexington, Kentucky: University Press of Kentucky. 1982.

Harknett, Richard J. "State Preferences, Systemic Constraints, and the Absolute Weapon," in T. V. Paul, Richard J. Harknett and James J. Wirtz, eds, *The Absolute Weapon Revisited: Nuclear Arms and the Emerging International Order* (Ann Arbor: University of Michigan Press, 1998), 47–72.

Hart, B. H. Liddell. *Strategy*. New York: Frederick A. Praeger, 1968.

Haslam Jonathan. *No Virtue Like Necessity: Realist Thought in International Relations since Machiavelli*. New Haven: Yale University Press, 2002.

Herken, Gregg. *Brotherhood of the Bomb: The Tangled Lives and Loyalties of Robert Oppenheimer, Ernest Lawrence, and Edward Teller*. New York: Henry Holt, 2002.

Herken, Gregg. Cardinal Choices: Presidential Science Advising from the Atomic Bomb to SDI. Oxford: Oxford University Press, 1992.

Herken, Gregg. *Counsels of War.* (New York: Knopf, 1985).

Herken, Gregg. "The Not-Quite-Absolute Weapon: Deterrence and the Legacy of Bernard Brodie," Roman Kolkowicz, ed., *Dilemmas of Nuclear Strategy* (London: Frank Cass & Co., 1987), 15–24.

Herken, Gregg. *The Winning Weapon: The Atomic Bomb in the Cold War, 1945–1950.* New York: Alfred A. Knopf, 1980.

Hirsch, Susan. Letter to Brodie, Feb. 28, 1962, Bernard Brodie Papers (Collection 1223), Department of Special Collections, Charles E. Young Research Library, UCLA.

Hisashi Owada, "Peaceful Change," *Max Planck Encyclopedia of Public International Law*, Section 3, www.mpepil.com/sample_article?id=/epil/entries/law-9780199231690-e1452&recno=19&, citing I.L. Claude Jr., *Swords into Plowshares: The Problems and Progress of International Organization*, 4th ed. (New York: Random House, 1971).

Holst, Johan Jorgen. *Norwegian Military Review* (*Norsk Militaert Tidsskrift*), trans. N. Bertelsen, Volume 5 (1967), Bernard Brodie Papers (Collection 1223), Department of Special Collections, Charles E. Young Research Library, UCLA.

Howard, Michael. "Brodie, Wohlstetter and American Nuclear Strategy." *Survival* 34, No. 2 (Summer 1992), 107–116.

Howard, Michael. Letters to Bernard Brodie, August 23, 1974; September 18, 1974; September 23, 1974, Bernard Brodie Papers (Collection 1223), Department of Special Collections, Charles E. Young. Research Library, UCLA.

Hubel, Gordon. Letters to Bernard Brodie, March 25, 1959; February 22, 1960; July 29, 1964, Bernard Brodie Papers (Collection 1223), Department of Special Collections, Charles E. Young. Research Library, UCLA.

Huntington, Samuel P. "Review: Strategy in the Missile Age by Bernard Brodie," *The American Political Science Review* 54, No. 2 (June 1960), 505–6.

Huntington, William. "Clausewitz and Strategy in the Missile Age: A Critique of Bernard Brodie's Strategic Thought," Unpublished Paper Submitted to Foundations of National Security Strategy, National War College, October 9, 1990, 1–6.

Hutchins, Robert M. "Scholarly Opinions on Atomic Energy—and its Control," *New York Times*, June 9, 1946, 6.

Iklé, Fred Charles. "When the Fighting has to Stop: The Arguments about Escalation," *World Politics* 19, No. 4 (July 1967), 692–707.

Jomini, Baron Henri-Antoine, *Art of War.* G. H. Mendell and W. P. Craighill, trans. (Philadelphia: Lippicott, 1892).

Jomini, Baron Henri-Antoine, *The Art of War: A New Edition with Appendices and Maps*, Translated from the French by Capt. G. H. Mendell, Corps of Topographical Engineers, U. S. Army, and Lieut. W. P. Craighill, Corps of Engineers, U. S. Army. Philadelphia: J. B. Lippincott & Co., 1862.

Kahn, Herman. Letters to Bernard Brodie, February 22, 1962; October 3, 1963, Bernard Brodie Papers (Collection 1223), Department of Special Collections, Charles E. Young Research Library, UCLA.

Kahn, Herman. "Major Implications of a Current Non-Military Defense Study" (P-1497-RC), RAND, November 7, 1958.

Kahn, Herman. *On Escalation: Metaphors and Scenarios.* New York: Frederick A. Praeger, 1965.

Kahn, Herman. *On Escalation: Metaphors and Scenarios.* New York: Transaction Publishers, 2009 (latest reprint).

Kahn, Herman. *On Thermonuclear War.* Westport, CT: Greenwood Press, 1978.

Kahn, Herman. *Thinking About the Unthinkable in the 1980s.* New York: Simon and Schuster, 1984.

Kahn, Herman. *Thinking About the Unthinkable.* New York: Avon Library, 1966.

Kahn, Herman. *Thinking About the Unthinkable.* New York: Horizon Press, 1962 (first print).

Kaplan, Fred and Martin J. Sherwin. *The Wizards of Armageddon.* Stanford, CA: Stanford University Press, 1991.

Kaplan, Fred. *1959: The Year Everything Changed.* Hoboken, NJ: John Wiley & Sons, 2000.

Kaplan, Fred. *The Wizards of Armageddon.* New York: Simon and Schuster, 1983.

Ken Booth, "Bernard Brodie," in John Baylis and John Garnett, eds, *Makers of Nuclear Strategy.* London: Pinters Press, 1991.

Kissinger, Henry A. and Bernard Brodie, eds, *Bureaucracy, Politics, and Strategy*, Security Studies Paper No. 17. Los Angeles: University of California, 1968.

Knorr, Klaus. Letters to Bernard Brodie, January 22, 1964; March 2, 1964, Bernard Brodie Papers (Collection 1223), Department of Special Collections, Charles E. Young Research Library, UCLA.

Kolkowicz, Roman, ed. *Dilemmas of Nuclear Strategy*. London: Frank Cass, 1987.

Leonard, L. Larry. "Review: Escalation and the Nuclear Option," *Current Thought on Peace and War*, Summer 1967, Bernard Brodie Papers (Collection 1223), Department of Special Collections, Charles E. Young Research Library, UCLA.

Lewis, Charles Lee. "Review of *Sea Power in the Machine Age*," *The Mississippi Valley Historical Review* 28, No. 2 (September 1941), 273–4.

Lynn Montross, *War Through the Ages*. New York: Harper, 1960.

McDonnell, Captain Robert H. "Clausewitz and Strategic Bombing," *Air University Quarterly Review* VI, No. 1 (Spring 1953), 43–54.

McGray, Douglas. "The Marshall Plan," *Wired* 11, No. 02 (February 2003), www.wired.com/wired/archive/11.02/marshall.html.

McNamara, Robert. "The Military Role of Nuclear Weapons: Perceptions and Misperceptions," *Foreign Affairs* 62 (1983): 59–81.

Menand, Louis. "Fat Man: Herman Kahn and the nuclear age," *New Yorker*, June 27, 2005.

Mochalov, Vladimir. Introduction to the Russian Edition, *Strategy in the Missile Age*. Moscow: Soviet Ministry of Defense, 1961; English translation of Russian introduction as preserved in the Bernard Brodie Papers at the UCLA special collections.

Montross, Lynn. *War Through the Ages*. New York: Harper and Bros., 1946.

Montross, Lynn. *War Through the Ages*, 3rd ed. New York: Harper and Row, 1960.

Morgenthau, Hans. *Politics among Nations*, 6th ed.. New York: Knopf, 1985.

Nelson, Jean Ware. Letter to Brodie, May 2, 1960, Bernard Brodie Papers (Collection 1223), Department of Special Collections, Charles E. Young Research Library, UCLA.

Nelson, Keith L. "Review: War and Politics," *Pacific Historical Review* 45, No. 1 (February 1976), 152.

Ogburn, William Fielding, ed., *Technology and International Relations*. Chicago: University of Chicago Press, 1949.

Osgood, Robert E. "Review: Strategy in the Missile Age by Bernard Brodie," *The Journal of Modern History* 32, No. 4 (December 1960), 426.

Pacific Historical Review, "Review of *A Guide to Naval Strategy*, *Pacific Historical Review* 13, No. 4 (December 1944), 484.

Paret, Peter. "Carl von Clausewitz: Biographical article for the International Encyclopedia of the Social Sciences," Center for International Studies, Princeton University, from September 16, 1963.

Paret, Peter. "Guerre et Politique selon Clausewitz," *Revue Francaise de Science Politique* V, No. 2 (Avril–Juin 1955): 291–314.

Paret, Peter. Letters to Bernard Brodie April 23, 1967; April 25, 1964; May 31, 1964; November 7, 1963; November 13, 1963; September 11, 1974; September 22, 1975, Bernard Brodie Papers (Collection 1223), Department of Special Collections, Charles E. Young. Research Library, UCLA.

Paret, Peter. "Napoleon and the Revolution in War," in Peter Paret, Gordon Alexander, and Felix Gilbert, eds, *Makers of Modern Strategy: From Machiavelli to the Nuclear Age*. Princeton: Princeton University Press, 1986, 123–42.

Paret, Peter. "The Political Ideas of Clausewitz," Paper Submitted to the Annual Meeting of the American Historical Association, December 29, 1962, 1–9.

Parks, Eric R. Letter to Brodie, n.d., Bernard Brodie Papers (Collection 1223). Department of Special Collections, Charles E. Young. Research Library, UCLA.

Paul, T. V., Richard J. Harknett and James J. Wirtz, eds, *The Absolute Weapon Revisited: Nuclear Arms and the Emerging International Order*. Ann Arbor: University of Michigan Press, 1998.

Phillips, Thomas R., ed. *Roots of Strategy: A Collection of Military Classics*. Harrisburg, PA: Military Service Publishing Co., 1940.

Porro, Jeffrey D. "The Policy War: Brodie vs. Kahn," *The Bulletin of the Atomic Scientists* 38, No. 6 (June/July 1982), 16–20.

Posvar, Wesley W., Chancellor of the University of Pittsburgh. Letter to Brodie, September 24, 1968, Bernard Brodie Papers (Collection 1223). Department of Special Collections, Charles E. Young. Research Library, UCLA.

Princeton University Press Editorial Board. Minutes from 13–14 June 1964 Meeting of the Editorial Board, Princeton University Press, Bernard Brodie Papers (Collection 1223), Department of Special Collections, Charles E. Young. Research Library, UCLA.

Princeton University Press. Contract for Clausewitz, February 28, 1974, Bernard Brodie Papers (Collection 1223), Department of Special Collections, Charles E. Young. Research Library, UCLA.

Princeton University, Public Announcement, April 10, 1964, Department of Public Information, Princeton University, Bernard Brodie Papers (Collection 1223), Department of Special Collections, Charles E. Young Research Library, UCLA.

R. Miriam Brokaw, Letter to Brodie, September 14, 1973, Bernard Brodie Papers (Collection 1223), Department of Special Collections, Charles E. Young. Research Library, UCLA.

Reagan, Ronald. Speech on the Strategic Defense Initiative, December 28, 1984. A transcript of President Reagan's speech is available online at the website of NuclearFiles.org: www.nuclearfiles.org/menu/key-issues/missile-defense/history/reagan_on-strategic-defense-iniative.htm.

Reid, Julian. "Foucault on Clausewitz: Conceptualizing the Relationship between War and Power," *Alternatives: Global, Local, Political* 28, No. 1 (January 1, 2003), http://findarticles.com/p/articles/mi_hb3225/is_1_28/ai_n28987201/?tag=content;col1.

Romer, Alfred. "Review of *Sea Power in the Machine Age*," *Isis* 34, No. 3 (Winter 1943), 230–1.

Ropp, Theodore. "Review of *Sea Power in the Machine Age*," *The American Historical Review* 47, No. 4 (July 1942), 821–2.

Rosen, S. McKee. "Review of *Sea Power in the Machine Age*," *The American Journal of Sociology* 48, No. 2 (September 1942), 292.

RUSI. "Review: Escalation and the Nuclear Option," Royal United Service Institution, *RUSI Journal*, May 1967, Bernard Brodie Papers (Collection 1223), Department of Special Collections, Charles E. Young Research Library, UCLA.

Saxon, David S. Letter to Brodie, July 18, 1977, Bernard Brodie Papers (Collection 1223). Department of Special Collections, Charles E. Young. Research Library, UCLA.

Schelling, Thomas. *A Tribute to Bernard Brodie and (Incidentally) to RAND*, RAND Paper P-6355, Santa Monica: RAND, July 1979, www.rand.org/content/dam/rand/pubs/papers/2006/P6355.pdf.

Schlatter, Richard. "Thomas Hobbes and Thucydides." *Journal of the History of Ideas*, Vol. 6, No. 3 (June 1945), 350.

Schmidt, Brian C. "Realism as Tragedy: Review of *The Tragedy of Great Power Politics* by John J. Mearsheimer," *Cambridge Review of International Studies* 30, No. 3 (July 2004).

Schmidt, Brian C. *The Political Discourse of Anarchy: A Disciplinary History of International Relations.* Albany: SUNY Press, 1998.

Schroeder, Paul. "Historical Reality vs. Neo-realist Theory," *International Security* 1 (Summer 1994). Schelling, Thomas. Brodie (1910–1978): A Tribute to Bernard Brodie and (Incidentally) to RAND," *International Security* 3, No. 3 (Winter 1978/79), 23.

Shy, John. "Jomini," in Peter Paret, ed. *Makers of Modern Strategy: From Machiavelli to the Nuclear Age.* Princeton: Princeton University Press, 1986.

Shy, John. "Jomini," in Peter Paret, Gordon A. Craig, and Felix Gilbert, eds, *Makers of Modern Strategy.* Oxford: Oxford University Press, 2000, 143–85.

Singer, Max. Letter to Brodie, Feb. 22, 1962, Bernard Brodie Papers (Collection 1223), Department of Special Collections, Charles E. Young Research Library, UCLA.

Singer, Max. Letter to Brodie, November 12, 1964, Bernard Brodie Papers (Collection 1223), Department of Special Collections, Charles E. Young Research Library, UCLA.

Singer, Max. Letter to Brodie, November 4, 1963, Bernard Brodie Papers (Collection 1223), Department of Special Collections, Charles E. Young Research Library, UCLA.

Smith, George H. E. "Review of *Sea Power in the Machine Age*," *The American Political Science Review* 35, No. 5 (October 1941), 1002–3.

Smith, Peter D. *Doomsday Men*. New York: Macmillan, 2007.

Smith, Peter D. *Doomsday Men*. New York: Penguin, 2008 (paperback edition).

Snyder, William P. and John A. MacIntyre, Jr., "Bernard Brodie: America's Prophetic Strategic Thinker," *Parameters* XI, No. 4 (1981), www.carlisle.army.mil/usawc/parameters/Articles/1981/1981%20 snyder%20and%20macintyre.pdf.

Speier, Hans. Letters to Bernard Brodie, November 19, 1954; November 30, 1954, Bernard Brodie Papers (Collection 1223), Department of Special Collections, Charles E. Young. Research Library, UCLA.

Steiner, Barry H. *Bernard Brodie and the Foundations of American Nuclear Strategy*. Lawrence, KS: University Press of Kansas, 1991.

Steiner, Barry. "Using the Absolute Weapon: Early Ideas of Bernard Brodie on Atomic Strategy," *Journal of Strategic Studies* 7, No. 4 (1984), 365–93.

Steiner, Barry. "Using the Absolute Weapon: Early Ideas of Bernard Brodie on Atomic Strategy," ACIS Working Paper No. 44 (January 1984), Center for International and Strategic Affairs, UCLA.

Strachan, Hew. *Clausewitz's On War: A Biography*. New York: Atlantic Monthly Press, 2007.

Strausz-Hupé, Robert. "Review of *The Absolute Weapon by Bernard Brodie*," *Annals of the American Academy of Political and Social Science* 249, Social Implications of Modern Science (January 1947), 177–8.

Stuart, Reginald C. "Clausewitz and the Americans: Bernard Brodie and Others on War and Policy," in *War and Society: A Yearbook of Military History*, Volume 2. Brian Bond and Ian Roy, eds. New York: Holmes and Meier, 1977, 166–72.

Tellis, Ashley J. "Reconstructing political realism: The long march to scientific theory," *Security Studies* 5, No. 2, 1995.

The Key Reporter. "Review: Escalation and the Nuclear Option," *The Key Reporter*, Spring 1967, Bernard Brodie Papers (Collection 1223), Department of Special Collections, Charles E. Young Research Library, UCLA.

Thomas, Roy E. Letter to Brodie, August 29, 1969, Bernard Brodie Papers (Collection 1223), Department of Special Collections, Charles E. Young. Research Library, UCLA.

Time Magazine, "ATOMIC AGE: Absolute Weapon?" *Time*, June 10, 1946, www.time.com/time/magazine/ article/0,9171,793035,00.html.

Trachtenberg, Marc, ed., *The Development of American Strategic Thought: Writings on Strategy, 1945–1951*. New York and London: Garland Publishing, 1987.

Trachtenberg, Marc, ed., *The Development of American Strategic Thought: Writings on Strategy, 1952–1960*. New York and London: Garland Publishing, 1988.

Trachtenberg, Marc, ed., *The Development of American Strategic Thought: Writings on Strategy, 1961–1969, and Retrospectives*. New York and London: Garland Publishing, 1988.

Trachtenberg, Marc. *History and Strategy*. Princeton: Princeton University Press, 1991.

Trachtenberg, Marc. "Strategic Thought in America, 1952–1966," *Political Science Quarterly* 104, No. 2 (Summer 1989), 301–34.

Waltz, Kenneth N. *Man, the State, and War*. New York: Columbia University Press, 1954.

Waltz, Kenneth N. "The Emerging Structure of International Politics," *International Security* 18, No. 2 (Fall 1993).

Waltz, Kenneth. "The Spread of Nuclear Weapons: More May Better," *Adelphi Papers*, No. 171. London: International Institute for Strategic Studies, 1981, www.mtholyoke.edu/acad/intrel/waltz1.htm.

Watts, Barry D. *The Foundations of U.S. Air Doctrine: The Problem of Friction in War*. Maxwell AFB, Alabama: Air University Press, December 1984.

Wildrick, Craig D, Capt. "Bernard Brodie: Pioneer of the Strategy of Deterrence," *Military Review*, October 1983, 39–45, http://usacac.army.mil/cac2/militaryreview/index.asp.

Williams, Michael C. *The Realist Tradition and the Limits of International Relations*. Cambridge, UK: Cambridge University Press, 2005.

Wolfe, Thomas W. "The Levels of Nuclear Strategy," *The Reporter*, January 12, 1967, 63–4.

Wolfe, Thomas W. Comments on 'Escalation and the Nuclear Option,'" RAND Memo to Brodie, March 16, 1965, Bernard Brodie Papers (Collection 1223), Department of Special Collections, Charles E. Young Research Library, UCLA.

Wolk, Herman S. "Politicians, Generals, and Strategists," *Air University Review*, January–February 1974, www.airpower.au.af.mil/airchronicles/aureview/1974/jan-feb/wolk.html.

Wright, Quincy, ed. *A Foreign Policy for the United States*. Chicago: University of Chicago Press, 1947.

Wright, Quincy. "Modern Technology and the World Order," in William Fielding Ogburn, ed., *Technology and International Relations* (Chicago, IL: University of Chicago Press, 1949). 177–98.

Young, Elizabeth. "On War in Europe," *The Guardian*, March 31, 1967, Bernard Brodie Papers (Collection 1223), Department of Special Collections, Charles E. Young Research Library, UCLA.

Zellen, Barry. "Bernard Brodie: A Clausewitz for the Nuclear Age." *Security Innovator*, January 1, 2009, http://securityinnovator.com/index.php?articleID=15954&sectionID=43.

Zellen, Barry. "Herman Kahn: A Jomini for the Nuclear Age." *Security Innovator*, January 2, 2009, http://securityinnovator.com/index.php?articleID=15955&sectionID=43.

Zellen, Barry. "Order in an Age of Absolute War: Brodie, Clausewitz and the Case for Complexity," *Security Innovator*, February 1, 2009, http://securityinnovator.com/index.php?articleID=15988&sectionID=43.

Bernard Brodie's Works (Chronological)

Books

Sea Power in the Machine Age (Princeton: Princeton University Press, 1941)

A Layman's Guide to Naval Strategy (Princeton: Princeton University Press, 1942. Subsequent editions were published by Princeton University in 1943, 1944, and 1958, and by Frederick A. Praeger in 1965. The book was retitled—*A Guide to Naval Strategy*—beginning with the 1944 edition in 1947, an updated French language edition was published under the title *La Strategie Navale, et Son Application dans la Guerre 1939-1945* (Paris: Payot, 1947)

The Absolute Weapon: Atomic Power and World Order (New York: Harcourt, Brace, 1946), editor and contributor.

Strategy in the Missile Age (Princeton: Princeton University Press, 1959).

From Crossbow to H-Bomb (New York: Dell, 1962, revised edition published by Indiana University Press in 1973), co-authored with his wife, Fawn M. Brodie.

La Guerre Nucléaire (Paris: Editions Stock, 1965).

Escalation and the Nuclear Option (Princeton: Princeton University Press, 1966).

War and Politics (New York: MacMillan, 1973).

National Security and International Stability (Cambridge: Oelgeschlager, Gunn & Hain, 1983, co-edited by Brodie with Michael D. Intriligator and Roman Kolkowicz and posthumously published).

Papers, Reports, Lectures, and Chapters

"The Atomic Bomb and American Security," New Haven, CT: Yale Institute of International Studies, Memorandum 18, November 1945.

"The Security Problem in the Light of Atomic Energy," 22nd Norman Wait Harris Memorial Foundation Lecture, July 1946, published in Quincy Wright, ed., *A Foreign Policy for the United States* (Chicago: University of Chicago Press, 1947), 89–96.

"The Atomic Bomb and the Armed Services," Washington, DC: Library of Congress, Legislative Reference Service, Public Affairs Bulletin 56, May 1947 (with Eilene Galloway).

"Foreign Oil and American Security," New Haven, Conn.: Yale Institute of International Affairs, Memorandum 23, September 1947.

"The Security Problem in Light of Atomic Energy," in Quincy Wright, ed., *A Foreign Policy for the United States* (Chicago: University of Chicago Press, 1947).

"New Techniques of War and National Policies," in William Ogburn, ed., *Technology and International Relations* (Chicago: University of Chicago Press, 1949).

"National Security Policy and Economic Stability," New Haven, CT: Yale Institute of International Studies, Memorandum 33,1950.

"Must We Shoot from the Hip?" RAND Working Paper, September 4, 1951.

"Characterizations of a Sound Strategy," Naval War College Lecture, March 17, 1952.

"Changing Capabilities and War Objectives," Air War College Lecture, April 17, 1952, Bernard Brodie Papers, Box 12, UCLA Library Special Collections.

"Tactical Effects of H-Bombs," unpublished RAND Working Paper, November 7, 1952.

"Political Consequences of the H-Bomb," unpublished RAND Working Paper, November 7, 1952.

"Attitudes Toward the Use of Force," RAND Paper P-360, December 1952 (revised December 1953).

"The Heritage of Douhet," RAND Research Memorandum No. RM-1013, December 31, 1952.

"Commentary on the Force Employment Study," RAND Informal Working Paper, January 9, 1953.

"A Slightly Revised Proposal for the Underemployment of SAC in an H-Bomb Era," unpublished RAND Working Paper, January 23, 1953.

"U.S. Political Objectives in a Context of Strategic Bombing," RAND internal working document, February 19, 1953.

"A Commentary on the Preventive-War Doctrine," unpublished RAND paper, June 11, 1953.

"The Next Ten Years," with C.J. Hitch and A.W. Marshall, RAND internal working document, December 30, 1954.

"Influence of Mass Destruction Weapons on Strategy," Lecture to the Naval War College, February 6, 1956.

"Nuclear Weapons and Changing Strategic Outlooks," Lecture to the U.S. Army War College on February 20, 1956.

"Nuclear Weapons and Changing Strategic Outlooks," RAND Paper No. P-811 (a composite of his February 6 and February 20 lectures).

"Is There a Defense?", RAND Research Memorandum, no. RM-1781, August 16, 1956.

"Implications of Nuclear Weapons in Total War," Santa Monica, Calif.: RAND Corporation, Research Memo, RM-1842, December 17, 1956 (republished, with nominal changes, as RAND Paper P-1118, July 8, 1957, as prepared for publication in the Fall 1957 edition of the *Royal Canadian Air Force Staff College Journal*).

"Some Strategic Implications of the Nuclear Revolution," RAND Paper P-1111, 1957.

"The Anatomy of Deterrence," Santa Monica, CA: RAND Corporation, Memo 2218, 1958.

"The Meaning of Limited War," Santa Monica, CA: RAND Corporation, Memo 2224, 1958.

"Alternative Strategic Policies II," RAND Informal Working Paper, March 27, 1958.

"The Anatomy of Deterrence," RAND Research Memorandum, RM-2218, July 23, 1958.

"The Meaning of Limited War," RAND Research Memorandum, RM-2224, July 30, 1958.

"Unlimited Weapons Choices and Limited Budgets," Berkeley lecture, November 18, 1958.

"Disarmament Goals and National Security Needs," Washington State talk, March 5, 1959.

"Strategic Objectives and the Determination of Force Composition," RAND Working Paper, June 9, 1959.

"Provocation Works on People," RAND Working Paper, June 12, 1959.

"The Rejection of the Airborne Alert: Another Facet of the 'Provocation' Problem," RAND Working Paper, February 8, 1960.

"A Comment on the Hoag Doctrine," RAND internal working document, 1962.

"Some Preliminary Observations on Escalation," RAND internal working document, July 16, 1962.

"A Critique of the Doctrine of Conventional War in Europe (CWE)," RAND Paper, September 24, 1962.

"A Proposal for the Projection of American Attitudes towards French Nuclear Policies," RAND Research Memorandum RM-3343-ISA, October 1962, with Nathan Leites.

"What Price Conventional Capabilities in Europe?" Santa Monica, Calif.: RAND Corporation, Memo P-2696, February 1963.

"Afterthoughts on CWE from the Meeting (with Herr Erler) of April 16," RAND Informal Working Paper, April 22, 1963.

"AFAG Talk: Political Impact of U.S. Force Postures," RAND Corporation Study, May 28, 1963.

"The Issue of Strategic Superiority: A Comment," RAND Informal Working Paper, July 19, 1963.

"The Missing Middle—Tactical Nuclear War," RAND Working Paper, May 8, 1964.

"Some Considerations Governing Escalation," RAND Working Paper, September 4, 1964.

"The Intractability of States: A Distinctive Problem," RAND Paper P-2970, September 1964.

"The American Scientific Strategists," RAND Paper P-2979, October 1964 also published in shorter form as a chapter under the slightly abbreviated title "The Scientific Strategists," in Robert Gilpin and Christopher Wright, eds, *Scientists and National Policy-Making* (New York: Columbia University Press, 1964).

"New Preface for Paperback Edition of *Strategy in the Missile Age*, RAND Paper, P-3033, December 1964.

"The Next Ten Years," RAND Working Paper, December 30, 1964 with Charles J. Hitch and Andrew W. Marshall.

"General Andre Beaufre on Strategy: A Review of Two Books," RAND Paper, P-3157, June 1965.

"Escalation and the Nuclear Option," RAND Research Memorandum, RM-4544-PR, June 1965.

"Chapter 15: What Price Conventional Capabilities in Europe?" in Henry Kissinger, ed., *Problems of National Strategy* (New York: Frederick A. Praeger, 1965), 313–26.

"Learning to Fight a Limited War," in William P. Gerberding and Bernard Brodie, eds, *The Political Dimensions in Strategy: Five Papers*, Security Studies Paper Number 13 (Los Angeles: UCLA Security Studies Project, 1968), 26–35.

"Missile Defense Against China?" in William P. Gerberding and Bernard Brodie, eds, *The Political Dimensions in Strategy: Five Papers*, Security Studies Paper Number 13 (Los Angeles: UCLA Security Studies Project, 1968), 26–35.

"Defense Strategy in its Political Context," in William P. Gerberding and Bernard Brodie, eds, *The Political Dimensions in Strategy: Five Papers*, Security Studies Paper Number 13 (Los Angeles: UCLA Security Studies Project, 1968), 36–47.

"Students and the Military-Industrial Complex," in William P. Gerberding and Bernard Brodie, eds, *The Political Dimensions in Strategy: Five Papers*, Security Studies Paper Number 13 (Los Angeles: UCLA Security Studies Project, 1968), 33–5.

"Defense Strategy in its Political Context," Paper Presented to the Fifth International Wehrkunde Conference, Sponsored by the Verlag Europaisch Wehrkunde, Munich, Germany, February 10–11, 1968 (a draft of this speech with the working title, "Nuclear Strategy in its Political Context," February 1968 paper for 'Munich Conference,'" is available in Box 20 of the Bernard Brodie Papers, UCLA Library Special Collections, a copy of which is reprinted in Marc Trachtenberg's *The Development of American Strategic Thought: Writings on Strategy, 1961–1969* (New York: Garland Press, 1988), 353–68.

"Strategy," in David L. Sills, ed., *The International Encyclopedia of the Social Sciences*, Vol. 15 (New York: MacMillan, 1968), 218–87.

"Conclusion: The Future of Deterrence," in *The Future of Deterrence in U.S. Strategy*, edited by Bernard Brodie, UCLA Security Studies Project, May 20, 1968.

"Changing Attitudes Towards War," Paper Presented at the Studies in Violence Symposium, UCLA, June 1–2, 1968, and published in *Bureaucracy, Politics, and Strategy* (UCLA Security Studies Paper No. 17, 1968), co-edited by Brodie and Henry Kissinger.

"Ending a War: Is the Korean Lesson Valid for Vietnam?" in *Bureaucracy, Politics, and Strategy* (UCLA Security Studies Paper No. 17, 1968) and also published as "Paying in Full for a Limited War," *Los Angeles Times*, October 17, 1968.

"Theories on the Causes of War," UCLA Faculty Lecture Series, "War and the Human Race," November 11, 1968, also included in *Bureaucracy, Politics, and Strategy* (UCLA Security Studies Paper No. 17, 1968).

"Technology, Politics, and Strategy," Paper Presented to the Tenth Annual Conference of the Institute for Strategic Studies at St. Catherine's College in Oxford, September 19–22, 1968, also presented in *Bureaucracy, Politics, and Strategy* (UCLA Security Studies Paper No. 17, 1968).

"Technology, Politics, and Strategy," *Adelphi Papers* 9, No. 55 (1969), 21–9.

"Technology, Politics, and Strategy," in *Problems of Modern Strategy* (London: Institute for Strategic Studies, Studies in International Security, 1970 and New York: Frederick A. Praeger, 1970).

"Strategy and National Interests . . . Reflections for the Future," New York: National Strategy Information Center, Strategy Paper No. 7, 1971.

"The Impact of Technological Change on the International System: Reflections on Prediction," *Change and the Future of the International System*, David S. Sullivan and Martin J. Sattler, eds. (New York: Columbia University Press, 1972), 1–15.

"How Much Is Enough? Guns Versus Butter Revisited," California Seminar on Arms Control and Foreign Policy, August 1975.

"Introduction," *Towards a New Defense for NATO: The Case for Tactical Nuclear Weapons*, National Strategy Information Center, Agenda Paper No. 5 (New York, National Strategy Information Center, July 1976), 1–9.

"The Development of Nuclear Strategy," ACIS Working Paper, No. 11 (Los Angeles: UCLA, 1976).

"Fourteen Informal Writings from the Unpublished Work of Bernard Brodie, 1952–1965," RAND Unbound Collection, 1980.

"The Development of Nuclear Strategy," in *National Security and International Stability* (Cambridge: Oelgeschlager, Gunn & Hain, 1983, eds. Bernard Brodie, Roman Kolkowicz, and Michael D. Intriligator).

"The Atomic Bomb and American Security," reprinted in the 1989 reader, Philip Bobbitt, Lawrence Freedman, and Gregory F. Treverton, eds, *U.S. Nuclear Strategy: A Reader* (London: Macmillan, 1989), 64–94, originally published by the Yale Institute of International Studies as Memorandum 18 in November 1945.

Articles

"Our Ships Strike Back," *Virginia Quarterly Review*, 21 (Spring 1945), 186–206.

"The Atomic Bomb and American Security," New Haven, CT: Yale Institute of International Studies, Memorandum 18, November 1945.

"New Tactics in Naval Warfare," *Foreign Affairs* 24, no. 2 (January 1946), 210–23.

"The Atomic Dilemma," *The Annals of the American Academy of Political and Social Science* 249 (January 1947), 32–41.

"The Battle For Leyte Gulf," *Virginia Quarterly Review*, 23 (Summer 1947), 455–60.

"War Department Thinking on the Atomic Bomb," *Bulletin of the Atomic Scientists* 3 (June 1947), 150–5, 168.

"Navy Department Thinking on the Atomic Bomb," *Bulletin of the Atomic Scientists* 3 (July 1947), 177–80, 198–9.

"A Critique of Army and Navy Thinking on the Atomic Bomb," *Bulletin of the Atomic Scientists* 3 (August 1947), 207–10.

"How Strong Is Britain?" *Foreign Affairs* 26, no. 3 (April 1948), 432–49.

"The Atom Bomb as Policy Maker," *Foreign Affairs* 27, no. 1 (October 1948), 17–33.

"Strategy As a Science," *World Politics*, 1 (July 1949), 467–88.

"Strategic Implications of the North Atlantic Pact," *The Yale Review*, 39 (December 1949), 193–208.

"Strategic Bombing: What it Can Do," *Reporter* 3 (August 1950), 28–31.

"Military Demonstration and Disclosure of New Weapons," *World Politics* 5, no. 3 (April 1953), 281–301.

"The Heritage of Douhet," *Air University Quarterly Review* 6 (Summer 1953), 64–69, 121–7.

"Nuclear Weapons: Strategic or Tactical?" *Foreign Affairs* 32, no. 2 (January 1954), 217–29.

"Unlimited Weapons and Limited War," *The Reporter*, 11 (18 November 1954), 16–21.

"Some Notes on the Evolution of Air Doctrine," *World Politics* 7, no. 3 (April 1955), 349–70.

"Strategy Hits a Dead End," *Harper's*, 211 (October 1955), 33–7.

"Nuclear Weapons and Changing Strategic Outlooks," *Bulletin of the Atomic Scientists*, February 1957.

"A Psychoanalytic Interpretation of Woodrow Wilson," *World Politics*, 9 (April 1957), 413–22.

"More About Limited War," *World Politics*, 10 (October 1957), 112–22.

"Scientific Progress and Political Science," *The Scientific Monthly* 85, no. 6 (December 1957), 315–19.

"The Anatomy of Deterrence," *World Politics* 11, no. 2 (January 1959), 173–91.

"Defense Policy and the Possibility of Total War," *Daedalus* 91, no. 4 (Fall 1962), 733–48.

"What Price Conventional Capabilities in Europe?" *Reporter* 28 (May 1963), 25–9, 32–3.

"Morals and Strategy: Distinguishing Virtue from Ignorance in Problems of National Defense," *Worldview Magazine*, Carnegie Council for Ethics in International Affairs, September 1964, 4–8.

"The McNamara Phenomenon," *World Politics*, 17 (July 1965), 672–86.

"Review of *Introduction to Strategy* and *Dissuasion et Strategie* by Andre Beaufre," *Survival* 7 (August 1965), 208–10.

"How Not to Lead an Alliance," *The Reporter*, March 9, 1967, 18–24.

"Missile Defense Against China?" *Los Angeles Times*, September 17, 1967.

"Students and the Military--Industrial Complex," *UCLA Daily Bruin,* December 1, 1967.

"Learning to Fight a Limited War," *Los Angeles Times*, December 3, 1967, G7.

"Paying in Full for a Limited War," *Los Angeles Times*, October 17, 1968, H7 (also published as "Ending a War: Is the Korean Lesson Valid for Vietnam?" in *Bureaucracy, Politics, and Strategy* (UCLA Security Studies Paper No. 17, 1968).

"Theories on the Causes of War," UCLA Faculty Lecture Series, War and the Human Race, November 11, 1968, and also included in *Bureaucracy, Politics, and Strategy* (UCLA Security Studies Paper No. 17, 1968).

"Technology, Politics, and Strategy," *Adelphi Papers* 9, No.: 55 (1969), 21–9 (also published in *Bureaucracy, Politics, and Strategy* (UCLA Security Studies Paper No. 17, 1968) and *Problems of Modern Strategy*, London: Institute for Strategic Studies, Studies in International Security, 1970, and New York: Frederick A. Praeger, 1970.

"Why Were We So (Strategically) Wrong?" *Foreign Policy*, 5 (Winter 1971–1972), 151–61.

"Review: On Clausewitz: A Passion for War," *World Politics* 25, no. 2 (January 1973), 288–308.

"How Much Conventional Force Do We Need?" *Foreign Service Journal* (April 1973), 18–22.

"On the Objectives of Arms Control," *International Security* 1, no. 1 (Summer 1976), 17–36.

"The Development of Nuclear Strategy," ACIS Working Paper, No. 11. Los Angeles: UCLA, 1976.

"In Quest of Unknown Clausewitz: A Review of *Clausewitz and the State* by Peter Paret, *International Security* 1 (Winter 1977), 62–9.

"Review of Clausewitz and the State, by Peter Paret," Journal of Interdisciplinary History 8 (Winter 1978), 572–4.

"The Development of Nuclear Strategy," *International Security* 3, no. 4 (Spring 1978), 65–83.

Index